9781405196949-1

D1749772

The Wiley Blackwell Encyclopedia of Gender and Sexuality Studies

Wiley Blackwell Encyclopedias in Social Science
Consulting Editor: George Ritzer

Published

The Wiley Blackwell Encyclopedia of Globalization
Edited by George Ritzer

The Wiley Blackwell Encyclopedia of Social and Political Movements
Edited by David A. Snow, Donatella della Porta, Bert Klandermans, and Doug McAdam

The Wiley Blackwell Encyclopedia of Health, Illness, Behavior, and Society
Edited by William C. Cockerham, Robert Dingwall, and Stella Quah

The Wiley Blackwell Encyclopedia of Consumption and Consumer Studies
Edited by Daniel Thomas Cook and J. Michael Ryan

The Wiley Blackwell Encyclopedia of Family Studies
Edited by Constance L. Shehan

The Wiley Blackwell Encyclopedia of Race, Ethnicity, and Nationalism
Edited by John Stone, Rutledge M. Dennis, Polly S. Rizova, Anthony D. Smith, and Xiaoshuo Hou

The Wiley Blackwell Encyclopedia of Gender and Sexuality Studies
Editor-in-Chief: Nancy A. Naples, Associate Editors: renée c. hoogland, Maithree Wickramasinghe, and Wai Ching Angela Wong

Forthcoming

The Wiley Blackwell Encyclopedia of Social Theory
Edited by Bryan S. Turner, Chang Kyung-Sup, Cynthia Epstein, Peter Kivisto, William Outhwaite, and J. Michael Ryan

The Wiley Blackwell Encyclopedia of Urban and Regional Studies
Edited by Anthony M. Orum, Marisol Garcia, Dennis Judd, Bryan Roberts, and Pow Choon-Piew

The Wiley Blackwell Encyclopedia of Environment and Society
Edited by Dorceta E. Taylor, Kozo Mayumi, Jun Bi, Paul Burton, and Tor A. Benjaminsen

Related titles

The Blackwell Encyclopedia of Sociology
Edited by George Ritzer

The Concise Encyclopedia of Sociology
Edited by George Ritzer and J. Michael Ryan

The Wiley Blackwell Encyclopedia of Gender and Sexuality Studies

Editor-in-Chief

Nancy A. Naples

Associate Editors

renée c. hoogland

Maithree Wickramasinghe

Wai Ching Angela Wong

Volume I

A–D

WILEY Blackwell

This edition first published 2016
© 2016 John Wiley & Sons, Ltd.

Registered Office
John Wiley & Sons Ltd, The Atrium, Southern Gate, Chichester, West Sussex, PO19 8SQ, UK

Editorial Offices
350 Main Street, Malden, MA 02148-5020, USA
9600 Garsington Road, Oxford, OX4 2DQ, UK
The Atrium, Southern Gate, Chichester, West Sussex, PO19 8SQ, UK

For details of our global editorial offices, for customer services, and for information about how to apply for permission to reuse the copyright material in this book please see our website at www.wiley.com/wiley-blackwell.

The right of Nancy A. Naples to be identified as the author of the editorial material in this work has been asserted in accordance with the UK Copyright, Designs and Patents Act 1988.

All rights reserved. No part of this publication may be reproduced, stored in a retrieval system, or transmitted, in any form or by any means, electronic, mechanical, photocopying, recording or otherwise, except as permitted by the UK Copyright, Designs and Patents Act 1988, without the prior permission of the publisher.

Wiley also publishes its books in a variety of electronic formats. Some content that appears in print may not be available in electronic books.

Designations used by companies to distinguish their products are often claimed as trademarks. All brand names and product names used in this book are trade names, service marks, trademarks or registered trademarks of their respective owners. The publisher is not associated with any product or vendor mentioned in this book.

Limit of Liability/Disclaimer of Warranty: While the publisher and author have used their best efforts in preparing this book, they make no representations or warranties with respect to the accuracy or completeness of the contents of this book and specifically disclaim any implied warranties of merchantability or fitness for a particular purpose. It is sold on the understanding that the publisher is not engaged in rendering professional services and neither the publisher nor the author shall be liable for damages arising herefrom. If professional advice or other expert assistance is required, the services of a competent professional should be sought.

Library of Congress Cataloging-in-Publication data is available for this book.

ISBN 9781405196949 (hardback)

Cover image: Clockwise from top left: Artists of street theater group ASSA (Ankara Cinema and Art Atelier) during a demonstration on International Women's Day © Piero Castellano/Pacific Press/LightRocket via Getty Images; Banyana beat Mali, Women's Championship match, South Africa, 2010 © Gallo Images/Alamy; Young girl from Oaxaca © Jennifer Bickham Mendez; Demonstration over same-sex marriages, Taipei, Taiwan, 2015 © Sam Yeh/AFP/Getty Images

Set in 10/12pt Minion by SPi Global, Chennai, India
Printed and bound in Singapore by Markono Print Media Pte Ltd

1 2016

Contents

Volume I

Editors — vii
Contributors — ix
Lexicon — xxxvii
Introduction and Acknowledgments — xlix

Gender and Sexuality Studies A–D — 1

Volume II

Gender and Sexuality Studies E–F — 497

Volume III

Gender and Sexuality Studies G–I — 931

Volume IV

Gender and Sexuality Studies J–R — 1471

Volume V

Gender and Sexuality Studies S–Y — 2051

Index of Names — 2619
Index of Subjects — 2633

Editors

EDITOR-IN-CHIEF

Nancy A. Naples is Board of Trustees Distinguished Professor of Women's, Gender, and Sexuality Studies and Sociology at the University of Connecticut. Her publications focus on the intersection of gender, sexuality, race, political activism, and citizenship in comparative perspective and feminist praxis. She is author of *Feminism and Method: Ethnography, Discourse Analysis, and Activist Research* (2003) and *Grassroots Warriors (1998)*; and co-editor of *Border Politics: Social Movements, Collective Identities and Globalization* (2015), *The Sexuality of Migration* (2010) by Lionel Cantú, and *Women's Activism and Globalization: Linking Local Struggles with Transnational Politics* (2002). She is also series editor for *Praxis: Theory in Action* published by State University of New York Press.

MANAGING EDITOR

J. Michael Ryan is Assistant Professor of Sociology at the American University in Cairo (Egypt). He has previously taught courses at Facultad Latinoamericana de Ciencias Sociales (FLACSO) in Quito, Ecuador and the University of Maryland in the United States. His publications focus on issues related to gender, sexualities, globalization, and consumer culture. He is editor of *Essential Concepts in Sociology* (forthcoming), and co-editor of *The Concise Encyclopedia of Sociology* (with George Ritzer, 2011), *The Wiley Blackwell Encyclopedia of Consumption and Consumer Studies* (with Daniel T. Cook, 2015) and *The Wiley Blackwell Encyclopedia of Social Theory* (with Bryan S. Turner, et al., forthcoming).

ASSOCIATE EDITORS

renée c. hoogland is Professor of English at Wayne State University in Detroit, where she teaches literature and culture after 1870, critical theory, cultural studies, and visual culture. She has published widely on American and British literature, film, feminist and queer theory, visual culture, and critical theory. hoogland is the author of *Elizabeth Bowen: A Reputation in Writing* (NYUP, 1994) and *Lesbian Configurations* (Columbia UP/Polity, 1997). Her most recent book is *A Violent Embrace: Art and Aesthetics after Representation* (UPNE, 2014). hoogland is also the editor of *Criticism: A Quarterly for Literature and the Arts* and the Senior Editor in Chief of a 10-volume handbook series on gender forthcoming with Macmillan.

Maithree Wickramasinghe is Professor at the Department of English and the Founding Director of the Centre for Gender Studies at the University of Kelaniya, Sri Lanka. She is Visiting Professor at the University of Sussex, UK. Her research interests include gender mainstreaming, sexual and gender-based violence, women and development as well as feminist research methodology. Her publications include *Feminist Research Methodology: Making Meanings of Meaning Making* (2010), and *From Theory to Action: Women, Gender and Development* (2000). She has worked extensively on transforming research into policy, programs, and evaluation.

Wai Ching Angela Wong is Vice-Chair and Associate Professor of the Department of Cultural and Religious Studies and Co-Director of the Gender Research Centre at The Chinese University of Hong Kong. Her publications include *Gender and Family in East Asia* (2014), *Chinese Women and Hong Kong Christianity: An Oral History* (2010), "Our Stories Our Bodies: Narrating Female Sexuality in Hong Kong," *Mainstreaming Gender in Hong Kong Society* (2009), and *The Poor Woman: A Critical Analysis of Asian Theology and Contemporary Chinese Fiction by Women* (2002).

ADVISORY EDITORS

Jennifer Bickham Mendez, The College of William and Mary, USA

Tom Boellstorff, University of California, USA

Catherine Hundleby, University of Windsor, Canada

Eva Magnusson, Umeå University, Sweden

Pardis Mahdavi, Pomona College, USA

Amrita Pande, University of Cape Town, South Africa

Maria del Pilar Grazioso, University of the Valley of Guatemala, Guatemala

Mansah Prah, University of Cape Coast, Ghana

Damien Riggs, Flinders University, Australia

Cecilia M. B. Sardenberg, Federal University of Bahia, Brazil

Tonia St. Germain, Oregon State University, USA

Bronwyn Winter, The University of Sydney, Australia

Contributors

Sarah H. Abercrombie, *Radford University, USA*

Martha Ackelsberg, *Smith College, USA*

Katie L. Acosta, *Georgia State University, USA*

Maeve Adams, *Manhattan College, New York, USA*

Michele A. Adams, *Tulane University, USA*

Joni Adamson, *Arizona State University, USA*

Shweta Majumdar Adur, *California State University, Fullerton, USA*

Lara Aasem Ahmed, *The American University in Cairo, Egypt*

Brittnie Aiello, *Merrimack College, USA*

Jami Ake, *Washington University in St. Louis, USA*

Angela Dziedzom Akorsu, *University of Cape Coast, Ghana*

Bonita Aleaz, *University of Calcutta, India*

Nada Mustafa Ali, *University of Massachusetts Boston, USA*

Keith Allan, *Monash University, Australia*

Christopher T. Allen, *University of Massachusetts Lowell, USA*

Mallary Allen, *Concordia College, USA*

Jason Alley, *University of California, Santa Cruz, USA*

Rangita de Silva de Alwis, *Global Women's Leadership Initiative, USA*

Metti Amirtham, *Holy Cross Social Centre, India*

Padma Anagol, *Cardiff University, UK*

Eric Anderson, *University of Winchester, UK*

Kim Anderson, *Wilfrid Laurier University, Canada*

Hazel Andrews, *Liverpool John Moores University, UK*

Michael Anhorn, *Independent Scholar*

Y. Gavriel Ansara, *University of Surrey, UK*

Nikó Antalffy, *Macquarie University, Australia*

Allison K. Arnekrans, *Central Michigan University, USA*

Rina Arya, *University of Wolverhampton, UK*

Victor Asal, *University at Albany, State University of New York, USA*

Chris Ashford, *Northumbria University, UK*

Carol J. Auster, *Franklin & Marshall College, USA*

Marianne Ayers, *East Carolina University, USA*

Lucy E. Bailey, *Oklahoma State University, USA*

Carmen Bain, *Iowa State University, USA*

Karen L. Baird, *Purchase College, State University of New York, USA*

Christina N. Baker, *Sonoma State University, USA*

Joanne Baker, *James Cook University, Australia*

Maureen Baker, *University of Auckland, New Zealand*

Ria E. Baker, *Houston Graduate School of Theology, USA*

Jessica Baltman, *Binghamton University, USA*

Shakuntala Banaji, *London School of Economics and Political Science, UK*

Maks Banens, *University of Lyon, France*

David P. Barash, *University of Washington, Seattle, USA*

Del Barczak, *University of Adelaide, Australia*

Jeffrey Bardzell, *Indiana University, USA*

Shaowen Bardzell, *Indiana University, USA*

Drucilla K. Barker, *University of South Carolina, USA*

Clare Bartholomaeus, *Flinders University of South Australia, Australia*

Linda Bartolomei, *University of New South Wales, Australia*

Jenna Basiliere, *Indiana University, USA*

Judith R. Baskin, *University of Oregon, USA*

Kattie Basnett, *Rice University, USA*

Leah Bassel, *University of Leicester, UK*

Kellie Bean, *Lyndon State College, USA*

Brigitte H. Bechtold, *Central Michigan University, USA*

Julia C. Becker, *Philipps-University Marburg, Germany*

Erin Bell, *University of Lincoln, UK*

Sara C. Bender, *Central Washington University, USA*

Rita Béres-Deák, *Central European University, Hungary*

Israel Berger, *The University of Sydney, Australia*

Michele Tracy Berger, *University of North Carolina at Chapel Hill, USA*

Günseli Berik, *University of Utah, USA*

Mary Bernstein, *University of Connecticut, USA*

Silvia Bettez, *University of North Carolina at Greensboro, USA*

Pamela J. Bettis, *Washington State University, USA*

Meghna Bhat, *University of Illinois at Chicago, USA*

Małgorzata Bieńkowska, *University of Białystok, Poland*

David B. Bills, *University of Iowa, USA*

Jessica E. Birch, *Indiana University South Bend, USA*

Carolyn Birnie-Porter, *Saint Mary's University, Canada*

C. J. Bishop, *University of Saskatchewan, Canada*

Hanne Blank, *Emory University, USA*

Jacob Clark Blickenstaff, *Pacific Science Center, USA*

Leslie Rebecca Bloom, *Roosevelt University, Chicago, USA*

John R. Blosnich, *Center for Health Equity Research and Promotion, VA Pittsburgh Healthcare System, USA*

Robyn Bluhm, *Michigan State University, USA*

Klaus Boehnke, *Jacobs University Bremen, Germany*

Rachel R. Bogan, *The City University of New York, USA*

Laura de Bonfils, *European Institute for Gender Equality, Lithuania*

Sharon A. Bong, *Monash University, Malaysia*

Pascal Borry, *KU Leuven, Belgium*

Aleksandar Bošković, *University of Belgrade and Institute of Social Sciences, Serbia*

Jennifer W. Bouek, *Brown University, USA*

Dina Bowman, *University of Melbourne, Australia*

Susan B. Boyd, *Professor Emerita, Allard School of Law, University of British Columbia, Canada*

Alexis L. Boylan, *University of Connecticut, USA*

Mary Brabeck, *New York University, USA*

Abigail Bray, *University of Western Australia, Australia*

Thomas Breda, *Paris School of Economics, France*

Rose M. Brewer, *University of Minnesota Twin Cities, USA*

Chris Brickell, *Otago University, New Zealand*

Jo Bridgeman, *Sussex Law School, University of Sussex, UK*

Deborah Brock, *York University, Toronto, Canada*

Madeline Brodt, *University of Massachusetts Boston, USA*

Erin Brown Bell, *Wayne State University, Detroit, USA*

Kath Browne, *University of Brighton, UK*

Attila Bruni, *University of Trento, Italy*

Lisa D. Brush, *University of Pittsburgh, USA*

Anne Bubriski-McKenzie, *University of Central Florida, USA*

Stephanie L. Budge, *University of Louisville, USA*

Rosemarie Buikema, *Utrecht University, The Netherlands*

Denise Buiten, *University of Notre Dame Australia, Australia*

Julia C. Bullock, *Emory University, USA*

Adrienne Burgess, *Fatherhood Institute, UK*

Anders Burman, *Lund University, Sweden*

Shawn Meghan Burn, *California Polytechnic State University, USA*

Ann Burnett, *North Dakota State University, USA*

Claudia L. Bushman, *Claremont Graduate University, USA*

Jill M. Bystydzienski, *Ohio State University, USA*

Denton Callander, *University of New South Wales, Australia*

Marina Calloni, *University of Milano-Bicocca, Italy*

Marta B. Calás, *University of Massachusetts Amherst, USA*

Julie Ann Harms Cannon, *Seattle University, USA*

Rose Capdevila, *Open University, UK*

Maria Carbin, *Umeå University, Sweden*

Jessica Carlisle, *University of Manchester, UK*

Stephen P. Casazza, *Radford University, USA*

Menoukha Case, *SUNY Empire State College, USA*

R. Casey Davis, *Independent Scholar*

Annalisa Casini, *Université libre de Bruxelles, Belgium*

Victoria Cass, *Johns Hopkins University, USA*

Peter Cava, *Georgia State University, USA*

Shelley Cavalieri, *University of Toledo College of Law, USA*

Courtney Caviness, *University of California, Davis, USA*

Karli June Cerankowski, *Stanford University, USA*

Stephanie Chaban, *University of Ulster, UK*

Eliza Chandler, *Ryerson University, Toronto, Canada*

Wendy Chapkis, *University of Southern Maine, USA*

Maria Charles, *University of California, Santa Barbara, USA*

Kay A. Chick, *Penn State Altoona, USA*

Joseph Man Kit Cho, *The Chinese University of Hong Kong, People's Republic of China*

Joan C. Chrisler, *Connecticut College, USA*

Emily K. Clarke, *University of Wisconsin–Madison, USA*

Krystal Cleary, *Indiana University, USA*

Sharyn Clough, *Oregon State University, USA*

Catherine Clune-Taylor, *University of Alberta, Canada*

David Coad, *University of Valenciennes, France*

Augustus Bonner Cochran III, *Agnes Scott College, USA*

Ilana Cohen, *Brandeis University, Waltham, USA*

Tracy J. Cohn, *Radford University, USA*

Wade M. Cole, *University of Utah, USA*

Marianne Coleman, *University of London, UK*

Kathleen Connellan, *University of South Australia, Australia*

Laura Connelly, *University of Leeds, UK*

Susan Conradsen, *Berry College, USA*

John A. Conteh, *Wright State University, USA*

Janet M. Conway, *Brock University, Canada*

Kay Cook, *RMIT University, Australia*

Alexander Cooper, *Central European University, Hungary*

Lisa Cosgrove, *University of Massachusetts Boston and Harvard University, USA*

Anne N. Costain, *University of Colorado, USA*

W. Douglas Costain, *University of Colorado, USA*

Christina Coto, *Argosy University, USA*

Betsy Crane, *Widener University, USA*

Christa Craven, *College of Wooster, USA*

Mary Crawford, *University of Connecticut, USA*

Barbara Creed, *University of Melbourne, Australia*

Jocelyn Crowley, *Rutgers University, USA*

Carolyn Cunningham, *Gonzaga University, USA*

Heather D. Cyr, *Southern Connecticut State University, USA*

Francine J. D'Amico, *Syracuse University, USA*

Sarah D'Andrea, *The Graduate Center, CUNY, USA*

Drude Dahlerup, *Stockholm University, Sweden*

Arpita Das, *The Asian-Pacific Resource and Research Centre for Women, Malaysia*

Lester M. Davids, *University of Cape Town, South Africa*

Georgiann Davis, *University of Nevada, Las Vegas, USA*

Keith E. Davis, *University of South Carolina, USA*

R. E. Davis, *College of the Mainland, Texas, USA*

Shannon N. Davis, *George Mason University, USA*

Stephen J. Davis, *Yale University, USA*

Tracy Davis, *Western Illinois University, USA*

Laura Deane, *Flinders University of South Australia, Australia*

Lisa DeLance, *University of California, Riverside, USA*

Timothy J. Demy, *US Naval War College, USA*

Amanda Denes, *University of Connecticut, USA*

Helma G.E. de Vries-Jordan, *University of Pittsburgh at Bradford, USA*

C. Nana Derby, *Virginia State University, USA*

Tara F. Deubel, *University of South Florida, USA*

Alexis Dewaele, *Ghent University, Belgium*

Marylynne Diggs, *Clark College, USA*

Heather Dillaway, *Wayne State University, USA*

Muriel Dimen, *New York University, USA*

Adrienne D. Dixson, *University of Illinois, Urbana-Champaign, USA*

Amy Dobson, *University of Queensland, Australia*

Danielle Docka-Filipek, *Otterbein University, USA*

Kathleen Doll, *Chapman University, USA*

Lena Dominelli, *Durham University, UK*

Michèle D. Dominy, *Bard College, USA*

Carmela Muzio Dormani, *CUNY Graduate Center, USA*

Steven Douglas, *Monash University, Australia*

Anat Drach-Zahavy, *University of Haifa, Israel*

Gregg Drinkwater, *University of Colorado, USA*

Julie L. Drolet, *University of Calgary, Canada*

Murray Drummond, *Flinders University of South Australia, Australia*

Pat Dudgeon, *University of Western Australia, Australia*

Clemence Due, *University of Adelaide, Australia*

Catherine N. Dulmus, *University at Buffalo, USA*

Danielle Dumaine, *University of Connecticut, USA*

Alice H. Eagly, *Northwestern University, USA*

John Eden, *University of New South Wales, Australia*

Leigh H. Edwards, *Florida State University, USA*

Sophia Efstathiou, *Norwegian University of Science and Technology (NTNU), Trondheim, Norway*

Elisabeth Eide, *Oslo and Akershus University College, Norway*

Christopher J. Einolf, *DePaul University, Chicago, USA*

John W. Ellis-Etchison, *Rice University, USA*

Moha Ennaji, *University of Fès, Morocco*

Michelle Erai, *University of California, Los Angeles, USA*

Michelle Casarella Espinoza, *Alliant International University, USA*

Laurie Essig, *Middlebury College, Vermont, USA*

Claire Etaugh, *Bradley University, USA*

Breanne Fahs, *Arizona State University, USA*

Panteá Farvid, *Auckland University of Technology, New Zealand*

Sandra L. Faulkner, *Bowling Green State University, USA*

Katalin Fábián, *Lafayette College, USA*

Abby L. Ferber, *University of Colorado, Colorado Springs, USA*

Nicole Capriel Ferry, *Washington State University, USA*

Stephen T. Fife, *University of Nevada, Las Vegas, USA*

Janaina Figueira, *University of Melbourne, Australia*

Noha Fikry, *The American University in Cairo, Egypt*

Leta Hong Fincher, *Tsinghua University, China*

Johanna B. Fine, *Center for Reproductive Rights*

Victoria Flanagan, *Macquarie University, Australia*

Heather Kohler Flynn, *Sonoma State University, USA*

Kate Foord, *Melbourne, Australia*

David Forstadt, *Medaille College, USA*

Johanna E. Foster, *Monmouth University, New Jersey, USA*

Susan Franceschet, *University of Calgary, Canada*

Elena Frank, *Arizona State University, USA*

Suzanne Franzway, *University of South Australia, Australia*

Heather Fraser, *Flinders University of South Australia, Australia*

David Frederick, *Chapman University, USA*

Nicole L Freiner, *Bryant University, USA*

Erica J. Friedman, *The Graduate Center, City University of New York, USA*

Cameron Kiely Froude, *University of Connecticut, USA*

Sara Fry, *New York University, USA*

Jessica J. Fulton, *Durham VA Medical Center, USA*

Donna R. Gabaccia, *University of Toronto, Canada*

Sonnet D. Gabbard, *Ohio State University, USA*

Audrey Gadzekpo, *University of Ghana, Ghana*

Christine Ward Gailey, *University of California, Riverside, USA*

Maria M. Galano, *University of Michigan, USA*

José E. García, *Catholic University of Paraguay, Paraguay*

Trevor G. Gates, *State University of New York at Brockport, USA*

Amber Gazso, *York University, UK*

Giulia Garofalo Geymonat, *University of Lund, Sweden*

Sanjukta T. Ghosh, *Castleton State College, Vermont, USA*

Gloria Giarratano, *Louisiana State University Health Sciences Center New Orleans, USA*

Holly Giblin, *Flinders University of South Australia, Australia*

Theodore K. Gideonse, *University of California, Los Angeles, USA*

Brenda I. Gill, *Alabama State University, USA*

Harjant Gill, *Towson University, Maryland, USA*

Jungyun Gill, *Stonehill College, USA*

Michael Gill, *Syracuse University, USA*

Patti Giuffre, *Texas State University, USA*

Judith Glazer-Raymo, *New York, USA*

Jacob W. Glazier, *University of West Georgia, USA*

Petra Glover, *University of West London, UK*

Dorota Golańska, *University of Łódź, Poland*

Rachelle S. Gold, *North Carolina Central University, USA*

Jamie L. Goldenberg, *University of South Florida, USA*

Alyssa Goldstein, *University of Massachusetts Amherst, USA*

Casey Golomski, *University of Massachusetts Boston, USA*

Stephanie Gonzalez-Guittar, *Valdosta State University, USA*

Linda Gordon, *New York University, USA*

Devon R. Goss, *University of Connecticut, USA*

Brendan Gough, *Leeds Beckett University, UK*

Gorkey Gourab, *International Centre for Diarrhoeal Disease Research, Bangladesh*

Amanda Gouws, *University of Stellenbosch, South Africa*

Jacqueline Granleese, *University of East Anglia, UK*

Sandra A. Graham-Bermann, *University of Michigan, USA*

Heidi Grasswick, *Middlebury College, USA*

Sheila Greene, *Trinity College, Republic of Ireland*

Pauline Greenhill, *University of Winnipeg, Canada*

Sandra Grey, *Victoria University of Wellington, New Zealand*

Alison I. Griffith, *York University, Toronto, Canada*

Danielle Griffiths, *University of Manchester, UK*

Mark D. Griffiths, *Nottingham Trent University, UK*

Elizabeth Groeneveld, *Old Dominion University, USA*

Nancy Gropper, *Bank Street Graduate School of Education, USA*

Rita M. Gross, *University of Wisconsin–Eau Claire, USA*

Katja M. Guenther, *University of California, Riverside, USA*

Lia D. Guerra, *St. Mary's University, USA*

Cari Gulbrandsen, *University of Calgary, Canada*

Samanthi J. Gunawardana, *Monash University, Australia*

Barbara Gurr, *University of Connecticut, USA*

Samar Habib, *School of Oriental and African Studies (SOAS), UK*

Ulla Hakala, *University of Turku, Finland*

Beatrice Halsaa, *University of Oslo, Norway*

Mary Hames, *University of the Western Cape, South Africa*

C. Winter Han, *Middlebury College, USA*

Farzana Haniffa, *University of Colombo, Sri Lanka*

Karen B. Hanna, *University of California, Santa Barbara, USA*

Alison Happel-Parkins, *University of Memphis, USA*

Tara Harney-Mahajan, *University of Connecticut, USA*

Wendy Harcourt, *International Institute of Social Studies, Erasmus University, The Netherlands*

Anita Harris, *Deakin University, Australia*

Denishia Harris, *University of Connecticut, USA*

John Harris, *University of Manchester, UK*

Mechthild Hart, *DePaul University, USA*

Courtney C. C. Heard Harvey, *South University, USA*

Narin Hassan, *Georgia Institute of Technology, USA*

Brianne Hastie, *University of South Australia, Australia*

Sarah L. Hastings, *Radford University, USA*

Susan Hawthorne, *James Cook University, Australia*

Nikki Hayfield, *University of the West of England (UWE), UK*

Brenda Hayman, *University of Western Sydney, Australia*

Jeff Hearn, *Örebro University, Sweden*

Robert B. Heasley, *Indiana University of Pennsylvania, USA*

Madeline Heilman, *New York University, USA*

Kenneth J. Heineman, *Angelo State University, USA*

Jan Paul Heisig, *WZB Berlin Social Science Center, Germany*

Susan Hekman, *The University of Texas at Arlington, USA*

Kevin Henderson, *University of Massachusetts Amherst, USA*

Tereza Hendl, *University of Sydney, Australia*

Alexandra Hendley, *Murray State University, USA*

Louis van den Hengel, *Maastricht University, The Netherlands*

Kathryn Henne, *Australian National University, Canberra*

Laura V. Heston, *University of Massachusetts Amherst, USA*

Chris Hickey, *Deakin University, Australia*

Encarnación Hidalgo-Tenorio, *University of Granada, Spain*

Angel M. Hinzo, *University of California, Davis, USA*

Keiko Hirao, *Sophia University Graduate School of Environmental Studies, Japan*

Maaya Kuri Hitomi, *University of Saskatchewan, Canada*

Jessica P. Hodge, *University of St. Thomas, Minnesota, USA*

Ulrika Holgersson, *University of Lund, Sweden*

Tora Holmberg, *Uppsala University, Sweden*

M. Morgan Holmes, *Wilfrid Laurier University, Canada*

Martin Holt, *University of New South Wales, Australia*

Sharon Horne, *University of Massachusetts, USA*

Carla Houkamau, *The University of Auckland, New Zealand*

Lola D. Houston, *University of Vermont, USA*

Alex Hrycak, *Reed College, USA*

Thomas K. Hubbard, *The University of Texas at Austin, USA*

April Hudson, *Texas State University, USA*

Edward F. Hudspeth, *Henderson State University, Arkadelphia, USA*

Elizabeth Huffaker, *University of Washington Bothell, USA*

Matthew W. Hughey, *University of Connecticut, USA*

Anne Laure Humbert, *European Institute for Gender Equality, Lithuania*

Mary E. Hunt, *Women's Alliance for Theology, Ethics and Ritual (WATER), USA*

Heather McKee Hurwitz, *University of California, Santa Barbara, USA*

Liisa Husu, *Örebro University, Sweden*

Janet Hyde, *University of Wisconsin–Madison, USA*

Chrys Ingraham, *Purchase College, State University of New York, USA*

Jennifer C. Ingrey, *University of Western Ontario, Canada*

Kristen Intemann, *Montana State University, USA*

Dan Irving, *Carleton University, Canada*

Lisa Isherwood, *University of Winchester, UK*

Viginta Ivaškaite-Tamošiune, *European Institute for Gender Equality, Lithuania*

Meagan Jacobs, *University of Cape Town, South Africa*

Joyce Jacobsen, *Wesleyan University, USA*

Diederik F. Janssen, *Independent Researcher, The Netherlands*

Rusi Jaspal, *De Montfort University, UK*

Daniela Jauk, *University of Graz, Austria*

Erik Jensen, *Miami University, USA*

Jing Jiang, *Bowling Green State University, USA*

Janet Elise Johnson, *Brooklyn College, City University of New York, USA*

Kimberly P. Johnson, *Tennessee State University, USA*

Angela Lewellyn Jones, *Elon University, USA*

Rene A. Jones, *Medaille College, USA*

Anelis Kaiser, *University of Bern, Switzerland*

Nyokabi Kamau, *Kenya*

Natalie Kate Kamber, *Deakin University, Australia*

Akane Kanai, *Monash University, Melbourne, Australia*

Melinda D. Kane, *East Carolina University, USA*

Nazneen Kane, *Mount St. Joseph University, USA*

Dredge Byung'chu Käng, *Emory University, USA*

Venetia Kantsa, *University of the Aegean, Greece*

Julia Kaplinska, *Miami University, USA*

Katharina Karcher, *University of Cambridge, UK*

Ellyn Kaschak, *San Jose State University, USA and the University for Peace, Costa Rica*

Noriko Kawahashi, *Nagoya Institute of Technology, Japan*

Britt-Inger Keisu, *Umeå University, Sweden*

Maura Kelly, *Portland State University, USA*

Emily Huddart Kennedy, *Washington State University, USA*

Sujay Kentlyn, *Evergreen Life Care, West Gosford, Australia*

Elizabeth Kerekere, *University of Wellington, New Zealand*

Yael Keshet, *Western Galilee Academic College, Israel*

Ursula Kessels, *Freie Universität Berlin, Germany*

Sahar Khamis, *University of Maryland, USA*

Niaz Morshed Khan, *International Centre for Diarrhoeal Disease Research, Bangladesh*

Sharful Islam Khan, *International Centre for Diarrhoeal Disease Research, Bangladesh*

Neha Khetrapal, *Macquarie University, Australia*

Kareem Khubchandani, *The University of Texas at Austin, USA*

Dustin Kidd, *Temple University, USA*

Linda Kiernan, *Trinity College, Republic of Ireland*

Wong Kin-yuen, *Hong Kong Shue Yan University, People's Republic of China*

Christa Knellwolf King, *Sultan Qaboos University, Oman, and University of Queensland, Australia*

Gary Kinsman, *Laurentian University, Canada*

Amy van Kirk, *University of Missouri–Kansas City, USA*

Mark Kiss, *University of Saskatchewan, Canada*

Sally L. Kitch, *Arizona State University, USA*

Andrzej Klimczuk, *Warsaw School of Economics, Poland*

Magdalena Klimczuk-Kochańska, *University of Warsaw, Poland*

Keith Klostermann, *Medaille College, USA*

Kai Kohlsdorf, *University of Washington, USA*

Simone Kolysh, *CUNY Graduate Center, New York, USA*

Elena Kosterina, *University of Massachusetts Boston, USA*

Kendall Kozai, *University of San Francisco, USA*

Elias Krell, *Vassar College, USA*

Andrea Krizsan, *Central European University, Hungary*

Samantha Kwan, *University of Houston, USA*

Michelle N. Lafrance, *St. Thomas University, Canada*

Judith Lakämper, *Wayne State University, USA*

Sharon Lamb, *University of Massachusetts Boston, USA*

Sarah A. Lamer, *University of Denver, USA*

Jennifer E. Lansford, *Duke University, USA*

Joseph De Lappe, *Open University, UK*

Rüdiger Lautmann, *University of Bremen, Germany*

Lisa Lazard, *Open University, UK*

Nathalie Lebon, *Gettysburg College, USA*

Jin-kyung Lee, *University of California, San Diego, USA*

Robyn Lee, *Brock University, Canada*

Theresa Man Ling Lee, *University of Guelph, Canada*

Melinda A. Lemke, *The University of Texas at Austin, USA*

Emma Lesser, *University of Connecticut, USA*

Irene Riobóo Lestón, *European Institute for Gender Equality, Lithuania*

Arlene Lev, *University at Albany, State University of New York, USA*

Roy J. Levin, *Porterbrook Clinic, UK*

Susan Levine, *University of Cape Town, South Africa*

Donald P. Levy, *Siena College, New York, USA*

Ellen Lewin, *University of Iowa, USA*

Rachel Lewis, *George Mason University, USA*

Vek Lewis, *The University of Sydney, Australia*

Adela C. Licona, *University of Arizona, USA*

Stephanie A. Limoncelli, *Loyola Marymount University, USA*

Cirila P. Limpangog, *Victoria University, Australia*

Annulla Linders, *University of Cincinnati, USA*

Lakshmi Lingam, *Tata Institute of Social Sciences, Hyderabad, India*

Taylor Livingston, *University of North Carolina at Chapel Hill, USA*

Barbara Ellen Logan, *University of Wyoming, USA*

Emanuela Lombardo, *Universidad Complutense de Madrid, Spain*

Liza Lorenzetti, *University of Calgary, Canada*

C. Laura Lovin, *University of Strathclyde, Scotland*

Michael Lowe, *Drexel University, Philadelphia, USA*

Hwei-syin Lu, *Tzu Chi University, Hualien City, Taiwan*

Aliza Luft, *University of Wisconsin–Madison, USA*

Zakiya Luna, *University of California, Santa Barbara, USA*

Justin Lynn, *California State University, USA*

Steven Jay Lynn, *Binghamton University, USA*

Emily J. Macgillivray, *University of Michigan, USA*

Sarah Maddison, *University of New South Wales, Australia*

Daniel C. Maguire, *Marquette University, Milwaukee, USA*

Manissa M. Maharawal, *CUNY Graduate Center, USA*

Mary-Margaret Mahoney, *University of Connecticut, USA*

Andrea Major, *University of Leeds, UK*

Priscilla Marie Maldonado, *Quinnipiac University, USA*

Josephine Maltby, *Sheffield University Management School, UK*

Anna Rita Manca, *European Institute for Gender Equality, Lithuania*

Francesca Manzi, *New York University, USA*

Susan Markens, *Lehman College and The Graduate Center, City University of New York, USA*

Jill Marshall, *University of Leicester, UK*

Lisa Maruca, *Wayne State University, USA*

Frances E. Mascia-Lees, *Rutgers University, New Brunswick, USA*

Hiroaki Matsuura, *University of Oxford, UK*

Alyssa J. Matteucci, *University of Pennsylvania, USA*

Siobhán M. Mattison, *Boston University, USA*

Hamid Mavani, *Claremont Graduate University, USA*

Alexander Maxwell, *Victoria University of Wellington, New Zealand*

Elizabeth Maynard, *McGill University, Canada*

Ama Mazama, *Temple University, USA*

Jean M. McAvoy, *Open University, UK*

Marguerite M. McCarty, *Medaille College, USA*

Karen M. McCormack, *Wheaton College, USA*

Judith A. McDonald, *Lehigh University, USA*

Nikki McGary, *University of Connecticut, USA*

Justin McGuinness, *American University of Paris, France*

David McInnes, *University of Western Sydney, Australia*

Joanna McIntyre, *University of Queensland, Australia*

Jennifer McMahon-Howard, *Kennesaw State University, USA*

Lynda Measor, *University of Brighton, UK*

Peace A. Medie, *University of Ghana, Ghana*

Brinda J. Mehta, *Mills College, USA*

Elva F. Orozco Mendoza, *Drexel University, USA*

Calvin Mercer, *East Carolina University, USA*

Terri L. Messman-Moore, *Miami University, USA*

Jill Theresa Messing, *Arizona State University, USA*

Helene Meyers, *Southwestern University, USA*

Letitia Meynell, *Dalhousie University, Canada*

Wendy Michaels, *University of Newcastle, Australia*

B. Paige Miller, *University of Wisconsin–River Falls, USA*

Cindy Faith Miller, *Arizona State University, USA*

David I. Miller, *Northwestern University, USA*

Khadijah O. Miller, *Norfolk State University, USA*

Shaeleya Miller, *California State University, USA*

Manasee Mishra, *IIHMR University, India*

Valentine M. Moghadam, *Northeastern University, USA*

Haideh Moghissi, *York University, Canada*

Patricia Mohammed, *University of the West Indies, Trinidad*

Joseph Molleur, *Cornell College, USA*

Barbara Molony, *Santa Clara University, USA*

Jane Montague, *University of Derby, UK*

Roy Moodley, *University of Toronto, Canada*

Louise Morley, *University of Sussex, UK*

Kasey Lynn Morris, *University of South Florida, USA*

Todd G. Morrison, *University of Saskatchewan, Canada*

Véronique Mottier, *University of Cambridge, UK and University of Lausanne, Switzerland*

Anna Muraco, *Loyola Marymount University, Los Angeles, USA*

Mary Murray, *Massey University, New Zealand*

Amber Jamilla Musser, *Washington University in St. Louis, USA*

Naama Nagar, *University of Wisconsin–Madison, USA*

Joane Nagel, *University of Kansas, USA*

Victoria M. Nagy, *La Trobe University, Australia*

Supriya M. Nair, *Tulane University, USA*

Nancy A. Naples, *University of Connecticut, USA*

Catherine Nash, *Brock University, Canada*

Misaki N. Natsuaki, *University of California, Riverside, USA*

Elly Jean Nielsen, *University of Saskatchewan, Canada*

Harriet Bjerrum Nielsen, *Centre for Gender Research, University of Oslo, Norway*

Yolanda Flores Niemann, *University of North Texas, USA*

Asimina Ino Nikolopoulou, *Northeastern University, USA*

Ramesh Mario Nithiyendran, *University of New South Wales, Australia*

Ruth Nina-Estrella, *University of Puerto Rico, Río Piedras Campus, Puerto Rico*

Ligia Nobrega, *European Institute for Gender Equality, Lithuania*

Rachel E. Nolan, *University of Connecticut, USA*

Sonny Nordmarken, *University of Massachusetts Amherst, USA*

Caroline Norma, *RMIT University, Australia*

Claire M. Norris, *Xavier University of Louisiana, USA*

Kristine L. Nowak, *University of Connecticut, USA*

Camille Nurka, *Independent Scholar*

Caryl Nuñez, *University of Connecticut, USA*

Roel van den Oever, *VU University Amsterdam, The Netherlands*

Leslie W. O'Ryan, *Western Illinois University, USA*

Ryan S. Ogilvy, *United States Air Force, Biomedical Science Corps, USA*

Marta Olasik, *University of Warsaw, Poland*

Domitilla Olivieri, *Utrecht University, The Netherlands*

Hiroshi Ono, *Hitotsubashi University, Japan*

Peter Ørebech, *UIT Arctic University of Norway, Norway*

Julio Orozco, *Oregon State University, USA*

Jennifer K. Page, *Northwestern Oklahoma State University, USA*

Marek Palasinski, *University of Derby, UK*

Catherine Helen Palczewski, *University of Northern Iowa, USA*

Michal Palgi, *University of Haifa, Israel*

Ingrid Palmary, *University of the Witwatersrand, South Africa*

Amrita Pande, *University of Cape Town, South Africa*

Vanessa R. Panfil, *Old Dominion University, Virginia, USA*

Carole Pateman, *University of California, Los Angeles, USA*

Smita M. Patil, *Indira Gandhi National Open University, India*

Adele Pavlidis, *Griffith University, Australia*

Susan C. Pearce, *East Carolina University, USA*

Nicholas Pedriana, *University of Wisconsin–Whitewater, USA*

Elizabeth Peel, *University of Worcester, UK*

Natalie M. Peluso, *Concordia College, USA*

Miriam Pensack, *Université Paris I/Panthéon-Sorbonne, France*

Christina Morris Penn-Goetsch, *Cornell College, USA*

Alejandra Pérez, *University of Washington Bothell, USA*

Devin M. Pinkston, *Valparaiso University, USA*

Adriana Piscitelli, *State University of Campinas, Brazil*

Carine Plancke, *Roehampton University, UK*

Liedeke Plate, *Radboud University Nijmegen, The Netherlands*

Alison Plumb, *Independent Scholar*

David Plummer, *Griffith University, Australia*

Raluca Maria Popa, *Central European University, Hungary*

Crystal Powell, *University of Cape Town, South Africa*

Camilla Power, *University of East London, UK*

Jennifer Power, *La Trobe University, Australia*

Vivian Price, *California State University, Dominguez Hills, USA*

Bruce Prideaux, *Central Queensland University, Australia*

Rosslyn Prosser, *University of Adelaide, Australia*

Amira Proweller, *DePaul University, USA*

Doyle K. Pruitt, *Keuka College, USA*

Jyoti Puri, *Simmons College, USA*

Dongxiao Qin, *Western New England University, USA*

Freyja L. Quick, *University of Surrey, UK*

Christine L. Quinan, *Utrecht University, The Netherlands*

Rosemary Radford Ruether, *Claremont School of Theology and Claremont Graduate University, USA*

Hilary Radner, *University of Otago, New Zealand*

Ellie Ragland, *University of Missouri, USA*

Mahbubur Rahman, *International Centre for Diarrhoeal Disease Research, Bangladesh*

Muhammad Aziz Rahman, *Australian Catholic University, Melbourne, Australia*

Senthorun Raj, *The University of Sydney, Australia*

V. G. Julie Rajan, *Rutgers University, New Jersey, USA*

Katherine Ramos, *University of Houston, USA*

Vicky Randall, *University of Essex, UK*

Elizabeth Ransom, *University of Richmond, USA*

Holly M. Reed, *Valparaiso University, USA*

Pamela C. Regan, *California State University, Los Angeles, USA*

Joanna Regulska, *University of California, Davis, USA*

Jolanta Reingarde, *European Institute for Gender Equality, Lithuania*

Larissa Remennick, *Bar-Ilan University, Israel*

Christina Richards, *Nottinghamshire NHS Trust Gender Clinic, UK*

James T. Richardson, *University of Nevada, USA*

Stephanie J. Richmond, *Norfolk State University, USA*

Damien W. Riggs, *Flinders University of South Australia, Australia*

Susan Harris Rimmer, *Australian National University, Canberra, Australia*

Susanne Rippl, *Technische Universität Chemnitz, Germany*

William J. Robertson, *University of Arizona, USA*

Brandon Andrew Robinson, *The University of Texas at Austin, USA*

Christine M. Robinson, *James Madison University, USA*

Monique N. Rodriguez, *St. Mary's University, Texas, USA*

Katrina Roen, *University of Oslo, Norway*

Nicola Rollock, *University of Birmingham, UK*

Brandon Ronne, *Chapman University, USA*

Paul Roscoe, *University of Maine, USA*

David Rosen, *Independent Scholar*

Lisa H. Rosen, *Texas Woman's University, USA*

Sue V. Rosser, *San Francisco State University, USA*

Geraldine Rossiter, *Union Institute & University, USA*

Silke Roth, *University of Southampton, UK*

Barbara Katz Rothman, *City University of New York, USA*

Leonie Rowan, *Griffith University, Australia*

David L. Rowl, *Valparaiso University, USA*

David A. Rubin, *University of South Florida, USA*

Linda J. Rubin, *Texas Woman's University, USA*

Anne Sisson Runyan, *University of Cincinnati, USA*

Dawn M. Rutecki, *Indiana University, USA*

Janette Rutterford, *Open University Business School, UK*

Kanchana N. Ruwanpura, *University of Edinburgh, UK*

J. Michael Ryan, *The American University in Cairo, Egypt*

Robyn Ryle, *Hanover College, USA*

Maya Sabatello, *Columbia University, USA*

Macarena Sáez, *American University Washington College of Law, USA*

Anna Dodson Saikin, *Rice University, USA*

Nida Sajid, *Rutgers University, USA*

Emily R. Cabaniss Sam, *Houston State University, USA*

Danielle V. Samuels, *University of California, Riverside, USA*

Teela Sanders, *University of Leeds, UK*

Gagan Sandhu, *Chapman University, USA*

Varunee Faii Sangganjanavanich, *The University of Akron, USA*

Michelle San Pedro, *University of Connecticut, Storrs, USA*

Gustavo Gomes da Costa Santos, *Federal University of Pernambuco, Brazil*

Nancy Santucci, *Rutgers University, USA*

Lauren M. Sardi, *Quinnipiac University, USA*

Casey Saunders, *Purchase College, State University of New York, USA*

Daniel G. Saunders, *University of Michigan School of Social Work, USA*

Kevin W. Saunders, *Michigan State University, USA*

Ann M. Savage, *Butler University, USA*

Marian Sawer, *Australian National University, Australia*

Graham Scambler, *University of Surrey, UK*

Londa Schiebinger, *Stanford University, USA*

Mimi Schippers, *Tulane University, USA*

Linda Schlossberg, *Harvard University, USA*

Sigrid Schmitz, *University of Vienna, Austria*

Tammy S. Schultz, *Marine Corps War College, Virginia, and Georgetown University, USA*

Carolyn Schwarz, *Goucher College, USA*

Terri Scott, *Chapman University, USA*

Denise A. Segura, *University of California, Santa Barbara, USA*

Priscilla Rose Selvaraj, *Ohio University, USA*

Lakshmen Senanayake, *Colombo, Sri Lanka*

Mary Cay Sengstock, *Wayne State University, USA*

José Fernando Serrano-Amaya, *Colombia, Australia*

Svati P. Shah, *University of Massachusetts Amherst, USA*

Shirley Shalev, *Harvard Medical School, USA*

Lisa Sharlach, *University of Alabama at Birmingham, USA*

Alankaar Sharma, *University of Minnesota–Twin Cities, USA*

Simona Sharoni, *State University of New York at Plattsburgh, USA*

Rhonda Sharp, *University of South Australia, Australia*

Rhonda Vonshay Sharpe, *Bucknell University, USA*

Susan E. Short, *Brown University, USA*

Carisa R. Showden, *University of North Carolina at Greensboro, USA and University of Auckland, New Zealand*

Helene A. Shugart, *University of Utah, USA*

Amy Shuman, *Ohio State University, USA*

Eva Sierminska, *LISER (Luxembourg Institute of Socio-Economic Research), Luxembourg*

Kalinga Tudor Silva, *University of Peradeniya, Sri Lanka*

Louise Bordeaux Silverstein, *Yeshiva University, USA*

Solange Simões, *Eastern Michigan University, USA*

April Sizemore-Barber, *University of California, Berkeley, USA*

Anneke Smelik, *Radboud University Nijmegen, The Netherlands*

Linda Smircich, *University of Massachusetts Amherst, USA*

Christine A. Smith, *University of Wisconsin–Green Bay, USA*

Kate E. Snyder, *University of Louisville, USA*

Anit Somech, *University of Haifa, Israel*

Jamie M. Sommer, *Stony Brook University, New York, USA*

Udi Sommer, *Tel Aviv University, Israel*

Anna Sorensen, *University of California, Santa Barbara, USA*

Natalie Spagnuolo, *York University, Canada*

Tamsin Spargo, *Liverpool John Moores University, UK*

Lynne Stahl, *Cornell University, USA*

Daniela Stehlik, *Australian National University, Australia*

Alison Stone, *The University of Lancaster, UK*

Gila Stopler, *College of Law and Business, Israel*

Carolyn Strange, *Australian National University, Australia*

Mangala Subramaniam, *Purdue University, USA*

Oriel Sullivan, *University of Oxford, UK*

J. E. Sumerau, *University of Tampa, USA*

Eva-Maria Svensson, *University of Gothenburg, Sweden*

Kendal Swanson, *Duke University, USA*

Caroline L. Tait, *University of Saskatchewan, Canada*

Maria Tamboukou, *University of East London, UK*

Christelle Taraud, *Université Paris I/Panthéon-Sorbonne, France*

Malaena Taylor, *University of Connecticut, USA*

Nik Taylor, *Flinders University of South Australia, Australia*

Robert Teixeira, *Ontario College of Art and Design University, Canada*

Selvy Thiruchandran, *Women's Education and Research Centre, Sri Lanka*

Gwynn Thomas, *State University of New York at Buffalo, USA*

Sue Thomas, *Pacific Institute for Research and Evaluation, USA*

Valorie Thomas, *Pomona College, USA*

Martha E. Thompson, *Northeastern Illinois University, USA*

Ryan Richard Thoreson, *New York, USA*

Robert J. Thornton, *Lehigh University, USA*

Irmgard Tischner, *University of the West of England, UK*

Rosalba Todaro, *Centro de Estudios de la Mujer, Chile*

Erin Tolley, *University of Toronto, Canada*

Michelle Tolson, *Siem Reap Citizens for Health, Educational and Social Issues (SiRCHESI), Cambodia*

Stacy Torres, *New York University, USA*

Jemma Tosh, *University of Chester, UK*

Eileen M. Trauth, *Pennsylvania State University, USA*

Manon Tremblay, *University of Ottawa, Canada*

Iris van der Tuin, *Utrecht University, The Netherlands*

Sarah E. Ullman, *University of Illinois at Chicago, USA*

Vindhya Undurti, *Tata Institute of Social Sciences, India*

Meg Upchurch, *Transylvania University, USA*

Jane M. Ussher, *University of Western Sydney, Australia*

Stephen Valocchi, *Trinity College, Hartford, USA*

Tiina Vares, *University of Canterbury, New Zealand*

Connie de la Vega, *University of San Francisco, USA*

Jessica Velasquez, *University of Washington Bothell, USA*

Mieke Verloo, *Radboud University, The Netherlands*

Elizabeth Victor, *William Paterson University, USA*

Sonja Vivienne, *University of Queensland, Australia*

Lisa Wade, *Occidental College, USA*

Miranda R. Waggoner, *Florida State University, USA*

Lisa K. Waldner, *University of St. Thomas, USA*

Christine Walsh, *University of Calgary, Canada*

Lena Wängnerud, *University of Gothenburg, Sweden*

Leah R. Warner, *Ramapo College of New Jersey, USA*

Sam Warner, *Salford University, UK*

Julia Wartenberg, *Independent Scholar*

Ryan J. Watson, *University of Arizona, USA*

Ann Weatherall, *Victoria University of Wellington, New Zealand*

Doris Weichselbaumer, *University of Linz, Austria*

Karen Weingarten, *City University of New York, USA*

Christina Welch, *University of Winchester, UK*

Carl Wellman, *Washington University in Saint Louis, USA*

Nicole Westmarland, *Durham University, UK*

Emily E. Wheeler, *University of Massachusetts Boston, USA*

Adam White, *University of Winchester, UK*

Pamala Wiepking, *Erasmus University Rotterdam, The Netherlands*

James D. Wilets, *Nova Southeastern University, USA*

Thomas Wiley, *Colgate University, USA*

Graham Willett, *University of Melbourne, Australia*

Daniel K. Williams, *University of West Georgia, USA*

Marian R. Williams, *Appalachian State University, USA*

Martina Williams, *University of Nottingham, UK*

Abbey Willis, *University of Connecticut, Storrs, USA*

Justin M. Wilson, *Western Illinois University, USA*

K. J. Wininger, *University of Southern Maine, USA*

Bronwyn Winter, *The University of Sydney, Australia*

Julie A. Winterich, *Guilford College, USA*

Elizabeth Wirtz, *Purdue University, USA*

Aimee Wodda, *University of Illinois at Chicago, USA*

Kristina B. Wolff, *Gender Research Institute at Dartmouth College, USA*

Arthur Laing Ming Wong, *The Chinese University of Hong Kong, People's Republic of China*

Wendy Wood, *University of Southern California, USA*

Susan W. Woolley, *Colgate University, USA*

Linda Worrall-Carter, *Her Heart, Melbourne, Australia*

Wynne Wright, *Michigan State University, USA*

Diane Kholos Wysocki, *University of Nebraska at Kearney, USA*

Reyn Yoshiura, *Chapman University, USA*

Arshia U. Zaidi, *University of Ontario Institute of Technology, Canada*

Jonathon Zapasnik, *Australian National University, Australia*

Patricia Zavella, *University of California, Santa Cruz, USA*

Madeline Zavodny, *Agnes Scott College, USA*

Yuejen Zhao, *Department of Health, Northern Territory, Australia*

Wang Zheng, *University of Michigan, USA*

Lal Zimman, *University of California, Santa Barbara, USA*

Carole Zufferey, *University of South Australia, Australia*

Lexicon

Art, Literature, and Culture

Anthropological Perspectives on Sex 78
Archetype 110
Bollywood 185
Camp 209
Children's Literature and Gender 252
Cognitive Critical and Cultural Theory 293
Fairy Tales 579
Feminist Art Practice 767
Feminist Film Theory 807
Feminist Magazines 819
Feminist Utopian Writing 901
Gay Male Literature 935
Gaze 940
Geisha 942
Gynocriticism 1233
Heterosexual Imaginary 1261
Hip-Hop/Rap 1287
Images of Gender and Sexuality in Latin America 1371
Images of Gender and Sexuality in Southern Africa 1380
Images of Gender and Sexuality of Māori 1376
Lesbian Cultural Criticism 1514
Lesbian Performance 1527
Lesbian Popular Music 1529
Monstrous-Feminine 1727
Oral Tradition 1810
Performance Art 1844
Popular Culture and Gender 1868
Pornography, Feminist Legal and Political Debates on 1877
Queer Anglophone Literature 1961
Queer Literary Criticism 1965
Queer Performance 1974
Representation 2025
Riot grrrl 2046
Sex and Culture 2080
Taboo 2303
Visual Culture 2399
Visual Culture and Gender 2403
Women as Cultural Markers/Bearers 2445
Women as Producers of Culture 2458
Women's Writing 2589

Body Practices

Contraception and Contraceptives 358
Cosmetic Surgery in the United States 365
Embodiment and the Phenomenological Tradition 520
Fashion 591
Female Genital Cutting 609
Footbinding 920
Sadomasochism, Domination, and Submission 2051
Sex Reassignment Surgery 2095
Sex Selection 2102
Skin Lightening/Bleaching 2247
Tattooing and Piercing 2305

Demography

Fertility Rates   911
Heterosexual Marriage Trends in the West   1265
Life Expectancy   1612

Economics

Economic Globalization and Gender   511
Entrepreneurship   537
Feminist Economics   788
Free Trade Zones   922
Gender and Development   968
Gender Audit   946
Gender Budget   961
Global Restructuring   1221
Informal Economy   1415
Microcredit and Microlending   1697
Poverty in Global Perspective   1905
Privatization   1914
Sex Tourism   2104
Structural Adjustment   2284
Sustainable Livelihoods   2298
Women in Development   2449
Women's Banking   2557

Education

Curriculum Transformation   396
Educational Testing and Gender   515
Feminist Pedagogy   844
Gender Equity in Education in the United States   993
Gender Inequality in Education   1046
Higher Education and Gender in the United States   1270
Mentoring   1691
Non-Sexist Education   1777
Sex Education in the United Kingdom and United States   2092
Sex Segregation and Education in the United States   2097
Single-Sex Education and Coeducation   2243

Environment/Ecology

Climate Change and Gender   280
Deep Ecology   416
Ecofeminism   502
Environment and Gender   539
Environmental Disasters and Gender   544
Environmental Justice   548
Environmental Politics and Women's Activism   550
Female Farming Systems   605
Hunger and Famine   1354
Mother Nature   1731

Family/Household

Adultery, Cultural Views of   21
Arranged Marriages (in South Asia)   112
Cohabitation and *Ekageikama* in the Kandyan Kingdom (Sri Lanka)   301
Commitment Ceremonies   321
Division of Labor, Domestic   454
Dowry and Bride-Price   476
Extended Families   576
Families of Choice   582
Fictive Kin   918
Household Livelihood Strategies   1322
Kinship   1489
Lesbians as Community Other Mothers   1538
Mail-Order Brides   1619
Matriarchy   1649

Matrilineal and Matrilocal Systems   1655
Monogamy, Biological Perspectives on   1722
Parenting in Prison   1836
Polygamy, Polygyny, and Polyandry   1866
Same-Sex Families   2053
Same-Sex Marriage   2055
Single-Parent Households   2241
Surrogacy   2296
Work–Family Balance   2593

Feminisms

Anglophone Caribbean Feminism   71
Bifurcated Consciousness   161
Black Feminist Thought   180
Borderlands   187
Capitalist Patriarchy   213
Discursive Theories of Gender   445
Feminism and Postmodernism   707
Feminism and Psychoanalysis   716
Feminism in North Africa   688
Feminism in Northeast Asia   694
Feminism in South Africa   729
Feminism in Southeast Asia   735
Feminism, Aboriginal Australia and Torres Strait Islands   618
Feminism, Anarchist   623
Feminism, Black   626
Feminism, Chicana   630
Feminism, Chinese   632
Feminism, Cultural   637
Feminism, Eighteenth-Century Britain   642
Feminism, Existential   647
Feminism, French   649
Feminism, Indo-Caribbean   654
Feminism, Islamic   658
Feminism, Latina   661
Feminism, Lesbian   666
Feminism, Liberal   669
Feminism, Material   671
Feminism, Materialist   676
Feminism, Multiracial   678
Feminism, Nineteenth-Century United States   683
Feminism, Postcolonial   702
Feminism, Poststructural   712
Feminism, Radical   726
Feminisms and Argumentation   743
Feminisms, First, Second, and Third Wave   745
Feminisms, Marxist and Socialist   749
Feminisms, Postmodern   753
Feminist Art   762
Feminist Consciousness in Historical Perspective   771
Feminist Disability Studies   783
Feminist Epistemology   794
Feminist Methodology   821
Feminist Perspectives on Whiteness   846
Feminist Standpoint Theory   867
Feminist Theories of the Body   878
Feminist Theories of Experience   883
Intersectionality   1439
Matrix of Domination   1660
Mestiza Consciousness   1693
Postfeminism   1891
Sex-Radical Feminists   2123
Sex Versus Gender Categorization   2116

Gender

Gangs and Gender   931
Gay Male Pornography   938
Gender as a Practice   1153
Gender as Institution   1052
Gender Belief System/Gender Ideology   949
Gender Bender   951
Gender Bias   953
Gender Blind   959
Gender, Definitions of   966
Gender Development, Theories of   977
Gender Identification   1023
Gender Identities and Socialization   1026

Gender Neutral   1065
Gender Oppression   1067
Gender Outlaw   1069
Gender Performance   1071
Gender Role Ideology   1159
Gender Stereotypes   1164
Gender Transgression   1167
Gender Variance   1169
Gender Violence   1172
Gendered Space   1189
Gendered Time   1191
Genderqueer   1196
Girls' Peer Cultures   1212
Hegemonic Masculinity   1255
Hijra/Hejira   1281
Human Rights and Gender   1326
Human–Animal Studies   1350
Hypermasculinity   1361
Identity Politics   1365
Initiation Rites   1424
Internet and Gender   1433
Masculinism   1625
Masculinities   1627
Maternal Activism   1640
Maternalism   1645
Military Masculinity   1714
Misogyny   1718

Monogamy, Sociological Perspectives on   1724
Niddah   1769
Normalization   1783
Phallocentrism and Phallogocentrism   1848
Privilege   1916
Psychology of Objectification   1956
Reproductive Choice   2027
Sisterhood   2245
Stone Butch   2274
Third Genders   2311
Third World Women   2314
Tomboys and Sissies   2319
Trans Identities, Psychological Perspectives   2328
Trans Theorizing   2331
Transgender Health and Healthcare   2333
Transgender Politics   2346
Transphobia   2357
Transvestitism   2362
Two-Spirit   2364
Violence Against Women in Global Perspective   2386
Women in Non-Traditional Work Fields   2451
Women Travelers   2466
Yoruba Culture, Religion, and Gender   2606

Gender, Politics, and the State

Amazons   53
Community Other Mothers   345
Feminist Theories of the Welfare State   892
Gender, Politics, and the State in Australia and New Zealand   1077
Gender, Politics, and the State in Central and Eastern Europe   1082
Gender, Politics, and the State in East Asia   1093
Gender, Politics, and the State in Latin America   1104
Gender, Politics, and the State in Northern Africa   1116
Gender, Politics, and the State in South Asia   1127
Gender, Politics, and the State in Southern Africa   1133

Gender, Politics, and the State in the United States and Canada   1138
Gender, Politics, and the State in Western Europe   1144
Gender, Politics, and the State in Aboriginal Australia and Torres Strait Islands   1073
Gender, Politics, and the State: Indigenous Women   1099
Gender, Politics, and the State, and the Māori   1112
Gender, Politics, and the State: Overview   1122
Nationalism and Gender   1737
Status of Women Reports   2266
Suffrage   2293

Health

Abortion and Religion   13
Adolescent Pregnancy   19
Alternative Medicine and Therapies   47
Androgen Insensitivity Syndrome   66
Birth Control, History and Politics of   175
Breast Cancer   194
Breastfeeding in Historical and Comparative Perspective   199
Cardiac Disease and Gender   218
Complementary and Alternative Medicine   351
Dieting   430
Disease Symptoms, Gender Differences in   450
Drug and Alcohol Abuse   490
Eating Disorders and Disordered Eating   499
Female Orgasm   612
Fetal Alcohol Syndrome   914
Global Gag Rule   1218
Health Disparities   1246
Health, Healthcare, and Sexual Minorities   1250
Hormone Replacement Therapy   1318
Male Circumcision   1621
Medicine and Medicalization   1671
Menarche   1678
Menopause   1680
Midwifery   1699
Occupational Health and Safety   1797
Premenstrual Syndrome (PMS)   1910
Reproductive Health   2030
Sexually Transmitted Infections   2225
Sterilization   2268
Traditional Healing   2326
Wet Nursing   2419

History

Amazons, Dahomey   57
Courtly Love   367
Feminist Movements in Historical and Comparative Perspective   827
History of Women's Rights in International and Comparative Perspective   1289

Immigration, Colonialism, Globalization

Asylum and Gender   128
Asylum, Challenges Faced by Sexual Minorities   123
Asylum, Sexual Orientation and   133
Colonialism and Gender   303
Colonialism and Sexuality   314
Feminization of Migration   905
Immigration and Gender   1394
Immigration, Colonialism, and Globalization   1388
Refugees and Refugee Camps   2004
Xenophobia and Gender   2597

Institutions/Organizations

Athletics and Gender   137
Athletics and Homosexuality   142
Feminist Organizations, Definition of   842
Feminist Theories of Organization   887
Institutional Micropolitics   1428
Leadership and Gender   1504
LGBT Activism Among Māori   1569
LGBT Activism in Australia and New Zealand   1541
LGBT Activism in Eastern Africa   1551
LGBT Activism in Eastern and Central Europe   1557
LGBT Activism in Latin America   1563
LGBT Activism in Native North America   1578

LGBT Activism in North America   1583
LGBT Activism in Northern Africa   1588
LGBT Activism in South Asia   1590
LGBT Activism in Southeast Asia   1595
LGBT Activism in Southern Africa   1600
LGBT Activism in the Caribbean   1546
LGBT Activism in the Middle East   1573
LGBT Activism in Western Europe   1605
Sexual Violence and the Military   2210
UN Decade for Women   2367
Volunteerism and Charitable Giving   2408
Women in Combat   2441
Women's and Feminist Activism in Aboriginal Australia and Torres Strait Islands   2470
Women's and Feminist Activism Among Māori   2504
Women's and Feminist Activism in Australia and New Zealand   2475
Women's and Feminist Activism in East Asia   2485
Women's and Feminist Activism in Eastern Africa   2489
Women's and Feminist Activism in Eastern and Central Europe   2494
Women's and Feminist Activism in Latin America   2499
Women's and Feminist Activism in the Native United States and Canada   2513
Women's and Feminist Activism in Northern Africa   2518
Women's and Feminist Activism in the United States and Canada   2539
Women's and Feminist Activism in Russia, Ukraine, and Eurasia   2524
Women's and Feminist Activism in Southeast Asia   2529
Women's and Feminist Activism in Southern Africa   2534
Women's and Feminist Activism in the Caribbean   2480
Women's and Feminist Activism in the Middle East   2508
Women's and Feminist Activism in West Africa   2545
Women's and Feminist Activism in Western Europe   2548
Women's and Feminist Organizations in South Asia   2553
Women's Centers   2559

Labor

Child Labor in Comparative Perspective   234
Comparable Worth/Work of Equal Value   348
Division of Labor, Gender   456
Dual Labor Market   493
Emotion Work   525
Employment Discrimination   531
Family Wage   589
Feminization of Labor   903
Gender Wage Gap   1175
Glass Ceiling and Glass Elevator   1214
Global Care Chain   1216
Head of Household and Supplementary Earner   1241
Health Careers   1243
Hostile Work Environment in the United States   1320
Maquiladora   1623
Occupational Segregation   1799
Prostitution/Sex Work   1933
Sex Work and Sex Workers' Unionization   2118
Transnational Labor Movements   2351

Law, crime, and social policy

Abortion, Legal Status in Global Perspective on   1
Affirmative Action   24
Age of Consent in Historical and International Perspective   30
Anti-Miscegenation Laws   87

Child Custody and the Father Right Principle 229
Child Prostitution 241
Civil Rights Law and Gender in the United States 274
Clitoridectomy, Female Genital Cutting Practices, and Law 288
Convention on the Elimination of All Forms of Discrimination against Women (CEDAW) 362
Criminal Justice System and Sexuality in the United States 371
Customary Laws 399
Dowry Prohibition Act 482
Fathers and Parenting Interventions 600
Feminist Jurisprudence 812
Fetal Rights 916
Fundamentalism and Public Policy 925
Gender and the Death Penalty in Comparative Perspective 964
Gender Redistributive Policies 1155
Hate Crimes and Hate Crime Law 1235
Human Rights, International Laws and Policies on 1330
Incest, Social Practices and Legal Policies on 1399
Obscenity Laws in the United States, Canada, and Europe 1793
Parental Leave in Comparative Perspective 1832
Population Control and Population Policy 1872
Rape Law 1989
Sexual Harassment Law 2166
Sexual Orientation and the Law 2181
Sexuality and Human Rights 2217
Sodomy Law in Comparative Perspective 2262
Victim Blaming 2379
Yogyakarta Principles 2604

Media and Communication

Alternative Media 43
Chick Flicks 227
Children's Literature and Sexuality 256
Discourse and Gender 441
Genderlect 1193
Images of Gender and Sexuality in Advertising 1367
Language and Gender 1497
Media and Gender Socialization 1662
Men's Magazines 1676
Non-Sexist Language Use 1779
Sexism in Language 2131

Methodology

Archaeology and Genealogy 109
Feminist Ethnography 796
Feminist Literary Criticism 816
Feminist Objectivity 838
Feminist Publishing 855
Gender Analysis 943
Gender Bias in Research 955
Gender Difference Research 983
Outsider Within 1816
Queer Methods and Methodologies 1969
Reflexivity 1999
Sex Difference Research and Cognitive Abilities 2085
Sex-Related Difference Research 2125
Sexology and Psychological Sex Research 2133
Strong Objectivity 2282

Movements

Age of Consent and Child Marriage in India   26
Anarchism and Gender   59
Anti-Globalization Movements   82
Anti-Racist and Civil Rights Movements   96
Arab Spring Movements   107
Backlash   149
Disability Rights Movement   439
Fatherhood Movements   595
Gay and Lesbian Pride Day   933
Gender and History of Revolutions in East Asia   998
Gender and History of Revolutions in Eastern and Central Europe   1005
Gender and History of Revolutions in Northern Africa   1015
Greenham Common   1229
Intersex Movement   1443
Lesbian and Gay Movements   1516
Menstrual Activism   1682
Occupy Movements   1801
Personal is Political   1846
Pro-choice Movement in the United States   1918
Pro-Life Movement in the United States   1925
Refugee Women and Violence Against Women   2001
Right-Wing Women's Movements   2040
Self-Help Movements   2074
Transgender Movements in International Perspective   2337
Transgender Movements in the United States   2341
United States' Women's Movements in Historical Perspective   2369
Violence Against Women, Movements Against   2392
Women's Health Movement in the United States   2563
Women's Movements: Early International Movements   2567
Women's Movements: Modern International Movements   2573

Philosophy/Ethics

Ethic of Care   558
Ethics, Moral Development, and Gender   560
Indigenous Knowledges and Gender   1405
Mind/Body Split   1716
Non-Violence   1781
Women's Ways of Knowing   2584

Political Economy

Beauty Industry   157
Feminization of Poverty   907
Technosexuality   2309

Politics

Activist Mothering   17
Anti-Poverty Activism   92
Body Politics   182
Communism and Gender in the United States   337
Communism in Eastern Europe   323
Communism in Russia   328
Community and Grassroots Activism   341
Consciousness-Raising   356
Declaration of Sentiments   414
Declaration of the Rights of Women   413
Democracy and Democratization   418
Feminist Activism   759
Feminist Sex Wars   865

Femocrat   909
Gender Equality   990
Gender Indices   1036
Gender Justice   1056
Gender Mainstreaming   1062
Governance and Gender   1223
International Women's Day   1431
Lesbian and Womyn's Separatism   1536
NGOs and Grassroots Organizing   1765
Pacifism, Peace Activism, and Gender   1826
Political Participation in Western Democracies   1855
Politics of Representation   1857
Radical Lesbianism   1983
Reproductive Justice and Reproductive Rights in the United States   2035
Universal Human Rights   2375
A Vindication of the Rights of Woman   2384
Womanism   2434
Women's Political Representation   2580
Women's Worlds Conference   2586

Psychology

Alpha Male   41
Appearance Psychology   102
Child Sexual Abuse and Trauma   249
Cognitive Sex Differences, Debates on   298
Depression   423
Diagnostic and Statistical Manual of Mental Disorders (DSM), Feminist Critiques of   428
Empowerment   534
Feminist Family Therapy in the United States   804
Feminist Psychotherapy   851
Gender Development, Feminist Psychoanalytic Perspectives on   973
Gender Dysphoria   987
Gender Identity, Theories of   1030
Gender Schema Theory   1162
Homosexual Reparative Therapy   1312
Lesbian, Gay, Bisexual, and Transgender Psychologies   1522
Masculinity and Femininity, Theories of   1632
Oedipal Conflict   1805
Post-Traumatic Stress Disorder   1884
Postmodern Feminist Psychology   1900
Psychological Theory, Research, Methodology, and Feminist Critiques   1939
Psychology of Gender: History and Development of the Field   1944
Rape and Re-Victimization, Treatment of   1993
Recovered Memories   1997
Self-Esteem   2071
Sexual Objectification   2179

Religion/Spirituality

Animality and Women   76
Buddhism   201
Christianity, Gender and Sexuality   259
Christianity and Homosexuality   263
Creation Stories   369
Daoism   411
Feminine and Masculine Elements   616
Feminist Christology   769
Feminist Theology   876
Gyn/Ecology   1231
Hinduism   1282
Islam and Gender   1458
Islam and Homosexuality   1463
Judaism and Gender   1471
Judaism and Sexuality   1475
Kibbutz/Kibbutzim   1485
Menstrual Rituals   1686
Monasticism   1720
Mormonism   1729
Mysticism   1733
Nuns, Including Taiwan Buddhist   1786
Open and Affirming Religious Organizations   1808
Pacifism, Quakers, and Gender   1821

Religious Fundamentalism   2020
Sects and Cults   2066
Shaker Religion   2232
Shakti Shanti   2234
Shaman Priestesses   2236
Shari'a   2237
Shinto   2239

Wicca   2425
Witches   2427
Woman-Centeredness   2431
Womanist Theology   2439
Women-Church   2468
Women's Dirges   2561
Yin-Yang   2601

Science and Technology

Assisted Reproduction   119
Biochemistry and Physiology   166
Clinical Trials and Experimental Science, Bias against Women in   283
Cyber Intimacies   401
Cyborg Manifesto   407
Digital Divide   433
Domestic Technology   465
Eugenics, Historical and Ethical Aspects of   565
Family Planning   584
Feminist Design in Computing   776
Feminist Studies of Science   870
Gendered Innovations in Science, Health, and Technology   1181
Genetics and Racial Minorities in the United States   1199

Genetics Testing and Screening   1206
Information Technology   1419
Medical and Scientific Experimentation and Gender   1667
Neuroscience, Brain Research, and Gender   1754
Neuroscience, Brain Research, and Sexuality   1759
Scientific Motherhood   2060
Scientific Sexism and Racism   2061
Sexuopharmaceuticals   2227
Steroids   2270
Traditional and Indigenous Knowledge   2322
Women in Science   2462

Sexuality

Asexual Activism   114
Asexuality   116
Bathhouses   150
Bear Culture   155
Bisexuality   177
Celibacy   221
Chastity   225
Child Sex Offenders   246
Cisgender and Cissexual   267
Comfort Women   317
Coming Out   319
Cybersex   405
Desexualization   426
Epistemology of the Closet   554
The Hite Report on Female Sexuality   1306

Imaginary   1386
Internet Sex   1437
Intersexuality   1448
Intimacy and Sexual Relationships   1451
Kathoey   1483
Kinsey Scale   1487
Kothi   1491
Ladyboys   1495
Lesbian Continuum   1512
Lesbian Stereotypes in the United States   1531
Lesbos   1540
Masturbation   1638
Metrosexual   1695
Passing   1839
Pink Triangle   1850

Plastic Sexuality   1853
Polyamory   1862
Queer Space   1977
Regulation of Queer Sexualities   2009
Religion and Homophobia   2016
Romantic Friendship   2048
Same-Sex Sexuality in India   2057
Senior Women and Sexuality in the United States   2078
Sex Toys   2109
Sex Trafficking   2111
Sexual Addiction   2142
Sexual Fetishism   2161
Sexual Freedom, Feminist Debates in the United States on   2163
Sexual Identity and Orientation   2171
Sexual Instinct and Sexual Desire   2174
Sexual Minorities   2176
Sexual Scripts   2200
Sexual Slavery   2202
Sexual Subjectivity   2205
Sexualities   2212
Socialization and Sexuality   2257
Strap-On Sex   2276
Tearoom Trade   2307
Transsexuality   2360
Virginity   2397

Sexuality, Politics, and the State

Communism and Gender in China   329
"Don't Ask, Don't Tell" Policy in the United States   470
Intimate Citizenship   1453
Nationalism and Sexuality   1741
Sexual Citizenship in East Asia   2151
Sexual Citizenship in the Caribbean   2146
Sexual Contract   2159
Sexual Regulation and Social Control   2192
Sexual Rights   2196
Sexualizing the State   2220

Stratification and Inequality

Aging, Ageism, and Gender   34
AIDS-Related Stigma   38
Eurocentrism   574
Gender Inequality and Gender Stratification   1050
Heteronormativity and Homonormativity   1257
Heterosexism and Homophobia   1259
Homelessness and Gender   1308
Hybridity and Miscegenation   1359
Lookism   1616
Sex Discrimination   2089
Sexism   2129
Stratified Reproduction   2280
Tokenism   2317
White Supremacy and Gender   2421

Theory

Biological Determinism   173
Capabilities Approach   211
Compulsory Heterosexuality   354
Critical Race Theory   384
Earner–Carer Model   497
Economic Determinism   509
Essentialism   556
Individualism and Collectivism, Critical Feminist Perspectives on   1410
Nature–Nurture Debate   1744
Nomadic Subject   1773
Nomadic Theory   1775
Orientalism   1813
Patriarchy   1841

Positionality   1882
Postcolonialism, Theoretical and Critical Perspectives on   1886
Private/Public Spheres   1912
Purity Versus Pollution   1957
Queer Theory   1978
Relations of Ruling   2014
Social Constructionist Theory   2249

Social Identity   2251
Social Role Theory of Sex Differences   2254
Stigma   2272
Strategic Essentialism   2278
Structuralism, Feminist Approaches to   2286
Subaltern   2291
Womanist   2437

Violence

Battered Women   152
Bullying   204
Domestic Violence in the United States   467
Dowry Deaths   480
Elder Abuse and Gender   518
Emotional Abuse of Women   527
Eugenics Movements   570
Femicide   614
Gender-Based Violence   1177
Genocide   1208
Honor Killing   1314
Human Trafficking, Feminist Perspectives on   1345
Infanticide   1412
Intimate Partner Abuse   1456

Leftist Armed Struggle, Women in   1507
Militarism and Gender-Based Violence   1701
Militarism and Sex Industries   1710
Nazi Persecution of Homosexuals   1750
Rape Culture   1985
Self-Defense and Violence against Women in the United States   2069
Sexual Assault/Sexual Violence   2144
Sexual Coercion   2157
Sexual Terrorism   2208
Suttee (Sati)   2300
Victimization   2381
War, International Violence, and Gender   2411
Women Suicide Bombers (LTTE, Sri Lanka)   2429

Introduction and Acknowledgments

The academic field of gender and sexuality studies is an interdisciplinary field of scholarly inquiry that explores and interrogates the operations of gender and sexual diversity across all realms of life. Gender and sexuality studies do not stop at what most people experience as their "natural" identities, but rather proceed by questioning precisely what appears to be natural, given, and self-evident about ourselves – in the world at large, within the various collective structures and institutions that constitute societies (family, school, neighborhood, city, state, nation, and so on), in our private and personal lives, and in our sense of identity and embodiment.

Described as such, the reach of gender and sexuality studies appears limitless. Since gender and sexual diversity, in intersection with other categories of difference (e.g., race, class, ethnicity, able-bodiedness), pervade almost every aspect of life; there is no academic discipline that has nothing to say about gender and sexuality, even if some realms of study (the humanities, the social sciences) have traditionally played a more dominant role in the development of this interdisciplinary field. At the same time, gender and sexuality studies, even if they play out differently over time and cross-culturally, know no regional boundaries. This means that the field of gender and sexuality studies today is truly global in its outlook. This has not always been the case: as in so many other respects, the so-called West (Western Europe, the United States, Canada, and Australia) has dominated, and to some extent still does, dominate the realms of knowledge and modes of knowing that are generated within academia, including university-based gender and sexuality studies.

The goal we set for the *Encyclopedia of Gender and Sexuality Studies* was to reflect the wide range of topics, debates, and approaches to this exciting interdisciplinary, and increasingly, global field, while yet being forced to work with the unequal power relations that have historically marked the relations between "the West" and "the rest." While the 719 entries included in this encyclopedia may not be able to cover the entire field of gender and sexuality studies as it continues to develop in virtually all parts of the world, we hope we have captured both its complexity and its international scope.

One way in which we have sought to achieve the latter is by highlighting the contributions of scholars in gender and sexuality studies in different parts of the world. With 621 lead authors and 16 advisory and associate editors from 28 different countries, the encyclopedia reaches beyond national boundaries to comprehend theoretical questions, critical debates, and key terms that are relevant to a variety of scholars in the field across the globe – albeit often in different ways and to different effects. Jointly, the five volumes make clear how differences among and between genders and diverse sexualities are socially constructed and embedded in structures of power and of discourses that reproduce inequalities and provide the basis for distinct forms of local resistance, social movements, and political activism. The volumes, taken as a whole, further testify to the fact that the field of gender and sexuality studies has a long history that predates many twentieth-century social movements, feminist and queer publications, and political and cultural events that are often cited as pivotal to its formation and institutionalization as an academic field.

One of the challenges we faced along the way included how to define geographic regions and do justice to the diversity of scholarship and concerns within such regions. We also strived to ensure that disciplinary and interdisciplinary frames are fairly represented and attend to the theoretical range of feminist and queer approaches without privileging Western or Northern epistemologies. Even if we have not always succeeded in achieving the latter goal, given the hegemony of these approaches, we have taken care to make visible the limits of relevant entries by tempering the claims to universality. We have taken inspiration from intersectional theory to reflect the ways in which gender and sexuality are inflected by race, caste, religion, indigeneity, colonialism, nationality, cultural context, and other structures of difference and inequality.

The themes of the *Encyclopedia* range from art, literature, culture, education, economics, labor, family, science, religion, psychology, health, political economy, law, and ethics to inequality, identity, body practices, social movements, violence, human rights, immigration, colonialism, and globalization. We also make evident the ways in which culture and politics shape constructions of gender and sexuality by paying attention to the role of the state, militarism, material culture, and discourse. The organization of the *Encyclopedia* reflects contemporary approaches to gender and sexuality, while simultaneously preserving the history of the field in its many permutations.

We could not have accomplished this massive undertaking without the expertise and insight of associate editors renée c. hoogland (The Netherlands/USA), Maithree Wickramasinghe (Sri Lanka), and Angela Wong (Hong Kong); and advisory editors Tom Boellstorff, Jennifer Bickman Mendez, Parvis Mahdavi, and Tonia St. Germain (USA); Catherine Hundleby (Canada); Eva Magnusson (Sweden); Amrita Pande (South Africa); Maria del Pilar Grazioso (Guatemala); Mansah Prah (Ghana); Damien Riggs and Bronwyn Winter (Australia); J. Michael Ryan (Egypt/USA); and Cecilia Sanderberg (Brazil). My special thanks to renée c. hoogland for her contributions and insightful editorial comments to this introduction.

The quality of any interdisciplinary publication depends on the expertise of authors who are willing to share their knowledge in such a way that readers from different backgrounds, with diverse academic training, and from different parts of the world can learn from them. Many of my colleagues at the University of Connecticut and other academic sites around the world have generously taken on the equally important role of anonymous reviewer, often providing quick turn-around time to facilitate the demanding production deadlines. I am very grateful for their willingness to review entries and for their careful attention to the international and interdisciplinary goals of the *Encyclopedia*.

Managing editor Mike Ryan is the most amazing collaborator who has taken on an additional role as advisory editor to add his own expertise to the project. Editorial assistant Jenniann Colon joined me at the beginning of the project and assisted in organizing headwords or entries, identifying authors, and maintaining files. M.J. Taylor followed Jenniann in her position and was intricately involved in all aspects of the production process, including communicating with authors and editing entries. Graduate assistants Brenna Harvey and Judith Lakämper offered additional support during crucial times. The College of Liberal Arts and Sciences at University of Connecticut provided the funds to hire my wonderful editorial assistant and supported me in my other role as Director of Women's, Gender, and

Sexuality Studies. Justin Vaughan commissioned the work and encouraged us through the many changes in editors and professional staff that are inevitable with such a long-term endeavor.

Nancy A. Naples
University of Connecticut, USA
September 17, 2015

A

Abortion, Legal Status in Global Perspective on

JOHANNA B. FINE
Center for Reproductive Rights

Abortion laws vary considerably throughout the world. Currently, more than 60 percent of the world's people live in countries where induced abortion is permitted either for a wide range of reasons or without restriction as to reason. In contrast, more than 25 percent of all people reside in countries where abortion is generally prohibited. Another roughly 14 percent of the world's population resides in countries that permit abortion to preserve a woman's health.

While evidence shows that women who seek to terminate their pregnancies will do so regardless of the legality of abortion, the legal status of abortion is an important indicator of women's ability to access abortion services in safe or unsafe conditions. In countries with restrictive abortion laws, which criminalize this reproductive health service in most circumstances, many women resort to traveling to other countries to obtain legal abortion services, seeking illegal, clandestine abortion services or self-inducing an abortion. In these situations, women with financial resources may be able to travel abroad to obtain safe and legal abortion services or can afford to pay a healthcare professional to perform an illegal but safe abortion. However, other women may attempt to self-induce abortion or be forced to turn to untrained providers in unhygienic conditions to terminate their pregnancies, with attendant risks to their health and lives.

Moreover, the criminalization of abortion on broad grounds creates a chilling and stigmatizing effect that may discourage women from seeking safe abortion services even in the limited circumstances in which abortion is permitted and may inhibit the availability of information about legal abortion services. Consequently, some women may erroneously assume that they are not entitled to legal abortion services.

In countries with restrictive abortion laws, healthcare providers may be unwilling to provide abortion services, even in the limited circumstances for which they are legal, for fear of criminal sanction or as a result of the chilling effect and stigma generated by such restrictive laws. These factors may also lead healthcare providers to narrowly interpret abortion laws, further limiting women's access to this reproductive health service. Another consequence of restrictive abortion laws is that healthcare providers may lack

The Wiley Blackwell Encyclopedia of Gender and Sexuality Studies, First Edition. Edited by Nancy A. Naples.
© 2016 John Wiley & Sons, Ltd. Published 2016 by John Wiley & Sons, Ltd.

training in safe abortion procedures or the most recent technologies for performing this service. Additionally, they may have insufficient information about the circumstances in which abortion is permissible. Moreover, fear of prosecution may cause healthcare providers to deny care to women who experience complications from unsafe abortions or even miscarriages.

Legal restrictions on abortion do not reduce the number of abortions. Instead, they increase the number of women seeking illegal and unsafe abortion services, which leads to increased maternal morbidity and mortality. Each year, an estimated 22 million abortions are performed unsafely, and approximately 47,000 women die from unsafe abortion complications, accounting for 13 percent of all maternal deaths. Additionally, an estimated 5 million women suffer permanent or temporary disability as a result of unsafe abortion. Nearly all unsafe abortions occur in the developing world where most countries with restrictive abortion laws are located. As such, maternal morbidity and mortality resulting from abortion is high in countries and regions characterized by restrictive abortion laws, such as Latin America and Africa. Conversely, it is low in regions with liberal abortion laws, such as Europe.

Abortion laws appear in multiple legal sources, including statutes enacted by legislatures, regulations created by administrative agencies, and court decisions. Many of these laws and policies apply concurrently. Although abortion is a medical procedure, it has historically been addressed in penal codes and characterized as a crime. As such, most countries, even those with liberal abortion laws, have penal code provisions that delineate the circumstances in which abortion is a crime. Procuring an abortion generally carries criminal sanctions for the abortion provider and the woman who procures abortion services. For example, in the Philippines and Peru, both the abortion provider and the woman who procures an abortion are subject to punishment. Moreover, in some countries, such as El Salvador, a person who helps a woman to obtain an abortion through economic or other forms of support can be punished with imprisonment. However, many penal codes recognize exceptions under which performing an abortion does not carry any criminal penalties.

Additionally, penal code provisions regulating abortion are increasingly being supplemented or replaced by public health statutes, court decisions, and other laws and regulations specific to reproductive healthcare. For example, in 2010, Spain adopted a law on sexual and reproductive health that recognizes the right to abortion without restriction as to reason. This law repealed the provision of the penal code that punished women for illegally procuring abortions.

Table 1 classifies the abortion laws of 199 countries and, where populations exceed 1 million, semi-autonomous regions, territories, and jurisdictions of special status, into four categories that demonstrate the range of legal restrictions on abortion from most to least restrictive. Notably, in some countries with federal systems, such as Mexico, the United States, and Australia, individual territories or states within the country regulate abortion. In these circumstances, disparities among the legal status of abortion exist throughout the country. For purposes of Table 1, the classification of these countries reflects the legal status of abortion for the largest group of people.

Each country in Table 1 is categorized on the basis of a literal reading of abortion statutes, regulations, and court decisions in that country. There follows a description of each category.

Table 1 Categories of abortion laws from most to least restrictive

I. TO SAVE THE WOMAN'S LIFE OR PROHIBITED ALTOGETHER *Countries printed in bold make an explicit exception to save a woman's life*	II. TO PRESERVE HEALTH *(also to save the woman's life).* *Countries printed in bold recognize an exception to preserve a woman's mental health*	III. SOCIO-ECONOMIC GROUNDS *(also to save a woman's life and health)*	IV. WITHOUT RESTRICTION AS TO REASON
Afghanistan	Algeria	Barbados	Albania PA
Andorra	Argentina R	**Belize** F	Armenia PA
Angola	Bahamas	Cyprus R/F	Australia ◆
Antigua & Barbuda	Benin R/I/F	Fiji R/I/F/PA	Austria*
Bangladesh	Bolivia R/I	Finland R/I/F/+	Azerbaijan
Bhutan R/I/+	**Botswana** R/I/F	Great Britain F	Bahrain
Brazil R/+	Burkina Faso R/I/F	Hong Kong R/I/F	Belarus
Brunei Darussalam	Burundi	Iceland R/I/F/+	Belgium*
Central African Rep.	Cameroon R	India PA/R/F	Bosnia Herzegovina PA
Chile ×	Chad F	Japan SA/R	Bulgaria
Congo (Brazzaville)	**Colombia** R/I/F	Saint Vincent & Grenadines R/I/F	Cambodia* PA
Côte d'Ivoire	Comoros	Taiwan SA/PA/I/F	Canada°
Dem. Rep. of Congo	Costa Rica	Zambia F	Cape Verde
	Djibouti		China° S
	Ecuador R1		Croatia PA
	Equatorial Guinea SA/PA		Cuba PA
			Czech Rep. PA
Malta ×	Monaco R/I/F/××		Kosovo‡ PA/S
Marshall Islands U	Morocco SA		Kyrgyzstan
Mauritania	**Namibia** R/I/F		Latvia PA
Mexico ◆/R/F	**Nauru**		Lithuania PA
Micronesia U	**New Zealand** I/F		Luxembourg*
Myanmar	Niger F		Moldova PA
Nicaragua ×	**Northern Ireland**		Mongolia∞
Nigeria	Pakistan		Montenegro
Oman	Peru		Mozambique PA/S
Palau U	Poland PA/R/I/F		Nepal S
Panama PA/R/F	Qatar F		Netherlands ^
Papua New Guinea	Rep. of Korea SA/R/I/F/+		Norway PA
Paraguay	Rwanda R/I/+		Portugal‡ PA
Philippines	**Saint Kitts & Nevis**		Puerto Rico ^
San Marino	**Saint Lucia** R/I		Romania*
Sao Tome &			Russian Fed.
			Serbia PA

(continued overleaf)

Table 1 (Continued)

I. TO SAVE THE WOMAN'S LIFE OR PROHIBITED ALTOGETHER Countries printed in bold make an explicit exception to save a woman's life	II. TO PRESERVE HEALTH (also to save the woman's life). Countries printed in bold recognize an exception to preserve a woman's mental health	III. SOCIO-ECONOMIC GROUNDS (also to save a woman's life and health)	IV. WITHOUT RESTRICTION AS TO REASON
Dominica	Principe		Singapore***
Dominican Republic	Senegal		Slovak Rep. PA
Egypt	**Soloman Islands**		Slovenia PA
El Salvador×	Somalia		South Africa
Gabon	**South Sudan**		Spain* PA
Guatemala	Sri Lanka		Sweden**
Guinea-Bissau	Sudan R		Switzerland
Haiti	Suriname		Tajikistan
Honduras	Syria SA/PA		Tunisia○
Indonesia	Tanzania		Turkey‡ SA/PA
Iran F	Timor-Leste PA		Turkmenistan
SA/R/F	Tonga		Ukraine
Iraq	**Tuvalu**		United States^
Ireland	Uganda		♦/PA
Kiribati	**United Arab Emirates** SA/PA		Uruguay PA
	Maldives SA		Uzbekistan
	Eritrea	**Samoa**	Dem. People's Rep. of Korea°
	Ethiopia R/I/F/+	Saudi Arabia SA/PA	Denmark PA
	Gambia	**Seychelles**	Estonia
	Ghana R/I/F/+	R/I/F/+	France*
	Grenada	Sierra Leone	Fmr. Yugoslav Rep. Macedonia PA
	Guinea R/I/F	**Swaziland** R/I/F	Georgia PA
	Israel R/I/F/+	**Thailand** R/F	Germany*
	Jamaica	Togo R/I/F	Greece PA
	Jordan	**Trinidad & Tobago**	Guyana†
	Kenya	Vanuatu	Hungary
	Kuwait SA/PA/F	Zimbabwe R/I/F/××	Italy§
	Lesotho R/I/F		Kazakhstan
	Liberia R/I/F		
	Liechtenstein +		
	Malaysia		

Laos	Venezuela	Mauritius	
Lebanon	**West Bank &**	R/I/F/PA	
Libya	**Gaza Strip**		
Madagascar	**Yemen**		
Malawi			
Mali R/I			
			Vietnam°

Source: Categories of abortion laws from most to least restrictive (Center for Reproductive Rights 2015). Reproduced by permission of the Center for Reproductive Rights.

GESTATIONAL LIMITS KEY

All Countries in Category IV have gestational limits of 12 weeks unless otherwise indicated. Gestational limits are calculated from the first day of the last menstrual period, which is considered to occur 2 weeks prior to conception. Where laws specify that gestational age limits are calculated from the date of conception, these limits have been extended by 2 weeks.

§ Gestational limit of 90 days
∞ Gestational limit of 3 months
* Gestational limit of 14 weeks
^ Law does not limit pre-viability abortion
† Gestational limit of 8 weeks
** Gestational limit of 18 weeks
° Law does not indicate gestational limit; regulatory mechanisms vary
‡ Gestational limit of 10 weeks
*** Gestational limit of 24 weeks

INDICATIONS

R   Abortion permitted in cases of rape
R1 Abortion permitted in the case of rape of a woman with a mental disability
I   Abortion permitted in cases of incest
F   Abortion permitted in cases of fetal impairment
SA Spousal authorization required
PA Parental authorization/notification required
+   Abortion permitted on additional enumerated grounds relating to such factors as the woman's age or capacity to care for a child
S   Sex selective abortion prohibited
x   Legislation eliminated all exceptions to prohibition on abortion; availability of defense of necessity highly unlikely
xx Legislation explicitly permits abortion only to protect the physical health of a woman
U   Law unclear
◆   Federal system in which abortion law is determined at state level; classification reflects legal status of abortion for largest group of people

I CATEGORIES OF ABORTION LAWS

To save a woman's life or prohibited altogether

According to the most recent research, the 66 countries in Category I of Table 1 have the most restrictive abortion laws. These countries only permit this reproductive health service to save a woman's life, or they prohibit abortion altogether. These countries account for 25.5 percent of the world's population and are primarily located in the Global South, with the exception of several countries in eastern Asia that have liberal abortion laws. Moreover, a handful of countries in Europe, including Ireland, Andorra, and Malta, fall into this category.

The penal codes of many of these countries, such as Tanzania and Brazil, explicitly indicate that abortion providers are exempt from punishment if they perform an abortion in order to save the life of a woman. Other countries, such as Haiti and Senegal, may not include such explicit language, but may permit abortion if a woman's life is at risk on the basis of the criminal law defense of "necessity." Many penal codes excuse liability if a criminal act is performed in order to save one's own life or the life of another person. In these circumstances, while the law does not expressly authorize abortion on these grounds, this service could be performed on the basis that it was necessary to save a woman's life. However, the success of this defense is difficult to predict because it is generally theoretical and requires a fact-specific analysis of the situation. Moreover, the defense is only applicable to avoid criminal liability. As such, a woman or abortion provider must face criminal charges before they can invoke this defense.

The availability of the necessity defense is highly unlikely in Chile, El Salvador, Malta, and Nicaragua. Each of these countries at one time permitted abortion services on limited grounds, but deliberately eliminated all exceptions to abortion bans from their penal codes, thereby prohibiting this service entirely.

To preserve health

A second category of abortion laws includes the 58 countries that permit abortion to protect a woman's health, as well as to save her life. The countries in this category comprise approximately 13.8 percent of the world's population and are mostly located in the Global South, with a few exceptions, such as Poland, New Zealand, and Northern Ireland. Most of the countries that permit abortion to protect a woman's health authorize abortion on "health" or "therapeutic" grounds generally. Some countries, such as Peru or Rwanda, require that the potential threat to the health of a woman is permanent, serious, or grave. Additionally, Monaco and Zimbabwe explicitly only recognize a threat to a woman's physical health as grounds for procuring an abortion. Other countries, such as Ghana and Colombia, embrace a more expansive health exception and explicitly permit abortion if a woman's physical or mental health is at risk. Moreover, some former British colonies, such as Gambia and Trinidad and Tobago, have retained Great Britain's former abortion law, which did not explicitly authorize abortion under any circumstances, but was interpreted in the 1938 *Rex v. Bourne* decision to permit legal abortion if continuing the pregnancy would render the woman a "mental wreck." As such, these countries permit abortion if a woman's mental or physical health is at risk.

Among the countries in Category I, the interpretation of a mental health justification for abortion varies. Some countries may consider the psychological distress that results from rape or incest, or a woman's socioeconomic circumstances. In New Zealand, for example, the law takes into account pregnancies that result from a sexual violation, in addition to the age of the girl or woman, in determining whether a woman can undergo an abortion.

On socioeconomic grounds

A third category of abortion laws include the 13 countries that permit abortions for socioeconomic reasons and comprise approximately 21.3 percent of the world's population. The countries that fall into this category are scattered throughout the world. Socioeconomic reasons for abortion are generally considered within the framework of women's health. For example, the laws of Great Britain and several former British colonies, such as Zambia and Belize, consider the "actual or reasonably foreseeable environment" in determining whether a pregnancy endangers a woman's physical or mental health. These abortion laws are generally interpreted liberally and permit women to procure abortions for factors such as their age, marital status, or economic status. Additionally, the laws of some countries in this category specifically list such factors. For example, Finland's abortion law, in addition to authorizing abortion on health grounds, takes into account whether the care of a child would place considerable strain on a woman and her family, as well as whether she conceived before the age of 17 or after the age of 40, among other circumstances.

In each of the three aforementioned categories, many countries also permit abortions for specific indications, such as if the pregnancy resulted from rape or incest, or in cases of fetal impairment. Table 1 contains a list of indications although some countries may also permit abortion on additional grounds that do not explicitly appear in Table 1. For example, Israel, in addition to permitting abortion on health grounds, authorizes abortion if the woman is younger than the age of marriage or older than 40 years of age.

Without restriction as to reason

The fourth category of abortion laws, which includes 62 countries, is the least restrictive, and countries in this category permit abortion without restriction as to reason. The countries in this category are mostly located in the Global North, including most countries in North America and Europe, as well as most countries in central and eastern Asia. These countries, which include China, the world's most populous country, comprise 39.5 percent of the world's population. In these countries, the woman, rather than her healthcare provider, makes the decision about whether or not to terminate a pregnancy. Many countries, including the United States, South Africa, and Canada, recognize that a woman has the right to choose to terminate her pregnancy and that excessive interference with this choice violates her constitutional rights.

Most of the countries in category IV establish a gestational limit during which a woman can terminate her pregnancy without restriction as to reason. Thereafter, a woman can normally procure abortion services on specified grounds. For example, in Denmark, a woman may procure an abortion without restriction as to reason during the initial 12 weeks of gestation. Subsequently, abortion is available in cases of fetal impairment, on specified socioeconomic grounds, or if a pregnancy results from a criminal act or poses a risk to a woman's life or health.

A uniform method for calculating gestational age does not exist. Generally, the gestational limit for abortion is calculated from the first day of a woman's last menstrual period, which is considered to occur 2 weeks prior to conception. The abortion laws of some countries, however, such as Montenegro, calculate the gestational limit for abortion from the estimated date of conception. In many countries, the law does not specify which method of calculation to use, and therefore the law may be applied differently depending on the method of calculation that the abortion provider uses.

Most of the countries in this category have a gestational limit of 12 weeks during which a woman may obtain an abortion without restriction as to reason. A few countries, such as Guyana and Portugal, have adopted shorter gestational limits of 8 and 10 weeks, respectively. Other countries have longer gestational limits. For example, in Singapore, a woman may terminate a pregnancy without restriction as to reason until the 24th week of pregnancy, and in Sweden, the gestational limit is 18 weeks. Moreover, some countries, such as the Netherlands, do not limit pre-viability abortions. The term "viability" refers to the chances of pre-term survival. However, an accepted definition of this term or agreement among healthcare professionals with respect to the gestational age at which viability is possible does not exist. As such, the determination of viability may vary depending on the context. In other countries, such as China, the law does not indicate a gestational limit. Among these countries, the regulatory limit for determining the gestational limit for an abortion varies.

Notably, despite the categorizations in Table 1, abortion laws may be interpreted more liberally or restrictively than a literal reading of the law would suggest, depending on factors such as individual circumstances, the views of government officials and providers, and public support for abortion rights. As such, these country classifications do not necessarily indicate the extent to which abortion services are actually available or permitted in practice. For example, while India permits abortion on socioeconomic grounds, many women are unable to access safe abortion services because of the law's inadequate implementation. Conversely, although Great Britain's abortion law only authorizes abortion on socioeconomic grounds, in practice, the liberal interpretation of the law has made abortion services freely available.

II TRENDS

Liberalization

Overall, in considering abortion laws in a global context, a clear trend toward the liberalization of abortion laws has emerged. Following World War II, abortion was highly restricted throughout the world. Since the 1950s, a global trend toward easing abortion restrictions has ensued, beginning with abortion laws in central and eastern Europe, moving to other industrialized countries throughout Western Europe and North America, and then expanding throughout the world more broadly. During this time, only a handful of countries have tightened restrictions on abortion. The liberalization of abortion laws using legal means has generally been achieved by amending criminal bans to specify certain circumstances in which there is no legal penalty for abortion. Thus, countries in the first wave of liberalization, in central and eastern Europe, saw the introduction of specific circumstances in which abortion carried no criminal sanction.

The liberalization of abortion laws has resulted from a recognition that the public health impact of abortion is directly linked to its legal status, and the identification of women's access to safe and legal abortion services as a human rights issue. Since the adoption of the International Conference on Population and Development (ICPD) Programme of Action in 1994 when 179 governments worldwide recognized reproductive rights as human rights and committed to address unsafe abortion as a public health concern, international and regional human rights bodies have increasingly addressed abortion as a human rights concern. Human rights bodies have called on states to liberalize abortion laws and ensure women's access to legal abortion services. Specifically, the Protocol to the African Charter on Human and People's Rights on the Rights of Women in Africa, which the African Union adopted on July 11, 2003, explicitly addresses abortion as a human right. Article 14(2) of the protocol states that "States Parties shall take all appropriate measures to ... protect the reproductive rights of women by authorizing medical abortion in cases of sexual assault, rape, incest, and where the continued pregnancy endangers the mental and physical health of the mother or the life of the mother or the fetus."

In the wake of these developments, countries have increasingly relied on human rights principles in liberalizing their abortion laws. For example, several West African francophone countries, including Benin, Guinea, and Togo, enacted laws that increase the legal availability of abortion following a series of regional meetings among government officials, legislators, and other interested parties that resulted in a draft model law addressing reproductive health issues. The draft law codified many of the provisions of the ICPD Programme of Action and other international instruments.

Moreover, throughout Latin America, human rights norms have guided several high courts in liberalizing abortion laws. For example, in 2006, the Colombian Constitutional Court overturned the country's abortion ban on the grounds that the lack of explicit exceptions failed to respect a woman's human rights, and ruled that this reproductive health service must be permitted in circumstances in which the pregnancy threatens a woman's life or health, in cases of incest or rape, and in cases in which the fetus has malformations incompatible with life. Argentina's Supreme Court, in a 2012 decision decriminalizing abortion in all cases of rape, recognized that international and regional human rights obligations require governments to offer a victim of rape the opportunity to terminate her pregnancy. Prior to this ruling, the interpretation of the rape exception in Argentina's abortion law was unclear. The Penal Code only explicitly permits abortion in cases of rape of a mentally disabled woman, although a growing body of provincial jurisprudence, protocols, and national health regulations has interpreted this provision to permit abortion in all cases of rape. Argentina's law also permits abortion in circumstances to preserve a woman's health or life. In 2012, in Brazil, the Supreme Court relied on human rights arguments in decriminalizing abortion in cases in which the fetus has anencephaly, a severe anomaly that causes the fetus to lack parts of the brain and is inconsistent with survival. Brazil also permits abortion to save a woman's life and in cases of rape.

Barriers to abortion services

Despite this trend in the liberalization of abortion laws across the globe, several barriers render abortion services difficult to access or inaccessible in practice in many countries. These obstacles result from gaps in the implementation of abortion laws or the imposition of procedural barriers, introduced through law or policy, which limit the availability of abortion services. Such barriers particularly impact low-income, rural, and young women, as well as women with low levels of education.

Many countries throughout the world have failed to adequately implement their abortion laws, which compromise the ability of many women to access safe and legal abortion services. Several countries lack regulations that establish procedures for obtaining legal abortion services or otherwise fail to ensure that they are providing the necessary resources to guarantee that safe abortion services are available, accessible and acceptable in practice, and of good quality. Such resources may include trainings for healthcare providers about the law and methods for providing abortion services, public awareness campaigns to educate the population about the abortion law, and provision of adequate facilities and personnel to provide abortion services throughout a country, particularly in rural areas.

For example, in 2002, Nepal amended its National Code, Muluki Ain, to permit abortion without restriction as to reason during the first 12 weeks of pregnancy and thereafter on specific grounds, unless a woman seeks to terminate a pregnancy because of the sex of the fetus. The previous law was interpreted to prohibit abortion altogether. The liberalization occurred as a result of the recognition of the public health impact of unsafe abortion, which led to high rates of maternal mortality; the fact that women were being imprisoned for procuring illegal abortions; and a growing women's rights movement in the country. However, despite the change in the law, its lack of implementation prevented many women from accessing safe and legal abortion services. Notably, in the 2009 case of *Lakshmi Dhikta v. Government of Nepal*, Nepal's Supreme Court ruled that Nepal's abortion law had not been sufficiently implemented because the cost of legal abortion services rendered it impossible for a woman to procure an abortion. In its decision, the Supreme Court ordered the government to develop a comprehensive abortion law that establishes a legal framework for access to abortion services, which includes the establishment of a fund to cover the cost of abortions for women who are unable to pay for this service.

In addition to the lack of implementation of abortion laws, some women may also be unable to obtain abortion services because of burdensome procedural barriers placed in the way of such services. For example, in many countries, women do not have access to information about available abortion services or receive inaccurate information about such services, which denies women the opportunity to make informed decisions. For instance, in November 2013, the Russian Federation passed a law banning any advertisement about abortion services. This law followed legislation adopted in 2011 that required 10 percent of any advertisements by abortion providers to erroneously describe the dangers of abortion to women's health and prohibited the description of abortion as a safe procedure, despite evidence to the contrary. Moreover, in many countries, the criminalization of abortion or stigma surrounding this reproductive health service inhibits the free exchange of information about abortion services, rendering them difficult for women to access.

Moreover, in several countries, such as the United States and Hungary, women must receive inaccurate information about abortion services in the context of counseling requirements, which mandate that they receive counseling before undergoing an abortion. While in some instances the information provided to women attempts to be neutral in explaining the possible risks of abortion, in many circumstances the counseling can be intended to discourage women from undergoing an abortion by providing inaccurate information. For instance, in the United States, several states mandate inaccurate counseling about negative mental health consequences of abortion.

Additionally, the laws of some countries establish waiting or reflection periods during which women must wait one to several days before they can undergo an abortion. For example, in 2009, the Slovak Republic introduced a 48-hour waiting period before women can obtain abortion services, among other procedural barriers to abortion access.

Mandatory waiting periods delay women's access to safe, legal abortion services and consequently make abortion more dangerous. While abortion is one of the safest medical procedures performed today, risks of complications increase as the pregnancy progresses. Mandatory waiting periods increase the gestational age at which the induced pregnancy termination occurs, thereby also increasing the risk associated with the procedure. Moreover, these mandatory delays demean women as competent decision-makers.

Furthermore, some countries limit the range of abortion methods available to women, thereby hindering their access to this reproductive health service. For example, in 2007, the US Supreme Court upheld a ban on a particular method of second-trimester abortion. Several countries also restrict women's access to medications for nonsurgical abortion. In some countries, medical abortion may be unavailable because of the lack of regulatory registration or approval of essential medicines (World Health Organization 2012). Other countries prohibit misoprostol, a medication that was originally marketed to prevent gastric ulcers but is also a safe and effective means of pregnancy termination. This medication, which can be stored at room temperature and administered by non-physicians, has increased women's access to safe abortion services in many resource-limited settings. Nevertheless, in 2002, the Philippines' Food and Drug Administration issued a circular prohibiting the distribution, sale, and use of misoprostol.

Other procedural barriers that impede women's access to legal abortion services include third-party consent and notification requirements. For example, the abortion laws of some countries, such as Saudi Arabia and Japan, require that a woman obtain the consent of her spouse before she can procure an abortion. In some instances, such consent may be bypassed. Many countries throughout the world, including Greece, Taiwan, and Mauritius, require that girls notify or obtain the consent of a parent or guardian before procuring an abortion. However, several countries, such as Italy and Denmark, permit a medical committee or court to authorize an abortion if a parent refuses. Moreover, some laws require the approval of another physician or physicians, or a hospital committee in order for a woman to procure an abortion. For example, Ireland's 2013 Protection of Life During Pregnancy Act requires that two doctors confirm that a physical threat to a woman's life exists in order for her to procure an abortion. In cases in which the pregnancy poses a risk of suicide, three doctors, including one obstetrician and two psychiatrists, must verify this risk before a woman can procure legal abortion services. Additionally, other countries mandate court approval before a woman undergoes an abortion. In Rwanda, the penal code requires that a woman secure a court order in order to procure an abortion in cases of rape, incest, or forced marriage. Furthermore, some countries, such as Poland, require that a public prosecutor confirm that a pregnancy resulted from an unlawful act, such as rape or incest, before a woman can legally terminate her pregnancy. These consent and notification requirements can often be waived if a woman's life is at risk, but they nonetheless impede women's access to safe and legal abortion services.

Restrictions on the types of medical facilities in which abortions can be performed and narrowly defining the range of healthcare providers that can offer this service also limits the accessibility of abortion. Many countries, such as Argentina, only permit registered medical practitioners to perform abortion services, even though mid-level health providers, such as trained nurses and midwives, can offer this service. Several countries, such as Zambia and Kuwait, for example, restrict the performance of abortion services to specific facilities, such as hospitals or similar authorized institutions. Notably, in 2004, South Africa amended its Choice on Termination of Pregnancy Act in order to permit nurses, as well as medical practitioners and registered midwives, to perform abortions during the first 12 weeks of pregnancy. This amendment also decentralized regulatory control over facilities that can provide abortion services, in order to permit local officials to approve such facilities and increase women's access to services. Restrictions on the types of healthcare providers and facilities that can offer abortion services impede the geographic distribution of services and reduce their availability, posing a significant barrier to access for many women.

Another obstacle to abortion access facing women is limited funding. For example, Bulgaria's constitutional court held that while the constitution requires coverage for medically necessary abortion, abortion for school and university students, and in cases of pregnancies that result from rape or incest, women are not constitutionally entitled to free abortion services beyond these circumstances. Additionally, in the United States, a patchwork of federal policies restrict funding for abortion in federal health insurance programs. Several groups of women, including federal employees, military service women, and women enrolled in Medicaid (a health insurance program for families and individuals with low income and resources) are denied coverage for abortion except in cases of life endangerment or for pregnancies resulting from rape or incest. Moreover, women in the Peace Corps, a volunteer program run by the US government, are denied coverage even in these circumstances. While US states have the discretion to use their own funds to provide abortion coverage in a broader range of circumstances to low-income women enrolled in Medicaid, many do not. Additionally, the recently enacted healthcare coverage law singles out abortion in *private* health insurance policies, allowing states to ban abortion coverage in the new state-based marketplaces created for small business and individuals. In states that do not enact such bans, insurers offering abortion coverage in these marketplaces must segregate the funds used to cover abortion services from the funds used for all other covered services, thereby singling out and stigmatizing abortion services from other healthcare services.

The unregulated practice of conscientious objection among healthcare providers and others is another barrier to legal abortion services. National laws and regulations govern the right to refuse to perform services, such as abortions, because of moral or religious objections. These laws and regulations vary in the scope of limits of conscientious objection and invite differing interpretations. In various contexts, nurses, judges, physicians, and healthcare institutions have invoked this principle in refusing to provide legal abortion services to women. As such, a growing body of jurisprudence is delineating the justifiable limits on the exercise of conscientious objection in this context. For example, the Colombian Constitutional Court has clarified that conscientious objectors have a duty to refer women to non-objecting providers in order to enable them to exercise their right to legal healthcare services, such as abortion. Moreover, the court held that hospitals and other institutions cannot invoke a right to conscientious objection and clarified that only healthcare providers directly involved in the provision of services to which they conscientiously object can exercise this right.

In considering these procedural barriers to abortion services, it is important to note that activists and advocates opposed to abortion often seek to impose these barriers in order to limit women's access to legal abortion services. Moreover, despite the global trend toward the liberalization of abortion laws, movements to restrict abortion are active in many countries and have the support of influential religious authorities. Notably, several of these movements collaborate across countries and regions and are increasingly using similar strategies in order to restrict women's access to this reproductive health service.

SEE ALSO: Abortion and Religion; Human Rights, International Laws and Policies on; Pro-Choice Movement in the United States; Reproductive Health; Reproductive Justice and Reproductive Rights in the United States; Stigma

REFERENCE

World Health Organization. 2012. *Safe Abortion: Technical and Policy Guidance for Health Systems*, 2nd ed. Accessed July 20, 2015, at http://apps.who.int/iris/bitstream/10665/70914/1/9789241548434_eng.pdf.

FURTHER READING

Boland, Reed. 2010. "Second Trimester Abortion Laws Globally: Actuality, Trends and Recommendations." *Reproductive Health Matters*, 18(36): 1–23.

Boland, Reed, and Laura Katzive. 2008. "Developments in Laws on Induced Abortion: 1998–2007." *International Family Planning Perspectives*, 34(3): 110–120.

Center for Reproductive Rights. 2014a. "A Global View of Abortion Rights." Accessed July 20, 2015, at www.worldabortionlaws.com.

Center for Reproductive Rights. 2014b. "Questions and Answers: Understanding the World's Abortion Laws Map." Accessed July 20, 2015, at www.worldabortionlaws.com.

Center for Reproductive Rights. 2015. "World's Abortion Laws." Accessed July 20, 2015, at www.worldabortionlaws.com.

Cook, Rebecca J., and Bernard Dickens. 1978. "A Decade of International Change in Abortion Law: 1967–1977." *American Journal of Public Health*, 68(7): 637–644.

Cook, Rebecca J., and Bernard Dickens. 1988. "International Developments in Abortion Laws: 1977–88." *American Journal of Public Health*, 78(10): 1305–1311.

Cook, Rebecca J., and Bernard Dickens. 1999. "International Developments in Abortion Law from 1988 to 1998." *American Journal of Public Health*, 89(4): 579–586.

Finer, Louise, and Johanna B. Fine. 2013. "Abortion Law Around the World: Progress and Pushback." *American Journal of Public Health*, 103(4): 585–589.

Guttmacher Institute. 2012. *Making Abortion Services Accessible in the Wake of Legal Reforms: A Framework and Six Case Studies*. Accessed 20 July, 2015, at https://www.guttmacher.org/pubs/abortion-services-laws.pdf.

Rahman, Anika, Laura Katzive and Stanley K. Henshaw. 1998. "A Global Review of Laws on Induced Abortion, 1985–1977." *International Family Planning Perspectives*, 24(2): 56–64.

Sedgh, Gilda, et al. 2012. "Induced Abortion: Incidence and Trends Worldwide from 1995 to 2008." *The Lancet*, 370(9816): 625–632.

Zampas, Christina, and Jaime M. Gher. 2008. "Abortion as a Human Right: International and Regional Standards." *Human Rights Law Review*, 2: 249–294.

Abortion and Religion

DANIEL C. MAGUIRE
Marquette University, Milwaukee, USA

Ethics has as its primary goal the discovery of what befits or does not befit life in its various manifestations. The world religions all contain elements of a moral philosophy and ethics, usually expressed in poetry, ritual, and symbol. Religion, definitionally, is *the response to the sacred*, whether that *sacred* is defined theistically (as, for example, in the Abrahamic religions, Judaism, Christianity, and Islam) or non-theistically as in Buddhism, Taoism, and Confucianism. Religions find their common ground in reverence and awe and concern for the preservation of life; therefore issues such as birth and death are of prime concern for all the world religions.

Abortion thus appears as an ethical issue in various religions.

There is no one unanimous view bonding all religions on the liceity of abortion. Opinions range from very conservative – permitting no abortions for any reason – to more permissive views, especially for early abortions. Very often there are a variety of views within a given individual religious tradition. There is also variation in the intensity of emotive response to the issue. Thus, for example, liberalization of abortion rights in India has unfolded without turmoil (Coward, Lipner, and Young 1991). For many conservative Christians, however, resistance to abortion assumes an urgent moral primacy, and yet most Protestant denominations support abortion in certain cirumstances (Harrison 1983). Again, showing the diversity within an individual religion, the hierarchy in Roman Catholicism hold the most rigid position against abortion, the Second Vatican Council dubbing it an "unspeakable crime" (Abbot 1966, 286). Still, a majority of Catholic theologians and people allow many instances of permissible abortion and can cite a long series of authorities supporting their view (Noonan 1970; Dombrowski and Deltete 2000).

In understanding the position of any religion on abortion, it is thus important not to look for a single "official" position in any religion, even in the most hierarchical religions. It is notoriously difficult to say with certainty how much the teachings of officials of the various religions relate to fertility decisions. Many factors are involved in fertility choices. Practice varies according to such things as poverty, education levels, the status of women, and competing, well-ensconced customs and traditions. The Roman Catholic hierarchy opposes both contraception and abortion, and yet France was the first country to experience a transition from high fertility to replacement levels or lower. Italy (which hosts the Vatican) and Spain have two of the three lowest fertility rates in the world (Cohen 1993). The basic fact is that no human society or no religious tradition can escape the need for fertility management. As Harold Dorn says with elemental logic: "No species has ever been able to multiply without limit. There are two biological checks upon a rapid increase in numbers – a high mortality and a low fertility. Unlike other biological organisms [humans] can choose which of these checks shall be applied, but one of them must be" (Dorn 1969, 275). The responses of the world religions to this fateful choice are as varied as those religions themselves.

BUDDHISM

At first blush, it would seem that Buddhism is in principle opposed to all feticide. Indeed, the first of the five fundamental precepts of Buddhism is to abstain from all killing. As Thai Buddhist scholar Parichart Suwanbubbha says: "That sounds like absolutist ethics and would seem to end all discussion of a just and moral abortion decision" (Suwanbubbha 2003, 153). However, it is not clear whether abortion of a fetus would constitute "killing," since there is no agreed upon belief that life begins at conception. In Buddhism, other principles step into the ethical dialogue such as the importance of avoiding the moral nemeses of *greed, hate,* and *delusion.* Although in Buddhism there is a "morally negative view of abortion," says Suwanbubbha, "intention is key" (Maguire 2010). Thus, abortion for good intentions is accepted by many Buddhists.

Buddhists are not alone in finding ways to escape the insensitivity of inflexible moral absolutes. As William LaFleur says: "The 'interpretation' of seemingly unambiguous commands and precepts goes on all the time in religion" (LaFleur 1992, 12).

In allowing for exceptions, ritual and myth often ease the tension. In Japanese Buddhism, in response to the demand for some liturgy to assuage the distress of having had an abortion, temples have responded by providing a rite known as *mizuko kuyo*, where the *mizuko*, the "child" that was aborted can be honored and commended to the care of *Jizo*, a sacred figure who lovingly takes care of the aborted being in its otherworld journey. The mood of the ritual is joyous because the aborted fetus is seen not so much as being terminated "as it is being put on hold, asked to bide its time in some other world" (LaFleur 1992, 26–27). The *mizuko* then is deemed to be in a kind of limbo, a state of temporary repose, awaiting return to another world. Some hope that the *mizuko* will return to the family that aborted it when circumstances make it possible to welcome its return to the family.

HINDUISM

As with Buddhism, Hinduism combines a seemingly absolute prohibition with allowance of abortion. The *Dharma sastras* forbid the abortion even of an illegitimate child. This is further complicated by the common belief that at the moment of conception both physical and spiritual life enters the human embryo. Conception is the result of a divine act. "Conception is the moment when the soul enters the body along with the indiviudal's past *karma*" (Jain 2003, 135). Thus, the embryo has an identity and a history and this would seem to make it inviolable. And yet, context again plays its dialogical part in Hindu ethics. The moral law, the *dharma*, must be appropriate to circumstances, and circumstances change. Thus, the "small family norm" which is now appropriate to an overcrowded world, including contraception and abortion when needed, "is in no way opposed to the Hindu concept of *dharma*" (Jain 2003, 139). The culture of India, permeated as it is by religion, does not block this malleability and that is why in India today, according to Jain (2003), "abortion is available practically on demand."

ABRAHAMIC RELIGIONS

Judaism, Christianity, and Islam, though sharing an Abrahamic root, illustrate the variety of religious views of abortion. As in Hinduism and Buddhism, there are serious prohibitions of abortion in Judaism. Jeremy Cohen points out that "forcing one's pregnant wife to abort" is seen as a heinous crime in some of the significant literature. If a man were to do that, "it would have been better were he never created" (Cohen 1992, 213). And yet, Laurie Zoloth (2003, 38) writes: "Abortion appears as an option for Jewish women from the earliest sources of the Bible and Mishnaic commentary." In fact, Zoloth says, if the mother's physical or mental health is at risk "the abortion is not only permitted, it is mandated" (2003, 37–38). The moral status of the fetus is a key issue. In Judaism "the fetus is not an ensouled person." In the first 40 days of pregnancy the conceptum is considered "like water." Even in the last trimester, the fetus has a lesser moral status (Zoloft 2003, 39). This idea of "delayed ensoulment" appears in other religions also.

In Christianity, abortion was not widely discussed until the Middle Ages. Delayed ensoulment was broadly accepted throughout Christian history. The early embryo/fetus was thought to have a vegetative soul. This was succeeded by an animal soul. But only when the fetus was "formed" could God infuse a spiritual soul, and only at that point did the fetus attain the moral status of a person. Prior to this, therapeutic abortion could be permitted. There was debate as to when the fetus became "ensouled." Some held it happened after 40 days of pregnancy; some said it happened at 80 or 90 days into the pregnancy. In practice, "quickening," detectable movement of the fetus in the woman, was taken as the arrival of personal status for the fetus. Early abortion was permissible for many reasons, such as to save the woman's life, to end a pregnancy conceived outside of marriage, or if the girl was betrothed to one man but pregnant by another (Noonan 1970; Gudorf 2003).

In Islam, there is also a great diversity of views on abortion. Legal positions range from total prohibition of all abortion to unqualified permission for abortion up to 120 days into the pregnancy. However, even after 120 days exceptions are allowed where the mother's life is in danger, the pregnancy is harming an already suckling child, or where the fetus is expected to be deformed (Omran 1992; Shaikh 2003). Islam also holds that the moral status of the fetus depends on its age. Only when the fetus is sufficiently developed can God's angel breathe spirit into the fetus. There is strong support in the traditions of Islam for all forms of contraception, for as Sa'diyya Shaikh says, "In Islam there is a prioritization on the quality of life rather than a large quantity of lives" (Shaikh 2003, 117).

CHINESE RELIGIONS

In Confucianism and Taoism there is an ancient appreciation of the need for balancing population and resources. Hans Fei (297–233 BCE) said that if every family has five children and the children all have five children soon "there are too few resources to support the number of people" (*A Collective Exegesis of Han Fei Tzu* 1974, 1040–1041). In these traditions, this is a matter of national interest and the ruler is charged with preventing population excess. As Geling Shang says, "having children had more to do with the national interests than with personal ones, and the government was expected to have a role in such matters" (Shang 2003, 231). The modern "one child" policy is not discontinuous with ancient Chinese culture. Abortion was a serious moral issue. As Shang says, "abortion was not encouraged, although there was no explicit code to prohibit it" (Shang 2003). If circumstances indicated a need for interruption of pregnancy, this was countenanced in a spirit of tolerance and compassion. Again, as in other religions, the fetus was not given full personal status and thus feticide was not seen as on a par with the murder of a born person. The supremacy of the notion of harmony in Chinese religions encouraged such attitudes.

RELIGIOUS NATALISM

Religiously encouraged natalism is commonplace in cultures generally. As John Mbiti has written, in many African cultures marrying and having children is seen as a religious duty. To be childless is regarded "as stopping the flow of life … and hence the diminishing of humankind upon earth" (Mbiti 1991, 98). This natalism has moved into legislation in places as diverse as Nigeria, Latin America, and the Philippines. And yet, in indigenous religions, in spite of strong cultural pressure and illegality, in practice, necessity eases the severity of absolutized prohibitions and no ban is met with full compliance.

WHERE RELIGION AND DEMOGRAPHIC SCIENCE CAN MEET

There are many views and debates on population policy but on one thing there is broad agreement. As Anrudh Jain of the Population Council writes: "The link between education, particularly girls' education, and fertility decline has been established and appreciated for many years" (Jain 1998, xiii). Religions generally favor education, and education diminishes unwanted pregnancies and thus abortion. Here, indeed, science and religion have compatible interests.

SEE ALSO: Abortion, Legal Status in Global Perspective on; Reproductive Health; Reproductive Justice and Reproductive Rights in the United States

REFERENCES

A Collective Exegesis of Han Fei Tzu. 1974. Shanghai: Shaanghae People's Press.

Abbott, Walter M., ed. 1966. *The Documents of Vatican II*. New York: Herder and Herder.

Cohen, Jeremy. 1992. *Be Fertile and Increase, Fill the Earth and Master It: The Ancient and Medieval Career of a Biblical Text*. New York: Cornell University Press.

Cohen, Joel E. 1993. *How Many People Can the Earth Support?* New York: W.W. Norton.

Coward, Harold, Julius Lipner, and Katherine Young. 1991. *Hindu Ethics, Purity, Abortion, and Euthanasia*. Delhi: Sri Saiguru.

Dombrowski, Daniel A., and Robert Deltete. 2000. *A Brief, Liberal, Catholic Defense of Abortion*. Urbana: University of Illinois Press.

Dorn, Harold F. 1969. "World Population Growth: An International Dilemma." Reprinted in *Science: Readings in Conservation Ecology*, edited by George W. Cox. New York: Appleton-Century-Crofts. First published 1962.

Gudorf, Christine. 2003. "Contraception and Abortion in Roman Catholicism." In *Sacred Rights: The Case for Contraception and Abortion in World Religions*, edited by Daniel C. Maguire, 55–78. New York: Oxford University Press.

Harrison, Beverly. 1983. *Our Right to Choose*. Boston: Beacon Pess.

Jain, Anrudh, ed. 1998. *Do Population Policies Matter? Fertilitiy and Politics in Egyt, India, Kenya, and Mexico*. New York: The Population Council.

Jain, Sandhya. 2003. "The Right to Family Planning, Contraception, and Abortion: The Hindu View." In *Sacred Rights: The Case for Contraception and Abortion in World Religions*, edited by Daniel C. Maguire, 129–144. New York: Oxford University Press.

LaFleur, William R. 1992. *Liquid Life: Abortion and Buddhism in Japan*. Princeton: Princeton University Press.

Maguire Daniel C. 2010. *Ethics: A Complete Method for Moral Choice*. Minneapolis: Fortress Press.

Mbiti, John. 1991. *Introduction to African Religion*. New York: Heinemann.

Noonan, John T. Jr., ed. 1970. *The Morality of Abortion: Legal and Historical Perspectives*. Cambridge, MA: Harvard University Press.

Omran, Abdel Hahim. 1992. *Family Planning in the Legacy of Islam*. London: Routledge.

Shaikh, Sa'diyya. 2003. "Family Planning, Contraception, and Abortion in Islam: Undertaking *Khilafah*." In *Sacred Rights: The Case for Contraception and Abortion in World Religions*, edited by Daniel C. Maguire, 105–128. New York: Oxford University Press.

Shang, Geling. 2003. "Excess, Lack, and Harmony: Some Confucian and Taoists Approaches to Family Planning and Population Management: Tradition and the Modern Challenge." In *Sacred Rights: The Case for Contraception and Abortion in World Religions*, edited by Daniel C. Maguire, 217–236. New York: Oxford University Press.

Suwanbubbha, Parichart. 2003. "The Right to Family Planning, Contraception and Abortion in Thai Buddhism." In *Sacred Rights: The Case for Contraception and Abortion in World Religions*, edited by Daniel C. Maguire, 145–166. New York: Oxford University Press.

Zoloth, Laurie. 2003. "Each One an Entire World: A Jewish Perspective on Family Planning." In *Sacred Rights: The Case for Contraception and Abortion in World Religions*, edited by Daniel C. Maguire, 21–54. New York: Oxford University Press.

Activist Mothering

SUSAN CONRADSEN
Berry College, USA

Although the term "activist mothering" itself did not originate until the late 1980s (Naples 1988), mothers have been active in social justice movements for a long time on a variety of issues including the movement for moral reform (which addressed prohibition, child labor laws, educational reforms, etc.), the settlement house movement, suffrage, labor reform, the abolitionist movement, anti-lynching campaigns, civil rights, the environmental movement, and the women's movement. Motherhood has often radicalized women to fight for the welfare of their children and the betterment of their community, and these activists have frequently called upon the symbolic power of the mother identity for legitimacy and inspiration for others to join their cause. However, maternal activism has often been overlooked as activism and dismissed as "just mothers" performing their domestic responsibilities, protecting their children. This has been inadvertently reinforced by some mothers' own interpretation of their activism as simply doing what needed to be done, i.e., not viewing their own efforts for social change as social activism.

There are three frameworks that scholars have applied to maternal activism: liberal feminism, maternalism, and feminist care theory. Liberal feminism emphasizes equal rights and egalitarianism and calls for justice and equity; maternalism focuses on women's essentialist nature as caregivers and the importance of maternal love and duty; and feminist care theory argues that caring for all people (children included) is a collective social responsibility and a public good (Tucker 2004). These frameworks shed light on the different paths mother-activists find themselves on as they develop into activists (Logsdon-Conradsen and Allred 2010). For example, studies of activist mothers of children with disabilities show how initially their motivation to advocate for disability rights stemmed from their identity as a mother taking care of their own child, but grew to include the larger community and advocating for political change (Panitch 2012). Motherhood organizations also tend to blend these frameworks and pick and choose what strategies and politics work best for their objectives within their contexts. Thus they may utilize a maternalist rhetoric to appeal to mothers and reduce the likelihood of backlash, but operate on principles of justice and a feminist ethic of care. Recognizing this, matricentric feminism was termed to distinguish twenty-first-century activist mothering as both a distinct motherhood movement and theory that encompasses these three complementary frameworks (O'Reilly 2011).

Scholars have labeled the recent increase in the formation of many motherhood organizations and maternal activism the "21st-century motherhood movement" and there is now a plethora of blogs, articles, websites, and books describing the various types of activism falling under this umbrella. Issues being tackled by activist mothers include those related to becoming a mother (e.g., pregnancy discrimination, childbirth practices/midwifery, breastfeeding rights), family/work life (e.g., paid sick leave, welfare reform, families with special needs, the maternal wall, mother–daughter project), violence (e.g., militarism, gun laws, police brutality, trafficking), the environment (e.g., eco-moms, environmental justice, toxic chemicals, superfunds), school reform (e.g., playground revolution, schoolyard gardens, curriculum reform, anti-bullying), and more. Activist mothers address issues at many levels including local (e.g., Mothers of East Los Angeles; Lois Gibbs and the Love Canal), regional (e.g., the Green Belt Movement; Mourning Mothers of Iran; Mothers of the Plaza de Mayo), and international (e.g., Peace X Peace; Mothers Acting Up). They also may focus exclusively on a specialized issue such as Moms on the Move (MOMS), which addresses special needs families, or they may focus on a few areas simultaneously such as Mainstreet Moms: Organize or Bust (MMOB), which targets three areas – promoting democracy through voting activism, addressing climate change, and protecting children's privacy from military recruiters. Like other activism, it is manifested through technology such as Facebook, Twitter, YouTube, online communities, and blogs, as well as via traditional grassroots strategies and public demonstrations (e.g., nurse-in for breastfeeding rights, Million Mom March).

Activist mothering is clearly multifaceted and covers a wide range of social issues. The commonality is that for activist mothers, their role and work as a mother empowers them to engage in social issues and effect change; their identity as a mother is the launching point into activism. It also has the ability to unite women from disparate backgrounds to work together on a common goal; this is part of the power of this movement. For instance, Peace X Peace is an online activist network with members from over 110 countries whose intent is to harness maternal energy to promote peace and develop peacebuilders around the world. The words of their CEO, Kimberly Weiche, summarize the belief of many mother activists (regardless of their targeted issue), "Everything that isn't peace is the antithesis of mothering. If mothers don't join together for peace, who else will?" (Liepold 2011, 680).

SEE ALSO: Community and Grassroots Activism; Environmental Justice; Ethic of Care; Feminist Activism; Maternalism; Nationalism and Gender; Pacifism, Peace Activism, and Gender; Personal is Political

REFERENCES

Liepold, Mary L. 2011. "Peace X Peace: Global Motherhood for the Twenty-First Century." In *The 21st Century Motherhood Movement: Mothers Speak Out on Why We Need to Change the World and How to Do It*, edited by Andrea O'Reilly, 670–681. Bradford, Ontario: Demeter Press.

Logsdon-Conradsen, Susan C., and Sarah L. Allred. 2010. "Environmental Mother-Activism: A Framework for Understanding Its Development and Manifestations." *Ecopsychology*, 2(3): 141–146.

Naples, Nancy. 1988. *Grassroots Warriors: Activist Mothering, Community Work, and the War on Poverty*. New York: Routledge.

O'Reilly, Andrea. 2011. "Introduction: Maternal Activism as Matricentric Feminism: The History, Ideological Frameworks, Political Strategies and Activist Practices of the 21st Century Motherhood Movement." In *The 21st Century Motherhood Movement: Mothers Speak Out on Why We Need to Change the World and How to Do It*, edited by Andrea O'Reilly, 1–36. Bradford, Ontario: Demeter Press.

Panitch, Melanie. 2012. *Disability, Mothers, and Organization: Accidental Activists*. Hoboken: Taylor & Francis.

Tucker, Judith S. 2004. "Motherhood and Its Discontents: The Political and Ideological Grounding of the 21st Century Mothers Movement." *Association for Research on Mothering Conference on Motherhood and Feminism*, Toronto, October 23.

Adolescent Pregnancy

NIKKI McGARY
University of Connecticut, USA

Adolescent pregnancy refers to when a young woman becomes pregnant some time during her adolescence. The adolescent stage of human development follows the onset of puberty, and comes before adulthood. According to the United Nations (UN) and the World Health Organization (WHO), global rates of adolescent pregnancy have decreased over the past two decades, but adolescent pregnancy still remains a social problem worldwide. The WHO (2014) reports that 16 million births a year are born to girls ages 15 to 19 years old. The UN Population Fund (UNFPA 2013) reported that there were 2 million births by adolescents under the age of 14. The Guttmacher Institute (2010) reports that adolescent women compose one fifth of all women of reproductive age worldwide, and that early marriage and early childbearing are most common among women who are poor with little education.

Adolescent pregnancies often result in greater risk for maternal and infant health (WHO 2014). Approximately 3 million girls ages 15–19 have unsafe abortions each year (WHO 2014), and 70,000 adolescent girls die each year in developing countries because of pregnancy and birthing complications (UNFPA 2013). Moreover, nations' economies are negatively affected as a result of adolescent pregnancy because governments either provide financial support for the adolescent mothers who need it, and/or they do not have as big a workforce (see, for example, Holness 2014; UN 2014).

Rates of adolescent pregnancy vary around the world. According to the WHO (2014), the majority of adolescent pregnancies are to women in lower- and middle-income countries. The highest adolescent birth rates among the developed countries were in the United States, Belarus, Bulgaria, Romania, and the Russian Federation; and the lowest adolescent birth rates were in the Netherlands and Japan (Singh and Darroch 2000). The WHO (2014) reports that 50 percent of all adolescent births worldwide occur in only seven countries, namely Bangladesh, Brazil, the Democratic Republic of Congo, Ethiopia, India, Nigeria, and the United States. Proportionately, only 2 percent of all births in China are to adolescents, whereas it is 18 percent in Latin America and the Caribbean, and over 50 percent in sub-Saharan Africa (WHO 2014).

Singh and Darroch (2000) argue that factors that have contributed to the declining rates in developed countries include "increased importance of education, increased motivation of young people to achieve higher levels of education and training, and greater centrality of goals other than motherhood and family formation." In a global review of adolescent pregnancy, Holness (2014) cites that Dutch and Scandinavian countries offer national sex education programs and accessible family planning clinics, which likely contributes to lower adolescent pregnancy rates. In Latin America and the Caribbean, the needs for family planning are not met, which has meant that there has not been such a significant decrease in the rate of adolescent pregnancies over the past 20 years.

Another important factor is sexual violence against young women and girls. UNICEF (2014a) reports that 150 million girls worldwide have been raped or forced to engage in other sexual acts, and the proportion of girls who are sexually assaulted varies by region (UN Women 2014). UNICEF (2014b) suggests that a large factor that contributes to the high rates of violence against girls is a result of social attitudes concerning the gender roles and undervaluing of women and girls. Other forms of violence include the sexual exploitation of girls through sex trafficking. Although it is very difficult to find accurate statistics regarding sex trafficking because of general underreporting and the fact that sex trafficking is hidden by its very definition, it is estimated that approximately 4.5 million women and girls are sold into slavery each year (UN 2014; UNICEF 2014b).

Child marriage is another factor that contributes to adolescent pregnancy. UN Women (2014) reports that 700 million women alive today were married before they were 18 years old, and 250 million of those were married before they were 15. These adolescents are less able to engage in safe sex, which makes them particularly vulnerable to pregnancy and sexually transmitted infections and diseases (UN Women 2014). Alongside an emphasis on access to contraception, there is also a scholarly emphasis on the need for comprehensive reproductive health education for reducing rates of adolescent pregnancy (see, for example, Kirby, Laris, and Rolleri 2007). The UNFPA makes the powerful argument that an attempt to decrease adolescent pregnancy rates should not focus on young women's behavior. Rather, nations should prioritize the education of young women, banning child marriage, changing family norms, and improving social attitudes toward women (UNFPA 2013).

SEE ALSO: Abortion and Religion; Abortion, Legal Status in Global Perspective; Age of Consent and Child Marriage in India; Age of Consent in Historical and International Perspective; Birth Control, History and Politics of; Poverty in Global Perspective; Reproductive Health

REFERENCES

Guttmacher Institute. 2010. "Facts on the Sexual and Reproductive Health of Adolescents in the Developing World." Accessed October 14, 2014, at http://www.guttmacher.org/pubs/FB-Adolescents-SRH.pdf.

Holness, Nola. 2014. "A Global Perspective on Adolescent Pregnancy." *International Journal of Nursing Practice*. DOI: 10.1111/ijn.12278.

Kirby, Douglas B., B. A. Laris, and Lori A. Rolleri. 2007. "Sex and HIV Education Programs: Their Impact on Sexual Behaviors of Young People Throughout the World." *Journal of Adolescent Health*, 40(3): 206–217.

Singh, Susheela, and Jacqueline E. Darroch. 2000. "Adolescent Pregnancy and Childbearing: Levels and Trends in Developed Countries." *Family Planning Perspectives*, 32(1): 14–23.

United Nations (UN). 2014. "'Motherhood in Childhood,' New UN Report, Spotlights Adolescent Pregnancy." Accessed October 14, 2014, at http://www.un.org/apps/news/story.asp?NewsID=46373#.VCL9I_mwJcR.

United Nations Children's Fund (UNICEF). 2014a. "Hidden in Plain Sight: A Statistical Analysis of Violence and Children." Accessed October 14, 2014, at http://files.unicef.org/publications/files/Hidden_in_plain_sight_statistical_analysis_EN_3_Sept_2014.pdf.

United Nations Children's Fund (UNICEF). 2014b. "Summary: Hidden in Plain Sight: A Statistical Analysis of Violence and Children." Accessed October 14, 2014, at http://www.unicef.org/publications/files/Hidden_in_plain_sight_statistical_analysis_Summary_EN_2_Sept_2014.pdf.

United Nations Population Fund (UNFPA). 2013. "State of World Population 2013: Motherhood in Childhood." Accessed October 14, 2014, at http://www.unfpa.org/swp.

UN Women. 2014. "Facts and Figures: Ending Violence Against Women." Accessed October 14, 2014, at http://www.unwomen.org/en/what-we-do/ending-violence-against-women/facts-and-figures.

World Health Organization (WHO). 2014. "Adolescent Pregnancy." Accessed October 14, 2014, at http://www.who.int/maternal_child_adolescent/topics/maternal/adolescent_pregnancy/en/.

FURTHER READING

Bearinger, Linda H., Renee E. Sieving, Jane Ferguson, and Vinit Sharma. 2007. "Global Perspectives on the Sexual and Reproductive Health of Adolescents: Patterns, Prevention, and Potential." *The Lancet*, 369(9568): 1220–1231.

Luker, Kristin. 1996. *Dubious Conceptions: The Politics of Teenage Pregnancy*. Cambridge, MA: Harvard University Press.

Ward, Martha C. 1995. "Early Childbearing: What is the Problem and Who Owns It?" In *Conceiving the New World Order: The Global Politics of Reproduction*, edited by Faye Ginsburg and Rayna Rapp. Berkeley: University of California Press.

Adultery, Cultural Views of

STEPHEN T. FIFE
University of Nevada, Las Vegas, USA

Marriage and other committed relationships typically include an explicit or implicit expectation and commitment to sexual and emotional loyalty to one's partner. This commitment serves to protect the unique bond between partners and regulates interactions with people outside the committed relationship. Adultery refers to a violation of the commitment to sexual fidelity within marriage. In comparison, infidelity is defined more broadly to include a variety of behaviors constituting a violation of fidelity to one's partner. Infidelity occurs when sexual and/or emotional intimacy is diverted away from the primary relationship without the partner's consent. Infidelity applies to diverse forms of committed relationships, including dating, cohabiting, heterosexual, homosexual, as well as marriage. Other terms that have been used to describe infidelity include affair, cheating, unfaithful, extramarital sex, extramarital coitus, extradyadic sex, and extradyadic relationship.

Traditionally, adultery/infidelity referred specifically to sexual relations with someone outside a marriage or committed relationship. However, infidelity may be subjectively defined, and contemporary definitions of infidelity include a wider variety of behaviors and relationships. Hertlein, Wetchler, and Piercy (2005) proposed three types: physical, emotional, and Internet infidelity. Although there are instances when an extradyadic relationship is limited to only one type of infidelity, affairs often involve more than one type.

Physical infidelity is the most recognizable type of infidelity and includes any kind of sexual behavior or physical affection that violates the commitment to exclusivity in the primary relationship. This could include behaviors such as holding hands, kissing, fondling, petting, genital stimulation, oral sex, anal sex, and intercourse.

Emotional infidelity is more common than physical infidelity and also takes a variety of forms. Emotional infidelity is defined as sharing emotional intimacy and connection with another person in violation of the commitment to the primary relationship. An emotional affair could include developing an emotionally intimate friendship, spending excessive amounts of time with another, or sharing intimate details of one's life with someone other than the committed partner.

In addition to infidelity that involves face-to-face interaction, technological advances in recent decades have created new avenues by which a betrayal of one's partner can occur. Internet or cyber infidelity takes place through the use of technology via the Internet or cell phones and may include sexual or emotional features. Certain characteristics unique to the Internet may contribute to online affairs: accessibility, affordability, anonymity, approximation, acceptability, ambiguity, and accommodation (Hertlein and Stevenson 2010). Internet infidelity may involve flirting with someone through email or text, cybersex (or sex over the computer using words and/or video), sexting (sending sexually explicit words or pictures via text), or viewing pornography online. It may also occur through chat rooms, social networking sites (e.g., Facebook), Skype, video chat applications on cell phones, or online virtual worlds or games such as Second Life and World of Warcraft. There are even websites with the express purpose of facilitating affairs, with millions of users in countries across the globe.

Although infidelity may be understood as a violation of the commitment to exclusivity, there are cultural variations regarding values, attitudes, and expectations of fidelity in committed relationships. Historically, many societies have strong social and legal constraints against adultery, often including severe consequences (such as public flogging, stoning, or death). In many countries, adultery is sufficient grounds for divorce. Additionally, the majority of world religions (e.g., Judaism, Christianity, Islam) condemn adultery. Although attitudes regarding sexual permissiveness shifted in the 1920s and

1960s, a vast majority believes that adultery is wrong. A cross-national study of 24 countries found that only 4 percent of respondents believe that marital infidelity is "not wrong at all." Other research comparing individuals from the United Kingdom, United States, Ireland, Germany, Sweden, and Poland found that 82–94 percent believed that adultery is wrong.

In spite of strong legal, social, and religious constraints, statistics indicate that the prevalence of infidelity is relatively high, with 20–25 percent of Americans committing adultery at some point in marriage (Atkins, Baucom, and Jacobson, 2001). However, there are relationships in which sexual fidelity is not expected, such as swinging, open, or polyamorous relationships. Even in these relationships, there are usually "rules" established regarding sexual relations, and infidelity can still occur.

Gender is also an important variable in understanding infidelity. There is a historical and cross-cultural double standard that supports greater permissiveness by men. Wiederman (1997) found that 22.7 percent of men and 11.6 percent of women reported having extramarital sex. However, this gender difference may be shrinking with younger generations. Other differences include the finding by Glass and Wright (1985) that men are more likely to commit "sexual-only" infidelity, and women are more likely to commit "emotional-only" infidelity.

In addition to gender, there are other variables associated with infidelity. For example, individuals in first marriages are less likely to cheat than cohabiting couples, remarried couples, and singles. Lower levels of marital satisfaction are positively correlated with the incidence of adultery. However, religiosity is inversely correlated with infidelity, with more frequent religious attendance being associated with lower incidence.

Experts agree that infidelity is one of the most destructive events that can occur in a committed relationship, and it is one of the most difficult relationship problems to treat in therapy. Because of the significance of the betrayal, infidelity often causes substantial emotional and relationship distress. The trauma of finding out that one's partner has cheated often precipitates loss of trust, depression, anxiety, extreme anger, insecurity, decreased self-esteem, and symptoms of post-traumatic stress disorder (PTSD) (e.g., emotional reactivity, obsessive thoughts, flashback, nightmares,). Many relationships do not survive the damage caused by infidelity. Although the impact of infidelity can be severe, many couples desire to stay together and attempt to heal. Some engage in this work on their own or utilize self-help literature. Others seek support and assistance from friends, family members, or clergy. Still others seek professional help from a marriage or relationship counselor.

SEE ALSO: Cyber Intimacies; Double Standard; Internet Sex; Polyamory

REFERENCES

Atkins, David, Donald Baucom, and Neil Jacobson, 2001. "Understanding Infidelity: Correlates in a National Random Sample." *Journal of Family Psychology*, 15: 735–749.

Glass, Shirley P., and Thomas L. Wright. 1985. "Sex Differences in Type of Extramarital Involvement and Marital Dissatisfaction." *Sex Roles*, 12: 1101–1120.

Hertlein, Katherine, and Armeda Stevenson. 2010. "The Seven 'As' Contributing to Internet-Related Intimacy Problems: A Literature Review." *Cyberpsychology: Journal of Psychosocial Research on Cyberspace*, 4(1): article 1.

Hertlein, Katherine, Joseph Wetchler, and Fred Piercy. 2005. "Infidelity: An Overview." *Journal of Couple and Relationship Therapy*, 4(2/3): 5–16.

Wiederman, Michael W. 1997. "Extramarital Sex: Prevalence and Correlates in a National Survey." *Journal of Sex Research*, 34: 167–174.

FURTHER READING

Peluso, Paul, ed. 2007. *Infidelity: A Practitioner's Guide to Working with Couples in Crisis*. Philadelphia: Routledge.

Springer, Janis. 2012. *After the Affair*, 2nd ed. New York: HarperCollins.

Widmer, Eric D., Judith Treas, and Robert Newcomb. 1998. "Attitudes Toward Nonmarital Sex in 24 Countries." *Journal of Sex Research*, 35(4): 349–358.

Affirmative Action

DEVON R. GOSS
University of Connecticut, USA

Affirmative action refers to efforts aimed at increasing opportunities for women and people of color within the United States. The practice has been one of the most successful policies for addressing gender and racial inequalities, especially within education and employment. Affirmative action necessitates continuous and proactive (i.e., "affirmative") actions to increase the numbers of women and people of color through a multi-tiered approach that includes training, admissions, recruitment, and retention. Therefore, women and people of color's race and gender should be evaluated positively by both private and public institutions and organizations. These actions are seen as a partial correction to deep structural inequalities that are pervasive throughout society.

Affirmative action has been most often discussed in regard to people of color, especially African Americans, in contemporary times. Most of the scholarly attention has followed this trend, focusing on affirmative action based on racial and ethnic identities and disregarding gender-based affirmative action programs. However, some argue that women are the main beneficiaries of affirmative action programs in the United States, despite the misconception that affirmative action primarily deals with race (Beeman, Chowdhry, and Todd 2000).

The need for affirmative action stems from unequal treatment based on race and gender within education and the workplace, as well as a lack of opportunities for women and people of color starting early in life, and impacting social networks, resources, and training. Affirmative action is often seen as an outgrowth of social movements aimed at racial and gender equity. Due to widespread racial and gender discrimination that has occurred within the United States, people of color and women formed coalitions and social movements in order to challenge discrimination and segregation. These movements, including the civil rights movement and the feminist movement, were ultimately successful in putting laws into place in the 1950s and 1960s that prohibited discrimination in policies and practices throughout the United States. State-specific and national organizations aimed at promoting equality, such as the National Organization of Women, spawned from these movements and now play an important part in advocating for affirmative action.

Affirmative action was introduced to the American public by President John F. Kennedy in a 1961 Executive Order, wherein he ensured that applicants for government employment were not being denied consideration on the basis of color, creed, race, or national origin (Rai and Critzer 2000). The Equal Pay Act was passed in 1963 by Congress, and demanded that men and women earn equal pay for equal work. Additionally, Title VII of the Civil Rights Act of 1964 banned employment discrimination based on race and sex. These laws explicitly outlawed two of the major issues plaguing gender equality in the workplace – discriminatory hiring and pay practices – and represented a significant win for liberal feminist movements and organizations. Moreover, the creation of the Committee on Equal Employment Opportunity allowed an explicit mechanism for women and people of color to bring complaints regarding discrimination. The concept of affirmative action also flourished outside of the United States, particularly through international bodies and organizations. For example, the United Nations General Assembly adopted the Convention on the Elimination of All Forms of Discrimination against Women (CEDAW) in 1979. The CEDAW included specific language supporting affirmative action for women, and acted as the impetus for laws and programs supporting affirmative action in numerous countries.

These laws resulted in a significant increase of women and people of color in positions of power in society. For example, throughout the 1970s, the number of women students and faculty increased throughout all fields in higher education (Zamani-Gallaher et al. 2009). Despite the significant gains made by passing these laws supporting affirmative action, their overall effectiveness has been limited. The 1970s brought the collapse of highly paid union jobs that women were expected to gain access to in the wake of affirmative action, stalling upward mobility for working-class women. Additionally, many scholars report evidence of a glass ceiling, an unseen and unreachable barrier to advancement for both women and people of color, in many professions (Cotter, Benard, and Paik 2001). Finally, the perception of women's obligations to their families, particularly their role as mothers, influences their ability to be hired, their potential income, and their perceived success on the job (Correll, Benard, and Paik 2007).

In addition, there has been a history of strong opposition to affirmative action that has influenced the shape and strength of contemporary affirmative action policies. Reasons for opposition to affirmative action include beliefs about meritocracy, rejecting government regulation of businesses, and fear of the long-term effect on the institutions of marriage and the family. Opponents have utilized the legal system to challenge affirmative action policies, resulting in many high-profile Supreme Court cases. These cases have resulted in the prohibition of a quota system (e.g., setting aside a certain number of cases for women or people of color) but have allowed race or gender to be considered among other factors in admissions or hiring procedures.

SEE ALSO: Employment Discrimination; Gender Wage Gap; Glass Ceiling and Glass Elevator; Sex Discrimination

REFERENCES

Beeman, Mark, Geeta Chowdhry, and Karmen Todd. 2000. "Educating Students about Affirmative Action: An Analysis of University Sociology Texts." *Teaching Sociology*, 28(2): 98–115.

Correll, Shelley J., Stephen Benard, and In Paik. 2007. "Getting a Job: Is There a Motherhood Penalty?" *American Journal of Sociology*, 112(5): 1297–1338.

Cotter, David A., Joan M. Hermsen, Seth Ovadia, and Reeve Vanneman. 2001. "The Glass Ceiling Effect." *Social Forces*, 80(2): 655–681.

Rai, Kul B., and John W. Critzer. 2000. *Affirmative Action and the University: Race, Ethnicity, and Gender in Higher Education*. Lincoln: University of Nebraska Press.

Zamani-Gallaher, Eboni M., Denise O'Neil Green, M. Christopher Brown II, and David O. Stovall. 2009. *The Case for Affirmative Action on Campus*. Sterling: Stylus.

FURTHER READING

Anderson, Terry H. 2005. *The Pursuit of Fairness: A History of Affirmative Action*. New York: Oxford University Press.

Pierce, Jennifer. 2012. *Racing for Innocence: Whiteness, Gender, and the Backlash against Affirmative Action*. Stanford: Stanford University Press.

Age of Consent and Child Marriage in India

PADMA ANAGOL
Cardiff University, UK

Anti-colonial struggles for a long time have been narrowly interpreted in terms of self-determination for equal rights in the political and economic realms in the making of sovereign nation-states. However, the long and impressive historical literature on the institution of Indian child marriage starting from the 1960s has unpicked the intimate relationships between sexual politics and sexual identities in the formation of new nationalist subjectivities both in the metropole (Britain) and the colony (India) displaying the power of the cultural realms in nationalist struggles. A close examination of debates generated over child marriage and the related age of consent issues in late nineteenth-century India reveal challenges to, and finally, the accommodation of feudal patriarchal familial practices in colonial India.

The institution of child marriage was common throughout India, cutting across religious, caste, and geographical lines. Behramji Malabari, a prominent social reformer, had started a campaign for the protection of women's rights and as early as 1884, utilizing the Imperial Census of India, he revealed shocking statistics for the widespread existence of infant and child marriages in India. In an article titled "Figures, If You Please" in his privately owned English newspaper *The Indian Spectator*, he claimed that out of a total of 81,600,000 Hindu females, 1,932,000 girls of 9 years old and younger were married, and 4,395,000 girls in the 10–14 year age group were married. He further calculated that about 3,800,000 girls were married to adult men between 30 and 50 years of age. Malabari painted a grim picture for the future of such girl wives whom he predicted would be widows well before their time.

At this stage it is pertinent to ask what prompted Indian parents to marry their daughters at such an early age. Both western-educated Indian intellectuals and orthodox Hindu clerics offered an explanation for the Indian practice of child marriage in religious terms. Citing Hindu scriptures, it was claimed that the *garbhadhan* ("gift of the womb" or impregnation) ritual mandated sexual intercourse between the husband and his girl-bride on the onset of her first menstrual cycle, failing which the patrilineal family of the girl would commit the sin of embryo-killing, resulting in calamitous spiritual consequences for both families. Since physiologically speaking, it was difficult to ascertain when a girl reached menarche, Hindu families married them off at an earlier age sometimes even in the cradle. Often the pre-pubertal girl-bride grew up in her mother's home but on some occasions she was sent to her in-law's house soon after the marriage. In theory, the impregnation of her womb – as the *garbhadhan* ceremony literally indicated – took place after the onset of her first menstruation. However, in practice, the late nineteenth-century vernacular and English language press published sensational accounts of widespread pre-pubertal consummation of marriage and accompanying gory details of the injuries sustained by the girl-wife.

Malabari's campaigns in both India and Britain raised awkward questions about the well-being of Indian girls which were partially prompted by the sensational law suit brought by a 35-year-old man called Dadaji Bhikaji from Bombay for the restitution of conjugal rights from his 19-year-old wife, Rakhmabai. The bourgeois sexual norms of Victorian society were imbricated in the discussions over the feasibility of allowing restitution of conjugal rights in India. Restitution of conjugal rights was an ecclesiastical and antiquated provision which had been imported into Anglo-Indian law despite having been discarded by the Matrimonial Clauses Act of 1884 in Britain as a barbaric accretion. There were several law suits and Rakhmabai was initially acquitted on the grounds that she had been married without her consent as a child and that her marriage had never been consummated but on Dadaji Bhikaji's appeal, the British judge succumbed to the widespread hostile reaction of Indians and ordered her to reside with her husband. Rakhmabai flatly refused, opting for prison instead. The various trials provoked transnational controversy including the British, vernacular, and Anglo-Indian press. Eventually the case was resolved by Rakhmabai making a financial settlement for her release from her husband. Barely had the case settled when yet another marriage scandal broke out, but this time in eastern India. In July 1890, a 35-year-old Hindu husband, Hari Maiti was accused of murdering his 10-year-old wife Phulmani Dasi (henceforth Phulmani) through forced coitus. The coroner's report conclusively proved that Phulmani had suffered horrific sexual injuries and hemorrhaged to death as a result of coerced pre-pubertal sex.

Together, the Rakhmabai and Phulmani cases unleashed a powerful debate in an electrified transnational setting covering both Britain and India. Aware of the mantle of the "civilizing mission" that the imperial government wore, it promptly issued a circular in 1890 to local governments requesting their opinion regarding the appropriateness of bringing in legislation to address the question of protection of the welfare of girls and women in India. As a consequence of government intervention, a large body of opinion was sought and collected from the "natural leaders" of Indian society such as princes, medical doctors, lawyers, eminent educationalists, and representatives of Hindu and Muslim clergy. A significant omission, however, was the opinion of Indian women whose welfare was being debated and legislated upon. The resulting discourses which preceded the legislation challenged the very premise of Hindu religious practices, the British role in India, the morality of Indian society, and brought to the fore opposing views of sexuality from Britain and India. Citing eugenic theories of race, medical authorities condemned the degraded morality of Indian men which they said had resulted in the degeneration of the Indian race through the birth of sickly children of underage mothers. Resting on the back of medical opinion, the government asserted that India could not modernize itself without emulating the moral values of "civilized" Europeans. On March 19, 1891, the Age of Consent Bill was passed by the Supreme Legislative Council of India which raised the age of consent for heterosexual and penetrative sex for girls from 10 (this was the age set by a previous legislation in 1860) to 12. It declared sexual intercourse illegal with a girl below the age of 12, both married and unmarried, and an offender could be jailed for a maximum of 10 years or transportation for life.

While the imperial state congratulated itself for its humanitarian act of protecting girls from bodily sexual harm, within India it was interpreted as a gross violation of the private lives of colonial subjects and a wanton aim of controlling the body of the Indian girl, which Indian men felt was their domain. Thus the debates over the age of consent only succeeded in radicalizing and boosting the nationalist movement against the social reform movements. At the heart of the debate was the core question as to who controlled Indian female sexuality? Was it the husband, or the family, or the woman, or was it the colonial state? Nowhere else is this made clearer than the manner in which official and Indian reformist and orthodox opinion honed in on the "age" of consent rather than the girl or woman's consent for sex. Mrinalini Sinha has studied how reformist and orthodox Indian men shared similar definitions of female consent. Both official and indigenous male discourses shared the viewpoint that female consent was based on the reproductive function of women, or the age at which girls could be deemed biologically mature to produce healthy children without endangering themselves or the health of the race. The government relied purely on medical experts to pronounce its judgment regarding the correct age at which Indian women reached puberty. Medical authorities suggested that Indian girls came of age at 12 years and any earlier evidence of menstruation was regarded as proof of the debased sexual morality of Hindu society, wherein artificial methods were cited as having induced younger girls to menstruate well before their bodies were ready to do so.

What was evident in the discussions between imperial officials, medical authorities and indigenous proponents and opponents to the Bill was that none of the main parties in the legislative debate saw female sexuality as being independent of the reproductive function of women. Further evidence of how both supporters and opponents to the Bill viewed the husband as the controller of female sexuality in India was provided in their reservations about the marital rape clause in the Exception to Section 375 of the Indian Penal Code. Bengali opponents to the Bill argued that the Criminal Amendment Act of 1885 in Britain had excluded the marital rape clause on the grounds that through marriage an English woman had automatically surrendered her sexual rights and consent to her husband. Taking the argument further it was shown how in contrast the proposed legislation in India was an infringement of the Indian husband's rights to certain patriarchal privileges. Thus the issue of marital rape brought by the Phulmani case enraged Indian orthodoxy and reformist camps equally because of its embedded proposal that if the government went ahead with the Bill of raising the age of consent for legally permissive sex, then female sexuality in India would henceforth be independent of the husband's control. That henceforth, any Indian husband would be treated on a par with any common rapist was anathema to the boldest and most radical reformer. Geraldine Forbes has contended that indigenous men masked their real intentions by putting forth spurious claims that Indian female sexuality came of age earlier than other countries due to the tropical climate and hence norms of Indian sexual respectability could only be complied with by early marriage of girls and the handing over of their sexual rights to the husband.

The male control of female sexuality was brilliantly outlined by the astute and dazzling cold logic of the lawyer and nationalist leader, Bal Gangadhar Tilak, who led the opposition in western India. Tilak argued that in Indian and Hindu tradition, the holy books did not consider the Indian woman as a "person." Hindu religious scriptures did not conceive of independence for a woman, having sanctioned that as a child (daughter) she would be under the control of her father, as a woman (post puberty, i.e., as wife and mother) under the control of her husband, and in her dotage (grandmother) under the control of her son, thus showing that in Indian traditions the woman was never an "agent." Tanika Sarkar has studied the Bengali opposition to the Age of Consent Bill and concluded that the indigenous opponents saw the proposed Bill as the first breach of Hindu autonomy. The revivalists and nationalists, she argued, understood clearly that the public arena was not the battleground for the test between competing notions of manhood (British manliness versus Bengali effeminacy) but that domestic social arrangements embedded in conjugality, consumption of marriage, and divorce were being eroded by the British. The consequent defense of Indian traditions by Bengali men is read by her as a political strategy to guard the "home" – their last bastion of self-rule – and thus gave rise to a militant nationalism in Bengal. Reading the British and Indian male preoccupation with the biological imperative of the "age" of puberty rather than with "consent" or compatibility, Himani Bannerji has correctly deduced that, together, the official, medical, and indigenous discourses saw the Indian female as "little more than a body and a reproductive system to be regulated and investigated."

But what about the sexual double standards in Indian society which appears obvious even in a superficial reading of the debates on child marriage? Did anyone talk about them? Anagol has argued that just because women's views were not solicited by the state does not mean that Indian women stayed silent. Anagol has argued that modern feminism came to India through women's participation in the nineteenth-century child marriage controversy. Indian women from the state of Maharashtra utilized their own Marathi Women's Press to challenge the assumptions of sexual double standards embedded in colonialist and indigenous discourses on child marriage. The politicization of Indian women's identities came through collective meetings and petitioning, use of law courts for redressal of marital grievances and taking their campaigns to the "mother country," Britain, to publicize their woes. Indian women inverted male strategies by turning the lens from a discussion of what the texts (the religious books called *shastras*) said about legitimacy or illegitimacy of child marriage to context (i.e., their own experiences of being "child-brides" and "child-wives"). New coinages in the feminist vocabulary is detected by Anagol in the crucial decades of the 1880s and 1890s when the "condition of Indian womanhood" (*strivarg*) and the solidarity of a woman's collective (*bhaginivarg*) was debated furiously by women leaders such as Pandita Ramabai, Lakshmibai Deshmukh, Kashibai Kanitkar, and Rakhmabai. Women participants called for a higher age of consent – not for prepubertal sex as enlightened men were doing, but for marriage – and their stance was far more radical than their menfolk evidenced in their call for divorce where incompatible marriages existed. Anagol's conclusions suggest that if Indian patriarchy felt it was under siege, it was not due to the colonial state's posturing as the protector of Indian child-wives and mothers but by the threat posed by the assertive words and deeds of their own womenfolk.

In recent years, the insights provided by queer theory and studies of childhood have led to the revisiting of the older debates from the point of view of the "boy child" as well as the girl child. Ishita Pande has called for a dialogue between feminist scholars and childhood studies on India to problematize interpretations of the child as "innocent," "victimized," or lacking in agency and in need of protection. Some areas waiting for further study are the conceptions in Indian Islamic traditions and Muslim society of the girlchild and her protection. Equally, how the Indian institutions of infant and child marriage normalized child sexual abuse also awaits urgent attention.

SEE ALSO: Child Sexual Abuse and Trauma

FURTHER READING

Anagol, Padma. 2006. "Women as Agents: Contesting Discourses on Marriage and Marital Rights." In *The Emergence of Feminism in India, 1850–1920*, 181–218. Aldershot: Ashgate.

Anagol, Padma. 2010. "Feminist Inheritances and Foremothers: The Beginnings of Feminism in Modern India." *Women's History Review*, 19(4): 523–546.

Bannerji, Himani. 1998. "Age of Consent and Hegemonic Social Reform." In *Gender and Imperialism*, edited by Clare Midgley, 21–44. Manchester: Manchester University Press.

Burton, Antoinette. 1998. "From Child Bride to 'Hindoo Lady': Rukhmabai and the Debate on Sexual Respectability in Imperial Britain." *American Historical Review*, 103(4): 1119–1146.

Pande, Ishita. 2013. "'Listen to the Child': Law, Sex, and the Child Wife in Indian Historiography." *History Compass*, 11(9): 687–701.

Sarkar, Tanika. 1993. "Rhetoric against Age of Consent: Resisting Colonial Reason and Death of a Child-Wife." *Economic and Political Weekly*, 28(36): 1869–1878.

Sinha, Mrinalini. 1995. "Nationalism and Respectable Sexuality in India." *Genders*, 21: 30–57.

Age of Consent in Historical and International Perspective

THOMAS K. HUBBARD
The University of Texas at Austin, USA

The controlling concept behind "age of consent" or "statutory rape" laws is the assumption that young people below a certain age have insufficient judgment, psychological maturity, or powers of resistance to be able to give informed consent to sexual intimacy with another person. Currently, the age of consent in almost all states of the United States ranges between 16 and 18, with some of the largest and most influential jurisdictions setting the age at the higher end (18 in California and Florida; 17 in Illinois, New York, and Texas). In contrast, about two thirds of European states (surveyed in Graupner 2004) set the minimum age at 14 (e.g., Austria, Germany, Italy) or 15 (France, Sweden). Little correlation exists between the minimum legal age for sexual activity and the actual average age of first intercourse (see the figures in Parker, Wellings, and Lazarus 2009, 229–231).

That so many young persons choose to explore their sexuality at ages below the legally mandated minimums problematizes the laws' effectiveness and wisdom in the eyes of many critics. Scholars of gender and sexuality are actively involved in the debates, weighing the utility of these laws for agendas of child protection versus the repressive effects of the laws in privileging parental or state control over adolescents' sexual self-determination and bodily autonomy. Although contemporary age of consent legislation does not distinguish on the basis of a young person's gender, this indifference was not the case historically. Scholarship is only beginning to contribute to the question of how younger adolescents may experience precocious sexuality differently based on gender and orientation.

The earliest recorded legislation on the topic is found in the definition of rape in the Statutes of Westminster (1275), which does not, however, stipulate a specific minimum age, only leaving it implied that it was identical to the minimum age of female marriage, which at the time was 12. The offense was merely considered a misdemeanor, becoming a felony first in 1576 (and only for "carnal knowledge" of a female under 10). Under the influence of this English common law tradition, American states adopted the same standard of 10 or 12 (7 in Delaware), again only with application to girls. More influential on the European continent was the French Napoleonic Code, which specified the age of 11. These ages fall well short of puberty, particularly when we consider that nutrition and conditions of life in premodern societies resulted in later menarche than is common in the contemporary West.

The considerably higher ages of consent that prevail in modern law have their roots in the late nineteenth century: in 1885 Victorian reformers, alarmed by sensationalistic journalism about "white slavery" rings enticing young girls into lives of prostitution, raised the age to 16 in Britain and Ireland. In the same year and in response to similar concerns, the Woman's Christian Temperance Union (WCTU) advocated an age of 18 in the United States, and over the course of the following decades succeeded in raising the age to 16 or 18 in most American states. While early minimum ages of marriage (and consent) may have appeared practical in an agrarian economy where most marriages were arranged and female children were often considered a burden, the rapid urbanization and industrialization of both the United Kingdom and United States stimulated new concerns over exploitation of child labor in ways that could be morally as well as physically enervating.

However, American historians have pointed out that the actual enforcement of these laws in the Progressive Era (1900–1930) often had the effect of reinforcing patriarchal structures of control over female bodies. Many families, especially immigrant parents accustomed to the arranged marriages still common in the rural societies of Southern Europe or Mexico, used the laws to manipulate their own "wayward" daughters. In an influential examination of juvenile justice records of this period, Schlossman and Wallach (1978, 68) concluded, "girls were prosecuted almost exclusively for 'immoral' conduct, a very broad category that defined all sexual exploration as fundamentally perverse and predictive of future promiscuity, perhaps even prostitution." Girls received longer reformatory sentences for these social misdemeanors than boys did for actual criminal conduct. This policing of adolescent female sexuality cannot be divorced from the broader agenda of social purity movements like the WCTU, which was to eliminate all forms of "vice" by the extension of criminal law into stricter regulation of alcohol, drugs, obscenity, gambling, sodomy, and even the conduct of adult heterosexual women; in the same period vagrancy, disorderly conduct, and prostitution laws were widely used as a basis for incarcerating adult women prone to even uncompensated promiscuity or sexual independence. Prosecution particularly targeted young women of working-class, immigrant, or African American backgrounds; penal rehabilitation aimed to train them in the middle-class domestic skills and habits expected of women by the largely white Protestant middle-class reformers. The attention to deterrence of teen pregnancy among poor immigrant populations also cannot be separated from the eugenicist preoccupations of some early birth control advocates.

Neither the statutes nor their practical enforcement showed much concern with regulating the sexual expression of minor males, except to the extent that statutory rape laws were sometimes used to compel a young man into early marriage as a safe alternative to prosecution. However, this changed with a second wave of US legal reforms beginning in the 1970s and 1980s (see Cocca 2004). Concerned with dissecting and deconstructing systemic inequities of power within the patriarchal family and reforming long-standing constructions of "consent" within rape law, some 1970s feminists were alarmed by what they perceived as the pervasive incestuous abuse of children, to which they assimilated all intergenerational relationships. In a curious alliance with social conservative groups alarmed over general promiscuity in the wake of the sexual revolution of the 1960s and the growing visibility of a gay subculture in the 1970s, feminist reformers pushed for legislative changes to promote gender-neutral language in legal codes pertaining to sexual assault. The drive for extending statutory rape "protections" to minor males was further fueled in the 1980s by a wave of well-publicized, though later debunked, allegations of widespread pedophile abductions (seared into every family's consciousness with ubiquitous images of missing children on milk cartons), ritual abuse of both male and female children in Satanic cults and otherwise innocent-appearing day-care centers, and iatrogenically induced "recovered memories" of incestuous abuse by parents and close relatives. Moral fears of rampant sexual license, particularly among gay males, were aggravated further by the new and at first poorly understood epidemic of AIDS. The male child thus came to be as much an object of sexual surveillance as the female child had been since the early 1900s.

In addition to adopting gender-neutral language, state legislatures in the United States have continued to adopt higher ages of consent and more severe punitive sanctions against adults who become sexually involved with minors below the legal age. At the dawn of the twenty-first century came new concerns about clerical abuse of boys in the Catholic Church and the vulnerability of children to contact by outsiders through the new social technology of the Internet. As Cocca (2004) has documented, state legislatures addressed these laws with little or no expert testimony, but in reaction to popular anxieties and the model of what other state legislatures had already done. Far from having any influence in arresting such legislative trends, a careful meta-analysis published in the top-ranked academic journal *Psychological Bulletin* (Rind, Tromovitch, and Bauserman 1998) that showed more positive than negative impacts of early age-discrepant relationships on boys' development (in marked contrast with girls) was so unwelcome as to receive unanimous censure by both houses of the US Congress, an action unprecedented in the history of social science.

The second major thrust of US legislative reform beginning in the 1970s was to adopt "age-span" provisions allowing for consensual sex between teens as long as their respective ages are not separated by more than 2–6 years, depending on the state. For example, in Florida 16- or 17-year-olds may consent to sexual contact with a partner up to the age of 23 (in Delaware up to the age of 30), but 18 is the operative age of consent for contact with anyone older. In Texas, 14-year-olds may consent to sex with someone no more than three years older, 15- and 16-year-olds with someone no more than four years older. These arbitrary provisions are seldom well understood even by young people themselves. They are not founded on any credible social science suggesting that sexual relations among adolescent partners close in age are less harmful or potentially traumatic than those with a partner above a certain age. They instead appear to be founded on what are essentially moral valuations about sex between equally naïve teen partners being less bad than sex between a teen and a more experienced adult, which is assumed to be inherently exploitive. However, critics maintain that such age-span provisions undermine the philosophical premise of statutory rape law, which holds that no "informed consent" can exist below a legislatively determined age: why is a Texas 14-year-old informed enough to consent to intercourse with a 17-year-old, but not with an 18- or 19-year-old (who might actually be more capable of providing support in the event of pregnancy)?

The legislative changes of recent decades have had a profound effect in terms of mass incarceration of American adults and even an alarming number of juveniles (since even the age-span provisions do not apply below a certain age) for sexual involvement with a minor: Zimring (2004, 35–37) has observed an 800 percent increase in the number imprisoned for such offenses between 1980 and 1997. Moreover, restrictions upon sex offenders after completing their prison terms have grown far more severe in the last 10–15 years, with community notification now almost universally mandated under "Megan's Law" as well as residency limitations (barring an offender from living within a certain distance of parks, schools, and other public facilities). In many jurisdictions, these restrictions have had the effect of making it nearly impossible for one-time sex offenders (including those who offended while still juveniles) to find affordable housing or avoid community harassment. The premise behind these safeguards, which are applied to no other class of felon, is that sex offenders are incurable deviants uniquely prone to reoffend, despite Department of Justice statistics establishing that recidivism for sexual offenses is in fact lower than for other classes of criminal offense.

These trends in recent American legislation have found some echo in Canada, which in 2008 raised its national age of consent from 14 (which it had been since 1890) to 16. Influenced by Western non-government organizations (NGOs) concerned over sex tourism, many Asian countries have raised their effective age of consent. Some European states that used to have a relatively low age of consent have also recently changed it to 16 (the Netherlands in 2002, Spain in 2013). However, the social and political factors that proved so potent in American legislation have for the most part exerted less influence in Europe. Since European states legislate such criminal issues at the federal level, special commissions and expert testimony by sexologists, educators, and criminologists have tended to carry more weight (see Waites 2005 for the United Kingdom). Rather than adopting the kind of age-span criteria common in American states, European law instead prefers special provisions protecting those under 18 from prostitution or abuse by persons in a position of authority. The punishment for offenders tends to be far less draconian in Europe (where 1- to 2-year sentences for non-coercive relations are common, compared to frequent sentences of 10–20 years or more in most US states), with a stronger emphasis on therapy and social reintegration of minor-attracted adults.

Age of consent is a complex social construction grounded in multiple factors, including traditional but wholly unscientific valuations of child independence and responsibility, availability of institutional education, a society's need for reproductive capacity, marital patterns, male bonding structures, and initiation into adulthood. It may be useful to ground any debate over the most rational age for recognizing responsible sexual decision-making in a broader anthropological and historical framework, while at the same time recognizing the specificity of each society's adaptive needs. In an influential ethnographic survey of "maidenhood" practices in a range of pre-industrial societies, Whiting (2006, 282–305) has noted that spans of medium to long duration (i.e., 3–4 years) between menarche and marriage are often accompanied by tolerance or even encouragement of some form of sexual experimentation before marriage, whereas societies that place a high value on bridal virginity tend to marry females close to the time of menarche. Ancient Athens (the most prosperous and successful of the Greek city-states) and Rome also generally arranged marriages when girls were between 12 and 15; this pattern appears particularly strong among the upper classes, who had the greatest ability to find suitable partners. While girls' "consent" to such arrangements was not always operative, these practices do at least suggest that a broad range of pre-industrial societies, including some that were complex, literate, and socially stratified, regarded their female children as mature enough for sexual activity at or soon after menarche.

Males, although typically marrying later, had considerable latitude for adolescent sexual freedom in classical times. Upper-class youths found slave girls of their own or neighboring households readily available, as the plots of numerous Hellenistic or Roman comedies attest. Greek ceramic decorations commonly show scenes of beardless (i.e., still adolescent) youths interacting with female prostitutes and older men courting their favor for pederastic liaisons, as well as youths their own age or younger. Textual and visual evidence clearly establishes that freeborn Greek youths from the age of puberty could spurn advances from adult suitors they did not like, or accept those who pleased them. Indeed, being able to hold one's own in negotiation with an adult suitor and maintaining proper standards of selectivity were seen as key tests of character development.

The critical question that contemporary social critics must address when considering a higher age of consent is what renders American teens more vulnerable in sexual interactions than their counterparts in other modern or historical cultures that permit sexual self-determination at an age closer to physiological puberty. A second, but important, question is whether comparatively high ages of consent may unduly restrict the opportunities of sexual-minority youth to explore their preferences with older and more experienced partners who can provide useful guidance in how to chart identity in a non-supportive social environment.

SEE ALSO: Adolescent Pregnancy; Child Sexual Abuse and Trauma; Eugenics, Historical and Ethical Aspects of; Menarche; Sexual Regulation and Social Control

REFERENCES

Cocca, Carolyn E. 2004. *Jailbait: The Politics of Statutory Rape Laws in the United States*. Albany: SUNY Press.

Graupner, Helmut. 2004. "Sexual Consent: The Criminal Law in Europe and Outside of Europe." *Journal of Psychology and Human Sexuality*, 16(2/3): 111–171. DOI: 10.1300/J056v16n02_10.

Parker, Rachael, Kaye Wellings, and J. V. Lazarus. 2009. "Sexuality Education in Europe: An Overview of Current Policies." *Sex Education*, 9: 227–242. DOI: 10.1080/14681810903059060.

Rind, Bruce, Philip Tromovitch, and R. Bauserman. 1998. "A Meta-Analytic Examination of Assumed Properties of Child Sexual Abuse Using College Samples." *Psychological Bulletin*, 124: 22–53. DOI: 10.1037/0033-2909.124.1.22.

Schlossman, Steven, and Stephanie Wallach. 1978. "The Crime of Precocious Sexuality: Female Juvenile Delinquency in the Progressive Era." *Harvard Educational Review*, 48: 64–92.

Waites, Matthew. 2005. *The Age of Consent: Young People, Sexuality, and Citizenship*. Basingstoke: Palgrave Macmillan.

Whiting, John. 2006. *Culture and Human Development*. Cambridge: Cambridge University Press.

Zimring, Franklin. 2004. *An American Travesty: Legal Responses to Adolescent Sexual Offending*. Chicago: University of Chicago Press.

FURTHER READING

Hubbard, T. K., ed. 2010. "Special Issue: Boys' Sexuality and Age of Consent." *Thymos*, 4: 95–192. DOI: 10.3149/thy.402.95, 10.3149/thy.402.99, 10.3149/thy.402.103, 10.3149/thy.402.113, 10.3149/thy.402.126, 10.3149/thy.402.149, 10.3149/thy.402.168.

Hubbard, T. K., and Beert Verstraete, eds. 2013. *Censoring Sex Research: The Debate over Male Intergenerational Relations*. Walnut Creek: Left Coast Press.

Aging, Ageism, and Gender

STACY TORRES
New York University, USA

While awareness of age as a gendered dimension of inequality is not entirely new to feminist scholarship, old age in particular has been understudied and undertheorized. When age does make the list of interlocking oppressions under consideration, it tends to appear after the big three (race, class, and gender) and is treated more as an "etcetera" category than a site of analysis in its own right (Calasanti and Slevin 2006). And while its use as a category is subject to debate even by those who study age, age remains a meaningful category as a social organizing principle for age-graded, age-stratified societies and one bound up with issues of power. Understanding the ways age intersects with gender draws our attention to the simultaneous social construction of age and gender and those social contexts in which age rises in salience for aging women and men and disadvantages them over time. This entry begins with a discussion of the parallels between social constructions of age and gender, takes up some ideas for incorporating age into intersectional frameworks, and later focuses on late-life poverty and the body as two sites in which women face particular disadvantage and ageism as they grow older.

Old age as a political location is ripe for feminist analysis because in many respects growing older is fundamentally a women's issue. In terms of sheer demographics, women live longer than men, and older women aged 65 and older outnumber elderly men by three to two. Thus any changes to existing social policies regarding retirement and healthcare, among others, will primarily affect elderly women. Given the rapid aging of the US population and the "graying" of other industrialized countries around the world (e.g., Japan, Western Europe) facing the dual challenges of aging populations and falling fertility rates, it is important for gender theorists to focus their attention on age as a significant aspect of gender experience and inequality on both a macro and micro level.

The theoretical foundation that feminists have laid for viewing gender as a social construction and as the site of interlocking oppressions provides a roadmap for conceptualizing age in a similar way (Reinharz 2002). Both age and gender share a taken-for-granted quality that makes them fitting counterparts. Like gender, age too suffers from having to disentangle itself from biology and specifically chronology (Laz 2002; Neugarten and Neugarten 2002). Sociologists have complicated our understanding of gender (and race) as social constructs, not biological givens, and we can examine the social nature of age and move beyond understanding age as simple chronology. Anthropologists further demonstrate the ways that gender and attitudes toward aging are shaped by cultural differences. In some societies, for example, the elderly play an important role as healers, sages, and decision-makers. In others, status decreases with age, and elderly women are the least well respected, especially in cultures that reward youth and beauty (Cruikshank 2009). Adapting some of the theoretical frameworks that gender scholars have developed can also enrich our understanding of gendered age. For example, building on the work of gender theorists Candace West and Don Zimmerman (1987), Cheryl Laz (2002) has written about age using an ethnomethodological framework and views age as a "managed accomplishment." She has taken West and Zimmerman's concept of "doing gender" (how gender is constituted or contested in interaction) and applied this framework to examine how age is enacted and performed in different contexts. This framework facilitates an analysis of how the salience of age varies across particular social contexts, and considering this micro-level variation allows us to capture the meanings created in interaction. Rather than simply a number, age becomes "a process and the outcome of ongoing interactional work" (Laz 2002, 131).

At first glance the experience of growing older seems straightforward enough, but its reality grows more complicated when we consider how intersections of race, class, and gender shape age and how age in conjunction with dimensions such as race, class, sexuality, and disability – to name just a few – structures gender over the life course. Prior scholarship on intersectional analyses of gender has laid important groundwork for including age and understanding how age relations intersect with other power relations, such as race, class, and gender, to privilege certain women over others in particular contexts. For example, Jennifer Utrata (2011) has found that in the context of Russian single-mother-headed families, single mothers and grandmothers "do gender and age" in ways that often privilege younger women and pressure grandmothers into providing the bulk of care work (including childcare) to help their daughters advance their careers and future marriage prospects, thereby securing their own financial security in late life, though some of these older women adhere to more modern discourses of femininity that emphasize leisure and taking care of one's self in old age.

When we view gender through the lens of age, two arenas emerge as sites where age intersects with gender to disadvantage men and women in different ways. Gender differences in late-life poverty and sites like the body deserve further attention from the distinct location of old age and can serve as new areas of inquiry and fertile ground for a distinctly feminist perspective on aging. Gender plays a large part in determining the ways that people thrive and suffer in old age. Longevity is a blessing and a curse for women. While older women are better at cultivating and maintaining social ties than their male counterparts and have a much lower risk of social isolation than men despite higher rates of living alone, they face significant economic disadvantages in old age. Because women live longer, they have more years to accumulate health problems and must find ways to patch together support despite living on fixed, and often meager, incomes. Compared with men 65 and older, they consistently face higher poverty rates. For example, in 2011 the poverty rate for women over 65 was 10.7 percent, compared with 6.2 percent for older men. And poor young women are not the only ones who become poor old women. Due to the wage gap and discontinuous work histories resulting from leaving and reentering the labor force more frequently due to unpaid caregiving, women receive substantially lower take-home pay and lifetime Social Security and pension benefits than men in old age. But women who remain single and live alone suffer the most economically in old age. Sharing a household allows for combining resources, but older women have higher rates of living alone (37 percent of women aged 65+ compared with 19 percent of same-aged men). These rates increase with age, and almost half of women 75 and older live alone. Women's poverty rates spike upon widowhood. They are almost three times more likely than older men to be widowed as a result of living longer, their tendency to marry older men, and a lower likelihood of remarriage. Taking into consideration intersections of race and gender with age paints an even bleaker picture for some groups of older women of color. Black women become widows in greater numbers and at younger ages, and poverty in certain demographic groups is much higher than average. Deborah Carr (2010) has noted that older women of color who live alone face significantly higher poverty rates than their white, male counterparts: 38 percent of black women and 41 percent of Hispanic women living alone are poor compared with 9 percent of white men living on their own. While women face greater economic threats to their well-being, men face greater difficulties staying integrated into social networks that keep them connected and provide social support. For example, widowers typically lose their connection to the social circles that their wives nurtured for years before they died. And white, widowed, older men face the greatest risk of suicide. The suicide rate for white men over the age of 80 is six times the overall suicide rate and three times higher than that of same-aged African American men.

The body serves as another area where increased attention to age can enrich our understanding of how age structures privilege and disadvantage individuals in different contexts. While feminists have turned their attention to the body as a site of feminist inquiry, much of the focus thus far has been on younger bodies (such as in the work of Susan Bordo, for example Bordo 2003/1993). Prior scholarship on the body and embodiment has taken up issues such as cosmetic surgery, eating disorders, and the pressure on younger women to conform to a thin, typically white, Western ideal of physical beauty. But much territory is left uncovered when it comes to examining the social significance of both men's and women's bodies as they age, and the gendered associations that accompany such changes as men's and women's bodies become further removed from the cultural ideal (i.e., assessments of old women's bodies as unattractive and old men's loss of physical strength as emasculating). Slevin (Calasanti and Slevin 2006, 252) argues that as a marker of age, the body serves as a "concrete site where ageism occurs." While little is known about how older men and women view their aging bodies and the unique pressures they face to fit the same bodily standards that afflict younger people and their perceptions of their bodies, Calasanti and Slevin's (2006) study of older lesbian women's embodied experiences helps address this dearth of scholarship.

Slevin interviewed old, white, economically privileged lesbians over 60 about their perceptions of their bodies and appearance, sexuality, and how ageism manifested itself in their daily lives, and found that despite a commitment to resisting and challenging hegemonic gender norms of attractiveness, gender socialization and ageist stereotypes remain powerful and far-reaching for this group. Many of these women negotiated ageism by using strategies such as resisting any self-identification as "old" and attempting to discipline their bodies through weight control and exercise that allow them to "pass" as younger.

Gloria Steinem (1983, 230) wrote that "Women may be the one social group that grows more radical with age." She poses an interesting hypothesis, and in thinking through whether women as a social group grow more radical as they grow older, it is important to consider which women grow more radical. Social dimensions like race, class, ethnicity, sexuality, disability, and others shape age and thus people's responses to their experiences of old age. Certain women may grow "more radical" with age, particularly those who have experienced the most privilege in their lives prior to entering old age. For example, an affluent, white woman may not have to deal with ageist stereotypes, discrimination, or reduced economic resources until reaching old age and therefore might only then become more radical in her outlook and political ideas. In contrast, other women who have had longer, more varied histories with struggle on multiple levels may not become more radical, simply because they have had their resilience continually tested, and such challenges may have forced them to become more "radical" earlier in their life trajectories. These same women may also come from communities that value the wisdom and experience that can accumulate by the time a woman reaches old age, allowing her to reap these benefits later in the life course. The work of Patricia Hill Collins (2000/1990) proves instructive here and stands as a promising model for ways we might integrate theories of gender with a life-course perspective on the experience of women in later life. Although Collins (2000/1990) does not explicitly take up the discussion of age, *Black Feminist Thought* provides insight into how we can conceptualize black women's experiences in old age, about which there is a paucity of research. Her in-depth examination of black women's thought and experience suggests that the survival strategies black women have developed during their lifetimes may have particular usefulness as they age. Perhaps a lifetime of multiple oppressions has better prepared black women for some of the indignities of old age. The stronger bonds they have forged as a result of living in segregated communities, sharing certain experiences due to this structural reality, and having to strategize together, passing on knowledge and earning wisdom among themselves about survival in a racist society, all serve them in old age.

Age is a complex dimension of gender that is not simply "added" on. Examining the contexts in which age is particularly salient helps bring into relief the ways privilege and disadvantage shift across time and space and are inherently linked to an individual's social location and his or her position along intersections of age, race, class, gender, and countless other social dimensions. Ultimately, negative ageist stereotypes hurt everyone by instilling fear and dread of growing older, and increased attention to age can help counter these stereotypes and make each of us aware of the situations in which we experience both the privileges and burdens of aging.

SEE ALSO: Embodiment and the Phenomenological Tradition; Intersectionality

REFERENCES

Bordo, Susan. 2003. *Unbearable Weight: Feminism, Western Culture, and the Body*. Berkeley: University of California Press. First published 1993.

Calasanti, Toni M., and Kathleen F. Slevin, eds. 2006. *Age Matters: Realigning Feminist Thinking*. New York: Routledge.

Carr, Deborah. 2010. "Golden Years? Poverty among Older Americans." *Contexts*, 9(1): 62–63.

Collins, Patricia Hill. 2000. *Black Feminist Thought: Knowledge, Consciousness, and the Politics of Empowerment*. New York: Routledge Classics. First published 1990.

Cruikshank, Margaret. 2009. *Learning to Be Old: Gender, Culture, and Aging*. Lanham, MD: Rowman & Littlefield.

Laz, Cheryl. 2002. "Act Your Age." In *Disciplinary Approaches to Aging. Volume 3: Sociology of Aging*, edited by Donna Lind Infeld, 131–150. New York: Routledge.

Neugarten, Bernice L., and Dail A. Neugarten. 2002. "Age in the Aging Society." In *Disciplinary Approaches to Aging. Volume 3: Sociology of Aging*, edited by Donna Lind Infeld, 281–299. New York: Routledge.

Reinharz, Shulamit. 2002. "Friends or Foes: Gerontological and Feminist Theory." In *Disciplinary Approaches to Aging. Volume 3: Sociology of Aging*, edited by Donna Lind Infeld, 179–200. New York: Routledge.

Steinem, Gloria. 1983. *Outrageous Acts and Everyday Rebellions*. New York: Holt.

Utrata, Jennifer. 2011. "Youth Privilege: Doing Age and Gender in Russia's Single-Mother Families." *Gender & Society*, 25(5): 616–641.

West, Candace, and Don H. Zimmerman. 1987. "Doing Gender." *Gender & Society* 1(2): 125–151.

AIDS-Related Stigma

NYOKABI KAMAU
Kenya

Stigma generally refers to prejudice, discounting, discrediting, and discrimination directed at people perceived not to be fitting into a certain normative culture. Anyone can be stigmatized if they do not "fit." Some of the issues used to stigmatize people include nationality, race, political affiliation, level of education, ethnicity, gender, class, sexuality, religion, preferences including clothing, food, and language. In the context of HIV and AIDS, stigma has become more pronounced, as those with HIV suffer the double stigma of being seen to have brought it on themselves through immorality.

The stigma of HIV and AIDS has been more pronounced by the moralistic theologies perpetuated by religions that have criminalized any kind of sexuality that does not occur within the norms of a heterosexual, monogamous marriage. As HIV has been branded as mainly sexually transmitted, those infected are seen as having sinned and therefore suffer the shame and stigma that is associated with sin. In the early years of HIV, vulnerability to infection was understood solely in terms of whether one was sexually promiscuous, and those infected were regarded as not living up to the high moral standards set by religious groups. This became the source of the stigma associated with HIV infection, with the artificial separation of the infected "them" from the uninfected "us."

Sexuality is intricately linked to practically every aspect of people's lives, from pleasure, power, politics, and recreation, to disease, violence, and war (Tamale 2005). To understand the complexity of HIV and AIDS it is worthwhile to look at the historical background on current attitudes about sexuality, especially in the African continent, where HIV and AIDS have had the biggest toll. Hunter (2003) provides a background to the origins of the shame that became associated with sex in Africa long before AIDS. The colonial masters viewed the colonized as uncivilized and with untamed sexual desires, which required control and taming. According to Hunter (2003): "Victorians thought that tropical climates acted as breeding grounds for disease, inflamed passions and negated reason … primitive peoples, they believed, were simply more tolerant of filth and STDs because of their unrestrained sexuality, both symptoms of non-western and moral decay" (Hunter 2003, 169). The general view of colonizers was that "Africans and their sexuality were savage."

From colonial times, the topic of sexuality became taboo because no one wanted to be viewed as a "savage." This was especially so for those who converted to the colonizer's religion, which had strict moral rules and regulations on sexuality. The Victorian/Western culture, though more open about sex compared with African cultures, tended to demonize it more (Foucault 1978). This demonization has contributed to much of the shame and stigma associated with sex and sexuality and, by extension, with those infected with or affected by HIV and AIDS.

The stigma and shame associated with a sexually transmitted illness makes those infected or affected (especially women) feel "worthless, undesirable and uneasy about their own as well as their children's health and futures" (Shelby and Ciambrone 2003, 38). In their study, Shelby and Ciambrone (2003) interviewed 37 HIV-positive women in the United States, many of whom had internalized the shame and stigma associated with HIV and AIDS. They viewed themselves as "abnormal and dirty, filthy … less of a good person … like the leprosy in the Bible" (Shelby and Ciambrone 2003, 39).

Stigma and sexuality is gendered, as women and girls in particular face more restrictions with regard to how they can enjoy sex. On this, Hunter (2003) notes that missionaries "had always viewed African women as the repository of the evil and dark side of African culture because of natural attitudes towards sexuality" (2003, 171). Colonial doctors, on the other hand, were not interested in African women. They concentrated their efforts on determining male fitness for work (Hunter 2003). It was only after World War II that these doctors, "charged with a new responsibility to maintain large and productive forces in the colonies became concerned that women's birth and fertility rates had declined" (Hunter 2003, 171). African women's sexuality only became of interest in the context of reproduction. Any other kind of sexuality has since been viewed with suspicion, hence leading to stigmatization of women and girls seen to have any kind of sex outside of the reproductive mode. In recent years, with HIV and AIDS presenting a major challenge to the world, stigma has been directed to those infected because of linking sex with immorality.

There are four characteristics of AIDS that make it more stigmatized than other terminal illnesses: (1) it can take years before any physical signs appear; (2) because of the disease's "multi-layer latency," it makes people think they are invulnerable; (3) it is passed on through the "most personal, most sensitive and most secretive of behaviours – sexual relations"; (4) it eventually kills. In addition, the initial responses to the disease were shrouded with political propaganda. Admitting to infection in a country was seen as a lack of patriotism, as this could discourage investors, especially tourists, or even have citizens of the country denied entry into the developed ones, which have always reported lower infection rates. Up to now, the United States and Australia do not admit migrants or even students who are infected with HIV. This is a real challenge given that there are millions of young people born with the virus who are of college age, as they have to live with the stigma of a disease whose connection with sexual immorality they cannot even understand.

SEE ALSO: Health, Healthcare, and Sexual Minorities; Religious Fundamentalism; Sexual Regulation and Social Control; Sexually Transmitted Infections; Stigma

REFERENCES

Foucault, Michel. 1978. *The History of Sexuality: An Introduction*, vol. 1, translated by R. Hurley. London: Penguin.

Hunter, Susan. 2003. *Who Cares? AIDS in Africa*. Houndmills: Palgrave.

Shelby, R. Dennis, and D. Ciambrone. 2003. *Women's Experiences with HIV/AIDS: Mending Fractured Selves*. New York: Haworth Press.

Tamale, S. 2005. "Eroticism, Sensuality and 'Women's Secrets' Among the Baganda: A Critical Analysis." *Feminist Africa*, 5: 5–36.

FURTHER READING

Arnfred, Signe. 2004. "'African Sexuality'/Sexuality in Africa: Tales and Silences." In *Re-thinking Sexualities in Africa*, edited by Signe Arnfred, 59–78. Uppsala: Nordic African Institute.

Campbell, Catherine, Yugi Nair, and Sbongile Maimane. 2006. "AIDS Stigma, Sexual Moralities and the Policing of Women and Youth in South Africa." *Feminist Review*, 83: 132–138.

Kamau, Nyokabi. 2006. "Invisibility, Silence and Absence: A Study of the Account Taken by Two Kenyan Universities of the Effects of HIV and AIDS on Senior Women Staff." *Women Studies International Forum*, 29: 612–619.

Kenyatta, Jomo. 1938. *Facing Mount Kenya: The Tribal Life of the Gikuyu*. London: Secker and Warburg.

McFadden, Patricia. 2003. "Sexual Pleasure as Feminist Choice." *Feminist Africa: Changing Cultures*, 2: 50–60.

Parker, Richard, and Peter Aggleton. 2003. "HIV and AIDS-related Stigma and Discrimination: A Conceptual Framework and Implications for Action." *Social Science and Medicine*, 57: 13–24.

Alpha Male

JENNIFER K. PAGE
Northwestern Oklahoma State University, USA

Alpha male is a term applied to men whose personality traits and behavior toward others display dominance or superiority. Originally used in zoological studies about animal hierarchies, when applied to human males the term comprises not only leadership, but also success in business, athletics, and the pursuit of sexual partners. The characteristics required to achieve success in these fields are actually quite similar to those needed to achieve dominance in animal hierarchies. The alpha male in an animal community usually demonstrates strength and intelligence superior to that of other males in the group; as a result, he is charged with protecting and managing the group, including procreating with many females within the group to ensure its survival. The alpha male enjoys privilege and authority over all other members of the group, including other males – sometimes called beta males – who submit to the alpha's displays of aggression and intimidation. For human males, displaying superior strength, intelligence, or sexual prowess does not necessarily lead to positions of power, but it does result frequently in admiration and deference from others in the alpha male's community.

Perhaps most essential to the alpha male's persona is the frequency of his sexual encounters and variety of his partners. For non-human alphas, mating with multiple females is a biological imperative to ensure the group's survival in general and the alpha's genetic durability in particular, but the human alpha seeks sexual contact for other reasons – namely, bodily pleasure and the desire to have more sexual experience than other males in his community. In pursuing multiple females, alpha males demonstrate above-average confidence, aggression, and cleverness. Tallying many successful sexual encounters validates the alpha's heterosexuality – an essential component of hegemonic masculinity, the dominant ideals of masculine behavior in a particular culture – and his desirability as a partner above his peers (Connell 2005). The alpha also uses his sexual successes as a means of gaining approval and privilege from other men. By narrating his conquests for other men, the alpha establishes a reputation as the best and most desirable man in his community, thus gaining the respect or envy of other men. Perhaps equally important as the frequency of his sexual encounters is the perceived beauty of the alpha male's partners; beautiful women are perceived as more challenging, more difficult to seduce, or potentially more intimidating than average-looking women, and so having intercourse with many beautiful women increases the apparent value of the alpha's sexual experiences. In retelling his conquests, the alpha male objectifies his partners and devalues potential emotional ramifications of these encounters.

Many of the personality traits which help alphas succeed sexually are also applicable to other competitive areas traditionally dominated by men, such as business and professional sports. In their professional roles, alphas tend to be persistent, demanding, confident, and direct. These characteristics, though essential to the alpha male's persona, are actually not linked to biological sex, and as a result, some question whether alpha females or homosexual alpha males exist. Kate Ludeman and Eddie Erlandson (2006) suggest that alpha females, with dominant, persistent, aggressive personality traits, do exist in the business sphere, though they are decidedly outnumbered by alpha males. Despite sharing many of the same behaviors and attitudes, it would be inaccurate to call female business executives alpha females due to the sexual implications of alpha maleness; the patriarchal system that condones male hypersexuality also condemns female hypersexuality. Whereas the alpha male's heterosexual savvy upholds long-standing ideals of masculinity, a woman following these same standards deviates from socially prescribed gender norms and is not usually rewarded with privilege and respect (Kimmel 2008). Similarly, while homosexual men may also exhibit dominant personality traits and be known for their sexual prowess, categorizing them as alpha males would be problematic. The alpha male's behavior, especially in regard to the pursuit of female sex objects, is a product of masculine gender ideals, and specifically hegemonic masculinity, which privileges heterosexuality. Though procreation is not a motive for the alpha male's sexual identity, his reputation as dominant, powerful, and sexually authoritative is based in part on his ability to gain the acquiescence, or willing submission, of supposedly weaker females. Because gay male sex does not carry the same inherent objectification of women, it does not quite fit the alpha male model. Hegemonic masculinity and all its ideals, however, are not stagnant; gender ideals shift based on cultural sentiment, and it is possible that the heterosexual imperative of idealized masculinity may be negotiable in future generations. In fact, the passage of the Marriage (Same Sex Couples) Act of 2013 in England and Wales, which allows same-sex couples to legally wed, and the US Supreme Court's decision to overturn the Defense of Marriage Act (2013) suggest that the Western zeitgeist about homosexuality is slowly shifting toward acceptance and creating new implications for gender stereotypes and standards, including the concept of the alpha male.

Although the alpha male is a conspicuous fixture in anglophone cultures, certain alpha characteristics are also apparent in other cultures around the world. David Gilmore (1990) explains that in many patriarchal cultures, numerous sexual conquests are a measure of an individual man's dominance over his peers. In "circum-Mediterranean" cultures in particular, the sexual or romantic pursuit of women has long been a prerequisite for social acceptance (Gilmore 1990). Superior physical strength and competitive skill are other alpha characteristics that are also prized by many non-Western cultures. Many Micronesian and African peoples perceive men's ability to best others in staged combat or to withstand intense pain to be indicative of their physical superiority to women and other men who cannot achieve the same feat. The demonstration of sexual and other physical competencies, then, is recognized as a traditional marker of masculine superiority.

The alpha male is typically glorified in popular culture, particularly in sports, films, and music, which reinforces to average men that this category is enviable. The resilience of this personality type is apparent in the continuing financial success of action films, such as the James Bond franchise, first started in 1962. Action stars portray the authoritative, aggressive, seductive nature that defines alpha males, and the success these films enjoy is indicative of the veneration Western culture places on the alpha male type. The alpha male is celebrated more conspicuously by the "Alpha Male Award," given during the "Guys Choice" awards, produced by Spike TV, a cable television network that targets male viewers. Receiving this award in June 2013 was Burt Reynolds, whose previous acting roles embodied ideals of hegemonic masculinity (Spike TV 2013). These and other celebrations of the alpha male proliferate the mythologized appeal of this particular portrayal of masculinity.

SEE ALSO: Gender Stereotypes; Hegemonic Masculinity; Hypermasculinity; Patriarchy

REFERENCES

Connell, R. W. 2005. *Masculinities*, 2nd ed. Berkeley: University of California Press.

Gilmore, David D. 1990. *Manhood in the Making: Cultural Concepts of Masculinity*. New Haven: Yale University Press.

Kimmel, Michael. 2008. *Guyland: The Perilous World Where Boys Become Men*. New York: HarperCollins.

Ludeman, Kate, and Eddie Erlandson. 2006. *Alpha Male Syndrome*. Boston: Harvard Business School Press.

Spike TV. 2013. "Guys Choice: Award for Alpha Male." Accessed July 12, 2013, at http://www.spike.com/guys-choice/alpha-male.

FURTHER READING

Boehm, Christopher. 2000. "Conflict and the Evolution of Social Control." *Journal of Consciousness Studies*, 7(1–2): 79–101.

Kimmel, Michael. 2010. *Misframing Men: The Politics of Contemporary Masculinities*. New Brunswick, NJ: Rutgers University Press.

Alternative Media

ERIN BELL
Wayne State University, USA

Alternative media, also known as independent media, offers a diverging point of view (as pertaining to politics, sexuality, economics, or almost any other locus of interest) and more diverse content than the mainstream media. As the term suggests, alternative media typically aims to report upon news and events ignored by the conventional reportage of the world, hence providing an "alternative" to the commonly disseminated media rhetoric in a given location. Some experts also suggest that alternative journalists often persuade their audiences to move from passive spectatorship to a state of political activism. In order to explicate the manner in which women and men are represented within alternative media, it is essential to differentiate it from the mainstream, especially as pertaining to gender and sexuality.

The term mainstream is usually applied to the values and cultural artifacts associated with dominant culture. Mainstream media, then, refers to the multiple channels of mass communication such as newspapers, magazines, television reportage, films, and new media (social networking websites, online journals, blogs, video-sharing hubs, and podcasts) that function within the prescribed dominant values of a nation. These forms of media maintain governing ideologies rather than minority opinions. Despite strides toward a more equitable society in which persons of all genders, races, ages, and sexualities are treated equally, patriarchal ideologies and male figures (Caucasian, heterosexual males, to be specific) still remain dominant in most Western societies' legal, economic, and political strata, so it is those patriarchal values that are therefore embedded within mainstream media and sustained within the scope of its information and imagery.

If the mainstream media is equated with this singular viewpoint, then the alternative media is steeped in multiplicity and diversity of voices, viewpoints, and subject matter. Within a global context, the alternative press often challenges the viewpoints of totalitarian and oppressive regimes, offering a counterpoint to the repressive, government-controlled media of a nation. Members of the alternative media, in fact, protest against a variety of rules, regulations, behaviors, and ideologies that they consider to be oppressive. While some print forms of alternative media in the United States, such as the journal *Adbusters*, for example, offer an anti-consumer viewpoint by lampooning commonly circulated advertisements that oftentimes perpetuate stereotypical images of women and men, the *Alternative Radio* program offers a weekly hour of on-air coverage of current events not typically covered by commercial stations. Pirate radio stations, underground newspapers, and independent films each protest against what are considered oppressive political regimes, sexist practices and policies, and many other polemical issues, while educating the public on modes and methods to counter such hegemonic practices.

Apropos concerns of sexuality and gender, it is important to consider that feminist theorists have long voiced their criticisms of the mainstream media, including television and film, due to its perpetuation of phallogocentrism (also called phallocentrism). Phallogocentrism is a term typically credited to French theorist Jacques Derrida (1978), who with other deconstruction theorists argued that Western literature, and in this case Western media, privileges the masculine, or the phallus, in the construction of Western systems of knowledge, meaning, and culture. Feminists and deconstructionists maintain that language, even at the very level of syntax and vocabulary, is centered and biased toward a male point of view. As language is a key component of media, what Westerners understand as "objective" knowledge within this media discourse is not particularly neutral.

Indeed, many critics argue that media is particularly culpable of presenting the phallogocentric point of view. As Laura Mulvey, one of feminism's most well-known film critics, explained, one manner in which filmic media maintains this view is by employing "the male gaze," as she denotes it (Mulvey 1989). Using psychoanalytical theory, Mulvey demonstrates that in American mainstream cinema (and arguably television, advertising, and other print re-presentations), the eye of the camera through the director's focus places viewers into a masculine subject position, thereby rendering the female film figure as a passive object. The male gaze of film and other modes of media is quite problematic, for if women are always portrayed as object rather than subject, and if media assist in the management of society's manner of understanding the world, then arguably, mainstream film reestablishes sexist messages to the world and presents a skewed understanding of the roles of gender and sex.

Referencing Mulvey's account, it follows that televised and print images (in both programming and advertising) continue to draw upon stereotypes and stock images of women and men, and of heterosexuals and homosexuals, allowing for very little deviation from the set norms. Often, female characters are portrayed in the role of the victim, and accounts of violence against females on both television and film are quite numerous. Feminists have enumerated many other objections to mainstream media, including the fact that women are still often underrepresented in the positions of power.

If the mainstream is biased toward a rather singular viewpoint, alternative media, on the other hand, is steeped in plurality. Whether print, online, or cinematic, alternative or independent media sets out to counter many of mainstream media's aforementioned biases and flaws, including its dependence upon patriarchal values and its focus upon economic gain. Alternative media challenges hegemonic views of the world by reporting upon lesser known topics and stories but also by providing its audiences with a variety of minority voices and opinions.

Examples of alternative print media date back to the era of Johannes Gutenberg's printing press; once dissenters against the popularly held beliefs and political systems of the time could more easily circulate their ideas by way of movable type, they did so. There are examples of alternative print media from the fifteenth century on, and the last few centuries are no different. *Adbusters* was cited earlier, but there are many alternative magazines and newspapers that relate specifically to gender and sexuality. Feminist activists including Gloria Steinem famously founded *Ms. Magazine* in the early 1970s; its first regular issue was published in 1972, offering articles on abortion, the Equal Rights Amendment, and other significant political issues relating to women. *Ms.* employs an advertising-free model, thereby freeing its contributors from would-be advertisers' interests. In the 1990s, both *Bitch* and *Bust* magazines were launched, offering feminist critique upon a variety of popular culture subjects.

In addition to feminist print media, there are numerous lesbian, gay, bisexual, and transgender (LGBT) interest magazines including *The Advocate*, *OUT*, and *Instinct*. While some of these publications rely upon advertising to generate revenue, their subject matter is centered round topics frequently ignored by the mainstream media including gay rights, health and family issues, and popular culture as pertaining to sexuality. In addition to the variety of professionally published alternative magazines and newspapers, some writers and reporters have enacted a "do-it-yourself" (DIY) approach to distributing their discourse. These non-commercial publications, called zines, usually cover unconventional subject matter and are self-published with the use of a photocopier, or in more recent years in an online format.

The tradition of Hollywood films has been critiqued by numerous feminist scholars, most notably by Laura Mulvey (1989) and Teresa de Lauretis (1987). While both Mulvey and de Lauretis are apprehensive of the images of women and men re-presented in the tradition of the Hollywood cinematic film, it is de Lauretis who argues that alternative films can evade the use of the male gaze, if not negate it. Though avant-garde films have been in circulation since the inception of cinematography, today there is a growing number of both female and LGBT directors within the independent film community. This development is significant because it counters the male gaze, but also because alternative film often celebrates subject matter that is rejected or ignored by mainstream Hollywood. Take, for example, *Boys Don't Cry* (1999), directed by Kimberly Peirce and co-written by Andy Bienen. The independent film documents the short life of Brandon Teena, a transgender teen who was murdered. Likewise, the black and white art film *Go Fish* (1994) explores lesbian relationships, while *Hedwig and the Angry Inch* (2001) presents a transitional character who must endure a set of challenges that mirror what many members of the transgender community encounter. While these films garnered an amount of financial and professional success, the subject matter covered is so atypical to mainstream cinema that the films still fall within the alternative paradigm.

While a plethora of commercial radio stations broadcast across the globe, most require commercial success to sustain their listenership. Alternative radio, however, is not usually dependent on advertisers, but may rely upon public donations or government funding. Though the critically acclaimed *Alternative Radio* show previously referenced does circulate to a global audience, there are many other forms of alternative radio that demonstrate a considerably lower audience. Community radio and low-power FM stations typically are non-profit and non-commercial and, due to their low wattage, may have a relatively small audience. That being said, these non-commercial stations are known for presenting nonconformist discourse, including programs that present content relating to gay rights, women's issues, and other gender-related subject matter.

One final channel of alternative media worth consideration is housed in the limitless expanse of the new media. Due to the prevalence of computer technology and its relative ease of use, online forms of alternative media are numerous and create an ideal vehicle for the transmission of many revolutionary discourses. Social media is often used as a form of protest, and in fact has been employed to facilitate rebellion, as demonstrated in the events of the Arab Spring. Here, social media was used successfully to communicate and organize protests and civil resistance against oppressive regimes in the Middle East. Social media has been used in a variety of domestic pursuits as well. Web logs, or blogs, are written by authors too numerous to count, and contain subject matter on topics ranging from women balancing work, life, and maternity to teens coping with coming out of the closet. Discussion boards and listservs also allow users to post messages relating to gender rights, support groups, and social activities geared toward specific interest groups.

There is extensive scholarship and cultural theory that focuses on mainstream media and critiques its perceived biases and shortcomings; the literature on the topic is plentiful and comes from a variety of disciplines. For decades, feminists, Marxists, poststructuralists, and other scholars have questioned the veracity and efficacy of mainstream media in the Western world because of its alignment with patriarchy and capitalism. Because alternative media does not typically ascribe as much value to financial success, it usually demonstrates less of an alliance with capitalistic concerns. The independent filmmaker, for example, many times produces her film simply for "art's sake," or to promote a specific feminist agenda, not necessarily to generate a profit. Alternative media, then, is not only a viable conduit of information, but also a rich ground for protest against the dominant patriarchal messages in the mainstream scope.

French Marxist theorist Guy Debord, in his book titled *The Society of the Spectacle*, for example, argues that authentic social life has been replaced by its representation, and the mass media, according to Debord, is society's "most glaring superficial manifestation" (2010, par. 24), assisting in the "totalitarian management of the conditions of existence" (2010, par. 24). Put more simply, Debord argues that mainstream media perpetuates the production of images that are not reflections of authentic social life.

Jean Baudrillard, a French philosopher and cultural theorist, also addresses mainstream media in his text titled *Simulacra and Simulation* (1994). This book posits that the symbols and signs present in contemporary mainstream media have created a precession of simulacra, which here are defined as imitations, substitutes, images or representations of life and/or "reality." Media culture, including contemporary advertisements, films, magazines, and online media, is complicit with this re-presentation of "reality" and is, as Baudrillard writes, the precession of simulacra. Television, in its situation comedies, for example, re-presents images of the family which are taken by some viewers to be portrayals that are in some fashion true to life. However, these portrayals are mere simulacra, copies of some ideal of family life (often based upon gender stereotypes) that never actually existed. The mainstream's adherence to stereotypes and simulacra is one of the many issues that necessitate alternative media.

Conventional media's symbiotic relationship with economic gain, i.e., its focus on creating profit, is also typically cited as the grounds for the requirement for alternative forms of media. Because of mainstream media's dependence on financial success and its concomitant relationship with commercials, product placement, and other forms of advertising, it is essentially more concerned with making a profit than providing non-biased content. American literary critic and Marxist theorist Fredric Jameson (1991) argues that the media is partially complicit with society's servitude to capitalism. According to Jameson and other Marxist theorists, television programming and advertising are often interchangeable and difficult to distinguish from one another. By Jameson's account, mainstream media is not only a mode of extending dominant capitalist values and ideals, in a sense the media *is* those dominant ideals. Alternative media, by contrast, is not as driven by financial gain or commercial success. It is important to note that alternative media is not the opposite of mainstream media in this regard. That is, many alternative media are financially solvent. However, the impetus for their work is not simply economic success but, rather, community education.

There is a significant amount of research and theory dedicated to the study of mainstream media and its perpetuation of ideologies, yet alternative media is a locus that warrants further scholarly investigation. Though Italian philosopher Antonio Gramsci (1971) writes extensively about the potentiality of alternative media in the struggle over hegemony, as the sites of alternative media continue to expand, contemporary scholars might interrogate how Internet-based modes of alternative media present specific possibilities for radical dissent.

SEE ALSO: Feminisms, Postmodern; Feminism, Poststructural; Feminist Art Practice; Feminist Film Theory; Feminist Magazines; Gay Male Literature; Gender Stereotypes; Images of Gender and Sexuality in Advertising; Phallocentrism and Phallogocentrism; Sexism in Language

REFERENCES

Baudrillard, Jean. 1994. *Simulacra and Simulation*, trans. Sheila F. Glaser. Ann Arbor: University of Michigan Press.
Debord, Guy. 2010. *The Society of the Spectacle*. Detroit: Black and Red.
de Lauretis, Teresa. 1987. *Technologies of Gender: Essays on Theory, Film, and Fiction*. Bloomington: Indiana University Press.
Derrida, Jacques. 1978. *Writing and Difference*. Chicago: University of Chicago Press.
Gramsci, Antonio. 1971. *Selections from the Prison Notebooks of Antonio Gramsci*. New York: International Publishers.
Jameson, Fredric. 1991. *Postmodernism, or, The Cultural Logic of Late Capitalism*. Durham, NC: Duke University Press.
Mulvey, Laura. 1989. *Visual and Other Pleasures*. Bloomington: Indiana University Press.

FURTHER READING

Atton, Chris. 2002. *Alternative Media*. Thousand Oaks, CA: Sage.
Bailey, Olga G., Bart Cammaert, and Nico Carpentier. 2008. *Understanding Alternative Media*. Buckingham: Open University Press.
Kenix, Linda Jean. 2011. *Alternative and Mainstream Media: The Converging Spectrum*. London: Bloomsbury.
McLuhan, Marshall. 1994. *Understanding Media: The Extensions of Man*, with introduction by Lewis H. Lapham. Cambridge, MA: MIT Press.
Watson, James, and Anne Hill. 2003. *Dictionary of Communication and Media Studies*. Oxford: Oxford University Press.

Alternative Medicine and Therapies

JOSÉ E. GARCÍA

Catholic University of Paraguay, Paraguay

Alternative medicine is a generic concept that comprises a set of different practices and procedures whose essential purpose is to provoke some kind of curative action at the physiological or behavioral processes of the organism to relieve symptoms or discomfort. Alternative medicine does not constitute a unified body of techniques and procedures, as one of its main characteristics is the wide variety of forms and styles encompassed by the phrase. However, the acceptance of these different modalities of intervention is far from being unanimous, and is often controversial. Indeed, a frequent objection to alternative medicine is the absence of scientific and experimental evidence that supports its purported validity and effectiveness. This means that forms of alternative medicine not only fail in attempts at experimental verification through the common methodological procedures used in the replication of scientific theories, but also that they are conceived in such a way that their concepts evade a clear, precise, and unequivocal definition.

The main objective of alternative medicine is to produce a change or improvement in health that helps to diminish the suffering of the patient and to generate a qualitative improvement in his/her health and well-being. For its application, adherents rely on specific forms of therapies, which are also called alternatives, including techniques and procedures used to promote healing. Other related concepts are those of natural medicine and herbal medicine, which refer to remedies such as those found in plants, natural substances, or preparations developed without the mixture of chemical compounds or artificially synthesized products in the laboratory. They can be applied topically or taken as dietary supplements. Traditional medicine makes use of healing resources whose origins are located in millennial cultures spread in different parts of the world, and are an integral part of the folklore and traditions in countries or defined historical periods. Among these should also be included indigenous medicine. Alternative medicine includes remedies for the prevention and treatment of diseases developed in ancient civilizations, such as the Egyptian, Chinese, Indian, Babylonian, Assyrian, Tibetan, and pre-Columbian American. Traditional Chinese medicine and the Ayurveda of India are the most well-known varieties. Much of today's alternative medicine incorporates concepts from multiple cultures.

Denominations that receive this varied range of applications to some of the problems inherent in human health also require a greater degree of precision, especially when they are considered as a general concept. To qualify as "alternative," these approaches do not need to adhere to an essentialist or metaphysical criterion, but to the more simple fact that their effectiveness still lacks experimental validation. In other words, this means that such treatments have simply not been subjected to systematic empirical validation and, if some of them have been minimally assessed, have also failed to demonstrate effectiveness at a scientific and statistically acceptable level. Because of the lack of conclusive evidence in scientific research, many forms of alternative medicine cannot be reliably applied in the field of healthcare. Academics suggest that applying alternative medicine in the place of scientific medicine would be the same as substituting alchemy for chemistry or astrology for astronomy (Stickler 2001). Some critics (Greek and Greek 2002) claim that there is simply no such thing as alternative medicine, but only scientifically proven evidence-based data, and therapy and treatments that have not been scientifically proven.

Advocates of alternative medicine argue that medical science is "reductionist." This charge refers to the alleged denial of other ontological levels of reality and the fact of epistemological diversity in science. Balboni and Balboni (2011) consider that the reductionist model in academic health sciences has prompted criticism and protests from people who are looking to revive holistic points of view, in harmony with the foundations of more traditional medicine. In principle, alternative medicine could become a part of the established scientific knowledge if it could achieve a verifiable and methodologically rigorous confirmation of its postulates. Typically, practitioners of alternative medicine use it in parallel with or as a replacement for scientifically validated approaches. In cases where it is applied in combination with academic conventional medicine, we must speak of complementary medicine or complementary and alternative medicine.

Many of the techniques of today's alternative medicine come from traditional Chinese medicine, whose remote origins are lost in time and projected earlier than the Shang dynasty in 1766 BCE, when writing was invented. In fact, traditional Chinese medicine covers a very broad range of strategies developed through millennia. The most common practices are the *tui na* (therapeutic massage), acupuncture, moxibustion (a technique to stimulate the circulatory system), cupping therapy (suction cups applied on the skin to cause a local congestion and eliminate the air contained inside), phytotherapy (treatments based on herbal products and substances of animal or mineral origin), and meditation exercises such as *qi gong* and *tai chi chuan*. Acupuncture involves the insertion of needles into the body to restore the lost balance and health of the patient. The needles are very thin and pierce the surface of the skin at specific points along the channels of energy known as meridians or collaterals. This is used for cases of back pain, osteoarthritis, nausea and vomiting caused by chemotherapy, pregnancy or pain after surgery, chronic pain, analgesia, dental pain, temporomandibular pain, rehabilitation in cerebrovascular accidents, fibromyalgia, rheumatic diseases, weight loss, asthma, neck pain, recurrent headaches, addictions, post-herpetic neuralgia, and the treatment of smoking. Despite isolated positive results, the effectiveness of these treatments has not been conclusively established (Ramey and Sampson 2001). Acupressure works by pressure at certain points in the body, the palms of the hands, soles of the feet, and the pinna. It is based on the principle that vital energy runs through the meridians and can be blocked in some places. Pressure applied on these points unblocks its circulation. All forms of therapy used in traditional Chinese medicine attempt to help the body to return to its natural state of harmony and balance of yin and yang (Xue and O'Brien 2003).

Another form of Asian traditional medicine that has found many adherents in the Western world is Ayurveda. Coming from India, this is a medical system based on the *Atharva Veda*, one of the sacred texts of Hinduism composed between 1500 and 1000 BCE. During the seventh and sixth centuries BCE, there was a systematic development of Ayurvedic forms of intervention. Ayurveda consists principally in the practice of diets and the consumption of herbal medicines. It is used in the treatment of psoriasis, vitiligo, arthritis, hypertension, cholesterol, diabetes, asthma, depression, epilepsy, and chronic fatigue. Ayurveda also includes influences from China, such as the use of diagnosis by pulse, acupuncture, and moxibustion.

Certainly, the spectrum of alternative medicine is not limited to these forms of Asian traditional medicine. Medical practices of indigenous peoples of the Americas, for example, rest in the action of the shamans, who obtained help from entities of the spiritual realm to cure physical and psychological disease. The native peoples living in North, Central, and South America conceived health according to a holistic approach comprising the physical, spiritual, mental, emotional, social, and environmental aspects. For this reason, indigenous medicine is always more preventive than curative. Natural medicine uses herbal remedies with a low level of processing and a very basic preparation that includes maceration, infusion, or cooking.

Its purpose is both to cure and prevent. The various ethnic groups in Central and South America also developed their systems of indigenous medicine based on the knowledge and uses of different varieties of plants, some of them with narcotic, hallucinogenic, and euphoric properties.

Despite its precedents many centuries ago, the use of the concept of alternative medicine is a product of the twentieth century CE. This transition in the West can be traced to the eighteenth century, when an increase in alternative medicine approaches occurred due to a growth in world trade and the inefficiency of scientific medical solutions available at the time. Natural healers proclaimed their treatments better than those prescribed in professional medicine (Bivins 2007). The irruption of curative processes with the use of magnets or the energy of the human body was proposed as the theory of animal magnetism, introduced by the German physician Franz Anton Mesmer (1734–1815). The mystical doctrines promoted by the Swedish philosopher and scientist Emanuel Swedenborg (1688–1772) in the eighteenth century aimed to assert the predominance of a higher spiritual reality, pretending to balance body harmony by appealing to unseen forces as the causal agent (Haller 2010). Other practices such as Spiritism, homeopathy, and Christian Science also became popular during the nineteenth century.

Of more recent origin is homeopathy. Created in 1796 by the German physician Samuel Hahnemann (1755–1843), homeopathy relies on the use of special preparations to reproduce the symptoms that the patient suffers. Its basic tenet is that something that causes the symptoms can also heal them, provided that the dose is low. Its application is performed with acute illnesses such as flu, cough, diarrhea, and migraine as well as chronic diseases such as allergies, dermatitis, asthma, and rheumatism and throat, ear, gynecological, and urinary tract infections. Evaluation of the effectiveness of homeopathy reveals that the seemingly positive results may be due to other processes such as the placebo effect, the patient's willingness to please the practitioner, the expectations of this person, selective attention, or diagnostic errors (Atwood 2001).

Alternative therapies that work with the body ensure operation in a holistic and natural manner to promote health through the management of the muscular and skeletal body structure. They hope to strengthen the immune system, helping in the elimination of toxins and providing stimulation and relaxation (Chivers 2006). They include chiropractic, physiotherapy and occupational therapy, osteopathy, Alexander technique, yoga, Pilates method, Feldenkrais method, and zero balancing. Chiropractic seeks to detect, diagnose, and correct mechanically dysfunctional areas known as subluxations in the neuroskeletal system that also affect the nervous system. It applies manual treatments to correct the spinal adjustment and the soft tissues. Physiotherapy looks for development and recovery of the functionality and mobility of the individual. In this sense it is associated with occupational therapy that brings together techniques such as sensory integration, Bobath neurodevelopmental treatment, massage, mobilization and stretching, strengthening, and postural education. Osteopathy focuses on different forms of dysfunctions, hypermobility, hypomobility of the vertebral column, articulations, nervous system, muscular system, and viscera. Its main foundations are that the human body is a holistic system, that the structure of an organ directly influences its function, that the body is homeostatic or self-regulated, and that it possesses the ability of auto-healing. The Alexander technique is focused on problems arising from poor posture. It proclaims the control of muscle and mental tension during daily activities through self-education.

The Pilates method is an elaborated set of physical exercises that promote mind control for the domain of the body. The central purpose is to develop internal muscles and increase flexibility to achieve equilibrium in the body and give firmness to the vertebral column. It is useful for back pain and as a rehabilitation therapy. Feldenkrais method is a strategy for the reeducation of body movements with the aim of increasing mental and physical function, promoting awareness of one's own body, and the refinement of mobility. Its two modalities are self-awareness through movement and functional integration. It is used in the treatment of osteoarthritis, lumbago, osteoporosis, contractions, and cervical pain. Finally, yoga is an ancient discipline of physical, breathing (*pranayama*), and mental exercises that originated in India about 5,000 years ago. Intellectually, yoga is a tributary of Hinduism, Buddhism, and Jainism, in addition to other variants of Eastern meditation. It assumes there is an energy moving inside the body and that the more freely it circulates, the more healthy and balanced is the person. Yoga helps the attainment of consciousness of the body, deep concentration, and relaxation.

Those modalities classified as "energy therapies" claim that various kinds of therapies using different forms of energy can affect the human body and restore its altered levels. They include two main types: (1) biofield therapies and (2) bioelectromagnetic therapies (magnet therapy). Chromotherapy, or therapy of colors, is a type of biofield therapy that uses color or light to balance physical, spiritual, or emotional energy. Polarity therapy is a bioelectromagnetic therapy that assumes that all the energy of the human body is electromagnetic and that incorrectly dissipated life energy is the cause of illnesses. Magnetic theory practitioners argue that the electromagnetic fields of the human body can be balanced to the achievement of physical and mental health by means of the use of magnets to stimulate the action of nerves. Qi gong is rooted in Chinese philosophy and uses physical postures, exercises, meditation, and breathing practices to restore the free flow of *qi*, which is presumed responsible for the maintenance of health. Reiki, despite its Japanese name, is an energy therapy that has its origins in Tibet. Reiki practitioners channel a form of universal energy with their hands (Kurtz 2008), and they use this energy in their hands to heal their clients. It is claimed that reiki therapy significantly reduces stress and provides calmness and well-being. This energy is said to expand and project beyond the skin, so the therapist does not actually touch the patient to redirect lost equilibrium. Zero balancing therapy argues that most of the physical forces lie in the bones, due to their greater density. Zero balancing therapy is said to liberate the energy contained in the skeletal system and improve its flow in the body and the mind.

Of course, the practice of this large group of complementary and alternative approaches also appears closely linked with gender, proving to be a very persistent and fundamental element to understand its differential function. Professionals administering alternative approaches in their various manifestations as well as people searching for treatment are mostly female. In the developed world, middle-aged women belonging to the middle class and well educated are its most frequent users. The use of these services has increased since the early 1980s, associated with some philosophical theories but also responding to the influence of feminist ideas, which have seen such holistic and spiritual treatments as more consistent with the new trends for women's healthcare. Feminist approaches to epistemology have been particularly critical of the analytical and rational thinking of science, which they associate with an androcentric or masculinist approach, and of which university medicine is a direct product. Feminist approaches to science stress the importance of intuition, subjectivity, and greater openness toward recognition of emotions as characteristics of the thought of women. The holistic, person-centered, and preventive practices that are typical of alternative therapies are in line with this so-called gynocentric approach to science. The regular use of certain variants such as homeopathy, chiropractic, and osteopathy has been considerably feminized. When consumers are men, the use is more justified in terms of scientific rationality and the presumed practical effects. When they turn to alternative medicine, both men and women reproduce traditional gender identities. This also involves a supposedly more balanced relationship between the practitioner and the client, presuming the replacement of the asymmetry between doctor and patient that is common in conventional medicine.

The range of applications of alternative medicine and therapies also covers problems such as sexual dysfunction, for which the Ayurveda, homeopathy, traditional Chinese medicine, and nutritional therapy are some alternatives. These can be achieved through the use of herbs to stimulate the release of sexual drives, also interpreted in terms of the *qi* powers, or by the use of herbs combined with positions of yoga (Ayurveda). In cases such as erectile dysfunction, homeopathy has received some scientific credit as a means of intervention. Other specific difficulties associated with the menopause also receive treatments such as meditative breathing, special soya diets, and yoga. Massage techniques are also used in the cases of anaphrodisia and anorgasmia. Bach flowers in their different variants are recommended in the treatment of problems of male sexuality, such as weakening of libido and premature ejaculation.

Given the large number of existing approaches, both historical and modern, some agencies have called for the classification of different varieties of alternative medicine treatments. Among the available options, one of the most complete and influential has been proposed by the National Center for Complementary and Alternative Medicine of the United States. This institution classifies these practices into five broad categories: (1) alternative medical systems (acupuncture, Ayurveda, homeopathy, Native American healing practices, naturopathic medicine, Tibetan medicine, and traditional Chinese medicine); (2) mind–body interventions (art therapy, biofeedback, dance therapy); (3) biologically based therapies (diet, dietary supplements, herbal products, megavitamins); (4) manipulative and body-based methods (acupressure, Alexander technique, chiropractic, Feldenkrais method); and (5) energy therapies (qi gong, reiki, therapeutic touch, pulsed fields, magnetic fields). Other governmental or official entities, such as the World Health Organization, have also worked in the last few years on projects directed toward the development of appropriate classification systems for alternative medicines.

In short, alternative medicine covers an important range of approaches, techniques, and practices, ranging from traditional Chinese, Tibetan, and Ayurvedic medicine to homeopathy and energy techniques. Many of them have ancient origins and others have been developed in modern times. Their range of applications is broad and varied, from common health complications to problems associated with sexual behavior. The loss of religious faith and the tendency to blame science for environmental decline (García 1998), among other reasons, have generated an increasing inclination among Westerners toward mysticism and the search for spiritual shelters. The complex dynamics of gender and sexuality are also evident in the different understanding of alternative medicine and its uses. The main challenge that these techniques face is the lack of experimental validation of their postulates.

SEE ALSO: Buddhism; Complementary and Alternative Medicine; Feminist Epistemology; Feminist Studies of Science; Traditional and Indigenous Knowledge; Traditional Healing; Yin-Yang

REFERENCES

Atwood, Kimball C. 2001. "Homeopathy and Critical Thinking." *Scientific Review of Alternative Medicine*, 5: 149–151.

Balboni, Michael J., and Tracy A. Balboni. 2011. "Spirituality and Biomedicine: A History of Harmony and Discord." In *The Soul of Medicine: Spiritual Perspectives and Clinical Practice*, edited by John R. Peteet and Michael N. D'Ambra, 3–22. Baltimore: Johns Hopkins University Press.

Bivins, Roberta. 2007. *Alternative Medicine? A History*. New York: Oxford University Press.

Chivers, Maria. 2006. *Dyslexia and Alternative Therapies*. London: Jessica Kingsley.

García, José E. 1998. "El problema de las terapias alternativas" [The Problem of Alternative Therapies]. *Más Luz. Revista Iberoamericana de Psicología y Pedagogía*, 4: 163–173.

Greek, C. Ray, and Jean Swingle Greek. 2002. *Specious Science: How Genetics and Evolution Reveal Why Medical Research on Animals Harms Humans*. New York: Continuum.

Haller, John S., Jr. 2010. *Swedenborg, Mesmer, and the Mind/Body Connection: The Roots of Complementary Medicine*. West Chester, PA: Swedenborg Foundation.

Kurtz, Lisa A. 2008. *Understanding Controversial Therapies for Children with Autism, Attention Deficit Disorder, and Other Learning Disabilities: A Guide to Complementary and Alternative Medicine*. London: Jessica Kingsley.

Ramey, David W., and Wallace Sampson. 2001. "Review of the Evidence for the Clinical Efficacy of Human Acupuncture." *Scientific Review of Alternative Medicine*, 5: 195–201.

Stickler, Gunnar B. 2001. "'Alternative' Medicine: A Review of Studies Supported by Grants Awarded by the National Center for Complementary and Alternative Medicine." *Scientific Review of Alternative Medicine*, 5: 202–204.

Xue, Charlie Changlie, and Kylie A. O'Brien. 2003. "Modalities of Chinese Medicine." In *Comprehensive Guide to Chinese Medicine*, edited by Ping-Chung Leung, Charlie Changlie Xue, and Yung-Chi Cheng, 19–46. River Edge, NJ: World Scientific.

Amazons

MAEVE ADAMS
Manhattan College, New York, USA

According to ancient sources, the Amazons were a matriarchal community of ruthless women warriors with origins in Bronze Age Eurasia. According to mythology, Amazons were born of Ares, the god of war, and Otrera, the first Queen of the Amazons. In literature after the ancient period, the ancient Amazon became an archetype representing women who presume to usurp the power and privilege of men. At once admired for their bravery and reviled for their warlike nature, the mythological Amazon warriors were represented as a martial and moral threat to patriarchal society and values. Many of the names given to these women reflect anxieties about that threat. For example, Penthesilea, early queen of the Amazons, means she who brings grief (*penthos*) to the people (*laos*) and Androdameia, an Amazon who purportedly fought against the Greeks in the Attic Wars, means conqueror (*damao*) of men (*andros*). In Homer's *Iliad* (1999; first published 760–710 BCE), where the Amazons make their earliest known literary appearance, the Amazons are described as the equals of male soldiers and are listed among the monsters heroically vanquished by the hero Bellerophon (1999, 143, 289). Defeating an Amazon was a subject worthy of epic narrative.

Amazons did not merely threaten men and masculine values, they also challenged Greek conceptions of femininity and women's social roles. Inaugurating one popular myth, Hellanicus of Lesbos (~490–405 BCE) claimed that the name Amazon derived from the Greek word for breast (*mazos*) referring to the legend that the women warriors cut off their right breasts to make themselves more efficient and deadly archers. Modern historians have since dismissed Hellanicus of Lesbos's theory, insisting instead that the name may have come from several Eurasian languages. The image of the single-breasted woman who refuses to fulfill her social and biological function as a wife and mother nonetheless persisted as a key feature of the ostensibly unnatural Amazonian woman who contravened the norms of patriarchal society. According to legend, the Amazons mated with Scythians in order to populate their kingdom, but refused to live with men or take them as husbands. In other variations of that narrative, the Amazons either sent male children home with their fathers or abandoned them, leaving them to fend for themselves in the wild. Amazons refused conventional female responsibilities, choosing violence against men over the care of their homes and offspring. Amazons thereby rejected patriarchal society and its gendered division of labor.

After the fall of Rome in approximately 476 CE, the figure of the Amazon only became a subject of renewed interest beginning in the late Middle Ages and Renaissance, when neoclassicism led to the retrieval of lost Roman and Greek literature. In this period, the Amazon appears as a fictional character and leitmotif drawn from antiquity in retellings of ancient legends. Benoît de Sainte-Maure's *Roman de Troie* (1904–1912; first published ~1155–1160) tells the story of the Amazon Queen Penthesilea's role in the Trojan wars. Geoffrey Chaucer's "Knight's Tale," the first tale in his late fourteenth-century *Canterbury Tales* (2008; first published 1478), and William Shakespeare's *A Midsummer Night's Dream* (2004; first published ~1590–1596) both recount stories of Theseus' marriage to Hippolyte, sister of Penthesilea and queen of the Amazons. If Amazons could not be defeated on the battlefield, they could be subdued through enforced marriage as a more conventional means of patriarchal domination. From this point forward the Amazon is a persistent trope, but references to the Amazon undergo subtle but significant shifts over the course of history.

From the Renaissance through the early eighteenth century, Amazons appear in literature in two guises. Pervasive retellings of classical tales feature them as characters. They are invoked also through more indirect allusion, in texts where authors describe characters as having Amazonian qualities or tendencies in order to explain the unfamiliar and/or offensive ways of modern women who flout social, cultural, and sexual conventions. The figure of the Amazon is thus increasingly detached from her ancient origins, resulting in stories that simply compare modern female characters with the ancient warriors rather than tell stories about ancient mythological women. In Shakespeare's *Twelfth Night* (2004; first published ~1601), for example, Sir Toby Belch calls Maria, his partner in crime, Penthesilea, in apparent reference to her brazenness in carrying out a cruel prank against the gullible Malvolio (II.3.875). European travelers to foreign lands also invoked the figure of the Amazon to describe the unfamiliar behaviors of matriarchal communities in the colonized (or soon to be colonized world) and to give a familiar name to women who take the power of men. Captain Edward Cooke's *Voyage to the South Sea* (1712) famously offers an account of the naming of the River Amazon by fifteenth-century

Spanish explorer and conquistador Francis de Orellana after women warriors who lived near that river and who reminded him of the ancient archetype (Cooke 1712, 234).

A subtle shift begins to take place in the eighteenth century, inaugurating a distinctive phase in the history of the Amazon as a literary trope. Literature before this period often directly referenced Amazon women from ancient mythology. Eighteenth- and nineteenth-century literature, by contrast, more often invented their own modern Amazons who resembled the ancient originals only in the most general sense and whose crimes against patriarchal society reflect uniquely modern concerns about gender and power. This is apparent in literature that tells stories of particularly dangerous or degenerate European women who have become Amazonian. The popular and anonymously authored *Authentic Narrative of the Modern Remarkable Adventures, and Curious Intrigues, Exhibited in the Life of Miss Fanny Davies, the Celebrated Modern Amazon* (1786), casts a "modern Amazon" as its protagonist, telling a tragi-comic cautionary tale about a cross-dressing British prostitute who, eager to secure her fortune, becomes a criminal and steals money from men. Rehearsing contemporary concerns, the eighteenth-century Amazon was a female libertine who sought the sexual prerogative and financial liberty of men characteristic of modern civil society and its emergent capitalist marketplace.

Eighteenth-century representations of the Amazon thus helped to engender a shift in the meaning of the term Amazon. While the term originally referred to a character from Greek mythology, it increasingly became more figurative in its meaning. The term was steadily stripped of its ancient mythological associations, referring more often to any woman from any time who challenges masculine privilege and threatens to usurp his power. In the first edition of Samuel Johnson's *Dictionary of the English Language* (1755–1756), "Amazon" signifies the "race of women famous for their valour, who inhabited the Caucasus." Secondarily, it carries the metaphorical meaning of "a warlike woman; a virago." That lexical hierarchy of meanings persisted through seven editions of Johnson's dictionary published before his death in 1784. In 1775, however, William Perry published the *Royal Standard English Dictionary*, in which he pared down his definition of Amazon to "a masculine woman; a virago," making no mention of the ancient warriors. By the late nineteenth century, even dictionaries that claimed to reproduce Johnson's definitions had abandoned his hierarchy of meanings and the ancient history to which they referred. In the 1882 edition of *A Dictionary of the English Language: Founded on that of Dr. Samuel Johnson* (Latham 1882), for example, Johnson's secondary meaning became the only meaning: three entries on "Amazon," "Amazon-like," and "Amazonian" make no mention of the ancient women of the Caucasus. Having lost the reference to ancient history, "Amazonian" had become a mobile quality that could apply to any women who take on power or authority usually reserved for men.

For nineteenth-century writers, Amazons remained an object of derision, as in Elizabeth Gaskell's comic novella *Cranford* (1897), which presents its superstitious and rumor-mongering older female characters as "Amazons," who live in a town mysteriously lacking male inhabitants. In this period, however, the figure of the Amazon also became a subject of more earnest political philosophy and policy. In *Mother Right* (1967), Johann Jakob Bachofen (1815–1887) elaborated on the concept of the Amazon by theorizing the problem of "Amazonism" for Western political rationality. Amazonism, according to Bachofen, represents a social and moral degeneracy from which patriarchy has triumphantly progressed. Bachofen insisted that patriarchy tames the warlike proclivities of women living in matriarchal societies and thus frees humanity from anarchy, allowing for the full formation of peaceful civilization and modern culture. In his ethnographic report *Mission to Gelele, King of Dahome* (1893), Sir Richard F. Burton (1821–1890), official emissary of Queen Victoria, documented the existence of women warriors in Africa that he and other writers called Amazons. Burton claimed that "the existence of Amazons is the second great evil of the empire. The first is, or rather was, a thirst for conquest, which unlike the projections of civilised lands, impoverish and debilitate the country" (Burton 1893, 49). Burton's naming of the African Amazons recalls earlier travel writing, but Burton's usage of the figure is no mere passing reference. His extended ethnographic discussion and elaboration of the warlike tendencies he witnessed in these modern Amazons formed a cornerstone of his policy recommendations in his official missive to Queen Victoria, who was, as it happens, regularly referred to in literature of the period as an Amazon queen. By the nineteenth century, modern Amazons were not merely distinct from ancient Amazons, there were different kinds of modern Amazons and one political concern of modern imperialist society was how Queen Victoria, the Western Amazon, could effectively rule over the distinctively degenerate and uncivilized African Amazons. The Western political rationality of nineteenth-century Europe was thus conceived, in part at least, as a response to the problem of Amazonism – a problem with origins in antiquity that took unique forms in the nineteenth century.

In the twentieth century, feminist writers inaugurated a radical break with the foregoing traditions by retrieving the figure of the Amazon and, in particular, the Dahoman Amazon as a mascot for their efforts to overturn patriarchy. In the writing of Vernon Lee (pseudonym for Violet Paget, 1856–1953), the Amazon is an example of the New Woman, an androgynous woman with the economic freedom and social mobility of men. In her *Gospels of Anarchy* (1909), Lee invokes the warrior women of Dahomey, insisting that their participation in the kingdom's defense is evidence of an ideal, if rudimentary, equality that she argues should characterize the era to come. Emmet Densmore (1907) likewise uses the figure of the Dahoman Amazon as evidence that the gender equality that she imagines is evident in ancient societies should be a model for modern society. This view of the Amazon as a vehicle for a productive reformation of society and politics likewise led to the creation of Wonder Woman, the Amazon superhero of DC comics and daughter of Hippolyte, invented by the writer and psychologist William Moulton Marston (1893–1947) as the model of the liberated modern woman (Daniel 2000). The reversal of the tradition is so complete with Wonder Woman that not only is she no longer a threat to patriarchal imperialism, she has, as the sidekick and girlfriend of Captain Steve Trevor, become its greatest defender, preserving America's interests at home and abroad.

SEE ALSO: Archetype; Female Criminality; Feminist Movements in Historical and Comparative Perspective; Gender Belief System/Gender Ideology; Gender Identities and Socialization; Gender Stereotypes; Gender Transgression; Gender, Politics, and the State in Western Europe; Hegemonic Masculinity; Matriarchy; Patriarchy; Women in Combat

REFERENCES

Anon. 1786. *Authentic Narrative of the Modern Remarkable Adventures, and Curious Intrigues, Exhibited in the Life of Miss Fanny Davies, the Celebrated Modern Amazon*. London: R. Jameson.

Bachofen, J.J. 1967. *Myth, Religion, and Mother Right*, translated by Ralph Manheim. Princeton: Princeton University Press. First published 1861.

Benoît de Sainte-Maure. 1904–1912. *Le Roman de Troie*, edited by Léopold Constans, 6 vols. Paris: Firmin-Didot.

Burton, Sir Richard Francis. 1893. *Mission to Gelele, King of Dahomé*. London: Tylson and Edwards. First published 1864.

Chaucer, Geoffrey. 2008. *The Canterbury Tales*. Oxford: Oxford University Press.

Cooke, Edward. 1712. *A Voyage to the South Sea, and Round the World, Perform'd in the Years 1708, 1709, 1710, and 1711*, vol. 1. London: B. Lintot and R. Gosling.

Daniel, Les. 2000. *Wonder Woman: The Complete History*. New York: DC Comics.

Densmore, Emmet. 1907. *Sex Equality: A Solution of the Woman Problem*. New York: Funk and Wagnalls.

Gaskell, Elizabeth Cleghorn. 1897. *Cranford and Other Tales*. London: Smith. First published 1851.

Homer. 1999. *Iliad*. Cambridge: Harvard University Press.

Johnson, Samuel. 1755–1756. *A Dictionary of the English Language*. London: W. Strahan.

Latham, Robert Gordon. 1882. *A Dictionary of the English Language: Founded on that of Dr. Samuel Johnson*. London: Longman.

Lee, Vernon. 1909. *Gospels of Anarchy*. New York: Brentano.

Perry, William. 1775. *The Royal Standard English Dictionary*. Edinburgh: David Willison.

Shakespeare, William. 2004. *A Midsummer Night's Dream*. New York: Washington Square Press.

Shakespeare, William. 2004. *Twelfth Night*. New York: Washington Square Press.

FURTHER READING

Adams, Maeve. 2010. "Amazons, Anarchic Women and the De/construction of Imperial Authority in Nineteenth-Century Colonial Literature." *Nineteenth-Century Gender Studies*, 6.1.

Blok, Josine. 1995. *The Early Amazons: Modern and Ancient Perspectives on a Persistent Myth*. New York: Brill Academic.

Mayor, Adrienne. 2014. *The Amazons: Lives and Legends of Warrior Women Across the Ancient World*. Princeton: Princeton University Press.

Amazons, Dahomey

CHRISTINE WARD GAILEY
University of California, Riverside, USA

When the French began their conquest of the West African kingdom of Dahomey in the late nineteenth century, they encountered a regiment of women soldiers. The French military dubbed them "Amazons" after the society of women warriors in Greek myth, and ultimately defeated and massacred them. The so-called Dahomey Amazons have entered into contemporary discussions about whether inclusion of women in military combat positions is requisite to achieving gender equity. The circumstances that framed the creation and operation of this regiment, however, have not been part of today's debates.

From the 1700s to the late 1800s Dahomey was a tribute-based state that collected in-kind and in-service taxes from the patrilineal villages that comprised the society. The kingdom was deeply engaged in the Euro-American slave trade; the royal coterie depended on the labor of captives to work lands and supply services. The state conducted annual slave raids that conscripted village men for the expeditions, but this labor service was temporary, generally for 2–3 months.

The regiment of women participated in these slave raids, but women soldiers were conscripted for life. They comprised the only standing army. Framing the institution of the women warriors is the transformation of gender relations associated with the creation of social classes and institutions for extracting goods and services from producing communities. The selection of women for the regiment and the way in which they were incorporated into the state apparatus reflect aspects of what happened to patrilineality, marriage, motherhood, and sexuality in a class and state formative process. The regiment of women is one instance of the emerging royal class deploying an idiom of kinship while distancing itself from kinship obligations to the rest of society.

Besides concubines, the king of Dahomey had several categories of sometimes thousands of wives. The first were the wives of the king who became his official sexual partners. The royal compound in the capital, Abomey, had an intricate internal ranking and the ranked wives and other women attached to the state operated a parallel bureaucracy within the compound. These women led lives of luxury, but they exercised no power outside of the compound. Official wives of the king were crucial to cement his political alliances, but their sons by the king were barred from succession. Princesses enjoyed sexual license regardless of marital status, but they remained at his disposal: he situated some in the polygynous compounds of male bureaucrats to act as spies. Others he permitted to marry, but if their husbands were not part of the bureaucracy, the men had to live in Abomey; their children were forbidden to inherit patrilineally.

The second group of "wives of the king" had no sexual relations with the king. These women moved to various parts of the kingdom and served as revenue generators for the state, selling sexual favors and relaying a hefty portion of the receipts once a year. At the same time, these women could, at strategic times, accuse male clients of rape. State agents invariably found the accused men guilty and the punishment for impinging on the king's right to his wife's sexual potential was conscription. Symbolically, the conduct of these wives of the king created conflict locally, casting aspersions about the reliability of any rape target's testimony.

The third group of "wives of the king" was the women's regiment, housed in the king's compound in Abomey. These women were not his sexual partners and, unlike the state sex workers, had to remain celibate. Of the estimated 4,000 women warriors, some had been expelled from their patrilineal compounds as adulteresses. A few were designated as criminals, the definition of "crime" being somewhat elastic and often at odds with customary local practices. Most, however, represented a tax in women from local communities. Bosman (1705) reported that every three years a delegation of bureaucrats from Abomey would visit local villages and demand the unmarried adolescent girls – an age cohort about 13 years old. Accompanied by state agents, the young women walked to the capital. They were not raped or harmed, as they were "reserved" for the king. Upon arrival at Abomey, some were retained for state service, while the rest were allowed to return to their home villages and continue their lives. Symbolically, physically, and geographically, the "tax in women" expressed the king's assertion of control over all unmarried women: the social reproduction of local communities was due to his largesse. In theory it was an honor to be chosen as one of the king's wives, but Bosman reported that some of the young women committed suicide.

The young women retained for state service were inducted as "king's wives." Some were assigned to domestic work in the royal compound; others were accorded official wife status, trained as state sex workers, or tapped for military service. Once recruited, the women warriors trained continuously under the command of male bureaucrats. They developed a reputation both in and outside Dahomey for ferocity in battle. When the regiment, or parts of it, left the compound, the soldiers were preceded by slaves ordered to strike down anyone in their path. Their training called for death rather than retreat or surrender.

The women warriors of Dahomey demonstrate the ways emerging state apparatuses assert control over women's reproductive functions. All of the women designated as king's wives or concubines forfeited control over their reproductive potential and sexuality. The exponential increase in polygyny by the emerging ruling class transformed the meaning of wifehood as the state claimed reproductive futures of thousands of women. The women warriors, alienated from their kin communities and celibate for life, had no reproductive future but that of state expansion, and no lives outside patriarchal surveillance.

SEE ALSO: Patriarchy; Sexual Slavery; Women in Combat

REFERENCES

Bosman, Willem. 1705. *A New and Accurate Description of the Coast of Guinea, Divided into the Gold, the Slave, and the Ivory Coasts*. London: J. Knapton.

FURTHER READING

Diamond, Stanley. 1951/1996. "Dahomey, the Development of a Proto-State in West Africa: An Essay in Historical Reconstruction." *Dialectical Anthropology*, 21: 121–216.
Gailey, Christine Ward. 1984. "Women and Warfare: Shifting Status in Precapitalist State Formation." *Culture*, 4(1): 61–70.

Anarchism and Gender

MARTHA ACKELSBERG
Smith College, USA

Anarchism is both a political theory and a social movement that aims to abolish hierarchy and structured relations of domination and subordination in society, and to create a society based on equality, mutuality, and reciprocity in which each person is valued and respected as an individual. This social vision is combined with a theory of social change that insists that means must be consistent with ends and that people cannot be *directed* into a future society, but must create it themselves, recognizing, thereby, their own abilities and capacities. For anarchists, domination in all its forms – whether exercised by governments, religious institutions, economic institutions, or gendered/familial institutions – is the source of social evil. While anarchism shares with many socialist traditions a radical critique of economic domination and an insistence on the need for the restructuring of society on a more egalitarian basis, it differs from Marxism in its critique of the state, and of hierarchical authority relationships in general. Anarchism did not develop – as theory or practice – specifically to address issues of male domination over women. Nevertheless, because anarchists recognized that hierarchical authority relations have many separate (albeit interrelated) dimensions, anarchism has provided important resources for gender-based critiques of authoritarian relationships, and for movements for gender and sexual liberation.

MAJOR TRENDS

There are two major strands of anarchist theory and practice, commonly referred to as individualist and collectivist or communalist, based in the works of four founding theorists. William Godwin (England, 1756–1836) published his *Enquiry Concerning Political Justice* in 1793, in which he argued the case against government and hierarchical authority based on principles of utility. Pierre-Joseph Proudhon (France, 1809–1865) rooted his visions of a mutualist, federative structure for society in peasant farming and artisan communities. Both Godwin and Proudhon emphasized individual autonomy in their writings, and most of those in the more individualist tradition (e.g., the German Max Stirner, and the Americans Josiah Warren and Benjamin

A. Tucker) have followed in their footsteps. Mikhail Bakunin (Russia, 1814–1876), a contemporary of Karl Marx and his competitor for the leadership of the First International, developed a collectivist, but sharply anti-statist vision. The last of the founding four was Peter Kropotkin (Russia, 1842–1921), trained as a geographer, who came to believe that Darwin's theory of the "survival of the fittest" depended on cooperation, rather than competition, *within* species, and developed his theory of mutual aid. Anarchists in the individualist tradition have had relatively little impact on social movements. But the more communalist tradition has served as a major competitor with Marxism for the allegiance of social activists, and has provided the grounding for considerable women's activism, beginning in the late nineteenth century and up to the present.

France, Italy, Switzerland, Argentina, Cuba, Japan, China, Russia, and the United States all saw the development of anarchist movements during the nineteenth and early twentieth centuries; but it was in Spain during this time that communalist anarchism developed to the greatest extent, both theoretically and as a social movement. The CNT (Confederación Nacional del Trabajo, the anarcho-syndicalist labor confederation), founded in 1911, counted close to 2 million members by the time of the outbreak of the Spanish Civil War (July 1936), and also provided the context for the creation of Mujeres Libres, an organization founded by anarchist women to address the subordination of women, both within Spain and within the anarchist movement itself.

As did socialists, activists in all these movements recognized that *economic* organization – and structures of power and dominance based on control over the means of production – was an important source of power and inequality. They agreed with Marx that those relationships of power and domination dehumanize both the powerful and the relatively powerless; and also that the only way out of such relationships is through the self-organization of the disempowered/subordinate: the process of organizing and struggling collectively changes people's perceptions of themselves, raises consciousness, empowers, and enables people to create a new reality.

Yet, they also differed from socialists on a number of important points. First, they did not "privilege" economics (or class) in the way that Marx had but, rather, insisted that the tendency toward power and domination could exist (and had to be addressed) independent of economic structures. Therefore, they insisted on confronting all forms of hierarchically structured power, not just that based in economic relations (directing themselves against the power of the state, the church, and of men over women). Equally importantly, they insisted that the relationship between means and ends in social struggles was absolutely critical: one cannot create an egalitarian society through authoritarian means. Since existing societies reinforce a sense of powerlessness, people need to come to a sense of their own power and capacities if they are to be able to participate as fully equal members of a new (egalitarian) society. The process for achieving such change is crucial: for anarchists, the revolutionary process must create an egalitarian society in its practices, whether in union movements or in neighborhood forms of resistance. At the same time (and perhaps a bit paradoxically), anarchist theorists and activists were also aware that "you can't improvise a revolution." People had to prepare themselves for it. For some anarchists – most notoriously in Russia, the United States, France, and Italy – direct action meant revolutionary violence, "propaganda by the deed" in the form of bombs and assassinations. Yet, in other contexts (notably

Spain and Argentina, and with the Industrial Workers of the World in the United States, among others), even though there were assassinations and violence, direct action took on significantly different meanings.

UNDERSTANDINGS OF GENDER AND GENDERED RELATIONSHIPS

The particular ways in which strategies of direct action were understood had profound implications for women, and for gendered relations more generally. Even within a movement that was, in theory, committed to overcoming the domination of men over women, and in which there was some attention to the unionization of women and to equalization of wages, the dominant understanding in virtually every country was that "workers" were men, whose wives were at home looking after their children and households.

There was, in fact, a divergence among anarchist writers, both about the place of women within working-class organizations and about the nature of women's subordination. One stream of thought, drawing on the works of Proudhon, treated women essentially as wives and mothers, whose major contribution to society would come through their domestic roles. A second stream, which had its roots in the works of Bakunin and Kropotkin, argued that women and men were equals, and that the key to women's (as well as workers') emancipation lay in women's full incorporation into the paid workforce on equal terms with men. Nevertheless, there were also those within the movement (Emma Goldman, for example, in the United States; Soledad Gustavo and Federica Montseny in Spain) who argued that, even if it were possible to incorporate women into unions and the workforce on equal terms with men, that would be insufficient to assure their emancipation. On this view, women's subordination was as much a cultural as an economic phenomenon, and would require specific attention to their education, and their treatment within home and family: women would have to undertake an internal emancipation to come to know their own value, to respect themselves, and to refuse to become psychic or economic slaves to their male lovers. And many writers argued that women's subordination was also rooted in the double standard of sexual morality: that, too, would have to change if women were to become equal partners in the creation of a new society.

While some anarchists followed Proudhon in insisting that, even in anarchist society, the authority of husband/father within the family must be preserved, others insisted that this authority must be resisted, and replaced by more egalitarian relationships. Some advocated asceticism, chastity, and monogamy; others advocated gender equality and free love.

Both male and female writers argued that control of fertility was critical both to women's full development and emancipation and to the empowerment of workers as a class. A variety of anarchists in the United States, Spain, Argentina, France, and Italy argued that individual women and working-class families, in general, suffered from the creation of more children than they could readily support. They insisted that access to information about sexuality and birth control could free women from the fear of unwanted pregnancy (thus enabling them to enjoy sexual relations more fully) and from the burdens of bearing and rearing large numbers of children; and could enable the working class to escape the downward pressure on wages that resulted from high levels of reproduction.

Nevertheless, while there was a great deal of writing about the value and importance of sexual emancipation for both sexes, it is also clear that more traditional expectations of chastity and monogamy continued in force, particularly for women. Relatively few anarchist men actually practiced what they preached in relation to sexual freedom for "their" women. Even in the midst of revolutionary changes, relatively few women in any of these contexts were willing to risk the social ostracism that followed from flouting more traditional sexual mores. Finally, with relatively few exceptions, early twentieth-century anarchist writers assumed the normative character of heterosexuality. While some Spanish anarchists writing in the 1920s and 1930s argued that strictures against homosexuality should be loosened, these were minority voices, which found ever fewer opportunities for expression once the Civil War began.

WOMEN ANARCHISTS AND ANARCHIST WOMEN'S MOVEMENTS

While women have been involved in many working-class movements, anarchist understandings of the multifaceted operations of power, and of the multiple grounds for resisting it, have provided particularly fertile ground for the development of explicitly women's, and feminist, activism.

In the United States, France, and Spain, the communist/collectivist anarchist focus on direct action opened important spaces for women's participation and engagement. While there were substantial numbers of women in these countries who worked for pay outside their homes, union organizations (including anarchist and anarcho-syndicalist unions) tended to focus primarily on male workers, seeing women as temporary workers who would leave the workplace once they married, and who would be particularly difficult to organize. Thus, in situations where working-class organization focused almost entirely on workplace-based union organizing, women tended to be ignored.

However, women did take active roles in community-based activism, whether in "quality of life protests" (challenging the rising costs of coal, food, or housing) in many Spanish cities, in the Paris Commune of 1870/1871, and in providing critical community support for workplace strikes, for example in Lowell and Lawrence, Massachusetts in the early years of the twentieth century. In each of these contexts, anarchist understandings of social change provided a framework for the incorporation of women as active participants in ways that more traditional workplace-based strategies for social change did not.

Aside from engaging in largely male-led anarchist organizations, some anarchist women also developed specific analyses of women's subordination – whether within the larger society or within anarchist organizations. Soledad Gustavo, Teresa Claramunt, and Federica Montseny in Spain, Emma Goldman, Lucy Parsons, and Voltairine de Cleyre in the United States, Madeleine Pelletier and Louise Michel in France, María Roda and others in Italy and the United States, He Zhen in China, Fumiko Kaneko in Japan, Juane Rouco Buela and the editorial group of *Nuestra Tribuna* and Josefa Martínez and other members of the editorial group of *La Voz de la Mujer*, both in Buenos Aires, were among early anarchist women writers who explicitly addressed the situation of women. Goldman, for example, collaborated with Margaret Sanger to offer birth control to working women, and often spoke and wrote about what would be necessary to overcome women's subordination. The group of women in Buenos Aires – largely immigrants from either Spain or Italy – that published *La Voz de la Mujer* in 1896–1897 recognized a double oppression of women, as workers and as women. They criticized the hierarchical structure of traditional marital relationships (even among anarchists) and the oppression of women as workers. They advocated free love, though (as was the case in Spain and the United States as well) leaving aside virtually any attention to questions of domestic labor.

Although there were strong and active anarchist women addressing men's domination of women in a variety of locations, it was in Spain that women's anarchist organizing achieved its greatest popular reach and effect. There, building on years of writing and organizing, women within the anarchist movement began explicitly addressing what they termed the "triple enslavement" of women – to ignorance, to capital, and to men. Between 1934 and 1936, groups of women anarchists formed in Barcelona, Madrid, and elsewhere; in April 1936, one of these groups published the first issue of *Mujeres Libres*, a magazine written and edited by women and addressed to working-class women (there were to be 14 issues before the end of the Civil War in February 1939). In August 1937, the organization Mujeres Libres was officially founded. It eventually mobilized between 20,000 and 30,000 women to address that triple enslavement.

Both the magazine and the organization were by and for women. This was the case not because they did not trust men, nor because there were no men ready to commit themselves to women's equality, but because of their (anarchist) commitment to direct action: only through their own autonomous, self-directed actions could women come to recognize their own capacities. As Lucía Sánchez Saornil, one of the founders of the organization, wrote in 1935: "It is not he [the male *compañero*] who is called upon to set out the roles and responsibilities of the woman in society, no matter how elevated he might consider them to be. No, the anarchist way is to allow the woman to act freely herself, without tutors or external pressures; that she may develop in the direction that her nature and her faculties dictate."

In the context of the Spanish Civil War, Mujeres Libres had two major goals: *capacitación* (roughly translated as empowerment, or coming to awareness of one's capacities) and *captación* (mobilization of women into the anarchist/libertarian movement).

Capacitación was at the center of virtually all their programs, and clearly followed from the long-standing anarchist commitment to "preparation" and direct action. They offered education and literacy programs at all levels; employment/apprenticeship programs – in both rural and urban areas – as a kind of practical education; consciousness-raising and help in the context of unions (education for "critical consciousness," even vis-à-vis their movement comrades); education and support around motherhood and childrearing; education about sexuality, birth control, anti-prostitution, and opposing the sexual double standard; education of the young; and public relations/media: they created a magazine and had an extensive program of publications (books, informational pamphlets, and exhibitions), a radio program, and a public speaking program. They understood organizational autonomy to be critical to all these activities, because only through their own self-directed action could they come to see themselves as capable and competent – and could the men, as well, recognize the women as equal partners.

As had been the case in Argentina, however, while male anarchists might have been supportive of women's organizing and mobilizing in theory, major anarchist movement organizations were rather less supportive in practice of the activities of women who wished to define their own priorities. Thus, most movement organizations were more interested in Mujeres Libres' activities to mobilize women (*captación*) than in its educational/empowerment work. As the Spanish Civil War progressed, Mujeres Libres' activities were increasingly limited; and, at the end of the war, most activists went into exile to escape Francoist persecution. Although a small group continued "Mujeres Libres in Exile" in southern France and even published a few issues of a journal, the end of the war effectively put an end to the activities of Mujeres Libres.

THE CONTEMPORARY MOVEMENT

Anarchist emphases on direct action and on creating change though putting into practice new forms of social organization have been inspirational to many contemporary movements, most notably the communes and collectivist activism of the New Left, "participatory budgeting" in Latin America, anti-globalization/World Trade Organization protests starting in the late 1990s through the Occupy and Indignados protests of 2011–2012, the Zapatista movement in Mexico, but also, perhaps most dramatically, the civil rights movement, the second-wave women's liberation movement, and the gay and other liberation movements that have grown out of them. In fact, although much left-wing feminist activism in the United States and Western Europe drew officially on Marxist socialism for its theoretical grounding, anarchism's multifaceted understanding of oppression/domination and the emphasis on self-direction in reality provide a more accurate reflection of what Barbara Epstein (1991) has termed the "prefigurative politics" that characterizes these movements. Many of them, wittingly or unwittingly, have adopted the anarchist perspective that "we make the road by walking." It is, perhaps, not coincidental that women are well represented as activists in all of these movements. Nevertheless, it is also the case that – true to much historical experience – (male) activists in these movements have often been less willing to foreground gender issues in the struggles.

At the same time, however, anarchist perspectives continue to be reflected in contemporary theorizing. The embrace – and elaboration – by contemporary feminist and critical studies scholars of the term intersectionality, for example, can be seen as a clear outgrowth of anarchist (and anarchist-feminist) insistence that the sources of domination/subordination in society are multiple, and must be considered and responded to in relation to one another, and not separately.

SEE ALSO: Feminism, Anarchist; Feminist Activism; Gender Equality; Occupy Movements; Women's Movements: Modern International Movements

REFERENCE

Epstein, Barbara. 1991. *Political Protest and Cultural Revolution*. Berkeley: University of California Press.

FURTHER READING

Ackelsberg, Martha. 2005. *Free Women of Spain*. Oakland, CA: AK Press.
Avrich, Paul. 1988. *Anarchist Portraits*. Princeton: Princeton University Press.
Ferguson, Kathy E. 2011. *Emma Goldman*. Lanham, MD: Rowman & Littlefield.
Goldman, Emma. 1970. *Anarchism and Other Essays*. New York: Dover Books.
Graeber, David. 2002. "The New Anarchists." *New Left Review*, 13 (January/February): 61–73.
Kaplan, Temma. 1977. *Anarchists of Andalusia, 1868–1903*. Princeton: Princeton University Press.
Leighton, Marian. 1990. "Anarcho-Feminism and Louise Michel." *Our Generation*, 21 (Summer): 22–29.
Molyneux, Maxine. 1986. "No God, No Boss, No Husband: Anarchist Feminism in Nineteenth-Century Argentina." *Latin American Perspectives*, 13(1): 119–145.
Nash, Mary. 1995. *Defying Male Civilization*. Denver: Arden Press.

Androcentrism

JOANNE BAKER
James Cook University, Australia

Androcentrism is the perspective that positions men and the masculine point of view at the center of social, historical, and political thought. The word derives from the Greek prefix *andro-* for man, male, or masculine. Psychoanalytic scholars such as Derrida (1978) and Lacan (1977) have used the term phallocentrism to emphasize the way in which the penis (or phallus) acts as the representation of male dominance.

Androcentrism sees the male experience as the universal or norm and so what is not male becomes "other." Simone de Beauvoir's *The Second Sex* (2009/1949) explicitly theorized the definition and differentiation of woman as the "other" to the male as human. Thus, perspectives and practices associated with masculinity are accorded the status of universality, while those associated with femininity are associated with deviance from the norm.

Androcentrism is propagated in a variety of ways. The use of masculine language through writing and speech to refer to both men and women is indicative of androcentrism. Masculine nouns and pronouns (such as "mankind," "man," or "he") are used as the human default. "Guys" is a common form of modern address used in Western countries to refer to both men and women. This practice has led to the call for the use of more gender-neutral and gender-inclusive language (for example, using words like "humankind," "person," "he or she"). Similarly, the default cultural image in Western society for "man" and for "human being" is usually the same. The figure of a man – usually a stick figure without the addition of shapes to indicate a dress or long hair – is considered to be a normative representation of humankind, rather than an image of a woman.

Androcentrism is also spread through formal and informal customs and via patriarchal social, religious, and political institutions founded on privileging male (paternal) lineage. It is reproduced through socialization and the normalization and greater value that is placed on masculine traits and behaviors. Girls and boys are socialized into the values associated with each sex and taught not to transgress them. Masculinity is associated with aggression, instrumentality, and self-interest. In contrast, femininity is associated with self-sacrifice, nurture, and communalism. People are expected to display the perspectives and behaviors that accord with the values attributed to their sex. The bodies, traits, experiences, and achievements associated with men are normalized and valued. Thus, while the qualities associated with masculinity such as competitiveness tend to be prized, they are likely to be problematized when they are aspired to or exhibited by girls and women. A competitive woman may thus be criticized for her aggression or ambition but the same attitude is praised in a boy or man.

An androcentric social order places limits on female social participation. The qualities associated with femininity have been regarded as rendering women unsuitable for positions of leadership or political or intellectual life in the public realm, for example. Work associated with the private, domestic sphere, such as cleaning and childrearing, has been considered as more appropriately "female." Women have been rendered largely absent from historical records and excluded from positions of religious influence, scholarship, and the advancement of knowledge.

This has significant consequences for the status and lived experience of girls and women who occupy marginal positioning and are primarily viewed through their perceived difference from the male sex as a result of the androcentric worldview.

The term androcentrism and its identification of a societal orientation to the masculine has thus been an important analytic concept for feminists. Feminist sociologist and writer Charlotte Perkins Gilman published one of the earliest explicit analyses of androcentrism with *Our Androcentric Culture, or The Man Made World* in 1911. Gilman argued that women are primarily understood through their relationship with and difference to men, rather than as discrete beings in their own right: "She has held always the place of a preposition in relation to man. She has been considered above him or below him, before him, behind him, beside him, a wholly relative existence" (1911, 20). She asserted that what was presented as human experience was, more accurately, male experience. Catharine MacKinnon (1982) also highlighted the significance of androcentrism to epistemology. She argued that what counts as objective knowledge derives from masculine interests and perspectives and termed this the "male epistemological stance" (1982, 537).

Androcentrism is informed by the belief not only that men and women are different but also that men and masculinity are superior to women and femininity. For Sandra Lipsitz Bem, "the cultural debate about sexual inequality must be reframed so that it addresses not male–female difference but how androcentric social institutions transform male–female difference into female disadvantage" (1993, 176–177). Therefore, the centering or focus on men inherent in androcentrism is of concern not only because of its neglect or exclusion of women, but also because it advances a hierarchy in which men and masculinity are systemically valued more than women and femininity.

SEE ALSO: Androgyny; Gender Identities and Socialization; Gender Neutral; Masculinity and Femininity, Theories of; Phallocentrism and Phallogocentrism

REFERENCES

Beauvoir, Simone de. 2009. *The Second Sex*, trans. Constance Borde and Sheila Malovany-Chevallier. New York: Knopf. First published 1949.

Bem, Sandra Lipsitz. 1993. *The Lenses of Gender: Transforming the Debate on Sexual Inequality*. New Haven: Yale University Press.

Derrida, Jacques. 1978. *Writing and Difference*. Chicago: University of Chicago Press.

Gilman, Charlotte Perkins. 1911. *Our Androcentric Culture, or The Man Made World*. New York: Charlton Co.

Lacan, Jacques. 1977. "The Signification of the Phallus." In *Écrits: A Selection*, trans. Alan Sheridan. New York: Norton.

MacKinnon, Catharine A. 1982. "Feminism, Marxism, Method, and the State: An Agenda for Theory." *Signs*, 7(3): 515–544.

FURTHER READING

Harding, Sandra. 1991. *Whose Science? Whose Knowledge? Thinking from Women's Lives*. Ithaca: Cornell University Press.

Androgen Insensitivity Syndrome

WILLIAM J. ROBERTSON
University of Arizona, USA

Androgen insensitivity syndrome (AIS), also sometimes referred to as androgen resistance and formerly known as testicular feminization syndrome, is the biomedical name for a group of associated symptoms resulting from a cell's inability to respond to androgenic ("masculinizing") hormones. AIS, an X-linked genetic mutation, can occur regardless of a person's karyotype (chromosomal make-up), but it is only clinically significant in individuals with Y chromosomes due to its effects on the body's masculinization processes. Thus, a person with a 46,XX karyotype will likely not experience problems from AIS because it will not impair typical feminization processes. The vast majority of people diagnosed with AIS have a 46,XY karyotype. The incidence of AIS varies depending on the population as well as on its severity, but is thought to affect between 2 and 5 per 100,000 people with 46,XY karyotype (NCBI 2014).

HISTORY

Anecdotal evidence of AIS dates back over 200 years (Hughes and Deeb 2006) and includes speculation that women including Queen Elizabeth I of England and Joan of Arc were affected by the condition. John McClean Morris (1953) provided the first clinical descriptions of AIS in the mid-twentieth century after reviewing 82 cases of patients, and Lawson Wilkins (1950) demonstrated AIS's pathophysiology by giving a 46,XY female patient daily doses of testosterone to which her body failed to show any signs of virilization.

Morris (1953) first named the condition "testicular feminization syndrome" based on the observation that the testes were producing estrogen-like hormones that led to genital feminization. The condition was later renamed AIS because of the recognition of the body's resistance to androgens (Oakes et al. 2008).

TYPES

There are three categories of AIS, each determined by the level of genital masculinization. Complete Androgen Insensitivity Syndrome (CAIS) refers to the total inability of cells to respond to androgens. This non-responsiveness prevents masculinization of the body (i.e., development of a penis and scrotum in utero and secondary sex characteristics at puberty), leading to the development of a phenotypically female body, with external genitalia appearing typically female, as the androgens are aromatized into estrogen. Symptoms usually do not appear until puberty, and may include atrophied or herniated internal testes, infertility, and vaginal hypoplasia.

Partial Androgen Insensitivity Syndrome (PAIS) refers to a limited ability for cells to respond to androgens. The body's partial responsiveness to androgenic hormones impairs full masculinization of the body such that external genitalia are often ambiguous from partial masculinization. PAIS is often diagnosed at birth due to the appearance of ambiguous genitalia. Because of the body's ability to partially process androgens, phenotypes can range from slightly under-masculinized male to slightly over-masculinized female. Symptoms may include gynecomastia, underdeveloped prostate, micropenis, infertility, and feminized secondary sex characteristics in male phenotypes, and internal testes, labial fusion, and enlarged clitoris in female phenotypes.

Mild Androgen Insensitivity Syndrome (MAIS) refers to the least limited ability for cells to respond to androgens. People with MAIS have a typical male phenotype, as cells are able to process enough androgenic hormones such that genital development is unaffected. MAIS typically presents as mild impairment to spermatogenesis (the production of mature sperm cells). People with MAIS can also develop mild gynecomastia and slightly feminized secondary sex characteristics.

CLINICAL DIAGNOSIS
AND MANAGEMENT

Diagnosis of AIS depends on which type of AIS is present, but generally diagnosis begins with an observation of atypical or impaired development, including ambiguous genitalia at birth, descending testes and the development of abdominal hernias in early childhood, or impaired spermatogenesis post-puberty. Diagnosis of AIS is sometimes confirmed through androgen receptor (AR) gene sequencing, though a mutation in this gene is not always present (Hughes and Deeb 2006).

Clinical management of patients with AIS also depends on which type of AIS is present. Typically it includes management of symptoms, but has also included sex/gender assignment, gonadectomy, and hormone therapy, among others. A joint consensus statement issued in 2006 by the Lawson Wilkins Pediatric Endocrine Society and the European Society for Pediatric Endocrinology (Hughes et al. 2006) recommended the following guidelines for clinical management of intersex children, including children with AIS:

- sex/gender assignment in newborns be avoided before evaluation by an expert;
- evaluation and management occur at an institution with an interdisciplinary team experienced with intersex conditions;
- all children receive a sex/gender assignment;
- communication with patients and families be open and honest, and patients and families be included in decision-making;
- address patient and family concerns with respect and in strict confidence.

SEE ALSO: Biochemistry and Physiology; Intersex Movement; Intersexuality; Sex Versus Gender Categorization

REFERENCES

Hughes, Ieuan A., and Asma Deeb. 2006. "Androgen Resistance." *Best Practice & Research Clinical Endocrinology & Metabolism*, 20(4): 577–598. DOI: 10.1016/j.beem.2006.11.003.

Hughes, Ieuan A., C. Houk, S. F. Ahmed, P. A. Lee, and LWPES1/ESPE2 Consensus Group. 2006. "Consensus Statement on Management of Intersex Disorders." *Archives of Diseases in Childhood*, 91(97): 554–563.

Morris, John McClean. 1953. "The Syndrome of Testicular Feminization in Male Pseudohermaphrodites." *American Journal of Obstetrics and Gynecology*, 65: 1192–1211.

National Center for Biotechnology Information (NCBI). 2014. Androgen Insensitivity Syndrome. Accessed November 6, 2014, at http://www.ncbi.nlm.nih.gov/books/NBK1429/.

Oakes, Meghan B., Aimee D. Eyvazzadeh, Elisabeth Quint, and Yolanda R. Smith. 2008. "Complete Androgen Insensitivity Syndrome – A Review." *Journal of Pediatric & Adolescent Gynecology*, 21: 305–310. DOI: 10.1016/j.jpag.2007.09.006.

Wilkins, Lawrence. 1950. *The Diagnosis and Treatment of Endocrine Disorders in Childhood and Adolescence*. Springfield: Charles C. Thomas.

FURTHER READING

Dreger, Alice D. 2000. *Hermaphrodites and the Medical Invention of Sex*. Cambridge, MA: Harvard University Press.

Fausto-Sterling, Anne. 2000. *Sexing the Body: Gender Politics and the Construction of Sexuality*. New York: Basic Books.

Intersex Society of North America (ISNA). 2015. Androgen Insensitivity Syndrome (AIS). Accessed January 24, 2015, at http://www.isna.org/faq/conditions/ais.

Karkazis, Katrina. 2007. *Fixing Sex: Intersex, Medical Authority, and Lived Experience*. Durham, NC: Duke University Press.

Kessler, Suzanne J. 1998. *Lessons from the Intersexed*. New Brunswick: Rutgers University Press.

Parker, Philip M. 2007. *Androgen Insensitivity Syndrome: A Bibliography and Dictionary for Physicians, Patients, and Genome Researchers*. San Diego: ICON Health Publications.

Androgyny

KRISTINE L. NOWAK and AMANDA DENES
University of Connecticut, USA

Androgyny is a third gender category which exists in the absence of a clear classification or identification as either male or female, and can be either biological or psychological.

As illustrated below, androgyny can be understood from both biological and psychological perspectives. It has been defined as the center of the continuum between masculinity and femininity, the presence of both masculinity and femininity, or the absence of either (Bem 1974; Spence, Helmreich, and Stapp 1975). Sex category assignment (classifying a person male or female) is one of the first things people do in an interaction and this assignment carries assumptions and cultural norms for appropriate engagement. The inability to make that determination increases uncertainty about how to speak and behave in an interaction because sex category fundamentally structures and influences the way people communicate and make meaning (Lakoff 1987; West and Zimmerman 1991). Because of this, androgynous others can be objectified (seen as less human) and perceived to be less credible and likeable (Nowak and Rauh 2008), and people are generally more uncertain and uncomfortable in situations where they cannot confidently categorize a person as either male or female.

Biological androgyny is associated with intersex, which is a broad medical term that encompasses many diagnoses, but generally refers to individuals whose bodies do not clearly fall into the biological categories of male and female, including individuals born with both male and female genitalia, also called hermaphroditic. It is estimated to apply to less than 2 percent of all live births (Blackless et al. 2000; Karkazis 2008). Biological sex is determined on the basis of genitalia and generally thought to be binary (male or female), though biological androgyny provides a third possible category.

Psychological androgyny is also a third possible category of gender and used to describe a person who is difficult to categorize as male or female because of either the absence of masculinity or femininity (Locksley and Colten 1979), or the presence of both (Spence, Helmreich, and Stapp 1975). Defining androgyny as the center of the continuum between masculinity and femininity makes the questionable assumption that masculinity is the opposite of femininity (Nowak and Rauh 2008; Nowak, Hamilton, and Hammond 2009) and ignores people who have both masculine and feminine characteristics. It is not surprising that androgyny is difficult to define and measure because it is based on gender, which is itself a fluid socially constructed concept that lacks the clear dichotomy or meaning across societies that is generally associated with biological sex, though it represents an important area of research.

Moving beyond the definition of androgyny, there is debate about how to measure it. While biological sex is generally operationalized as binary (male or female), gender and sex categorization are based on the application of socially defined criteria resulting from stereotypes and not all people fit into one of those two categories. Gender is not binary and is better described (and measured) on a continuum. There are debates on whether (1) femininity and masculinity operate on separate continua, (2) individuals can be both highly feminine *and* highly masculine, and (3) individuals' femininity or masculinity is relative and can vary in different contexts.

The Bem Sex-Role Inventory (BSRI) facilitated empirical research on psychological androgyny (Bem 1974). The BSRI viewed femininity and masculinity as separate constructs, and the items measured individual identification with prevailing cultural definitions of socially desirable depictions of masculinity and/or femininity (Hoffman and Borders 2001). Individuals with high differences between their endorsement of feminine and masculine characteristics were sex-typed (feminine or masculine), while individuals with low difference scores (endorsing both feminine and masculine characteristics) were labeled androgynous. Early work focused on androgyny as a *balance* between femininity and masculinity and was calculated as the absolute difference between individuals' femininity and masculinity scores (Bem 1974), which failed to differentiate between individuals that were either high or low on both femininity and masculinity. These measures were very controversial because (1) they were based on cultural norms of femininity and masculinity in the 1970s, which have changed; (2) the measures involved the linking of gender and biological sex; and (3) there were problems with factor analyses and methodological issues related to the computation of androgyny scores. These and other limitations are discussed by Hoffman and Borders (2001) and elsewhere.

Another popular measure of androgyny was the Personal Attributes Questionnaire (PAQ), which argued that only individuals scoring high on measures of both masculinity and femininity should be labeled androgynous (Spence, Helmreich, and Stapp 1975). It classified individuals into one of four categories based on their scores on the femininity and masculinity scales: feminine (high feminine–low masculine), masculine (high masculine–low feminine), androgynous (high feminine–high masculine), or undifferentiated (low feminine–low masculine).

Androgyny and gender research has begun using technology to explore aspects of gender that are not feasible offline (Blascovich and Bailenson 2011) and this is likely to continue in the future. Online interactions using visualization software and computer displays provide a forum for researchers to explore the codes of gender and sex where they can manipulate and explicitly test visual indications of masculinity and femininity while controlling for other factors. The ability to systematically separate biological sex from socially determined and perceived gender allows for the examination of perceptions and attributions of different aspects of masculinity and femininity, including visual and social attributions and perceptions (Nowak, Hamilton, and Hammond 2009; Blascovich and Bailenson 2011; Fox, Bailenson, and Tricase 2013).

SEE ALSO: Feminist Theories of the Body; Gender, Definitions of; Gender Difference Research; Gender Dysphoria; Gender Identities and Socialization; Gender Identity, Theories of; Gender Neutral; Gender Stereotypes; Internet and Gender; Intersexuality; Language and Gender; Masculinities; Masculinity and Femininity, Theories of; Media and Gender Socialization; Sex Versus Gender Categorization; Third Genders

REFERENCES

Bem, Sandra L. 1974. "The Measurement of Psychological Androgyny." *Journal of Consulting and Clinical Psychology*, 42(2): 155–162.

Blackless, M., et al. 2000. "How Sexually Dimorphic Are We? Review and Synthesis." *American Journal of Human Biology*, 12: 151–166.

Blascovich, Jim, and Jeremy Bailenson. 2011. *Infinite Reality: Avatars, Eternal Life, New Worlds, and the Dawn of the Virtual Revolution*. New York: HarperCollins.

Fox, Jesse, Jeremy N. Bailenson, and Liz Tricase. 2013. "The Embodiment of Sexualized Virtual Selves: The Proteus Effect and Experiences of Self-Objectification via Avatars." *Computers in Human Behavior*, 29: 930–938. DOI: 10.1016/j.chb.2012.12.027.

Hoffman, Rose Marie, and L. DiAnne Borders. 2001. "Twenty-Five Years after the Bem Sex-Role Inventory: A Reassessment and New Issues Regarding Classification Variability." *Measurement and Evaluation in Counseling and Development*, 34: 39–55.

Karkazis, Katrina. 2008. *Fixing Sex: Intersex, Medical Authority, and Lived Experience*. Durham, NC: Duke University Press.

Lakoff, George. 1987. *Women, Fire, and Dangerous Things: What Categories Reveal about the Mind*. Chicago: University of Chicago Press.

Locksley, Anne, and Mary Ellen Colten. 1979. "Psychological Androgyny: A Case of Mistaken

Identity?" *Journal of Personality and Social Psychology*, 37(6): 1017–1031.
Nowak, Kristine L., Mark A. Hamilton, and Chelsea C. Hammond. 2009. "The Effect of Image Features on Judgments of Homophily, Credibility, and Intention to Use Avatars in Future Interactions." *Media Psychology*, 12(1): 50–76. DOI: 10.1080/15213260802669433.
Nowak, Kristine L., and Christian Rauh. 2008. "Examining the Perception Process of Avatar Anthropomorphism, Credibility and Androgyny in Static and Chat Context." *Computers in Human Behavior*, 24(4): 1473–1493.
Spence, Janet T., Robert Helmreich, and Joy Stapp. 1975. "Ratings of Self and Peers on Sex Role Attributes and their Relation to Self-Esteem and Conceptions of Masculinity and Femininity." *Journal of Personality and Social Psychology*, 32(1): 29–39.
West, Candace, and Don H. Zimmerman. 1991. "Doing Gender." In *The Social Construction of Gender*, edited by Judith Lorber and Susan A. Farrell, 13–37. Newbury Park, CA: Sage.

FURTHER READING

Nowak, Kristine. 2003. "Sex Categorization in CMC: Exploring the Utopian Promise." *Media Psychology*, 5(1): 83–104.
Nowak, Kristine L. 2015. "Examining Perception and Identification in Avatar-Mediated Interaction." In *The Handbook of the Psychology of Communication Technology*, edited by S. S. Sundar, 89–114. Hoboken, NJ: Wiley-Blackwell.
Reeves, Byron, and Clifford Nass. 1996. *The Media Equation: How People Treat Computers, Television, and New Media Like Real People and Places*. Stanford, CA: CSLI.

Anglophone Caribbean Feminism

SUPRIYA M. NAIR
Tulane University, USA

The history of gender and feminism is a commonly conflicted one, but within the Caribbean it is particularly fraught given the contexts of native genocide, European settlement, African slavery, Asian servitude, and almost continuous waves of migration. When Christopher Columbus wandered into the Bahamas in 1492, he set off a catastrophic chain of events that left multiple legacies on the archipelago and influenced in specific ways its colonial and postcolonial histories. Indigenous peoples were driven into the interior or decimated in number. Enslaved black men and women from Africa were brought across the Atlantic on ships of the Middle Passage and forced to labor in horrendous conditions, raising tropical crops like sugarcane for imperial profit. After Emancipation in the mid-nineteenth century, destitute populations from traditional societies in India and China were brought to replace slave labor. Diverse European powers struggled for supremacy over various islands, producing an array of cultural, political, and linguistic differences. For many in the Caribbean, overcoming these destabilizing and traumatic conditions shared by both men and women was perceived as the primary goal in the struggle for freedom and independence. Consequently, with the end of European empire and the rise of black nationalism after the world wars, the male leaders who took over from the whites subordinated women's issues to what they believed were more urgent individual and national crises following centuries of debasement. Therefore, in addition to battling these issues of historic significance to the region, women's rights, gender equity, and sexual politics in the Caribbean have additionally had to struggle to clear a space for themselves.

When modern feminists attempted to bring issues like domestic violence and rape into the public sphere, they were seen as upstaging more crucial national independence and social justice movements that demanded cooperation rather than conflict between sexes. Instead of being granted equal importance in the struggle for full human rights on the islands, women's issues were domesticated and rendered invisible in the separate-spheres, middle-class ideology borrowed from Victorian times. While colonialism affected gender relations between white and non-white communities, colonized male subjects were perceived as being deprived of the traditional rights of men, which were usurped by white masters. One of the most popular tropes of Caribbean and Latin American resistance borrowed from Shakespeare's *The Tempest* was Caliban, the slave, who was constructed as a sexual threat to the white woman, Miranda (Lamming 1991). Some Caribbean male writers tended to embrace rather than challenge the sexism. Anglophone Caribbean fiction tends to portray white women in problematic ways, as either the white man's chaste, coveted property or as oversexed objects lusting after black and brown men. Women authors were not exempt from circulating stereotypes, and Charlotte Brontë's *Jane Eyre* (2001/1848) infamously presented the white Creole woman, Bertha Mason, as a drunken lunatic, an account that was challenged a century later by Dominican author Jean Rhys (1999/1966). None of this rhetoric took into consideration that non-white women, particularly slaves and indentured servants, had been targets of rape and other forms of sexual and physical violence from both white and non-white men for centuries. In more troubling ways, the image of the sexualized and hypermasculine man was constructed as a reaction to the supposed castration of colonization, with male violence as the cathartic reaction to the loss of masculinity in models of masculinity that not only remained unchallenged, but became more virulent. Jamaica Kincaid's *My Brother* (1997), which describes her brother's death from AIDS in 1996, includes a critique of this rhetoric but also engages in anti-maternal discourse about her mother.

In a controversial afterword to *Out of the Kumbla*, an anthology on Caribbean women writers, Sylvia Wynter (1990) famously challenged the grounds of both feminism and womanism as debated in the academy. Despite womanism as a third world approach that was meant to mitigate the hostility between sexes assumed to be more characteristic of first world feminism, where men became the enemy to be routed rather than companions in struggle, Wynter suggests that Caribbean womanism is a necessarily questionable enterprise in a system where all black or non-white people were dehumanized. As Hortense Spillers (1987) argued in the African American context, Wynter implies that the slave ship obliterated the finer points of gender distinction more prevalent in middle-class, white European cultures. While she questions Caliban's "non-desire" "for his own mate" in the popular invocation of Shakespeare's characters in Caribbean writing (1990, 360), Wynter identifies Miranda's role in the colonial triad as that of fellow imperialist with her father, Prospero, rather than as a possible sympathizer of the enslaved Caliban or his absent mother, Sycorax. Thus, according to Wynter, race rather than gender was the more significant category of difference in the rhetoric and discourse of slavery and empire. Spillers went on to defend African American women from the "matriarchal" stereotypes applied to what Patrick Moynihan (1965) would label the pathological structure of black families where the women were presumably stronger than the men, and so did feminists in the Caribbean context of female-headed households and single women. But what came to be known as the male marginalization thesis continues to haunt women's demands for equality. The thesis rests on the pervasive demonization of black men from slave times to the contemporary period, asserting that in such contexts women were not the only or even primary victims of injustice and social deprivation.

In an article titled "Blacklash," Orlando Patterson (1993), a black sociologist of Jamaican descent, also claimed that gender relations in the black context were troubled, but was more concerned with the "collective psychosis" of young black men, whose disproportionate number of deaths, embrace of suicidal violence, lack of employment, drop-out rates, and other disturbing statistics challenged the idea that African American women, for instance, suffered a double oppression (on the grounds of gender and race). The argument was made in the Caribbean even earlier in 1986, with the publication of Errol Miller's *Marginalization of the Black Male*. The controversy that erupted over his claims was discussed in later collections, and several feminist scholars across disciplines challenged what seemed to them the overhasty ascription of "matriarchal power" status to struggling women in the Caribbean, especially since the label was less a tribute to women's multiple strategies for survival and their undeniable strength and more a negative stereotype that robbed them of their history of labor and achievement. As Dr. Joycelin Massiah, then the regional program director for UNIFEM (United Nations Development Fund for Women), demands in an assessment of gender equality in the Caribbean, "how did a region which was in the vanguard of commitment and action in the seventies, eighties and early nineties find itself, at the turn of the century, unable to articulate a comprehensive programme of action towards the achievement of gender justice?" (2003, xvi).

Not just in the contemporary period but even during slavery female subjects were assumed to have had it better than men, since they did not perform the most intense physical labor and were able to gain favors from white men through sexual relations. In one of the earliest slave narratives by a woman, *The History of Mary Prince* (1831; Salih 2004), Prince's disclosure of sex in exchange for money was kept as discreet as possible, concealing what were common consequences of prostitution and pauperization of women that continue today in the feminization of poverty. Despite legendary figures such as Maroon Nanny in Jamaica, women's roles in Caribbean slave revolts were also forgotten, and they were seen as little more than props rather than as main actors in Caribbean history. In the literary field, although women writers like Una Marson, Phyllis Shand Allfrey, Erna Brodber, Beryl Gilroy, Merle Hodge, Maryse Condé, Paule Marshall, Jean Rhys, and Sylvia Wynter wrote from the 1930s onward, it was not until the 1970s and 1980s that women's writing was conceived of as a separate category, partly influenced by similar developments in the Anglo-American academy. When George Lamming complained of the invisibility of Caribbean writers in the 1950s, he was not including women writers in this picture of neglect.

While women have been writing for centuries, only an occasional woman writer appeared in earlier anthologies or literary criticism of Caribbean writing, and it was not until 1988 that a major conference focusing on anglophone Caribbean women writers was held, leading to one of three major literary anthologies on women writers and women's issues that were published in or after 1990. The collection that came out of this conference, *Caribbean Women Writers* (Cudjoe 1990), remains one of the most significant contributions, with both critical and creative writing. This was one of the first collections on women writers that paid attention to non-anglophone islands and includes sections on hispanophone, francophone, and Dutch-speaking contexts, along with discussions of Creole languages. Writers like Lorna Goodison, Marlene NourbeSe

Philip, and Afua Cooper addressed the particular tribulations of writing as women, each rejecting the "voicelessness" that women's histories were consigned to and providing a specific context for modern women's, if not radical feminist, writing. The distinction is a significant one, since Evelyn O'Callaghan is reluctant to set aside too purist a space for the Caribbean "woman version," and refuses the confrontational politics and binary oppositions of Western approaches. Despite a certain "*something*" that apparently unites women as a group, O'Callaghan also points out both their differences from each other and their similarities with themes and styles of male writers (1993, 8–9; emphasis in text). Some scholars are reluctant to make too quick a move from feminism to gender studies, which tends to destabilize gender binaries and challenge essentialist constructions of womanhood.

However, this is not to say that fiery feminist portrayals were absent in the Caribbean, as Michelle Cliff's works, for example, demonstrate. Feminist critic Paula Morgan was to observe, "in 1994 I also concluded a cross-cultural study of a substantial cross-section of African, African American and Caribbean women's novels with the comment that, for the most part, they deliver a devastating judgment on their male characters. A substantial cross-section is depicted as weak or blindly egoistic; if they are strong, they are inclined to be vicious and cruel or complacent, authoritarian and unwilling to listen, or vain and foolish" (2004, 290–291). She wonders, therefore, if "gender create[s] an alien and alienating barrier which cannot be breached" (2004, 291). While women's rights legislation and even women leaders suggest that the women's movement has come a long way, Caribbean gender history is yet to deliver a euphoric account of success.

Nevertheless, sociologist Rhoda Reddock (1998) believes that the feminist movement has been constantly evolving in the Caribbean, from religious affiliations in the nineteenth century, to political and trade union membership in the 1970s, to more radical feminist identification in the 1980s, which saw women more focused on issues specific to their sex. The UN Decade for Women from 1975 to 1985 inspired a series of scholarly, developmental, educational, and activist measures. As Reddock and other feminist scholars have discussed, women's organizations focused on a range of causes including education, wage equity, maternity and family, domestic abuse and sexual violence, childcare, married women's property, and inheritance and reproductive rights. More recent work has expanded the initial focus on slavery and Afro-Caribbean contexts to the multi-ethnic differences in the Caribbean and to critiques of the heterosexist emphasis of women's activism. Indian and Chinese gender relations, for instance, have a different set of parameters from black families, and women's literature also includes same-sex relationships.

SEE ALSO: Feminism, Indo-Caribbean; LGBT Activism in the Caribbean; Sexual Citizenship in the Caribbean; Sexualities; UN Decade for Women; Women's and Feminist Activism in the Caribbean

REFERENCES

Brontë, Charlotte. 2001. *Jane Eyre*, edited by Richard J. Dunn. New York: Norton. First published 1848.

Cudjoe, Selwyn R., ed. 1990. *Caribbean Women Writers: Essays from the First International Conference*. Wellesley, MA: Calaloux Publications.

Kincaid, Jamaica. 1997. *My Brother*. New York: Farrar, Straus and Giroux.

Lamming, George. 1991. *The Pleasures of Exile*. Ann Arbor: University of Michigan Press. First published 1960.

Massiah, Joycelin. 2003. "Preface." In *Gender Equality in the Caribbean: Reality or Illusion*, edited by Gemma Tang Nain and Barbara Bailey, ix–xviii. Kingston, Jamaica: Ian Randle.

Miller, Errol. 1994. *Marginalization of the Black Male: Insights from the Development of the Teaching Profession*, 2nd ed. Kingston, Jamaica: Canoe Press, University of the West Indies. First published 1986.

Morgan, Paula. 2004. "Under Women's Eyes: Literary Constructs of Afro-Caribbean Masculinity." In *Interrogating Caribbean Masculinities: Theoretical and Empirical Analyses*, edited by Rhoda E. Reddock, 289–308. Mona, Jamaica: The University of the West Indies Press.

Moynihan, Patrick. 1965. *The Negro Family: The Case for National Action* ["The Moynihan Report"]. Washington, DC: US Department of Labor.

O'Callaghan, Evelyn. 1993. *Woman Version: Theoretical Approaches to West Indian Fiction by Women*. New York: St. Martin's Press.

Patterson, Orlando. 1993. "Blacklash: The Crisis of Gender Relations Among African Americans." *Transition*, 62: 4–26.

Reddock, Rhoda. 1998. "Women's Organizations and Movements in the Commonwealth Caribbean: The Response to Global Economic Crisis in the 1980s." *Feminist Review*, 59 (Summer): 57–73.

Rhys, Jean. 1999. *Wide Sargasso Sea*, edited by Judith Raiskin. New York: Norton. First published 1966.

Salih, Sara, ed. 2004. *The History of Mary Prince: A West Indian Slave*. London: Penguin. First published 1831.

Spillers, Hortense J. 1987. "Mama's Baby, Papa's Maybe: An American Grammar Book." *Diacritics*, 17(2): 64–81.

Wynter, Sylvia. 1990. "Beyond Miranda's Meanings: Un/silencing the 'Demonic Ground' of Caliban's 'Woman'." In *Out of the Kumbla: Caribbean Women and Literature*, edited by Carole Boyce Davies and Elaine Savory Fido, 355–372. Trenton, NJ: Africa World Press.

FURTHER READING

Alexander, Jacqui, M. 2005. *Pedagogies of Crossing: Meditations on Feminism, Sexual Politics, Memory, and the Sacred*. Durham, NC: Duke University Press.

Anim-Addo, Joan, ed. 1996. *Framing the Word: Gender and Genre in Caribbean Women's Writing*. London: Whiting and Birch.

Bailey, Barbara, and Elsa Leo-Rhynie, eds. 2004. *Gender in the 21st Century: Caribbean Perspectives, Visions, and Possibilities*. Kingston, Jamaica: Ian Randle.

Barriteau, Eudine, ed. 2003. *Confronting Power, Theorizing Gender: Interdisciplinary Perspectives in the Caribbean*. Mona, Jamaica: The University of the West Indies Press.

Barrow, Christine, ed. 1998. *Caribbean Portraits: Essays on Gender Ideologies and Identities*. Kingston, Jamaica: Ian Randle.

Clarke, Edith. 1999. *My Mother Who Fathered Me: A Study of the Families in Three Selected Communities in Jamaica*. Mona, Jamaica: The University of the West Indies Press. First published 1957.

Edmondson, Belinda. 1999. *Making Men: Gender, Literary Authority, and Women's Writing in Caribbean Narrative*. Durham, NC: Duke University Press.

Kanhai, Rosanne, ed. 2011. *Bindi: The Multifaceted Lives of Indo-Caribbean Women*. Mona, Jamaica: The University of the West Indies Press.

Kempadoo, Kamala. 2004. *Sexing the Caribbean: Gender, Race, and Sexual Labor*. New York: Routledge.

Lamming, George. 1972. *Water with Berries*. New York: Holt, Rinehart and Winston. First published 1971.

Mahabir, Joy, and Mariam Pirbhai, eds. 2013. *Critical Perspectives on Indo-Caribbean Women's Literature*. New York: Routledge.

Mohammed, Patricia, ed. 2002. *Gendered Realities: Essays in Caribbean Feminist Thought*. Mona, Jamaica: The University of the West Indies Press.

Momsen, Janet H., ed. 1993. *Women and Change in the Caribbean: A Pan-Caribbean Perspective*. Kingston, Jamaica: Ian Randle.

O'Callaghan, Evelyn. 2004. *Women Writing the West Indies, 1804–1939: "A Hot Place, Belonging to Us."* Abingdon, Oxon: Routledge.

Shepherd, Verene, Bridget Brereton, and Barbara Bailey, eds. 1995. *Engendering History: Caribbean Women in Historical Perspective*. Kingston, Jamaica: Ian Randle.

Smith, Faith, ed. 2011. *Sex and the Citizen: Interrogating the Caribbean*. Charlottesville: University of Virginia Press.

Tinsley, Omise'eke Natasha. 2010. *Thiefing Sugar: Eroticism Between Women in Caribbean Literature*. Durham, NC: Duke University Press.

Animality and Women

KATTIE BASNETT
Rice University, USA

Women have often been animalized subjects susceptible, by way of their symbolic animalization, to forms of social, political, and physical violence normally reserved for animals. Debates about women's political enfranchisement have historically been linked to similar debates about animals. Various theoretical orientations capture the ideological continuity between the marginalization of women and animals, including posthumanism, feminist theory, animal theory, and ecocriticism. Scholarship on the topic is often interdisciplinary, emerging from the humanities and from social and hard sciences, including literature, cultural studies, history, philosophy, religious studies, anthropology, evolutionary biology, bioethics, and cognitive science.

Much contemporary scholarship, like that of literary posthumanist Cary Wolfe (2003) and continental philosopher Jacques Derrida (1995), designates the symbolic equation of marginal groups (e.g., women) with animals for the purposes of marginalization, a consequence of humanistic ideology, specifically its species bias or speciesism. Speciesism exists on a continuum of ideological violence alongside other -isms including racism, sexism, and ethnocentrism. Because the animal is the ultimate species-"Other" exempt from the kinds of ethical and political protections afforded to human beings, such as human rights, other marginal individuals and groups can be symbolically attached to the category of animality for the purposes of exploitation, violence, or disenfranchisement. Contemporary feminist-vegetarian critical theorist Carol J. Adams (2011) argues that one consequence of speciesism is a "sexual politics of meat" inherent in Western culture. She reads fast-food ads and other cultural images in which highly sexualized women are portrayed as pieces of meat for consumption, or in which animal food products are feminized and sexualized as indicative of what Derrida (1995) terms carno-phallogocentrism, or the unsettling relationship between carnivorousness, male sexual virility, and violent, hypersexual attitudes toward women and animals. From a feminist ecocritical perspective, Adams and Josephine Donovan (2006) note how common terms like "chick," "cow," and "henpecking" are all animalizing, sexist terms applied exclusively to women.

The animalization of women has historically made feminism, animal rights, and ecological activism natural partners. The women's rights and animal rights movements in nineteenth-century Britain arose in tandem, and feminist figures (e.g., Frances Power Cobbe and Mona Caird) played leadership roles in both. Historian Harriet Ritvo (1987) and literary critic Lisa Surridge (2005) have shown how Victorian animal rights propaganda explicitly correlated violence toward animals with abuse of human beings, especially women, thereby directly connecting the goals of animal rights and women's rights groups.

The philosopher of science, feminist, and posthumanist Donna Haraway (2003) has proclaimed thinking and writing about companion animals as inherently feminist, as such work reinforces the feminist project of expanding ways of relating to and living with others in ways that liberate us from typologies, binaries, relativisms, and universalisms. Like the poet and professional dog trainer Vicki Hearne (1986), who has written on the philosophical and practical issues of human–animal communication, French feminist philosopher Luce Irigaray (2004) sets animals apart as uniquely situated to both understand and respond to the call of need from humans. Animals (usually domestic) have frequently been cited as agents in women's empowerment, particularly their renegotiation of heteronormative gender and sexual proscriptions. Literary critic Marjorie Garber (1997) has argued that relationships with animals are uniquely independent of hardline gender and sexual conventions. Viewing cross-species relationships as bisexual, Garber offers them as a model for how we might self-describe and relate apart from culturally constructed ideas about what behaviors are proper to or between individuals on the basis of sex, gender, or species.

Within the past two decades, the amount of scholarship problematizing the ideological underpinnings of the marginalization of women and animals has increased with the rise of posthumanism, animal theory, and ecocriticism. Simultaneously, mainstream texts, including *Dogs and Their Women* (Cohen and Taylor 1989), a photographic collection of women and their dogs, have emerged to document how new understandings of love, loyalty, friendship, intimacy, sexuality, self, and self-acceptance are gained by women through canine companions.

SEE ALSO: History of Women's Rights in International and Comparative Perspective; Human–Animal Studies; Universal Human Rights

REFERENCES

Adams, Carol J. 2011. *The Sexual Politics of Meat: A Feminist-Vegetarian Critical Theory*. New York: Continuum.

Adams, Carol J., and Josephine Donovan, eds. 2006. *Animals and Women: Feminist Theoretical Explorations*. Durham, NC: Duke University Press.

Cohen, Barbara E., and Louise Taylor. 1989. *Dogs and Their Women*. Boston: Little Brown.

Derrida, Jacques. 1995. "'Eating Well,' or the Calculation of the Subject." In *POINTS …: Interviews, 1974–1994*. Stanford: Stanford University Press.

Garber, Marjorie. 1997. *Dog Love*. New York: Touchstone.

Haraway, Donna. 2003. *The Companion Species Manifesto: Dogs, People, and Significant Otherness*. Chicago: Prickly Paradigm Press.

Hearne, Vicki. 1986. *Adam's Task: Calling Animals by Name*. New York: Alfred A. Knopf.

Irigaray, Luce. 2004. "Animal Compassion." In *Animal Philosophy: Essential Readings in Continental Thought*, edited by Matthew Calarco and Peter Atterton. New York: Continuum.

Ritvo, Harriet. 1987. *The Animal Estate: The English and Other Creatures in the Victorian Age*. Cambridge, MA: Harvard University Press.

Surridge, Lisa. 2005. *Bleak Houses: Marital Violence in Victorian Fiction*. Athens: Ohio University Press.

Wolfe, Cary. 2003. *Animal Rites: American Culture, the Discourse of Species, and Posthumanism*. Chicago: University of Chicago Press.

FURTHER READING

Derrida, Jacques. 2008. *The Animal That Therefore I Am*, edited by Marie-Louise Mallet. New York: Fordham University Press.

Derrida, Jacques. 2009. *The Beast and the Sovereign*, vol. 1. Chicago: University of Chicago Press.

Gaarder, Emily. 2011. *Women and the Animal Rights Movement*. New Brunswick: Rutgers University Press.

Hamilton, Susan, ed. 2004. *Animal Welfare and Anti-Vivisection 1870–1910*. New York: Routledge.

Haraway, Donna. 1991. *Simians, Cyborgs, and Women: The Reinvention of Nature*. New York: Routledge.

Haraway, Donna. 2008. *When Species Meet*. Minneapolis: University of Minnesota Press.

Kemmer, Lisa A., and Carol J. Adams. 2011. *Sister Species: Women, Animals, and Social Justice*. Champaign: University of Illinois Press.

McHugh, Susan. 2011. *Animal Stories: Narrating Across Species Lines*. Minneapolis: University of Minnesota Press.

Peterson, Barbara, Brenda Peterson, and Deena Metzger. 1999. *Intimate Nature: The Bond Between Women and Animals*. New York: Ballantine.

Weil, Kari. 2012. *Thinking Animals: Why Animal Studies Now?* New York: Columbia University Press.

Wolfe, Cary. 2003. *Zoontologies: The Question of the Animal.* Minneapolis: University of Minnesota Press.

Wolfe, Cary. 2010. *What is Posthumanism?* Minneapolis: University of Minnesota Press.

Wolfe, Cary. 2011. *Before the Law: Humans and Other Animals in a Biopolitical Frame.* Chicago: University of Chicago Press.

Anthropological Perspectives on Sex

CAMILLA POWER
University of East London, UK

That sex in all human cultures is the subject of beliefs and customs, rules, and norms is perhaps the fundamental difference between humans and non-humans. Yet, the particular ideas people hold about sex vary greatly both across and within cultures. Beliefs about sex concern who can have sex with whom, and when; and how bodily fluids and substances interact in this most intimate of human experiences, affecting the wider gendered world of ritual and economic activities. Customs involve norms and traditions, but can also include practices for evading restrictions on behavior.

An anthropology of sex faces the difficulty of finding data on what people say about sex, what people think about it, and then, if possible, what they really do. The fieldworker's own projections, interests, and identity add more obscuring layers. While this is the case for virtually any area of research, the subjectivities involved in sex must be especially elusive. An example is found in the acrimonious Mead–Freeman controversy where Mead's work with Samoan teenage girls in the 1920s was challenged after her death by Freeman several decades later. Discrepancies arose from the differing perspectives of the two researchers, while testimonial of Mead's earlier informants also shifted in response to increasing Samoan exposure to Christianity and American culture in the intervening period following World War II. A respectable Christian grandmother cannot be expected to tell the same stories as she did in her adolescence, nor, given Samoan "joking" practices, were those stories likely to be gospel truth.

Anthropology grew up as a modern fieldwork discipline with questions about universals and variation of human sexual behavior at its heart. It emerged from a Victorian period when lawyers, ethnologists, anthropologists, and sociologists such as Bachofen, McLennan, Maine, Morgan, and Westermarck sifted the evidence on early stages of human society, sexuality, and forms of marriage. Despite patriarchal standards of moral prudery, some of these early scholars speculated boldly, notably in the Bachofen-Morgan thesis of sexual promiscuity, group marriage, and the priority of matrilineal clans in early kinship. Developed by Engels, this remarkably asserted women's equality and sexual freedom at human origins. Other origin "myths" from Durkheim, Freud, and, later, Lévi-Strauss placed the incest taboo, as a rule of exogamy, central to human morality and kinship.

With his rich ethnography of sexual life among the matrilineal Trobrianders of Melanesia, Malinowksi (1929) attacked speculations about the origins of marriage. He also challenged the universality of Freud's notion of sexual complexes arising from the psychological tensions within the nuclear family. In *Sex and Repression* (1927), he put this to the test with a comparison of sexual life history between European "father-right" and Trobriand "mother-right" societies demonstrating the lack of repression, latency period, or Oedipal conflict in Melanesia. Sex before marriage was entirely normal for Trobriand adolescents, centered on the institution of the *bukumatula*, or bachelor hut, which girls could visit freely, while Trobriand children happily played sex games among their repertoire of activities imitating adults.

The Trobriands material supported an association of matrilineal ideology with women's sexual equality and freedom from coercion or double standards. Malinowski argued the importance of interpreting data on beliefs within a wider understanding of sociological structures, enabling the ethnographer to build a whole picture of the world from an indigenous perspective. His early study *Baloma* (1954/1916) gave a detailed account of the cycle or journey of ancestral spirits. A female *baloma* of a woman's maternal kindred caused pregnancy by inserting a rejuvenated spirit child (*waiwaia*) into her body as she bathed in certain lagoons or the sea. With badgering, the Trobrianders acknowledged that only women who had had sex would get pregnant, so a man was needed to open the way for the spirit. Malinowski explored the view that "unchaste girls" were particularly susceptible to being approached by a *baloma*. Yet, he reports, unmarried girls took precautions to avoid exposure by not bathing at high tide, rather than by avoiding sex. Malinowksi discarded his earlier idea that Trobrianders had a "primitive ignorance" of the physiology of paternity, adopting a more sophisticated position on the ideology as elaborate assertion of rights of the maternal kindred over a child and of the fundamental clan structure. A mother's husband was involved as the one who "received the child in his arms" but remained a "stranger" from outside the clan.

Malinowski struggled to understand that what he termed "the correct physiological view" was a folk belief of exactly the same standing as the Trobrianders' – no more nor less a cultural construction. He well recognized Christian morality as associated with the institution of a patrilineal and patriarchal family (1929, 159). For the Trobrianders, physiological paternity sanctified by God the Father and God the Son was "talk of the missionaries." They refuted it, observing that unmarried girls were having sex all the time, and were "overflowing" with semen, yet rarely got pregnant (1929, 160). Malinowksi persisted with imagery of "a seed being planted in the soil and the plant growing out of the seed" (1954/1916, 223). Delaney (1986) compares this "embryological view" to that of patriarchal Turkish peasants who assert the male role in reproduction as generative and causative. It does not correspond to the scientific finding of an equal genetic contribution from each parent, only itself established in the early twentieth century with Mendelian genetics.

The Western preoccupation with paternity, in the form of a doctrine of "One Sperm, One Fertilization," has featured prominently in accounts of human evolution and the sexual division of labor. "Man the hunter" brings home the bacon to his faithful mate, trading investment for sex with paternity certainty. This "standard model" pervades evolutionary psychology to such an extent that Western views on male sexual jealousy and possessiveness are assumed to be universals (Beckerman and Valentine 2002, 3). The idea that no man is willing to let another man share sexual access to a wife is soon followed by assumptions about women's natural tendency to monogamy.

Such axioms have been challenged by the prevalence across much of lowland South America of beliefs admitting that one child may have several fathers (Beckerman and Valentine 2002, 4). The array of ideologies allowing for "partible paternity" derives from the idea that one sexual act is simply not enough to conceive a child. For the Kulina of Western Brazil, conception is a process requiring numerous acts of sexual intercourse: men must "work hard," they say (Pollock 2002, 52). The fetus is built up by accumulation of semen and, when it forms, it blocks the flow of menstrual blood from the uterus. More than one man can contribute to the seminal growth of the fetus, and since both men and women have affairs, this is normal. Kulina women participate in a public ritual when they are "hungry for meat," going together from house to house in the village to sing provocatively, ordering men to hunt (Pollock 2002, 53). Women bang sticks on the house door to show they will be sex partners for the men of the house that night if they are successful. They choose men who are in the sexually permitted category of affines, but must not choose their own husband for such a hunt. This ritual, besides other informal affairs, guarantees most, if not all children have more than one "father."

Sex also acts as an economic force of production in the traditions of the Canela of Central Brazil who celebrated several festivals and ceremonies involving publicly validated sex outside marriage, besides other less formal occasions. Crocker (1994, 144) relates how Canela research assistants initially denied the existence of extramarital sex practices, having learned through bitter experience not to reveal these to outsiders. He had brought with him medical volumes with explicit plates of internal and external body parts. Women soon began crowding around, enjoying the fun of pointing to and naming genital and reproductive parts in a typical atmosphere of Canela sexual joking while Crocker himself gradually lost his inhibitions. As he gained people's trust, he began to find out about the goings on during annual ceremonies like Red and Black moiety day (Crocker 1994, 145). Each moiety group, painted in traditional designs, would sit quietly on either side of a fence too high to see over. Discreetly, men would be informed if they had been chosen as partner by a woman of the opposite moiety. As the groups filed off into the woods, each woman would catch the eye of the man she had chosen. Once partners had paired up, men would hunt in the woods, bringing back game to their partner who then decided if she wanted sex. This meat would be used in a ceremonial meat-pie exchange between a woman and her mother-in-law, marking the latter's acceptance of her daughter-in-law's right to take part in sex with others apart from her spouse both in public ritual and private trysts.

Born into households organized around matrilines, Canela children have their mother's husband as social father, his brothers as classificatory fathers and men who have inseminated their mother during pregnancy as "contributing" fathers (Crocker and Crocker 1994, 83). Pregnant women will pick good hunters as contributing fathers, and these men are meant to give semen without hesitation, or the mother might miscarry. When she gives birth, her husband's mother usually "catches" the child, and then asks the mother to name the contributing fathers, for the sake of the child's health. Those men enter a state of seclusion known as *couvade*, observing food and sex taboos to avoid pollution of the child's blood since they share in this substance. After 40 days, the social and contributing fathers gather at the mother's house to share a meat-pie ceremony. They mime abstention from the meat, while the mother's uncle lectures them in their responsibilities to the child. Should the child get sick, they are publicly accountable for keeping food and sex taboos.

Partible paternity ideologies thrive among groups like the Canela or Bari where uxorilocality and matriline tendencies prevail, and women have freedom to choose extra fathers, making no secret of their identity. A secondary father among the Bari of Venezuela has positive effects on a child's chance of surviving to adulthood. The idea of partible paternity can persist even in groups where patriliny and virilocality dominate, although husbands are likely to police women's sexual activity, and sexual jealousy can threaten the interests of women and children. Among the Curripaco of Venezuela, for instance, the child of a woman who has had sex with men of different patrikin will be deemed *mapachica* – a mixture of species.

In the Congo basin, Mbendjele forest hunters also consider pregnancy to be a process requiring continuous "work" from husband and wife. Men view this as rivalry with "women's biggest husband," the moon (Lewis 2008, 299). By putting in sperm every day, "we men cut the moon from women" (2008, 303). Governing sexual and economic exchange is *ekila*, a polysemic concept revolving around moon, blood, sex, fertility, health, meat, taboo, hunting luck, and sharing properly. To maintain strong *ekila*, a husband and wife must cooperate in observing all proscriptions affecting how they share his meat, what species they eat and with whom (and when) they have sex (Lewis 2008, 300–301). When a woman is menstruating, she is *ekila*; her husband cannot go hunting, or the animals will smell him. A "great hunter" who slept around would ruin his *ekila*. This is an example of a principle found regularly in African and many other hunter-gatherer groups of mystical intertwining of production (hunting) with reproduction (menstruation, pregnancy, and childbirth). Menstrual blood on the one hand and the blood of game on the other are never allowed to mix, yet, there is profound connection and conflation between male and female spheres.

A number of cultures which assert male superiority ritually through secret initiation societies, for instance, the Amazonian Mehinaku, the Gahuka-Gama and other Highland New Guinea groups, or numerous Australian Aboriginal traditions, may express this through severe aversion to menstrual blood. Paradoxically, male secrets imitate aspects of menstruation in ritual. Further contradictions appear between sexual desire or behavior, and ideology of pollution. Gimi men in New Guinea profess horror of contact with menstrual blood, these notions being elaborated in their entire cosmology. Yet, songs celebrate the eroticism of menstrual blood: sexual intercourse often took place inside menstrual huts built to isolate women for the period during the month when they supposedly represent danger to the community. Similar fantasies pervade the *Love Songs of Arnhem Land* (Berndt 1978). Again, strict prohibitions applied at menstruation, and women were meant to stay in seclusion, yet, the songs celebrate sex with menstruating and/or deflowered girls, including both ritually sanctioned coitus and hidden or illicit assignations, in both cases with classificatory kinsmen.

Another example of antithesis of menstrual blood as a powerful and dangerous contaminant opposed to semen as the most valued generative substance comes from the Sambia of Highland New Guinea (Herdt 1984). While girls grow up naturally as their bodies develop a "menstrual blood organ" (*tingu*), Sambia boys must be nurtured through initiation stages, only becoming men by imbibing semen. Their semen organs (*keriku-keriku*) cannot produce this most valued commodity internally, so a boy must accumulate semen through ritual fellatio, having oral sex with an older bachelor youth of the correct affinal kinship category. Semen is drunk on analogy with breast milk as a nurturing substance, and is itself a source of breast milk. A young husband "feeds" his wife semen with oral sex before he dares to risk genital–genital contact, and by this means he strengthens the baby via his wife's breast milk. Herdt interprets Sambia kinship and affinal relations in terms of a cycle of semen transactions. Ritual homosexual contacts transferring semen involve potential enemies who may become affines in the first generation and then kin in the second.

Much contemporary research has shifted the focus to sexual transactions in a globalized world, rather than embedded in traditional kinship frameworks. With topics as variegated as suppression of lesbian sensibilities during Ann Summers parties; cosmetic surgery in the Colombian narco-economy; action research with and by sex workers; exchanges of violence in the life of Salvadorean *travestis*; or urban gay geographies, it remains difficult to disentangle sexual beliefs, customs, and ideologies from the economic materialities of the bodies having sex.

SEE ALSO: Adolescent Pregnancy; Adultery, Cultural Views of; Double Standard; Gender Belief System/Gender Ideology; Gender Equality; Initiation Rites; Kinship; Matrilineal and Matrilocal Systems; Oedipal Conflict; Taboo

REFERENCES

Beckerman, Stephen, and Paul Valentine, eds. 2002. *Cultures of Multiple Fathers: The Theory and Practice of Partible Paternity in Lowland South America*. Miami: Florida University Press.
Berndt, Ronald. 1978. *Love Songs of Arnhem Land*. Chicago: University of Chicago Press.
Crocker, William, and Jean Crocker. 1994. *The Canela: Bonding through Kinship, Ritual, and Sex*. Fort Worth: Harcourt Brace College Publishers.
Delaney, Carol. 1986. "The Meaning of Paternity and the Virgin Birth Debate." *Man*, 21: 494–513.
Herdt, Gilbert. 1984. "Semen Transactions in Sambia Culture." In *Ritualized Homosexuality in Melanesia*, edited by Gilbert Herdt, 167–210. Berkeley: University of California Press.
Lewis, Jerome. 2008. "Ekila, Blood, Bodies and Egalitarian Societies." *Journal of the Royal Anthropological Institute*, 14: 297–315.
Malinowski, Bronislaw. 1927. *Sex and Repression in Savage Society*. London: Routledge and Kegan Paul.
Malinowski, Bronislaw. 1929. *The Sexual Life of Savages in North-Western Melanesia*. London: Routledge.
Malinowski, Bronislaw. 1954. "Baloma: Spirits of the Dead in the Trobriand Islands." In *Magic, Science and Religion*. New York: Doubleday Anchor. First published 1916.
Pollock, Donald. 2002. "Partible Paternity and Multiple Maternity among the Kulina." In *Cultures of Multiple Fathers*, edited by Stephen Beckerman and Paul Valentine, 42–61. Miami: Florida University Press.

FURTHER READING

Donnan, Hastings, and Fiona Magowan. 2010. *The Anthropology of Sex*. New York: Berg.
Gregor, Thomas. 1985. *Anxious Pleasures: The Sexual Lives of an Amazonian People*. Chicago: University of Chicago Press.
Shankman, Paul. 1996. "The History of Samoan Sexual Conduct and the Mead-Freeman controversy." *American Anthropologist*, 98: 555–567.

Anti-Globalization Movements

JANET M. CONWAY
Brock University, Canada

In response to the pervasive claim by global elites that "there is no alternative" to neoliberal globalization, a widespread globally dispersed popular revolt coalesced in the late 1990s under the banner of the anti-globalization movement. Although marked by a great diversity of struggles and a range of understandings of globalization, the movement was united in its opposition to neoliberal strategies of privatization, deregulation, free trade, and deep cuts to government services. They contested growing corporate power and control in all domains of social and ecological life and its undermining the exercise of popular democratic sovereignty through nation-states. "Anti-globalization" is a problematic moniker in that these movements are opposed to US-led, corporate-dominated neoliberal globalization, not to increased global interconnectedness, and often see themselves promoting alternative globalizations. Thus, some activists prefer "global justice" or "alter-globalization," but "anti-globalization" continues to be the most internationally recognized way of naming this globally extensive and diverse phenomenon.

Since the origin of the term with reference to the 1999 protests in Seattle that shut down the World Trade Organization (WTO) meetings, the anti-globalization movement has been conceived in two major ways. The first refers to a worldwide eruption of popular resistance to neoliberal globalization – not a single movement but a "movement of movements" with diverse roots, North and South, global in scope, and in formation since the 1980s. It is constituted by both vibrant transnational networks and myriad local- and national-scale resistances. It is increasingly densely networked through the Internet, the World Social Forum process, and periodic mobilizations at symbolic sites of global governance – summits of the International Monetary Fund (IMF), World Bank, WTO, G8, and now G20.

The second usage refers more narrowly to the predominantly white, anarchist-inspired student and youth movements whose direct action tactics successfully shut down the WTO in Seattle. In a series of mass actions around elite summits in the Global North from the late 1990s to the present, their practices of direct democracy, horizontalism, and diversity of tactics are the focus of one strand of anti-globalization scholarship.

The anti-globalization movement has produced a large and diverse scholarly literature across the social sciences, drawing on multiple theoretical and analytical traditions, focusing on different empirical sites and attending to a range of problematics.

Within this diverse field, the literature is somewhat bifurcated according to the two conceptualizations outlined above, and relatedly in terms of geographic focus on the Global North, Global South, or the North–South axis, and between place-based studies and those focused on transnational networks and spaces. In recent years, there have been significant attempts to analyze the anti-globalization movement as a coherent phenomenon, to situate it in relation to longer-term historical developments, such as those in the world system, global capitalism, Western or global modernity, global democratization or global network society.

The anti-globalization movements entered popular consciousness during the Seattle protests against the WTO in November 1999, which mobilized more than 50,000 people predominantly from the United States but including significant international participation, notably from the Global South. Over several days, throngs marched, protested, lobbied, and conferred in an alternative "people's summit" in a carnivalesque atmosphere. About 15,000 of the protesters, mostly students and youth, organized with the intent to shut the WTO meetings down through mass non-violent direct action. They were met with intense police violence and the declaration of martial law but their tactics caught police and politicians off guard and the WTO meetings ended in disarray. The use of direct action and, more controversially, a "diversity of tactics" including property destruction and self-defense against police violence, which departed from strict codes of non-violence, provoked intense debate in the broader movement. The events of Seattle and the subsequent wave of counter-summit protests have produced a growing volume of work, much of it by activist scholars (Burton-Rose, Yuen, and Katsiaficas 2004), as well as more social scientific work involving participant surveys, organizational mapping, and cross-national comparisons of protest events. In the years following Seattle, a number of anthologies appeared, including case studies of key organizations, transnational networks, and campaigns that were understood as constituting the anti-globalization movement (Bandy and Smith 2005; Della Porta and Tarrow 2005; Kaldor 2001–2012).

The youth movements have also demonstrated great creativity: aesthetically in the visual culture of the protests; mediatically, in their prolific cultural production of and about the movement and their use of digital and social media technologies and platforms; organizationally, in their practices of consensual decision-making, leaderlessness, and self-organization; and politically-philosophically in their utopian search for postcapitalist ways of life through the construction of alternative communities in the present. The novelty of their practices on all these fronts has attracted attention from scholars who note similarities with the popular movements of 2011 in the Arab world, anti-austerity movements in Europe, and Occupy Wall Street. Analytically, many situate these practices in relation to political traditions of anarchism and autonomism (Graeber 2009), while others have connected them with processes of individuation associated with modernization.

The events of Seattle established a pattern of summit protests that continues into the present, despite the chilling effects of 9/11, widespread anti-terrorism laws, the increased securitization of summit sites, and the criminalization of protesters. However, as important as these protests are, it is critical not to conflate them with the diverse and pluralistic politics and practices of the worldwide movement of movements against neoliberal globalization. The summit protests of the Global North, with their particular politics and cultures of activism, are specific to the Global North.

Mass popular resistance to neoliberal globalization had been in formation in diverse place-based struggles around the world for a decade prior to the Seattle protests. In the Global South, movements resisting structural adjustment programs (SAPS) and the burden of third world debt had been underway since the early 1980s. They protested against the privatization of state-owned resources and public services and organized in the free trade zones. Women especially have been at the forefront of reorganizing social life for survival and subsistence in both urban shantytowns and rural villages. Also originating in the 1980s, popular movements arose against the mega-development projects of the World Bank, financed through loans that brought SAP conditionality, environmental degradation, the displacement of peoples, and destruction of subsistence economies. The communities of the Narmada valley in India are a well-known example. Local populations are increasingly confronting multinational corporations directly. The Ogoni people in Nigeria have been engaged in a decades-long struggle with Shell that is simultaneously an environmental justice, indigenous rights, anti-corporate, and pro-democracy movement. Localized struggles against extractivism have proliferated and intensified over the last decade, often with indigenous peoples in the lead, and are increasingly networked at every scale.

Realities of exploitation and resistance to neoliberalism exploded onto the world stage with the Zapatista uprising in Chiapas, Mexico on January 1, 1994. Timed to coincide with the coming into effect of the North American Free Trade Agreement (NAFTA), it brought together many strands: resistance to structural adjustment and interconnected demands for land reform, indigenous rights, and cultural autonomy, decrying the loss of national sovereignty and demanding a renewal of Mexican democracy. Through their brilliant and erudite spokesperson, Subcomandante Marcos, the Zapatistas waged their revolution over the Internet and in the international media, generating a global outpouring of solidarity. Zapatismo became a global political force and an important phenomenon in the early consolidation of the anti-globalization movement (Midnight Notes 2001).

Meanwhile in the Global North, a Canada-based struggle against free trade with the United States had begun in the mid-1980s and led to the formation of cross-border networks like the Hemispheric Social Alliance. The increasingly internationalized anti-free trade movement was key to the 1998 defeat of the Multilateral Agreement on Investment (MAI) at the OECD and was a significant element in the early anti-globalization manifestations. The anti-free trade movement won another major victory in the 2005 defeat of US President George Bush's plan for a Free Trade Area of the Americas.

Although rooted in localized realities and spawning a wide range of community-based resistance and survival strategies, movements were increasingly networked internationally as the 1990s progressed. Peasants organizing against genetically modified (GM) foods, patenting of seeds and other life forms, and land grabbing by states and corporations for export-oriented monocropping has been networked since 1993 through Via Campesina, a transnational North–South network and now the largest social movement in the world. The Jubilee 2000 movement to cancel third world debt coalesced in the late 1990s as a massive North–South campaign, in which Northern partners mounted critical public education campaigns, lobbied Northern governments, financed Southern organizing, and engaged in direct pressure on the World Bank, IMF, and other emerging institutions of neoliberal global governance. The Jubilee movement was a significant constituency in the June 1999 anti-G8 demonstrations in Cologne, Germany and in the subsequent anti-globalization demonstrations. Jubilee South, a network of Global South anti-debt movements born of Jubilee 2000, remains a prominent presence at the World Social Forum and in current actions, such as the 2012 climate justice mobilizations at the Rio+20 United Nations (UN) conference in Brazil.

Through the late twentieth century but accelerating through the 1990s, UN conferences were critical sites for growing convergence and mounting opposition to neoliberalism among non-governmental organizations (NGOs) from all over the world. Although the official processes were profoundly contradictory, the parallel summits provided for unprecedented contact among NGOs, many of which are connected to broader popular movements in their home countries. Women's, environmental, human rights, dalit, and indigenous peoples' movements articulated to the anti-globalization movement and the World Social Forum process all have had significant points of contact with the UN processes.

The UN has been central to the consolidation of a global feminist movement, marked by the explosion of feminist NGOs, the appearance of durable transnational feminist networks, and the global proliferation of grassroots feminisms (Naples and Desai 2002). Through the 1990s, an increasingly militant transnational feminism opposed to neoliberalism and articulated to the emerging anti-globalization movement appeared (Moghadam 2013). One new expression is the World March of Women, a now permanent mobilizing process and key organizational participant in the World Social Forum. The World March currently has more than 70 national coordinations, organizes major international actions every five years, and is active in transnational anti-globalization alliances.

Perhaps the most important development in the international consolidation of the anti-globalization movement has been the appearance of the World Social Forum (WSF). Building on the momentum created by the Seattle protests, the WSF was initiated by Brazilian organizations as an alternative to the World Economic Forum, to which the groups and movements of civil society worldwide opposed to neoliberalism were invited to communicate their struggles, strategies, and alternatives. Under the banner "Another world is possible," the first WSF was held in January 2001 in Porto Alegre, Brazil. Its stunning success led to the WSF becoming a permanent process of mobilization, with social forums being organized on every continent, from local to regional scales, and with regular global gatherings that continue to attract tens of thousands, sometimes over 100,000, participants. The WSF has been the key site for cultivating transnational and inter-movement alliances, the most recent example being the global climate justice movement. Women's groups and feminist networks have been key actors in organizing and populating social forums from the beginning, although they persistently struggle for visibility and voice. Feminism as a political current of radical thought and practice has remained rather submerged – both in the anti-globalization movement and in studies of the movement (Eschle and Maiguashca 2010). A WSF was held annually for seven years and since has become biennial. It moves regularly to different sites across the Global South, expanding the geographic and cultural reach of the anti-globalization movement as an umbrella political identity to localized struggles against neoliberal globalization (Santos 2006; Conway 2013).

SEE ALSO: Economic Globalization and Gender; Feminist Activism; Global Restructuring; Occupy Movements

REFERENCES

Bandy, Joe, and Jackie Smith. 2005. *Coalitions across Borders: Transnational Protest and the Neoliberal Order*. Lanham, MD: Rowman & Littlefield.

Burton-Rose, Daniel, Eddie Yuen, and George Katsiaficas. 2004. *Confronting Capitalism: Dispatches from a Global Movement*. New York: Soft Skull Press.

Conway, Janet. 2013. *Edges of Global Justice: The World Social Forum and its "Others."* New York: Routledge.

Della Porta, Donatella, and Sidney Tarrow, eds. 2005. *Transnational Protest and Global Activism*. Lanham, MD: Rowman & Littlefield.

Eschle, Catherine, and Bice Maiguashca. 2010. *Making Feminist Sense of the Global Justice Movement*. Lanham, MD: Rowman & Littlefield.

Graeber, David. 2009. *Direct Action: An Ethnography*. N.p.: AK Press.

Kaldor, Mary, ed. 2001–2012. *Global Civil Society Yearbook*. Thousand Oaks, CA: Sage.

Midnight Notes. 2001. *Auroras of the Zapatistas: Local and Global Struggles of the Fourth World War*, 2nd ed. Jamaica Plain, MA: Autonomedia.

Moghadam, Valentine M. 2013. *Globalization and Social Movements: Islamism, Feminism and the Global Justice Movements*, 2nd ed. Lanham, MD: Rowman & Littlefield.

Naples, Nancy A., and Manisha Desai. 2002. *Women's Activism and Globalization: Linking Local Struggles and Transnational Politics*. New York: Routledge.

Santos, Boaventura de Sousa. 2006. *The Rise of the Global Left: The World Social Forum and Beyond*. London: Zed Books.

FURTHER READING

Chesters, Graeme, and Ian Welsh. 2006. *Complexity and Social Movements: Multitudes at the Edge of Chaos*. New York: Routledge.

Juris, Jeffrey S. 2008. *Networking Futures: The Movements against Corporate Globalization*. Durham, NC: Duke University Press.

Maeckelbergh, Marianne. 2009. *The Will of the Many: How the Alterglobalisation Movement is*

Changing the Face of Democracy. New York: Pluto Press.
Munck, Ronaldo. 2007. *Globalization and Contestation: The New Great Counter-Movement.* London: Routledge.
Reitan, Ruth. 2007. *Global Activism.* New York: Routledge.

Anti-Miscegenation Laws

SALLY L. KITCH
Arizona State University, USA

US COLONIES AND STATES

Anti-miscegenation (racial mixing) laws, also known as miscegenation laws, have shaped and regulated marriages throughout history in many places in the world. Such laws targeted marriages between persons of different races, primarily between blacks and whites, in the mainland British colonies and the United States between 1634 (in Maryland) and 1967, when the last anti-miscegenation laws were declared unconstitutional by the Supreme Court. Anti-miscegenation laws shaped the racial regime in the United States over four centuries by naturalizing notions of racial difference and hierarchy, suggesting that white racial purity could and should be protected, and asserting that race is a material, biological category that can be measured. The laws contrasted the presumed naturalness of same-race marriages with the allegedly illicit sexuality of miscegenous relationships that even marriage could not legitimize (Pascoe 2009, 7–8, 12).

The laws predated by more than a century the term *miscegenation,* which reflected the laws' gendered racial intent. The term was coined during the election campaign of 1864, when several rogue southern Democrats penned cartoons and leaflets that associated political freedom for black men, sought by Republicans, with rampant sex between emancipated black men and white women (Kitch 2009, 137). Anti-miscegenation laws became more plentiful after the Civil War. By 1915, 28 states barred and invalidated all marriages between Negroes and whites. By the 1940s, as eugenicist fears of white "hypodescent" through racial dilution escalated and the "threat" of intermarriage with Asian immigrants or Native Americans increased, 41 out of 48 states passed anti-miscegenation laws. In 1967, 16 states still had anti-miscegenation laws on their books (Kitch 2009, 279n4). Although ostensibly gender neutral, these laws revealed their biases, as discussed below, through their focus on interracial marriage rather than extramarital sex and their role in promoting the doctrine of white supremacy.

Indeed, "it was by analogy to the 'natural' difference of sex that 'miscegenation' became so deeply grounded in the 'natural' difference of race" (Pascoe 2009, 28).

Anti-miscegenation laws reinforced the black–white racial binary central to US racial thinking since at least the nineteenth century, even though some states prohibited marriages between whites and other groups, including Native Americans (Maine in 1821) and Malays and the Chinese (western states in the 1880s and 1890s). In such cases, other racialized groups were often stand-ins for the African Americans who were less prevalent in those regions.

Anti-miscegenation laws were declared constitutional by US courts before 1967 on the shaky grounds that they applied equally to all races and to both sexes and were therefore not discriminatory. Because judges and justices defined miscegenation as illicit sex, it was presumed exempt from the legalities of contracts, choice, and civil rights usually associated with marriage and citizenship. Thus, anti-miscegenation laws appeared to be the very model of constitutional equality despite their denial of Fourteenth Amendment protection for interracial couples (Pascoe 2009, 3–4). The *Loving v. Virginia* Supreme Court Decision in 1967 exposed the faulty logic of the laws' legal heritage by recognizing both their differential effects, based on a specific characteristic – race – that did not pass strict constitutional scrutiny, and their purpose to promote white supremacy (Leslie 2014, 1105–1106). The Supreme Court's decision in 2014 not to rule on the constitutionality of same-sex marriage exposes another feature of the *Loving* decision, however. That is, *Loving* was handed down after mixed-race marriages were widely accepted in the Northeast and Midwest and only 16 states still banned them. It could be argued that the court waited for a similar tipping point as only 14 states prohibited same-sex marriage by the time of their 2015 ruling that granted same-sex couples throughout the United States the right to marry (see also Gabriel 2014).

The *Loving* decision did not recognize the gender biases inherent in anti-miscegenation laws, despite evidence that they affected primarily two gendered racial groups – non-white men and white women – and depended on an analogy between racial difference and allegedly natural, God-given gender differences. In addition, while supporting white supremacy, the laws enforced white male control over racial identity and status and the transfer of power and rights across generations.

The historical roots and evolution of anti-miscegenation laws further reveal their gendered foundations.

Status-of-the-mother laws (*partus sequitur ventrum*), passed between 1662 (Virginia) and the 1740s (South Carolina) and beyond, proclaimed that children inherited the racial status of their mothers, no matter who their fathers were. Such laws helped to expand the enslaved population through the systematic rape of black women by their white masters, particularly after 1807, when the United States banned the importation of slaves from abroad. Anti-miscegenation laws basically ensured that status-of-the-mother laws would outlive slavery, since they too targeted legitimate reproductive relationships between white women and black men, prevented the progeny from such unions from being classified as white, and exempted white men's extramarital sexual access to black women from scrutiny and censure.

Status-of-the-mother laws did not allow white women to bequeath their racial status or citizenship to their children, however. Indeed, any white woman who produced a mixed-race child was classified as black herself in states like Maryland and Virginia for many years. The one-drop rule discussed below further ensured that any legitimate mixed-race child produced by a white woman and a black man would not be classified as white. The rule was designed in part to reduce claims to white status or property by women's mixed-race descendants, while white men's property and status were protected by the continued claim that black women could produce only black children.

Racial distinction based on blood, which led to the one-drop rule still considered valid by some Americans, might seem a gender-neutral classification system. In practice, however, it had distinctly gendered implications. First, using blood as a measurement for racial categorizing, starting in earnest in the 1830s, was motivated by the preceding two centuries of racial mixing, which was propagated mostly through white men's rape of black women. It was primarily that form of miscegenation which rendered skin color and hair texture unreliable indicators of racial difference.

Second, the mechanisms for determining racial classifications were often different for men and women. Through the 1840s in both northern and southern states, for example, racial blood measurements were frequently tempered by considerations of actual skin color and reputation, despite laws promoting precise measurements, such as one eighth "Negro" or Indian blood (one great-grandparent), that allegedly disqualified an individual for white rights and privileges. A man's reputation typically meant his "reception into society" and "having commonly exercised the privileges of a white man," even if his ancestors were black. But a woman's reputation usually meant her history of private associations with men. Consorting with black men could render a woman black or mulatto for social purposes, even if all of her blood ancestors were white.

Such discretion disappeared during the years immediately before and following the Civil War. After the 1857 *Dred Scott* Supreme Court decision, blackness was increasingly defined by a single drop of black blood, which tainted all who bore it with the "deepest degradation," according to the Court. In 1896, the *Plessy v. Ferguson* Supreme Court ruling upheld racial segregation based on the one-drop rule (Kitch 2009, 131, 133, 116). Despite that decision, the one-drop rule remained gendered as well as raced because enforcement against crossing the color line continued to target the black men and white women who were the most likely interracial pairs to marry. White men's extramarital sex and reproduction with black women mostly escaped sanction.

Because it focuses on race, the term *white privilege* obscures the doctrine's gendered foundations. Actually, the legal and cultural manipulations that produced and reinforced white supremacy in the United States should be understood as the promotion of white racial superiority through the suppression and manipulation of black and white women's sexual behavior, reproductive agency, and civil rights. Status-of-the-mother laws established the gendered foundations of white supremacy by allowing white men, but not white women, to bequeath their racial status to their children and by declaring that black women could only produce black children. In addition, the burgeoning influence of eugenics in the nineteenth and early twentieth centuries identified white women (but not white men) as the "guardians" of white racial blood. To fulfill that role, eugenicists admonished white women to avoid anything, including education, careers, and birth control, that interfered with the transmission (via white men) of their pure racial blood to the next generation. Strict gender role differentiation and male dominance were the primary eugenic tools for preserving white racial purity and racial differentiation. That white males were the primary beneficiaries of the economic, political, and social privileges being maintained by white supremacy further exposes the doctrine's gendered foundations (Kitch 2009, 123–125, 147–154, 175–180). In protecting white supremacy, therefore, anti-miscegenation laws reinforced a gendered racial regime.

BRITISH COLONIAL ISLANDS

The regulation of interracial marriage and, to a lesser extent, sexual relationships in mainland North American British colonies and eventual states differed from the approach taken by British colonials in the New World island colonies, including Bermuda, Jamaica, Barbados, Antigua, the Bahamas, and about 15 others. Indeed, with the exception of Antigua, none of those colonies enacted anti-miscegenation legislation (and Antigua's was not enforced) (Murphy and Spear 2011, 74n23). In addition, regulations that did exist regarding sexual relations, concubinage, prostitution, or rape initially recognized a gradation of racial categories rather than imposed a strict black–white binary on people of various racial ancestries. And rather than the one-drop rule that at times classified as black any mainlander with a single non-white great-great-grandparent, islanders who were "removed three Degrees [generations] from the Negro Ancestor" could be re-classified as white. An eighteenth-century Jamaican law identified such persons as seven eighths white and indistinguishable from other white persons (Wilson 2002, 148; Newman 2010, 589).

This contrast cannot be explained by religious laxity, because many island colonials were staunchly religious, or solely by geography, the supply of white women, or any other single characteristic. Rather, the contrast between the islands and the mainland exemplifies numerous features of the specific histories of colonial projects at various times and in various places, and by "the ideologies and anxieties that shaped" the colonists' existence. At the same time, several shared circumstances produced similar patterns of regulation of the interracial reproduction that was so crucial to the formation of empire (Ray 2013, 191).

Several conditions on the islands effectively made anti-miscegenation laws superfluous. First, most interracial sexual relationships between white men and colonized women of color, including indigenous women (except in Bermuda) and imported African slaves, occurred outside of marriage. Such relationships, which were often coerced and served to reinforce white European male privilege and white supremacy, were not the focus of mainland anti-miscegenation laws either. Second, relationships between white European women and island men of color were extremely rare, and the threat of intermarriage between those groups was almost non-existent. Thus, that dreaded circumstance, which most motivated anti-miscegenation laws on the mainland, was absent. Instead, as on the mainland, any man of color accused of rape or fornication with a white woman was subject to harsh punishment. In addition, white men were universally allowed more violations of whatever interracial sex code was in place than were white women. Such disparities "speak volumes about the raced and gendered nature of colonial power" (Ray 2013, 191–195).

As slavery became more entrenched and more identified with African-ness, however, circumstances changed. Although miscegenous behavior was rarely punished, the progeny of mixed-sex relationships who might threaten white dominance faced increased restrictions in order to keep "'humble the whole coloured race'" (Livesay 2010, 86). In the same spirit, white women's infractions were regarded as more damaging to themselves and the community than either fornication or incontinence (pre-marital sex) by women of color. The latter distinction reflected women of color's increased identification as property, even in locations (such as Bermuda) where they were initially allowed to participate fully in religious rites and even to marry, with the governor's permission (required for all couples) (Kopelson 2013, 483).

If there was one defining factor affecting interracial sexual mores and regulations across island colonial societies, it was probably demographics. Unlike the European men on the mainland, most white male colonists on the islands were unmarried or widowed, and they were often vastly outnumbered by slaves. For example, Dominica in 1787 consisted of 1,236 free Europeans and nearly 15,000 enslaved Africans (Newman 2010, 588–589). The combination of unfettered white men and plentiful enslaved or otherwise objectified women of color promoted island cultures that tolerated, even celebrated, interracial dalliances, concubinage, and rape without worries about the intergenerational transmission of property or power that marriages entail. That attitude changed as the mixed-race population expanded. Toward the end of the eighteenth century, islands in the British West Indies, for example, began imposing limitations on personal wealth and employment opportunities of mixed-race persons and enacting laws to increase economic opportunities for whites (Livesay 2010, 85–95). Thus white supremacy was maintained on the islands by punishing the children for the mixed-race sexual boundary crossings of the fathers.

OTHER EXAMPLES

Governments around the world have regulated marriages for centuries. In France, for example, various laws prohibited marriages between whites and non-whites between 1723 and 1833. The 1935 Nuremberg laws forbade marriages between Aryans and non-Aryans in Nazi Germany. Apartheid-era laws in South Africa prevented whites and non-whites from marrying between 1949 and 1985. Even today, laws in Saudi Arabia prohibit Saudi women from marrying non-Arab and non-Muslim men. In keeping with anti-miscegenation laws' complicity with precepts of male dominance, only Saudi men over age 25 can apply for a government permit to marry a non-Arab woman.

Each of these legislated prohibitions has a specific relationship with the regulatory regime of its own national and historical context. At the same time, the laws are interrelated in their recognition that it is marriage – not sex – between groups that can undermine property rights and upset sanctioned racial or ethnic hierarchies. In particular, the laws all recognize that empowering women of any race to make unregulated reproductive decisions in the context of marriage and inheritance presents the greatest threat to male control of property, racial identities, and social stratification.

SEE ALSO: Gender Stereotypes; Same-Sex Marriage; Sex and Culture; Women as Cultural Markers/Bearers

REFERENCES

Gabriel, Arana. 2014. "The Bigots Finally Go Down: How Anti-Gay Haters Officially Lost the Marriage Fight." Accessed September 7, 2015, at http://www.salon.com/2014/10/08/the_bigots_have_finally_lost_how_anti_gay_haters_officially_got_beat_in_marriage_fight/

Kitch, Sally. 2009. *The Specter of Sex: Gendered Foundations of Racial Formation in the United States*. Albany: SUNY Press.

Kopelson, Heather Miyano. 2013. "Sinning Property and the Legal Transformation of Abominable Sex in Early Bermuda." *The William and Mary Quarterly*, 70(3): 459–496.

Leslie, Christopher R. 2014. "Embracing *Loving*: Trait-Specific Marriage Laws and Heightened Scrutiny." *Cornell Law Review*, 99(5): 1077–1130.

Livesay, Daniel. 2010. "Children of Uncertain Fortune: Mixed-Race Migration from the West Indies to Britain, 1750–1820." Dissertation, University of Michigan.

Murphy, Kevin, and Jennifer Spear, eds. 2011. *Historicizing Gender and Sexuality*. Hoboken: Wiley-Blackwell.

Newman, Brooke. 2010. "Gender, Sexuality and the Formation of Racial Identities in the Eighteenth-Century Anglo-Caribbean World." *Gender & History*, 22(3): 585–602.

Pascoe, Peggy. 2009. *What Comes Naturally: Miscegenation Law and the Making of Race in America*. New York: Oxford University Press.

Ray, Carina. 2013. "Interracial Sex and the Making of Empire." In *A Companion to Diaspora and Transnationalism*, edited by Ato Quayson and Girish Daswani, 190–211. Hoboken: Wiley-Blackwell.

Wilson, Kathleen. 2002. *The Island Race: Englishness, Empire, and Gender in the Eighteenth Century*. London: Routledge.

Anti-Poverty Activism

AMBER GAZSO
York University, UK

Anti-poverty activism includes any individual, group, or institutional participation in activities and behaviors with the end goal of achieving economic equality or preventing economic inequality. Advocacy and protest are common forms of anti-poverty activism, with advocacy and protest being verbal or physical acts in recommendation of greater income equality or objection to poverty. Creating awareness of the need for change or for preventing change, if not achieving actual change, through advocacy and protest are important elements of anti-poverty activism.

There is considerable debate about the definition of poverty in the United States and Canada which makes it difficult to universalize an understanding of poverty shared among all activists. However, a useful way to understand anti-poverty activism is activism in response to perceived poverty or an individual or group's sense that some people are experiencing economic insecurity relative to the majority of other persons in society. Perceived relative poverty can be understood in any of the following ways: incomes below government low income measures (e.g. low income cut-offs in Canada or the poverty threshold in the United States); incomes that do not afford some people the basic necessities of life including food, shelter, and clothing; or incomes that do not permit an individual or family to afford the same quality of food, shelter, and clothing relative to families who earn average incomes.

There are many reasons that motivate people to engage in anti-poverty activism: personal and familial experiences, individual morals and/or beliefs in social justice, altruism, religious faith, and so on. This motivation is differently informed by and linked to gender, race/ethnicity, class, citizenship, sexuality, ability, and religious affiliation. The broad yet simple idea that the perceived poverty of others is unfair, morally wrong, and socially unjust can be pinpointed as a major motivator behind advocacy and protest among many anti-poverty activists.

Perceptions of the unfairness of the economic harms created through the relationships between capitalism and neoliberalism underlie a great deal of anti-poverty activism. US and Canadian societies are capitalist political economies and predominantly operate as welfare states organized according to the ideology and economic doctrine of neoliberalism. Neoliberalism emphasizes the free market, a reduced role of government, individual responsibility and freedom, and self-sufficiency. Those who act in response to poverty believe that income inequality is not the fault of individuals alone, and should not be facilitated by neoliberal economic and social policies nor tolerated as a given in capitalist societies. Activism is additionally fueled by the contradictions between capitalism and social democracy in each nation. The United States and Canada are nations that are governed through a free voting electorate and recognition of individual civil, social, and political rights and freedoms. Many persons who engage in activism in response to poverty believe that all persons should have a reasonable standard of living, that being able to afford food, clothing, and shelter is a simple and basic human right. People's experiences of poverty in Canada and the United States are often perceived as morally and ethically wrong because they violate individual freedoms, economic and social rights protected by law, for example the US Bill of Rights and the Canadian Charter of Rights and Freedoms.

Anti-poverty activism is also pursued through a narrower focus on the unfairness or unjustness of poverty experienced by specific groups of people. For example, groups may protest against poverty experienced by refugees and how this is linked to their being disentitled from support from the welfare state. Others may demand awareness and change concerning the connections between race and poverty. Activism may be about how Aboriginal peoples' poverty is linked to historical and ongoing practices of colonialism or how poverty experienced by black citizens is connected to historical and ongoing systemic racism. For some, eradicating the low income experienced by women who have survived domestic violence is a reason for anti-poverty activism. Still others may advocate for the elimination of poverty experienced by those who face "double" or "multiple jeopardy" in their daily lives (e.g. non-white women who are disabled).

Strategies of anti-poverty activism occur at multiple interconnected levels in Canadian and US society: individual, interactional, institutional, and global. At the individual and interactional level, a person can advocate for or protest change in their own economic situation in interaction with others either explicitly or implicitly. Take the example of caseload interviews among welfare (or social assistance in Canada) recipients and case workers. An individual on welfare may explicitly argue for improvements in the amount and type of benefits they receive on the basis of several reasons. Another individual may "play the system" by implicitly protesting changes that would exacerbate their poverty. They may present themselves as appearing to follow rules and regulations when they are not (e.g. falsely reporting a legally mandated job search) to the extent that this obfuscation makes a difference in their personal economic situations (e.g. their continued receipt of welfare benefits). Individual activism is also performed by people who are not experiencing poverty. For example, persons employed by non-profit organizations who mediate on behalf of welfare recipients to find affordable housing or access other services to which the recipients are entitled are engaged in anti-poverty activism.

Individuals can also collaborate with others in activism against poverty. At the group level, anti-poverty activism involves several people coming together as a collective dedicated to reducing poverty or preventing policy changes that may exacerbate poverty. Not all members of anti-poverty groups are individually impoverished. Participants in activism can be poor themselves or supporters of social justice for the poor and can be incredibly diverse in terms of their gender and sexuality, education levels, employment status, incomes, and racial/cultural backgrounds. Group level activism against poverty can be small or large scale protest events that occur one time or are part of an ongoing campaign of protests. Group level activism can also be achieved through loose or formal organization. Some activists might share a common goal of eradicating poverty but loosely organize their protest or advocacy efforts through word of mouth or communication through social media. Others may occupy a public space that represents their efforts and are more formally organized and recognized. These mostly non-profit and non-governmental organizations have an Internet presence and vary municipally, regionally, and nationally across Canada (e.g. Ontario's Coalition Against Poverty; the Regina Welfare Rights Centre (now closed); Canada Without Poverty) and the United States (e.g. Action for Boston Community Development; Heartland Alliance; American Poverty.org). The existence of agencies and centers additionally make clear that anti-poverty activism is a social institution. Notably, so too do public protests demonstrate the group and institutional levels of anti-poverty activism.

Law suits against regulations in social assistance or welfare policies on the argument that they discriminate or infringe constitutional rights of persons additionally illustrate the institutionalization of anti-poverty activism. Notable Supreme Court cases include *Gosselin v. Quebec (Attorney General)* 4 S.C.R. 429, 2002 SCC 84 (Canada) and *Dandridge v. Williams* 397 U.S. 47 (United States) and in provincial or district level courts, *Falkiner v. Director, Income Maintenance Branch*, 2000 CanLII 15904 (Ontario, Canada) and *LeBron v. Florida Dept. of Children and Families* No. 11-15258 (Florida, United States). Anti-poverty activism in these cases involves individual interactions and relations around the unfairness of poverty, on the part of individuals and their legal representatives, coming into direct contact with the institution of law. In total, the sheer number of organizations devoted to eradicating poverty and the pairing of anti-poverty activism with court challenges demonstrate that anti-poverty activism is part of the larger social structure of US and Canadian societies.

At the global level, anti-poverty activism is engaged in when Americans and Canadians organize together with other transnational anti-poverty organizations such as Oxfam, the United Nations Development Programme, and Action Aid International to protest poverty in their own nation or in other developed or developing countries. As well, anti-poverty activism can be simultaneously local and global. A recent US case is the Occupy Wall Street Movement, a social movement that began in September 2011 in New York City and involved activism, mostly public protests, against the social and economic inequality created by the majority of wealth being concentrated in the hands of 1 percent of the population. By October, this activism had spread to several US, Canadian, European, and Asian cities.

Anti-poverty activism can be separate from or embedded in other activism agendas at multiple levels. Groups that protest changes to welfare such as the Welfare Warriors in the United States often do so because these changes are perceived to exacerbate the low income experienced by people. The Hunger Action Network of New York State advocates for ending hunger and the perceived root cause of hunger, poverty. In Canada, Idle No More is an indigenous movement protesting neocolonialism and poverty as one effect of these practices. A recent gathering of anti-poverty activists at City Hall in Hamilton, Ontario, protested cuts to social assistance, specifically the elimination of special discretionary benefits (e.g. coverage of dental care costs).

Anti-poverty activism may result in creating or preventing change. It is difficult to pinpoint a cause–effect relationship between efforts of anti-poverty activists and changes achieved or prevented without detailed rigorous study. However, from the perspective that social actors (e.g. politicians, other government officials, policy analysts) are exposed to public discourses about poverty, a direct connection between repeals of change or new policies and the advocacy and protest of anti-poverty activists is plausible. For example, in the province of British Columbia, Canada, new social assistance regulations introduced in 2002 included a time limit to social assistance receipt. Once benefit recipients had accessed two out of five years, they were to be expelled from the caseload or experience reduced benefits. Anti-poverty activists in British Columbia rallied around the unfairness of this new legislation. Two months before this deadline was to take effect for the first group of recipients who had maxed out their time on social assistance (2004) the government introduced new exemption criteria. These criteria, in effect, weakened the enforcement of time limits especially because case workers were given discretion in how they applied them. In both Canada and the United

States, there are numerous other examples of government anti-poverty agendas that materialized following government reviews of social assistance or welfare programs in which anti-poverty activists were invited to participate.

The anti-poverty activism of today is linked to the early histories of charity in Canada and the United States. During the industrializing period and/or the period of colonial settlement, charity or the helping of others, often financially, stemmed from similar beliefs in social justice. For example, early charitable efforts to feed people through community soup kitchens were in response to an awareness that food insecurity is because of impoverishment. The main difference between charitable responses to poverty, even those of today, and anti-poverty activism is that charitable organizations do not necessarily advocate for change or to prevent change. Rather, they primarily respond to the social conditions of poverty.

Feminists have long had a strong commitment to anti-poverty activism. Though feminisms differ in their focus, they have shared the major goal of achieving social equality between women and men and recognition of social reproduction. Feminist research has strongly established that women are more likely to be poorer than men, nonwhite women are more likely to be poorer than white women, and single mothers will more often raise children in low income than single fathers. The general consciousness raising efforts of feminist anti-poverty activists have made the poverty of women particularly resonate as a social problem demanding change.

As an area of academic scholarship, anti-poverty activism is studied for its origins, goals, and impacts but especially how activism interconnects with other institutions, social movements, and discourses. To name just a few examples: Naples and Desai (2002) explore how reducing poverty can be a central or supplementary goal of women who organize, sometimes transnationally, against the inequalities created through processes of globalization. Clayson (2010) uses the case of Texas to make a convincing case that anti-poverty activism in the United States emerged in tandem with the Civil Rights movement. Finally, Newman (2012) unravels how gendered activism is performed in a neoliberal social climate and the power relations embedded in these relationships.

SEE ALSO: Activist Mothering; Anti-Racist and Civil Rights Movements; Feminist Activism; Indigenous Knowledges and Gender; NGOs and Grassroots Organizing

REFERENCES

Clayson, William S. 2010. *Freedom is Not Enough: The War on Poverty and the Civil Rights Movement in Texas.* Austin: University of Texas.

Naples, Nancy, and Manisha Desai, eds. 2002. *Women's Activism and Globalization: Linking Local Struggles and Global Politics.* Kentucky: Routledge.

Newman, Janet. 2012. *Working the Spaces of Power: Activism, Neoliberalism and Gendered Labour.* London: Bloomsbury Publishing.

FURTHER READING

Idle No More. 2013. "Idle No More: Waskuhwee." Accessed July 14, 2015, at http://www.idlenomore.ca/.

Occupy Wall Street. 2013. "Occupy Wall Street: The Revolution Continues Worldwide." Accessed July 14, 2015, at http://occupywallst.org/.

Ontario Coalition Against Poverty. 2013. "Ontario Coalition Against Poverty." Accessed July 14, 2015, at http://www.ocap.ca/.

Statistics Canada. 2013. "Low Income Cut Offs." Accessed July 14, 2015, at http://www.statcan.gc.ca/pub/75f0002m/2009002/s2-eng.htm.

US Department of Health and Social Services. 2013. "2013 Poverty Guidelines." Accessed July 14, 2015, at http://aspe.hhs.gov/poverty/13poverty.cfm.

Anti-Racist and Civil Rights Movements

EMMA LESSER and MATTHEW W. HUGHEY
University of Connecticut, USA

The civil rights movement, considered to have lasted from the mid-1950s through the early 1970s, used a variety of political strategies to fight against racist injustices and infringements of rights faced by people of color (especially African Americans) in the United States. Each strategic approach was derived from a particular anti-racist ideology, and thus attracted specific constituencies of activists. The differences between each subgroup of the movement engendered unique social norms, challenges, and support systems based on gender, race, class, sexual orientation, and religion.

Throughout the early and middle parts of the twentieth century, scholarship on anti-racist and civil rights movements focused on the relationship between social structure and political behavior. That is, scholars examined connections between economics, class and status, community organization, formal organization, and bureaucracy, in order to explain the ideologies, aims, and motivations of some movements in relation to whether they were reformist or revolutionary, secular or religious, pragmatic or ideological, nationalist or communist, peaceful or violent.

In the 1970s, many social movement theorists altered tack and narrowed the scope of investigation to the process of mobilization – how social groups organize resources, recruit supporters, and navigate political environments in order to develop and flourish. By the 1990s, another strand of scholarship began to focus on the construction of meaning, the formation of shared identities, and the encouragement and magnification of emotions in civil and human rights activities. Accordingly, current scholarship has all but abandoned the early attention on variation in the social structure and political orientation of movements, but has retained an interest in both mainly as by-products of group mobilization and social movement framing (see Walder 2009).

Early social movement students of anti-racist and civil rights movements concentrated on the use of non-violence. Non-violence was one of the primary ideologies utilized within the movement. Non-violence, largely influenced by the Indian protestor Mahatma Karamchand Gandhi, used peaceful protests and lack of physical response to attacks in order to highlight the violence of racist perpetrators (particularly the police force) and the victimhood of black people in a white-supremacist society. The beginning of the Montgomery bus boycott in 1955 is an early example of non-violent protest. The boycott was kicked off with a symbolic event whereby Rosa Parks, a black woman, would not give up her seat in the front of a segregated bus. While Parks's actions were the culmination of long-term planning and organizing in the black community of Montgomery, Alabama, mainstream literature (as well as colloquial representations of history) has typically treated this as a stand-alone, random act of rebellion. Well-known non-violent organizations include the Southern Christian Leadership Conference (SCLC), whose first president was Dr. Martin Luther King, Jr., and the Student Non-Violent Coordinating Committee (SNCC) (until its later years).

Some of these non-violent organizations, particularly SNCC and the Congress of Racial Equality (CORE), included in their ideologies an interest in interracial organizing. CORE trained many white activist allies to work in the movement, and SNCC, along with other organizations, coordinated the Mississippi Freedom Summer (a summer-long project to register systematically disenfranchised black citizens to vote) in which approximately 90 percent of the volunteer activists were white.

Black nationalism is frequently perceived as the opposite of non-violence – although in later years their approaches and ideologies became more closely aligned. The majority of literature on the movement treat these approaches as polar opposites because nationalists often promoted militant protection of black communities and households, and believed that non-violence was fundamentally incapable of preventing violent attacks against black people. Later work has emphasized their common denominators and variation in terms of how members constructed a shared sense of belonging and purpose, embraced collective identities of black-as-beautiful, and relied upon varied emotional appeals: from the human suffering of poverty to the quest for equality in intimate relations (see Snow et al. 1986).

While there were several ways in which these organizations differed, the academic treatment of them has in many ways limited an understanding of the complexity of movement organizing. In contrast to the interracial organizing of some of the non-violent groups, nationalists sought out a separatist, self-determined, black-led movement. The Black Panther Party for Self-Defense (BPP) is perhaps the best known nationalist organization from the movement.

While more mainstream research provided a substantial understanding of the movement, certain voices were being left out of the narrative. In the 1970s and through the 1980s, a new wave of research drew attention to the experiences and impact of marginalized people within civil rights activism. Highlighting these activists meant shifting the academic vision of the movement away from large-scale, legislative victories to grassroots activism. Having a new group of scholars focus on these activists has offered a far more well-rounded picture of the inner workings of the movement, particularly as they pertain to sexual and gender identity politics within activist organizing.

Marginalized groups within black communities (namely heterosexual, lesbian, and bisexual women, and gay and bisexual men) fought not only against racism, but against sexism and/or homophobia, which came from across the color line and from within the organizations to which they belonged. In the earlier years of the movement, these activists worked within existing structures and ideologies, but later on, some developed their own intersectional politics that would account for multiple oppressions and place the needs and interests of marginalized activists at the center.

Within non-violent organizations, women were crucial players as organizers and leaders. Charles Payne (1990) – whose scholarship uncovering the impact of marginalized activists has been crucial to our understandings of the movement – argues that "men led, but women organized," since much of the fieldwork (work done out in communities to gain support and participants for the movement) was carried out by women. Because women predominated fieldwork positions, they were able to bring the interests of the community to the attention of formal leaders. These women were "bridge leaders" – those who connected the needs of the common people to leadership decisions, and who were the main recruiters for the movement (Robnett 1996, 1663–1664). Fieldwork often allowed for more decision-making by women on a day-to-day basis.

Though the majority of women in non-violent organizations in the movement were organizers and recruiters, many women also held crucial leadership roles. Jo Ann Robinson, the president of the Women's Political Council (WPC) – an organization for black women's civil rights – beginning in 1950, was one of the main leaders of the Montgomery bus boycott. Ella Baker was a vital leader and organizer in SCLC. Baker established the ideology of non-hierarchy for SCLC, which attempted to keep all members of the organization in equal power and made more room for women's opinions to be heard. Baker also began initiating women-centered programs within SCLC as early as the late 1950s (Payne 1990, 9). Baker was the interim director for SCLC in the absence of John Tilley. Other women had leadership roles within SCLC, such as Septima Clark, who was on the executive staff of the organization. Clark was also the primary founder of the Highlander Folk School, a literacy and voter-registration preparation school for the black community. Fannie Lou Hamer, an instrumental organizer for the Mississippi Freedom Summer, not only did formal organizing, but her dedication to the movement mobilized many others to become involved in the Freedom Summer. Hamer was also the vice-chair of the Mississippi Freedom Democratic Party (a political party that worked to include black voters in Mississippi's political discourse). Carole F. Hoover became the executive assistant at SCLC in 1964 when Wyatt T. Walker relocated, leaving Hoover partly in charge.

While women were heavily involved in the movement, their involvement did not come without challenges. Though Septima Clark was one of the most important leaders in SCLC, her abilities as a member of the executive staff were often called into question due to her gender. Though Carole F. Hoover was left partially in charge of SCLC, she was not afforded all of the pertinent information necessary to conduct her job sufficiently – information to which men in lower positions were privy (Robnett 1996, 1672). Though several women were able to attain leadership in non-violent organizations, most were relegated away from the formal leadership roles taken primarily by men (Robnett 1996, 1667). Though women could understand the struggle against sexist oppression within their organizations, many women policed one another about speaking out against sexism and challenging the gendered hierarchy of the movement because they feared it would detract from the goal of togetherness of black people (Robnett 1996, 1669).

Despite social regulations to keep frustrations of sexist oppression hushed, women-centered groups such as the National Council of Negro Women (NCNW) and the Women's Political Council (WPC) together worked to mobilize black women and to articulate their specific interests. For example, Pauli Murray was an activist in multiple civil rights organizations and a vocal advocate for black women's rights. At the March on Washington for Jobs and Freedom in 1963 (one of the largest rallies for civil rights, at which Dr. Martin Luther King, Jr. delivered his "I Have a Dream" speech), Murray spoke explicitly about the exclusion of women in the movement. And in 1963 Murray delivered her speech, "The Negro Woman in the Quest for Equality," at the National Council of Negro Women's Leadership Conference. Murray was also one of the only lesbian leaders to be open about her sexual orientation during the movement.

In non-violent organizations, gay identity was frequently seen as potentially divisive, and therefore destructive, to the movement's goals. Bayard Rustin, who did much of the early planning for SCLC and was the executive director for the March on Washington, was one of the best known openly gay leaders. In his own writing, Rustin says, "My being gay was not a problem for Dr. [Martin Luther] King [Jr.] but a problem for the movement" (Carbado 2003, 292). Though Rustin was openly gay, he was encouraged to limit discussion of his sexuality for the purpose of the movement's progression. Well-known black lesbians who were involved in the movement include Audre Lorde, Alice Walker, and Barbara Smith.

Economic class status also affected experiences of participants, organizers, and leaders in the movement. The poorer black women were often seen as apolitical, passive followers, whereas the more economically well-off women were perceived as more aware of political struggle and strategies (Barnett 1993, 165). However, many poor and lower-working-class women were important actors in organizing. The Montgomery bus boycott was initiated and sustained by both educated and working black women in the WPC. Georgia Gilmore was a cook and domestic worker who single-handedly organized the Club From Nowhere, a fundraising group organized to gain financial support for the Montgomery bus boycott (Barnett 1993, 168).

Increased academic attention to the gender politics within the movement has illuminated how non-violent organizations engendered particular forms of masculinity. Though, in general, men had more access to formal leadership positions within these organizations, some poor men with lower levels of education were given "bridge-work" roles, similar to women (Robnett 1996, 1688). Non-violent tactics were met with ambivalence by some of the men involved in these organizations. Some felt emasculated by not being allowed to protect the women of their community (Wendt 2007, 543). While non-violence was sometimes perceived as lack of masculinity, for some, non-violence was the epitome of self-control and courage, and thus boosted masculine identities (Wendt 2007, 548).

Interracial organizing, particularly the inclusion of white anti-racist allies, in the movement was a strategic move to show that black liberation was a human rights cause, not "just" a black cause. The Mississippi Freedom Summer is a prime example of the integration of white allies; almost 90 percent of the volunteers were white. Of these white volunteers, as many as two thirds were Ashkenazi Jews (meaning Jews of European descent). A common explanation for the overwhelming representation of Ashkenazi Jews is the firsthand experience of being cultural outsiders, even seen as an outside "race," particularly in a newly post-Holocaust period. Jewish women were involved in greater numbers than Jewish men; a few notable activists including Melanie Kaye/Kantrowitz and Rita Schwerner Bender (an activist in her own right, but also the widow of the CORE fieldworker Michael Schwerner, murdered in 1964 by the Ku Klux Klan (KKK) for his involvement in the movement). Jewish activists were often less visible within the movement because many of them easily blended in with other whites. Furthermore, some Jewish activists intentionally concealed their difference because they did not want to fit into the stereotypes held by other activists, and many feared announcing their Jewishness in a region where the KKK was active (Schultz 2001, 22). Despite the importance of white involvement to non-violent organizations during the 1960s, SNCC became far more nationalist and militant in its later years and asked white activists to leave the organization.

Like non-violent groups, nationalist organizations were rife with gender- and sexuality-based discrimination. There were many accounts of abuse and battery of female Panthers by the male leaders (Spencer 2008, 100). In the earlier years, the Black Panther Party (BPP) often stated in its newspaper, *The Black Panther*, that the role of women in their organization was merely to be supportive of the black men. Also in the earlier life of the organization, there were very few female members. Some of the heterosexual male Panthers expected women in the organization to provide them with sexual favors, a practice

Panther Eldridge Cleaver condoned and termed "pussy power" (Spencer 2008, 104).

In the BPP, women were vital organizers and leaders. Elaine Brown was a member of the BPP and leader of the organization from 1974 to 1977. During her time leading the organization, Brown promoted many women to leadership positions. She also took an explicitly anti-sexist stance, angering some of the male Panthers who believed feminism was too closely aligned with white ideals and interests. Tareka "Matilaba" Lewis chided the BPP for its lack of female membership and insisted on joining. Lewis frequently contributed to *The Black Panther*, including writing a poem about the necessity of men and women working as equals within the organization. In 1969, female Panther June Culberson also wrote about gender oppression in *The Black Panther*, publicly challenging gender hierarchies within the BPP. Kathleen Cleaver (née Neal) was a former SNCC activist recruited to the Panthers by Eldridge Cleaver (whom she later married) to organize on behalf of the BPP's co-founder Huey P. Newton, who was facing criminal charges for his militancy. Neal initiated fundraising programs, organized demonstrations protesting Newton's charges, and was the prime contact for the press.

Under the guidance of women, the BPP began openly discussing sexuality and gender, and created programs specifically designed for women and children. Many of these female-oriented programs within the BPP opened up new leadership roles for women. The Intercommunal Youth Institute (IYI) (later renamed the Oakland Community School), a program that provided children of ages two through 11 with free school tuition, health care, dorms, and meals, was directed by Brenda Bay and later by Erika Huggins. Within the BPP, female Panthers organized the Pantherettes, a subgroup of the organization with its own female leadership structure. As far as can be seen from Panther documents, the Pantherettes lasted no later than 1968, at which point women were far more integrated into the organization structure of the BPP. The United States FBI Counter Intelligence Program (COINTELPRO), a federally regulated program that used often illegal tactics to dismantle groups and leaders that threatened the stability of the sociopolitical climate of the United States, was devastating to the BPP. However, COINTELPRO's targeting of predominantly male Panthers opened many leadership roles to women, and thus the female Panthers were vital to the continued existence of the BPP (Spencer 2008, 103).

In its later years, the BPP began to shift its stance on gender equality and framed sexism as counter-revolutionary. In 1969, the Panthers asserted that men and women are equals. A year later, co-founder Huey P. Newton ordered that the BPP must recognize and respect both women's and gay liberations. He wanted the BPP to "unite with [women and gay men] in a revolutionary fashion," and believed that gay men may be the "most oppressed people in the society," and therefore potentially the vanguard of the revolutionary forces (Newton 2002/1970, 158). The BPP cited global instances of women fighting alongside men in other struggles, including those in Palestine and Zimbabwe (Lumsden 2009, 908). Because the BPP was a nationalist organization, the inclusion of women as militant protectors of their communities challenged standard gender roles. Images of black women holding both guns and children directly confronted expectations of femininity by combining traditional images of motherhood with militance (Lumsden 2009, 901). Angela Davis, a female icon and leader in the BPP, also contested gender norms, and was highly visible in doing so because of her stature in the BPP community and the media writ large.

Nationalism produced forms of expected black masculine performances that were dependent upon militant protection of black communities. In the earlier years of the BPP, masculinity was often discussed in contrast to non-violence. Black nationalist icon Malcolm X saw non-violence as passive and effeminate, and Newton and Bobby Seale (the other co-founder of BPP) rejected non-violence as degrading to black masculinity. Those forced to use defensive violence often had a sense of masculine pride over being able to protect their community – a stark contrast to racist stereotypes of black male powerlessness (Wendt 2007, 544). While militant masculinity bolstered the identities of many male Panthers, it often reinstated subordination of black women and gay and bisexual men (Wendt 2007, 544, 557).

Through the 1980s and 1990s, those who had been fighting in the movement continued to express their concern for the rights of marginalized black populations. Similarly, academics became committed to examining non-dominant narratives and identities that existed within, and extended beyond, the movement's classical period. The queer movement as well as womanism, a combination of nationalism and rights for women that takes into account the specific social locations and experiences of black women, focused on using intersectional approaches in activism and academia in the continued fight for freedom for black people.

SEE ALSO: Civil Rights Law and Gender in the United States; Human Rights, International Laws and Policies on; Identity Politics; Universal Human Rights

REFERENCES

Barnett, Bernice McNair. 1993. "Invisible Southern Black Women Leaders in the Civil Rights Movement: The Triple Constraints of Gender, Race, and Class." *Gender & Society*, 7(2): 162–182.

Carbado, Devon W., and Donald Weise, eds. 2003. *Time on Two Crosses: The Collected Writings of Bayard Rustin*. San Francisco: Cleis Press.

Lumsden, Linda. 2009. "Good Mothers with Guns: Framing Black Womanhood in the Black Panther Party." *Journalism and Mass Communication Quarterly*, 86(4): 900–922.

Newton, Huey P. 2002. *The Huey P. Newton Reader*, edited by David Hilliard and Donald Weise. New York: Seven Stories Press. First published 1970.

Payne, Charles. 1990. "Men Led, but Women Organized: Movement Participation of Women in the Mississippi Delta." In *Women in the Civil Rights Movement: Trailblazers and Torchbearers, 1941–1965*, edited by Vicki L. Crawford, Jacqueline Anne Rouse, and Barbara Woods, 1–11. Brooklyn: Carlson Publishing.

Robnett, Belinda. 1996. "African-American Women in the Civil Rights Movement, 1954–1965: Gender, Leadership, and Micromobilization." *American Journal of Sociology*, 101(6): 1661–1693.

Schultz, Debra L. 2001. *Going South: Jewish Women in the Civil Rights Movement*. New York: New York University Press.

Snow, David A., E. Burke Rochford, Jr., Steven K. Worden, and Robert D. Benford. 1986. "Frame Alignment Processes, Micromobilization, and Movement Participation." *American Sociological Review*, 51(4): 464–481.

Spencer, Robyn Ceanne. 2008. "Engendering the Black Freedom Struggle: Revolutionary Black Womanhood and the Black Panther Party in the Bay Area, California." *Journal of Women's History*, 20(1): 90–113.

Walder, Andrew G. 2009. "Political Ideology and Social Movements." *Annual Review of Sociology*, 35: 393–412.

Wendt, Simon. 2007. "'They Finally Found Out that We Really Are Men': Violence, Non-Violence and Black Manhood in the Civil Rights Era." *Gender & History*, 19(3): 543–564.

FURTHER READING

Collier-Thomas and V. P. Franklin, eds. 2001. *Sisters in the Struggle: African American Women in the Civil Rights-Black Power Movement*. New York: New York University Press.

Collins, Patricia Hill. 1990. *Black Feminist Thought: Knowledge, Consciousness, and the Politics of Empowerment*. New York: Hyman.

Davis, Angela Y. 1983. *Women, Race, and Class.* New York: Vintage Books.

Ling, Peter and Sharon Monteith, eds. 2004. *Gender and the Civil Rights Movement.* New Brunswick: Rutgers University Press.

McGuire, Danielle L. 2010. *At the Dark End of the Street: Black Women, Rape, and Resistance – a New History of the Civil Rights Movement from Rosa Parks to the Rise of Black Power.* New York: Vintage Books.

Umoja, Akinyele Omowale. 2013. *We Will Shoot Back: Armed Resistance in the Mississippi Freedom Movement.* New York: New York University Press.

Appearance Psychology

NIKKI HAYFIELD and IRMGARD TISCHNER
University of the West of England, UK

Appearance psychology is the exploration of how our physical appearance can have psychological consequences which shape our lives (Rumsey and Harcourt 2012). Most mainstream appearance psychology has been located within health psychology. Here, the focus has been how appearance can become a concern for those with congenital (e.g., birthmarks, cleft lip and/or palate, skin conditions) or acquired (e.g., burns, scars) visible differences or "disfigurements," alongside the development of interventions and provision of care (for an overview, see Rumsey and Harcourt 2012). More recently a body of research, focused predominantly on women, has used mainly quantitative measures to explore "body image." Some of this research has included comparisons of heterosexual and lesbian, gay, and (occasionally) bisexual body image and (dis)satisfaction (see Clarke, Hayfield, and Huxley 2012 for a summary and critical review of this research).

There is also a small body of research within (and beyond) social psychology that has explored how our appearance is a key part of our lived identities. A number of scholars have highlighted that appearance is often dismissed as frivolous and a topic of triviality. However, appearance psychology is an important area in relation to gender and sexuality because these identities are in part constructed and performed through dress and appearance. Some scholars have recognized that clothing and appearance are one way in which individuals construct and perform their personal and (sub)cultural identities. Some of these individual and group identities may "stand out" more so than others (for example, the appearances associated with "Goth"/"Emo" identities) and be more apparent than those often taken-for-granted and deeply culturally embedded identities such as gender. Notwithstanding the level of consciousness and overtness of this identity work, others are potentially reading our gendered and sexual identities (accurately or otherwise) through how we look. In this entry we draw on (mainly) psychological sources to provide an overview of appearance in relation to gender and sexual identities.

GENDER AND APPEARANCE

Appearance is a highly gendered issue. Women, and women's bodies, are "to be looked at" more so than men's bodies, and the cultural ideal of (heterosexual) "femininity" is that women should be slim, toned, and preferably devoid of any body hair (e.g., Bordo 1993). The ideal "masculine" body, on the other hand, is generally seen as tall, strong, and lean but muscular (with a "six-pack") (e.g., Gill 2008). Research suggests that men and women worry about different areas of their physical appearance. Certainly in Western industrialized societies, research indicates that men are mainly concerned with penis size, body weight, and height, while women predominantly focus on the appearance of their stomachs, hips, and thighs in addition to their body weight (Fawkner 2012). Worrying about one's appearance and body dissatisfaction, and the resulting psychological distress (e.g., lower self-esteem), is considered to be more prevalent in women than men (Fawkner 2012), and these form major areas of interest in mainstream appearance psychology (Rumsey and Harcourt 2012).

Therefore, it is not surprising that women are also the main focus in the extensive psychological literature on mainstream mass media and links to its effects on body image. The gendered differences in levels and foci of body dissatisfaction have been extensively reported on, and are well summarized by Fawkner (2012). However, these do not reflect the whole picture of gendered appearance issues and it is important to draw attention to the difference in the "quality" of gendered appearance pressures, rather than their extent, and to the findings of critical and feminist psychological studies. One major difference seems to be the extent to which men/women are defined through their bodies and appearance generally. Women's and men's bodies are construed in different ways, inscribed with different meanings, and produce different possibilities for subjectivities and "ways of being." This gendering of appearance is intertwined with constructions of sexed/gendered identities and can also be understood in the discursive context of Cartesian dualism, dominant in contemporary Western societies, and the culturally entrenched hierarchical binaries of mind/body, man/woman, culture/nature, rational/irrational (Malson 1998; Bordo 1993). Within this context "women" are discursively produced and regulated through the ways in which their bodies and physical appearance are socially constituted much more so than "men." Men seem to have a greater diversity of resources to draw on in their construction of their masculine identities – what Coles calls "mosaic masculinities" (Coles 2008; Tischner 2013) – rather than being fairly monolithically limited to their bodily features. In building such "mosaic masculinities," men can draw on non-physical elements of hegemonic masculinities such as competitiveness, or more specifically academic and professional/financial success, all of which are not considered feminine attributes.

In contemporary Western societies, one of the socially defining physical characteristics, for both women and men, seems to be body size. Murray (2005) calls it the "collective knowingness" about fat individuals, a socially produced and generally accepted "knowledge" about fat men and women which "allows" us to make (broadbrush and inherently incorrect) judgments about an individual's personality and social identity, based on their body size. Most of these attributes are not positive in nature. In addition to these judgments, the definitions of femininity and masculinity seem to be particularly influenced by body fat. While the masculine body, as stated above, is allowed or even required to be of a certain, generous size, this relates more to the idea of being taller and stronger than women, but it should be muscular and certainly not fat (Tischner 2013). Both physical body fat and openly emotionally worrying about one's appearance have the potential to feminize – or demasculinize – men. Interestingly, however, fat also seems to defeminize women in Western industrialized nations, where the doctrines of femininity demand a (perhaps curvy but) small, slim, and toned body. One of the few areas where the defeminizing effect of body fat seems to bear advantages for women is in the working environment of male-dominated domains. Here, fat women are more likely to be seen as "one of the lads" and thus perceived to be more capable in their jobs than thinner or slimmer women (Tischner 2013). This seemingly positive positioning presents itself as a double-edged sword, however, as women can only ever be positioned in the binary categories of "feminine" or "capable."

In summary, appearance, and body size in particular, are issues discussed in both mainstream and critical/feminist psychology, and both potentially risk constructing women as the sole victims of an appearance-focused society in ways that belie the complexities of the relationship between gender and appearance. Body and appearance dissatisfaction seem to be more prevalent in women than men, and women are defined more through their physical appearance than men. However, this relationship between appearance and psychological well-being on the one hand, and appearance and gender identity/subjectivity on the other hand, can appear too reductionist and simplistic if relayed in the short space available in this entry. The picture of the psychology of appearance in regard to gender is complex and dynamic, and women (as well as men) are not merely subjected to, or victims of, the influences of society. Individuals are implicated in the construction and reconstruction of appearance standards, and the various consequences of it, through their use of discourses of femininity/masculinity, as well as their day-to-day "performances" of being a woman/man; individuals can also contest, resist, and mock normative appearance conventions and pressures in ways that expand the possibilities of appearance and embodied identities, though such efforts often have significant social impediments and can be individually and collectively dangerous (Butler 1999).

SEXUALITY AND APPEARANCE

Gender and appearance are underpinned by normative expectations of masculine and feminine bodies. Body size is one example of how "traditional" notions of gender are disrupted through the processes of "demasculinization" and "defeminization," which often result in penalty for the individuals whose bodies enact these disruptions. Similarly, normative expectations regarding sexuality and appearance are also understood through a lens of masculinity and femininity, and scholars have highlighted the near impossibility of disentangling the frequently naturalized links between sexuality and gender.

Since, and possibly predating, the theorizing of early sexologists in Europe and the United States, the identities of gay men and lesbians within Western societies have been associated with notions of gender inversion (Clarke, Hayfield, and Huxley 2012). This relationship has been linked to what Butler (1999) has termed the "heterosexual matrix." The matrix calls attention to the male/female and hetero/homosexual binaries, understood as discursive constructions of mutually exclusive opposites. In the framework of the matrix, sex, gender, and sexuality are all understood to be interlinked. The dominant and stable model is that of the (feminine) heterosexual female woman and the (masculine) heterosexual male man. Homosexuality is positioned as directly opposite to this dominant heterosexual model and therefore homosexual women become associated with masculinity, and homosexual men with femininity. It is clear to see how such an understanding maps onto appearance, so that the masculine "butch" lesbian and the feminine "effeminate" and "camp" gay man are the opposite of the feminine heterosexual woman and the masculine heterosexual man (Butler 1999). However, these inversion theories and the heterosexual matrix that arises from them are unable to accommodate bisexuality.

In fitting with the heterosexual matrix and the persistent legacy of inversion theories of gender, the cultural image of "the lesbian" within Western cultures is often understood to be that of masculinity, embodied through clothing, short hairstyles, and comfortable or "lesbian shoes." The image of "the gay man" is one who takes meticulous care of his appearance in a way more commonly associated with femininity (including less notably visible characteristics such as an effeminate walk and a high voice). These "appearance norms" are often understood to go beyond simply an adornment of the body and instead are considered to be embodied, hence outer appearance is understood to be an authentic visible expression of an inner self (Riley and Cahill 2005; Clarke and Spence 2012). However, as noted, gender inversion theories of sexuality and appearance are overly simplistic, imbued with a history of pathology around gender and sexual nonconformity, and overlook the nuances, diversity, and frequent intentional politicization of lesbian and gay appearance. Recognized lesbian and gay appearance "types" include a multitude of alternative "looks" and subjectivities (e.g., gay hypermasculinities such as bears and leathermen, and hyperfemininities such as femme and lipstick lesbians), as well as subtle signifiers of same-sex attraction such as brands, the positioning of jewelry, and not only what is worn, but also how it is worn. Notably, bisexual people remain seemingly invisible, with no distinctive appearance norms associated with bisexual identities (Huxley and Hayfield 2012; Hayfield 2013; Hayfield et al. 2013).

To "dress the part" associated with one's sexuality can perform various functions, and there are many reasons why lesbians and gay men in Western societies have sometimes chosen to conform to the respective "appearance norms" associated with these identities. First, many lesbians and gay men have rejected the dominant norms of gender-conforming heterosexual appearance and presented what they consider to be their authentic sexuality to the wider world through their appearance (Clarke and Spence 2012; Huxley and Hayfield 2012). This has not only served as a form of self-expression but also enabled gay men and lesbians to "come out" to each other; thus it has enabled the creation and maintenance of collective communities. These communities have often been safe places away from the historically oppressive and hostile climates of sexist and homophobic heterosexual mainstream societies, and these sites have at times been critical in organizing political action against heterosexism, homophobia, injustice, and inequality (Hutson 2010; Huxley and Hayfield 2012).

In addition to functioning as a way to fit in and belong among lesbians and gay men, lesbian and gay appearance norms can also be recognizable to heterosexual people. A number of (mainly US) research studies have focused on assessing the accuracy of heterosexual and lesbian and gay perceptions of appearance. This has often been done through photographs and video clips and the findings have, perhaps unsurprisingly, indicated that lesbians and gay men are sometimes more accurate in their abilities in this area. In fitting with the lack of dress and appearance norms for bisexual people, most research of this type has overlooked bisexuality as a category, or has found that bisexuality is seemingly unrecognizable and mainly invisible (Clarke, Hayfield, and Huxley 2012; Hayfield 2013).

Qualitative research in the United Kingdom has identified that heterosexuals may dismiss the appearance norms of lesbians and gay men as being purely stereotypes. While they may do so as a discursive rhetoric in order to present themselves as liberal citizens engaged in equality, and what they view as the "lack of difference" between lesbians and gay men and heterosexuals, this does also suggest that they overlook not only difference, but also the functions of shared visual identity. Heterosexual people may also be less able to assess sexuality through appearance due to the nuances of dress and appearance discussed above (Clarke, Hayfield, and Huxley 2012; Hayfield 2013). However, it is also important to note that social models of gender and sexuality have become increasingly complex and, accordingly, recent research indicates that lesbian and gay appearance norms have been becoming less distinctive and more diverse. This has been attributed in part to what is perceived to be an increased social acceptance of non-heterosexual sexualities and to the mainstreaming of certain aspects of lesbian looks such as tattoos and piercings (Clarke and Spence 2012; Huxley, Clarke, and Halliwell 2013).

There are of course implications that arise from dressing in ways which make sexuality apparent to others. Due to an understanding that lesbians, for example, are violating gender norms through failing to conform to the rules of femininity, they tend to be assessed as (heterosexually) unattractive. Lesbians and gay men who are visible through their appearance are more likely to be open to prejudice and discrimination by hostile heterosexuals. In contrast, bisexual men and women, who are effectively excluded from the binary understandings that dominate notions of gender inversion theories, have no similar appearance norms to lesbians and gay men; together with those who do not elect to conform to the respective appearance norms, they may struggle to feel a part of lesbian, gay, and bisexual spaces. In summary, individual appearance is experienced and negotiated in social contexts where gender and sexual markers are loaded with social and political implications, and where appearance has enormous consequences for individual well-being and life opportunities.

SEE ALSO: Gender Belief System/Gender Ideology; Lesbian, Gay, Bisexual, and Transgender Psychologies; Queer Performance; Queer Theory

REFERENCES

Bordo, Susan. 1993. *Unbearable Weight: Feminism, Western Culture, and the Body*. Berkeley: University of California Press.

Butler, Judith. 1999. *Gender Trouble: Feminism and the Subversion of Identity*, 10th anniversary ed. London: Routledge.

Clarke, Victoria, Nikki Hayfield, and Caroline J. Huxley. 2012. "Lesbian, Gay, Bisexual and Trans Appearance and Embodiment: A Critical Review of the Psychological Literature." *Psychology of Sexualities Review*, 3(1): 47–66.

Clarke, Victoria, and Katherine Spence. 2012. "I Am Who I Am? Navigating Norms and the Importance of Authenticity in Lesbian and Bisexual Women's Accounts of Their Appearance Practices." *Psychology & Sexuality*, 4(1): 25–33.

Coles, Tony. 2008. "Finding Space in the Field of Masculinity: Lived Experiences of Men's Masculinities." *Journal of Sociology*, 44(3): 233–248.

Fawkner, Helen J. 2012. "Gender." In *The Oxford Handbook of the Psychology of Appearance*, edited by Nichola Rumsey and Diana Harcourt, 175–189. Oxford: Oxford University Press.

Gill, Rosalind. 2008. "Body Talk: Negotiating Body Image and Masculinity." In *Critical Bodies – Representations, Identities and Practices of Weight and Body Management*, edited by Sarah Riley, Maree Burns, Hannah Frith, Sally Wiggins, and Pirkko Markula, 101–116. Basingstoke: Palgrave Macmillan.

Hayfield, Nikki. 2013. "'Never Judge a Book by its Cover?': Students' Understandings of Lesbian, Gay, and Bisexual Appearance." *Psychology & Sexuality*, 4(1): 16–24.

Hayfield, Nikki, Victoria Clarke, Emma Halliwell, and Helen Malson. 2013. "Visible Lesbians and Invisible Bisexuals: Appearance and Visual Identities among Bisexual Women." *Women's Studies International Forum*, 40(1): 172–182.

Hutson, David J. 2010. "Standing OUT/Fitting IN: Identity, Appearance and Authenticity in Gay and Lesbian Communities." *Symbolic Interaction*, 33(2): 213–233.

Huxley, Caroline, Victoria Clarke, and Emma Halliwell. 2013. "Resisting and Conforming to the 'Lesbian Look': The Importance of Appearance Norms for Lesbian and Bisexual Women." *Journal of Community and Applied Social Psychology*, 24(3): 205–219.

Huxley, Caroline, and Nikki Hayfield. 2012. "Non-Heterosexual Sexualities: The Role of Sexual Identity in Appearance and Body Image." In *Oxford Handbook of the Psychology of Appearance*, edited by Nichola Rumsey and Diana Harcourt, 190–202. Oxford: Oxford University Press.

Malson, Helen. 1998. *The Thin Woman: Feminism, Post-Structuralism and the Social Psychology of Anorexia Nervosa*. London: Routledge.

Murray, Samantha. 2005. "(Un/Be)coming Out? Rethinking Fat Politics." *Social Semiotics*, 15(2): 154.

Riley, Sarah C. E., and Sharon Cahill. 2005. "Managing Meaning and Belonging: Young Women's Negotiation of Authenticity in Body Art." *Journal of Youth Studies*, 8(3): 261–279.

Rumsey, Nichola, and Diana Harcourt, eds. 2012. *Oxford Handbook of the Psychology of Appearance*. Oxford: Oxford University Press.

Tischner, Irmgard. 2013. *Fat Lives: A Feminist Psychological Exploration*. Abingdon: Routledge.

Arab Spring Movements

SAHAR KHAMIS
University of Maryland, USA

The term "Arab Spring" or "Arab Awakening" refers to the massive wave of political upheavals and citizen revolts which have been sweeping many parts of the Arab region since 2011 (Khamis and Vaughn 2011). This wave started in Tunisia, with the young man who set himself on fire to protest his poverty and harsh living conditions, as well as the humiliation and degradation he suffered. His story became symbolic of the plight of many others across the Arab region, who suffered from economic distress, as well as social marginalization and lack of dignity, freedom, and political participation, under long-term, repressive, dictatorial regimes. Therefore, the "flames" of the Tunisian revolution were said to set the whole region on fire, as this wave of rebellion and protest spread to Egypt, followed by Libya, and, subsequently, Syria, Yemen, and Bahrain. However, each of these countries witnessed different developments and, ultimately, had varying outcomes, based on a myriad of political, social, and economic factors.

The Arab Spring revolutions have been characterized as grassroots, across the board, bottom-up, horizontal, leaderless tides of political transformation and social reform. The largely loose structure of these movements was subsequently viewed as a double-edged sword. On the one hand, it increased the level of public participation, grassroots involvement, and civic engagement (El Nawawy and Khamis 2013). On the other hand, it left a power vacuum, because of the absence of centralized, structured leadership. This was blamed for some of the setbacks witnessed in some of the Arab Spring countries, such as Egypt, which relapsed into military dictatorship; Libya, which suffered from chaos and tribal strife; and Syria, which has an ongoing, violent war, resulting in an exceptionally severe humanitarian crisis.

Two demographic groups were especially visible in their roles and leadership during the Arab Spring movements: youth and women. The significance of youth stems from the fact that over 70 percent of the overall population in the Arab world today are under 30 years of age. Naturally, this is the age group that is most dynamic, passionate about change and reform, capable of organizing and mobilizing, and more technologically savvy. This last point is of special importance since the Arab Spring movements have also been characterized by the significant role of new media, especially social media, which have been effectively utilized by the young protesters and activists to enact political change. This phenomenon is commonly known as "cyberactivism" (Howard 2011), which refers to the use of online communication to advance a cause which is difficult to advance offline, such as paving the way for political transition, as witnessed in the Arab world since 2011.

The young activists relied on social media to achieve three main goals: mobilization, documentation, and education. Mobilization refers to the use of social media to help people organize, coordinate, and network, such as using Twitter to orchestrate minute-by-minute on the ground protests. Documentation refers to the use of social media to provide evidence of governmental corruption and violations of human rights, such as using cell phone cameras to capture incidents of police brutality and harassment of protestors, a phenomenon commonly known as "citizen journalism" (Bennett 2008). Education refers to increasing awareness about current social and political problems, in the hope of resolving them, as in the case of brainstorming and deliberating about key issues via political blogs (El Nawawy and Khamis 2013).

As for women, they had an equally visible role, as hundreds of thousands of Arab women throughout the region, including in some of the most traditional, conservative countries, like Yemen and Bahrain, took to the streets, alongside men, calling for an end to dictatorship and repression and demanding dignity and freedom (Khamis 2011; Radsch 2012). In doing so, they were not confining themselves to stereotypical gender roles, such as nurturing or supporting men in their struggle for freedom. Rather, they assumed non-stereotypical gender roles by being in the front lines of resistance, risking their own lives, and exposing themselves to the dangers of arrest or assault. The Arab spring unveiled many examples of brave Arab women, who risked not only their reputation, but also their physical safety for the sake of reform (Al-Malki et al. 2012). This culminated in the selection of Tawakkul Karman, the Yemeni journalist and human rights activist, as the first Arab woman to be awarded the Nobel Peace Prize in 2011, which was seen as a nod to the Arab Spring movements in general, and the role that women played in them in particular (Khamis 2011).

The Arab Spring movements granted Arab citizens, especially youth and women, unprecedented opportunities to increase their visibility, exercise their leadership, and execute their activism, mainly through the deployment of new forms of communication, such as social media, to spread their messages and support their causes.

SEE ALSO: Alternative Media; Empowerment; Feminism, Islamic; Women's and Feminist Activism in Northern Africa; Women's and Feminist Activism in the Middle East

REFERENCES

Al-Malki, Amal, David Kaufer, Suguru Ishizaki, and Kira Dreher. 2012. *Arab Women in Arab News: Old Stereotypes and New Media*. Doha: Bloomsbury Qatar Foundation.

Bennett, W. Lance. 2008. "Changing Citizenship in the Digital Age." In *Civic Life Online: Learning How Digital Media Can Engage Youth*, edited by W. L. Bennett, 1–24. Cambridge: MIT Press.

El Nawawy, Mohammed, and Sahar Khamis. 2013. *Egyptian Revolution 2.0: Political Blogging, Civic Engagement, and Citizen Journalism*. New York: Palgrave Macmillan.

Howard, Philip N. 2011. *The Digital Origins of Dictatorship and Democracy: Information Technology and Political Islam*. Oxford: Oxford University Press.

Khamis, Sahar. 2011. "The Arab 'Feminist' Spring?" *Feminist Studies*, 37(3): 692–695.

Khamis, Sahar, and Kathryn Vaughn. 2011. "Cyberactivism in the Egyptian Revolution: How Civic Engagement and Citizen Journalism Tilted the Balance." *Arab Media and Society*, 14. Accessed August 13, 2015, at http://www.arabmediasociety.com/?article=769.

Radsch, Courtney. 2012. "Unveiling the Revolutionaries: Cyberactivism and the Role of Women in the Arab Uprisings." James A. Baker III Institute for Public Policy of Rice University. Accessed August 13, 2015, at http://bakerinstitute.org/publications/ITP-pub-CyberactivismAndWomen-051712.pdf.

Archaeology and Genealogy

MARIA TAMBOUKOU
University of East London, UK

Archaeology and genealogy are two interrelated strands in Michel Foucault's work shaping its methodological and theoretical directions. As Foucault simply put it in one of his lectures at Berkeley in 1983, "genealogy is the aim of the analysis and archaeology is the material and methodological framework," further adding that, "I never stopped doing archaeology. I never stopped doing genealogy." But how exactly are archaeology and genealogy interwoven in Foucault's analytics?

In theorizing and discussing Foucault's work, Gilles Deleuze (1992) has pointed out that in *The Archaeology of Knowledge*, Foucault made the distinction between discursive and non-discursive formations but dealt exclusively with the former. *The Order of Things*, the book that made Foucault famous in 1966, is presented in its subtitle as "an archaeology of the human sciences." Foucault looked into the history of a range of empirical sciences in the Renaissance and the classical age, including biology, economics, and language, but he did not explicitly discuss his approach. It was in his *Archaeology of Knowledge*, published three years later, that Foucault made a meticulous exposition of his archaeological method, particularly looking into the discursive construction of systems of thought and knowledge, what he called epistemes. Drawing on his previous work in *Madness and Civilization* (1961), *The Birth of the Clinic* (1963), and *The Order of Things* (1966), what Foucault maintained is that there are specific rules, taxonomies, and classifications that define the grounds, disciplinary boundaries, and histories of the various epistemes under scrutiny; the task of the archaeological method is therefore to excavate accumulated layers of discursive formations in order to reveal discontinuities, contingencies, and ruptures in what seems to be "natural" or "necessary" in the history of sciences, ideas, and concepts. In this context the subject is also decentralized in the archaeological approach since many of these formations are unconscious and not necessarily derived from or driven by an overriding mind.

The weak link of the archaeological method, however, was the neglect of non-discursive formations and the role of power relations in mobilizing transitions between systems of thought, in short the famous power/knowledge couplet, which is at the heart of Foucault's genealogical turn. Genealogy took up the thread where archaeology left it loose in Foucault's analytics, namely, accounting for the contingencies and non-linear formations of discursive regimes in the history of ideas and systems of thought. Thus, against what are seen as traditional types of history, Foucault has proposed the Nietzschean theme of genealogy. This is what he calls the form of his reflection on the nature and development of modern power. A key Nietzschean insight for Foucault is that truth cannot be separated from the procedures of its production. The philosopher's task is therefore to criticize, diagnose, and demythologize "truth phenomena." Consequently, genealogy is concerned with the processes, procedures, and apparatuses whereby truth and knowledge are produced, in what Foucault calls the discursive regime of the modern era.

Instead of asking in which kinds of discourse we are entitled to believe, Foucault's genealogies pose the question of which kinds of practices, linked to which kinds of external conditions, determine the different knowledges in which we ourselves figure. In engaging with the Kantian idea of illuminating the present, Foucault introduces skepticism about universalist dogmas of truth, objectivity, and pure scientific reason, and interrogates the supposed interconnections between reason, knowledge, progress, freedom, and ethical action. Within this problematic, Foucault also attempts to see differently the role of the thinking subject, by primarily recognizing the historical dimension of all human reality. While Kant was preoccupied with the question of how a free moral subject can exist within the deterministic world of science, Foucault rejects the theme of a fixed human nature, which acts on abstract impartial moral principles, regardless of the network of the surrounding social practices and relations.

In elaborating new answers to Kantian questions, Foucault moves to an analysis of the different discursive and non-discursive ways in which the subject emerges in history. Genealogy conceives human reality as an effect of the interweaving of certain historical and cultural practices, which it sets out to trace and explore. What is significant in the Foucauldian approach is exactly this conceptualization of human reality as practices or technologies, which are to be analyzed and deconstructed from within. Instead of seeing history as a continuous development of an ideal schema, genealogy is oriented to discontinuities. Throughout the genealogical exploration there are frequent disruptions, uneven and haphazard processes of dispersion, that call into question the supposed linear evolution of history. In this context of reversal, our present is not theorized as the result of a meaningful development, but rather as an episode, a result of struggle and relations of force and domination. Genealogy is the history of such fights, their deep strategies, and the ways that interconnect them. While, however, genealogy focuses on the war of discourses and power relations, it does not stop there. By revealing discontinuities in the supposed continuous development of history, Foucault's genealogical project also implies a discontinuity in the present social formations. Genealogy is attempting to go further, by tracing possible ways of thinking differently instead of accepting and legitimating what are already the "truths" of our world. The aim is to provide a counter-memory that will help subjects recreate the historical and practical conditions of their present existence.

SEE ALSO: Queer Theory

REFERENCES

Deleuze, Gilles. 1992. *Foucault*, trans. Sean Hand. Minneapolis: University of Minnesota Press.

Foucault, Michel. 1965. *Madness and Civilization*, trans. R. Howard. New York: Pantheon.

Foucault, Michel. 1971. *The Order of Things: An Archaeology of the Human Sciences (unidentified collective translation)*. New York: Pantheon.

Foucault, Michel. 1973. *The Birth of the Clinic: An Archaeology of Medical Perception*, trans. A. Sheridan Smith. New York: Pantheon.

Foucault, Michel. 1976. *The Archaeology of Knowledge*, trans. A. Sheridan Smith. New York: Harper.

Foucault, Michel. 1983. "The Culture of the Self." Lecture at Berkeley. Michel Foucault, Audio Archive, Library, University of California, Berkeley. Accessed July 4, 2015, at http://www.lib.berkeley.edu/MRC/onlinemedia.html#foucault.

Archetype

MARGUERITE M. McCARTY and KEITH KLOSTERMANN
Medaille College, USA

This Greek-rooted word which means *the original pattern or model of which all things of the same type are representations or copies*, represents ideal or perfect examples of both the animate (i.e., humans compared to a wise owl, timid rabbit, joker, hero) and the inanimate (i.e., table, chair, lamp).

Although use of the word is not documented until 1545, 2000 years prior, Plato's "theory of forms" begins the formation of the concept "archetype." This legendary theory suggests that all objects have an idealized form such as one table is representative of all other tables that ever were and ever will be, or has a specific "tableness." The table that the baby's high chair is pulled up to, and the table that this same "baby" has at his or her wedding meal share the same innate qualities, characteristics, and forms. Humans experience a variety of innate emotions (i.e., fear, sadness, shame) and express a multitude of personality traits (i.e., humbleness, arrogance, loyalty). Although more complicated and nuanced, the human experience can be compared to Plato's theory in that all human emotion and the expression of personality traits have similarities regardless of whoever is feeling or expressing. This feeling and expression transcends gender, location, time, and cultural diversity. Fear felt by a fifteenth-century Indian man of royal status shares some of the same qualities of fear felt by a twenty-first-century French woman living in poverty.

Gender and sexuality archetypes have a ubiquitous, multicultural historical presence. A few examples include the Bible's Adam and Eve, Aristotle's "Metaphysics," Pythagorean Table of Opposites (male is aligned with straight, good, light and woman is aligned with crooked, bad, darkness), the Chinese Yin (female, dark) and Yang (male, light), and the Indian god "Shiva" who has both male and female attributes. In each of these examples, the female is associated with what each culture deems dark and mysterious, while the male represents light and morality. The male is associated with attributes that illicit higher prestige and value within each culture. Scholars argue that modern patriarchal gender stereotypes can be traced throughout the world's history due, in part, to these long-standing gender and sexuality archetypes.

Beginning in the twentieth century, the universality and commonality of the human experience was explained by the compilation of archetypes within the human psyche. Carl Jung (1875–1961) is most often associated with the concept which he links to his life-long work in the field of psychoanalysis. He used the term to describe his theory of the human psyche which suggests primal and universal emotional experiences shared by humankind in what he called a "collective unconsciousness." According to Jungian theory, archetypes are original imprints given to humans at birth which represent feelings, personality traits, virtues, and cultural, social, and religious patterns. Overarching these innate archetypes are the female "anima" which is eros or emotion, and the male "animus" which is logos or reason. Psychotherapists working from a feminist theoretical orientation help clients to create a more robust expression of what it means to be a man or a woman utilizing the socially constructed expectations of what it means to be male or female along with the feminine and masculine archetypes.

Together with the fascination of archetypes from the philosophy, gender and sexuality, and psychology disciplines, archetypes are often used in the creation of literary characters. The "sly fox" is present in many children's books while the classic good/evil combination of the Dr. Jekyll and Mr. Hyde personality split is common in books and movies. The hero, the mother, the villain, and the damsel in distress are all archetypal literary characters. Symbolism in stories also derives from archetypes such as the evil snake, poison apple, or magical sword. These reoccurring characters, themes, patterns, and symbols are considered universal. Literary critics believe that since archetypes originate before, during, and after the life cycle, these archetypes will evoke similar reactions in all readers and viewers. Feminist archetypal literary criticism draws from women's studies, psychology, history, the arts, and anthropology. From this lens, archetypes are understood as the psyche's way to respond to essential life experiences. Texts are analyzed to determine the impact of gender archetypes in relation to the author's culture and time period.

The current research about archetypes is found among the disciplines of psychology, philosophy, gender studies, anthropology, and literature. The human quest to understand archetypes within the context of humankind is continually written about and discussed among scholars.

SEE ALSO: Appearance Psychology; Fairy Tales; Gender Belief System/Gender Ideology; Gender, Definitions of; Gender Identity, Theories of; Gender Role Ideology; Language and Gender; Masculinity and Femininity, Theories of; Psychology of Gender: History and Development of the Field

FURTHER READING

"Archetype." Accessed January 30, 2014, at: http://www.merriam-webster.com/dictionary/archetype.

Enns, C. Z. 1994. "Archetypes and Gender: Goddesses, Warriors, and Psychological Health." *Journal of Counseling & Development*, 73: 127–133. DOI: 10.1002/j.1556-6676.1994.tb01724.x.

Jung, C. G., and R. F. C. Hull. 2012. "Four Archetypes." (From Vol. 9, Part 1 of the *Collected Works of C. G. Jung*). Princeton: Princeton University Press. Accessed January 30, 2014, at: http://connectny.eblib.com/patron/FullRecord.aspx?p=832709.

Lauter, E., and Rupprecht, C. 1985. *Feminist Archetypal Theory*. Knoxville: University of Tennessee Press.

Santas, Gerasimos. 2010. *Understanding Plato's Republic*. Malden, MA: Wiley-Blackwell.

Arranged Marriages (in South Asia)

ARSHIA U. ZAIDI
University of Ontario Institute of Technology, Canada

In all societies across the globe marriage is an undeniable institution that binds people legally and socially into a lifelong union. However, within this institution are cross-cultural variations in how marriage happens; some are based on love, and others are arranged. In recent times, there has been internationally growing concern about the cultural practice and custom of arranged marriages. Arranged marriages are common in parts of Asia, Africa, and the Middle East, with West and South Asians falling in the majority with regard to the practice of arranged marriages. The institution and practice of arranged marriages is heavily rooted in the patriarchal structure of the South Asian subcontinent and is most commonly associated with the South Asian population. With a rise in detraditionalization or modernization of the South Asian family's collectivist cultural norms, values, and practices, this way of marriage has ignited new dialogue between older and younger generations. It should also be noted that despite modernization, there are still immigrant South Asian families in the West who hold strong beliefs in favor of the practice (Talbani and Hasanali 2000; Zaidi and Shuraydi 2002). Arranged marriages persist, and are very much perceived as the sociocultural norm in South Asian families.

The tradition of mate selection in the form of arranged marriages, in which parents or families and/or family friends, not the two persons involved, select and negotiate the individual's life partner with their consent, is not new and dates back to the British aristocracy to maintain political and economic affairs. Here, social interaction between the two candidates is minimal. The South Asian shame-oriented culture focuses on the ideology of collectivism, which emphasizes how individual decisions may affect significant others in the larger familial context. Individuals belonging to these cultures develop a less rigid and/or autonomous view of self. The arranged marriage is not concerned with love, needs, and/or desires of the individuals involved; rather, it is based on familial and social compatibility.

It is important to note that the traditional custom of arranged marriages is not universal and comes with variations depending on the country/region, religious affiliation, ethnicity, education, and family one belongs to. For example, in some countries, families, and cultures there may be more flexibility; the bride and groom may be able to see, interact, meet, and/or date before the marriage, where in other cases they may not see or meet each other until after the marriage ceremony has taken place. According to Samad (2010), the notion of arranged marriages with time and location is evolving and adapting to the new milieu. In recent times, technology (i.e., via Internet matrimonial matchmaking websites) is being used to assist with the matchmaking process.

It is also important to point out that there is a gender power differential with regard to arranged marriages. South Asian women, compared with men, are the ones affected most by such marriages, especially those belonging to conservative households. While South Asian men have arranged marriages, they fall in the minority group compared with South Asian women (Zaidi and Shuraydi 2002). Lalonde and colleagues (2004, 507) assert that "the tendency of research to focus on female respondents is probably a reflection of the observation that greater socialization demands are placed on daughters compared to sons."

The significance of arranged marriages is that they bring utility and functionality to the South Asian family in more ways than one. For example, arranged marriages in the South Asian family play an important role in the preservation of family honor or *izzat* in these shame-oriented cultures. These arrangements function to minimize sexuality by governing individuals' autonomy through policing personal matters, especially for women (Mehrotra, Morck, Shim, and Wiwattanakantang 2011). The arranged marriage functions to fulfill specific family objectives that may not otherwise be attainable in a love-based marriage. A love-based marriage may simply become an unnecessary liability for the family and create more problems. In arranged marriage settings, social status, caste or biraderi, and education level of families and bride and groom are all factored in to the process of making a decision to marry.

As South Asians transcend borders and immigration to the West continues, the South Asian diaspora flourishes and arranged marriages are on the decline. In recent times there has been a lot of negotiation, debate, and discussion surrounding arranged marriages between South Asian parents and their children. Research indicates that there are various forms and continuums of arranged marriages, which shy away from the traditional definition, that are being adopted to accommodate South Asian youth in the mate selection process (Stopes-Roe and Cochrane 1990; Zaidi and Shuraydi 2002; Samad 2010).

There are many social explanations that are attributed to such a change; some scholars point to modernization (Adams 2010), others to ideational factors (Thornton 2005), and some to Westernization (Srinivas 2002). While the sociocultural context of an individual may influence modernization, ideational factors and Westernization with respect to perceptions of arranged marriages through electronic media (Internet, telecommunications, mobile devices, online social networking sites), according to Dhariwal and Connolly (2013), have become major influencing factors changing attitudes toward arranged marriages and encouraging romantic partnerships.

The rigid customary definition of arranged marriages continues to be in a state of flux to accommodate the interests of tradition, South Asian youth, and parents. Today, in heritage and host societies there is more flexibility, conversation, and negotiation amongst the generations when talk about marriage occurs in the household (Zaidi and Shuraydi 2002). Regulation of arranged marriages, where tradition meets modernity, needs to be assumed to facilitate the process and avoid further conflicts so that everyone involved in the marriage process lives happily ever after.

SEE ALSO: Courtly Love; Dowry and Bride-Price; Immigration and Gender; Immigration, Colonialism, and Globalization

REFERENCES

Adams, Bert N. 2010. "Themes and Threads of Family Theories: A Brief History." *Journal of Comparative Family Studies*, 41(4): 499–505.

Dhariwal, Amrit, and Jennifer Connolly. 2013. "Romantic Experiences of Homeland and Diaspora South Asian Youth: Westernizing Processes of Media and Friends." *Journal of Research on Adolescence*, 23(1): 45–56.

Lalonde, Richard N., Michaela Hynie, Manjit Pannu, and Sandeep Tatla. 2004. "The Role of Culture in Interpersonal Relationships: Do Second Generation South Asian Canadians Want a Traditional Partner?" *Journal of Cross-Cultural Psychology*, 35(5): 503–524.

Mehrotra, Vikas, Morck, Randall, Shim, Jungwook, and Wiwattanakantang, Yupana. 2011. "Adoptive Expectations: Rising Sons in Japanese Family Firms." February 28. 10.2139/ssrn.1777548.

Samad, Yunas. 2010. "Forced Marriage Among Men: An Unrecognized Problem." *Critical Social Policy*, 30(2): 189–207.

Srinivas, M. N. 2002. "Changing Institutions and Values in Modern India." In *Collected Essays*, 443–454. Oxford: Oxford University Press. First published 1962.

Stopes-Roe, Mary, and Raymond Cochrane. 1990. *Citizens of this Country: The Asian-British*. Philadelphia: Multilingual Matters.

Talbani, Aziz, and Parveen Hasanali. 2000. "Adolescent Females between Tradition and Modernity: Gender Role Socialization in South Asian Immigrant Culture." *Journal of Adolescence*, 23(5): 615–627.

Thornton, Arland. 2005. *Reading History Sideways: The Fallacy and Enduring Impact of the Developmental Paradigm on Family Life*. Chicago: University of Chicago Press.

Zaidi, Arshia U., and Muhammad Shuraydi. 2002. "Perceptions of Arranged Marriages by Young Pakistani Muslim Women Living in a Western Society." *Journal of Comparative Family Studies*, 33(4): 495–514.

Asexual Activism

JOSEPH DE LAPPE
Open University, UK

Asexual activism is linked to the recent emergence of online asexual communities, and to the expanding role both within and without those communities in promoting asexual identities and orientation. Owing to asexual activism, there has been an increase in public awareness of asexual identities and orientations. It is also linked to challenges to the sexual imperative, which is the often tacitly taken for granted assumption, and related beliefs, that it is impossible to lead a healthy life without being sexually active.

Asexual activism is one of a group of emerging, contemporary sexual and gender social movements that have been facilitated by the Internet. Prior sexual and gender social movements, such as the gay and lesbian movements in the United States and United Kingdom, were often facilitated by the physical migration of homosexual men and lesbians to urban and cosmopolitan areas where gay ghettos enabled critical masses to form.

This has been particularly marked in the emergence and expansion of digital online communities such as AVEN (The Asexual Visibility and Education Network). These communities have expanded in less than two decades from memberships of hundreds to estimates of 100,000 for the current English-speaking online communities. The last decade in particular has seen a proliferation of asexual websites, forums, and blogs across the Internet. This lends a particular character to asexual activism. It means that asexual activism, while a sexual and gender social movement, is also a digital social movement in its character and concerns.

Like most social movements, asexual activism has three strands: a contentious strand (public acts of engagement, protest and/or unity to promote asexual aims); a lifestyle strand (events which seek to promote asexuality either within or without the asexual community); and an identity strand (the dissemination of information through various means about asexual identities and orientation). It is important to recognize that the strands are not distinct in practice. It can be a matter of perspective as to whether a particular action is more concerned with contending an issue or promoting a particular lifestyle. However, separating the strands remains useful as it facilitates distinguishing particular trends in asexual activism.

Within the contentious sphere, asexual activism has been concerned with challenging the sexual imperative, with challenging the perception (particularly biomedical) of asexual orientation as a pathologized condition, and with establishing a relationship for asexuality (A-Pride) within the wider Pride/LGBT*Q+ umbrella.

The challenge to the sexual imperative is a core component of asexual activism. The importance of challenging the idea that asexual people cannot be fully healthy, or fully human, because they do not engage in sexual activity runs across all three strands of asexual activism. In order to challenge the perception of asexual orientation as a pathologized condition, asexual activists have sought to promote better research, often conducting research themselves. They also do this by promoting such research online, organizing events such as the Asexuality Conference 2014 in Toronto, or, by seeking to take an active, consulting role so that the concerns of the asexual community are included. A notable example of this was the active, consulting role that AVEN took in changes from the DSM-4 to the DSM-5 concerning hypoactive sexual desire disorder (a much disputed mental disorder based on low or non-existent sexual desire).

Over the last decade, asexual activists have been increasingly visible at local, national, and international Pride events, particularly in North America and Europe. There is a broad section of asexual activism, and related asexual communities, who see themselves as connected to the LGBT*Q+ umbrella, and as learning from the experiences of older sexual and gender social movements. They view A-Pride as part of the larger Pride social movement. However, this remains a contentious issue within asexual activism because not all asexuals define themselves as LGBT*Q+. Given that many asexuals still define as heterosexual (in terms of gender, romantic, sensual, aesthetic, and/or some sexual attraction), there are also some within the wider Pride movement who have misgivings as to the inclusion of asexual activists.

Within the lifestyle sphere, asexual activists have organized events at local, national, and international levels that enable members of the asexual community to come together.

Often this has been done with the intention of promoting an asexual lifestyle as positive and healthy, but there is often an implicit criticism of what many asexuals feel is the overt hyper-sexualization of contemporary life. Some asexual activists feel that the hyper-sexualization of contemporary life not only encourages but expects individuals to engage in sexual behavior. Such beliefs are closely aligned to challenges to the sexual imperative. Both aspects of the lifestyle strand – the promotion of an asexual lifestyle and critique of hyper-sexualization – are prevalent on the Internet, particularly with individual activists with a presence on sites such as YouTube and Tumblr.

Within the identity sphere, asexual activists have provided examples of the broadening ways by which asexual orientations can be combined with gendered identity and gender, romantic, sensual, aesthetic, and/or some sexual attraction. These are usually in the form of personal biographies that serve as "case studies" with which others who might be questioning their own asexual orientation may compare their own histories. They can then judge which particular combination of their own asexual, a-motive, and a-gendered identities is most similar. Again, this may happen at local, national, or international events, but it is particularly prevalent on the Internet, as befits a digital social movement. This form of identity activism has had two main impacts. First, it has enabled far more people to consider their own potential asexual identities, especially those who might for one reason or another have been or felt isolated from such information. Second, for some asexual activists, the proliferation of asexual, a-motive, and a-gendered identities radically challenges the sexual imperative by challenging the preeminence of sexual orientation.

SEE ALSO: Asexuality; Romantic Friendship

FURTHER READING

Bogaert, Anthony F. 2012. *Understanding Asexuality*. Lanham: Rowman & Littlefield.

Carrigan, Mark. 2011. "There's More to Life Than Sex? Difference and Commonality Within the Asexual Community." *Sexualities*, 14(4): 462–478. DOI: 10.1177/1363460711406462.

Asexuality

KARLI JUNE CERANKOWSKI
Stanford University, USA

Asexuality is most simply defined as a sexual orientation that identifies people who do not experience sexual attraction. This definition was developed by the Asexual Visibility and Education Network (AVEN), an online community established in 2001, hosted at asexuality.org. It is only since 2004 that asexuality has really gained the attention of the public. Much of the work of scholars and activists at that time sought to establish asexuality as a legitimate and healthy orientation. Still to this day, many doubt its existence, dismissing it as a medical condition in need of treatment or as a failure to reach sexual maturation. For example, asexuality has often been lumped in with Hypoactive Sexual Desire Disorder (HSDD) or other disorders of low desire. Asexuality is also commonly dismissed as closeted homosexuality or as a symptomatic response to past sexual trauma. Scholars and activists have since worked to refute these ideas and to understand how asexuality can bring about more complex understandings of intimacy, desire, and human sexuality. Although skepticism remains, the increasing prevalence of the asexual community is beginning to shift cultural attitudes toward asexuality.

The worldwide growth and visibility of the asexual community is a twenty-first-century phenomenon made possible by

Internet social networking. AVEN provides resources for self-identified asexuals, individuals who are questioning their asexuality, and friends and family members who are interested in learning more. AVEN also hosts a community forum, where members participate in online discussion threads on a variety of topics. The AVEN website was created in 2001 by David Jay, who was a college student at the time and remains one of the main public figures advocating on behalf of understanding and acceptance of asexuals. AVEN is predated only by the Yahoo! group, Haven for the Human Amoeba, created in October 2000. While the group is still active, AVEN boasts the largest online community and set of resources for asexuals and their allies. Since 2001, the AVEN community has grown – and continues to grow – exponentially; the forums now register more than 62,000 users.

In addition to the AVEN website, many other online venues host the asexual community. For example, one can find digitized zines, blogs, Tumblr sites, journals, podcasts, and video blogs all over the web. The proliferation of asexual discussion online has broadened the scope of asexuality, introducing more complex definitions that account for the spectrum of asexual expression in relation to topics like masturbation, libido, desire, attraction, disability, autism spectrum, race, intimacy, and LGBTQ community. For example, asexuality can be more complexly defined along a spectrum that includes categories like "demisexual," "gray-A," and "semisexual." In general, these terms may refer to people who experience sexual attraction infrequently, who prefer developing intimate emotional connections before engaging in sex, who experience a low sex drive, or who may experience little to no sexual attraction but engage in sexual activity under certain circumstances.

Understandings of asexuality have also been complicated along lines of diversity. People with disabilities, for example, have grappled with a different set of challenges, as disabled people already face a stigma of desexualization. Scholar Eunjung Kim (2014) has analyzed how disability and asexual activist communities engage in a process of "mutual negation," in which disabled people advocate for recognition as sexual beings while asexual people advocate for the "normalcy" of asexuality, emphasizing that it is not a disability or a disorder. In turn, each of these groups exclude the other from their activism, but many bloggers and activists have intervened to argue for the inclusion of disabled asexuals in both communities. Similarly, activists and community members have also engaged with the connection between asexuality and autism or Asperger's syndrome, seeking inclusion for a wide range of asexual expression.

The discourse around asexuality and ability also connects to medical concerns about asexuality. Sometimes people try to discredit asexuality's existence by characterizing it as a symptom of a disorder like a hormonal imbalance or as a mental health issue resulting from trauma. While AVEN suggests that anyone who experiences asexuality as a "problem" should seek out the advice of a doctor or therapist, it also discourages an understanding of asexuality as a disorder and advocates for a healthy identification with asexuality that is not to be pathologized or medicalized. One challenge Kim (2010) points out with this model is that it can be hard to assess the cause of distress in an asexual person. Whether one experiences asexuality as a "problem" may be due to any variety of factors, internal or external, medical or non-medical.

In addition to these various activist outlets, the mainstream movement for asexuality has been recognized in the media through television appearances on shows like *Montel*

Williams, *The View*, and *20/20* as well as through Internet and print media such as *The Huffington Post*, *The New York Times*, and *The Atlantic*. While asexuality has become increasingly notable in the United States, it has also received attention from media around the world. For example, stories on asexuality have appeared in the *New Zealand Herald*, Canadian editions of the *Epoch Times*, including the French language *Époque Times*, and on the Swiss television station *TeleZüri*. These media appearances have largely increased the visibility and understanding of asexuality in the broader population, but they have not gone without criticism. In particular, some activists and scholars have criticized them for making a spectacle of asexuality (Cerankowski 2014) or for representing asexuality as a largely "white" movement (Owen 2014). The critique leveled at a lack of racial diversity in representations of the asexual community has also been raised through blogs and Tumblr sites for discussion for people of color who experience race-based discrimination that is used to discredit their asexuality. For example, cultural stereotypes about the hypersexualization of black men and women have been employed to dismiss black asexuals when they come out to their peer groups. Further, the characteristically white and otherwise normalized asexuals who appear in media have been described by various community members as "unassailable asexuals," or people who are no different than the mainstream norm except for being asexual. Their perceived "unassailability" allows them to leverage their privileges of race, ability, and beauty to make asexuality more digestible for a general audience.

With the growth of media visibility, scholars have likewise become more interested in the topic. Some of the first essays on asexuality were published by social psychologist Anthony Bogaert (2004), who analyzed data to produce the oft-cited statistic that at least 1 percent of the population may be asexual. Bogaert (2006) also advocated for asexuality as a valid sexual orientation, calling it a "fourth orientation" akin to heterosexuality, homosexuality, and bisexuality. Following Bogaert's work, other psychologists, sociologists, and clinical scientists produced studies attempting to understand asexuality as a sexual classification as well as a social category. In 2010, Cerankowski and Milks published an article suggesting that this scholarship offered a good foundation for making sense of asexuality, but that the study of asexuality needed to be expanded to include more perspectives through the lens of feminist and queer theories of sexuality. Following this call, several scholars in the social sciences, biological sciences, and humanities began to study asexuality from perspectives that incorporate feminist and queer analysis as well as critical race and disability studies. This work has been published in several academic journals and in two edited volumes: *Asexualities: Feminist and Queer Perspectives* (Cerankowski and Milks 2014) and *Asexuality and Sexual Normativity: An Anthology* (Carrigan, Gupta, and Morrison 2014). Diverse perspectives on asexuality are also reaching a popular audience through the documentary film *(A)sexual* (2011) and with the publication of the books *Understanding Asexuality* (2012) by Anthony Bogaert and *The Invisible Orientation: An Introduction to Asexuality* (2014), written by prominent asexual activist and video blogger Julie Decker.

The trajectory of the scholarly developments on asexuality as well as the shift in media representation and asexual activism mirror what David Jay has called the "three phases" of the asexual movement. The first phase involved simply establishing the community through the creation of the website and encouraging more discussion of asexuality. The second phase moved asexuality into the media spotlight in order to increase its visibility. In an interview with *The Atlantic*, Jay suggests that we have now moved into the third phase, which he describes as "more mature" as it moves beyond mere visibility and aims to challenge beliefs about how we define a "normal" sex life. Such is the ongoing project of much of the scholarship and cultural objects being produced on asexuality today.

SEE ALSO: Celibacy; Critical Race Theory; Desexualization; Sexual Identity and Orientation; Sexual Instinct and Sexual Desire

REFERENCES

(A)sexual. 2011. [Film] Directed by Angela Tucker. New York: Arts Engine.
Bogaert, Anthony. 2004. "Asexuality: Prevalence and Associated Factors in a National Probability Sample." *The Journal of Sex Research*, 41: 279–287.
Bogaert, Anthony. 2006. "Toward a Conceptual Understanding of Asexuality." *Review of General Psychology*, 10: 241–250. DOI: 10.1037/1089–2680.10.3.241.
Bogaert, Anthony. 2012. *Understanding Asexuality*. New York: Rowman & Littlefield.
Carrigan, Mark, Kristina Gupta, and Todd G. Morrison, eds. 2014. *Asexuality and Sexual Normativity: An Anthology*. New York: Routledge.
Cerankowski, Karli June. 2014. "Spectacular Asexuals: Media Visibility and Cultural Fetish." In *Asexualities: Feminist and Queer Perspectives*, edited by Karli June Cerankowski and Megan Milks, 139–161. New York: Routledge.
Cerankowski, Karli June, and Megan Milks. 2010. "New Orientations: Asexuality and Its Implications for Theory and Practice." *Feminist Studies*, 36: 650–664.
Cerankowski, Karli June, and Megan Milks, eds. 2014. *Asexualities: Feminist and Queer Perspectives*. New York: Routledge.
Decker, Julie. 2014. *The Invisible Orientation: An Introduction to Asexuality*. New York: Carrel Books.
Kim, Eunjung. 2010. "How Much Sex is Healthy? The Pleasures of Asexuality." In *Against Health: How Health Became the New Morality*, edited by Anna Kirkland and Jonathan Metzl, 157–169. New York: New York University Press.
Kim, Eunjung. 2014. "Asexualities and Disabilities in Constructing Sexual Normalcy." In *Asexualities: Feminist and Queer Perspectives*, edited by Karli June Cerankowski and Megan Milks, 249–282. New York: Routledge.
Owen, Ianna Hawkins. 2014. "On the Racialization of Asexuality." In *Asexualities: Feminist and Queer Perspectives*, edited by Karli June Cerankowski and Megan Milks, 119–135. New York: Routledge.

Assisted Reproduction

SHIRLEY SHALEV
Harvard Medical School, USA

Human reproduction has gone through fundamental shifts over the past four decades as an increasing number of prospective parents have been using diverse methods of assisted reproduction with the hope of overcoming various fertility challenges. The growing consumption of assisted reproduction has considerably transformed the conceptualization of kinship and parentage, and has led to profound ethical and social implications for women's health, reproductive rights, and sexuality. According to the Centers for Disease Control and Prevention (CDC), assisted reproductive technology (ART) may generally include a variety of medical procedures that allow for the removal of eggs from the ovaries, fertilization with sperm, and transfer of the resulting embryos to the uterus (CDC 2011). The first baby to be conceived through in vitro fertilization (IVF) was Louise Brown in 1978, and it is estimated that since then over 5 million babies have been born through ART worldwide (Kashir et al. 2012).

Scientific developments in assisted reproduction have vastly expanded the range of reproductive options available to individuals and couples who are facing a variety of medical, social, or personal difficulties to conceive their offspring. Infertility is known to affect about 12 percent of women of childbearing age in the United States (CDC 2011). According to the National Survey of Family Growth (NSFG), it was estimated that in 2002, 7.3 million American women of childbearing age (15–44 years) had experienced impaired fecundity (Chandra et al. 2005, Macaluso et al. 2010). However, in addition to the medical challenges of infertility, some prospective parents are seeking a variety of assisted reproduction practices due to sexual orientation, marital status, personal preferences, or other social circumstances. For example, single individuals, gay or lesbian couples are increasingly using sperm or egg donation (as well as surrogacy) in order to have a child in spite of lacking a partner, or having a same-sex partner.

These new forms of assisted reproduction that were made possible by ART also reflect the separation of sexual intercourse from reproduction (as pregnancy can be initiated without preceding intercourse) along with the fragmentation of the unity of reproduction (Ragoné 1997), as a number of individuals can be involved in the creation of a new life (e.g., genetic mother, genetic father, gestational carrier, social mother, social father) by providing gametes, pregnancy, or upbringing. Thus the conception of a baby may occur between individuals who are unrelated to one another, and in some cases even unknown to one another, as many sperm or egg donors prefer to preserve their anonymity (depending on the particular laws and regulations of each country). Hence, to some extent, it seems that the growing use of assisted reproduction has also shifted the context of human conception from sexual intercourse to the Petri dish at the laboratory, as human embryos are often created in the professional setting of the clinic. This process is also associated with greater medical intervention as assisted reproduction practices usually include a number of medical procedures, such as the fertilization of eggs with sperm, the transfer of embryos to the womb, and often the cryopreservation of the remaining embryos.

The medical practices that are typically associated with assisted reproduction are considered fairly expensive and thus might be less accessible for certain populations, depending on country and state legislation and healthcare coverage. These practices are also known to be emotionally stressful and physically challenging as they typically involve the administration of hormones and drugs (to stimulate the ovaries to produce multiple eggs), anesthesia, and surgical practices (e.g., egg retrieval) that carry a number of potential risks and health complications (such as cramping, infection, and bleeding). It could therefore be argued that women are the ones who are mainly subjected to the possible health risks and long-term effects that are typically associated with different assisted reproduction practices, since in most cases they undergo the vast majority of ART-related medical procedures (also in different cases of infertility in men). Moreover, the use of such reproductive procedures can potentially carry the risk of multiple pregnancies, and in some cases may be associated with gestational diabetes, cesarean section, premature birth, and possible harm to the infant. Indeed, infertility treatments are often associated with preterm deliveries, which occur in 95.9 percent of triplet pregnancies and 53.8 percent of twin deliveries (Ombelet et al. 2005), and are known for their overall contribution to multiple births as 30–50 percent of twin pregnancies and at least 75 percent of triplet pregnancies occurred after infertility treatments (Blondel and Kaminski 2002).

Therefore, there is a great need for further detection, monitoring, management, and policy development regarding the diagnosis and treatment of infertility and its implications, which are estimated to exceed an annual cost of US$5 billion (Macaluso et al.

2010). Moreover, the fertility industry seems to be rapidly expanding as sperm banks, egg donation programs, and fertility clinics are constantly offering reproductive services to prospective parents who are often seeking local fertility treatments within their own country (based on its particular fertility policies and regulations), or in some cases, extending their search for reproductive services beyond national borders with the hope of overriding different cultural, financial, or legal constraints that may apply to their situation in their home country (e.g., the option of surrogacy is banned in some countries for gay couples). The global commerce of various reproductive services has created a new marketplace in which potential egg donors, sperm donors, and surrogate mothers can offer their detailed profiles and provide specific information about their genetic traits, ethnic background, educational achievements, and aesthetic characteristics (e.g., height, eye color, hair type) that may greatly affect their price in the booming fertility market.

However, the commerce of human gametes seems to differ greatly between men and women, as egg donation carries far greater risks to the donor than sperm donation, and its cost tends to be much higher than that of sperm donation (in countries that allow commercial gamete donation). Moreover, the medical procedures involved in egg retrieval could potentially lead to hormonal changes, infection, and different levels of ovarian hyperstimulation syndrome (OHSS) that in some cases may require hospitalization and lead to additional health risks to the female donor (hence it is also often suggested that the number of repeated donations from a single egg donor be fairly limited). A recent study on medical complications among oocyte donors suggests that 30.3 percent had experienced some degree of OHSS, 11.6 percent required hospitalization, and 26.4 percent reported new menstrual cycle changes (Kramer, Schneider, and Schultz 2009). These potential harms to oocyte donors thus illuminate some of the ethical challenges that might be involved in this practice, and shed light on the deep concern over potential exploitation of underprivileged women (from both developed and developing countries) who turn to egg donation merely as a result of financial difficulties.

The growing demand for egg donation is also associated with the dramatic increase in advanced maternal age, as older women may experience more difficulties using their own oocytes and be in greater need of oocyte donation. Indeed, egg donation was used in about 12 percent of all ART cycles in 2009, and became fairly common among women over 40 years of age. Almost 92 percent of all ART cycles among women over 48 years of age involved egg donation (CDC 2011). The growing phenomenon of late maternity is also demonstrated by the substantial increase in maternal age at first pregnancy as one in five women in the United States had her first child after the age of 35 years (ASRM 2003). While women over 30 years of age accounted for 5 percent of total first pregnancies in 1975, their number had increased to 24 percent of total first pregnancies in 2006 (Macaluso et al. 2010). This growing phenomenon of advanced maternal age may also involve additional risks for both mother and child, as older women may potentially experience more complications during pregnancy that may also affect their baby and possibly lead in some cases to preterm birth, low birth weight, and fetal morbidity and mortality (Salihu et al. 2003). In addition to these concerns regarding the safety of pregnancy at advanced maternal age, it has also been suggested that older parenthood may potentially pose other ethical and psychological challenges for the well-being of older women and their children (Caplan and Patrizio 2010).

The reproductive possibilities created by assisted reproduction for older parenthood can be also associated with women's health, lifestyle, and career choices, as they could potentially carry far-reaching implications for their family planning and marriage plans. These implications may even become more profound as recent medical advances allow the possibility of cryopreservation of unfertilized eggs, which gives women the option to determine the identity of their preferred sperm provider (e.g., sperm donor or a life partner) at a later stage in their lives. Oocyte cryopreservation can therefore be appealing for diverse female cohorts whose fertility might potentially be at risk (e.g., female cancer patients, women with significant illness, certain women going into the military), and also for women who wish to delay childbearing for a variety of personal reasons (e.g., due to career considerations or lack of a male partner). This reproductive practice has broad social implications for women's ability to secure a genetic tie to their offspring despite postponing childbirth to a later stage in their lives. Also, this assisted reproductive option may potentially challenge the commonly perceived notion regarding the time period that typically marks women's ability to conceive (often referred to as a kind of "biological clock") as it opens up the possibility of preserving their ability to bear their own genetic child at a later chronological age.

Another demonstration of assisted reproduction may involve various forms of surrogacy as some prospective parents opt for surrogacy services due to diverse fertility challenges (e.g., the designated mother's inability to carry a pregnancy to term, or due to the lack of a female partner in cases of homosexual couples). While traditional surrogacy is formed around the notion that the surrogate is genetically related to the baby (providing both oocyte and uterus), there is no such genetic relation between the surrogate and the baby in cases of gestational surrogacy (in which the surrogate offers the uterus only). In those cases, the gestational mother is typically inseminated with an embryo created by IVF that is either genetically related to both designated parents (using both their gametes), to only one of them (designated father's sperm with donor egg or designated mother's egg with donor sperm), or to none of them. Although gestational surrogacy resolves some of the tough challenges of traditional surrogacy, it still remains a controversial reproductive practice that raises many ethical, legal, and social concerns as it touches on broader issues regarding women's autonomy, right for parenthood, reproductive freedom, social justice, and human rights.

While there are countries that allow both types of surrogacy, some permit the use of gestational surrogacy alone, and others ban the practice of surrogacy altogether. Different countries have thus regulated the practice of surrogacy in diverse ways, either by restricting it for altruistic reasons with the hope of eliminating the financial motivation underlying many surrogacy cases (and related concerns for potential exploitation of surrogates), by allowing commercial surrogacy for those who can afford it, or by drafting other regulations that specify the particular conditions in which it is permissible.

Hence assisted reproductive practices vary widely in the ways in which they are regulated in different countries around the world, depending on different legal and social frameworks. They further illuminate the power of public policy to shape various forms of assisted human reproduction, and also their overall consumption, cost, or level of commercialization. Lastly, these ever-evolving reproductive options also shed light on the changing landscape of contemporary women's lives as they navigate through ample new reproductive challenges, choices, and possibilities.

SEE ALSO: Kinship; Medicine and Medicalization; Reproductive Health; Sexualities

REFERENCES

ASRM. 2003. American Society for Reproductive Medicine. *Age and Fertility: a Guide for Patients*. Birmingham, AL: American Society for Reproductive Medicine.

Blondel, Béatrice, and Monique Kaminski. 2002. "Trends in the Occurrence, Determinations, and Consequences of Multiple Births." *Seminars in Perinatology*, 26(4): 239–249.

Caplan, L. Art, and Pasquale Patrizio. 2010. "Are You Ever Too Old to Have a Baby? The Ethical Challenges of Older Women Using Infertility Services." *Seminars in Reproductive Medicine*, 28(4): 281–286.

CDC. 2011. Centers for Disease Control and Prevention, American Society for Reproductive Medicine, Society for Assisted Reproductive Technology. *2009 Assisted Reproductive Technology Success Rates: National Summary and Fertility Clinic Reports*. Atlanta: US Department of Health and Human Services.

Chandra, Anjani, Gladys Martinez, William D. Mosher, Joyce C. Abma, and Jo Jones. 2005. "Fertility, Family Planning, and Reproductive Health of U.S. Women: Data from the 2002 National Survey of Family Growth." *Vital Health Statistics*, 23(25): 1–160.

Kashir, Junaid, Celine Jones, Tim Child, Suzannah A. Williams, and Kevin Coward. 2012. "Viability Assessment for Artificial Gametes: the Need for Biomarkers of Functional Competency." *Biology of Reproduction*, 87(5): 1–11.

Kramer, Wendy, Jennifer Schneider, and Natalie Schultz. 2009. "US Oocyte Donors: a Retrospective Study of Medical and Psychosocial Issues." *Human Reproduction*, 24(12): 3144–3149.

Macaluso, Maurizio, Tracie J. Wright-Schnapp, Anjani Chandra, Robert Johnson, Catherine L. Satterwhite, Amy Pulver, and Lori A. Pollack. 2010. "A Public Health Focus on Infertility Prevention, Detection, and Management." *Fertility and Sterility*, 93(1): 16.e1–10.

Ombelet, Willem, Petra De Sutter, Josiane Van der Elst, and Guy Martens. 2005. "Multiple Gestation and Infertility Treatment: Registration, Reflection and Reaction: the Belgian Project." *Human Reproduction*, 11(1): 3–14.

Ragoné, Helena. 1997. "Chasing the Blood Tie." In *Situated Lives*, edited by Louise Lamphere, Helena Ragoné, and Patricia Zavella, 110–127. New York: Routledge.

Salihu, M. Hamisu, M. Nicole Shumpert, Martha Slay, S. Russell Kirby, and R. Greg Alexander. 2003. "Childbearing Beyond Maternal Age 50 and Fetal Outcomes in the United States." *Obstetrics and Gynecology*, 102(5): 1006–1014.

FURTHER READING

American Society for Reproductive Medicine. 2011. *Assisted Reproductive Technologies: a Guide for Patients*. Accessed August 30, 2013, at http://www.asrm.org/uploadedFiles/ASRM_Content/Resources/Patient_Resources/Fact_Sheets_and_Info_Booklets/ART.pdf.

Sullivan, Elizabeth A., Fernando Zegers-Hochschild, Ragaa Mansour, O. Ishihara, J. de Mouzon, K. G. Nygren, and G. D. Adamson, 2013. "International Committee for Monitoring Assisted Reproductive Technologies (ICMART) World Report: Assisted Reproductive Technology 2004." *Human Reproduction*, 28(5): 1375–1390.

Asylum, Challenges Faced by Sexual Minorities

RACHEL LEWIS
George Mason University, USA

AMY SHUMAN
Ohio State University, USA

International interest in the subject of lesbian, gay, bisexual, transgender, and intersex (LGBTI) refugees and asylum seekers has grown exponentially during the past decade. Since the United Nations Refugee Agency published its official guidelines on claims relating to sexual orientation and gender identity in 2008, a number of countries have introduced new training manuals for the adjudication of LGBTI asylum cases. Although sexual orientation and gender identity have been grounds for political asylum since the mid- to late 1990s, not all courts accept sexuality or gender as meeting the qualifications of membership in a particular social group. Further, courts vary in what they are willing to admit as evidence of both sexual identity and sufficient fear of persecution.

Like all political asylum applicants, LGBTI refugees must prove both that they have a "well-founded fear of persecution" and that they are members of a particular social group. Article 1 of the 1951 Refugee Convention provides the following definition of a refugee:

> Any person who ... owing to well-founded fear of being persecuted for reasons of race, religion, nationality, membership of a particular social group or political opinion, is outside the country of *his* nationality and is unable or, owing to such fear, is unwilling to avail *him*self of the protection of that country; or who, not having a nationality and being outside the country of *his* former habitual residence as a result of such events, is unable or, owing to such fear, is unwilling to return to it. (Emphasis added)

The primary challenge to LGBTI asylum claims lies in the fact that the 1951 Refugee Convention was designed to protect individuals from racial, religious, or political persecution, and the category "particular social group" included neither women nor individuals persecuted for their sexual orientation or gender identity. Although sexual orientation and gender identity have been included in the category "membership of a particular social group" since the mid- to late 1990s, it is still the case that the closer one's application conforms to the traditional model of the male activist fleeing an oppressive political regime, the more likely one is able to obtain asylum (Bohmer and Shuman 2008).

In 1993, Attorney General Reno's consideration of the Toboso-Alfonso case established the precedent for determining that persecution of homosexuals should be considered as persecution of a particular social group (thus warranting consideration for political asylum). However, LGBTI applicants have faced obstacles proving their sexual orientation, demonstrating that they faced and will face persecution on account of their sexual orientation, and arguing against the idea that they should hide or change their sexual orientation to avoid persecution. Proving sexual orientation has presented obstacles for asylum applicants who do not conform to the immigration officials' expectations for homosexual appearance and behavior. Officials sometimes accepted an individual's claim to be gay but determine that lack of conformity to stereotypical gay appearance protected someone from being persecuted. These issues were considered in the precedent setting case of Geovanni Hernandez-Montiel, a Mexican, identified as attracted to men who began dressing and behaving as a woman at age 12. The Board of Immigration Appeals (BIA) denied asylum because, the official determined, dressing like a female and/or as a male prostitute was not an immutable characteristic (Landau 2004, 112). In reversing the BIA decision, the Ninth Circuit Court categorized the applicant as belonging to the group of "gay men with female sexual identities," a phrase that opened up the possibility of individual self-definition, rather than immutable characteristics, to justify an asylum application. The court noted that, "[S]exual identity goes beyond sexual conduct and manifests itself outwardly, often through dress and appearance" (Landau 2004, 115). Even when applicants' claims as sexual minorities are accepted, and even when they can prove that their countries of origin have laws against homosexuality, courts have not often accepted that sexual minorities have a "well-founded fear of being persecuted." For many years, courts in some countries (the United Kingdom, for example) argued that individuals could choose to remain discreet and thus avoid persecution. The issue of discretion was part of a larger category of immutability, the idea that political asylum was offered for conditions that were considered unchangeable or that a person should not be obligated to change (for example, religion). Sexual orientation has been argued to be immutable, but courts still tend to accept only narrowly defined categories that meet the officials' preconceptions.

Women's and lesbians' claims for asylum are often dismissed as insufficiently meeting the Refugee Convention requirements. Lesbians' and bisexual women's ways of displaying sexuality and other experiences, including forms of persecution, are often quite different from those of gay men, and do not conform to immigration officials' preconceptions and expectations. In many political asylum hearings, individuals have been interrogated regarding the degree of visibility of their sexual orientation, and lesbians are often declared to be insufficiently visible, measured by expectations of gay men. In lesbian asylum cases, courts frequently disregard the interrelation of gender and sexual identity in narratives of lesbian persecution (Lewis 2013). Moreover, courts still have a tendency to equate the lack of documented evidence of human rights abuses against lesbians in country-of-origin reports with an absence of persecution (Neilson 2005; UK Lesbian and Gay Immigration Group 2010; Lewis 2013). The result is that it is often difficult for lesbians to produce successful asylum claims when their experiences are perceived by judges to be "too private," the assumption being that they can return to their countries of origin and be "discreet" about their sexual orientation. As Bohmer and Shuman (2008, 241) observe, "The belief of the asylum authorities that someone can avoid harm by not flaunting their sexual orientation is more likely to be a problem for lesbian asylum seekers because women are less likely to engage in targeted public activities."

Although a number of countries (for example, the United Kingdom, the Netherlands, the Czech Republic, and Australia) have recently rejected the "discretion" requirement, or the notion that LGBTI asylum applicants can return to their country of origin and be "discreet" about their sexual orientation or gender identity, a growing number of lesbian and gay asylum claims are now being refused on the grounds that the applicant's claimed sexual orientation is disbelieved (Jansen and Spijkerboer 2011; UKLGIG 2010). As the UK Lesbian and Gay Immigration Group (2010) has reported, for example, in the year 2009–2010, between 98 and 99 percent of all lesbian and gay asylum claims were rejected at the initial interview stage, compared with a 73 percent rejection rate for other asylum claims. The emphasis on credibility, requiring gay and lesbian applicants to prove their sexual orientation, demands a high level of socially visible sexual practices and creates the illusion that discretion is an option to avoid persecution. In the 2010 UK Supreme Court decision *HJ (Iran) and HT (Cameroon)*, for example, Lord Rodger concludes that only those individuals who are "practicing homosexuals," or who choose to "live openly," constitute a particular social group for the purposes of the refugee convention. Those who adopt what he refers to as a "voluntary choice of discretion" do not qualify as convention refugees (Webels 2012, 71). By assuming a scenario of "natural discretion" and "voluntary concealment," the Supreme Court ruling gives immigration officials increasing power to interrogate asylum applicants about the visibility of their sexual orientation in a way that lends itself to negative credibility assessments.

The privileging of credibility in LGBTI asylum claims continues to pose significant challenges for lesbian asylum seekers. Although the discretion requirement is no longer explicitly stated in most countries' asylum policies, it remains implicit in the treatment of lesbian asylum cases and is evident in terms of the increasing burden of proof placed on lesbian asylum applicants to make their sexual orientation visible. Indeed, the problems of claiming asylum are often compounded for lesbian and bisexual women, who may be asked to "prove" their sexual orientation and who are frequently disbelieved, especially if they have children or have been married. In her recent work with lesbian refugees in the United Kingdom, Claire Bennett (2013) has observed the hypersexualization of lesbian and bisexual women in the political asylum process. While one of the women Bennett interviewed was interrogated about whether or not she "used sex toys," and which sexual positions she liked to adopt in bed, another woman was questioned about the novels of Oscar Wilde and "which [lesbian] shows she watched." Judges also told some of the women Bennett interviewed that they did not "look like" lesbians, that lesbians "don't have children," and that all lesbians "enjoy the gay scene" and like to go on "Pride marches." Failure to conform to these heteronormative stereotypes about lesbian identity meant that the women were disbelieved, their asylum claims denied.

Recent work on LGBTI asylum claims in Europe and Canada has shown that bisexual and transgender identities tend to be similarly judged in relation to heteronormative assumptions about gender and sexuality in the political asylum process. While transgender and intersex identities are commonly misunderstood by immigration officials and conflated with sexual orientation, bisexual asylum applicants are deemed unworthy of protection because of the notion that it is possible for them to return to their country of origin and assume a heterosexual orientation (Rehaag 2009; Jansen and Spijkerboer 2011).

Laurie Berg and Jenni Millbank (2013) have noted the lack of attention to transgender refugee claims in the scholarship on political asylum, with the exception of literature focusing on the United States. In their analysis of how transgender identities are incorporated into the category of "particular social group" (PSG), they have observed that transgender asylum claims are relatively successful in terms of establishing credibility regarding gender identity. They suggest that this is due to the privileging of visual markers of difference and gender performance within the political asylum process, as well as the minority status of transgender applicants. As they write, "If trans claimants are seen by adjudicators as distinctively embodied (unlike women, who are everywhere, and the unencoded gay body which may be 'discrete' and pass as straight, or indeed be straight in a deceptive posture) their very exoticism assuages the implicit floodgates fears in PSG analysis" (2013, 131). While transgender asylum applicants tend to be more successful in establishing credibility than gay and lesbian asylum seekers, the reasoning behind this success is often the result of misunderstanding on the part of immigration officials about the differences between sexual orientation and gender identity. Berg and Millbank have noted that transgender claims are frequently treated as a "subset" of sexual orientation claims, leading to inappropriate applications of country of origin reports in documenting transgender persecution. This has the potential to exclude transgender claimants who identify as heterosexual from refugee protection and marginalize forms of persecution experienced by gay and lesbian claimants who do not engage in practices of cross-gender identification. For this reason, there is a clear need to establish transgender asylum claims as a separate identity category within refugee law.

The categories LGBTI are themselves problematic for asylum seekers whose experiences as sexual minorities do not match the preconceptions of immigration officials. The lack of documentation of intersex applicants may point to different cultural attitudes ranging from acceptance to persecution; intersex is not necessarily stigmatized in the same way as sexual orientation. The categories of sex worker and sex trafficking also complicate consideration for political asylum. Many individuals report rejection, or worse, by their families, unlike other political asylum applicants who report relying on networks of support for their escape and travel to a place of greater safety. Recent documentation by ORAM, the Organization for Refuge, Asylum, and Migration, reports that sexual minorities find very little protection, including an almost complete lack of police protection. They report that LGBTI individuals in Mexico, Uganda, and South Africa are often isolated, with no social networks, leaving them "vulnerable to violence and unable to secure even the basics: food, shelter, and a livelihood" (ORAM 2013, 9). Many LGBTI refugees have experienced violence as a response to their visibility. They do not have the networks that would establish their participation in a "particular social group," and instead of evidence of their public performances of their sexuality, they report the opposite, efforts to conceal their sexuality as a matter of safety. These conditions of vulnerability in the world weaken, rather than strengthen, their claims for political asylum. Many different sorts of organizations are involved in assisting LGBTI asylum applicants in the Global South, including lawyers, community action organizations, gay and lesbian organizations, and non-governmental organizations (NGOs) such as ORAM. However, scholarship on queer migration has not, for the most part, situated the challenges to LGBTI asylum claims in relation to issues of human rights and development. Those organizations that do address political asylum and LGBTI displacement have used social networks, films, and performance art to increase awareness about the protection gaps facing sexual and gender minority refugees (ORAM 2013). Future work on asylum, sexual orientation, and gender identity needs to connect queer migration in the Global South to questions of human rights and development.

SEE ALSO: Asylum and Gender; Asylum, Sexual Orientation and; Human Rights and Gender; Refugees and Refugee Camps; Sexuality and Human Rights; Universal Human Rights

REFERENCES

Bennett, Claire. 2013. "Claiming Asylum on the Basis of Your Sexuality: The Views of Lesbians in the UK." *Women's Asylum News*. January/February, 115: 1–4.

Berg, Laurie, and Jenni Millbank. 2013. "Developing a Jurisprudence of Transgender Particular Social Group." In *Fleeing Homophobia: Sexual Orientation, Gender Identity, and Asylum*, edited by Thomas Spijkerboer, 121–153. New York: Routledge.

Bohmer, Carol, and Amy Shuman. 2008. *Rejecting Refugees: Political Asylum in the Twenty-First Century*. New York: Routledge.

Jansen, Sabine, and Thomas Spijkerboer, eds. 2011. *Fleeing Homophobia: Asylum Claims Related to Sexual Orientation and Gender Identity in Europe*. Accessed August 7, 2015, at http://www.refworld.org/pdfid/4ebba7852.pdf.

Landau, Joseph. 2004. "Soft Immutability and Imputed Gay Identity: Recent Developments in Transgender and Sexual-Orientation-Based Asylum Law." *Fordham Urban Law Journal*, 32: 237–264.

Lewis, Rachel. 2013. "Deportable Subjects: Lesbians and Political Asylum." *Feminist Formations*, 25(2): 174–194.

Neilson, Victoria. 2005. "Homosexual or Female: Applying Gender-Based Asylum Jurisprudence to Lesbian Asylum Claims." *Stanford Law and Policy Review*, 16(2): 417–444.

Organization for Refuge, Asylum, and Migration (ORAM). 2013. *Blind Alleys: The Unseen Struggles of Lesbian, Gay, Bisexual, Transgender and Intersex Urban Refugees in Mexico, Uganda, and South Africa*. Accessed August 7, 2015, at http://www.alnap.org/resource/9783.

Rehaag, Sean. 2009. "Patrolling the Borders of Sexual Orientation: Bisexual Refugee Claims in Canada." *McGill Law Journal*, 53: 59–102.

UK Lesbian and Gay Immigration Group (UKLGIG). 2010. "Failing the Grade: Home Office Initial Decisions on Lesbian and Gay Claims for Asylum." Accessed August 7, 2015, at http://uklgig.org.uk/wp-content/uploads/2014/04/Failing-the-Grade.pdf.

UK Supreme Court. 2010. *HJ (Iran) and HT (Cameroon) v. Secretary of State for the Home Department*. Accessed August 7, 2015, at https://www.supremecourt.uk/cases/uksc-2009-0054.html.

UNHCR: The UN Refugee Agency. 2008. "UNHCR Guidance Note on Refugee Claims Relating to Sexual Orientation and Gender Identity." Accessed August 7, 2015, at http://www.justice.gov/sites/default/files/eoir/legacy/2014/08/15/UNHCR_Guidelines_Sexual_Orientation.pdf.

Webels, Janna. 2012. "HJ (Iran) and HT (Cameroon): Reflections on a New Test for Sexuality-Based Asylum Claims in Britain." *International Journal of Refugee Law*, 24(4): 815–839.

FURTHER READING

National Center for Lesbian Rights. 2006. "The Challenges to Successful Lesbian Asylum Claims." Accessed August 7, 2015, at http://www.nclrights.org/legal-help-resources/resource/the-challenges-to-successful-lesbian-asylum-claims/.

Asylum and Gender

SENTHORUN RAJ
The University of Sydney, Australia

Gender has increasingly become an important category of analysis in international refugee law. While the United Nation's (UN) Convention Relating to the Status of Refugees 1951 (Refugee Convention 1951) and the 1967 Protocol do not explicitly include gender as grounds for seeking asylum, both the United Nations High Commissioner for Refugees (UNHCR) and a number of states have recognized the need to protect women, girls, and sexual minorities from persecution. In doing so, legal and policy responses to asylum seekers have focused on the way gender intersects with the existing categories outlined in the Refugee Convention, the conceptual limits of defining persecution, the problem of causality, and the inadequacies of state protection.

Public policy discussions of gender often default to assumptions of women and men as a fixed category. Gender, however, is a difficult concept to define. Gender can be relationally and hierarchically defined: women are defined in terms of their lack (compared with men) and are subordinated to men. Gender is also a porous and performative category. Specifically, gender should be understood as the disparate social practices that constitute the identities, experiences, and roles that are typically associated with the binary category of sex (Butler 1990, 22–34). Gender works as a set of culturally and historically situated expressions that give shape to individual psyches and subjectivities. These dichotomous sexed/gendered identities are also tethered to binary notions of (homo/hetero) sexual orientation and erotic desire – an assumption that excludes intersex bodies that do not conform to these binary expectations.

Under the Refugee Convention 1951 a country is obliged to grant asylum to a refugee where they demonstrate a well-founded fear of persecution owing to race, religion, nationality, political opinion, or membership of a particular social group. Refugees must be outside their country of origin and unwilling or unable to seek protection from that country. The underlying principle is one of "non-refoulement." That is, states must not return people to places where their life or liberty would be threatened. How this is implemented in practice varies amongst countries.

Given the strictly circumscribed definition of a refugee, understanding the particular implications of gender in asylum law requires broader consideration of international human rights law. In recent decades, women's rights (and to a much lesser extent sexual orientation, gender identity, and intersex rights) have come to the attention of international decision-making forums. From the UN Decade for Women (1976–1985) to the UN Convention on the Elimination of All Forms of Discrimination Against Women 1979 (CEDAW), there has been an evolving recognition of the systemic violence and discrimination perpetrated against women in private (as well as public) life. In particular, the identification of domestic violence, poor reproductive healthcare, homophobia, limited education opportunities, and employment discrimination highlighted the precarious circumstances to which women continued to be subjected (Reilly 2009, 59–62). These persisting conditions of inequality, often manifested in the home, forcibly displace women and force them to seek asylum in countries that will grant them effective protection.

Asylum, however, remains difficult for women or other gender minorities to access. Sex, gender, or sexual orientation is not an enumerated ground of protection alongside the categories of race, nationality, religion, political opinion, or membership of a particular social group. UNHCR has acknowledged that refugee law provides scope for recognizing gender-specific claims within all the existing categories – especially within the particular social group. Gender is relevant to race-based claims when they involve the control of reproductive or sexual autonomy of a specific ethnic population. Women can be subject to punitive religious sanction when they repudiate scriptural demands. For example, religious persecution could manifest against Muslim women refusing to wear a veil or a Christian woman living in a same-sex relationship. Gender may also manifest in the category of political opinion where women challenge the putatively domestic roles that the state seeks to secure through its "family" policies or even where they publicly identify as a "feminist." Particular social identities can be politicized as transgressive. This could include women who refuse to get married and reproduce, or who are in a same-sex relationship, or who engage in sex work.

Most commonly, women or sexual minorities within a specific country have been considered sufficient to form a particular social group. In the cases of *Khawar v. Minister for Immigration and Multicultural Affairs* [2002] 187 ALR 574 in Australia and *Islam (AP) v. The Secretary of State for the Home Department; R v. Immigration Appeal Tribunal ex parte Shah (AP)* [1999] 2 All ER 545 in the United Kingdom, the appellate jurisprudence left open the possibility that a community as large as "women in Pakistan" could constitute a particular social group (PSG). Whether the group is large or whether the members share the experience of persecution uniformly is irrelevant to the social group characterization. Such a group is defined by an innate or fundamental characteristic, common to members of the group, which is not their risk of persecution. In gender identity claims, the slippage between sexual orientation and gender expression becomes more pronounced. In *Hernandez-Montiel v. Immigration and Naturalization Service* [2000] 225 F.3d 1088 (9th Cir. 2000), a US federal court opted to define the PSG more narrowly: "gay men with female sexual identities living in Mexico." Emphasis was placed on academic testimony in analyzing the specific cultural context: the "female" role performed by a man in a same-sex relationship is subject to heightened level of abuse. This case brought to the fore the conflation of sexual and gender identifications by framing the notion of sexual identity in more elastic terms to include dress, appearance, and other aesthetic typologies. Gender expression was collapsed into a sexual identity.

Defining a well-founded fear of persecution poses more problematic challenges for gender-based asylum claims. Historically, refugee jurisprudence and academic scholarship have characterized persecution as serious harms or abuses of human rights combined with the systemic failure of a state to remedy such acts (Hathaway 1991, 112). Persecution is more than "mere" discrimination. With an emphasis on state responsibility or activity, the definition has come to secure a distinction between public harm (perpetrated by the state) that warrants protection and private harm (perpetrated by non-state actors) that does not invoke protection obligations. This public/private distinction elides the way violence saturates intimate or gendered life. Specifically, the unwillingness or inability of the state to remedy violence against women such as familial or sexual violence, the "corrective" rape of lesbians, coerced marriages, and controlling female sexuality is tantamount to persecution.

UNHCR has recognized the need for more inclusive and culturally sensitive approaches to determine gender-based claims. Guidelines have been developed both internationally and within specific countries to assist decision-makers. Leading refugee barristers Rodger Haines and Jenni Millbank advocate for broader constructions of persecution that recognize the private, rather than strictly "public" context, through which women experience violence (Haines 2003, 327–338; Millbank 2003, 75–76). In *Nabulwala v. Gonzales* [2007] F.3d 1115 (8th Cir. 2007), a judicial review case in the United States, a Ugandan lesbian woman sought asylum having been the victim of sexual abuse orchestrated by her family when they discovered she was same-sex attracted. At the first instance her application was rejected because the serious harm she endured was perpetrated by family members. On review, the court noted that it was erroneous to define persecution in terms of a specific act by a government official; rather, private actors perpetrating harm with impunity satisfy the threshold of persecution under the Refugee Convention 1951. The state's refusal to intervene in domestic matters – spaces in which women typically experience violence – is a denial of basic human rights (Roberts 2002, 161).

In order to determine whether there is a "real chance" of persecution, decision-makers rely on both the plausibility of the applicant's personal testimony and the country of origin information reports they are able to access. For lesbian asylum seekers, the demand to conform to aesthetic or ethnocentric stereotypes becomes cumbersome. Cases such as *SW (Jamaica) v. Secretary for the Home Department* [2011] UKUT 00251 (24 June 2011) from the United Kingdom reveal how the idea of an "authentic" sexual identity is rendered through both public and private acts. In this particular case, the lesbian applicant from Jamaica had her sexuality authenticated by reference to her relationship history with other women and her participation in online social communities for same-sex-attracted women.

What counts as gender-specific persecution, however, is not easily delineated. While gender discrimination alone does not constitute persecution, identifying the seriousness of particular legal or policy measures that discriminate against women varies between jurisdictions. Particular legislative measures may have a disproportionate impact on women by nullifying or impairing their right and recognition of equality. Though as the Canadian Gender Guidelines on refugee assessment point out, asylum is not available to women solely on the basis that they are subject to a law or policy they dislike. However, restrictions on public participation or being subject to forced sterilization or other medical interventions (as is the case for many intersex infants) raises further considerations about what forms of discrimination will be considered "sustained" or "systemic" enough to warrant the grant of asylum. Domestic violence can be dismissed as an act of personal conflict rather than seen as exemplifying the abuse that occurs within a broader social structure in which women are subordinated to men. Persecution need not be experienced as a public display – it is insidiously banal.

Correspondingly, a refugee usually needs to demonstrate that a state has no adequate measures of protection. However, the criterion that is used to measure this particular level of "adequacy" varies on a case-by-case basis. For example, many jurisdictions recognize that a law that just prohibits sexual assault, for example, without proper implementation or enforcement, is insufficient state protection. State protection, however, need not be perfect. Additionally, given the Refugee Convention 1951 was designed to hold states accountable for their failure to protect refugees, in situations where a functional government cannot be held accountable (i.e., because of civil war or revolution), a person fleeing persecution may be denied asylum.

Refugees must also establish a nexus between the persecution they suffer and the relevant Convention characteristic (i.e., being a part of a particular social group). Causation, however, may be multifaceted. Asylum seekers need not demonstrate that they are persecuted solely for reasons of the protected category. Both *Khawar* and *Nabulwala* illustrate that persecution can be established through a combination of factors: state inaction combined with malicious violence perpetrated by non-state actors (i.e., family members). When considering non-state actors and the acts of violence they perpetrate, persecution can be causally established where the state commits, condones, acquiesces, or is otherwise unable to provide protection against such violence. Establishing the nexus between persecution and the relevant protected category can be difficult in the context of private harms. While persecutory intent of the non-state actor is not necessary, it is necessary to show that states withhold protection or allow these acts to continue with impunity because of the protected characteristic. In the US case *Pitcherskaia v. Immigration and Naturalization Service* (1997) 118 F.3d 641, a lesbian woman from Russia was subject to forced reparative "therapies" to "cure" her of her homosexuality. While the motivation of the act was to cure not punish, the Ninth Circuit Court held it still amounted to harm arising from persecution.

Using gender as a specific category of analysis in asylum claims also applies to men. In gay male asylum claims, the performance of gender becomes the cause of persecution and is also determinative of an applicant's credibility. For example, same-sex-attracted men in Mexico can be subjected to violence for failing to reproduce norms of heterosexual machismo and appearing "effeminate."

When making an asylum claim, gendered norms relating to aesthetics, fashion, and comportment are used by decision-makers to identify whether an applicant is gay and whether they would risk persecution if they were returned home. If a gay man presents as too effeminate or camp they are deemed to risk persecution. However, if they are athletic or "masculine" in appearance, decision-makers consider them unlikely to experience abuse or harassment (LaViolette 2007, 196). Undertaking an analysis of gender in asylum urges more reflection about other intersecting social differences, such as sexual orientation, race, class, age, marital status, and disability.

Procedural challenges also arise for women and other sexual minorities subject to sexual violence and trauma. In adversarial (and even inquisitorial) decision-making contexts, asylum seekers are required to disclose intimate information about rape, harassment, abuse, and their sexual practices or orientation. Many applicants lack legal and psychological support prior to being confronted with an interrogation. Such questions can generate evasive answers, confused responses, and non-linear testimony. While decision-makers impute this to a lack of credibility, many academic scholars have emphasized that the shame or stigma that surrounds such emotional questions can be internalized, making it difficult for asylum seekers to respond coherently to invasive questions (UNHCR 2002, 9). Alternatively, social psychological commentaries have elaborated that claimants should not be expected to express the sincerity of their experiences by conforming to social expectations of emotion or body language – such as crying when recounting a traumatic experience (Shidlo and Ahola 2013, 9). Credibility decisions are usually not reviewable by common law courts, as they are deemed questions of fact not law. Improper credibility assessment, therefore, can have adverse consequences for refugee claimants.

Gender provides a rich category of analysis when thinking about refugee law. From the definition of social groups to quantifying public/private experiences of persecution, asylum law has been strengthened by a critical focus on the way experiences of sexed or gendered harm impinge on the lives of women and other sexual or gender minorities. While this is an evolving area of law, policy, and practice, the proverbial "floodgates" have not yet been opened. In furthering the humanitarian purpose of the Refugee Convention 1951, more inquiries must be made about how asylum law accommodates questions of gender.

SEE ALSO: Convention on the Elimination of all Forms of Discrimination against Women (CEDAW); Heterosexism and Homophobia; Human Rights and Gender; Human Rights, International Laws and Policies on; Identity Politics; Queer Theory; Refugee Women and Violence Against Women; Refugees and Refugee Camps; Sexual Citizenship in East Asia; Sexualities; UN Decade for Women

REFERENCES

Butler, Judith. 1990. *Gender Trouble: Feminism and the Subversion of Identity*. New York: Routledge.

Haines, Rodger. 2003. "Gender-Related Persecution." In *Refugee Protection in International Law: UNHCR's Global Consultations on International Protection*, edited by Erika Feller, Volker Turk, and Frances Nicholson, 320–350. Cambridge: Cambridge University Press.

Hathaway, James. 1991. *The Law of Refugee Status*. Toronto: Butterworths.

LaViolette, Nicole. 2007. "Gender-Related Refugee Claims: Expanding the Scope of the Canadian Guidelines." *International Journal of Refugee Law*, 19(2): 169–214.

Millbank, Jenni. 2003. "Gender, Sex, and Visibility in Refugee Claims on the Basis of Sexual Orientation." *Georgetown Immigration Law Journal*, 18: 71–110.

Reilly, Nimah. 2009. *Women's Human Rights*. Cambridge: Polity.

Roberts, Anthea. 2002. "Gender and Refugee Law." *Australian Yearbook of International Law*, 22: 159–199.
Shidlo, Ariel, and Joanne Ahola. 2013. "Mental Health Challenges of LGBT Forced Migrants." *Forced Migration Review*, 42: 9–11.
United Nations High Commissioner for Refugees (UNHCR). 2002. Guidelines on International Protection: Gender-Related Persecution within the context of Article 1A(2) of the 1951 Convention and/or 1967 Protocol relating to the Status of Refugees. Accessed July 23, 2013, at http://www.unhcr.org/3d58ddef4.html.

Asylum, Sexual Orientation and

SENTHORUN RAJ
The University of Sydney, Australia

For the past two decades, many signatories to the United Nation's Convention Relating to the Status of Refugees 1951 (Refugee Convention 1951) and the 1967 Protocol have recognized the validity of sexual orientation asylum claims under the category of the "particular social group." Within the current scope of asylum jurisprudence, recognizing the sexual non-normativity or "queerness" of refugees who face a well-founded fear of persecution relies on causally relating narratives of possessing an authentic (homo)sexuality to specific incidents of state-related persecution.

The recognition of human rights relating to sexual and gender minorities remains a contested space under international law. No specific convention or treaty recognizes the human rights of gay, lesbian, bisexual, transgender, and intersex persons. Despite this, human rights discourse has increasingly evolved to recognize the ongoing violence, harassment, and discrimination faced by people on the basis of their sexual orientation and gender identity. On June 15, 2011, the United Nations Human Rights Council (HRC) passed a historic resolution expressing grave concerns at the human rights violations committed globally against individuals based on their sexual orientation and gender identity. In doing so, the HRC emphasized the principles of human dignity, equality, and non-discrimination that underscore the Universal Declaration of Human Rights 1948 (UDHR), the International Covenant on Civil and Political Rights 1966 (ICCPR) and the International Covenant on Economic, Social and Cultural Rights 1966 (ICESCR). In 2007 the Yogyakarta Principles were drafted by the International Commission of Jurists to promote international human rights obligations in relation to sexual orientation and gender identity. These international principles act as persuasive interpretations of binding human rights treaties and relate to gay, lesbian, and transgender people (although intersex is a notable omission from the document).

In the context of asylum, Article 23(A) of the Yogyakarta Principles identifies an obligation on states to:

> Review, amend and enact legislation to ensure that a well-founded fear of persecution on the basis of sexual orientation or gender identity is accepted as a ground for the recognition of refugee status and asylum.

Under Article 1A(2) of the Refugee Convention 1951, there are no categories for persecution on the basis of sexual orientation or gender identity specifically. In order to seek asylum, persons must be outside their country of origin, and must face a well-founded fear of persecution owing to their ethnicity, nationality, religion, particular social group, or political opinion.

While the articles outlined in the Yogyakarta Principles do not legally bind states to recognize sexual orientation in its domestic application of asylum law, a number of Anglophone jurisdictions have come to accept sexual orientation and gender identity as a valid basis of persecution under the Refugee Convention 1951 and the 1967 Protocol category of "particular social group" over the last two decades. In Australia, this category has taken its legal currency from *Morato v Minister for Immigration, Local Government and Ethnic Affairs (1992) 39 FCR 401*, where a (homosexual) person "belongs to or is identified with a recognizable or cognizable group within a society that shares some interest or experience in common." In the United States, *Matter of Toboso-Alfonso (1990) 20 I.&N. Dec. 819 (BIA 1990)* established the precedent that sexual orientation could constitute a valid social group. The United Kingdom had a somewhat delayed response compared with the United States and Australia when it came to recognizing LGBT claims: a sharp obiter dictum in *Islam (A.P) v Secretary of State for the Home Department of Regina v Immigration Appeal Tribunal and Another Ex Parte Shah (1999) 2 All ER 545* recognized the possibility of sexual and gender minorities constituting a particular social group. Despite the statutory variations relating to the grant of asylum in the United States, United Kingdom, and Australia, sexual and gender identity has been accepted in the common law as a peculiar characteristic fundamental to human conscience that should be protected. However, clearly delimiting sexual orientation and gender identity within the definition of a particular social group remains problematic.

Despite the statutory variations relating to the grant of asylum in the United States, United Kingdom, and Australia, sexual orientation has been accepted in the common law as a peculiar characteristic fundamental to human conscience that should be protected. However, clearly delimiting sexual orientation and gender identity within the definition of a particular social group remains problematic. The ongoing pursuit to find a common, reducible characteristic that is immutable to all those who identify as non-heterosexual obscures the complex identities and experiences of sexual and gender minorities who flee persecution. Refugee law scholars Catherine Dauvergne and Jenni Millbank argue that much of the jurisprudence in this area focuses upon sexuality by understanding the "social" as a universal characteristic innate to particular bodies (Dauvergne and Millbank 2003, 100). What this juridical reasoning obscures is the way in which the body is discursively constructed within the legal system. That is, queer bodies are not ontologically fixed. Failing to acknowledge the diasporic, non-Western position of the queer refugee body effaces sexual heterogeneity and the mediation of homophobic violence through different cultural and social relations. Sexuality is not reducible to a script of genital penetration, sexual object choice, or incidence of partners as is preferred by decision-makers; rather, it is an embodied response or process of orientation that manifests in particular locations.

Irrespective of this, administrative tribunals and primary decision-makers utilize stereotypical assumptions about what constitutes "legitimate" sex or "proper" relationships to recognize queer refugees from different national contexts. Administrative decision-making involves locating individual history within a much broader social context regarding the legitimacy of the asylum seeker's non-conforming sexuality or gender identity and the subsequent threat it presents. Tribunals seek to establish a "ring of truth" to a claim (Millbank 2009, 2). Effectively, this term reflects the way in which administrative decision-makers think that sexuality should be understandable as a discoverable "objective" truth. As cases such as *SW (Jamaica) v Secretary for the Home Department (2011)*

CG UKUT 00251 evince, sexual identity is rendered relevant through both public and private acts. In this case, the lesbian applicant from Jamaica had her sexuality authenticated by reference to her relationship history with other women and her participation in online social communities for same-sex attracted women.

Bisexuality adds a further critical challenge by countenancing the fluidity of sexual attraction. In *N98/23086 (1998) RRTA 3373 (8 July 1998)*, the applicant's same-sex attraction was dismissed as "experimentation." Instead of accepting his claim to now being attracted to men, his sexual identification was eclipsed by a decision-maker who believed he had not attempted to engage in enough heterosexual relations before being able to qualify as "really" gay. Moreover, in *V97/06483 (1998) RRTA 27 (5 January 1998)*, the applicant was rejected as being same-sex attracted because he had engaged in cross-sex activities and was therefore capable of "functioning as a heterosexual" (or at least bisexual). Refugee law works by authenticating cultural identity through a universalized genealogical narrative. For queer refugees, despite rhetoric to the contrary, sexual experiences continue to be thematized within indexes of biological essentialisms, genital penetration, consumption, and transgression for their sexual authenticity to become intelligible to an Australian legal imaginary. Thematizing experience in terms of positive and ongoing acts, however, ignores the ways in which queer identities can be culturally marked by inaction or difference (i.e., not getting married, failing to meet conventional gender roles, etc.).

Sexual orientation has also been extended to incorporate gender identity. Despite this broadened particular social group, judicial review and administrative decision-making in the United States, United Kingdom, and Australia reveals considerable anxiety about delineating between volitional aspects of gender and sexual expression and immutable sexuality or gender identities. The US case *Hernandez-Montiel v Immigration and Naturalization Service (2000) 225 F.3d 10484*, for example, does not explicitly recognize "transgender" or "transsexuality" as either a protected asylum category or an immutable part of individual identity. Alternatively, in *0805932 (2008) RRTA 879 (28 November 2008)*, an Australian case, the tribunal recognized a transgender claim from South Korea, noting the applicant (biologically male although taking estrogen hormones) exhibited a "blend" of gender qualities (while identifying predominantly as male). Although moving past immutability, the decision in this case rendered gender identity within a spectrum of (hetero)sexual attraction, or specifically for the applicant, a "female sexual taste" that was manifested in both his gender expression and choice of sexual partners (men). In a similar vein to *Hernandez-Montiel*, the tribunal bridged the distinction between sexual orientation and gender identity, noting that the particular social group in this case was "male homosexuals with transgender characteristics." However, by subrogating the applicant's gender identity or expression to a sexual orientation, the Australian Refugee Review Tribunal eclipsed the possibility of recognizing the unique position of gender minorities.

Procedurally, a critical problem for refugee decision-makers is negotiating cultural differences and the emotional experiences of those who seek asylum. In 2012, the United Nations High Commissioner for Refugees updated its policy guidelines to address the need for culturally sensitive decision-making that disavows the use of stereotypes (United Nations High Commissioner for Refugees 2012, 16). For example, the demand for queer asylum seekers to "come out" forces the narratives of claimants to meet ethnocentric and masculine expectations of sexual visibility. Given the inquisitorial emphasis of merits review, asylum seekers who fail to respond (or even understand) questions posed by decision-makers often lead to adverse inferences of credibility. Barrister S. Chelvan argues that the connection between difference, stigma, shame, and harm make disclosure about one's sexual orientation or gender identity difficult for applicants who live beyond the strict prescriptions of a heterosexual life and/or binary gender (Chelvan 2013, 27). Specifically, in a context of sexual orientation or gender expression – two intensely intimate features of a person's identity that are subject to policing in both public and private spheres – asylum seekers must navigate feelings of shame, demands for privacy, and a history of secrecy. Asylum seekers are often asked to "come out" and provide evidence of participation in a local community or previous/current relationships. Such evidentiary demands, however, ignore the compound reality of shame and stigma that coerces many asylum seekers into avoiding public spaces/situations where they could be identified. Alternatively, if they were in a relationship or in a community group, they could not disclose it to others for fear of violence or harassment. Adjudicators often fail to grasp the emotional "tells" of oral testimony because they refuse to imagine experiences of sexuality or gender identification that contest their pervasive stereotypes of what being "gay" looks/sounds like (Johnson 2011, 70). Instead of understanding the reasons for silence, decision-makers use it as a marker to impugn an asylum seeker's credibility.

Understanding what constitutes a "well-founded fear of persecution" relating to sexual minorities has also shifted. Until recently, common law countries such as Australia and the United Kingdom utilized a "discretion" test to limit the claims of sexual minorities. Specifically, this worked by limiting protection on the basis of homosexuality to consensual private sexual acts, rather than public manifestations of identity. The latter were apparently not an "inherent characteristic" of being homosexual. The emphasis on "discretion" has focused on the ways in which sexuality is managed in order to avoid persecution in public spaces. This often obscures the predominant ways in which queer women are subjected to violence in a domestic context. Correspondingly, in *Nabulwala v Gonzales (2007) 481 F.3d 1115*, a judicial review case in the United States, a Ugandan lesbian woman sought asylum having been the victim of sexual abuse orchestrated by her family when they discovered she was same-sex attracted. At the administrative stage her application was rejected because the serious harm she endured was perpetrated by family members. On review, the court noted that it was erroneous to define persecution in terms of a specific act by a government official; rather, private actors perpetrating harm with impunity satisfies the threshold of persecution under the Refugee Convention 1951.

Persecution, however, does not always need to be motivated by malice. Requiring a punitive dimension to persecution can leave many applicants without protection. In the US case *Pitcherskaia (1997) 118 F.3d 641*, the applicant had her claim refused because the attempts to "cure" her homosexuality were not done punitively. The persecutor's intent (i.e., lack of malice) works against the applicant's claim, and oddly becomes the determinative test for persecution, despite no legal precedent to suggest this. In a similar vein, in *Hernandez-Montiel* and *0805932*, both the relevant court and tribunal noted that the availability of reparative therapies were used not to "punish" the applicant but to "cure" what was perceived to be illness. In Australia, the High

Court has confirmed this underlying principle: persecution need not require enmity or malignity.

Drawing determinative conclusions or trends on sexual orientation and gender identity-based refugee claims is undesirable, if not impossible, given the limited accessibility to primary and administrative review decisions. From what data are available, it is clear that the scope for protecting sexual minority refugees is improving. Although this improvement is by no means universal, advocates, case workers, and decision-makers are giving greater attention to the fluidity of sexual identity and the culturally different dynamics of sexual experience. Moreover, given that many sexual minorities do not identify with ethnocentric labels such as "homosexual," "bisexual," "lesbian," and "gay," such refugee claims challenge immutable assumptions of sexual identity and intransigent beliefs about how such sexuality manifests.

Sexual orientation-based asylum claims continue to challenge assumptions about identity, persecution, credibility, and experience that underscore the grant of asylum. Identifying the inconsistencies and paradoxes is crucial in order to recognize the current limits that exist in status determination processes at a policy, administrative, and judicial level. Rather, the experience of violence is dynamic and has the capacity to shape identities and how individuals identify with a particular sexual orientation.

SEE ALSO: Gender Justice; Human Rights and Gender; Identity Politics; Sexualities

REFERENCES

Chelvan, S. 2013. "From Silence to Safety: Protecting the Gay Refugee?" *Counsel*, May: 26–28.
Dauvergne, Catherine, and Jenni Millbank. 2003. "Applicants *S396/2002* and *S395/2002*, a Gay Refugee Couple from Bangladesh." *Sydney Law Review*, 6: 97–124.
Johnson, Toni. 2011. "On Silence, Sexuality and Skeletons: Reconceptualising Narrative in Asylum Hearings." *Social & Legal Studies*, 20(1): 57–78.
Millbank, Jenni. 2009. "The Ring of Truth: A Case Study of Credibility Assessment in Particular Social Group Refugee Determinations." *International Journal of Refugee Law*, 18(1): 1–33.
United Nations High Commissioner for Refugees. 2012. *Guidelines on International Protection No. 9: Claims to Refugee Status Based on Sexual Orientation and/or Gender Identity Within the Context of Article 1A(2) of the 1951 Convention and/or 1967 Protocol Relating to the Status of Refugees.* Accessed July 23, 2013, at http://www.unhcr.org/509136ca9.pdf.

FURTHER READING

Millbank, Jenni. 2003. "Gender, Sex, and Visibility in Refugee Claims on the Basis of Sexual Orientation." *Georgetown Immigration Law Journal*, 18: 71–110.
Raj, Senthorun. 2011. "Affective Displacements: Understanding Emotions and Sexualities in Refugee Law." *Alternative Law Journal*, 36(3): 177–181.
Shidlo, Ariel. 2013. "Mental Health Challenges of LGBT Forced Migrants." *Forced Migration Review*, 42: 9–11.

Athletics and Gender

JENNIFER K. PAGE

Northwestern Oklahoma State University, USA

TRADITIONS AND STEREOTYPES ABOUT GENDER AND SPORT

As a social institution, sports and athletics have traditionally been associated with masculinity. Sport's implicit emphases on physical skill and competition recall conservative values of male superiority, strength, and aggression, and so sports are omnipresent in patriarchal societies in order to reinforce traditional gender roles. The Olympic Games held in ancient Greece, considered to be a classical example of sporting competition, featured the segregation of male athletes and female spectators: married women could not watch the games, but unmarried women were welcomed as viewers and later as competitors. Kyniska, a Spartan woman, was listed as a victor in the chariot race competitions in 396 and 392 BCE. Women's participation in sports has increased dramatically since the late nineteenth century, which has resulted in the complication of patriarchal, heteronormative gender ideas, especially regarding physical equality between the sexes.

Whether as participants or spectators, men are generally accepted into sporting communities, where they make friendships and engage in socially prescribed gender behavior. Traditional ideals of masculinity hold that emotional vulnerability and intimacy are feminine traits, therefore playing and discussing sports allows men to create friendships and other connections without compromising the stoicism that is privileged by hegemonic masculinity. Male athletes are often encouraged to play through injuries, which reinforces the stereotype that men should not show weakness or complain about physical discomfort; those men who do acknowledge their pain tend to be mocked or feminized by their teammates. The very act of engaging in contact sports, which require the body to be treated as a weapon in order to neutralize the threat of an opposing team, is perceived as masculine. The aggressive nature of contact sports reinforces the essentialist perception of masculinity, which suggests that men are biologically predisposed to enjoy and be skilled at physical contests for dominance. Men's contact sports glorify and reward aggressive, even violent behaviors, which are not socially permissible anywhere but in the sporting arena. On the other hand, patriarchal perceptions about women assume that they are weaker than men and not suited for physical competition; as a result, women have historically been allowed and later encouraged to engage in individual, non-contact sports, such as tennis, golf, swimming, and track and field.

Because of the long-standing perception of sports as a masculine outlet, women who participate in or watch sports are sometimes perceived as tomboys, or in the first half of the twentieth century, "mannish." Many early opponents of women's participation in sports argued that engaging in such strenuous activity would cause irreparable harm to a woman's delicate physiology and even her future children. In addition to biological fears, physical educators in the early twentieth century warned that women who engaged in the manly activities of sports would themselves start to behave as men, thus challenging patriarchal dictates for femininity. Part of this feared mannish behavior manifested in the stereotype of the female athlete as lesbian, which also challenged the normative heterosexual family structure. In order to combat the negativity associated with the stereotype of the masculine female athlete, sports reporters, officials, and even athletes themselves would emphasize their traditionally feminine physical beauty to overcompensate for their perceived masculinity in competition. This tendency to view female athletes as women first and athletes second continues today. Alysia Montaño, for example, is a contemporary American middle-distance runner who competes at international track and field competitions, such as the Olympic Games and World Championships, with a flower tucked in her hair to remind spectators that she is a lady *and* an athlete.

WOMEN AND TWENTIETH-CENTURY SPORTS

Whereas men have been the facilitators of sports since their inception, women's entrance into sports and athletics occurred much later. Upper-class British and American women began to pursue athletic interests in the late 1800s; these women had leisure time and financial means to enjoy individual sports and exercises such as croquet, archery, bicycling, and skating – athletic activities still traditionally associated with the wealthy. Women were also encouraged to participate in individual sports such as golf, tennis, and swimming – non-violent, non-competitive sports that would not portray the athletes as overly aggressive or "mannish." The first team sport women could play was basketball, starting in 1892, and for more than a century, basketball has consistently been the most popular sport among female student athletes. Just a few years later, in 1900, the first women competed at a modern-day Olympic Games in Paris. Twenty-two women athletes competed in tennis, sailing, croquet, golf, and equestrian competitions.

More and more women began to participate in sports in the early twentieth century, either recreationally or in college organizations, and by the 1920s, the growing number of female athletes was considered a threat to traditional ideas of femininity and the separation of gendered spheres. The majority of physical education instructors in 1923, a primarily male group, was opposed to intercollegiate sports for women, and other athletics administrators opposed women's participation in the 1928 Olympic Games (Messner 2007). Women's sporting opportunities were limited or eliminated entirely, and those women who could still play were now doing so under more restrictive rules than men's teams. Some of these restrictions are still in effect; for example, women's softball diamonds are smaller than men's baseball diamonds, and women play three sets in tennis matches while men play five sets.

Despite opposition and official restrictions in the first half of the twentieth century, many women excelled in athletics, challenging traditional notions of female weakness. In 1926, Gertrude Ederle became the first woman to swim across the English Channel, breaking the men's record time by almost two hours and proving to detractors that sex is not necessarily a deciding factor in an athlete's performance. Mildred "Babe" Didrikson's success on the golf green in the 1930s popularized the sport for men and women of all economic classes. When a large portion of male professional baseball players were called to military service during World War II, women athletes were specifically scouted to participate in the All-American Girls' Professional Baseball League (AAGPBL) to keep spectators satisfied. In 1958, Italian Maria-Teresa de Filippis became the first woman to drive in a European Grand Prix race. Kathy Switzer became the first woman to run the Boston Marathon as a numbered entry in 1967; previously, athletic officials would not allow women to run races longer than 2.5 miles. In 1973's "Battle of the Sexes," the young female tennis player Billie Jean King defeated the seasoned male professional Bobby Riggs in a game that was originally conceived to demonstrate men's athletic superiority over women. The breakthroughs and struggles continue for sporting women in the twenty-first century. Sadaf Rahimi, the first woman boxer to represent Afghanistan at the Olympic Games, had her invitation to the 2012 London Games revoked by the International Boxing Association due to concerns about her safety in the ring. Wojdan Ali Seraj Abdulrahim Shahrkhani is a judo competitor and one of only two women who represented Saudi Arabia at the 2012 Olympic Games; Shahrkhani was only able to compete after the International Olympic Committee and the Saudi Arabian Olympic Committee agreed that she wear a modified hijab, be accompanied by male chaperones, and be segregated from male athletes.

Even with female athletes' growing presence and success in athletics, administrators and sponsors continued to impose stereotypes of femininity in competition. Players for the AAGPBL were required to attend charm school lessons and be accompanied by chaperones who would enforce a curfew and morality standards. Dress codes, which required hair length below the collar and forbade the wearing of slacks and shorts, were also meant to emphasize the players' femininity to compensate for their athletic skill (Boutilier and SanGiovanni 1983). Media reports on female athletes also tended to emphasize the players' physical beauty or overt sexual appeal in a reflection of the period's typical patronizing or dismissive attitude toward sporting women.

The expansion of feminism and the women's liberation movement in the 1970s, however, brought about greater gender integration and sporting opportunities with the founding of the Association for Intercollegiate Athletics for Women and the implementation of Title IX regulations. The Women's Sports Foundation, founded by Billie Jean King in 1974, and the US Department of State's Sports Diplomacy Division are two groups that are lobbying for women's rights to participate in sports around the world, which can be a challenge in many countries that also stunt women's opportunities for education, professional growth, and political visibility.

TITLE IX

The passage of Title IX in 1972 marked a shift in the political response to gender discrimination in organized sport in America. The law, which did not take effect until 1975, mandated that educational institutions with sports and athletics programs must offer equal opportunities for participation to both male and female students. Part of providing equal opportunities for all athletes is ensuring that all team and individual sports have adequate funding, equipment, and practice space. Furthermore, educational institutions are supposed to ensure that the selection of sports offerings is representative of the students' interests. In other words, if a group of students is interested in playing a particular sport, the institution cannot deny their right to play the sport based on the athletes' sex. Educational institutions are allowed, however, to maintain separate male and female teams within the same sport provided that neither team is discriminated against or favored. If an institution does not offer both male and female teams for a single sport, interested members of the opposite sex must be allowed to try out for the team unless it is labeled a contact sport (e.g., boxing, wrestling, football, hockey).

Since the implementation of Title IX, American high schools and universities have seen a dramatic increase in female athletes; Michael Kimmel (2010) notes that in 1971 there were fewer than 300,000 female athletes in American high schools, but by 2005, this number had grown to 2.9 million. This growth is also apparent in American universities, where in the first few years of the new millennium over 600 new women's sports teams were added (Messner 2007). As a result of the greater athletic opportunities for young American women since the mid-1970s, more women are participating in competitive sports at a professional level than ever before, including in the Olympic Games and other international competitions.

Despite the fact that Title IX has been in effect for nearly four decades, the law has faced continuing opposition, and thousands of schools across the United States are not in compliance with its regulations (National Women's Law Center 2013). Many political figures and university coaches have argued that allowing equal funding for male and female sports teams would actually detract from larger, male-dominated teams' ability to attract and maintain the best athletes. From the 1976 lawsuit filed by the National Collegiate Athletic Association (NCAA) challenging Title IX's legality to the 2004 suit brought by the National Wrestling Coaches Association which charged that its regulations discriminate against male athletes, the law has been continually challenged, upheld, and reinterpreted.

GENDER AND SPORTS IN THE TWENTY-FIRST CENTURY

Despite Title IX regulations and the growing public awareness and acceptance of women in the sporting world, gender stereotypes and prejudices linger to reveal an inherent androcentrism in contemporary athletics. The language of sports itself suggests male exclusivity: women are still known as "female athletes," while the unmodified "athlete" is presumed to be male, and women's sports teams are named feminized versions of comparable male teams (e.g., "Lady Cardinals" or "Lady Bulldogs"). Women's sports receive far less financial support than male sports, and most female professional athletes tend to make only a small percentage of the salary their male counterparts do. Aside from the Ladies Professional Golf Association (LPGA, founded in 1950) and Women's Tennis Association (WTA, founded by Billie Jean King in 1974), most of the professional women's sporting leagues are underfunded and suffer from comparably low spectatorship. The Women's National Basketball Association (WNBA), National Women's Soccer League (NWSL), Women's Professional Football League (WPFL), and Professional Women's Bowling Association (PWBA) all receive far less media attention and sponsorship than their male counterparts, which proliferates the discriminatory perception of women's sports as less important and less interesting than men's sports. In fact, even the governing boards of many popular sports leagues are made up primarily of men, reducing the visibility women have at the leadership and administrative level of athletics as well.

The othering of women is apparent in continuing media portrayals of the female body as a locus of sexuality rather than skill and strength. Female athletes' bodies, rather than their athletic accomplishments, are often the subject of visual media, including *Playboy*, *Maxim*, and other magazines that target a heterosexual male audience. Olympians like Gabrielle Reece and Katarina Witt are among the numerous female athletes who posed nude for *Playboy* (2001 and 1998, respectively). The increasingly common inclusion of male athletes in nude photographs and magazines, however, suggests a shift in the way athletes of both sexes are perceived. *ESPN Magazine*'s body issue, which features nude images of prominent professional athletes of all races, ages, and body types, featured eight different cover images in July 2013: four male athletes and four female athletes. As photographers and editors sometimes argue, it is possible that spectators are starting to recognize the athletic body – independent of sex – as a triumph of human physicality; it is also possible that male athletes are now starting to be objectified and sexualized as female athletes have been for more than a century.

Though much of the research about contemporary sports focuses on women's issues, the perception and treatment of Western male athletes have also shifted in the last decade. Sports that have always emphasized hard hits and physical sacrifice, such as football, hockey, and boxing, are now placing greater importance on the health of the athletes than ever before. American high school and college football programs, particularly, have taken measures recently to protect players and prevent concussions and other serious injuries. At the professional level, National Football League (NFL) officials have taken actions to ensure that the game's hard-hitting nature does not become unnecessarily violent or dangerous to players.

The traditional association of male athletes with compulsory heterosexuality, too, is changing in America. In April 2013, Jason Collins, a free-agent National Basketball Association (NBA) center, was the first active player to come out publicly as gay. The National Hockey League (NHL) partnered with the You Can Play Project in early 2013 to develop a program that would combat homophobia in sports. Through training, counseling, and public service announcements, the NHL offers its support of gay rights and acceptance of gay players. Many straight allies in the NFL have also come out in support of gay rights, and in 2014, Michael Sam became the first openly gay player to be drafted by a professional team – the St. Louis Rams. With the attitude toward male athletes' sexuality changing, it is possible that key components of sports, such as hypermasculinity, misogyny, and discriminatory practices, may also change.

SEE ALSO: Athletics and Homosexuality; Biological Determinism; Women's Health Movement in the United States

REFERENCES

Boutilier, Mary A., and Lucinda SanGiovanni. 1983. *The Sporting Woman*. Champaign, IL: Human Kinetics.
Kimmel, Michael. 2010. *Misframing Men: The Politics of Contemporary Masculinities*. New Brunswick, NJ: Rutgers University Press.
Messner, Michael A. 2007. *Out of Play: Critical Essays on Gender and Sport*. Albany: SUNY Press.
National Women's Law Center (NWLC). 2013. "Title IX." Accessed June 20, 2015, at http://www.titleix.info.

FURTHER READING

Butler, Judith. 1998. "Athletic Genders: Hyperbolic Instance and/or the Overcoming of Sexual Binarism." *Stanford Humanities Review*, 6(2). Accessed June 20, 2015, at http://www.stanford.edu/group/SHR/6-2/html/butler.html.
Cahn, Susan K. 1994. *Coming on Strong: Gender and Sexuality in Twentieth-Century Women's Sport*. New York: Free Press.
International Olympic Committee (IOC). 2013. "Ancient Olympic Games." Accessed June 20, 2015, at http://www.olympic.org/ancient-olympic-games?tab=the-athlete
Jay, Kathryn. 2004. *More Than Just a Game: Sports in American Life Since 1945*. New York: Columbia University Press.
Messner, Michael A. 2002. *Taking the Field: Women, Men, and Sports*. Minneapolis: University of Minnesota Press.
Messner, Michael A., and Donald F. Sabo. 1994. *Sex, Violence and Power in Sports: Rethinking Masculinity*. Freedom, CA: The Crossing Press.
Sabo, Donald F., and Ross Runfola, eds. 1980. *Jock: Sports and Male Identity*. Englewood Cliffs, NJ: Prentice Hall.

Athletics and Homosexuality

ERIC ANDERSON and ADAM WHITE
University of Winchester, UK

INTRODUCTION

American footballer Michael Sam became an Internet sensation when he declared his sexual orientation as gay before the NFL draft. He was subsequently drafted by the St. Louis Rams before taking a position with the Dallas Cowboys. Unlike previous athletes who have come out at the end of their professional careers, Sam has been openly gay from the start. And, like the last several openly gay men to come out in the center of masculine sports, Sam was applauded by fans and the media, alike. Such accepting attitudes have not, however, always been evident. The experiences of openly gay athletes a generation before were significantly worse.

TWENTIETH-CENTURY SPORT

In the Western world organized sport largely originated as a product of the Industrial Revolution. It was used to produce brave, stoic, and self-sacrificing men; the type of men needed for both industry and war. Sport taught them to accept orders without question; to take risks; and to put their bodies in harm's way for the sake of the team (and its proxy of family). Sport also helped secure patriarchal privilege in a time of advancing first-wave feminism.

Before industrialization, competitive organized sport was a mere shell of what it would become in the first decade of the twentieth century. There was little need for sport in the agrarian world: there was little concept of leisure time for the working classes. Instead, farming men and women worked long hours together. Cancian (1987) argues that the roles of masculinity and femininity overlapped during this time.

However, after the economic migration of families from rural farming to urban factories in the latter half of the nineteenth and early decades of the twentieth century, gender spheres separated, with men going to work in factories and coal mines and women taking on increasingly domesticated roles. Throughout the advancing decades of the twentieth century femininity became the exclusive terrain of women, and its requirements saw women as increasingly emotionally and physically fragile while men were required to be the opposite.

Furthermore, because boys were separated from their factory-working fathers who worked long hours, culture became increasingly concerned that boys were becoming overly feminine; they (wrongfully) thought that this would lead to homosexuality. This belief was enhanced by increased visibility of homosexuality in new urban cities. Psychologist Sigmund Freud, for example, believed this was a result of boys being raised by their mothers and wrongly attributed this phenomenon (something he termed inversion) to the lack of male influence in the household. Masculine endeavors – like sport – was thus used as a tool in preventing boys from becoming effeminate, and thus gay.

Boys who excelled in sport typified masculinity and thus heterosexuality. "Real boys and men" were understood to be stoic, strong, aggressive, competitive, misogynistic, and homophobic; and this (traditionally) positioned them to gain cultural capital among their peers. Men who did not conform to such rigid ideals of masculinity were marginalized, policed, and socially excluded. Thus, this was a king-of-the-hill style hierarchy, where the orthodox jock is positioned at the top of the hill and symbolically pushes down those around him. Those who were subjugated continually strived to improve their position in this social stratification, something Anderson (2005) calls a jockocracy. Here, the primary methods to compete for social standing is to challenge others' masculinity or question their heterosexuality through homophobic discourse. As such, Hekma noted that gay men in sport "seen as queer and effeminate are granted no space whatsoever in what is generally considered to be a masculine preserve and a macho enterprise" (Hekma 1998, 2).

HOMOHYSTERIA

Before the 1980s, there was a paucity of research exploring the relationship between sport and homosexuality. As a result of the high cultural homophobia of that era, gay athletes remained hidden. Pronger (1990), for example, found a culture of verbal harassment, physical assault, and social exclusion of gay men, showing that it prevented them from coming out. The social ordering of men in this zeitgeist is best explained using inclusive masculinity theory (Anderson 2014) and its operating principle of homohysteria.

The central concept of homohysteria is to situate homophobia within the wider cultural, temporal, and institutional context. A homohysteric culture must have three key features: (1) understanding that a significant proportion of the population is gay; (2) antipathy toward homosexuality; and (3) the association of femininity with men's homosexuality (McCormack and Anderson 2014).

Anderson shows that all three of these variables existed in the 1980s. Accordingly, knowing that homosexuals "must be out there," but not wanting to be thought one of them, heterosexuals (and gay and bisexual men wishing to remain closeted) continually policed the behaviors of one another in the hunt for homosexuality. Men continually tried to identify who was gay, usually through the performance of femininity or otherwise association with feminine matters. Anything that did not conform to the orthodox jock mentality was seen as an indicator of homosexuality.

However, Anderson argues that as the cultural antipathy toward homosexuality changes to that of acceptance (as in the current epoch in the West), homohysteria decreases, and thus so will the necessity for male policing of gender behaviors and sexuality. Accordingly, as Western society's antipathy toward homosexuality began reducing in the 1990s, sports position as a bastion of homophobia started to crack.

CRACKS IN THE JOCKOCRACY

The picture of the early twenty-first century shows rapid cultural progress. In his research of 26 openly gay athletes, Anderson (2002) found positive coming-out stories and reported acceptance in American sports teams, but principally only for those with high athletic capital. Still, this was better than what was found a decade earlier, when Pronger (1990) was unable to find any openly gay athletes for his study. This hinted at social progress toward the inclusion of gay men in sport, but troubles remained.

In his 2002 study, all of the 26 athletes reported they were anxious about telling their teammates they were gay, as they perceived sport to be a homophobic institution (Anderson 2014). Gay athletes were concerned with being socially excluded, verbally abused, and physically beaten – even though none of these happened after coming out. On the contrary, athletes who came out framed their experiences as positive, with stories of acceptance. In fact, when asked if they would have changed anything, most mentioned how they had wished to come out to their teammates earlier.

Indeed, athletes in Anderson's 2002 study told some inspiring stories. For example, a sprinter named Gabriel explained how he came out to his team near the end of his senior year, and that this inspired one of his gay teammates to also come out. He said that during the state meet, at the year's end, the two heterosexual relay teammates wanted to show them their support, so they purchased rainbow socks for the four to wear. Together they ran, and won, the state championship wearing rainbow socks.

However, not all was as inclusive as the athletes thought. For example, for the above-mentioned athlete, upon further questioning, Anderson (2005) found stories of homophobia and denial from other teammates. Gabriel explained, "We had been around these guys for years, and someone had found out that we were gay and had a fit over it." The social exclusion Gabriel faced from some team members was not an irregularity, in fact, with the exception of only one participant, every story showed signs of homophobia. However, when this discrimination was highlighted to the athletes they still contended that their experiences were positive. Anderson (2005) theorized this as reverse relative deprivation. As such, these athletes thought their coming-out experience would be horrendous, anything short of this seemed therefore to be positive.

Anderson also found a great deal of heteronormativity. Principally, this came in the form of *don't ask, don't tell*. This was an unofficial policy in which heterosexual athletes were open and free to discuss their girlfriends, but gay athletes were not extended the same liberty to discuss their love or sexual lives. Gay athletes were also complicit in this heterosexism, claiming they did not want to make a big deal of their homosexuality or *force it upon* their heterosexual teammates.

Interestingly, all of the gay athletes who participated in the 2002 research were also central or key players among their teams; they were talented and therefore had high athletic capital. This meant that losing these athletes would be detrimental to the team's success. As a result, Anderson suggested that these athletes had a cloak of athletic capital to them which would help mediate harassment or victimization based upon their homosexuality. So, although there were some positive narratives expressed by athletes, these may in part be influenced by the athletic prowess these gay athletes have among their teams.

Even though these findings show significant heterosexism and some elements of homophobia, his findings were a noticeable improvement from the narratives of gay male athletes in the 1980s (Anderson 2005). Matters have continued to improve, and rapidly so, ever since.

TWENTY-FIRST CENTURY JOCKS

Today, Anderson argues that in many, perhaps most Western locales, the jockocratic system has not only started to crack; it has fallen apart. As the Anglo-American cultural antipathy toward homosexuality continues to decline, homohysteria has diminished in the Western world. According to his inclusive masculinity theory, as homohysteria dissipates, there should be a realigning of masculinity types. Whereas the jock ruled the day in times of high homohysteria, in times of low homohysteria, the stratification of men realigns to esteem various masculinities in a more equal manner. The result of this liberal cultural shift means that gay men are increasingly accepted – and Anderson (2014) shows that this has also been the case with the gay male athlete.

Anderson (2014) shows that gay athletes in the twenty-first century do not fear coming out to their teammates like gay men did just a decade ago. There are far fewer concerns regarding being physically assaulted, either on or off the field, and gay athletes certainly do not fear exclusion from their peers. Correspondingly, gay athletes no longer have the internal angst of worrying about coming out to their peers to the same degree as athletes used to have. For example, Tom, a high-school runner, said "I knew it wouldn't be a problem [coming out], why would it be?" (Anderson 2014, 60).

Anderson finds that, where athletes used to believe that sport had elevated levels of homophobia compared with society as a whole, today's athletes see their sports teams as safe spaces for gay men. Accordingly, whereas the gay athletes of the 1980s and 1990s needed to be athletically superior to open up about their sexuality, today's gay athletes do not need a cloak of athletic capital to protect them from victimization. Exemplifying this, in 2011 Anderson used the same methods to interview another 26 openly gay athletes. In this study, athletes were not central to the outcome of their team's success and they held considerably less athletic ability than those a decade earlier. This implies that gay male athletes no longer feel they need to be top in their team in order to have a successful coming out.

Anderson also finds that when a gay male athlete opens up about their homosexuality today, their teammates value the disclosure of a personal matter in a similar way to close friends sharing secrets. They feel privileged, honored, and trusted with the disclosure. Accordingly, many teammates respond by also disclosing personal information. For example, in research on a small soccer team in the United States, one heterosexual teammate commented that after Brent had come out, he was able to "spend lots of time talking about all types of deep or personal things … and now I can ask him stuff I've never been able to ask other gay guys" (Adams and Anderson 2011, 356).

The support network is also evident in the new ways heterosexual athletes view homophobic language and attitudes. Today's athletes see anti-gay discourse and attitudes both as archaic and immature (Anderson 2014). This means, athletes who deplore homophobia are vilified for what is seen as immature and homophobic behavior. Rather than having to battle against teammates, by coming out, gay athletes are increasing their network of allies through disclosure of their homosexuality.

Finally, Anderson (2014) shows that gay athletes today largely evade the conditions *don't ask, don't tell* on their teams. They openly talk about boyfriends, discuss homosexual sex, and chat about who they think is attractive. They are often encouraged into these conversations by their heterosexual teammates. For example, another teammate of Brent's, Steve, said, "I've always wondered if it feels good to be fucked. I asked Brent and now I know it does. I asked Brent all kinds of stuff about gay sex" (Anderson and Adams 2011, 356). This open discussion about sexuality not only affords heterosexual athletes to learn about a previously taboo subject, but also creates a culture of inclusion for gay sportsmen.

CONCLUSION

The story of the twenty-first century jock is significantly different from athletes of only a couple of decades ago in the Western context. The decreasing levels of cultural homohysteria have afforded gay athletes the ability to be open, accepted, and highly esteemed in contemporary sports teams. Regardless of their athletic ability, they are welcomed, valued, and oftentimes popular team members in sports across modern Anglo-American society.

Openly gay athletes today are not socially excluded by teammates and there is no evidence whatsoever that shows hostility toward openly gay athletes. The stories of some professional athletes – Tom Daley, Michael Sam, Robbie Rogers, Jason Collins, Gareth Thomas, Steve Davies (and many other openly gay sportsmen) – are just a few examples of how the sporting world is no longer the last bastion of homophobia.

It is important to recognize that this is based upon evidence in the Western world, including Australia, Canada, Europe, New Zealand, and the United States. There is little or no research other than in the countries mentioned previously to base our claims upon. Globally, athletes will have different experiences depending on the cultural and institutional levels of homohysteria where they are located. The story in Russia will be somewhat different from those in the Middle East or Africa. This does leave space for further research on the international experiences of openly gay athletes.

Finally, these results are drawn from the experiences of openly gay athletes; clearly, athletes who remain closeted do so out of fear. Thus it is important to note that inclusivity is rapidly spreading across the United States and within other Anglo-American cultures, but matters will vary depending on the cultures and institutions where sport is situated.

SEE ALSO: Athletics and Gender; Heterosexism and Homophobia; Masculinities; Socialization and Sexuality

REFERENCES

Anderson, Eric. 2002. "Gays in Sport: Contesting Hegemonic Masculinity in a Homophobic Environment." *Gender & Society*, 16(6): 860–877.

Anderson, Eric. 2005. *In the Game: Gay Athletes and the Cult of Masculinity*. New York: SUNY Press.

Anderson, Eric. 2011. "Updating the Outcome: Gay Athletes, Straight Teams, and Coming Out at the End of the Decade." *Gender & Society*, 25(2): 250–268.

Anderson, Eric. 2014. *21st Century Jocks: Sporting Men and Contemporary Heterosexuality*. Basingstoke: Palgrave Macmillan.

Anderson, Eric, and Adi Adams. 2011. "Exploring the Relationship between Homosexuality and Sport among the Teammates of a Small, Midwestern Catholic College Soccer Team." *Sport, Education and Society*, 17(3): 347–363. DOI: 10.1080/13573322.2011.608938.

Cancian, Francesca. 1987. *Love in America: Gender and Self-development*. Cambridge: Cambridge University Press.

Hekma, Gert. 1998. "'As long as They Don't Make an Issue of It…': Gay Men and Lesbians in Organized Sports in the Netherlands." *Journal of Homosexuality*, 35(1): 1–23. DOI: 10.1300/J082v35n01_01.

McCormack, M., and Eric Anderson. 2014. "The Influence of Declining Homophobia on Men's Gender in the United States: An Argument for the Study of Homohysteria." *Sex Roles*, 71(3–4): 109–120.

Pronger, Brian. 1990. *The Arena of Masculinity: Sports, Homosexuality and the Meaning of Sex*. New York: St. Martin's Press.

Backlash

KELLIE BEAN
Lyndon State College, USA

The backlash against feminism was first defined in *Backlash: The Undeclared War Against Women* by Susan Faludi (1991), and the term has inflected discussions of feminism ever since. Faludi identified the "backlash" as a widespread, deeply conservative media response to feminist progress during the Reagan era which sought to undermine the victories of the feminist movement by claiming women's equality was leading to their unhappiness. Within the media of the time, any choices by women that could be defined as anti-family, such as remaining single or putting off having children, were pathologized and blamed on feminism. Indeed, feminism created all kinds of new suffering, such as infertility, divorce, stress-related disorders, sexual confusion, infidelity, identity crises, hair loss, depression, the feminization of men, spinsterhood, and increased likelihood of rape. Faludi carefully defines the backlash as a trend, not a conspiracy; she describes the backlash as a media development that grew to have tremendous impact due not to a concerted strategy, but rather to a cultural zeitgeist already anxious about feminism's apparent successes.

The guiding assumptions behind the backlash were demonstrable not through sociological research or demographic data, but rather through a survey of popular film, television, gossip, and self-help books. For example, backlash messages that women were more miserable than ever, less healthy, badly behaved, or confused were coded into movies such as *Fatal Attraction*, where a single woman is driven to both homicidal and suicidal ideations through an unhappy liaison with a married man. Major news magazines, such as *Time*, featured cover stories on the film as if it were diagnostic of a genuine cultural phenomenon. In newspapers and magazines and on the evening news, women were warned of a "man shortage" and encouraged to abandon unattractive feminist goals, such as focusing on a career or attending college, in favor of family- and man-friendly choices. Perhaps the most famous backlash media event was the 1986 *Newsweek* cover story announcing that a woman over 40 years of age was "more likely to be killed by a terrorist than marry." This story began in a casual joke repeated by a *Newsweek* bureau reporter among colleagues, and became the defining data item of the backlash era. It is a hallmark of backlash reportage to offer up startling and unverifiable claims about women's lives under feminism and then treat these claims as fact.

The Wiley Blackwell Encyclopedia of Gender and Sexuality Studies, First Edition. Edited by Nancy A. Naples.
© 2016 John Wiley & Sons, Ltd. Published 2016 by John Wiley & Sons, Ltd.

These "facts" revealed a deep concern over the potential loss of masculine power embedded in traditional notions of marriage and family. The subjects around which backlash stories centered all suggest a desire for women to return to the home and resume their status as supportive of and subordinate to men. Such "facts" include: women working outside the home made children delinquent and women infertile; single women were more likely to be unhappy and suffer from neuroses; abortion led to more violence on television; and feminism has feminized men.

When a woman says, "I'm not a feminist, but …," we are seeing the lasting effects of the backlash; this phrase is a direct consequence of the backlash and while it is often appended to a statement of unalloyed feminist politics, women learned to question the term's usefulness and to resist the negative associations it carries. As the term was rendered problematic, its meaning seemed up for grabs, and a new trend emerged in the 1990s that locates feminism's pernicious influence on college campuses – inside women's studies departments and within women-centered curricula. Books such as *Who Stole Feminism: How Women Have Betrayed Women* (Hoff Sommers, 1994) and *The Morning After: Sex, Fear, and Feminism on Campus* (Roiphe, 1993) argue that feminist concerns, such as rape on campus, are overstated within feminist rhetoric and have been exploited to shift higher education away from its Enlightenment roots and toward a radical, pro-feminist ideology. As a continuation of the backlash argument, works such as these turn feminist success on its head; allowing women access to higher education has created a crisis on campuses, which impedes the rights of men and diminishes the value of traditional education.

Rhetorically refashioning the word against itself, the backlash drained much of the political seriousness out of the term "feminist" and by the mid-1990s one could claim to be second or third wave or any of a growing number of pre-fix feminisms, such as girlie-, pro-sex, do-me, anti- or post-feminist. This apparent diversity in fact points instead to a loss of meaning, and allows any issues of even the remotest connection to women's lives (not to mention empowerment) to be properly called "feminism."

In 2006, *Newsweek* issued an apology for its story on women and marriage. Since that time, a reassessment of the roots and inheritances of the backlash has taken place in the mainstream and on college campuses. Today, definitional coherence is of growing importance to a generation of women and men who identify feminism as less of a rhetorical stance and more of a call to action. Within social media, feminism is being recast again, this time as a movement growing out of and meaningful to lived experience and increasingly free of the either/or logic of anti- or post- or backlash approaches to the movement.

SEE ALSO: Empowerment; Feminisms, First, Second, and Third Wave; Higher Education and Gender in the United States; Postfeminism

REFERENCES

Faludi, Susan. 1991. *Backlash: The Undeclared War Against American Women*. New York: Random House.

Hoff Sommers, Christina. 1994. *Who Stole Feminism: How Women Have Betrayed Women*. New York: Simon and Schuster.

Roiphe, Katie. 1993. *The Morning After: Sex, Fear, and Feminism on Campus*. New York: Little, Brown.

Bathhouses

CHRIS ASHFORD
Northumbria University, UK

Bathhouses have long been associated with gay male sexuality and, particularly since the

1980s, with issues of public health and morality. While the term sauna might be commonly applied to these spaces in the United Kingdom and other parts of the world, the term bathhouse remains de rigueur in North America and much of Asia.

The bathhouse or sauna is a public sex venue (PSV) rather than a public sex environment (PSE), combining its original sauna, steam room, and (more recently) jacuzzi bath role with a sexual space. In contrast to the PSE of the public toilet, documented in Laud Humphreys's *Tearoom Trade*, the bathhouse offers a commercial sexual space, although it shares the tearoom characteristic of providing a legitimate cover for men to have sex with other men.

Typically, a bathhouse might have a relatively discreet outward appearance and patrons will be met with a check-in counter just inside the entrance. Often this is behind security glass or even bars and serves as a small anti-room before entering the bathhouse. This is where patrons may pay a membership fee as well as an admittance fee. In the North American context, patrons are typically asked whether they would like to rent a room or a locker (the locker is significantly cheaper) and are often asked to produce photographic identification, although Canada is seen as having a less stringent approach (Couture 2008, 3). Once inside the bathhouse, the sexualized spaces in the form of open orgy spaces, private rooms, mazes, public slings, and so on are "cruised" along with the "wet" spaces of the sauna and steam room.

Although generally regarded as an exclusively male sexual phenomenon, recent years have seen the emergence of lesbian bathhouse spaces, notably in Canada with Toronto's Pussy Palace and Halifax's SheDogs (Hammers 2009).

The appropriation of Turkish, Russian, and public baths as "gay spaces" in the United States, along with health resorts and spas, began in the late nineteenth and early twentieth centuries (Bérubé 2003, 34). At a time when sex acts between men were socially and legally prohibited, the bathhouse became one of a number of venues that offered the protection of anonymity, some privacy, and the illusion of legitimacy. Ultimately, the bathhouse was to evolve into a key community space.

As a new sense of sexual liberation emerged in the late 1960s, "orgy rooms" were installed. However, it was only in 1976 that a consenting adult sex bill went into effect in California, legalizing the sex that went on in these venues for the first time. Throughout the 1960s, 1970s, and 1980s, erotic murals were added to many bathhouses. The Bulldog Bathhouse murals survived its closure and can still be viewed in the GLBT Historical Society Archive in San Francisco.

The 1970s also saw entertainers appearing at bathhouses, notably Bette Midler, who began her career singing at the Continental Baths in New York City. This social dimension was accompanied by the installation of "fantasy" environments such as video rooms to recreate the movie theater, cells recreating prisons, along with glory holes that replicated the public toilet environment and mazes the bushes and parks of cruising grounds.

Bathhouses began to come under greater public health scrutiny in the 1970s as sexually transmitted infection (STI) rates dramatically rose among gay men. This led to health authorities and community organizations beginning to offer sexual health testing services in the bathhouse, a practice that continues to this day in bathhouses and saunas.

The emergence of HIV and AIDS was to lead to a significant shift in approach to bathhouses. In New York City, a Sanitary Code (regulation) amendment in 1985 provided for new controls on "high-risk sexual activity" and was introduced as an emergency measure (Elovitz and Edwards 1996). This resulted in bathhouse raids by law enforcement and health agents, and the closure of bathhouses when evidence was found of such activity. Curiously, the policy had the effect of reducing the signs of such activity – namely condoms and lubricant – and, in doing so, had the somewhat perverse effect of increasing the risk of STI transmission in these bathhouses.

In 1984, city officials in San Francisco took a similarly hard-line approach, ordering the closure of bathhouses in the city in the belief that these sites were significantly contributing to the spread of HIV through promiscuous sexual encounters. Disman (2003, 72) notes that many venues defied the ban at first and legal and regulatory battles reigned from 1985 to 1989. During this time the emphasis of commercial PSEs shifted from bathhouses to sex clubs, and the bathhouses of San Francisco became extinct, with "private" rooms banned in sex clubs and bathhouses alike. Bathhouses continue to be associated with sexual health concerns in North America, Europe, Australia, and, more recently, Asia.

SEE ALSO: Sexual Orientation and the Law; Sexual Regulation and Social Control; Tearoom Trade

REFERENCES

Bérubé, Allan. 2003. "The History of Gay Bathhouses." In *Gay Bathhouses and Public Health Policy*, edited by William J. Woods and Diane Binson. New York: Harrington Park Press.

Couture, Joseph. 2008. *Peek: Inside the Private World of Public Sex*. New York: Routledge.

Disman, Christopher. 2003. "The San Francisco Bathhouse Battles of 1984: Civil Liberties, AIDS Risk, and Shifts in Health Policy." In *Gay Bathhouses and Public Health Policy*, edited by William J. Woods and Diane Binson. New York: Harrington Park Press.

Elovitz, M. E., and P. J. Edwards. 1996. "The D.O.H. Papers: Regulating Public Sex in New York City." In *Policing Public Sex: Queer Politics and the Future of AIDS Activism*, edited by Dangerous Bedfellows. Boston: South End Press.

Hammers, Corie. 2009. "An Examination of Lesbian/Queer Bathhouse Culture and the Social Organization of (Im)Personal Sex." *Journal of Contemporary Ethnography*, 38(3): 308–335.

FURTHER READING

Bedfellows, Dangerous, eds. 1996. *Policing Public Sex: Queer Politics and the Future of AIDS Activism*. Boston: South End Press.

Freeman, Gary, ed. 2010. *The Fairoaks Project: Polaroids from a San Francisco Bathhouse 1978*. Photos by Frank Melleno. Los Angeles: drkrm/gallery.

Ko, Nai-Ying et al. 2008. "Condom Availability in Taiwanese Gay Bathhouses: The Right Things in the Wrong Places." *AIDS Education and Prevention*, 20(4): 338–346.

Leap, William L., ed. 1999. *Public Sex/Gay Space*. New York: Columbia University Press.

Wiel, Marcel. 2010. *Find Love in a Gay Bathhouse*. London: Homohappy Books.

Woods, William J., and Diane Binson, eds. 2003. *Gay Bathhouses and Public Health Policy*. New York: Harrington Park Press.

Wotherspoon, Garry. 1991. *City of the Plain: History of a Gay Sub-Culture*. Sydney: Hale & Iremonger.

Battered Women

JAMI AKE
Washington University in St. Louis, USA

"Battered women" became a recognizable term in the mid-1970s, increasingly used to describe women who were physically, psychologically, and/or sexually abused by their spouses or intimate partners. In the United States, the term emerged alongside growing social awareness of the systemic nature of domestic violence and grassroots organizing that ultimately became known as the Battered Women's Movement. This social movement, emerging as part of the larger feminist movements of the 1960s and 1970s, fostered an evolving feminist analysis of battering that located the origins of domestic violence in sexism and lodged critiques of patriarchal assumptions pervasive in culture and law that allowed such violence to continue unchecked.

As awareness of domestic violence grew in the 1970s and 1980s, activists working on behalf of battered women focused on meeting the immediate needs of abuse survivors, including the provision of emergency shelter, legal services, and other resources to ensure continued safety and independence, while also developing political strategies and coalitions at the community and state levels to change the widespread neglect of the problem.

THEORY

The focus on battered women as a specific population has shifted significantly over the last four decades. In the mid-1970s, scholars first began to turn their attention to the commonalities of battered women, with particular focus on the question of why battered women stayed in abusive relationships.

Adopting a psychological approach to answer this question, Lenore Walker (1977) observed a cycle of violence within abusive relationships that was characterized by a tension-building phase, followed by an "acute battering incident" (Walker 1977, 53), and a period of "contrite, forgiving, loving behavior" (1977, 54). Building on Martin Seligman's theory of learned helplessness, Walker suggested that this cyclic pattern of abuse leads to low self-esteem and passivity on the part of the abuse victim, who comes to view the violence as inevitable and inescapable. Walker's explanation helped give rise to the diagnosis known as battered women syndrome, a psychological condition resulting from the effects of such cyclical patterns of violence.

A decade after Walker's initial work, Edward Gondolf and Ellen Fisher (1988) countered the idea of battered women's learned helplessness, arguing that women in abusive relationships most often make rational choices of active help-seeking within the limits of their immediate contexts – efforts that in fact increased with the severity of violence.

More recently, Jill Davies and Eleanor Lyon's (2014) work has similarly framed battered women as survivors, calling critical attention to the unique circumstances of battered women as individuals and for the need to tailor "victim-defined" advocacy accordingly. Davies and Lyon observe that abusive partners often capitalize on life-generated risks (including vulnerabilities created by forms of oppression such as poverty, racism, and physical or cognitive disabilities) in exercising power and control over intimate partners, thus connecting intimate partner violence to larger social, political, and cultural forms of oppression.

LEGAL CHANGES

A great deal of early activism in the 1970s and 1980s focused on the unequal treatment of battered women in the legal system. Activists observed that law enforcement and the criminal justice system often treated those who abused their intimate partners differently from those who harmed strangers in otherwise similar assaults. Such discrimination had the result of further isolating battered women, leaving them little recourse to legal or state support. Many supporters of battered women's interests worked to rectify this unequal treatment by seeking state-sponsored solutions to the problem of battering, including improved legal protections, expanded statutes, and better informed officials within the legal system.

After a controlled experiment testing police response to battering incidents conducted by Lawrence Sherman in the early 1980s found arrest to be the best deterrent to future incidents of violence, mandatory arrest policies became a common feature of state and local domestic violence law in the United States. In addition, a series of civil law suits initiated by battered women whose appeals for help were ignored by police in the early to mid-1980s resulted in improved law enforcement protocols for protecting victims of abuse. Increasing access to civil orders of protection (also called restraining orders), the strengthening of coordinated community responses to intimate partner violence, and the innovation of specialized domestic violence courts in many places also signaled an increasingly robust criminal justice response to the problem of battering in the United States.

In many ways, the Violence Against Women Act (VAWA), first passed in 1994, achieved the goals of activists who advocated for a criminal justice approach to battering and other forms of gender-based violence. Among its many provisions, VAWA stipulated the participation of law enforcement in the programs its funding supports and created the Office on Violence Against Women within the Department of Justice. VAWA's subsequent reauthorizations (in 2000, 2005, and 2013) have expanded protections to undocumented people who are battered, Native Americans abused by non-tribal intimate partners, and LGBT survivors of violence.

As VAWA's inclusion of new populations suggests, an increasing attention to issues of intersectionality – the ways that individuals are constituted by multiple and interlocking identities – has led to an expanded understanding of battering as not limited to women or to heterosexual relationships and as a problem that affects male and transgender survivors.

Other countries have passed similar laws to protect battered women and prevent domestic violence. Such legislation includes the Intrafamily Violence Law, passed in 1994 in Chile; the Domestic Violence Act, passed in 1998 in South Africa; the Anti-Violence Against Women Act, passed in 2004 in the Philippines; and the Domestic Violence Act of 2005 in India.

In China, it is estimated that the rate of women suffering domestic abuse is about the same as in the United States, but the rate of actual reports in China is far lower. Although most provinces in China have laws against domestic abuse, they are often vaguely worded and do not include provisions for punishing offenders. There is no national law against domestic violence in China as of the writing of this entry, though the problem has been in the national conversation since 2012, when a battered woman left her famous husband, Li Yang, and posted pictures of her injuries on social media. Her act was considered heroic by many in China, where secrecy surrounding the issue is the norm. In Japan, where laws very similar to those in the United States have existed for decades, reports of domestic abuse handled by police increased by more than 20 percent from 2008 to 2009 because survivors are increasingly becoming comfortable with speaking out about their abuse, rather than adhering to the same kind of culture of secrecy around the issue.

In Uganda, men feel free to assault women in public, with complete impunity. However, in 2009, Uganda's former Vice-President, Specioza Kazibwe, Africa's highest-ranking female politician, spoke out about her own experience as a survivor of domestic abuse. Her comments have caused a stir in a society where the subject is largely taboo, but legislation toward preventing or criminalizing domestic abuse has yet to be proposed.

A law was passed in 2013 to outlaw domestic abuse in Saudi Arabia; however, women are banned from traveling outside of their homes without their male guardians, who are usually the perpetrators of such violence, so the effects of this law may be minimal at best. In many other countries, such as Pakistan, law enforcement authorities do not view domestic violence as a crime and usually refuse to register any cases brought to them.

Not all anti-violence activists endorse a criminal justice-centered approach to the problem. Critiquing legal approaches in which white, middle-class interests and versions of citizenship are often taken for granted, some activists have framed battering as one of many consequences of larger, structural inequalities that make some groups disproportionately vulnerable to intimate partner violence and disproportionately vulnerable to the negative effects of state-sponsored criminal justice solutions to it.

SEE ALSO: Domestic Violence in the United States; Gender-Based Violence; Gender Violence; Victimization

REFERENCES

Davies, Jill M., and Eleanor Lyon. 2014. *Domestic Violence Advocacy: Complex Lives/Difficult Choices*, 2nd ed. Washington DC: Sage.

Gondolf, Edward W., and Ellen R. Fisher. 1988. *Battered Women as Survivors: An Alternative to Treating Learned Helplessness*. Lexington: Lexington Books.

Walker, Lenore E. 1977. "Who Are the Battered Women?" *Frontiers: A Journal of Women Studies*, 2: 52–57.

Bear Culture

THEODORE K. GIDEONSE
University of California, Los Angeles, USA

Bear culture is a gay male subculture that originated in the United States and is particularly active in North America and Europe, with increasing presence in gay centers of South America and East Asia. While what defines a bear has always been debated by those who identify as one, archetypically gay bears are bearded, hirsute, and stocky. Bear culture encompasses other physical types named after other animals, including, among others: cubs, who are younger and often smaller bears; muscle bears, who are both muscular and thick; otters, thinner men who are hairy; polar bears, who are older and greying bears; and panda bears, who are bears of Asian descent. Bears are expected to perform hyper-masculine gendered behavior. Many bears see this behavior and the bear appearance as standing in opposition to what they consider to be a dominant gay culture that encourages a thin and hairless frame, fashion consciousness, and an effeminate affect. This differentiation includes both sexual and social segregation with distinct bars, festivals, social media sites, etc. By examining the cultural emergence of the bear community, the underpinnings of this differentiation can be understood.

The genealogy of the bear subculture can be traced to a confluence of subcultures and historical events in the mid-1980s. Since the advent of widespread gay culture in the first half of the twentieth century, masculine and feminine gay men have been polarized to varying degrees, with fairies and wolves in the early twentieth century, queens and leather men in the mid- to late twentieth century, and twinks and bears in the late twentieth and early twenty-first centuries. While many gay men have always drifted towards these extremes unconsciously, many have deliberately allied themselves with one or the other poles, often in deliberate opposition to the ideology of its opposite. The advent of bears in the mid- to late 1980s is seen partly as an extension of both the hippie-influenced Radical Faerie movement of the 1960s and the girth-and-mirth parties, "for big men and their admirers," that started at gay bars in the United States in the 1970s. Both were clearly resistant to the carefully performed and consumerist clone culture of that era. At the same time, bear culture also incorporates aspects of gay leather culture that reached its dominance and apex in the 1970s, especially in the fetishization of blue collar accoutrements. In addition, several writers have theorized that the advent of bear culture in the 1980s was a reaction to the AIDS epidemic, with a gay man's heft signaling that he was not sick. Bear culture exploded, as did all of gay culture, along with the Internet and mobile phones, with sites like Bear411 and BigMuscleBears and apps like Scruff and GROWLr providing both meeting places for bears and centers from which bear cultural tropes emanated.

Debates within bear culture about its values and meaning have been contentious since its inception. Who constitutes a bear is rarely agreed upon, with some claiming that bearness is a state of mind and simply based on self-identification and others believing that the definition should be not only rigid but carefully policed. Many bears see bear culture as inherently resistant not only to mainstream gay culture but also to mainstream culture's conception of how gay men look and behave. Hyper-masculine and often older bears are seen as contrary to superficial, youth-obsessed gay culture that is supposedly dominant in media portrayals; many bears see themselves as disruptive of gay stereotypes and celebrants of masculinity and brotherhood. At the same time, some bears criticize bears' performance of hyper-masculinity as a misogynistic reaction to the aspects of gay culture seen as feminine. These critics within the bear community also note that bear bars and events are as unwelcoming to women as they are to gay men perceived as twinks. As bear culture has spread across the world, encouraged by the Internet and circuit parties catering to bears like Lazy Bear and BEARCelona, these historical, political, and ideological issues have been subsumed by a globalized and shallower bear culture of circuit parties, internationally known bear bars, and global bear porn stars that have homogenized the image of iconic bears as typically white, muscular, dark haired, and middle class.

As broadly based and increasingly populated as bear culture is now, surprisingly little academic research has focused on bears, especially compared with the leather and drag subcultures. Two anthologies *The Bear Book* (Wright 1997) and *The Bear Book II* (Wright 2001) compile academic, historical, and testimonial works, while *Bears on Bears* (Suresha 2002a) features interviews with bears about bear culture. However, the anthropological and sociological analysis of bear culture, its formation, spread, diffusion, and gender politics have not yet resulted in full monographs and only a few peer-reviewed publications, while popular, consumer-oriented cultural analysis has been published by promoters and elders within bear culture. While gay men as a broad culture have higher rates of HIV, STDs, addiction, and depression, these and other health issues particular to bears have been understudied; this includes obesity, steroid misuse, and sleep apnea, among others.

While also under-analyzed, bear culture as represented in the arts, however, is increasing, with the animated American cable comedy *Chozen* (DeKernion 2014); feature films like the Spanish film *Cachorro* (or "Bear Cub") (Albaladejo 2004) and the American films *BearCity* (Langway 2010) and *BearCity 2* (Langway 2012); web series *Where the Bears Are* (Dietl 2012) and *Bulk* (Christopher, J. Julian 2011); comic books such as *Wuvable Oaf* (Luce 2008) and *Shirtlifter* (MacIsaac 2010); anthologies of erotica like *Bearotica* (Suresha 2002b) and *Bear Lust* (Suresha 2004); and bear-identified musical acts like Big Dipper, Matt Alber, and Bear Force 1.

SEE ALSO: Gender Performance; Masculinities; Masculinism

REFERENCES

Albaladejo, Miguel. 2004. *Bear Cub*. [Comedy, Drama.]
Christopher, J. Julian. 2011. *Bulk*. [Web. Romance, Drama.]
DeKernion, Grant. 2014. *Chozen*. [Animation, Comedy.]
Dietl, Joe. 2012. *Where the Bears Are*. [Web. Comedy, Mystery.]
Langway, Douglas. 2010. *BearCity*. [Comedy.]
Langway, Douglas. 2012. *BearCity 2: The Proposal*. [Comedy.]
Luce, Ed. 2008. *Wuvable Oaf. #1 #1*. San Francisco: Goteblüd Comics.
MacIsaac, Steve. 2010. *Shirtlifter. 1 1*. Long Beach: Drawn, Out Press.
Suresha, Ron Jackson. 2002a. *Bears on Bears: Interviews and Discussions*. Los Angeles: Alyson Books.
Suresha, Ron Jackson. 2002b. *Bearotica: Hot, Hairy, Heavy Fiction*. Los Angeles: Alyson Books.
Suresha, Ron Jackson. 2004. *Bear Lust: Hot, Hairy, Heavy Fiction*. Los Angeles: Alyson Books.
Wright, Les K. 1997. *The Bear Book: Readings in the History and Evolution of a Gay Male Subculture*. New York: Harrington Park Press.
Wright, Les K. 2001. *The Bear Book II: Further Readings in the History and Evolution of a Gay Male Subculture*. New York: Harrington Park Press.

FURTHER READING

Butler, Judith. 1990. *Gender Trouble: Feminism and the Subversion of Identity*. New York: Routledge.

Beauty Industry

SAMANTHA KWAN
University of Houston, USA

Every society has cultural ideals that define physical attractiveness. For example, today the feminine beauty ideal in the United States is taut and slender. In contrast, in some West African countries, the feminine beauty ideal is voluptuous and heavy set. Where beauty ideals come from is open to debate. On the one hand, some evolutionary psychologists argue that desirable characteristics, such as large breasts for women and broad shoulders in men, signify reproductive potential and the ability to protect offspring. On the other hand, some sociologists argue that beauty ideals are socially constructed, that is, they are by-products of humans and social institutions such as the mass media. A social constructionist argument maintains that the beauty industry plays a key role in creating these ideals.

Businesses that sell cosmetics, clothing, and related products comprise the beauty industry. Estimates indicate that the US cosmetics industry alone generates annual revenue of $50 billion. The beauty industry is also closely related to the diet industry, which produces a plethora of weight-loss products ranging from diet soda to appetizer suppressants, and also to the cosmetic surgery industry, which provides myriad surgical procedures (such as breast augmentation) and non-surgical procedures (such as Botox) to help consumers achieve their beauty goals.

Beauty industry businesses use advertisements to convince the public to purchase products. These advertisements market the message that purchasing a specific brand of, say, cosmetics or lingerie will increase a consumer's physical attractiveness, including sexual appeal. In this way, marketers create what scholars refer to as a "culture of lack." By telling consumers that their bodies are wanting in some way, consumers are encouraged to purchase goods and services to help fill this void. Critics have attacked the beauty industry for this and on other grounds.

Public interest groups, for instance, accuse the industry of selling products that endanger consumers' health. These critics maintain that some beauty products such as shampoos, lotions, and lipsticks contain unhealthy ingredients. For example, consumer advocates warn that parabens often found in cosmetics can cause allergic reactions and even breast tumors. The American Cancer Society has now encouraged large-scale studies to determine the effect of parabens on breast cancer risk.

Animal rights advocates also criticize the beauty industry for its use of animal testing, especially because the *Federal Food, Drug, and Cosmetic Act,* regulated by the US Food and Drug Administration (FDA), does not require animal tests to demonstrate the safety of cosmetics. These tests, performed mostly on mice, rats, rabbits, and guinea pigs, include skin and eye irritation tests, repeated force feeding, and "lethal dose" tests that force animals to ingest large quantities of a test chemical to determine the amount leading to death.

Feminist activists and scholars are also vocal critics of the beauty industry. In *The Beauty Myth*, third-wave feminist Naomi Wolf (1991) contends that, in the name of profit, the beauty industry creates unrealistic physical attractiveness ideals that the vast majority of women will fail to achieve. This is especially the case today as photo-manipulation techniques such as airbrushing are commonplace. Ultimately, Wolf concludes that preoccupation with beauty ideals is detrimental to women and girls. It can compromise their mental and physical health, as evident in lowered self-esteem and increased susceptibility to eating disorders.

Feminist activists and scholars also criticize beauty industry advertisements, asserting that they present a narrow image of physical attractiveness. Specifically, advertisements tend to depict thin, young, and able-bodied women alongside young, muscular, and able-bodied men. Advertisements tend to privilege height and "whiteness" as embodied in, for example, light skin and hair. By "symbolically annihilating" social groups such as heavy-set individuals, racial and ethnic minorities, and individuals with disabilities, these advertisements send the message that these groups are not valued and do not embody society's physical attractiveness ideal.

Feminist scholars further criticize beauty industry advertisements on the grounds that they objectify women by presenting them as sexual objects for a heterosexual male audience. For example, some advertisements do not depict a woman's whole body, but instead reduce her to specific body parts such as her lips, breasts, and legs. Female models also appear in sexually explicit positions and dressed in scantily clad attire. Moreover, some advertisements trivialize violence against women (or even make violence appear sexy) by staging men in these advertisements as cool, strong, and powerful, and women as submissive, willing, and passive victims. Some critics maintain that media objectification occurs with girls at increasingly younger ages, and warn that objectification can result in self-objectification that can lead to shame and appearance anxiety.

In light of these criticisms of the beauty industry, consumers are now demanding safer beauty products, are turning to cruelty-free companies that do not test on animals, and are campaigning for increased FDA regulation. Feminist groups are also pressing companies for more responsible advertisements that depict realistic beauty ideals and that do not derogate women and girls (and also men and boys). Resistance to the beauty industry is also evident in the celebration of body diversity.

SEE ALSO: Body Politics; Cosmetic Surgery in the United States; Dieting; Eating Disorders and Disordered Eating; Images of Gender and Sexuality in Advertising

REFERENCE

Wolf, Naomi. 1991. *The Beauty Myth: How Images of Beauty are used Against Women*. New York: William Morrow.

FURTHER READING

Bordo, Susan. 2003. *Unbearable Weight: Feminism, Western Culture, and the Body*, 2nd ed. Berkeley: University of California Press.
Fraser, Laura. 1998. *Losing It: False Hopes and Fat Profits in the Diet Industry*. New York: Plume.
Kilbourne, Jean. 1999. *Can't Buy My Love: How Advertising Changes the Way We Think and Feel*. New York: Touchstone.
Kilbourne, Jean. 2010. *Killing Us Softly 4: Advertising's Image of Women*. Northampton, MA: Media Education Foundation.
Levin, Diana E., and Jean Kilbourne. 2008. *So Sexy So Soon: The New Sexualized Childhood, and What Parents Can Do To Protect Their Kids*. New York: Ballantine Books.
Termini, Roseann B., and Leah Tressler. 2008. "American Beauty: An Analytical View of the Past and Current Effectiveness of Cosmetic Safety Regulations and Future Direction." *Food and Drug Law Journal*, 63: 257–274.

Berdache

ROBYN RYLE
Hanover College, USA

Berdache, or two-spirit, is a gender-variant category within some Native American tribal groups. The existence of berdache demonstrates the socially constructed nature of sex/gender systems across different cultures, in that two-spirit individuals are seen as neither male nor female, but an entirely different sex/gender category (Nanda 2000). The term "berdache" derives from early European explorers' encounters with two-spirit individuals. It was used by early French explorers, who adapted a Persian word, *bardaj*, which means an intimate male friend. As a word applied by outsiders and based on a misunderstanding of the nature of two-spirit individuals in Native American culture, berdache is generally seen as an offensive term. Two-spirit was coined in the 1990s by urban American Indians in order to emphasize the spiritual nature of this gender-variant role. However, the term two-spirit still reflects a binary gender system (male/female), which is not consistent with many Native American cultures with three or four sex/gender categories. The use of the terms two-spirit and berdache also disguises the important variation across Native American groups, collapsing the unique names for these roles (for example, *nádleehí* among the Navajo, *alyha* among the Mohave, *hetaneman* among the Cheyenne, etc.) under one label, which emphasizes similarities rather than differences (Epple 1998).

Early European explorers condemned berdache individuals they observed as sodomites, and up until the late nineteenth century little research was conducted on this aspect of tribal culture. Research in the early twentieth century saw this form of gender variance as an example of "institutionalized homosexuality," a social role that served as a structural outlet for individuals whose sexual preferences and gender expressions did not fit into the norms prescribed for their sex/gender (Whitehead 1981). This framework saw gender variance among Native American groups as a way for cowardly or failed men to avoid performing their masculine roles. Subsequent research approaches emphasized the spiritual role of berdache individuals, as well as their centrality rather than marginality to Native American cultures.

The existence of multiple sex/gender systems varies across Native American groups. Male gender-variant roles are more common than female gender-variant roles and have been documented in 110 to 150 societies. These roles are more common in the North American region extending from California to the Mississippi Valley, as well as the upper Great Lakes, the Plains and the Prairies, and the Southwest. Multiple sex/gender systems exist to a lesser extent among the Northwest Coast tribes and have not been well documented among eastern North American groups, though this may be because the roles existed but disappeared before they were recorded (Callender and Kochems 1983).

Despite variations in how gender-variant identities manifested and were understood in Native American cultures, there are some commonalities across different groups. Gender-variant individuals sometimes, but not always, dressed as the other sex. More important than dress to the gender-variant role was the occupation of berdache. The crucial way in which gender-variant individuals demonstrated their identity was through the adoption of the activities associated with the other sex. Recruitment to the berdache role often resulted from a young boy demonstrating interest in the implements and activities of women or from a girl's interest in male tools and activities. Among some groups, female gender variants took on the male warrior role, sometimes with great success. Male gender variants were often prosperous because they were seen as especially skilled and industrious in many women's crafts and domestic work.

Sexual behavior was not an important component of how this gender-variant role was understood. Among some groups, male gender variants had sexual relationships with men, while in other groups male berdache engaged in sexual relationships with both women and men. These relationships were not considered homosexual in the contemporary Western conceptualization of that term. Because berdache individuals were considered a third or fourth sex/gender category, sexual acts between them and a non-gender-variant individual were not seen as same-sex sexual behavior. A different set of norms applied to non-gender-variant individuals who engaged in same-sex sexual behavior. The sexual partners of berdache individuals were not viewed as gender variants themselves. In this particular sex/gender system, sexual behavior was a result of gender variation rather than a cause for it. Individuals became berdache because they wanted to live as another gender and not in order to be able to engage in sexual relations with someone of the same sex.

The association of the berdache role with sacred power was prevalent across many different Native American groups. Recruitment to the role sometimes took the form of a spiritual vision or dream. Among some groups, gender-variant individuals were believed to be endowed with special healing powers. In some tribes, berdache individuals filled unique ritual functions (Williams 1992; Jacobs, Thomas, and Lang 1997).

Female gender-variant roles occur more frequently among Native American cultures than among others, though less so than male gender-variant roles (Jacobs, Thomas, and Lang 1997). Estimates suggest female berdache occurred in only one quarter to one half of all the societies with male gender-variant roles. As with male berdache, the sexual relationships of female gender variants varied greatly.

Contemporary research on berdache traditions attempts to understand gender variance without imposing Western categories and beliefs about sexuality and gender (Epple 1998). The emphasis on gender and sexuality as the most salient aspects of berdache identities presumes that these are the most important traits associated with these statuses, though this may not be the case from the contemporary and historical perspective of Native American groups themselves.

SEE ALSO: Gender Variance; Sexualities; Third Genders; Two-Spirit

REFERENCES

Callender, Charles, and Lee Kochems. 1983. "The North American Berdache." *Current Anthropology*, 24(4): 443–456. (Commentary, pp. 456–70.)

Epple, Carolyn. 1998. "Coming to Terms with Navajo 'nádleehí': A Critique of 'Berdache,' 'Gay,' 'Alternate' and 'Two-Spirit'." *American Ethnologist*, 25(2): 267–290.

Jacobs, Sue-Ellen, Wesley Thomas, and Sabine Lang, eds. 1997. *Two-Spirit People: Native American Gender Identity, Sexuality, and Spirituality*. Urbana: University of Illinois Press.

Nanda, Serena. 2000. *Gender Diversity: Cross-cultural Variations*. Long Grove, IL: Waveland Press.

Whitehead, Harriet. 1981. "The Bow and the Burden Strap: A New Look at Institutionalized Homosexuality in Native North America." In *Sexual Meanings: The Cultural Construction of Gender and Sexuality*, edited by Sherry B. Ortner and Harriet Whitehead, 80–115. Cambridge: Cambridge University Press.

Williams, Walter. 1992. *The Spirit and the Flesh: Sexual Diversity in American Indian Culture*. Boston: Beacon Press.

Bifurcated Consciousness

JULIE ANN HARMS CANNON
Seattle University, USA

BIFURCATED CONSCIOUSNESS AND THE LIVES OF THE OPPRESSED

The concept of bifurcated consciousness has given scholars a way to address the duality of experiences among oppressed groups. More specifically, oppression is understood in the context of the dominant culture as well as identifying the everyday lived realities of the oppressed. Although initially used in analyzing the experiences of African Americans in the United States following the Civil War, bifurcation has also been used to identify the experiences of women in general and the experiences of diverse groups of women more specifically. The following addresses *double-consciousness* for African Americans as formulated by W.E.B. Du Bois, women and the *feminine mystique* for Betty Friedan, Dorothy Smith's *bifurcated consciousness* of women within sociology and sociological discourse, the *decentering* of African American women for bell hooks, the *outsider-within* for African American women as developed by Patricia Hill Collins, and Gloria Anzaldúa's *borderland* experienced by some Latinas. Indeed, when the fragmentation of the oppressed is reconciled with a deeper understanding of oppressive social structures and ideologies, the individual consciousness is transformed, creating both a more authentic sense of self/group and the deconstruction and reimagining of dominant ideologies and practices. Racism, sexism, heterosexism, classism, feminism, Western thought, and other sources of oppression are best changed from below, from those who experience them in their everyday lives.

DOUBLE-CONSCIOUSNESS IN THE WORKS OF W.E.B. DU BOIS

Although not specifically addressing gender issues, W.E.B. Du Bois was one of the first to develop what has come to be known as *bifurcated consciousness* as it relates to oppressed groups. This term was derived from the work of psychologist Oswald Kulpe in 1893: "the phenomenon of double consciousness or the divided self … characterized by the existence of a more or less complete separation of two aggregates of conscious process … oftentimes of entirely opposite character" (Introduction to *Souls of Black Folk* by Henry Louis Gates, Jr., 1989, xix). Du Bois used the term to describe the often painful condition of legally free African Americans living in the United States after slavery. The pervasive racism during his lifetime, and arguably today, left Du Bois to address what he termed, *double-consciousness*.

This gift of second sight left African Americans with the ability to understand both the laws that made them free as well as the societal practices and thought that left individuals imprisoned almost as surely as did slavery. According to Du Bois:

> It is a peculiar sensation, this double-consciousness, this sense of always looking at one's self through the eyes of others, of measuring one's soul by the tape of a world that looks on in amused contempt and pity. One ever feels his twoness – an American, a Negro; two souls, two thoughts, two unreconciled strivings; two warring ideals in one dark body, whose dogged strength alone keeps it from being torn asunder. (Du Bois, 1989, 3)

Accordingly, for Du Bois (1989) it is the aim of every individual, regardless of skin color, to seek "true self-consciousness," an understanding of the self from within rather than through the lens of the dominant culture. Interestingly, while double consciousness poses challenges and often pain for those experiencing its contradictions, Du Bois argues that it is not a weakness, it is a gift. The gift of "second sight" allows African Americans to see themselves through their own cultural lens as well as through the eyes of whites. However, while African Americans have a much clearer understanding of the dominant culture in general and their specific views of African Americans, the same cannot be said of whites. They do not develop a true understanding of African Americans because this knowledge is unnecessary for their survival. Therefore, while this "gift" allows African Americans to function within a racist society with a more complete knowledge of how they appear to whites, thus contributing to their ability to survive in a racist society, this same understanding or knowledge can lead to the internalization of both racism and shame. Thus, navigating between two cultures requires an understanding of both dominance and oppression. Further, it requires strength on the part of the oppressed to acknowledge the historical struggle of African Americans that speaks to a specific cultural worldview or truth, while simultaneously rejecting the views of whites as unfounded, stemming from a socially constructed ideology that perpetuates racism and the inferiority of African Americans.

FEMININE MYSTIQUE AND BIFURCATED CONSCIOUSNESS

Betty Friedan's powerful work, *The Feminine Mystique* (1997) facilitated the development of "woman consciousness" in the mid-twentieth century. During this time, many women who had been called to work during World War II because of the absence of men were sent back into the home in order for men to move into their rightful positions in the workforce. Many women who had enjoyed life outside the home as college students and as workers were now culturally denied these opportunities (although it should be noted that poor women and women of color have always worked, so the shift from work and education back to housewifery was more keenly felt by white working class and middle class women). During this time, many women still yearned for education and work outside the home, but culturally this was not the sanctioned role for women (Friedan 1997). Brief sojourns in both education and work were now viewed as opportunities to find a spouse and fulfill the cultural mandate of the gender binary, thus limiting women to the private sphere of the home, while men thrived in the public spheres of college and work.

Having had a taste of freedom and possibilities in education or a brief career life, many women became discontented housewives, mirroring the struggle of *double-consciousness* among free African Americans. Not surprisingly, a large number found themselves sinking into deep depressions that were seemingly abnormal given the societally prescribed roles women were encouraged to desire for themselves and others (Friedan 1997). It was difficult for women to process this pain in the light of their "successes" as women – obtaining the right husband, home, and children. This duality of "success" and "discontent" was termed *the feminine mystique* by Friedan (1997). Women had internalized the patriarchal ideology of the division of labor, but somehow it left them alone, warring with the constraints of the home and the individual desire to do something more. Many women sought medical help for this condition – although they had not named it as such for themselves. Doctors began prescribing medications to alleviate this abnormality and women were grateful. Unfortunately, the medications could not quench their desires for something more.

However, as women began to discuss their struggles with one another, they found out that they were not alone; indeed, it was very common for women to have aspirations beyond their husbands, homes, and children (Friedan 1997). The development of "women's consciousness" for some and "feminist consciousness" for others, led to the articulation of women's oppression within patriarchal society. Similarly to Du Bois, Friedan explained how rejecting the internalization of dominant cultural ideologies becomes a survival mechanism for the oppressed and facilitates the development of an identity that speaks to the experiences of women, particularly white middle-class and upper middle-class women.

Following the development of women's consciousness, Dorothy E. Smith began to formulate an understanding of women's dual position within the academy more generally, and sociology more specifically in her work, *The Everyday World as Problematic: A Feminist Sociology* (1987). Just as Du Bois named the cultural framework of white racism that led to the *double-consciousness* experienced by African Americans and Friedan named the ideological determinant of the feminine mystique the gendered expectations of women, Smith works to explain the everyday world of women as scholars and subjects of sociological research. Smith (1987) critiques the *relations of ruling* in sociology:

> We are looking at a gender organization of the apparently neutral and impersonal rationality of the ruling apparatus. The male subtext concealed beneath its apparently impersonal forms is integral not accidental. Women were excluded from the practices of power within these textually mediated relations of ruling. (Smith 1987, 4)

Interestingly, as Smith (1987) notes, she was not trained to see the gendered nature of the relations of ruling. The nature of this relationship came to her as she worked to pursue her academic life at the University of California, Berkeley while simultaneously carrying on with life as a single mother with two children. She made the case that these two worlds or "modes of consciousness could not coexist with one another" (Smith 1987, 7). In fact, trying to maintain both levels of consciousness was stressful and led to a *bifurcated consciousness* among women: "The strains and anxieties involved in putting and holding together work sites, schedules, and modes of consciousness that were not coordinated marked the separations institutionalized in a gender division of labor" (Smith 1987, 46).

Consequently, in the gendered world of sociology women were silenced. Their experiences did not relate to those of their male peers or faculty, thus women felt alienated and silenced in a discipline designed to account for masculine ways of knowing and explaining the world. But how does the silencing of women in sociology operate? How are women alienated and left with a bifurcated consciousness of their own everyday lived experience as well as in their experiences of the discipline of sociology? According to Smith (1987) it is not due to the "rough stuff" of active discrimination such as occurred with the medicalization of midwifery, or against those women seeking to become physicians. Instead, the discrimination takes on a subtler no less devastating form as it becomes ingrained within the organizational processes of institutions. She uses women's institutional exclusion from education as one example. Women are under-represented as part of the faculty in community colleges and universities, and also as officers of professional organizations. "We find in general that the closer positions come to policymaking or innovation in ideological forms, the smaller the proportion of women. Power and authority in the educational process are the prerogatives of men" (Smith 1987, 29).

For Smith, women had to be brought into the center of sociology as both researchers and as subjects. Sociology would need to begin from the everyday lived experiences of women. Given their outsider status, Smith (1987) calls for the creation of a sociology for women. However, a "sociology for women does not mean a sociology exclusively for women. It means a sociology that addresses society and social relations from the standpoint of women situated *outside* rather than within the relations of ruling" (Smith 1987, 46). It should be noted that this work was not to be engaged in solely by women. It was to be created by anyone who had the experience of standing outside of the relations of ruling, thus working to challenge the dominant discourse and creating a more inclusive space for those with alternative ways of knowing and experiencing the world.

BLACK FEMINIST THOUGHT AND CHICANA FEMINISM: OUTSIDERS' EXPERIENCES IN THE BORDERLANDS

Although Smith (1987) encourages sociology to broaden its perspective on who can produce knowledge and what constitutes knowledge, she only takes us as far as the male/female binary. More specifically, while she does acknowledge social class to some extent, she does not consider "whiteness" in the relations of ruling. For Smith, it is enough to begin from the position of women – although she acknowledges the importance of race as well, she explicitly states that this is not her work. bell hooks (1984), Patricia Hill Collins (2000), and Gloria Anzaldúa (2012) assert that while feminists such as Friedan and Smith have made an important start, they have silenced women of color and lesbians. Consequently, the oppressed are better equipped to create a feminism from below:

> Those of us who stand outside the circle of this society's definition of acceptable women; those of us who have been forged in the crucibles of differences – those of us who are poor, who are lesbians, who are Black, who are older know that *survival is not an academic skill ... For the master's tools will never dismantle the master's house.* (Lorde 2007, 112)

bell hooks and Patricia Hill Collins are African American feminists. However, their contributions to the field are somewhat different. First, hooks takes feminism to task for its limited focus on white women. Specifically, in *Feminist Theory: From Margin to Center*, hooks (1984) writes that "feminism in the United States has never emerged from the women who are most victimized by sexist oppression; women who are daily beaten down, mentally, physically, and spiritually – women who are powerless to change their condition in life" (hooks 1984, 1). More directly, she critiques Betty Friedan's work noting that it "actually referred to the plight of a select group of white, college educated, middle and upper-class, married white women – housewives bored with leisure, with the home, with children, with buying products, who wanted more out of life" (hooks 1984, 1). From these passages it is clear that African American women are *decentered* or left out of the women's movement. Additionally, she argues that the feminist struggle to obtain equality with men has alienated African American women. To centralize the struggle means recognizing the intersectionality of sex, race, and class oppression – for this reason African American men are more often recognized as comrades in the political struggle to end racism, rather than simply labeling them oppressors.

Patricia Hill Collins works to make black feminist thought more specific. In many ways she extends the earlier efforts of Dorothy Smith. She is working to create a more inclusive feminism and sociology. In *Black Feminist Thought: Knowledge, Consciousness, and the Politics of Empowerment* (2000) she presents a critical social theory that is written from the perspective of African American women. She argues that African American women have always been producers of knowledge, but that the forms and expressions this work has taken has existed outside the dominant discourse. She uses both historical and contemporary works to empower African American women. This work comes from the shared oppression experienced by African American women who have been excluded from the relations of ruling. Their *outsider-within* experiences are related to their "other" status or "assumptions on which full group membership are based – whiteness for feminist thought, maleness for Black social and political thought, and the combination for mainstream scholarship – all negate Black women's realities" (Collins 2000, 15). Similar to Du Bois, Collins argues that this outsider position lends itself to a unique vantage point for African American women, making them better able to discern power relationships within oppressive social dynamics. Central to the development of this thought are African American women intellectuals. However, the term intellectual is not limited to those who hold academic positions. Rather, Collins (2000) argues that all African American women share in the possibility of developing black feminist thought given their experiences as members of a subjugated group, or as outsiders-within. It is up to contemporary African American women intellectuals to reclaim the voices of those whose work remains outside the dominant discourse both within and outside of academia. More specifically Collins states: "Black women intellectuals are neither all academics nor found primarily in the Black middle-class. Instead, all U.S. Black women who somehow contribute to Black feminist thought as critical social theory are deemed to be 'intellectuals'" (Collins 2000, 15). Calling on the voices of women such as Anna Julie Cooper, Zora Neale Hurston, Audre Lorde, Ma Rainey, Bessie Smith, Maria Stewart, Sojourner Truth, Mary Helen Washington, Ida B. Wells-Barnett among many others, African American women work together to develop a "black women's consciousness" that more closely mirrors the everyday lived experiences of African Americans both historically and presently.

Offering a Chicana lesbian feminist critique of race, class, and gender oppression is Gloria Anzaldúa in *Borderlands/La Frontera: The New Mestiza* (2012). Similar to Smith's bifurcated consciousness and Collins' outsider-within, Anzaldúa writes of the alienating experiences of life lived on the border:

The Borderlands are physically present whenever two or more cultures edged each other, where people of different races occupy the same territory, where under, lower, middle and upper classes touch, where the space between two individuals shrinks with intimacy. (Anzaldúa 2012, 19)

These borders, literal and figurative, are sights for the development of both alienation and *mestiza consciousness*: "She has discovered that she can't hold concepts or ideas in rigid boundaries… Rigidity means death" (Anzaldúa 2012, 101). The new mestiza occupies multiple identities and transverses multiple borders simultaneously. Her sexuality, race, class, and gender are synthesized or joined; she has discovered herself, her consciousness. As a "border woman," Anzaldúa speaks of both joy and pain as she claims her intersectionality and the knowledge that "opened the locked places in me and taught me first how to survive and then how to soar" (2012, 19). Anzaldúa takes the idea of bifurcated consciousness further than the authors noted above. She identifies multiple points of rupture where her identity as a Chicana lesbian feminist is challenged. In terms of race she considers the potential of linking her native voice with her Chicana voice, and also her Chicano feminism in the context of white feminism. Additionally, in terms of sexuality she considers her lesbian voice as it is positioned within white feminism and Latina/o culture. Finally, there is the literal border between Texas and Mexico which she has to transverse physically and metaphorically in both her work and her identity. This complexity of consciousness facilitates the journey from standpoint feminism to a more intersectional feminism that works to identify all facets of individual and group consciousness.

SEE ALSO: Critical Race Theory; Feminist Standpoint Theory; Gender Identities and Socialization; Gender, Politics, and the State: Overview; Intersectionality

REFERENCES

Anzaldúa, Gloria. 2012. *Borderlands/La Frontera: The New Mestiza*. San Francisco: Aunt Lute Books. First published 1987.

Collins, Patricia Hill. 2000. *Black Feminist Thought: Knowledge, Consciousness, and the Politics of Empowerment*. New York: Routledge. First published 1990.

Du Bois, W.E.B. 1989. *The Souls of Black Folk*. New York: Bantam Books. First published 1903.

Friedan, Betty. 1997. *The Feminine Mystique*. New York: Norton. First published 1963.

hooks, bell. 1984. *Feminist Theory: From Margin to Center*. Boston: South End Press.

Lorde, Audre. 2007. *Sister Outsider*. New York: Crossing Press. First published 1984.

Smith, Dorothy E. 1987. *The Everyday World as Problematic: A Feminist Sociology*. Boston: Northeastern University Press.

FURTHER READING

Allen, Paula Gunn. 1986. *The Sacred Hoop: Recovering the Feminine in American Indian Traditions*. Boston: Beacon Press.

de Beauvoir, Simone. 2011. *The Second Sex*. New York: Vintage Books. First published 1949.

Friedan, Betty. 1981. *The Second Stage*. New York: Summit Books.

hooks, bell. 2015. *Ain't I a Woman: Black Women and Feminism*. New York: Routledge. First published 1981.

Millett, Kate. 1969. *Sexual Politics*. New York: Ballantine Books.

Moraga, Cherríe. 1983. *Loving in the War Years: Lo Que Nunca Paso Por Sus Labios*. Boston: South End Press.

Tong, Rosemarie. 2009. *Feminist Thought*. Philadelphia: Westview Press.

Biochemistry and Physiology

DAVID A. RUBIN
University of South Florida, USA

Biochemistry uses molecular methods to study chemical processes in organic systems.

Physiology is the study of integrated function among organisms, organs, cells, and molecules in bionetworks and ecosystems. Long-standing arguments about nature versus nurture and essentialism versus constructionism notwithstanding, biochemistry and physiology explain some – though not all – of the many dimensions of sex and gender. To outline these explanations, first it is important to note that historically the scientific study of male and female differences and bodies has been shaped by gender biases, or ungrounded and culture-specific assumptions about the nature of masculinity and femininity (Fausto-Sterling 1985). Instances where gender ideology has inflected research design, data collection, or the interpretation of results include descriptions of the egg and the sperm in twentieth-century biology textbooks (Martin 1991), estimates of mathematical ability among boys and girls (Fausto-Sterling 2000), and the scientific classification of the steroids estrogen and testosterone as female and male hormones, respectively (Oudshoorn 1994). These examples show that science is not a pure "mirror of nature," but rather an interpretive grid through which people narrativize various phenomena using the epistemological resources available in particular times and places (Keller 2010). Science is situated knowledge, always partial, incomplete, dynamic, open to revision, and contested (Haraway 1988). Nowhere is this more apparent than in the biochemistry and physiology of sex and gender.

While the degree to which feminist critiques have impacted scientific practice is difficult to ascertain, contemporary research in biochemistry and physiology has advanced significantly beyond the monocausal explanations of sex and gender that once dominated these fields. Scientists have come to define sex as anatomically multidimensional and molecularly polygenic, which is to say that any hope that the definition of sex would somehow ultimately boil down to a single, straightforward, and uniform binary formulation appears to be dwindling, if not altogether dashed. Scientists are also investigating the biochemical, physiological, and neurological aspects of gender (sense of self as masculine or feminine), but at present findings are incongruous and inconclusive.

The sex/gender distinction – which traditionally figures sex as biological and gender as social – can be traced to the mid-twentieth-century research of psychoendocrinologist John Money and his various collaborators (Money 1955). The distinction was adapted by British and American second-wave feminist scholars, who documented the historical and cultural contingency of gender inequalities in order to dismantle claims that women's subordination was biologically predestined. Money, on the other hand, used the term *gender role* to refer to the psychosocial imprinting of masculine and feminine forms of personhood, outlook, and behavior. Studying intersex individuals (whose chromosomal and/or hormonal makeup was found to be discordant with their gonadal, internal reproductive, or genital morphology), Money recognized that sex is multilayered. That is, he acknowledged that no single biological factor alone determines sex. However, though his research initially destabilized the idea that sex has a unitary basis, Money used the concept of gender role to make the potential masculinity or femininity of an intersex person the definitive gauge of how they should be sexed using surgical, hormonal, and psychological technologies of normalization, a gesture that paradoxically restabilized the binary conception of sex in the medical sciences (Rubin 2012). Over the past several decades, scientists and social scientists have reworked as well as challenged Money's theories (Kessler 1990; Diamond and Sigmundson 1997). Meanwhile, activist organizations such as the now-defunct Intersex Society of North America have voiced serious ethical concerns about his treatment paradigm.

Despite the skepticism about Money's research that surfaced in the 1990s, scientists today generally embrace his multilayered model of sex. Fetal sex in humans has five layers (chromosomal, hormonal, gonadal, internal reproductive, and genital), each of which can function independently of the others. Importantly, despite the extensive body of scientific literature on sex differences, none of these layers has been shown to be the absolute determinant of all the others. Transitions across the lifespan from infancy to adolescence and adulthood add a number of extra layers to human sex (e.g., sex of rearing, pubertal hormonal sex, pubertal morphology, and others), which has led to the recognition that sex is dynamic and morphs as individuals develop. Biochemists and physiologists study all of these markers as they interact with one another in processes of male, female, transsexual, transgender, and intersex development.

Intersex is an umbrella term for individuals born with what Western biomedicine deems to be non-standard sexual anatomies. Among recently labeled disorders of sex development (DSDs) in biomedical discourse, there are many diagnoses – including Klinefelter's syndrome, Turner's syndrome, androgen insensitivity syndrome (AIS), congenital adrenal hyperplasia (CAH), vaginal agenesis, hypospadias, and others – that fall under the intersex umbrella. Estimations of the frequency of intersex range from .018 to 1.87 per 100 live births (Blackless et al. 2000). Without denying that intersex variations are physiological, some scholars argue that the diagnostic criteria for intersex are overdetermined by social logics (Karkazis 2008). For instance, the figures just cited do not include those conditions that are not diagnosed until later in life, or those that remain undiagnosed throughout the life course. Beyond these empirical considerations, some people (including many medical professionals) still view intersex differences as pathological, when the most comprehensive studies indicate that the majority of intersex conditions pose few if any health risks (Fausto-Sterling 2000). For this reason, some scholars hypothesize that the medicalization of people with intersex is a Western cultural artifact, akin to yet distinct from the labeling of transgender and gender non-conforming behaviors and identifications as "disorders" (Preves 2003). However, while the meaning of intersex is contingent, defined in relation to what Western biomedicine and culture more broadly consider to be normative configurations of male and female anatomy, intersex embodiment cannot be said to be solely a product of sociocultural relationships. In short, intersex reveals that both biological differences and the interpretive lenses through which people understand those differences matter.

With growing recognition of the complexity of the biochemistry and physiology of intersex in particular and sex more generally, a bimodal model of sex development with "two curves corresponding to two typical functional outcomes, male and female," with myriad possible variations plotted along and between the path of each curve, has largely replaced a strictly binary model (Rosario 2009, 278). Furthermore, the lines between intersex and non-intersex anatomies appear to be blurring under the weight of growing scientific evidence. Nevertheless, physicians continue to place the most emphasis on genitalia, as ascertained at birth, to prognosticate sex assignment, which they mostly still frame as binary due to Western cultural pressures. Feminist and queer science studies scholars have observed that the equation of genitalia with sex writ large is reductionist, shaped by heteronormative and masculinist ideologies, and highlights the role of gendered social structures in the medical construction of sex (Kessler 1990). While some feminist theorists argue that sex is already gender (Butler 1990), biochemical and physiological research suggests that sex cannot be reduced to a mere discursive construction, even as what counts as "sex" in biological explanations is shaped, in part, by extra-biological – that is, by social and linguistic – forces. This point will be taken up below.

First, it is necessary to summarize current scientific accounts of sex. Sex variation (intersexuality) and sex change (transsexuality) have been documented in numerous species. In some reptiles and fish, environmental variables such as temperature determine sex, while for some invertebrates the location of the organism is the critical factor. In most mammals, sex development begins at the chromosomal level. After fertilization, in chromosomally male (XY) and female (XX) embryos the process proceeds identically, resulting in an "equipotential" pre-gonadal structure. This indifferent gonadal tissue can develop in a number of directions.

For years, scientists searched for the biological blueprint of male development. In 1990, they located a gene on the Y chromosome that induces the indifferent gonadal tissue to develop into testis. This gene was labeled SRY (Sex Reversal on the Y chromosome) (Berta et al. 1990). Often inaccurately called the "sex-determining" chromosome, the Y does not actually shape development in XX, XXX, or XO females, but does play a role for XY, XYY, and XXY males. Subsequent studies quickly hampered the initial excitement over the discovery of SRY when they revealed that SRY alone does not dictate male development. Rather than confirming the absolute dimorphism of sex, studies of the biology of intersex individuals led to the discovery of sex-determining genes on non-sex chromosomes, such as WT-1 on chromosome 11 (Hossain and Saunders 2001). WT-1 is critical for male gonadal formation, but is also associated with female genital development in some XY individuals (Mueller 1994). Moreover, there are intersex individuals with testes who do not have the SRY gene, which implies that other genes are likely involved in testes determination when SRY is not present (Rosario 2009, 274). Currently, "genes from chromosomes 9 (SF-1), 11 (WT-1), 17 (SOX-9), 19 (MIS), and the X chromosome (DAX-1) in addition to SRY on the Y chromosome (or sometimes the X)" are considered to be "essential for the usual development of testes and male internal and external genitalia" (Rosario 2009, 274).

Generally, once the fetal testis forms, it produces two hormones that encourage internal reproductive sex to differentiate in a male direction. Anti-Mullerian Factor (AMF) "eliminates the female developmental option by causing the paramesonephric ducts to degenerate," while fetal testosterone "repurposes the mesonephric ducts, influencing them to develop into the vas deferens, epididymis, and seminal vesicle" (Fausto-Sterling 2012, 21). However, some XY intersex individuals with AIS are unable to process these hormones, or can only process them partially, and their endocrine systems transform excess androgens into estrogens, which often leads to the feminization of internal reproductive sex and/or genitalia. As this example suggests, various factors modulate the expression of hormonal sex and other primary sex characteristics, and the possible developmental pathways are multiple.

While male development has been at the epicenter of biological research during the last century, female embodiment has not received the same level of attention. For a long time, scientists incorrectly assumed that female development was a passive process and the "default" pathway, rather than an active process like male development. However, recent research has challenged this premise. Scientists have discovered that female gonadal and genital formation is not monopolized by the X chromosome, but is rather a result of genes from many chromosomes acting in conjunction with hormonal processes (Richardson 2012). Ovarian differentiation is controlled by a polygenic network that includes WNT4, formerly solely associated with kidney development, FOXL2, RSPO1, and possibly other genes as well. Interestingly, XX humans who lack RSPO1 develop testes and internal and external male genitalia even though they lack SRY (Fausto-Sterling 2012, 20). In typical processes of female development, WNT4 and RSPO1 inhibit SOX9, which causes regression of both the mesonephric ducts and testes (DiNapoli and Capel 2008). Then estrogens stimulate the paramesonephronic ducts to form the uterine tubes, uterus, cervix, and upper vagina. Some researchers hypothesize that SRY also has the ability to inhibit RSPO1, pushing sex development in a male direction.

Taken together, such findings have deconstructed the older model of female development as passive. This has led some researchers to postulate that "the bipotential gonad is the battleground between two active and opposing signaling pathways" (DiNapoli and Capel 2008, 4; cited in Fausto-Sterling 2012, 20). The process of female gonadal and genital differentiation is still being studied, and much about the factors involved remains unknown. Nonetheless, there is growing recognition that gender bias must be critically displaced in order to arrive at more objective conclusions.

Displacing such gender bias has proven difficult. According to Sarah S. Richardson, it is a misnomer to label the X the "female chromosome." Indeed, the relationship between the X chromosome and female development is not analogous to the relationship between the Y and male development. Richardson (2012) shows that gender ideology has "sexed the X" as female in scientific discourse, resulting in the erroneous ascription of feminine behavior to certain chromosomal combinations but not others. "The still very contemporary view that the double X makes females unpredictable, mysterious, chimeric, and conservative, while the single X allows men to learn, evolve, and have bigger brains but also makes them the more risk taking of the two sexes, shows how conceptions of X chromosome structure and function often reflect and support traditional gender stereotypes" (2012, 927). The attribution of gender stereotypes to biological objects of study is a recurrent problem in scientific work, one that focalizes the importance of guarding against sexist and anthropomorphic readings of molecules and cells.

A similar critique can be applied to hormonal sex. Popular accounts continue to frame testosterone as a male hormone, and while males on average have higher levels of testosterone than females, this is not the case in all species (for instance, in hyenas), and all mammals actually produce varying levels of androgens and estrogens. While fetal testosterone is associated with testis formation, and adolescent and adult testosterone has been correlated with the development of male secondary sex characteristics in humans (the dropping and deepening of the vocal cords, body and facial hair growth, and skeletal and muscular changes, among other signifiers), testosterone cannot be said to cause, in any simple sense, maleness or masculinity. In biochemical studies of aggression, which is typically thought of as a male phenomenon, researchers have shown that while aggression and testosterone are correlated in mammals, their relationship is not purely causal. Rather, aggression has a "permissive effect" on testosterone (Sapolsky 1998). That is, aggression elevates testosterone levels, which means that behavior drives hormonal changes and that the social environment has a material effect on the biochemistry and physiology of individual bodies. According to Sapolsky, it has taken a long time to convince scientists of this because there is a strong bias in favor of reductionist biological explanations of complex behavioral phenomena.

Such bias is evident not only in studies of the layers of sex discussed above, but also in another potential layer called brain sex that has become a popular object of investigation in neurology and associated fields. Brain organization theory proposes that fetal exposure to steroid hormones permanently hardwires the brain along gendered lines, laying the foundation for what will become, as the child develops into an adult, what are considered to be stereotypically "masculine" or "feminine" patterns of personhood, interests, sexuality, cognition, temperament, and psychological health that differ by sex. Rebecca Jordan-Young (2011) has argued that brain organization theory relies on a number of problematic assumptions, most notably that the fetal brain can be divided along two distinct and mutually exclusive pathways of development. Furthermore, the brain sex hypothesis cannot be tested in a pure experimental fashion because of the ethical guidelines that structure research on human subjects. Brain sex can thus only be tested with quasi-experiments, which lack the rigorous controls of all the variables involved and inevitably include an interpretive element. In an expansive review of the quasi-experimental literature on brain sex, Jordan-Young (2011) concludes that current findings contradict one another and do not provide the theory with adequate support. Despite this critique, brain sex is treated in much scientific literature as an established empirical reality rather than a hypothesis that requires further investigation. With the disintegration of the binary model of sex initiated by biochemistry and physiology looming in the wings of the sciences, brain organization theory seems to promise to return stability to the binary by reformatting the psyche/soma dualism and locating sex/gender not in the body so much as in the neurocognitive mind.

As the examples of brain sex, sex chromosomes, and hormonal sex reveal, the definition of biological objects of study takes place, in part, through social and linguistic structures that frequently reinforce gender ideology. Another case in point is the language of "male development" and "female development," which not only homogenizes each sex, obscuring key variations within and between each category, but also makes it seem as if male–female differences are biologically absolute rather than products of contingent interactions between genes, neighboring tissues, and hormones that are modulated by time, the environment, and sociocultural influences as well. The shift from a binary to a bimodal model of sex development, where sex is understood as polygenetic and multifactorial, is likely to require the formulation of new critical vocabularies that are open-ended, dynamic, and flexible enough to acknowledge the irreducible complexity and biocultural diversity of sex and gender.

One of the most innovative interdisciplinary approaches to sex/gender that has taken up this challenge is called developmental systems theory. Pioneered by feminist and queer science studies scholars such as Fausto-Sterling, Keller, and Haraway, developmental systems theory investigates the infusion and intertwining of biological and cultural systems. In this way, the field actively recognizes the limitations of the nature/nurture binary, agitates against the disciplinary and epistemological divides between the humanities, social sciences, and hard sciences, and articulates the intra-activity and consubstantiality of biological, environmental, and sociocultural agents in the constitution of embodied forms of life (Wilson 2004; Barad 2007). From a developmental standpoint, though the slash commonly inscribed between sex/gender seems to imply a clear line of demarcation, the existence of such a line cannot be taken for granted. As Fausto-Sterling puts it, "Our bodies are too complex to provide clear-cut answers about sexual difference. The more we look for a simple physical basis for 'sex,' the more it becomes clear that 'sex' is not a purely physical category. What bodily signals and functions we define as male or female come already entangled in our ideas about gender" (2000, 4). For this reason, future research on the biochemistry and physiology of sex and gender is likely to be both enriched and contested by critical supplementation from developmental systems theory and queer feminist science studies.

SEE ALSO: Androgen Insensitivity Syndrome; Biological Determinism; Feminist Studies of Science; Gender, Definitions of; Genetics Testing and Screening; Intersexuality; Neuroscience, Brain Research, and Gender; Sexology and Psychological Sex Research

REFERENCES

Barad, Karen. 2007. *Meeting the Universe Halfway: Quantum Physics and the Entanglement of Matter and Meaning*. Durham, NC: Duke University Press.

Berta, Philippe et al. 1990. "Genetic Evidence equating SRY and the Testis-Determining Factor." *Nature*, 348: 448–450.

Blackless, Melanie et al. 2000. "How Sexually Dimorphic Are We? Review and Synthesis." *American Journal of Human Biology*, 12(2): 151–166.

Butler, Judith. 1990. *Gender Trouble: Feminism and the Subversion of Identity*. New York: Routledge.

Diamond, Milton, and H. Keith Sigmundson. 1997. "Sex Reassignment at Birth: Long-Term Review and Implications." *Archives of Pediatric and Adolescent Medicine*, 151: 298–304.

DiNapoli, L., and B. Capel. 2008. "SRY and the Standoff in Sex Determination." *Molecular Endocrinology*, 22(1): 1–9.

Fausto-Sterling, Anne. 1985. *Myths of Gender: Biological Theories about Women and Men*. New York: Basic Books.

Fausto-Sterling, Anne. 2000. *Sexing the Body: Gender Politics and the Construction of Sexuality*. New York: Basic Books.

Fausto-Sterling, Anne. 2012. *Sex/Gender: Biology in a Social World*. New York: Routledge.

Haraway, Donna. 1988. "Situated Knowledges: The Science Question in Feminism and the Privilege of Partial Perspective." *Feminist Studies*, 14(3): 575–599.

Hossain, Anwar, and Grady F. Saunders. 2001. "The Human Sex-Determining Gene SRY is a Direct Target of WT1." *Journal of Biological Chemistry*, 276: 16817–16823.

Jordan-Young, Rebecca. 2011. *Brain Storm: The Flaws in the Science of Sex Differences*. Cambridge, MA: Harvard University Press.

Karkazis, Katrina. 2008. *Fixing Sex: Intersex, Medical Authority, and Lived Experience*. Durham, NC: Duke University Press.

Keller, Evelyn Fox. 2010. *The Mirage of a Space Between Nature and Nurture*. Durham, NC: Duke University Press.

Kessler, Suzanne J. 1990. "The Medical Construction of Gender: Case Management of Intersexed Infants." *Signs: Journal of Women in Culture and Society*, 16(1): 33–38.

Martin, Emily. 1991. "The Egg and the Sperm: How Science Has Constructed a Romance Based on Stereotypical Male–Female Roles." *Signs*, 16(3): 485–501.

Money, John. 1955. "Hermaphroditism, Gender and Precocity in Hyperadrenocorticism: Psychologic Findings." *Bulletin of the Johns Hopkins Hospital*, 96: 253–264.

Mueller, R. F. 1994. "The Denys-Drash Syndrome." *Journal of Medical Genetics*, 32: 471–477.

Oudshoorn, Nelly. 1994. *Beyond the Natural Body: An Archeology of Sex Hormones*. New York: Routledge.

Preves, Sharon. 2003. *Intersex and Identity: The Contested Self*. New Brunswick: Rutgers University Press.

Richardson, Sarah S. 2012. "Sexing the X: How the X Became the 'Female Chromosome'." *Signs*, 37(4): 909–933.

Rosario, Vernon. 2009. "Quantum Sex: Intersex and the Molecular Deconstruction of Sex." *GLQ*, 15(2): 267–284.

Rubin, David A. 2012. "'An Unnamed Blank that Craved a Name': A Genealogy of Intersex as Gender." *Signs*, 37(4): 883–908.

Sapolsky, Robert M. 1998. *The Trouble with Testosterone and Other Essays on the Biology of the Human Predicament*. New York: Scribner.

Wilson, Elizabeth A. 2004. *Psychosomatic: Feminism and the Neurological Body*. Durham, NC: Duke University Press.

Biological Determinism

SHEILA GREENE
Trinity College, Republic of Ireland

Biological determinism refers to the idea that human behavior originates in biological entities or processes, either innate or constitutional. Most frequently, in recent years, the causal mechanism is seen to reside in the individual's genetic makeup, which acts on behavior through the brain or the hormones. Theories colored by biological determinism can be used to explain species-specific behaviors, group differences, or differences between individuals. As a scientific viewpoint it has been applied throughout history to many different human characteristics and behaviors and has been used, often contentiously, to explain differences between people, such as those associated with race.

Biological determinism has always had strong currency in the explanation of observed differences in behavior and capacities between men and women and in accounting for differences between people in their sexual orientations and behaviors.

In relation to sex and gender, statements indicative of a biological determinist position can be found as far back as the writings of ancient Greek philosophers. For example, Aristotle said, "As regards the sexes the male is by nature superior and the female inferior, the male ruler and the female subject," and the thirteenth-century theologian St. Thomas Aquinas stated that, "As regards individual nature, woman is defective and misbegotten."

Biological determinism became one of the main targets of the feminist movement in the twentieth century. At the turn of the century women found themselves pigeon-holed and constrained by widely held assumptions that they were biologically unfit for education, sporting activity, the world of business, and so on. Freud's assertion that "anatomy is destiny" was therefore rejected by early feminists. Simone de Beauvoir's view that "One is not born a woman but becomes one" became representative of the alternate feminist stance.

Much of the work of liberal feminist researchers in the twentieth century focused on demonstrating the minimal difference between the sexes and the considerable overlap in capacities (Maccoby and Jacklin 1974). Where differences were evident, feminists advanced social explanations. For example, feminist researchers argued that the relatively weaker performance of girls in mathematics was due to lack of opportunity and negative attitudes and expectations on the part of teachers and parents rather than an inbuilt incapacity to deal with spatial and numeric concepts. More radical feminist theorists totally rejected biologically based explanations for any form of behavior, seeing it as "biological essentialism," which inevitably sets limits on what women can be and do. As a result there has been a widespread rejection of any form of theory that includes biological elements. Alternatively, the body and its functions have been seen as texts where discourses about the body – often positioned as oppressive and unhelpful discourses – dictate what is experienced by the individual. More recently in feminist writing there has been a return to some form of acceptance of the material reality of the body, with material-discursive approaches and "the new materialism" becoming more popular.

In relation to sexuality a number of different positions on the social-biological continuum have been proffered. Explanations that favor biological determinants have been seen as both negative and positive by gay, lesbian, and transgender activists. Thus the claim by Hamer et al. (1993) to have identified the "gay gene" was embraced by some activists as evidence that homosexuality was innate and therefore should not be the target of discrimination any more than the color of a person's skin or hair. However, there have been difficulties in replicating this finding. Many different biological explanations of sexual orientation have been put forward ranging from genetic differences to prenatal differences in hormonal levels, but the general consensus is that while biological factors operating via the genes or prenatally may have a role, sexual orientation is determined by many different factors and may have different causal origins across the population.

In the modern period many scientists would see biological determinism as an untenable position because of the incontrovertible evidence that human behavior is strongly influenced by social and cultural factors. Thus very few biological or social scientists would identify as hardline biological determinists and what becomes a matter of dispute is the extent to which scientists emphasize the social or biological. However, recent developments in sociobiology, evolutionary psychology and the "new genetics" have bolstered biologically based explanations of male–female differences (e.g., Buss 1995). Reflecting the contemporary interest in neuroscience, brain differences in structure and function have been emphasized by some researchers (e.g., Baron-Cohen 2004) and roundly rejected by others (e.g., Fine 2010).

Biological determinism is not only critiqued by those who favor sociocultural determinants but by those who oppose the idea that all human behavior is determined, either by biological or by social factors. A counter-deterministic or non-deterministic view of human behavior emphasizes human agency and intentionality. This viewpoint foregrounds the capacity of human persons to act on the world and respond to it in ways that are novel, creative, and essentially unpredictable (Martin, Sugarman, and Hickinbottom 2010).

Feminist biologists such as Anne Fausto-Sterling (2012) regret the neglect of biology that has been a consequence of the rejection of biological determinism. She argues that any complete and adequate view of human behavior, including gender and sexual identity, must incorporate biology and that this can be done non-reductively. Dynamic developmental models have recently come to the fore, incorporating the new perspectives offered by findings at the intersection of biology and the psycho-social sciences, such as epigenetics, and recognizing the ongoing interconnectedness of biological, social, and psychological processes (e.g., Martin and Ruble 2009).

SEE ALSO: Essentialism; Gender Difference Research; Genetics Testing and Screening; Neuroscience, Brain Research, and Sexuality

REFERENCES

Baron-Cohen, S. 2004. *The Essential Difference: Men, Women and the Extreme Male Brain*. London: Penguin.

Buss, D. 1995. "Psychological Sex Differences: Origins through Sexual Selection." *American Psychologist*, 50: 164–168.

Fausto-Sterling, A. 2012. "Not Your Grandma's Genetics: Some Theoretical Notes." *Psychology of Women Quarterly*, 36: 411–418.

Fine, C. 2010. *Delusions of Gender: The Real Science behind Sex Differences*. London: Icon Books.

Hamer, D. H., S. Hu, V. L. Magnusson, N. Hu, and A. M. Pattatucci. 1993. "A Linkage between DNA Markers on the X Chromosome and Male Sexual Orientation." *Science*, 261(5119): 321–327.

Maccoby, E. E., and C. J. Jacklin. 1974. *The Psychology of Sex Differences*. Stanford: Stanford University Press.

Martin, C. L., and D. N. Ruble. 2009. "Patterns of Gender Development." *Annual Review of Psychology*, 61: 353–381.

Martin, J., J. H. Sugarman, and S. Hickinbottom. 2010. *Persons: Understanding Psychological Selfhood and Agency*. London: Springer.

Birth Control, History and Politics of

LINDA GORDON
New York University, USA

Birth control is neither modern nor medical, and for most of its long history was uncontroversial. As far back in history as evidence is available, every society tried to practice some form of reproduction control. They were not always successful, of course. Some methods were difficult to practice, such as male withdrawal before ejaculation. Other methods were dangerous, such as taking poisons or beating the abdomen. Abortion, the most common method, done by inserting an object into the uterus, could be painful and dangerous, though nowhere near as much as childbirth. These risky procedures stand as testimony to how important it was to so many to control childbearing. But in some communities women manufactured methods both harmless and effective, covering the cervix with animal skins and spermicidal pastes (Gordon 2002, ch. 1). For most of the centuries since written records were developed, these various birth control methods were accepted as legitimate.

Political debates about reproduction control became intense in the mid-nineteenth century, when European countries and US states began to ban it. At the time, abortion was the most widely practiced birth control method, and it was widely understood as an unfortunate necessity. In all three major western religions, abortion before "quickening" – the moment when a pregnant woman could feel a fetus stir – was a respectable, traditional practice.

The first anti-birth control campaigns, beginning early in the nineteenth century, were led by Protestant ministers in both the United States and Europe; Catholic priests were then the followers, not the leaders, of this reform. At this time people made little if any distinction between abortion and what we call contraception, and opponents condemned *any* attempts to control reproduction except through sexual abstinence. Their chief arguments emphasized not protecting fetuses but rather the immorality and danger to family life of allowing women to evade their God-and-Nature-ordained role as mothers. This first political campaign to prohibit birth control was in large part a backlash against changing possibilities and aspirations among women. Industry had brought many poor women into factory employment, which in turn increased their independence and decreased birth rates. More privileged women were clamoring for education and were venturing into public political debate, notably in women's rights and anti-slavery movements. At the same time some "regular" or allopathic physicians joined the anti-abortion campaign as a means of gaining control over obstetrics, a field previously dominated by midwives.

Among Western countries, prohibitions on birth control were most draconian in the United States. Still, even there abortion never disappeared and probably did not even decline. Commercial abortionists thrived and even advertised publicly. A class double standard grew larger: prosperous women could persuade private physicians to perform abortions in the guise of treatments for medical problems, while working-class women relied on midwives or specialized, commercial abortionists. Meanwhile the nineteenth-century development of thinner, stronger, and more flexible rubber changed birth control by making possible better condoms, cervical pessaries, and vaginal diaphragms. This was the first technological improvement in contraceptive practice.

Simultaneously, several concurrent factors – urban economies and compulsory education made large numbers of children more expensive, the number of women in the out-of-home labor force increased, and Victorian sexual prudery eroded – made the prohibitions on birth control less tolerable. As a result, before and after World War I, social movements for the legalization of birth control grew exponentially. Socialists and other Leftists led, advocating women's rights, sexual freedom, and the welfare of the working classes. Emma Goldman and Margaret Sanger in the United States, Annie Besant and Marie Stopes in England, Magnus Hirschfeld in Germany, Aletta Jacobs and Johannes Rutgers in the Netherlands, to name but a few, became propagandists for the cause.

As this pressure built, 1920s birth control activists resorted to three strategic compromises and alliances in order to gain broader support. First, since effective, manufactured contraception was now available, they distinguished contraception from abortion, and pushed for legalization of the former while accepting the continued prohibition on the latter. Second, they accepted medical control over contraception and supported legislation that gave physicians the authority to prescribe it when they deemed it appropriate. And third, birth controllers in many countries built alliances with eugenists, who supported the promotion of contraception to reduce populations deemed inferior. After World War II these alliances were extended to include population controllers, who sought to reduce poverty by reducing population growth and without challenging economic and political inequality. This third compromise, identifying birth control with eugenics and population control, produced blowback that continues today, making many people of color and colonized people suspicious of birth control as a racist and imperialist strategy.

In the 1960s two new developments changed the picture: the introduction of contraceptive hormones in pill form – the second technological change in contraception – and renewed women's movements. Reproductive rights occupied a major place in feminist agendas throughout the world, and the new feminists rejected all three of the compromises outlined above. They reconceived birth control, including abortion, as a human right, and succeeded in relegalizing abortion in many countries including the United States. Global feminisms, aided by governmental and NGO aid and education campaigns, produced radical declines in family size throughout the world. By 2010, sixty-three percent of married women worldwide used contraception (Doskoch 2013). The abortion rate declined accordingly until about 2003, when increasing poverty and migratory work patterns made childbearing more burdensome (Bankole, Singh, and Haas 1998; Guttmacher Institute 2012).

Feminist movements and women's increased independence, unsurprisingly, generated a backlash, in which a second anti-abortion campaign has been its most prominent feature. (In the United States this campaign has been recently called a "war on women" by birth control advocates, but this slogan is actually a misnomer: Men as well as women rely on birth control, especially as HIV/AIDS made condom usage widespread.) The Catholic Church began this second campaign, but was soon joined by Protestant evangelicals and Jewish and Islamic fundamentalists as well. In Europe and the United States these new religious conservatives, understanding that a platform of chastity outside of marriage and motherhood as women's destiny could gain no traction, focused primarily on the rights of the fetus. The greatest achievement of this anti-abortion campaign was the invention of the "Right-to-Life" slogan, which moved many groups into an anti-abortion-rights camp.

As a result, abortion remains central in political controversies worldwide. Still, outside of Africa, majorities throughout the world support its legalization. Catholics are not more conservative than non-Catholics: only one third oppose abortion in all cases, except in Africa and Philippines where anti-abortion opinion is stronger. Support for contraception is still higher, even among Catholics (Univision n.d. – there is a great need for data on Muslims' birth control attitudes and practices). Moreover, the discrepancies between publicly professed attitudes toward birth control and actual practices suggested that anti-birth control political victories produce change in rhetoric more than in practices.

SEE ALSO: Abortion and Religion; Abortion, Legal Status in Global Perspective on; Adolescent Pregnancy

REFERENCES

Bankole, Akinrinola, Susheela Singh, and Taylor Haas. 1998. "Reasons Why Women Have Induced Abortions: Evidence from 27 Countries." *International Family Planning Perspectives*, 24(3). Accessed July 23, 2015, at http://www.guttmacher.org/pubs/journals/2411798.html.

Doskoch, P. 2013. "Global Levels of Contraceptive Use by Married Women Have Risen, Especially in Developing Countries." *International Family Planning Perspectives*, 39(2): 103–104. Accessed July 23, 2015, at https://www.guttmacher.org/pubs/journals/3910313.html.

Gordon, Linda. 2002. *The Moral Property of Women: A History of Birth Control Politics in America*. Chicago: University of Illinois Press.

Guttmacher Institute. 2012. Facts on Induced Abortion Worldwide. Accessed July 23, 2015, at http://www.guttmacher.org/pubs/fb_IAW.html.

Univision. n.d. Voice of the People. Accessed July 23, 2015, at http://www.univision.com/interactivos/openpage/2014-02-06/la-voz-del-pueblo-matriz-1.

Bisexuality

LOLA D. HOUSTON
University of Vermont, USA

Bisexuality is generally thought of as the sexual or romantic attraction to more than one sex. While this definition encompasses much of the term's commonly shared meaning, it does not convey the extent and complexity, as well as the often contentious nature of the term. Bisexuality frequently denotes sexual orientation as well as sexual identity. As such, it can encompass both behavior and identification.

Discussion over the nature of bisexuality has incorporated a broad range of subject matter and attempted to draw on a wide span of human history and prehistory. The nature of sexuality and gender frequently figures in serious research as well as in social and political discussions. Disagreements over whether or not bisexuality is prevalent, or even exists at all, have frequently had a polarizing effect, with some suggesting that bisexuality is a kind of intermediate stage between heterosexuality and homosexuality, and others insisting that bisexuality stands on its own. These differences have persisted and, to some extent, reflect the complex nature of the term.

In an exploration of the origins of gender, Cucchiari (1981) offers a model of an early "gender-free" society in which the members are all inherently bisexual. While this theoretical model is useful for the examination of a specific institution – gender – it also lends itself to the idea that "everyone is bisexual," a claim heard with varying degrees of frequency among those professing to be bisexual (see Hutchins and Kaahumanu 1991; Ochs and Rowley 2005). The belief that we are all bisexual sometimes finds root in ancient history, with mixed results. Cantarella (1992) contests the common mythology that classical Greece and Rome enjoyed an uninhibited and unfettered sexuality, often imagined as a free and easy bisexual environment, making it possible to choose according to whim. Much of what constituted "bisexual" behavior in ancient Greece was tightly controlled by a set of social norms that were arranged around male desires and interests, with women excluded entirely. In ancient Rome, the code of masculinity largely dictated the nature of same-sex and opposite-sex encounters, making the idea of bisexuality again a matter of social, and male-centered, codes. In short, classical civilizations relied strongly on the idea that specific behaviors – which included sexual activities with members of the same and opposite sex – governed the interaction and thus the nature of sexual relations. In this sense, "bisexual" has a somewhat skewed meaning.

Non-Western cultures also are a source of both research and difference in the exploration of bisexuality. Herdt (1999) details the accounts of same-sex behaviors among the Sambia culture of Papua New Guinea. Here, young boys and young male adults are part of an initiation ritual into manhood that has the older emerging adult male obtaining specific sexual services from the younger boys. Following this process, the newly initiated young male finds a female bride and relinquishes all sexual contact with the same sex. Here too we find that the notion of "bisexual" is indefinite and is again organized around male sexuality.

Considerable work has also been done in Latin America and South Asia that suggests similarly ambiguous results around the idea of bisexuality. In Latin America, for example, roles are generally determined by the behavior of the participants, the active or dominant role being regarded as heterosexual and the passive or receptive role being regarded as homosexual (Kulick 1997).

Within today's social and cultural systems, the binary model predominates: there are male and female persons, biologies, and roles. As such, both the nature and understanding of sexual relations are organized around this implicit norm. Some researchers have argued that the fluid nature of human sexual contact requires a more expansive approach. One result of this binary thinking is that bisexuality becomes both invisible and difficult to define (Yoshino 2000). Sexual dichotomy is the socially accepted model, with the corresponding expectation that one must be sexually or romantically attracted to one or the other. While this in itself does not preclude the idea of bisexuality – a romantic or sexual attraction to a different sex – it sometimes confines it to a binary polarity.

Efforts to understand and clarify the nature of bisexuality have a long history in the area of sex research. In the 1940s, Alfred Kinsey and colleagues (1948) questioned the idea of the basic binary model, pointing out the fallacy of the simple hetero-/homosexual model of sexual activity. Even when adding in the notion of bisexuality, Kinsey felt that this was too limiting and did not adequately speak to the variety of human sexual activity. One outgrowth of this work was the development of the Kinsey Scale. In this model, the two poles of heterosexual and homosexual behavior are set apart and divided into six equal gradations. Each interval is described in terms of hetero- and homosexual behavior. Within each segment or gradation, the following vertical scale mapping is used: 0 = Exclusively heterosexual with no homosexual, 1 = Predominantly heterosexual with only incidental homosexual, 2 = Predominantly heterosexual but with more than incidental homosexual, 3 = Equally heterosexual and homosexual, 4 = Predominantly homosexual but with more than incidental heterosexual, 5 = Predominantly homosexual with only incidental heterosexual, 6 = Exclusively homosexual with no heterosexual.

When the data were collected, a subject professing to be bisexual would be represented in the precise "middle," or segment 3, where equal amounts of hetero- and homosexual behavior occur. The Kinsey Scale afforded early researchers a means to better understand the nature of the data they were actually collecting. It also focused exclusively on behavior. Subsequent researchers recognized that there were limitations to the Kinsey Scale, such as the realization that both behavior and attitude could change over time.

In the 1980s, Klein and Wolf (1985) made similar efforts to understand the nature of bisexuality. One result of this work was the development of the Klein Grid. In this system, the subject was queried not just about behavior, but also about emotions and fantasies, both past and present. A third temporal category allowed subjects to envision their "ideal." Klein's grid more precisely established the idea of what bisexual meant. To do this, a simple table was devised. In the left column, numerous characteristics of interest were listed as follows: sexual attraction, sexual behavior, sexual fantasies, emotional preference, social preference, heterosexual/homosexual lifestyle, and self-identification. Three additional columns were then added, titled "past," "present," and "ideal." For the first five characteristics, a simple scale of 1 to 7 was used, and mapped to the following: 1 = Other sex only, 2 = Other sex mostly, 3 = Other sex somewhat more, 4 = Both sexes, 5 = Same sex somewhat more, 6 = Same sex mostly, and 7 = Same sex only. The final two characteristics were mapped differently: 1 = Heterosexual only, 2 = Heterosexual mostly, 3 = Heterosexual somewhat more, 4 = Hetero-/Gay–Lesbian equally, 5 = Gay/Lesbian somewhat more, 6 = Gay/Lesbian mostly, and 7 = Gay/Lesbian only.

In this particular model, the notion of "bisexual" again situates the subject in the middle of the scale. The Klein Grid has also come under scrutiny in that it does not deal with factors such as partner age, differing variations of emotional preference, and the significance, if any, of sex and gender roles. To date, there is no one body of research or opinion that is accepted as a definitive measure of bisexuality.

Despite the lack of clarity as to the meaning of the term, bisexuality has garnered considerable attention and interest from those who are self-identified as bisexuals. In this respect, the term becomes a means to locate those of a similar persuasion, and to collaborate and share information, resources, and support. The increasing visibility of transgender persons has sometimes resulted in the term bisexual being a source of real confusion, both for those who practice it as transgender persons and for those who are cisgendered (those whose gender experience matches the gender assigned at birth). An individual of a particular sex or gender who is sexually and romantically attracted to those of the same *biological* sex may also be attracted to those of the same *gender* who themselves are of a *different* biological sex.

SEE ALSO: Kinsey Scale; Lesbian, Gay, Bisexual, and Transgender Psychologies; Sexual Identity and Orientation; Sexual Orientation and the Law; Sexualities

REFERENCES

Cantarella, Eva. 1992. *Bisexuality in the Ancient World*. New Haven: Yale University Press.

Cucchiari, Salvatore. 1981. "The Gender Revolution and the Transition from Bisexual Horde to Patrilocal Band: The Origins of Gender Hierarchy." In *Sexual Meanings: The Cultural Construction of Gender and Sexuality*, edited by Sherry B. Ortner and Harriet Whitehead, 31–79. Cambridge: Cambridge University Press.

Herdt, Gilbert H. 1999. *Sambia Sexual Culture: Essays from the Field*. Chicago: University of Chicago Press.

Hutchins, Loraine, and Lani Kaahumanu. 1991. *Bi Any Other Name: Bisexual People Speak Out*. Boston: Alyson.

Kinsey, Alfred C., Wardell Baxter Pomeroy, and Clyde E. Martin. 1948. *Sexual Behavior in the Human Male*. Philadelphia: W. B. Saunders.

Klein, Fred, and Timothy J. Wolf. 1985. *Bisexualities: Theory and Research*. New York: Haworth Press.

Kulick, Don. 1997. "The Gender of Brazilian Transgendered Prostitutes." *American Anthropologist*, 99(3): 574–585.

Ochs, Robyn, and Sarah Rowley. 2005. *Getting Bi: Voices of Bisexuals Around the World*. Boston: Bisexual Resource Center.

Yoshino, Kenji. 2000. "The Epistemic Contract of Bisexual Erasure." *Stanford Law Review*, 52(2): 353–461.

FURTHER READING

Fox, Ronald C. 2004. *Current Research on Bisexuality*. Binghamton: Harrington Park Press.

Garber, Marjorie B. 1995. *Vice Versa: Bisexuality and the Eroticism of Everyday Life*. New York: Simon and Schuster.

Ochs, Robyn, and H. Sharif Williams. 2014. *Recognize: The Voices of Bisexual Men*. Boston: Bisexual Resource Center.

Ortner, Sherry B., and Harriet Whitehead. 1981. *Sexual Meanings: The Cultural Construction of Gender and Sexuality*. Cambridge: Cambridge University Press.

Weinberg, Martin S., Colin J. Williams, and Douglas W. Pryor. 1994. *Dual Attraction: Understanding Bisexuality*. New York: Oxford University Press.

Black Feminist Thought

CARYL NUÑEZ
University of Connecticut, USA

Black feminist thought consists of the ideas, theory, and methods voiced by black women regarding the intersection of race, class, and gender primarily in the United States. Although black women had long been theorizing their unique experiences, the black feminist perspective developed out of the second-wave feminist teachings during the women's movement in the late 1960s. Women's liberation movements often focused on white women's struggles and actively silenced black women's voices, while the black liberation movement focused on black men and disregarded the struggles of black women. Consequently, it became necessary to confront racism in the women's movement and sexism in black liberation together. Black women were being pressured to join the women's liberation movement, but owing to the varying silencing tactics that kept the participation of women of color obscure in both movements, black feminists came together in the early 1970s to create the National Black Feminist Organization (NBFO). The NBFO was a space for black women freely to be themselves and endeavor towards empowerment on their own terms. Unfortunately, the NBFO did not have long-term success owing to the many challenges that black women faced and the fact that many black women had to work multiple jobs in addition to their political activism. Later, in 1977, the groundbreaking creation of "A Black Feminist Perspective" by the Combahee River Collective became a formative statement of black feminism on two fronts. The document claims the specific concerns of black feminists and makes explicit the tenets of intersectionality, namely that the primary systems of oppression are interlocking.

Scholars whose life work contributes to black feminism include Angela Davis, Beverly Guy-Sheftall, Patricia Hill Collins, Fannie Lou Hamer, bell hooks, Audre Lorde, Pauli Murray, Alice Walker, and Patricia Williams, among many others. Taking their work together, a definition of black feminism that fits well is "a process of self-conscious struggle that empowers women and men to actualize a humanist vision of community" (Collins 1990, 39). In this way, black feminism centers on collective consciousness within varying standpoints in order to work as a community toward social change. Addressing policy change meant that black feminists had to demystify the legal problems distinctive for black women. This is where the role of critical legal scholars such as Kimberle Crenshaw, Patricia Williams, and Paulette M. Caldwell play a unique role within black feminism. Advocating for change through a black feminist lens is to identify how systems of power are predicated on and seek to maintain socially constructed categories of class, race, and gender (Taylor 1998). Black feminists empowered themselves in the creation of black feminist thought by taking ownership of defining themselves and what feminism means to them. Largely drawing on the lived experience of black womanhood, black feminism centers the perspectives of black women in relationship to systems of oppression. Black feminists reject an additive analysis whereby racism and classism can be added to sexism (King 1988). They strive toward an understanding of the way black women experience simultaneous oppressions, which often work in tandem with one another. As a result, black feminism does not follow a hierarchy of oppressions or focus solely on race. In fact, the "ultimate goal of black feminism is to create a political movement that not only struggles against exploitative capitalism and … the racialized construction of sexuality, but that also seeks to develop institutions to protect what the dominant culture has little respect and value for – black women's minds and bodies" (Taylor 1998, 18).

Black feminist thought serves as a resistance strategy against patriarchal white supremacy. The purpose is to develop a theory to address and analyze the way race, gender, and class are intricately connected in black women's lives. In this way, black feminist thought is both theory and practice, or praxis. The explanatory power of black feminism is in the ability to engage the complicated histories of identity politics with the matrices of domination. Methodologically, traditional academic training can prove inadequate to study oppressed groups, who develop alternative forms of analysis and epistemological positions. The standards used to assess knowledge are not apolitical since power shapes who is believed and why (Collins 1990). As a result, broader epistemological frameworks are necessary when conducting black feminist research. Black intellectuals often have to respond to questions of their credibility of knowledge due to the oppressive processes of knowledge validation. This is why intersectionality is a suitable paradigm for black feminism because it shifts the affirmation of knowledge.

Patricia Hill Collins is one of the leading scholars of black feminist thought and she terms black women's awareness and ability to tap into their experiences for analysis as the development of a black feminist consciousness. Such self-awareness and analysis of social politics encouraged black feminism to resist tropes of womanhood that were also common in women's movements. Black feminism refuses to essentialize women as a catchall category. While women may experience discrimination on account of their gender, black feminist thought argues that differences matter, including racial, class, ethnic, and cultural differences. Black women's experiences are both similar to and different from those of white women and black men. Owning their experiences as sites of knowledge, standpoint feminism and feminist theories of experience resonate with black feminist thought. Although black feminist thought has recently become highly visible within feminist theory, this does not mean that it is not subjugated and distorted. Indeed, the very word "feminist" carries the weight of racism within mainstream feminist movements and many black feminists sought to adopt womanism, as termed by Alice Walker, as a more accurate representation of their politics. The politics of naming are important to black feminists, whose voices are often silenced.

While black feminism has its roots in activism and expanded into academia, the use of literature has provided infinite possibilities for black women writers such as *The Color Purple*, *Their Eyes Were Watching God*, *Coming of Age in Mississippi*, *Beloved*, and *Praise Song for the Widow*, to name just a few. Black feminism is organic and continues to thrive in online communities in collectives, blogs, and other social media platforms in addition to academic pursuits. Notable sites include For Harriet (www.forharriet.com), Black Girl Dangerous (www.blackgirldangerous.com), The Feminist Wire (www.thefeministwire.com), and The Crunk Feminist Collective (www.crunkfeministcollective.com).

SEE ALSO: Feminist Standpoint Theory; Feminist Theories of Experience; Intersectionality; Womanism

REFERENCES

Collins, Patricia Hill. 1990. *Black Feminist Thought: Knowledge, Consciousness, and the Politics of Empowerment*. New York: Routledge.
King, Deborah. 1988. "Multiple Jeopardy, Multiple Consciousness: The Context of a Black Feminist Ideology." *Signs*, 14(1): 42–72

Taylor, Ula Y. 1998. "Making Waves: The Theory and Practice of Black Feminism." *Black Scholar*, 28(2): 18–28.

FURTHER READING

Collins, Patricia Hill. 1996. "What's in a Name? Womanism, Black Feminism, and Beyond," *Black Scholar*, 26(1): 9–17.
Guy-Sheftall, Beverly. 1995. *Words of Fire: An Anthology of African-American Feminist Thought*. New York: New Press.
hooks, bell. 1982. *Ain't I a Woman: Black Women and Feminism*. Boston, MA: South End Press.
Ransby, Barbara. 2000. "Black Feminism at Twenty-one: Reflections on the Evolution of a National Community." *Signs*, 25(4): 1215–1221.
White, Aaronette M. 1999. "Talking Feminist, Talking Black: Micromobilization Processes in a Collective Protest Against Rape." *Gender & Society*, 13(1): 77–100.
Williams, Patricia. J. 1991. *The Alchemy of Race and Rights: Diary of a Law Professor*. Cambridge, MA: Harvard University Press.

Body Politics

WENDY HARCOURT
International Institute of Social Studies, Erasmus University, The Netherlands

Body politics is about the political struggle of people to claim control over their own biological, social, and cultural "bodily" experiences. Feminist practice and writing in the last 30 years have engaged in body politics, where bodies are understood as sites of cultural meaning, social experience, and political resistance (Grosz 1994). The three main entry points into body politics are: feminist theory on the body; international development policy related to bodies, namely health, sexuality, and reproduction; and popular writings on the female body as a site of political action. All three approaches challenge the normative construction of the gendered body in discourses around sexual relations, economics, health, and medical and biological scientific processes. The assumption is that by looking at how gendered bodies are constructed in different popular, scientific, economic discourses it is possible to challenge and change oppressive conditions (Harcourt 2009).

Ever since Michel Foucault (1976) explored resistance to systemic power on the body, Western feminist theory has aimed to retell narratives about female embodiment in order to unsettle presumed concepts of biological sex and gender. Judith Butler (1993) has been one of the most well known feminist theorists to raise questions about the gaps between values and interests of women's lives and those that inform dominant conceptual frameworks around the female body. Butler has challenged dominant views of embodiment in order to unpack how tradition and modernity are played out on the lived body. For example, the presumption that femininity is linked to a body having a uterus is one way in which heterosexual privilege is presented as the norm and women are defined as biologically (naturally) mothers. Other feminist theorists such as Inderpal Grewal and Caren Kaplan (1994) have contributed to this work, challenging the conceptual frameworks that bind male and female embodied experiences in dominant macro frameworks of politics, economics, culture, and society. In these feminist writings aspects of female embodiment (such as pregnancy, rape, and aging) become privileged sites of significance bearing on how female experience is lived (Shildrick 1997).

Another example of feminist theorizing on body politics is Donna Haraway's *A Cyborg Manifesto* (1992) that explores how Western science and politics inform racism and colonialism in the language of development and modernization. Her writing complements that of feminist theorists writing from their experience of the global South. Gayatri Chakravorty Spivak (1987, 1999) and Chandra Talpade Mohanty (2003) look at how the experience of female embodiment is informed by sexism, racism, misogyny, and heterosexism. Spivak points to sexist and racist imperialist structures that have made the high fertility of women from the global South a central focus of development policy. Following Spivak and Mohanty, feminist writings on body politics in colonialism have explored how bodies, sex, and race are intertwined in imperial and colonial medicine and science (Tamale 2011; Wieringa and Sivori 2012). These feminist writings show how the corporeal, fleshly, material existence of bodies is deeply embedded in political relations.

Development policy has been one field where body politics has been at the core of political struggles around gender equality, human rights, and public health. The 1990s series of United Nations (UN) conferences were key international events that consolidated gender and development practices around body politics. Feminists brought to the UN arena issues such as domestic violence; rape as a weapon of war; denial of sexual and reproductive rights; sexual oppression of women, children, homosexuals, and transgender people; racism that discriminates because of skin color; ageism that stereotypes and uses young bodies. Body politics in these struggles emerges as a strong movement of resistance and expansion of rights linking the political dimension of the body with a radical form of democracy (Hartmann 1995; Vargas 2005). Body politics in the UN debates joined the feminist counter-culture with policy that made visible many previously taboo issues challenging "traditions" that veil women, condone and institutionalize inequalities in the workplace, fail to challenge homophobia, and silence women in public spaces (Petchesky 2002; Harcourt 2009).

Feminist advocates have been successful in changing human rights and public health policy to include the body (World Health Organization 2006). The sexual and reproductive health and rights agenda (the right to choose a partner, to have or not to have children, to bodily integrity, to sexual and reproductive healthcare services) is now part of the mainstream global and national development agendas in the struggle to end poverty and social exclusion (Cornwall, Correa, and Jolly 2008).

In popular writing, feminists have reclaimed the lived experience of the female body as a vehicle for making and remaking the world (Bordo 1993). Female embodiment in these writings has become an important political terrain for feminist politics where the body is seen as a central way for women to claim power. From the Boston Women's Health Collective's bestselling manual *Our Bodies, Ourselves* (2005) (published in 50 languages) to Eve Ensler's play *The Vagina Monologues* (1996), female bodies are "reclaimed." Naming the vagina is presented as a tool of female empowerment where women reclaim a sense of pride and self-fulfillment through embracing feminine embodiment. Naomi Wolf's 2012 "biography" of the vagina combs through history in order to assert female courage and consciousness. Other popular forms of body politics look at body image and dieting in Western culture (Orbach 2009) and there have been several books contributing to the campaign to end female genital cutting among African societies and immigrant populations in Europe (Miré 2011).

Feminist analysis and practice shows how body politics is interwoven into social, colonial, ethical, and economic discourses. Social, cultural, and economic institutions and discourses shape and are being shaped by body politics as feminism challenges dominant norms, making body politics a key mobilizing force for gender equality, sexuality, and human rights in the last three decades.

SEE ALSO: Feminist Theories of the Body; Gender and Development; Third World Women

REFERENCES

Bordo, Susan. 1993. *Unbearable Weight: Feminism, Western Culture, and the Body*. Berkeley: University of California Press.

Boston Women's Health Collective. 2012. *Our Bodies, Ourselves*, rev. ed. Boston: Touchstone Press. http://www.ourbodiesourselves.org.

Butler, Judith. 1993. *Bodies That Matter*. London: Routledge.

Cornwall, Andrea, Sonia Correa, and Susie Jolly, eds. 2008. *Development with a Body: Sexuality, Human Rights and Development*. London: Zed Books.

Ensler, Eve. 1996. *The Vagina Monologues*. New York: Random House.

Foucault, Michel. 1976. *The History of Sexuality*, vol. 1. Harmondsworth, UK: Penguin.

Grewal, Inderpal, and Caren Kaplan. 1994. *Scattered Hegemonies: Postmodernity and Transnational Feminist Practices*. Minneapolis: University of Minnesota Press.

Grosz, Elizabeth. 1994. *Volatile Bodies: Towards Corporeal Feminism*. Bloomington: Indiana University Press.

Haraway, Donna. 1992. "A Cyborg Manifesto: Science, Technology, and Socialist-Feminism in the Late Twentieth Century." Accessed August 24, 2015, at http://faculty.georgetown.edu/irvinem/theory/Haraway-CyborgManifesto-1.pdf.

Harcourt, Wendy. 2009. *Body Politics in Development: Critical Debates in Gender and Development*. London: Zed Books.

Hartmann, Betsy. 1995. *Reproductive Rights and Wrongs: The Global Politics of Population Control*, rev. ed. Massachusetts: South End Press.

Miré, Soraya. 2011. *The Girl with Three Legs: A Memoir*. Chicago: Lawrence Hill Books.

Mohanty, Chandra. 2003. *Feminism Without Borders: Decolonizing Theory, Practicing Solidarity*. Durham, NC: Duke University Press.

Orbach, Susie. 2009. *Bodies*. New York: Picador.

Petchesky, Rosalind. 2002. *Global Prescriptions: Gender Health and Human Rights*. London: Zed Books in association with UNRISD.

Shildrick, Margrit. 1997. *Leaky Bodies and Boundaries: Feminism, Postmodernism and (Bio)ethics*. London: Routledge.

Spivak, Gayatri. 1987. *In Other Worlds: Essays in Cultural Politics*. New York: Methuen.

Spivak, Gayatri. 1999. *A Critique of Postcolonial Reason: Toward a History of the Vanishing Present*. Cambridge, MA: Harvard University Press.

Tamale, Sylvia, ed. 2011. *African Sexualities: A Reader*. Oxford: Pambazuka Press.

Vargas, Virginia. 2005. "Feminisms and the World Social Forum: Space for Dialogue and Confrontation." *Development*, 48(2): 107–110.

Wieringa, Saskia, and Horacio Sivori, eds. 2012. *The Sexual History of the Global South: Sexual Politics in Africa, Asia and Latin America*. London: Zed Books.

Wolf, Naomi. 2012. *Vagina: A New Biography*. London: Virago.

World Health Organization. 2006. *World Report on Violence and Health*. Geneva: World Health Organization.

FURTHER READING

Jolly, Susia, Andrea Cornwall, and Kate Hawkins, eds. 2013. *Women, Sexuality and the Political Power of Pleasure*. London: Zed Books.

Bollywood

SHAKUNTALA BANAJI

London School of Economics and Political Science, UK

Hindi commercial cinema has gained the name "Bollywood." This allusion controversially elides Bombay, its city of origin, with Hollywood, which has Western, imperialist connotations for some commentators.

Contrary to perceptions of Bollywood as monolithic, or a single genre, it is a vibrant and diverse cinema industry that produces distinct genres, including social, romance, comedy, action, gothic, family melodrama, and gangster/crime.

Films generally last about 3 hours. Most depict stock characters from the honorable hero and chaste heroine to the villain, the mother, mother-in-law, or crime boss. While songless films are gaining popularity, most contain skillfully choreographed dances, songs, and lavish sets and costumes. Frequent clothing changes play a crucial role in drawing attention to female bodies and, more recently, to male torsos. Star-crossed love, tensions between duty and personal desire, the criminal underworld, family, and corruption are common tropes.

Good guys who win in the end and "get the girl" were replaced some decades ago by nihilist anti-heroes, only to be superseded by heroes who show superhuman courage and adhere to apparently Indian traditions. Discursive and representational changes in Hindi films since India's economic neoliberalization in 1990 include increased attention to diasporic Indians as bearers of "authentic Indian values," a linking of Islam with global terrorism, visual tropes of wealth and consumption rather than poverty and development, and heroines who combine elements of Madonna and vamp.

Although subtexts of homosocial friendship and homoerotic love persist (Gopinath 2000), overt heterosexism is the norm, with rare transsexual, gay, and lesbian characters inserted for comic or sinister effect. Successful Hindi films often intertwine prejudiced depictions of religious or ethnic violence with romantic or sexual infatuation. The femininity of "evil" female characters is often thrown into question, as is the masculinity of male villains.

Studies using textual analysis and theoretical commentary have argued that Hindi films are based on good-versus-evil master narratives from Hindu epic plays (Mishra 2002), are escapist, pre-realist, anti-modern (Nandy 1998), patriarchal and/or ultra-nationalist, and generally ideologically reactionary (Kazmi 1999; Vasudevan 2000). These authors theorize Hindi films as pitting comforting rituals and tradition against an intruding and uncertain modernity.

Plausible critiques of Hindi films also see representations as constructing and contributing to inegalitarian imaginaries and cultures. They argue that nationalism, religion, and Hindutva, politically-motivated Hindu chauvinism (Chakravarty 1998), as well as caste, class, gender, patriarchy, and sexuality (Prasad 1998; Vitali 2008) are reinforced by camera techniques, dialogue, and narrative structures.

Textual closure is assumed to cue psychic closure. The endings of films, containing hegemonic reinforcements and/or erasures of class difference, ethnic, intergenerational and other conflicts, apparently affect audiences more than earlier sequences in which both male and female characters rebel against patriarchy, challenge authority, or provide alternatives to neoliberal social values.

These assumptions have meant that there is unremitting concern expressed about the *effects* of Hindi films, with calls for censorship, banning, or alternative representation. However, concerns are also countered by more celebratory accounts (Thomas 1985; Dwyer 2000) which focus on Hindi films' carnivalesque hybridity and emotional perceptiveness, suggesting their ability to sidestep conventional realist ideological binaries.

The relationship between Hindi films and audiences has been theorized more recently in reception studies based on sociological methods such as observation and interviewing (Banaji 2006; Rao 2007). These studies suggest that emotional–rational engagement with Bollywood is an active process. While the pleasures of conventional patriarchal romance, social conformity, and violent action sequences are evident, not all viewers respond to the ideological invitations of Hindi films in the same ways or to the same extent. Some groups of viewers are implicated more in ideological discourses of class, gender, and nation by their previous experience and intersecting social identifications, whereas those who feel alienated from central narratives by virtue of religion or class tend to focus on songs, costumes, mise-en-scène, stars, and sets. Enjoyment is also often linked to irritation and critique rather than to imitation and acceptance.

Hindi film narratives follow a limited range of pathways but the ideological meanings made from them vary significantly. Reception studies suggest that sequences at the beginning or in the middle of Hindi films are viewed multiple times, and may carry as much if not more psychic weight than those at the conclusion. Hence conformity and closure are not necessarily reflected in the meanings carried away by viewers.

However, Hindi films using themes of ethnicity and gender, history, religion, love, and violence also contribute to the highly authoritarian contexts in which many viewers live. As frequently as these films offer liberating and alternative narratives and goals, they also work alongside other media, and governmental and community discourses and dictates, to undermine feminist critiques of discriminatory values and practices such as Islamophobia, honor killing, marital rape, wife beating, and homophobia. Future scholarship would therefore do well to combine ethnographic methods and qualitative textual analysis with detailed historical and sociological evidence to theorize more precisely the dialectical relationship between sociopolitical and production contexts, audience subjectivity, and changing Hindi film representations.

SEE ALSO: Intersectionality; Misogyny; Patriarchy

REFERENCES

Banaji, Shakuntala. 2006. *Reading 'Bollywood': The Young Audience and Hindi Films*. Basingstoke: Palgrave Macmillan. DOI: 10.1057/9780230501201.

Chakravarty, Sumita S. 1998. *National Identity in Indian Popular Cinema: 1947–1987*. New Delhi: Oxford University Press.
Dwyer, Rachel. 2000. *All You Want is Money, All You Need is Love*. London: Cassell.
Gopinath, Gayatri. 2000. "Queering Bollywood: Alternative Sexualities in Popular Indian Cinema." *Journal of Homosexuality*, 39(3/4): 283–297. DOI: 10.1300/J082v39n03_13.
Kazmi, Fareed. 1999. *The Politics of India's Commercial Cinema: Imaging a Universe, Subverting a Multiverse*. New Delhi: Sage.
Mishra, Vijay. 2002. *Bollywood Cinema: Temples of Desire*. New York: Routledge.
Nandy, Ashis, ed. 1998. *The Secret Politics of Our Desires: Innocence, Culpability and Indian Popular Cinema*. New Delhi: Oxford University Press.
Prasad, M. Madhava. 1998. *Ideology of the Hindi Film: a Historical Construction*. New Delhi: Oxford University Press.
Rao, Shakuntala. 2007. "The Globalization of Bollywood: An Ethnography of Non-Elite Audiences in India." *The Communication Review*, 10(1): 57–76. DOI: 10.1080/10714420601168491.
Thomas, Rosie. 1985. "Indian Cinema: Pleasures and Popularity." *Screen*, 26(3–4): 116–131. DOI: 10.1093/screen/26.3-4.116.
Vasudevan, Ravi S., ed. 2000. *Making Meaning in Indian Cinema*. New Delhi: Oxford University Press.
Vitali, Valentina. 2008. *Hindi Action Cinema: Industries, Narratives, Bodies*. New Delhi: Oxford University Press.

Borderlands

DENISE A. SEGURA
University of California, Santa Barbara, USA

PATRICIA ZAVELLA
University of California, Santa Cruz, USA

In an often-cited statement, Chicana feminist lesbian poet and theorist Gloria Anzaldúa writes,

> The US–Mexico border *es una herida abierta* (an open wound) where the Third World grates against the first and bleeds. And before a scab forms it hemorrhages again, the lifeblood of two worlds merging to form a third country – a border culture. Borders are set up to define the places that are safe and unsafe, to distinguish us from them. (Anzaldúa 1987, 5)

Borderlands theory offers new ways of exploring relationships of power and domination, resistance and agency among women and men hitherto cast as marginalized others. Research utilizing borderlands theory has been increasing rapidly (Luibhéid and Cantú 2005; Segura and Zavella 2007). Notions of borderlands are complex and have been used by writers and theorists in widely disparate ways (Klahn 1997). In a literal sense, borderlands include the geopolitical space between national borders characterized by the ongoing movement of people, products, and ideas. One of the most influential thinkers about borderlands, Gloria Anzaldúa, argues that borderlands have multiple meanings (1987). She and others postulate the existence of social and psychic spaces that transcend the geopolitical border areas where women, men, and children adapt, resist, and innovate to cope with social inequalities based on cultural differences, poverty, racism, gender, and sexual differences.

Anzaldúa's work offered one of the first treatises on Chicana/o cultural forms of oppression, resistance, and empowerment which explains the spaces where Chicanas and other women of color in particular develop alternative intellectual, emotional, and spiritual agency. These expressions of agency integrate feelings of being "in between" socially legitimate cultures, languages, or places which simultaneously generate psychic processes of exclusion and identification with marginalized others as well as spiritual transformations that can lead to empowered selves. Within these borderland spaces, subjects voice their unique identities and develop forms of resistance, individual and collective. All of these social, political, spiritual, and emotional transitions transcend geopolitical space.

Our review of key theoretical and methodological characterization of borderlands in the social sciences identified a strong emphasis on transnational social formations, how migrants engage in economic, political, or sociocultural activities that transcend national borders and "deterritorialize," or span international boundaries. Researchers who use this approach often conduct field research in multiple sites – "sending" and "receiving" communities – to empirically demonstrate and theorize how deterritorialized processes unfold. Research emphasizing cultural studies approaches to borderlands theories tend to emphasize the ways in which new, hybridized identities are linked to multiple sites, both real and imagined. From this work arises a greater understanding of new emerging identities including undocumented women who learn to "*valerse por si misma/value oneself*" (Villenas and Moreno 2001), transgender migrants, and gay fathers, all whose identities are shaped by multiple processes. These borderlands approaches offer ways to identify some of the changes that historically disenfranchised subjects negotiate daily, how they adapt to structural transformations, contest or create representations of their identities in light of their marginality, and give voice to their complex human agency or what we refer to as "subjective transnationalism" (Segura and Zavella 2007).

One critical contribution of a borderlands perspective is its attention to the history of colonization and racialization of Mexicans. Intersections between Mexico and the United States have created specific social conditions for both Mexicanas/Mexicanos and Chicanas/Chicanos. The terms "Chicana" and "Chicano" refer, respectively, to women and men of Mexican descent in the United States who articulate a politicized consciousness. "Latina/o" is a broader term that typically refers to people of Latin American heritage, and also includes Mexicans. Latino is often used interchangeably with the term "Hispanic." Race, gender, sexuality, and class are negotiated in the daily lives of Chicanas within the context of the borderlands. By using the term borderlands, we contextualize and substantiate myriad Mexicana/Chicana experiences as forms of adaptation and resistance to linguistic and cultural differences. Borderlands provide fertile ground from which individual and collective action arises. For example, Mary Pardo's work (1998) on the mothers of East Los Angeles is a key text on Chicana/Mexicana collective action. In education, the work of Concha Delgado-Gaitan (2001) highlights the role of women to engage in collective advocacy for their children's education.

This leads us to consider the transnational nature of borderlands that emphasizes coalitions with other *mujeres* (women) across the US–Mexico geopolitical border. Borderlands feminist research interrogates and moves beyond nation-bound discourse. Borderlands feminist research works on developing binational approaches that include structural forces and women's individual and collective agency that integrate perspectives from the United States and the Global South of women on both sides of the US–Mexico border. For more than three decades, Chicanas and Latinas have been involved in international and transnational political efforts through solidarity movements and documenting women's activism outside the United States. As Chicanas and Latinas continue to do empirical research in transnational sites, the conditions under which they conduct their work lead to important questions. For example, how are Chicana and Latina scholars contributing to and critiquing the "globalization discourse?" As Chicanas and Latinas engage in transnational scholarship and activities, scholars are debating the implications to theory, epistemology, methodology, and activism.

Borderlands feminist research interrogates women's "subjective transnationalism," or their ongoing constructions of cultural identity and agency in the nebulous spaces where they live and work. Given economic realities, women are constantly negotiating economic and political spaces in both geographic and psychic borderlands. Much of this activity disrupts traditional notions of gender within households, local communities, and the state. Subjective transnationalism problematizes feelings that one is neither from "here" nor from "there," not at home anywhere. Subjective transnationalism also underscores the work women and other marginalized subjects do to develop ways to feel "at home" in multiple geographic locations where identity construction is deterritorialized as part of a borderlands mixture shifting racial-ethnic boundaries and gendered transitions in a global economy (Zavella 2011). In a recent *New York Times* (2014) survey, a wide majority of US residents (66 percent) said that most recent immigrants contributed to this country, up from 49 percent in 2010. The same poll reported a majority (55 percent) believed police should take an active role in identifying undocumented immigrants; three quarters of these respondents expressed this belief even if it meant that immigrants might not report crimes or volunteer information to the police. These conflicting views of migrants suggest shifts and also cleavages within communities regarding questions of legitimacy and the value of migrants and by extension other marginalized subjects. Such conflicting views form the context within which migrant women strive to create meaningful lives.

Subjective transnationalism also refers to women's spiritual agency and borderless *concientización* (politicized consciousness) that reclaims their political and sexual subjectivities and rejects domestic or state-sanctioned violence. Fregoso and Bejarano (2010), for example, argue that violence against women in Ciudad Juarez, the state of Chihuahua, and elsewhere express how a male-dominated state uses its power to reclaim women as subordinate objects. Women may take on breadwinner roles within families, for example, when their spouses are deported while children often become translators and intermediaries with state officials, taking on authority for helping families negotiate complex issues such as home rentals or health decisions. Reclaiming the voice of women and uncovering their paths to resist violence and assert their sexual subjectivities are critical borderlands in which growing numbers of researchers are now directing their feminist projects. These researchers include Gloria González-López (2007), who subverts conventional understandings of Mexican women's sexuality though an analysis of their "erotic journeys" across Mexico and the United States, and research collaborators Yvette Flores and Enriqueta Valdez Curiel (2009), who explore transnational differences in the ways domestic violence is interpreted and challenged. Such studies are critical in developing culturally sensitive intervention strategies.

Whether working in a social science or cultural studies frame, scholars find that sexuality is an integral part of borderlands subjectivities. In some instances, patriarchal, heteronormative, and racial discourses travel and become salient in new locales (Parrini et al. 2007; García 2012). In others, subjects seeking the autonomy to express their sexual identities construct new norms, relationships, or communities after migration that contend with colonial legacies (Alexander 2005; Ochoa 2010). Luibhéid (2013) and Luibhéid and Cantú (2005) argue that normative sexual regimes shape how, when, and where subjects are categorized in different legal or social statuses, often with devastating consequences, which become redefined through efforts to control illegal immigration. All of these scholars find that sexuality is interconnected to racism, class oppression, heteronormativity, and imperialism.

Borderlands theory makes gender and gender oppression central in studies of migration, Chicana/o-Latina/o studies, Latin American studies, and globalization. Key investigations include how family/work intersections operate, new family forms emerge, the role of social networks in adaptation, resistance, and empowerment as well as the rise of different modes of women's cultural expressions. A borderlands analysis contextualizes the many layers of violence that originate in structural dislocations that permeate family life as well as work sites and interpersonal relations. When women become the center of analysis, questions change and previously held assumptions become subjects of inquiry. For example, how are decisions made within households regarding who migrates and who remains behind? Under which circumstances do women migrate alone, with children, or support their children to migrate with or without other family members? In view of global interpenetration, how are new identities and social formations being reconstructed on either side of the borders by migrant women? How are these reconfigured identities and social formations being represented in cultural expressions and imaginaries in the United States, Mexico, and the Global South? Borderlands theory provides a space to bring together new research that inspires paradigm shifts. Scholarship framed within a borderlands perspective explores the range of women's experiences from reconstructions of "tradition" to contestations of racist, patriarchal, and/or heteronormative structures in work sites, families, popular culture, and the state.

Feminist borderlands projects interrogate the multiple meanings of borders and borderlands across four key dimensions: structural, discursive, interactional, and agentic. Structural dimensions of a feminist borderlands project critique the effects of globalizing economies, neoliberal state practices, and growing regional interdependence on women's life chances. Discursive elements of borderlands projects offer critiques of ideologies and practices that reinforce racializations and heteronormativity and resistance to unequal power relations. Interactional dimensions of borderlands projects interrogate the active accomplishments of unequal relations of race, class, gender, and sexualities. Women's agency to negotiate and claim space within the local and global "matrices of domination," for example, activist mothering or transborder organizing, are important borderlands projects. How women maneuver within structures of power that are often brutal, whether contesting personal or political abuse, discourses of state, or social violence are critical borderlands projects.

The dialectic between borderlands theory and borderlands projects are dynamic and often incorporate interdisciplinary approaches to reveal the poetics and performance of women's agency, crafting a tapestry of voice and resistance to nativist politics and silencing discourse as well as traditional gendered expectations at work, within homes, or in communities (Vélez-Ibáñez and Sampaio 2002; Lugo 2008; Rosas 2012). We also see border inspections as key sites for objectifying the "other" based on their race, gender, or sexual identities (Rosas 2006; Alvarez 2012; Luibhéid 2013). By exploring multiple sites of gendered control and contestation, borderlands research reveals the multifaceted representations, experiences, and identities that women create within the context of globalization and transnational migration. Within these structural and socially violent discourses, women continually challenge confining notions of citizenship and strive to develop resilience and create community within and across national borders.

SEE ALSO: Feminism, Chicana; Feminism, Latina; Feminism, Lesbian; Feminism, Multiracial; Intersectionality

REFERENCES

Alexander, M. Jacqui. 2005. *Pedagogies of Crossing: Meditations on Feminism, Sexual Politics, Memory, and the Sacred.* Durham, NC: Duke University Press.

Alvarez, Robert R., Jr. 2012. "Borders and Bridges: Exploring a New Conceptual Architecture for (US–Mexico) Border Studies." *The Journal of Latin American and Caribbean Anthropology*, 17(1): 24–40.

Anzaldúa, Gloria. 1987. *Borderlands/La Frontera: The New Mestiza.* San Francisco: Aunt Lute.

Delgado-Gaitan, Concha. 2001. *The Power of Community: Mobilizing for Family and Schooling.* New York: Rowman & Littlefield.

Flores, Yvette, and Enriqueta Curiel. 2009. "Conflict Resolution and Intimate Partner Violence among Mexicans on Both Sides of the Border." In *Mexicans in California: Transformations and Challenges*, edited by Ramón Gutiérrez and Patricia Zavella, 183–215. Urbana: University of Illinois Press.

Fregoso, Rosa Linda, and Cynthia Bejarano, eds. 2010. *Terrorizing Women: Feminicide in the Américas.* Durham, NC: Duke University Press.

García, Lorena. 2012. *Respect Yourself, Protect Yourself: Latina Girls and Sexual Identity.* New York: New York University Press.

González-López, Gloria. 2007. "'Nunca he dejado de tener terror': Sexual Violence in the Lives of Mexican Immigrant Women." In *Women and Migration in the US–Mexico Borderlands: A Reader*, edited by Denise A. Segura and Patricia Zavella. Durham, NC: Duke University Press, 224–246.

Klahn, Norma. 1997. "Writing the Border: The Languages and Limits of Representations." *Travesia*, 3(1–2): 29–55.

Lugo, Alejandro. 2008. *Fragmented Lives, Assembled: Culture, Capitalism, and Conquest at the US–Mexico Border.* Austin: University of Texas Press.

Luibhéid, Eithne. 2013. *Pregnant on Arrival: Making the Illegal Immigrant.* Minneapolis: University of Minnesota Press.

Luibhéid, Eithne, and Lionel Cantú, Jr., eds. 2005. *Queer Migrations: Sexuality, US Citizenship, and Border Crossings.* Minneapolis: University of Minnesota Press.

The New York Times. 2014. "The New York Times Poll," May 7–11. Accessed June 21, 2014, at https://www.documentcloud.org/documents/1160841-new-york-times-poll-on-immigration-may-7-11-2014.html.

Ochoa, Marcia. 2010. "Latina/o Transpopulations." In *Latina/o Sexualities: Probing Powers, Passions, Practices, and Policies*, edited by Marysol Asencio, 230–242. New Brunswick: Rutgers University Press.

Pardo, Mary. 1998. *Mexican American Women Activists: Identity and Resistance in Two Los Angeles Communities.* Philadelphia: Temple University Press.

Parrini, Rodrigo, Xóchitl Castañeda, Carlos Magis, Juan Ruiz, and George Lemp. 2007. "Migrant Bodies: Corporality, Sexuality, and Power among Mexican Migrant Men." *Sexuality & Social Policy*, 4(3): 62–73.

Rosas, Gilberto. 2006. "The Managed Violences of the Borderlands: Treacherous Geographies, Policeability, and the Politics of Race." *Latino Studies*, 4(4): 401–418.

Rosas, Gilberto. 2012. *Barrio Libre: Criminalizing States and Delinquent Refusals of the New Frontier.* Durham, NC: Duke University Press.

Segura, Denise A., and Patricia Zavella, eds. 2007. *Women and Migration in the US–Mexico Borderlands: A Reader.* Durham, NC: Duke University Press.

Vélez-Ibáñez, Carlos G., and Sampaio, Anna. 2002. *Transnational Latina/o Communities: Politics, Processes, and Cultures.* Lanham: Rowman & Littlefield.

Villenas, Sofia, and Melissa Moreno. 2001. "To *valerse por si misma* between Race, Capitalism, and Patriarchy: Latina Mother–Daughter Pedagogies in North Carolina." *Qualitative Studies in Education*, 14(5): 671–687.

Zavella, Patricia. 2011. *I'm Neither Here nor There: Mexicans' Quotidian Struggles with Migration and Poverty.* Durham, NC: Duke University Press.

Boys' Peer Cultures

DAVID PLUMMER
Griffith University, Australia

RITES OF PASSAGE

Major transitions in social status have traditionally been organized into rituals known as "rites of passage" (van Gennep 1960). The transition from childhood to manhood is no exception. Based loosely around biological maturation, puberty rites serve to emphasize the social significance of manhood, reinforce gender conformity, and impose order over a complex transition that can otherwise vary widely, over time, across cultures, and within cultures. In Gilmore's words, "boys have to be encouraged, sometimes actually forced, by social sanctions to undertake efforts toward a culturally defined manhood, which by themselves they might not do" (1990, 25). It is here, in defining acceptable manhood and policing norms, that peer groups are pivotal.

Traditional passage to manhood has three phases: (1) separation from childhood; (2) transition in "liminal" status; and (3) reincorporation into society as a "real" man. The rites are undertaken with other peers who are being initiated; boys are mentored by older men; and rites typically involve ritual challenges where the candidate "proves" his manhood and earns the right to be called a man. Two peer groups participate in the rites: younger initiates and older mentors.

Formal rites have now largely disappeared, but the transition is as important as ever and sanctions for transgression remain heavy (Mac an Ghaill 1994). The traditional transition has been replaced by adolescence, which is protracted compared with the short, intense rites of passage, but there are many parallels: rituals of separation, when parents say farewell to tearful children on their first school day; transition with peers and supervised by teachers and other mentors; formal challenges such as sporting competitions and examinations, and unofficial challenges by peers in the school ground; and finally, graduation into adulthood.

PEER PRESSURE

The balance between the roles of elder mentors and younger peers has shifted. Peer groups now play a much greater role in the passage to manhood while the role of elders is diminished. This shift is largely due to social change: more diverse families, not necessarily including older males; work and commuting pressures that take adults away from home for longer; moral panics that question the motives of men working with children; fewer male teachers and non-family role models; and comparatively short school hours. The result is greatly increased time for peer groups and reduced access to traditional sources of guidance. These shifts create a temporary power vacuum, which is quickly filled by peer groups (Plummer and Geofroy 2010).

The growing influence of peer groups has two notable consequences. First, a tug of war between peer groups and adult authority can emerge. In the words of Chevannes (1999, 24), "the peer group … exerts influences that are not only greater than the influence of parents, but which contradict those nurtured within the family." The result is a competing set of rules: the honor codes of peer groups (and gangs) and the rule of law. This polarization can result in conflict. Second, peer groups play a growing role in the passage to manhood. This affects the type of man that emerges. Future hegemonic masculinity will reflect present-day peer group norms if the peer group is the reference point.

Peer groups police masculinity. They scrutinize boys' gender enactment intensely; adjudicate each other's gender performance; and respond to subtle transgressions with sanctions. Serious transgressions can trigger punishments including marginalization, teasing, violence, and murder (Plummer 2005). Special attention is paid to physical development, appearance, and dress style; styles of speech, gestures, and gait; social interactions and group membership; and sexuality. Characteristics that can attract disapproval include lisping, being slightly built, certain wrist actions, clothing colors, not playing team sport, being studious, well spoken, and "teacher's pet," suspected of being gay, and so on (Martino 1999). Attracting sanctions and witnessing others being targeted encourages careful self-policing, which becomes second nature.

In addition to taboo behaviors that peers actively suppress, peer groups enforce a raft of gender obligations. Group loyalty and conforming to group gender norms are chief among these. Being strong, dominant, aggressive, and sexually successful are highly valued. Success in these areas bolsters boys' reputations and helps them climb the "pecking order."

SHIFTING GENDER ARRANGEMENTS

Feminism has rightly brought improvements in the roles and status of women; however, the unintended consequences for manhood are problematic. Gender is mutually exclusive: something feminine cannot also be masculine (at least not in the orthodox sense). However, norms can shift, so what is masculine today may not be so in another culture or time. Thus, if norms for women change, then masculinity will have to change too.

The impact of shifting gender norms is particularly evident in education (Plummer 2013). Previously, many subjects were considered "boys' subjects" and academic prowess was an important way to assert masculinity. However, an unintended consequence of greater *equality* is that educational achievement has lost its utility for defining manhood. Indeed, from the vantage point of peer groups, there is growing evidence that education is stigmatized as unmasculine. The consequence is that boys are seeking alternative means of proving their manhood.

In the absence of other guidance, peer groups are resorting to physical characteristics as a source of "truth" about manhood. Characteristics include (1) physical development, musculature, deepening voice, hair growth, penis size, and other secondary sexual characteristics, and (2) physical performance – what the masculine body can do: strength, aggression, risk-taking, and sexual domination (Flood 2008). This retreat from education toward a renewed emphasis on physicality may be referred to as a "retreat to the body" and the "rise of hard masculinity" (Plummer 2013).

The combination of peer group solidarity, reorientation toward physicality and risk, and intensified masculine taboos such as homophobia produces a vicious cycle. Masculine obligations and taboos in the hot-house atmosphere of peer groups encourage hypermasculine acting out. It is difficult for a boy to avoid risky activities because this undermines his reputation and group solidarity, potentially at his peril. When it comes to choosing between obeying the law or conforming to peer group expectations, group loyalty and the capacity for summary justice often prevail (Plummer 2005). Paradoxically, while peer groups can seem anti-social, possibly criminal, they are highly social and rule bound for members. Group codes are elaborate and regularly include anti-social and dangerous behaviors. At their most developed, peer groups form gangs with similar codes but greater intensity. Intense peer group dynamics may well explain the gender patterns underpinning conflict, extremism, and terrorism (Messerschmidt 1994).

On a more mundane level, shared peer codes are the basis for youth culture, which is passed from generation to generation in the school ground and on the street, often unmediated by opposing adults. Handing codes down at arm's length from adults is known as "rolling peer pressure." The paradoxical twist for modern society is that rather than elders handing down masculine codes during traditional rites of passage, young people now transmit codes of manhood to each other without adult mediation. These become the standards that the world is destined to live with.

SEE ALSO: Hegemonic Masculinity; Heterosexism and Homophobia; Hypermasculinity; Mentoring

REFERENCES

Chevannes, Barry. 1999. *What We Sow and What We Reap – Problems in the Cultivation of Male Identity in Jamaica*. Kingston, Jamaica: Grace Kennedy Foundation.
Flood, Michael. 2008. "Men, Sex, and Homosociality: How Bonds between Men Shape Their Sexual Relations with Women." *Men and Masculinities*, 10(3): 339–359.
Gilmore, David D. 1990. *Manhood in the Making*. New Haven: Yale University Press.
Mac an Ghaill, Mairtin. 1994. *The Making of Men*. Buckingham: Open University Press.
Martino, Wayne. 1999. "'Cool Boys', 'Party Animals', 'Squids' and 'Poofters': Interrogating the Dynamics and Politics of Adolescent Masculinities in School." *British Journal of Sociology of Education*, 20(2): 239–263.
Messerschmidt, James W. 1994. "Schooling, Masculinities and Youth Crime by White Boys." In *Just Boys Doing Business? Men, Masculinities and Crime*, edited by Tim Newburn and Elizabeth A. Stanko, 81–99. London: Routledge.
Plummer, David. 2005. "Crimes against Manhood: Homophobia as the Penalty for Betraying Hegemonic Masculinity." In *Perspectives in Human Sexuality*, edited by Gail Hawkes and John Scott, 218–232. South Melbourne: Oxford University Press.
Plummer, David. 2013. "Masculinity and Risk: How Gender Constructs Drive Sexual Risks in the Caribbean." *Sexuality Research and Social Policy*, 10(3): 163–174. DOI: 10.1007/s13178-013-0116-7.
Plummer, David, and Stephen Geofroy. 2010. "When Bad is Cool: Violence and Crime as Rites of Passage to Manhood." *Caribbean Review of Gender Studies*, 4. Accessed July 28, 2015, at https://sta.uwi.edu/crgs/february2010/journals/PlummerGeofroy.pdf.
van Gennep, Arnold. 1960. *The Rites of Passage*. Chicago: University of Chicago Press.

Breast Cancer

CAMERON KIELY FROUDE
University of Connecticut, USA

INCIDENCE, ETIOLOGY, AND RISK FACTORS

One million women are diagnosed with breast cancer every year and more than 410,000 will die from breast cancer. Female breast cancer incidence rates vary considerably across geographic regions, ranging from 20 per 100,000 in Eastern and Middle Africa to 90 per 100,000 in Western Europe. Breast cancer incidence overall has risen in most countries with rapid increases occurring in developed countries such as Australia, the United Kingdom, and the United States. The United States and Northern Europe have the highest incidence of breast cancer followed by Southern and Eastern Europe and South America. Asia has the lowest incidence of breast cancer. However, third-generation American-Japanese women are now at the same general risk as American women.

Incidence rates have also risen considerably in countries with historically lower rates such as Japan, Singapore, and urban areas of China. Breast cancer risk increases for women who move from regions with lower incidence to those with higher incidence, supporting the theory that lifestyle factors are an integral factor in breast cancer incidence rates. For example, the traditional Japanese diet of low fat and high soy has gradually become similar to the American diet, which emphasizes increased fat and less soy and fiber-enriched foods.

Improvements in the economy and increased numbers of women in the workforce have impacted the lifestyle of individuals living in countries with historically lower incidence rates. Diverse lifestyle factors provide a compelling explanation for the regional variation in breast cancer incidence. For example, women in developed countries have fewer children overall, have children at an older age, and are less likely to breastfeed, factors that increase risk for breast cancer.

Clinical and experimental data have revealed that the development of breast cancer involves a perpetual battle between tumor growth and individual resistance level. There are many other influencing factors present such as hereditary, damage to the cell DNA, and other genetic abnormalities. Although experts do not know everything that causes breast cancer, the US Center for Disease Control identified five categories of risk factors for breast cancer, including: menstruation, motherhood, hormones, lifestyle, family history, and genetics. There are some risk factors that cannot be changed, such as age, and risk factors that can be changed, such as smoking behaviors. Other risk factors that place an individual at greater risk for breast cancer include environmental factors.

In 2005, the World Health Organization (WHO) reported that prolonged exposure to estrogen is associated with a lifelong risk of breast cancer. Estrogen replacement therapy (ERT) has been the subject of many studies that have attempted to determine whether estrogen exposure is a causal agent in the development of breast cancer. One of the most publicized studies, known as the Million Women Study, tracked United Kingdom women between the ages of 50 and 64 who were administered ERT. The results of this study revealed that women who took any form of estrogen for 10 years or longer had a slightly increased risk of breast cancer. Reproductive factors associated with exposure to estrogen, such as menstruation before the age of 12 and menopause after the age of 55, also influence breast cancer risk.

Risk for breast cancer also increases when relatives have breast or ovarian cancer at a young age and/or the genes related to breast cancer, BRCA1 and BRCA2. These genetic risk factors, also known as mutations, are responsible for approximately 5–10 percent of breast cancer cases in women. The BRCA1 and BRCA2 help prevent cancer in ordinary cells by creating proteins that inhibit cells from growing abnormally; however, women who have BCRA mutations have a 60–80 percent risk of developing breast cancer. Other risk factors include aging, radiation treatment to the breast area, and breast cancer or other breast problems such as radial scars.

SYMPTOMS, DIAGNOSIS, AND STAGES

The majority of breast cancers begin in the ducts while some begin in the lobules. However, a minority of breast cancers develop from other breast tissues. Most breast lumps are benign, meaning not cancerous. These lumps are often caused by changes in the breast tissue, causing fibrosis or cysts. Some lumps are malignant tumors, a cluster of cancer cells that invade surrounding tissues or spread to other areas of the body. Although these lumps are not cancerous, women with benign lumps are at a higher risk of developing breast cancer. If the cancer cells have spread to the lymph nodes, there is a greater likelihood that the cells have metastasized.

Some women with early stage breast cancer may be asymptomatic, while others might present with a lump in the breast, nipple discharge, or other abnormalities. The most common symptom of breast cancer is a new lump or mass on or around the breast. Additional symptoms include breast swelling, skin irritation, dimpling, breast or nipple pain, nipple retraction, nipple or breast skin irritation, and nipple discharge other than breast milk.

Diagnosis of breast cancer relies primarily on biomedical tests, such as mammography, biopsy, X-ray, CAT scan, bone scan, or a positron emission tomography (PET) scan. Mammography remains the gold standard in breast screening. The National Cancer Institute reports that mammogram screening can reduce death caused by breast cancer by as much as 30 percent. These tests confirm the presence of cancer and determine whether cancerous cells have spread within the breast or to other parts of the body. Cancer can spread by the cancerous tissue invading the non-cancerous tissue, the bloodstream, or the lymph system. The progression of cancer, determined by testing the tumor and lymph nodes, is conceptualized as stages.

Stage 0 (carcinoma in situ) is when abnormal cells are found in the lining of the breast duct. Stage I is divided into two sub-stages, IA and IB. In stage IA, the tumor is 2 cm or smaller and has not spread outside the breast. In stage IB, no tumor is found in the breast or the tumor is 2 cm or smaller. Small clusters of cancer cells are found in the lymph nodes. Stage II is invasive breast cancer, requiring one of the following: the tumor has spread to the lymph nodes under the arm and measures less than 2 cm, breast cancer cells are found in the lymph nodes under the arm without a tumor in the breast, or the tumor in the breast is between 2 and 5 cm, but has not spread to the lymph nodes.

Stage III breast cancer is divided into the sub-stages IIIA, IIIB, and IIIC. A requisite for a stage IIIA tumor is that it is larger than 5 cm and has spread from one to three lymph nodes. Other stage IIIA tumors may be any size and spread into multiple lymph nodes. Stage IIIB cancer requires a tumor of any size that has spread to tissues near the breast and may have spread to lymph nodes. Inflammatory breast cancer is also categorized as a stage IIIB. Stage IIIC is a tumor of any size that has spread to 10 or more lymph nodes under the arm, to lymph nodes above and beneath the collarbone, or to lymph nodes within the breast and lymph nodes under the arm. In stage IV, the cancer has spread to other organs of the body, namely the lungs, distant lymph nodes, skin, bones, liver, and/or brain (Mayo Clinic 2012; National Cancer Institute 2012).

TREATMENT

Beginning in the late nineteenth century, Johns Hopkins was the leader in America's healthcare transformation and the model institution for medical reform worldwide. While practicing at Johns Hopkins, Dr. William Halsted created and disseminated the radical mastectomy. He argued that all women with early-stage breast cancer would be cured if the entire breast and surrounding tissue were removed. This debilitating surgery represented a milestone in the treatment of breast cancer and remained the treatment of choice into the early 1900s.

Following approaches used by American AIDS activists, in the late 1960s American breast cancer activists began staging peaceful protests in an effort to politicize breast cancer and garner media attention. The purpose of the protests was to increase the public's awareness of breast cancer and change the ways in which the medical community treated the disease. Concerns about overtreatment of breast cancer with mastectomy and lack of alternatives fueled the passage of legislation, which required that physicians provide unbiased, detailed information to patients concerning alternative treatment options.

Today there are different types of treatments for individuals with breast cancer. According to the National Cancer Institute, six types of standard treatments are used alone or in conjunction with one another to treat breast cancer: surgery, sentinel lymph node biopsy followed by surgery, radiation therapy, chemotherapy, hormone therapy, and targeted therapy. Physicians also may prescribe a variety of other medications in addition to, or in place of, chemotherapy and radiation. This prescribed class of drugs, known as targeted agents, blocks the growth of cancerous cells by interfering with the "targeted" molecules. Research has shown that some of these medications can help prevent breast cancer recurrence among women with early-stage breast cancer.

Some treatments are commonly used and others are being studied in clinical trials, a research study conducted to improve current treatments. Regardless of the type of treatment, medical care should be multidisciplinary in nature and healthcare professionals should include the patient and her family in the decision-making process.

ADVOCACY

International grassroots movements, focused on collaboration among individuals with cancer, developed in the latter part of the twentieth century. Some of these grassroots movements and organizations grew into worldwide cancer coalitions, such as the European Cancer Coalition and Breast Cancer Network Australia. Coalitions and networks such as these connect individuals with cancer to one another and to local resources. In some countries, these organizations not only provide resources to individuals with cancer but also shape the social and cultural meanings about cancer. For example, Reach for Recovery International, a non-medical organization created to help women adjust after a breast cancer diagnosis, began a group in South Africa in 1967. Since that time, Asian countries have adopted the Reach for Recovery International model, decreasing shame and stigma around a diagnosis of breast cancer and increasing women's power in the medical decision-making process.

In 1982, Nancy Brinker founded the Komen Foundation to increase the number of American women saved from breast cancer because of early detection. By 1985, Breast Cancer Awareness month was celebrated in America. Since the beginning of the twenty-first century, the pink ribbon has been an international icon and the most compelling marketing strategy of the breast cancer movement. Sulik (2012) argued that the pink ribbon culture has trivialized the social problem of breast cancer and reduced activism to mere consumerism shrouded in discourses of awareness.

Companies and organizations have adopted the pink ribbon, utilizing it as a marketing technique to sell products; many companies donate money to breast cancer whereas others do not. According to Sulik, the pink ribbon is not an innocuous accessory worn by breast cancer survivors and endorsed by institutions in the name of solidarity. The ribbon symbolizes a particular worldview, which is hinged on women's positive thinking, improved lives for women, and the belief in biomedicine's ability to cure breast cancer.

PREVENTION

There is no evidence-based, streamlined program offered for breast cancer prevention. However, women can reduce their risk of developing breast cancer by being physically active, maintaining a healthy body weight, eating a balanced diet, and moderating alcohol intake. Self-breast examinations and attending regular mammography screenings can also prevent breast cancer by detecting the disease at an early stage.

Cancer survival rates are inextricably connected to a country's health service development and efficiency to provide early diagnosis, treatment, and clinical follow-up (Sankaranarayanan et al. 2010). Disparities in breast cancer diagnosis, treatment, and mortality by race/ethnicity in the United States are well documented. It is established that compared with non-Hispanic whites, blacks, Hispanic whites, and Native Americans are more likely to be diagnosed with advanced breast cancer and have lower survival rates. Moreover, black and Hispanic white women are more likely to receive inappropriate treatments. Black women have adverse outcomes that are connected to lack of access to and utilization of screening and preventative services, medical care following diagnosis, and long-term follow-up care. Using data from 17 population-based registries, researchers evaluated disparities in breast cancer characteristics and outcomes by race and ethnicity. They found that Pacific Islander women, specifically Samoan women, experience the starkest disparities. Samoan women have significantly higher odds of presenting with late-stage disease, receiving inappropriate treatment for early-stage breast cancer, and had the highest risk of any group for mortality.

A population-based study measuring cancer survival in Africa, Asia, and Central America demonstrated that cancer survival was highest in countries where health services were well developed with advanced treatment centers, such as Hong Kong, South Korea, Singapore, and Turkey. Survival was intermediate in Costa Rica, mainland China, Thailand, India, Saudi Arabia, Pakistan, and Philippines, regions where cancer health services are moderately developed. The Gambia and Uganda had the lowest survival rates and also had poorly developed health services. The authors attributed high breast cancer survival rates in Hong Kong, South Korea, Singapore, and Turkey to these countries having established screening and early detection programs and accessibility to diagnostic services and treatment. The worldwide prevalence of cancer could be more effectively prevented through streamlined programming that addressed early detection, treatment, and healthy lifestyle choices.

SEE ALSO: Women's Health Movement in the United States

REFERENCES

Mayo Clinic. 2012. Breast Cancer Staging. Accessed July 5, 2014, at http://www.mayoclinic.com/health/breast-cancer-staging/BR00022/NSECTIONGROUP=2.

National Cancer Institute. 2012. Stages of Breast Cancer. Accessed July 5, 2014, at http://www.cancer.gov/cancertopics/pdq/treatment/breast/Patient/page2#Keypoint9.

Sankaranarayanan, Rajan, et al. 2010. "Cancer Survival in Africa, Asia, and Central America: A Population Based Study." *Lancet Oncology*, 11: 165–173.

Sulik, Gayle. 2012. *Pink Ribbon Blues: How Breast Cancer Culture Undermines Women's Health.* New York: Oxford University Press.

FURTHER READING

Berg, Wendy A., et al. 2012. "Detection of Breast Cancer with Additional Annual Screening Ultrasound or a Single Screening MRI to Mammography in Women with Elevated Breast Cancer Risk." *JAMA*, 307: 1394–1404.

Chalupka, Stephanie. 2011. "Selective Estrogen Modulators for the Primary Prevention of Breast Cancer." *AAOHN Journal*, 59: 48.

Coleman, Michael P., et al. 2008. "Cancer Survival in Five Continents: A Worldwide Population-Based Study (CONCORD)." *Lancet Oncology*, 9: 730–756.

Love, Susan. 2010. *Dr. Susan Love's Breast Book*, 5th ed. Cambridge, MA: De Capo Press.
Mukherjee, Siddhartha. 2011. *The Emperor of All Maladies*. New York: Scribner.

Breastfeeding in Historical and Comparative Perspective

TAYLOR LIVINGSTON
University of North Carolina at Chapel Hill, USA

Ideas about breast milk vary by culture. For instance, views on colostrum – the sticky yellow substance produced by breasts after birth (before milk production begins) – differ by culture. The biomedical view of colostrum is as a substance beneficial to infants because its fatty nature aids in the elimination of meconium from the infant's bowels. However, many cultures view the substance as unnecessary or harmful to newborns. For example, the Bilanta mothers in the Republic of Guinea-Bissau believe that colostrum can cause illness and even infant death. In cultures where colostrum is viewed negatively, breastfeeding is delayed until days 3–5 postpartum until white breast milk is produced.

In industrialized societies, women who are older, highly educated, married, and have a high income are more likely to breastfeed. In non-industrialized societies, most women breastfeed notwithstanding differences in education levels, income, age, and marital status (Riordan and Wambach 2009). This is possibly attributed to the fact that women in non-industrialized nations are less likely to have access to artificial infant foods (Liamputtong 2011).

While the World Health Organization (WHO) recommends that infants be exclusively fed breast milk for the first 6 months of life, few infants meet this recommendation. Most women around the world participate in mixed feeding, which involves feeding the infant breast milk in addition to other foods such as formula, tea, water, rice water, non-human animal milks, and other foods deemed culturally appropriate.

Until the domestication of plants and animals in the Neolithic age, most infants were breastfed by their mothers or other women. Predictions for a natural age of weaning of modern human populations based on evolutionary indicators range from 2.5 to 7 years of age (Dettwyler 1995). Most non-industrial societies wean their children between 2 and 4 years of age, while most children in the United States are weaned before 1 year of age. The lengths of time that infants are only fed breast milk are unknown. Archaeological evidence suggests mixed feeding occurred during the Neolithic given the discovery of pottery vessels used for infant feedings and horns used to feed animal milks and gruels (in cultures with a history of animal milk production and consumption).

The use of wet nurses, lactating women employed to feed another woman's infant, has a long social history in the West. Many ancient religious texts allude to wet nursing of infants. In the ancient Roman and Greek empires, wealthy women were likely to employ wet nurses. This practice remained, and expanded into the middle class in the Middle Ages. In the mid-1700s, it became popular for wealthy women to breastfeed their own children, although some women still employed wet nurses. Prior to the Industrial Revolution, many women began using cow and goat milks as infant foods, and began dry nursing (making a gruel of cereals mixed with water) infants. This was common among the wealthy and used as a means to feed orphans. The Industrial Revolution in the West brought a massive change to the way infants were fed. Most women initiated breastfeeding and fed for a short time, but quickly weaned to artificial infant foods in order to work outside of the home (Fides 1995). The Industrial Revolution also began the mass production of artificial infant foods – mainly homogenized cow's milk (formula) – and initiated the period known as scientific motherhood, where women were expected to rear their children according to the latest medical and/or scientific advice (Apple 2006). Due to the rise of scientific motherhood and the promotion and mass marketing of artificial infant foods by childcare "experts," such as doctors and public health officials, and companies, breastfeeding rates significantly declined. For instance, in the United States by the 1950s, over 75 percent of children were fed artificial infant foods (Riordan and Wambach 2009). Most of these infants were from wealthy or middle-class families, as rural and poor women did not have access to artificial infant foods. During the 1960s and 1970s in the West, as the ideals of scientific motherhood waned, breastfeeding rates began to increase largely as a result of the women's health movement and the spread of La Leche League International, a mother-to-mother breastfeeding support organization. During the 1980s, the mass marketing of artificial infant foods to international mothers living in conditions without access to clean water also increased breastfeeding rates. This controversy also spurred research comparing the benefits of breastfeeding with formula feeding. The findings of this research spurred large national public health campaigns to encourage women to breastfeed (Wolf 2013).

In non-Western cultures, breastfeeding and wet nursing were the dominant methods of infant feeding until World Wars I and II. During this period breastfeeding declined in non-Western areas as well, largely as a result of colonization. Colonial elites followed the feeding methods of their social class peers in their country of origin to further distance themselves from indigenous peoples. However, indigenous populations were willing to accept the use and promotion of artificial infant foods since colonial medicine often worked in treating health problems. After World War II, the rates of breastfeeding in colonial populations continued to decline due to the wide availability of artificial infant foods and closer contact with healthcare workers. In the 1970s, when breastfeeding rates in Western countries were rising, breastfeeding rates in non-Western countries stagnated due to the mass marketing of artificial infant foods, the migration of people from rural to urban areas, and women entering the workforce. Breastfeeding remains the most popular method of infant feeding; however, more women are mixed feeding than ever before (Riordan and Wambach 2009).

The spread of the HIV/AIDS epidemic has been an infant-feeding problem cross-culturally, as breastfeeding contributes to almost half of mother-to-child transmission of HIV in poor breastfeeding populations (Liamputtong 2011). In poor countries where HIV-positive mothers lack access to anti-retroviral treatment, breast milk can spread the virus. However, women in these poor countries usually lack access to clean water, and thus cannot safely supplement their infants with artificial infant foods. Further, breastfeeding protects against diarrheal and other infections that may lead to infant mortality. In order to combat these challenges, WHO began recommending in 2010 that mothers who are HIV-positive and are taking anti-retrovirals (ARVs) breastfeed their infants to at least 12 months of age. Mothers who are HIV-positive, not receiving ARVs, but lack "acceptable, feasible, affordable, sustainable, and safe" artificial infant-feeding substitutes are encouraged to exclusively breastfeed for the first months of life (WHO

2010). WHO also recommends that all mothers who are HIV-positive, regardless of treatment with ARVs, cease breastfeeding as soon as is feasible, taking into consideration local situations, mothers' circumstances, and risks of replacement feeding, in order to reduce the risk of HIV transmission.

SEE ALSO: Birth Control, History and Politics of; Medicine and Medicalization; Scientific Motherhood; Wet Nursing; Women's Health Movement in the United States

REFERENCES

Apple, Rima. 2006. *Perfect Motherhood: Science and Childrearing in America*. New Brunswick: Rutgers University Press.
Dettwyler, Katherine A. 1995. "A Time to Wean: The Hominid Blueprint for the Natural Age of Weaning in Modern Human Populations." In *Breastfeeding: Biocultural Perspectives*, edited by Patricia Stewart-Macadam and Katherine A. Dettwyler, 39–74. New York: Aldine de Gruyter.
Fides, V. 1995. "The Culture and Biology of Breastfeeding: A Historical Review of Western Europe." In *Breastfeeding: Biocultural Perspectives*, edited by Patricia Stewart-Macadam and Katherine A. Dettwyler, 101–126. New York: Aldine de Gruyter.
Liamputtong, Pranee, ed. 2011. *Infant Feeding Practices: A Cross-Cultural Perspective*. New York: Springer.
Riordan, Jan, and Karen Wambach, eds. 2009. *Breastfeeding and Human Lactation*. Boston: Jones and Bartlett.
Wolf, Joan B. 2013. *Is Breast Best: Taking on the Breastfeeding Experts and the New High Stakes of Motherhood*. New York: NYU Press.
World Health Organization (WHO). 2010. "Guidelines on HIV and Infant Feeding: Principles and Recommendations for Infant Feeding in the Context of HIV and a Summary of Evidence." Accessed June 15, 2015, at http://www.who.int/maternal_child_adolescent/documents/9789241599535/en/.

FURTHER READING

Blum, Linda. 1999. *At the Breast: Ideologies of Breastfeeding and Motherhood in the Contemporary US*. Boston: Beacon Press.
Maher, Vanessa, ed. 1992. *The Anthropology of Breastfeeding*. New York: St. Martin's Press.
Van Esterik, Penny. 1989. *Beyond the Breast–Bottle Controversy*. New Brunswick: Rutgers University Press.
Wolf, Jacqueline H. 2001. *Don't Kill Your Baby: Public Health and the Decline of Breastfeeding in the Nineteenth and Twentieth Centuries*. Columbus: Ohio State University Press.

Buddhism

RITA M. GROSS
University of Wisconsin–Eau Claire, USA

Buddhist texts and practices are dominated by two incompatible contrasting attitudes toward gender. The more normative view, proclaimed by many authoritative texts and teachers, is that the enlightened mind is beyond gender, neither male nor female, and that women and men have equal spiritual capacities. If that view were put into practice more frequently, Buddhist institutions and societies would be much more gender egalitarian than they are. The more popular view, held by many ordinary Buddhist practitioners, is that men have many advantages over women and that being a woman is significantly less desirable than being a man. This view dominates popular Buddhist thinking and is often used to explain and justify male dominance in Buddhist institutions and the male near-monopoly on Buddhism's most favored roles and activities. Because Buddhist institutional practices have followed the popular attitude more frequently than the normative attitude, women have always been seriously disadvantaged in Buddhist institutions such as monasteries and universities. Thus, birth or rebirth as a male is considered to be far more fortunate than female birth, despite the oft-quoted slogan that enlightened mind is beyond gender. Buddhists have done little to address or redress this deep contradiction between their ideals and the way their institutions work.

These two views regarding gender are found from the beginnings of the religion to the present day and in all forms of Buddhism. Early Buddhist texts, such as the *Therigatha (Songs of the Female Elders)*, demonstrate that women could become highly regarded teachers and attain the same status as men. Buddhism was one of the first religions to allow an alternative to domesticity and motherhood for women by allowing not only men but also women to renounce householder life and become celibate monastics. Other religions of the time envisioned no role for women other than marriage and motherhood. For women, or men for that matter, to live independently was almost impossible. Other texts narrate that the Buddha himself was reluctant to allow women to become monastics, the preferred lifestyle for serious practitioners in early Buddhism.

Some modern scholars doubt the authenticity of texts about the historical Buddha's reluctance to ordain women, suggesting that they are later interpolations of earlier texts. Others have argued that Buddhism, like many other religions, was more egalitarian in its earliest forms and gradually became much more male dominated. Still others have argued that, even if these theses are correct, male dominance has been contested in all forms of Buddhism and in all periods of Buddhist history. Many classical texts ridicule male dominance and portray women as representing all Buddhist ideals. Nevertheless, Buddhist institutions became very male dominated quite early in its history. Attitudes towards women also hardened into the popular view that female rebirth is less fortunate by far than male rebirth. This view, which is so offensive to many contemporary Buddhists, actually reflects the social disadvantages faced by women in the traditional cultures in which Buddhism was practiced. Contemporary Buddhist feminists have argued that traditional Buddhism recognized one key part of feminist analyses – life under male dominance is unpleasant for women – but that classical Buddhism failed to provide an adequate solution to that problem. Instead of advocating for social change, traditional Buddhists offered women spiritual advice on how to be reborn as men at some point in the future, thus improving their status and chances for a more fortunate existence. Modern feminists, of course, are not impressed by that solution to the problem of extreme male dominance.

Because monasticism and its requirement of celibacy are so dominant, many suppose that Buddhism must have a negative view of sexuality and regard it as something that should be avoided or something that damages those who engage in it. But this is not correct. Sexuality is regarded as one part of the whole complex of domestic conventional life. In early Buddhist analysis, domestic life is evaluated as being totally unable to bring lasting joy and peace, but always producing sorrow and disappointment eventually. This analysis emphasizes that domestic life is so time-consuming and distracting that one who is embedded in domesticity can never ponder life's deeper meanings or practice spiritual disciplines seriously. That is why the monastic lifestyle is regarded as preferable for serious Buddhist practitioners. The monastic lifestyle frees people of such demands, which is why it is thought to be more likely to bring lasting peace and wisdom. Buddhists have also always recognized that not all people are suited for monasticism and that to function, society must offer various options suited to humans of different capacities and interests. For those who choose a domestic lifestyle, sexuality and sexual pleasure are not regarded negatively. Sexuality is a problem only for monastics but not for people in general. In fact, in some later forms of Buddhism, sexual symbolism became very important and a couple in sexual union came to symbolize the tradition's norms and goals for the most accomplished practitioner, who could unify both wisdom and compassion. The effect of such symbols on the lives of ordinary practitioners is less clear. Sexual symbolism does not seem to have improved women's lives or brought them higher status or more self-determination.

Buddhism has always had a strong sex ethic which, at its core, is more about care that one's sexual activities do not cause harm to either one's partner or oneself than about rules. For laypeople, Buddhist sexual ethics have usually followed the norms of the local culture in which Buddhists live. Buddhists have engaged in monogamous, polygynous, and polyandrous marriages and in many forms of less binding sexual unions between women and men.

Homosexuality is generally frowned upon in many Asian cultures, and most Buddhist codes of sex ethics recommend using only sexual organs, not other organs or orifices, for sexual activity, whether between homosexuals or heterosexuals. The Dalai Lama, the world's best-known Buddhist authority, has recently stated that he does not disapprove of same-sex marriage for those who condone it, but that religious people should follow their own religion's rules regarding marriage norms. Because traditional Buddhist recommendations regarding sexual behavior do not condone homosexual practices, many Buddhists have been very disappointed by his pronouncements. Given these rules, it is difficult to know to what extent homosexual laypeople were able to forge satisfactory relationships in traditional Asian Buddhist cultures. Because sexual activity is forbidden to monastics, homosexual relationships were forbidden to monastics, though they were quite common among Japanese Buddhists at some times.

In contemporary times, Buddhism has spread around the world, including the Western world, where it is currently flourishing. Buddhists in both Asia and the West experience the same conflicts surrounding gender and sexuality that are found in other religions and societies regarding gender roles and gender identity. A strong worldwide Buddhist women's movement addresses the needs of both nuns and laywomen. Increasing women's opportunities for leadership, especially as spiritual teachers, is an important reform for Buddhist feminists. Among Western Buddhists, about half of their spiritual teachers are women, a situation unprecedented in previous forms of Buddhism. Among these spiritual teachers are many laywomen, also unprecedented in Buddhist history. Central issues for many Asian Buddhists include upgrading the status of nuns and introducing full monastic ordination for women into those forms of Buddhism in which it is lacking. Previously, nuns often lacked Buddhist knowledge and had very low status. In Southeast Asia and Tibet, the ordination of women was absent and efforts to introduce it into those forms of Buddhism are not yet fully successful. However, nuns' education has improved in all parts of the Buddhist world including those that still lack full ordination. Among Western Buddhists, the same options regarding gender and sexuality, including the open practice of homosexuality or transgender activities and lifestyles, that prevail in society at large are common, though Western Buddhists tend to be more liberal than society at large regarding these issues.

SEE ALSO: Celibacy; Heterosexism and Homophobia; Monasticism

FURTHER READING

Cabezon, Jose Ignacio, ed. 1992. *Buddhism, Sexuality, and Gender*. Albany: State University of New York Press.

Gross, Rita M. 1993. *Buddhism after Patriarchy: A Feminist History, Analysis, and Reconstruction of Buddhism*. Albany: State University of New York.

Paul, Diana Y. 1979. *Women in Buddhism: Images of the Feminine in the Mahayana Tradition*. Berkeley: Asian Humanities Press.

Rhys-Davids, C.A.F., and K.R. Norman, trans. 1989. *Poems of the Early Buddhist Nuns (Therigatha)*. Oxford: Pali Text Society.

Bullying

LISA H. ROSEN and LINDA J. RUBIN
Texas Woman's University, USA

Bullying is a subtype of aggressive behavior in which a victim is repeatedly targeted by negative actions on the part of another student or group of students. Although bullying behaviors can take many forms, including spreading rumors, teasing, and even physical attacks, three conditions must be met in order for behavior to be considered bullying: (1) the behavior is intended to harm the victim, (2) the behavior continues over time, and (3) a power asymmetry exists with the bully or bullies having more power than the victim (Nansel et al. 2001).

There is growing concern among parents, teachers, researchers, and policymakers about bullying, given the serious negative consequences that ensue for both bullies and victims. Victims of bullying are at increased risk for various forms of maladjustment, including both internalizing difficulties (e.g., anxiety, depression, and somatic complaints) and externalizing difficulties (e.g., delinquency and substance use) (Sullivan, Farrell, and Kliewer 2006). Aggressive behavior has also been associated with internalizing and externalizing problems, and children who bully others are more likely to face academic difficulties and engage in violent, delinquent behavior later in life (Coyne, Nelson, and Underwood 2011).

Boys are often believed to be involved in bullying to a greater extent than girls, both as victims and perpetrators. Analyses of data from a representative sample of American youth indicate that a substantial proportion of middle- and high-school students report moderate to frequent involvement in bullying. Thirteen percent of youth were identified as bullies, and 11 percent identified as victims, with boys reporting higher levels of both bullying and victimization than girls (Nansel et al. 2001).

A focus on physical aggression may be a possible reason why boys report higher levels of involvement in bullying than girls. Researchers frequently present students with a definition of bullying that includes both physically and socially aggressive behaviors without differentiating between them. That boys are more physically aggressive than are girls is a robust finding in the literature (Card et al. 2008). There are a number of possible reasons to explain why boys are more physically aggressive than girls, including that boys have more physical strength than girls and are socialized differently by parents and other adults. Whereas boys may be encouraged to be tough and dominant, physical aggression is more discouraged among girls.

Gender differences become less clear when social aggression is considered. Social aggression refers to behaviors intended to harm a peer's social status and relationships, and includes behaviors such as social exclusion and malicious gossip. Stereotypically, girls are believed to be more socially aggressive than boys, and this is widely reflected in media portrayals. Even preschoolers commonly view social aggression as predominantly female behavior (Giles and Heyman 2005). The belief that girls are more socially aggressive than boys has been referred to as *gender oversimplification of aggression*, and is inconsistent with some studies that found no gender difference in social aggression, some studies finding that girls are more socially aggressive, and others that boys are more socially aggressive (Swearer 2008). A meta-analysis found a significant difference in social aggression favoring girls, but the researchers concluded that this difference was so small as to be trivial (Card et al. 2008).

Researchers are now beginning to examine possible gender differences in cyberbullying. The experience of cyberbullying is important to investigate, given that the physical size differential between girls and boys is less relevant when the harmful behavior is inflicted through electronic communication tools. Many common cyberbullying behaviors (e.g., spreading insulting, humiliating, and/or threatening material on the Internet) resemble social aggression and have the same impact as offline bullying (Klein 2012). Cyberbullying creates an added complication for victims, as it follows children from the schools into the 24/7 world of cyberspace, often behind anonymous identities. Evidence of a gender difference in cyberbullying is mixed, and it is unclear whether there are meaningful gender differences in levels of cyberbullying (Underwood and Rosen 2011).

Another important avenue of research is examining gender differences in bullying roles. Many forms of bullying still take place in the school setting in front of other children. Girls are more likely to take the roles of defender of the victim and outsider. Boys, on the other hand, are more likely to take the roles of reinforcer and assistant of the bully, either encouraging the behavior or actively supporting the bully during the incident (Salmivalli et al. 1996).

Researchers and school officials are also beginning to focus on bullying targeted at sexual minority and gender non-conforming youth. Sexual minority youth report higher levels of bullying than heterosexual youth, and this peer maltreatment is often severe and unremitting (Tharinger 2008). Further, youth who identify as lesbian, gay, bisexual, or transgender (LGBT) often experience multiple forms of bullying (e.g., verbal taunts and physical attacks), also known as gay bashing, at much higher rates than non-LGBT youth. According to the Gay, Lesbian, and Straight Education Network's National School Climate Survey (2014), 74 percent of LGBT students were verbally harassed and 36 percent were physically harassed during the past year due to their sexual orientation (Kosciw et al. 2014). Students who identify as sexual minority youth are more likely to be considered gender non-conforming; however, many adolescents who identify as heterosexual express their gender in a manner that does not conform to traditional gendered stereotypes. Regardless of sexual orientation, youth who are viewed as violating societal gender norms are at increased risk for physical and social victimization (Toomey, Card, and Casper 2014). In 2013, over 55 percent of LGBT students were verbally harassed and nearly 23 percent were physically harassed because of their gender nonconformity (Kosciw et al. 2014). Some scholars suggest that such peer interactions can be viewed as a form of "gender policing," and boys who behave in what is believed to be a non-masculine fashion may be labeled using homophobic names or otherwise victimized. Boys who aggress against other boys based on sexual orientation or gender nonconformity may be downplaying another's masculinity to bolster their own. As such, there is an association between these forms of bullying and hegemonic masculinity in which aggressors consider themselves to embody more stereotypically masculine traits, such as being tough, unemotional, and dominant, than their victims (e.g., Tharinger 2008).

Prevention and intervention programs must take bullying and cyberbullying of all youth seriously and be gender sensitive in all aspects of training. In designing these programs and educating youth, schools should actively differentiate sexual harassment from bullying. Some researchers and policymakers believe that bullying and sexual harassment should be treated similarly, as both can be viewed as abuses of power. However, treating sexual harassment as bullying denies girls powerful legal rights, and also frames the situation as an interpersonal problem, rather than the result of cultural stereotypes of gender (Brown, Chesney-Lind, and Stein 2007). Schools must be advised to create a culture in which compassion and the courage to speak out against all forms of bullying are more highly valued than the status, recognition, and popularity associated with bullying (Klein 2012). Future researchers should examine strategies for reducing all forms of aggression and promoting prosocial behavior in boys and girls.

SEE ALSO: Boys' Peer Cultures; Gender Violence; Girls' Peer Cultures; Victimization

REFERENCES

Brown, Lyn M., Meda Chesney-Lind, and Nan Stein. 2007. "Patriarchy Matters: Toward a Gendered Theory of Teen Violence and Victimization." *Violence Against Women*, 13: 1249–1273.

Card, Noel A., Brian D. Stucky, Gita M. Sawalani, and Todd D. Little. 2008. "Direct and Indirect Aggression During Childhood and Adolescence: a Meta-analytic Review of Gender Differences, Intercorrelations, and Relations to Maladjustment." *Child Development*, 79: 1185–1229.

Coyne, Sarah M., David A. Nelson, and Marion Underwood. 2011. "Aggression in Children." In *The Wiley-Blackwell Handbook of Childhood Social Development*, 2nd ed., edited by Peter K. Smith and Craig H. Hart, 491–509. Chichester: John Wiley & Sons.

Giles, Jessica W. and Gail D. Heyman. 2005. "Young Children's Beliefs about the Relationship between Gender and Aggressive Behavior." *Child Development*, 76: 107–121.

Klein, Jessie. 2012. *The Bully Society: School Shootings and the Crisis of Bullying in America's Schools*. New York: New York University Press.

Kosciw, Joseph G., Emily A. Greytak, Neal A. Palmer, and Madelyn J Boesen. 2014. *The 2013 National School Climate Survey: the Experiences of Lesbian, Gay, Bisexual and Transgender Youth in Our Nation's Schools*. New York: Gay, Lesbian, Straight Education Network.

Nansel, Tonja R., Mary Overpeck, Ramani S. Pilla, W. June Ruan, Bruce Simons-Morton, and Peter Scheidt. 2001. "Bullying Behaviors Among US Youth: Prevalence and Association with Psychosocial Adjustment." *Journal of the American Medical Association*, 285: 2094–2100.

Salmivalli, Christina, Kirsti Lagerspetz, Kaj Björkqvist, Karin Österman, and Ari Kaukiainen. 1996. "Bullying as a Group Process: Participant Roles and their Relations to Social Status Within the Group." *Aggressive Behavior*, 22: 1–15.

Sullivan, Terri N., Albert D. Farrell, and Wendy Kliewer. 2006. "Peer Victimization in Early Adolescence: Association Between Physical and Relational Victimization and Drug Use, Aggression, and Delinquent Behaviors Among Urban Middle School Students." *Development and Psychopathology*, 18: 119–137.

Swearer, Susan M. 2008. "Relational Aggression: Not Just a Female Issue." *Journal of School Psychology*, 46: 611–616.

Tharinger, Deborah J. 2008. "Maintaining the Hegemonic Masculinity Through Selective Attachment, Homophobia, and Gay-Baiting in Schools: Challenges to Intervention." *School Psychology Review*, 27: 221–227.

Toomey, Russell B., Noel A. Card, and Deborah M. Casper. 2014. "Peers' Perceptions of Gender Nonconformity: Associations with Overt and Relational Peer Victimization and Aggression in Early Adolescence." *The Journal of Early Adolescence*, 34: 463–485.

Underwood, Marion K., and Lisa H. Rosen. 2011. "Gender and Bullying: Moving Beyond Mean Differences to Consider Conceptions of Bullying, Processes by Which Bullying Unfolds, and Cyber Bullying." In *Bullying in American Schools*, 2nd ed., edited by Dorothy L. Espelage and Susan M. Swearer, 13–22. New York: Routledge.

Butch/Femme

CHRISTINE A. SMITH
University of Wisconsin–Green Bay, USA

In the 1930s and 1940s in the United States, a visible lesbian culture emerged through bars and house parties, especially in working-class communities. Many working-class lesbian communities had strict rules in which a woman must assume either a butch or femme (sometimes written as fem) role and presentation (Lapovsky Kennedy and Davis 1993; Crawley 2001). Writers such as Levitt and Hiestand (2004) refer to butch and femme as "lesbian genders," which function culturally to structure expectations of personal identity, social interactions, and romantic play. Rather than simply imitating heterosexual roles of male/female, masculine/feminine, these identities transformed those roles to create a unique lesbian community (Lapovsky Kennedy and Davis 1993).

To be butch meant that a woman presented a masculine appearance and mannerisms. Butch can be style of dress, attitude, sexual stance, actions, and means of relating to the world. Butch lesbians often held traditionally male jobs and coupled romantically only with femmes (and vice versa). Their masculine presentation marked them as lesbian and, as a result, they were subject to frequent discrimination.

The term butch also signified the active or dominant partner in sexual relationships. The idea conceptualized a butch as a "top" and femme as a "bottom", although the rigidity of this dichotomy has been questioned. A stone butch was someone who was sexually untouchable by a femme partner.

Femmes adhered to more traditionally feminine forms of dress, hairstyles, and interests and, as a result, may have "passed" for heterosexual. While femmes tended to conform to traditional gender norms for women, their desire for other women made them transgressive.

Butch and femme were less prevalent among middle-class lesbians. As Lilian Faderman (1991) indicates, a visible lesbian culture was threatening for many middle- and upper-class lesbians, who had more class privilege to lose and saw butch and femme roles as undesirable. Middle-class lesbian organizations such as Daughters of Bilitis worked for lesbian acceptability through assimilation, and were critical of butch and femme lesbian sexual imagery (Smith 1989).

Race was another factor, especially in butch identity. Black butch lesbians instead sometimes identified as studs. While white butches were characterized by dress, including the 1950s "butch uniform" of white tee-shirt and jeans, black studs were more likely to dress in the more formal wear of black culture at the time, for example, in three-piece suits.

Butch and femme fell out of favor (at least publicly) in the 1970s as feminists began to critique gender relations. Butch/femme roles came to be seen as imitating heterosexual patriarchy (Jeffreys 1989). Butches were seen as embodying undesirable male characteristics and femmes were seen as adhering to traditional subservient female roles. Lesbian feminism saw the dichotomy of masculinity and femininity as contributing to women's oppression.

In the 1980s, lesbian communities, especially urban, middle and upper-middle class, began reclaiming these identities, but with greater performative aspects and with less class division. Crawley (2001) argues that this revival coincides with the decline of feminist activity in the 1980s, but it is unclear if these roles operate in opposition to feminism or as a form of social resistance to patriarchy in the absence of feminist activities. Additionally, some theorists began to reframe butch and femme in feminist terms. For example, femme lesbians' strength and power (as opposed to their image as passive) began to be recognized. Monique Wittig (1981) framed butch lives as transgressive as they represent the ability to escape social programming of traditional femininity.

As transgender acceptance in the queer community has increased, some butch-identified women have claimed male identity as female-to-male transmen. Some, such as Levitt and Hiestand (2004), argue that butch lesbians are part of the transgender community because of their gender transgression, and in their interviews of self-identified butches, several identified as transgender. However, others, such as Arlene Stein (2010), have written about the concern among some in the lesbian community that butches are now becoming (trans)men.

Currently, while identifying as femme indicates queerness, there seems to be much broader conceptualizations than in the past. Fewer lesbians strongly identify as butch or femme, nor do they request these specific labels in romantic partners. When lesbians do adhere to butch or femme identity labels, the majority identify as femme and seek femme partners (Smith and Stillman 2002), at least for white lesians.

For black lesbians, the terms "stud," "aggressive," and "dominant" are also used for those assuming a butch role. The stud/femme dynamic continues to be an important part of black lesbian culture.

Academically, theorists and writers continue to examine butch and femme as historical constructs as well as current expressions of the lesbian experience (see, for example, Gibson and Meem 2002; Coyote and Sharman 2011).

SEE ALSO: Gender Performance; Gender Transgression; Lesbian Performance; Masculinities; Stone Butch

REFERENCES

Coyote, Ivan, and Zena Sharman. 2011. *Persistence: All Ways Butch and Femme*. Vancouver: Arsenal Pulp Press.

Crawley, Sara L. 2001. "Are Butch and Fem Working-Class and Anti-Feminist?" *Gender and Society*, 15: 175–196.

Faderman, Lillian. 1991. *Odd Girls and Twilight Lovers: A History of Lesbian Life in Twentieth-Century America*. New York: Columbia University Press.

Gibson, Michelle, and Deborah T. Meem. 2002. *Femme/Butch: New Considerations of the Way We Want to Go*. Binghampton: Harrington Park Press.

Jeffreys, Sheila. 1989. "Butch and Femme, Now and Then." In *Not a Passing Phase: Reclaiming Lesbians in History, 1840–1985*. Edited by Lesbian History Group, 158–187. London: Women's Press.

Laprovsky Kennedy, Elizabeth, and Madeline D. Davis. 1993. *Boots of Leather, Slippers of Gold: A History of a Lesbian Community*. New York: Routledge.

Levitt, Heidi, and Katherine Hiestand. 2004. "A Quest for Authenticity: Contemporary Butch Gender." *Sex Roles*, 50: 605–621.

Smith, Christine, and Shannon Stillman. 2002. "Butch/Femme in the Personal Advertisements of Lesbians". *Journal of Lesbian Studies*, 6: 45–51.

Smith, Elizabeth. A. 1989. "Butches, Femmes, and Feminists: The Politics of Lesbian Sexuality". *NWSA Journal*, 1: 398–421.

Stein, Arlene. 2010. "The Incredible Shrinking Lesbian World and Other Conundra." *Sexualities*, 13: 21–32.

Wittig, Monique. 1981. "One is Not Born a Woman." *Feminist Issues*, 2: 48–54.

Camp

HELENE A. SHUGART
University of Utah, USA

Camp is an aesthetic sensibility that is historically anchored in strategic performances of gender or sexuality, especially at their intersection. Although camp is no longer necessarily tied to gender or sexuality in contemporary popular articulations, performance remains one of its defining features, and specific performative qualities associated with it have persisted across time, cultures, and contexts.

The origins of camp are strongly associated with gay male culture, so much so that many critics have defined it as a peculiarly "gay sensibility." Esther Newton (1993) asserts that a "camp/theatrical" sensibility is one of two major gay sensibilities, the other of which is an "egalitarian/authentic perspective": the distinction between them inheres in their respective relationships to bourgeois middle-class democratic ideology, wherein the former draws itself against those ideals – camp is, Newton asserts, fundamentally "a philosophy of transformations and incongruity" (1993, 73) – and the latter is drawn directly from them. The earliest uses of "camp" as an adjective are traced to the early twentieth century, and its popular association with gay male culture was soon thereafter secured in relation to Oscar Wilde, whose sardonic, arch, and ostentatious style came to define the aesthetic; in that case, they were identified with and mobilized in the persona of the "dandy," which Wilde epitomized. Those stylistic qualities and their performative potential subsequently evolved within gay male culture to include the phenomenon of drag, or the impersonation of (usually iconic) women by gay men, and they also influenced artifacts and design associated with gay male culture. Today, camp is widely available in popular culture and not necessarily, or at least directly, hinged to gay male culture; however, the qualities that characterize camp, irrespective of context or object, reflect its genesis in cultural politics and performances of gender and sexuality.

As noted, at its core, camp turns on performance. That performance may be of a person – drag performances of Judy Garland or Cher constitute classic, even cliché examples – or it may be of a concept (like femininity, more broadly and generically) or a bygone era (the 1950s, for example) or a style (such as disco). Accordingly, the qualities associated with camp follow directly from this performative imperative, which in turn reflect their underpinnings in gay male

The Wiley Blackwell Encyclopedia of Gender and Sexuality Studies, First Edition. Edited by Nancy A. Naples.
© 2016 John Wiley & Sons, Ltd. Published 2016 by John Wiley & Sons, Ltd.

culture. The first of these is *parody*, or theatricality – the explicit and obvious "sending up" of particular individuals, objects, or ideas, which has been tied to the act of passing, or drawing a line between one's "authentic" self and the performance expected or demanded within a given culture. A related yet distinct quality of *irony*, or incongruity – the "double entendre," or the notion that a hidden meaning undergirds the superficially available one seen – is integral to camp, and it is typically accomplished by the recontextualization of signs that signals the double meaning. *Excess*, sometimes manifested as spectacle, is another feature of camp: flamboyantly "over the top" performances frequently secure the incongruity and artifice that camp seeks to establish. Importantly, two other qualities typically characteristic of camp are *humor*, or playfulness – a disruption of the expected, the conventional, the "straight", and *nostalgia* – rather than mean or cynical, camp is generally offered in a spirit of affection, tenderness, or homage.

If relatively implicit, two other qualities have been associated with camp, which can also be traced to its genesis. The first of these is *elitism*, in terms of both social capital – Wilde's dandy, the prototype of camp, was steeped in white, Western, aristocratic privilege, and camp remained and arguably remains associated primarily with relatively wealthy white gay men – as well as cultural capital: one must have a vaunted point of reference from which to "camp," or a presumed elevated place from which to articulate (or appreciate) ironic or parodic claims. Elitism is especially apparent as relevant to male privilege, according to many critics (e.g., Robertson 1996) who note that women are excluded at least by the historical tradition if not the sensibility proper of camp. Women and/or femininity, they aver, frequently constitute the field or objects of camp but are not accorded agency: while women (or femininity) are frequently camped, certainly per its mobilization as drag, their own performative plays on gender and sexuality are conspicuously absent from received discussions, definitions, or apprehensions of camp. These patterns have led some critics to suggest that camp may feature at least an undercurrent of misogyny, despite the ostensibly affectionate impulses that inform it. Finally, despite Susan Sontag's (1964) notorious allegation that camp is apolitical, most critics have, to the contrary, suggested that camp is inherently *critical* or at least characterized by critical potential, per its performative nature: by definition, it resignifies or recontextualizes that which it takes up, and it often denaturalizes it – queers it, in the estimation of many – in significant ways.

However, Sontag's controversial contention may be gaining credibility in recent years, at least as relevant to the advent of "pop camp" or "camp lite," widely available in the contemporary mainstream, which many critics decry as an appropriation of camp rather than camp proper. This variation, they contend, is devoid of political and cultural critique, much less of an acknowledgment – implicit or otherwise – of its queer moorings. Rather, it turns on recycling the cultural detritus of history, rendered purely aesthetically and superficially via stock performative camp sensibilities of parody, irony, excess, humor, and nostalgia – for example, as evident in retro fashion trends, like avocado green kitchen appliances; tributes to past cultural icons, like *Charlie's Angels*; or evoking bygone eras and sensibilities, like those captured in *Mad Men*. If the popularization of camp suggests an apparent antidote to elitism, critics note that this incarnation is squarely situated in the logic of capitalism, or the conditions of production and consumption – hence widespread skepticism regarding its resistive potential.

SEE ALSO: Drag; Gender Performance; Queer Performance

REFERENCES

Newton, Esther. 1993. *Cherry Grove, Fire Island: Sixty Years in America's First Gay and Lesbian Town*. Boston, MA: Beacon Press.
Robertson, Pamela. 1996. *Guilty Pleasures: Feminist Camp from Mae West to Madonna*. Durham, NC: Duke University Press.
Sontag, Susan. 1964. "Notes on Camp." *Partisan Review*, 31(4): 515–530.

FURTHER READING

Babuscio, Jack. 1977. "Camp and the Gay Sensibility." In *Gays and Film*, edited by Richard Dyer, 40–57. London: BFI.
Booth, Mark. 1983. *Camp*. London: Quartet.
Cleto, Fabio, ed. 1999. *Camp: Queer Aesthetics and the Performing Subject*. Ann Arbor, MI: University of Michigan Press.

Capabilities Approach

SHELLEY CAVALIERI
University of Toledo College of Law, USA

The capabilities approach (sometimes referred to as the capability approach or the human development approach) is a theory of international development that focuses on building human capacity to pursue and achieve a range of outcomes. It provides both a theory of basic social justice and an approach for making quality-of-life comparisons and assessments across nations (Nussbaum 2000, 70–71; Nussbaum 2011, 18). Development economist Amartya Sen first articulated an early version of the theory in 1979 (Sen 1979); he and Aristotelian philosopher Martha Nussbaum have in parallel developed and expounded the theory since that time.

The hallmark of the capabilities approach is to consider societies through the lens of what each person is able to do and to be (Nussbaum 2011, 18). The capabilities approach is centered on equipping individuals with capability, which comprises the skills, freedoms, and primary social goods necessary to pursue their own life ends and visions of the good. Sen has referred to these individual ends as functionings and defines them as the various things a person may value doing or being, which can range from health and well-being to the pursuit of specific life goals and purposes (Sen 1999, 75). The model is conspicuously agnostic in its consideration of the kind of life an individual wishes to seek. It focuses on the capacity with which a society endows the individual to pursue his or her personally chosen goals and aspirations, and the array of options available to all individuals, not on the accomplishment of a particular set of mandated life choices (Sen 1999). Nussbaum has described the theory as having five central aspects (Nussbaum 2011, 18–19). First, the capabilities approach takes each person as an end; it does not focus on average opportunity, but opportunity for each person. Second, it is focused on choice or freedom, which people may choose whether and how to exercise. Third, the capabilities approach is pluralist about value and multifaceted in its content; the array of capabilities cannot be reduced to a single scale such as money. Fourth, it is concerned with entrenched social injustice and inequality, especially where these are consequences of systemic discrimination or marginalization. Fifth, it assigns to government and public policy the urgent task of improving quality of life for all people.

While these five tenets animate the work of both Nussbaum and Sen, their emphases within the capabilities approach differ. The capabilities approach is useful both as a social justice theory and for making comparisons regarding quality of life, and each theorist has concentrated on one of these functions. Nussbaum's angle on the capabilities approach attends more closely to the social justice theory aspects; she considers the role of human dignity in a manner befitting her role as an Aristotelian philosopher (Nussbaum 2011). In contrast, Sen looks at the capabilities approach as an economist, using it as a tool to compare countries based on the capabilities with which they endow their own citizens, both as a function of differences in the nation's wealth and as evidence of inequality within the nation's distribution of freedoms and opportunities. Furthermore, Nussbaum has articulated a specific list of central capabilities (Nussbaum 2011), whereas Sen has offered a small number of examples of capabilities that he views as crucial, but has not published a comprehensive list. These distinctions are rather technical, and what unifies the two theorists is far more substantial than what distinguishes them.

The capabilities approach stands in contrast to development theories that focus on aggregate measures of well-being, such as gross domestic product, to analyze the development of nations, and instead contemplates the capacities the society offers each individual to pursue his or her own ends. In contrast to the standard development approach, which assumes that economic growth and human development improvements will follow from proper arrangement of economic institutions in a nation, the capabilities approach demands that poor people's lives improve immediately as a precursor to economic development within the nation (United Nations Development Programme 2013). As a result, it influences international development efforts worldwide, most notably through the work of the United Nations Development Programme, which has observed that state investment in people's capabilities such as health, education, and nutrition have led to improvements in human development (United Nations Development Programme 2013). The United Nations has therefore shaped its Millennium Development Goals around benchmarks of development that align closely with the establishment of basic human capabilities such as health, nutrition, and education, and the eradication of hunger, poverty, disease, and gender discrimination.

The capabilities approach is relevant to gender and sexuality studies because of its focus on the capabilities of individuals. Rather than focusing on first theoretical principles undergirding any particular political system, the capabilities approach instead looks to the outcomes that a public policy approach can generate for each individual citizen. The approach's rejection of aggregate measures of well-being that might mask disparities in outcomes based on gender or sexuality means that it considers the lives of even disfavored individuals as relevant to the level of development a nation has achieved. When the capabilities approach is used to compare nations' development, the freedoms and capabilities of each individual matter far more than the welfare of the majority. To the extent that the well-being of and opportunities available to gender or sexual minorities is included when the capabilities approach is used to measure development, this model offers a promising way of improving the status of these groups.

SEE ALSO: Gender and Development; Women in Development

REFERENCES

Nussbaum, Martha C. 2000. *Women and Human Development: The Capabilities Approach (The Seeley Lectures)*. Cambridge: Cambridge University Press.

Nussbaum, Martha C. 2011. *Creating Capabilities: The Human Development Approach*. Cambridge, MA: Harvard University Press.

Sen, Amartya. 1979. "Equality of What? The Tanner Lecture on Human Values, Stanford University, May 22, 1979." Accessed 22 June, 2015, at http://www.tannerlectures.utah.edu.

Sen, Amartya. 1999. *Development as Freedom*. New York: Alfred A. Knopf.

United Nations Development Programme. 2013. *Human Development Report 2013: The Rise of the South: Human Progress in a Diverse World*. New York: United Nations Development Programme.

FURTHER READING

Deneulin, Séverine. 2009. *The Human Development and Capabilities Approach*. London: Earthscan.

Capitalist Patriarchy

MECHTHILD HART
DePaul University, USA

The term "capitalist patriarchy" represents a nodal point of a number of issues inserted into different theoretical frameworks or historical analyses of both "capitalism" and "patriarchy." These frameworks shape the particular meanings of these terms as well as their relationship to each other. They may therefore be seen as two separate systems that are in conflict with each other, or that complement or mutually reinforce each other. In addition, the particular sequencing of the terms may imply whether capitalism or patriarchy is considered the overarching system of oppression, and therefore responsible for the general structuring of social, political, or economic realities.

Two US writers, Zillah Eisenstein and bell hooks, and a group of German writers, originally referred to as the Bielefeld School, are most representative of the vast range of meanings and analyses of "capitalist patriarchy." They also illustrate how different theoretical-political agendas determine the particular toolkits they use for describing the "capitalist" and the "patriarchal" aspect of social reality, what particular reality, or realities, they focus on, and how their understanding of the history of old and new global capitalism influences their line of thinking.

Eisenstein (1979) originally used the term "capitalist patriarchy" in order to draw attention to a system of oppression that had been ignored or neglected by Marxist writers. Similar to other "socialist feminist" writers of the 1970s and 1980s, she investigated how capitalism functions in relation to the position of the housewife, the epitome of patriarchal relations, and how these relations are influenced by, and in turn influence, class relations. She therefore broke rank with other socialist feminists' insistence that capitalism is the primary source of exploitation, and that the housewife will either wither away, like the state, once women are on equal terms with male wage laborers, or that housework will be recognized as "real work" by receiving a wage, as demanded by the Wages for Housework movement of that time. Instead, Eisenstein sees patriarchy and capitalism as simultaneous, mutually reinforcing systems of oppression that stand in a "dialectical" relationship to each other. Where she does not part with socialist feminists, however, is in her ascription of patriarchy to "pre-capitalist" patriarchal family relations, leaving class as the main signifier of capitalism.

In her later writings Eisenstein broadens and "pluralizes" her analytical reach from her original emphasis on the United States to the operations of a "transnational capitalist" (1998) or "global capitalist racialized patriarchy" (2007). She thereby moved closer to the writings of Veronika Bennholdt-Thomsen, Maria Mies, and Claudia von Werlhof, the main writers of the Bielefeld School, who from the beginning viewed capitalist patriarchy in terms of a "world system" (Immanuel Wallerstein). Their writings nevertheless differ from Eisenstein's in two major ways: on the one hand, they debunk or turn "upside down" the Marxian myth of the primacy of class relations under capitalism; on the other, they also see capitalism as only the latest version of patriarchy.

In terms of the first difference, the writers describe how various forms of "subsistence production," that is, production oriented toward creating "use values" for immediate consumption rather than exchange on the market, have always been the very foundation of the commodity form of production, and therefore of capitalist class exploitation. Bennholdt-Thomsen (1988) and von Werlhof (1985) examined the fate of peasants and other non-waged "subsistence workers" in Mexico and Venezuela in the 1970s and describe how under the auspices of neoliberal global capitalism peasant men turned into landless paid laborers, and peasant women into landless unpaid "housewives." Land expropriation and enclosure, together with an import of the bourgeois notion of the housewife, therefore constituted the advanced, neoliberal version of early capitalism's plunder of the colonies and its peoples, and the creation of the bourgeois family.

Just as the peoples of the colonies were "naturalized back into nature" as uncivilized savages, the work of the housewife was labor made invisible, "naturalized," controlled, unfree, and above all, unpaid. This labor therefore underlies and supports the very capitalist division between the bourgeoisie and the proletariat. The bourgeois nuclear family is therefore not simply a leftover from pre-capitalist patriarchal times, but instead an inherently capitalist invention. Expropriation and forced labor of the colonies and its peoples was therefore inextricably linked to the expropriation of "women as the last colony" (Mies, Bennholdt-Thomsen, and von Werlhof 1988), turning them into "housewives" and pushing for the "housewifization" (von Werlhof) of, eventually, all wage labor. Today unstable, precarious forms of wage labor and new forms of forced labor, indentured servitude, and slavery therefore continue to spread not only in the neocolonies of the global South, but also in the centers of the global North.

In terms of the second difference from Eisenstein's theoretical framework, the Bielefelders place patriarchy at the front of the dual term because they consider it the overarching as well as the "deep structure" (von Werlhof) of capitalism. Von Werlhof therefore traces the beginnings of a patriarchal logic in the way prehistoric matriarchal societies underwent a process of "patriarchalization," a process that Mies sees as the origin of the patriarchal, asymmetrical sexual division of labor. Today this patriarchal logic has intensified to a level where neoliberal globalization means a globalization of war (Mies 2004).

Von Werlhof (2007) characterizes patriarchy as an "alchemical system," with Western civilization its "most violent project." She locates the origin of this system in the meaning of *pater arché*, the Greek origin of "patriarchy." *Pater arché* usurped and changed the meaning of "matriarchy," or "in the beginning was the mother" to patriarchy, or "in the beginning was the father," leading to an inverse of matriarchal thinking. Since fathers have no uterus, they need to resort to the control of women and their bodies, and to attempts at creating life without any mother-bodies. In the meantime, the male power to control and take life serves as a substitute for the female power to give life. Von Werlhof therefore summarizes the essence of the patriarchal logic as one of "'creation' through destruction" (2013). Mies (1986) uses the European witch hunts that lasted from the twelfth to the seventeenth century as a prime example of the interplay of expropriation, usurpation, and killing of female power because women's relative economic and sexual independence at that time had become too threatening for the emerging bourgeois order.

Von Werlhof connects the patriarchal efforts of finding ways of creating new life to the ancient search for the *Stein des Weisen*, the sorcerer's stone. This stone was believed to hold the secret of life, and therefore the power to produce life outside of a woman's body. Von Werlhof identifies this as the heart of the utopian patriarchal dream that is still being pursued today. Where fifteenth- or sixteenth-century alchemists like Paracelsus tried to find the "elixir of life" in order to create a "homunculus," modern scientist-alchemists try to create "mother machines" that let babies gestate and develop outside a woman's body. Likewise, life sciences try to create new life forms through the "algeny" (Jeremy Rifkin) of gene-slicing and transgenic manipulations (von Werlhof 2010). They thereby continue the work of the founding fathers of Western science who wanted to penetrate Mother Earth in order to wrest her secrets from her. The "biopiracy" of indigenous knowledge of plants and nature by so-called "life industries" (Mies and Shiva 1993) is only the latest version of the same violent relation to nature and life. These industries, like the life sciences, nevertheless still depend on live substances. Where the utopian patriarchal dream has only been partially realized, finance capitalism offers a virtual realization of this dream. By letting money "beget" money, financial speculators create life in its purest, most abstract form. Money is life.

In her chapter in *Women and Revolution*, edited by Lydia Sargent (1981), Azizah al-Hibri presents a strikingly similar theory in her response to Heidi Hartman's analysis of the partnership between patriarchy and capitalism. She places the male desire for immortality and the use of technology as a productive tool for the domination of the "female-nature-male Other" at the core of patriarchy, and therefore also of capitalism. At the "dawn of history" both woman and nature were recognized as having the power to "reproduce themselves," thereby giving them, but not men, the "key to immortality."

Gloria Joseph, another contributor to *Women and Revolution* (Joseph 1981), gives a preview of bell hooks's critique of capitalist patriarchy by emphasizing the interconnectedness of male domination and white supremacy. Racism must therefore be seen as an integral component of the development of US capitalism and imperialism. Although race functioned as the "great equalizer" for black men and women's labor under slavery, black men also "learned" from white men to "dominate, exploit, and oppress Black women," if only in an "ersatz manner."

bell hooks continues this argument but also more firmly links US imperialism and white supremacy to the history and logic of a predatory capitalist patriarchy within the black community. Despite employing a vastly different theoretical framework than the writers of the Bielefeld School, hooks nevertheless grounds her writings on "black masculinity" in a similar understanding of the predominance of patriarchy, and of capitalism evolving out of patriarchal white European colonialism and plantation slavery. She therefore uses the term "imperialist white supremacist capitalist patriarchy" (2004). She describes how many black men and women continue to live under the spell of two different images of patriarchy despite, or in conjunction with, the continued worsening of living conditions that cause havoc in black families. One is the image of the "benign" bourgeois patriarch, the other of the "dominator patriarch." The image of the bourgeois male head of household is associated with a sense of manhood by providing for and protecting the family. hooks describes how this image continues its seductive hold, particularly on women, and this despite the fact that it was not only imposed upon people with very different cultural traditions and family formations, but it also never had any chance of becoming a standard reality in black family life. Nevertheless, for men it lives on in the ownership of women and the fruits of their paid labor; and for women in the dream of a real man who provides and protects.

As hooks writes, the image of the "dominator patriarch" reigns supreme in the "gangsta culture." The dominator patriarch merges the capitalist ethos of greed with the patriarchal need to own and control women. Black men first moved from brute slave labor to low-paid racialized labor to facing increasing levels of unemployment, and now many of them are living on "borrowed time," just waiting to be imprisoned or murdered. Making money and seizing the power to kill does, however, promise a way out of victimhood, and of regaining a sense of manhood.

Eisenstein, hooks, and the writers of the Bielefeld School offer a variety of alternatives to capitalist patriarchy. Bennholdt-Thomsen and Mies (1999) describe how a new economics and politics needs to be based on "subsistence perspectives," and therefore on cooperative relations with others and with nature. A corresponding "subsistence politics" would give support to small peasant agriculture and oppose the genetic manipulation and patenting of life. It would also dissolve the hegemony of the wage-labor regime and recognize all forms of non-waged labor as well as non-hegemonic combinations of subsistence and wage labor, but now in the form of freely engaged-in, unforced labor. In addition, only a vibrant international network of popular movements could counter the problems of environmental destruction, poverty, and war. This would also require a sense of solidarity between men and women where adult men would guide young men in participating in unpaid subsistence work while stopping the increasing glorification of military-style violence in young men.

hooks likewise grounds her alternative vision in a call for undoing the effects of the death-affirming patriarchal foundation of white supremacy. This would require engaging in a long and creative process of self-recovery and healing, making young black men (especially) learn to love themselves and others. Part of this process also involves men becoming fathers by embracing the work of mothering and creatively using their capacity to nurture the spiritual and emotional growth of children.

In her earlier writings Eisenstein also touched upon the subject of children by outlining an alternative society where child-rearing has become a social responsibility. Her main suggestions for "revolutionary" strategies focused, however, on building connection among women, and across class divisions. In her later writings on race and the global spread of capitalism Eisenstein extends her call for forming cross-class connection to building "virtual sisterhoods" that would both acknowledge *and* transgress "the barriers of colonialism, racism, nationalism, and transnational capital" (1996).

Von Werlhof goes furthest in her suggestions by claiming that only an "alterna-depth," an alternative that reaches into the very depth of what it means to live with the earth, could put an end to the violent, deadly logic of modernity, and therefore of patriarchy. The beginnings of such a deep alternative can be found in both the history of pre-patriarchal matriarchy as well as in the remnants of matriarchal thinking and connecting that are either still alive or newly practiced on the margins of many societies. She therefore points to matriarchal studies as the most promising field for further research.

Its findings not only remove the patriarchal misinterpretations of matriarchy as the "rule of women," but also offer the vision of a world that is free of dominance, that nurtures and sustains life, and that cooperates with nature as a lived entity.

SEE ALSO: Division of Labor, Gender; Economic Globalization and Gender; Empowerment; Gender Belief System/Gender Ideology; Global Restructuring; Hegemonic Masculinity; Matriarchy; Patriarchy

REFERENCES

al-Hibri, Azizah. 1981. "Capitalism is an Advanced State of Patriarchy: But Marxism is not Feminism." In *Women and Revolution: A Discussion of the Unhappy Marriage of Marxism and Feminism*, edited by Lydia Sargent, 165–193. Boston: South End Press.

Bennholdt-Thomsen, Veronika. 1988. *Campesinos: Entre Producccíon de Subsistencia y de Mercado* [Peasants: Between Subsistence and Commodity Production]. Mexico: UNAM/CRIM.

Bennholdt-Thomsen, Veronika, and Maria Mies. 1999. *The Subsistence Perspective*. London: Zed Books.

Eisenstein, Zillah R., ed. 1979. *Capitalism and the Case for Socialist Feminism*. New York: Monthly Review Press.

Eisenstein, Zillah R. 1996. *Hatreds: Racialized and Sexualized Conflicts in the 21st Century*. New York: Routledge.

Eisenstein, Zillah R. 1998. *Global Obscenities: Patriarchy, Capitalism, and the Lure of Cyberfantasy*. New York: New York University Press.

Eisenstein, Zillah R. 2007. *Sexual Decoys: Gender, Race, and War in Imperial Democracy*. London: Zed Books.

hooks, bell. 2004. *We Real Cool: Black Men and Masculinity*. New York: Routledge.

Joseph, Gloria. 1981. "The Incompatible Ménage à Trois: Marxism, Feminism, and Racism." In *Women and Revolution: A Discussion of the Unhappy Marriage of Marxism and Feminism*, edited by Lydia Sargent, 91–107. Boston: South End Press.

Mies, Maria. 1986. *Patriarchy and Accumulation on a World Scale: Women in the International Division of Labour*. London: Zed Books.

Mies, Maria. 2004. *Krieg ohne Grenzen: Die neue Kolonisierung der Welt* [War without Borders: The Neocolonization of the World]. Cologne: Papy Rossa.

Mies, Maria, Veronika Bennholdt-Thomsen, and Claudia von Werlhof. 1988. *Women: The Last Colony*. London: Zed Books.

Mies, Maria, and Vandana Shiva. 1993. *Ecofeminism*. Halifax, NS: Fernwood.

von Werlhof, Claudia. 1985. *Wenn die Bauern wiederkommen* [When the Peasants Come Back]. Bremen: Periferia/Edition CON.

von Werlhof, Claudia. 2007. "Capitalist Patriarchy and the Negation of Matriarchy: The Struggle for a 'Deep' Alternative." In *Women and the Gift Economy: A Radically Different Worldview is Possible*, edited by Genevieve Vaughan, 139–153. Toronto: Innana.

von Werlhof, Claudia. 2010. *Vom Diesseits der Utopie zum Jenseits der Gewalt* [From This Side of Utopia to the Other Side of Violence]. Freiburg: Centaurus.

von Werlhof, Claudia. 2013. "Destruction through 'Creation' – the 'Critical Theory of Patriarchy' and the Collapse of Modern Civilization." *Capitalism Nature Socialism*, 24: 68–85. DOI: 10.1080/10455752.2013.846498.

FURTHER READING

Bennholdt-Thomsen, Veronika, Nicolas Faraclas, and Claudia von Werlhof, eds. 2001. *There is an Alternative: Subsistence and Worldwide Resistance to Corporate Globalization*. London: Zed Books.

von Werlhof, Claudia. 2008. "The Globalization of Neoliberalism, its Consequences, and Some of its Basic Alternatives." *Capitalism Nature Socialism*, 19: 94–117. DOI: 10.1080/10455750802348903.

von Werlhof, Claudia. 2009. "The Utopia of a Motherless World Patriarchy as 'War System.'" In *Societies for Peace*, edited by Heide Göttner-Abendroth, 29–44. Toronto: Innana.

von Werlhof, Claudia. 2011. *The Failure of Modern Civilization and the Struggle for a "Deep" Alternative*. Frankfurt am Main: Peter Lang.

Cardiac Disease and Gender

LINDA WORRALL-CARTER
Her Heart, Melbourne, Australia

MUHAMMAD AZIZ RAHMAN
Australian Catholic University, Melbourne, Australia

Cardiovascular diseases (CVD), which include coronary heart disease (CHD) and stroke, are the leading causes of mortality among both sexes globally. In 2012, 17.5 million people died due to CVD which is equivalent to three in every 10 deaths (WHO 2014). CVD is the biggest killer of women, which is responsible for one third of all female deaths globally, according to the World Health Organization. In fact, each year CVD causes a larger number of deaths in older women than in older men; in 2008, 7.5 million women over 60 years of age died compared with 6.6 million men of similar ages (WHO 2015).

Traditionally, women are under-represented in cardiac research, although CHD is the largest single cause of deaths among women. Most of the cardiac research informing practice and policies has included men only, as previously CHD was thought to be a predominantly "male disease," so gender perspectives have not been well studied. CHDs among women are characterized by lack of awareness, poor symptom recognition, atypical symptom presentation, treatment delay by healthcare providers because of poor symptom recognition, gender disparity in diagnosis and management, and, combined with poorer prognosis, there is a greater likelihood of disability and higher rates of illness and death than in men (National Heart Foundation of Australia 2011).

Women are largely unaware of their heart disease risk. Breast cancer is perceived to be the leading cause of deaths among women, whereas women are three times more likely to die of CHD (Australian Institute of Health and Welfare 2011). Studies report that women are not only unaware of CHD being the leading cause of deaths, but also most women do not know the risk factors for CHD (National Heart Foundation of Australia 2011). Women are more predisposed to developing acute coronary syndrome at an older age than men and are more likely to have hypertension, diabetes, hypercholesterolemia, and other severe comorbid conditions (Worrall-Carter et al. 2011). Although women are more likely to develop CHD over the age of 50 years, when this occurs in younger women it can be severe and carries an increased risk of mortality. Among the risk factors, diabetes and smoking exacerbate cardiovascular risk, especially in women. The presence of diabetes confers an approximately twofold increased risk of experiencing a wide range of CVDs (Emerging Risk Factors Collaboration 2010). Diabetes is associated with an increased incidence of sudden cardiac death and it has been postulated that diabetes leads to higher CVD and all-cause mortality in women than it does in men (Lee et al. 2012). While young and middle-aged women are less likely than men to develop CHD in the absence of diabetes, its presence has been found to equalize the risk by gender (Kalyani et al. 2014). Smoking also poses a significantly higher risk for women, with a greater increase in risk of atherosclerosis and acute myocardial infarction among female smokers than male smokers (Worrall-Carter et al. 2011). Moreover, even if women know the risk factors for CHD, they may be unaware of the links and associations due to those risk factors (Crouch, Wilson, and Newbury 2011).

Women with CHD are often more under-recognized, under-assessed, and under-treated than men. They are more likely to experience atypical symptoms, and delays in diagnosis and treatment are more likely to occur because of issues related to both patients and service providers (Kuhn et al. 2013). Women experiencing cardiac events often present with non-specific symptoms such as unusual fatigue, sleep disturbance, shortness of breath, weakness, anxiety, and chest discomfort, which pose a challenge for women to recognize their symptoms early. Women tend to put others' needs before their own (such as family needs) and tend to ignore those symptoms, which can cause significant delay during a critical period. In addition to this, risk of coronary events in women is significantly underestimated by health professionals, which leads to more conservative treatment and eventually contributes to poorer outcomes. Research has shown that women are more likely to have delayed treatment onset upon arrival at hospital emergency department (EDs), be allocated a lower triage scoring at ED, receive fewer diagnostic tests, be prescribed fewer medications, receive less aggressive treatment, and be discharged from hospital prematurely. Compared with men, women are also less likely to be referred to cardiac rehabilitation programs so have lower rates of participation, report lower health-related quality of life, and are more likely to live with CHD-related disabilities (Kuhn et al. 2015).

The social impact on women with CHD is often ignored (Worrall-Carter, Edward, and Page 2012). Women from lower socioeconomic groups in particular experience negative impacts on their general health because of gender inequities in the allocation of resources such as income, education, healthcare, nutrition, and political voice. Sociocultural factors cause delay in seeking care for women with CHD and differences in self-management behaviors contribute to poorer outcomes; in particular groups, such as indigenous women, these health differentials are more pronounced (Worrall-Carter, Edward, and Page 2012). Morbidity and mortality resulting from CHD among women adversely affects their families, particularly young children, which are often ignored in the literature.

International initiatives have been undertaken to address the challenges related to CHD in women. The very successful "Go Red for Women" campaign from the American Heart Association has been running in the United States for over a decade (American Heart Association 2015). The campaign was designed to empower women to take charge of their heart health through increasing awareness and encouraging them to understand their risks and make healthier choices to reduce them. Similar campaigns have also been adopted in other countries in recent years including the United Kingdom, European countries and, in the last 5 years, in Australia. However, there need to be more resources, as a funding paradox exists globally. More funding is allocated for cancer research and management than heart disease. Data from the United States (2011) shows that the largest proportion of donations goes towards breast cancer ($257.85 million); however, approximately 41,000 people die annually from breast cancer. However, heart disease kills over 596,000 people in the United States every year, but only receives $54.1 million in donations (*Medical Daily* 2014). Finally, guidelines have been developed to address inequity for management of CHD among women but knowledge translation from guidelines to practice remains suboptimal. Guidelines from the United States, Europe, and Australia emphasize the evidence-based practice for both genders. Studies show that, contrary to guideline-based recommendations, women receive fewer coronary interventions and have higher mortality rates than men (Kuhn et al. 2015).

In conclusion, cardiac disease among women needs to be a global priority. There need to be major public campaigns to increase awareness, education to address preventable risk factors, and an overall strategy to allow for equity for diagnosis and treatment based on implementation and adherence to guidelines. This will require more women to be represented in cardiac research and, more importantly, an increase in funding is imperative considering the burden of cardiac disease among women.

SEE ALSO: Disease Symptoms, Gender Differences in; Gender Inequality and Gender Stratification; Health Disparities

REFERENCES

American Heart Association (AHA). 2015. "Go Red for Women." Accessed August 9, 2015, at https://www.goredforwomen.org/#.

Australian Institute of Health and Welfare (AIHW). 2011. *Cardiovascular Disease: Australian Facts 2011*. Canberra: AIHW.

Crouch, R., A. Wilson, and J. Newbury. 2011. "A Systematic Review of the Effectiveness of Primary Health Education or Intervention Programs in Improving Rural Women's Knowledge of Heart Disease Risk Factors and Changing Lifestyle Behaviours." *International Journal of Evidence-Based Healthcare*, 9: 236–245. DOI: 10.1111/j.1744-1609.2011.00226.x.

Emerging Risk Factors Collaboration, N. Sarwar, et al. 2010. "Diabetes Mellitus, Fasting Blood Glucose Concentration, and Risk of Vascular Disease: A Collaborative Meta-Analysis of 102 Prospective Studies." *Lancet*, 375: 2215–2122. DOI: 10.1016/S0140-6736(10)60484-9.

Kalyani, R.R., et al. 2014. "Sex Differences in Diabetes and Risk of Incident Coronary Artery Disease in Healthy Young and Middle-Aged Adults." *Diabetes Care*, 37: 830–838. DOI: 10.2337/dc13-1755.

Kuhn, Lisa, Karen Page, Aziz Muhammad Rahman, and Linda Worrall-Carter. 2015. "Gender Difference in Treatment and Mortality of Patients with ST-Segment Elevation Myocardial Infarction Admitted to Victorian Public Hospitals: A Retrospective Database Study." *Australian Critical Care*, pii: S1036-7314(15)00005-3 [Epub ahead of print]. DOI: 10.1016/j.aucc.2015.01.004.

Kuhn, Lisa, Linda Worrall-Carter, John Ward, and Karen Page. 2013. "Factors Associated with Delayed Treatment Onset for Acute Myocardial Infarction in Victorian Emergency Departments: A Regression Tree Analysis." *Australasian Emergency Nursing Journal*, 16: 160–169. DOI: 10.1016/j.aenj.2013.08.002.

Lee, C., L. Joseph, A. Colosimo, and K. Dasgupta. 2012. "Mortality in Diabetes Compared with Previous Cardiovascular Disease: A Gender-Specific Meta-Analysis." *Diabetes and Metabolism*, 38(5): 420–427. DOI: 10.1016/j.diabet.2012.04.002.

Medical Daily. 2014. "The Diseases That Actually Kill Us and Where We Donate Our Money Aren't Always Aligned." Accessed August 9, 2015, at http://www.medicaldaily.com/diseases-actually-kill-us-and-where-we-donate-our-money-arent-always-aligned-300312.

National Heart Foundation of Australia. 2011. *Women and Heart Disease Forum Report*. Accessed August 9, 2015, at http://www.heartfoundation.org.au/SiteCollectionDocuments/Women-Heart-Disease-Forum.pdf.

Worrall-Carter, Linda, Karen-Leigh Edward, and Karen Page. 2012. "Women and Cardiovascular Disease: At a Social Disadvantage?" *Collegian*, 19: 33–37.

Worrall-Carter, Linda, Chantal Ski, Elizabeth Scruth, Michelle Campbell, and Karen Page. 2011. "Systematic Review of Cardiovascular Disease in Women: Assessing the Risk." *Nursing and Health Sciences*, 13: 529–535. DOI: 10.1111/j.1442-2018.2011.00645.x.

World Health Organization (WHO). 2014. "The Top 10 Causes of Death." Accessed August 9, 2015, at http://www.who.int/mediacentre/factsheets/fs310/en/.

World Health Organization (WHO). 2015. "10 Leading Causes of Death in Females." Accessed August 9, 2015, at http://www.who.int/gho/women_and_health/mortality/causes_death_text/en/.

Celibacy

DIEDERIK F. JANSSEN
Independent Researcher, The Netherlands

Celibacy (from Latin *cælibatus* and ultimately *cælebs* (obscure origin), unwedded or bachelor) refers generally to the unmarried state of, or singlehood option for, the legally marriageable, typically for religious reasons, and with variably central implications and connotations of sexual abstinence. Ancient and medieval grammarians connected the word *caelebs* to the "celestial" life led by celibates or their being on their way to heaven (*ad caelum*). Distinctions are common between vocational (e.g., clerical), separatist-secular (e.g., philosophical or activist), and other (e.g. "involuntary" or strictly demographic) uses for the term celibacy, and correspondingly between temporary and indefinite, mandated and facultative celibacies. Celibacy often implies a vow-based component of, or condition for, ordination and religious office. As such it is distinct from the mere circumstance of bachelordom or spinsterhood, and instead marked by conceptual, and often administrative, proximity to notions including sexual renunciation, abstinence, chastity, and asceticism. The term, in fact, is frequently taken to apply generally to sexual continence.

Customs and valuations of celibacy vary according to historical context (Abbott 1999), religious purpose (Olson 2008), and cultural setting (Sobo and Bell 2001). These often underlie distinct regimes of administrative dedication and religious charisma marking positions from Christian clerics and Sufi mystics to Hindu ascetics, Buddhist monks, eunuchs, seers, shamans, and prophets. Motivations for celibacy vary with underlying and historically shifting motivations for ascetic life, with doctrinal or scriptural primacy on reproduction for laity, and vitalist-conservationist connections of the sex act with depletion of the body's vital substances or with endangerment of the soul's resilience in the face of temptations. Depending on the weighing of these motives, celibacy assumes part instrumental, part symbolic efficacy.

Celibacy is the exception in both Judaism and Islam, being considered contrary to divine instruction and thus incompatible with orthodoxy. It is not central either, indeed often figures as contrary, to Daoist ethos, Confucianism, Shinto (Japan), African indigenous, and Native American religions. In the foregoing, sexual continence may be a periodic stipulation and as such tied to warrior preparations, hunts, initiations, shamanistic rituals, and occasional festivals. Celibacy has only a minor role in Vedic religion, and is more characteristic of newer religious groups including Buddhists (e.g., Zen and Korean Buddhism), Jains, and Ājīvikas (a fourth-century BCE heterodoxy). The Hindu and later Buddhist notion of *brahmacārya* entails the requirement of a "celibate" life, and more generally the cultivation of a pure or holy life, during the study of the Vedas or pursuit of Brahman. Abstinence is considered key to the transmutation, or sublimation, of sexual energy from *retas* ("sexual fluid") into higher states of energy, ultimately to *ojas* ("spiritual vigor"). Originally a permanent commitment, celibacy became deeply connected to the *āśrama* or male age grade or "vocation" system, where it names the first (student) grade particularly, although celibacy is recommended for the third and fourth grades (forest dweller and renouncer) as well. Only the householder is exempt; but even a Jain householder should limit sexual activity to certain times, stick to a single partner, and curb libidinal urges. Mahatma Gandhi's *brahmacārya* was notably unorthodox and experimental: as a married septuagenarian, he had his grandniece sleep naked in his bed as part of a spiritual self-test.

A noted cause for controversy and schism throughout the history of Christianity, sacerdotal, consecrated, priestly, or clerical celibacy (*sacerdotalis caelibatus*) is the renunciation of marriage implicitly or explicitly pursued by ordained ministers of the Latin Church, with the exception of permanent deacons. In the Holy See's Code of Canon Law celibacy figures as consequential to mandated observance of "perfect and perpetual continence for the sake of the kingdom of heaven" (Canon 277§1; www.vatican.va). Lively debates are ongoing about mandatory celibacy's apostolic origins, its ties to asceticism, and its historical relation to ecclesiastical power and wealth given the prevented drain of clerical assets to widows, sons, and other contenders associated with marital ties. In the early modern context, celibacy figured prominently in Reformation polemics over the question of the nature of the priesthood and the sacraments, both between Catholics and Protestants (prominently involving opinions by Luther, Erasmus, and Calvin) and within the Roman Catholic Church itself. Since the 1990s to date, clerical celibacy has come under intensified scrutiny given its presumed causal ties to clerical child sexual abuse around the mid-twentieth century.

As asceticism more broadly, celibacy presents a puzzle to evolutionary theorists. Lifelong vows of celibacy seem incongruent given that they present a case of costly, unreciprocated altruism in non-kin settings. From this perspective Richard Dawkins (2006) has considered celibacy "a minor partner in a large complex of mutually-assisting religious memes." In the postmillennial West, disparate contemporary contexts and frames for reflection on the "survival" of mandated celibacy, and on single lifestyles more broadly, include secularization and modernization of the Roman Catholic Church (urged onward by its sexual misconduct legacy, hesitant admission of women, and position on gay ministers), demographic trends (high age on first marriage and high divorce rates across the postindustrial West), global law reforms (for instance, the expanding option of same-sex marriage), shifting intellectual frames (including anti-normative approaches to coupledom: Cobb 2012), and the recent profiling of asexuality.

SEE ALSO: Asexuality; Chastity; Christianity, Gender and Sexuality; Nuns, including Taiwan Buddhist

REFERENCES

Abbott, Elizabeth. 1999. *A History of Celibacy*. Toronto: HarperCollins.

Cobb, Michael. 2012. *Single: Arguments for the Uncoupled*. New York: NYU Press.

Dawkins, Richard. 2006. *The Selfish Gene*. 30th anniversary ed. Oxford: Oxford University Press. First published 1976.

Olson, Carl, ed. 2008. *Celibacy and Religious Traditions*. New York: Oxford University Press.

Sobo, Elisa Janine, and Sandra Bell, eds. 2001. *Celibacy, Culture, and Society: The Anthropology of Sexual Abstinence*. Madison: University of Wisconsin Press.

FURTHER READING

Frassetto, Michael, ed. 1998. *Medieval Purity and Piety: Essays on Medieval Clerical Celibacy and Religious Reform*. New York: Garland.

Howard, Veena. 2013. *Gandhi's Ascetic Activism: Renunciation and Social Action*. Albany: SUNY Press.

Launderville, Dale. 2010. *Celibacy in the Ancient World: Its Ideal and Practice in Pre-Hellenistic Israel, Mesopotamia, and Greece*. Collegeville, MN: Liturgical Press.

Parish, Helen. 2009. *Clerical Celibacy in the West, c.1100–1700*. Farnham, Surrey: Ashgate.

Charivaris

PAULINE GREENHILL
University of Winnipeg, Canada

Charivari traditions have been documented in parts of Europe and North America from the Middle Ages to the present, with cognate customs found across the world. Some scholars prefer to limit the term to its medieval French meaning: a raucous, parading, house visit usually incited by weddings, a community deemed problematic (or *adultery*, or sexual relations, and/or procreation outside or before marriage). This form historically expressed disapproval of some aspect of *stigma* in the match, or even its apparent non-consummation and/or infertility. A charivari prompted by the latter is represented in the film *The Return of Martin Guerre* (directed by Daniel Vigne 1982).

Marriage charivaris conventionally dramatized popular objections to weddings between two older people; between an older and a younger person; involving a widow and/or widower – especially too soon after the previous spouse's death; and/or involving a racially mixed or religiously diverse couple. Charivariers often sought to exact a price – money, cigarettes, food, and/or drink, especially alcohol – for the couple's transgression of traditional expectations that marriage should be between two previously unmarried, fertile young people with common ethnoracial and religious heritages. A form of social coercion, this type of charivari could result in its recipients changing the actions receiving censure, or sometimes leaving the community. In the case of interracial marriages, the racially othered partner's life would be in danger. Susanna Moodie's *Roughing it in the Bush* (1852) demonstrates charivari's racism and sometimes deadly results. Her account of her experiences as a new immigrant in the area of what is now Peterborough, Ontario, Canada in the 1830s offers several descriptions of charivaris, including one in which the newlywed African-Canadian groom was murdered by the charivariers.

Other scholars would include in the rubric of charivari a number of noisy parading performances traditionally directed toward a variety of offenders against community morality and sensibility. Such events often comprised displays to censure browbeaten and/or cuckolded husbands, unmarried mothers, wife-beaters, but also unpopular politicians, officials, employers, and public servants. These objects of the people's ire were sometimes incorporated into the event themselves or in surrogates or effigies. Infrequently, charivariers might disguise themselves to avoid identification and thus legal repercussions for these sometimes very violent events.

Perhaps paradoxically, charivari is also used as a term for loud, usually late-night, surprise house visits from community members to newlyweds, but recently also for those celebrating a milestone wedding anniversary, accompanied by a *quête* (a request for a treat and/or money in exchange for the noisy performance) and/or pranks and tricks aimed at the couple, their house, and their property. Though in some ways identical to disapproval charivaris, this form expresses welcome to the newlyweds rather than censure of the marriage or anniversary. The association of this practice with non-consummation or infertility of a marriage continues in that a newlywed couple could be charivaried any number of times until the arrival of their first child. Again paradoxically, this welcome form often co-existed with the disapproval charivari at the same times and places.

The term is sometimes anglicized to "shivaree" or "chivaree," but a congeries of other terms are used for the custom and its cognates, including skimmington (ride), riding (the stang), *assouade*, *Rügebrauch*, *mattinata*, serenade, banjo or bango, and rough music. As the last words suggest, noise is crucial, even definitive. North American charivariers sometimes use a "horse fiddle," an instrument constructed from a plank of wood fitted with a crank that turns a toothed gear against a piece of metal, resulting in an ear-splitting vibration. Most charivari noisemakers, however, are not specially constructed but instead improvised from objects and materials readily at hand. Though domestic implements like pots and pans beaten with wooden spoons are popularly associated with the practice, their noise would generally be drowned out when gunshots or parts of farm implements banged together were added, as they often were. More recently, car horns and chainsaws are favored noisemakers in Canada.

The use of firearms, often accompanied by excessive use of alcohol by charivariers and newlyweds, sometimes led to homicide or even murder at these events. For example, in 1909 near Brookdale, Manitoba, Canada, a thirty-five-year-old widower who eloped with a much younger woman was charivaried by several young men who circled the couple's house firing a shotgun and beating on agricultural tools. The groom shot from an upstairs window with a rifle, striking one of the party who later died of peritonitis. Charivari murders were not only associated with firearms, however. In 1881 in what is now Ottawa, Ontario, Canada, on the wedding night of an elderly widower and younger widow, a succession of charivaris culminated in four young men apparently throwing stones, resulting in the groom's fatal head injuries.

These different forms of the practice are strongly gendered. Generally young men and older boys organized and perpetrated disapproval charivaris, but approval charivaris usually include women and men from more diverse age groups. That even welcoming charivaris sometimes lead to court cases is hardly surprising given the possibility of personal injury and damage to or destruction of property that can ensue from the traditional pranks and tricks. The latter often aim to highlight the couple's *sexuality*. Thus the bedroom and bathroom serve as targets, including such practices as short-sheeting the bed, tying bells beneath it, removing the mattress and displaying it elsewhere inside or outside the house, dyeing the linens in the bathtub with Jello, putting ketchup or chocolate on underwear, putting plastic wrap over the toilet, and a myriad others. Dealing with the aftermath of tricks associated with the bride's domain – the domestic spaces inside the house – is considered her responsibility alone; however, the groom often gets help the next day with pranks directed against his domain. Male friends and family, including the previous evening's charivariers, may arrive the next morning to help him round up livestock released during the charivari, reassemble farm equipment, or move machinery placed on a barn roof, for example. However, women often mitigated some of the unwelcome acts associated with the event itself, bringing food and drink, and/or organizing a collectively prepared gift for the newlyweds. The potentially negative content of the tricks at any individual charivari would in large part depend on local tradition. But when one or both of the newlyweds were known to be extreme tricksters at others' charivaris, they could expect to receive the same, or worse, at their own.

The stated purpose of the welcome charivari belies the sometimes rather problematic behavior and potential negative repercussions associated with it. Today's upper- and middle-class urban residents may find it difficult to be welcoming to late-night, uninvited guests – even family and friends – invading their house and turning its contents topsy-turvy – or worse. Currently, charivari is practiced primarily in rural areas. Explanations for this limitation cite urban noise ordinances that could make the tradition illegal. However, marriage-related charivari transmits concerns about community values and ideas more relevant to rural than to urban areas. These include the idea that women must always be prepared to be hospitable and expect the unexpected, and that connections between community members transcend all other considerations. It must be noted that the marriage charivari, welcoming or otherwise, presumes heterosexuality, traditional ideas of gender roles, and compulsory motherhood, among other conservative and conventional ideologies. However, progressive social protest groups often use charivari's historic noisemaking modes, including pots and pans beaten with wooden spoons, to draw attention to their causes, demonstrating the tradition's malleability.

SEE ALSO: Division of Labor, Domestic; Gender Role Ideology; Heterosexual Marriage Trends in the West; Images of Gender and Sexuality in Advertising; Sex and Culture; White Supremacy and Gender

FURTHER READING

Davis, Natalie Zemon. 1975. *Society and Culture in Early Modern France*. Stanford: Stanford University Press.
Dobash, Russell P., and R. Emerson Dobash. 1981. "Community Response to Violence against Wives: Charivari, Abstract Justice and Patriarchy." *Social Problems*, 28(3): 563–581.
Greenhill, Pauline. 2010. *Make the Night Hideous: Four English-Canadian Charivaris, 1881–1940*. Toronto: University of Toronto Press.
Le Goff, Jacques, and Jean-Claude Schmitt, eds. 1981. *Le Charivari*. Paris: École des Hautes Études en Sciences Sociales.
Pettitt, Tom. 2005. "Nuptial Pageantry in Medieval Culture and Folk Custom: In Quest of the English Charivari." *Medium Ævum Quotidianum*, 52: 89–115.
Rey-Flaud, Henri. 1985. *Le Charivari: les Rituels fondamentaux de la Sexualité*. Paris: Payot.

Chastity

DIEDERIK F. JANSSEN
Independent Researcher, The Netherlands

Deeply ingrained in Roman and later Christian concepts of the ideal woman, chastity (from Latin *castitas* "moral purity") denotes adherence to prescribed notions of sexual morality in relation to marriage, especially abstinence from premarital and extramarital escapades. Associated in particular with marriageable girls, brides, wives, nuns, widows, patron deities (Ceres, Artemis) and saints (Agnes of Rome), and the Blessed Virgin Mary, chastity figures forth a virtuous state of spiritual purity and attunement, with variable implications of sexual abstinence, virginity (*virginitas*), celibacy (*caelibatus*), modesty (*pudicitia*), or accession to conjugal (that is, legitimate procreative) duties (*iugalitas*). Depending on context and epoch, chastity resonates with more generic concepts such as continence (*continentia*), self-control (*temperentia*, *sophrosyne*), and sobriety (*sobrietas*). In Christianity, especially, these nuances informed and continue to inform struggles to establish, crystallize, and expound theological direction and ecclesiastical law. Disregard for chastity codes and violation of chastity expectations or vows fall under such rubrics as dishonor, impiety, illicitness, fornication, adultery, and debauchery.

Anthropologists have found some form of restriction upon extramarital sex for wives to be near universal, although moral concepts such as chastity vary widely. Codifications of chastity by way of commandments, canons, informal covenants, ceremonialized vows, pledges, or tests are readily associated with Abrahamic religions and their denominations such as the Church of Jesus Christ of Latter-Day Saints. However, comparable terms are attested in Buddhism, Daoism,

Hinduism, and Jainism. Late nineteenth-century German ethnologists gradually turned *Keuschheit des Weibes* from a largely theological and moral evolutionary into an ethnographic, philological, and folkloric motif. In anglophone anthropology, too, chastity's religious and cultic imprimatur has been a subject of book-length comparative inquiries for more than a century (Parsons 1913). Onomasiologically, terms comparable to *chastity* are attested across many non-Romance languages but with semantically, historically, and socially particular embeddings. Examples include Arabic *'irḍ* (a generic term also implying respect, honor) and Tamil *karpu* (connoting "service" to one's husband, with wider connotations of filial loyalty and self-sacrifice). Since the 1930s, "cultic" regard for female chastity has been an established research motif for sinologists studying China's Song, Yuan, Ming, and especially Qing dynasties, 960–1911 (Theiss 2004).

Chastity was the explicit focus of early Christian church fathers, patristic writers and theologians (prominently including St. Paul, Ambrose, Chrysostom, Jerome, Augustine, and Aquinas), but also moral philosophers including Spinoza, Hume, and Nietzsche. The Bible provided the spiritual and theological underpinnings for defining chastity, with the writings of the church fathers adding detailed expositions. In the Western Empire by the end of the fourth century CE, conjugal fidelity underwent a conceptual shift, transformed from an ancient guarantor of inheritance – that is, from a social obligation to kin groups – into a Christian virtue, a critical component of lay piety. Ideas originating from within Christianity during this period challenged the legitimacy of the institution of marriage and the role of sex in marriage, as part of larger debates concerning the place of sexuality in Man, Society, and Nature. This tied the chaste person's spiritual salvation to the moral/theological direction of a fledgling religion. Patristic writers commonly identified three distinct states of female chastity: virginity, marriage, and widowhood (*viduitas*). Throughout early patristic literature and later medieval commentaries, *castitas* emerged as a quality of the spirit and *virginitas* more of a physical technicality (Kelly 2000).

Defining, defending, and regulating conjugal chastity became one of the most urgent pastoral concerns of the emerging institutional church. Both virginity and paternity claims were hard to prove yet essential to feudal societies where the bulk of wealth was in private, aristocratic hands and passed on from father to son. Both the testing and demarcation of virtuous or chaste behavior in (prospective) wives reflected related concerns of ensuring and securing paternity. Tests of chastity have an accordingly extended presence throughout medieval folklore and imaginative writing, from Arabic to Welsh. In early modern Venice, illustratively, the patrician class placed high value on maintaining hereditary purity. Virginity was an asset, bought by husbands from fathers. *Castità* connoted a history not just of absolute sexual decorum, but of most influences that, in excess or even in moderation, could indicate its compromise: dancing, spicy foods, lascivious books, luxurious clothing. Prescriptive literature and pedagogical metaphor figured forth a highly precarious, uncorrupted mind, with marital fidelity, cleanliness, fasting, and regulated sleep. Premodern lore expectedly abounds in chastity's purported signs, correlates, tests, proofs, and ordeals.

Historians consider the existence of medieval chastity belts or girdles a popular myth proliferating predominantly in the nineteenth century, however (Classen 2007). With struggle over religion's standing continuing, chastity vows have taken on a degree of formal attention across various Christian denominations in the United States since the early 1990s. Ceremonial "purity balls," "virginity pledges," and "chastity rings" have seen a formal revival as part of evangelical-led sexual abstinence campaigns, marking a rhetorical shift from a negative focus on abstinence to calls to formative "purity" (Gardner 2011). They are widely reported as ineffectual.

SEE ALSO: Adultery, Cultural Views of; Celibacy; Christianity, Gender and Sexuality; Religious Fundamentalism; Virginity

REFERENCES

Classen, Albrecht. 2007. *The Medieval Chastity Belt: A Myth-Making Process*. New York: Palgrave Macmillan.
Gardner, Christine. 2011. *Making Chastity Sexy: The Rhetoric of Evangelical Abstinence Campaigns*. Berkeley: University of California Press.
Kelly, Kathleen Coyne. 2000. *Performing Virginity and Testing Chastity in the Middle Ages*. London: Routledge.
Parsons, Elsie Clews [John Main = pseud.]. 1913. *Religious Chastity: An Ethnological Study*. New York: Macaulay.
Theiss, Janet. 2004. *Disgraceful Matters: The Politics of Chastity in Eighteenth-Century China*. Berkeley: University of California Press.

FURTHER READING

Giovannini, Maureen. 1987. "Female Chastity Codes in the Circum-Mediterranean: Comparative Perspectives." In *Honor and Shame and the Unity of the Mediterranean*, edited by David D. Gilmore, 61–74. Washington, DC: American Anthropological Association.
Paige, Karen. 1983. "Virginity Rituals and Chastity Control during Puberty: Cross-Cultural Patterns." In *Menarche: The Transition from Girl to Woman*, edited by Sharon Golub. Lexington, MA: Lexington Books.
Salih, Sarah. 2001. *Versions of Virginity in Late Medieval England*. Woodbridge, Suffolk: D. S. Brewer.
Van Deusen, Nancy. 2008. *Chastity: A Study in Perception, Ideals, Opposition*. Leiden: Brill.

Chick Flicks

HILARY RADNER
University of Otago, New Zealand

The "chick flick" as a film genre covers a broad and fairly nebulous territory. While the term is associated with film reviewer and scholar B. Ruby Rich, informal usage predates her highlighting of the genre. The most powerful and pervasive use of the category posits it as a cinematic parallel to a literary form known as "chick lit," characteristic of late twentieth-century, primarily anglophone fiction frequently translated into many different languages and enjoying a global appeal. Generically diverse, both structurally and thematically, these fiction forms, including television programming from the same period as well as film, are united through their address of a female viewer, like the woman's film of classical Hollywood. Chick flicks distinguish themselves from earlier female-directed material through their ironic and self-conscious tone, their emphasis on consumer culture, and their affirmation of a sexually active feminine subject. Appropriating some of the values associated with second-wave feminism, both chick flicks and chick lit can be understood as a product of what has been variously described as postfeminism, what Elspeth Probyn calls "choiceoisie," and, more recently, neofeminism.

Largely associated with conglomerate Hollywood, the chick flick has generated an array of significant subgenres, also loosely defined, such as the "older bird film," which focuses on a mature woman (see, for example, *It's Complicated*, directed by Nancy Meyers in 2009); the wedding film, in which the narrative conceit revolves around an impending wedding (as in Gary Winick's 2009 *Bride Wars*); the smart-chick film, a variation on the indie smart film, exemplified by films like

Frances Ha (2012, dir. Noel Baumach); and the female event film such as *The Devil Wears Prada* (2006, dir. David Frankel), which depends upon preestablished awareness for a substantial first-weekend box office and is usually an adaptation of a previously popular chick lit novel.

Though a number of female directors are identified with the chick flick, including Nora Ephron, Nancy Meyers, and the independent director Nicole Holofcener, male directors such as Gary Marshall, Gary Winick, Michael Patrick King, Joel Zwick, and David Frankel have been equally, if not more, successful. Nonetheless, as a rule, chick flicks are the consequence of a personal investment by a woman who, for various reasons, believes in the project, whether it be the star, as in the case of Sarah Jessica Parker and *Sex and the City: The Movie* (2008, dir. Michael Patrick King); the director, as in the case of Phyllida Lloyd and *Mamma Mia!* (2008, dir. Phyllida Lloyd); the screenwriter, as in the case of Nia Vardolos, who also played the lead, and *My Big Fat Greek Wedding* (2002, dir. Joel Zwick); or the combined forces of a producer and studio president, as in the case of Wendy Finerman, Elizabeth Gabler, and *The Devil Wears Prada*.

The heyday of the chick flick occurred arguably in the 1990s and early twenty-first century in the wake of the success of Gary Marshall's *Pretty Woman* (1990), which did well at the international box office and to some degree offset the prejudices of conglomerate Hollywood, which saw females as comprising a niche audience. These chick flicks were often, but not always, romantic comedies. Films that did not fall clearly into the category, such as the career girl film *Legally Blonde* (2001, dir. Robertic Luketic), generally included strong romantic themes foregrounding heterosexuality and the anticipation of marriage. An emphasis on consumer culture was another prominent feature of these films. Subsequent to the 2008 US recession and the failure of *Sex and the City: The Movie* to generate a successful franchise, such films with their emphasis on fashion became less common, with generally fewer and fewer films made for a female audience, in keeping with conglomerate Hollywood's focus on the more profitable young male demographic and the family film in the face of declining DVD sales. An exception to this trend is the continued output of smart-chick films by independent directors, such as *The Bling Ring* (2013, dir. Sofia Coppola), *Blue Jasmine* (2013, dir. Woody Allen), and *Enough Said* (2013, dir. Nicole Holofcener), but with limited release in theaters, reaching their audience through festivals and broadcasting on cable networks as well as DVD and video on demand (VOD), with a very different economy of scale than the blockbuster. The teen franchises such as the five films (2008, 2009, 2010, 2011, 2012) in the Twilight Saga, based on the novels of Stephanie Meyer, and the Hunger Games, *The Hunger Games* (2012, dir. Gary Ross) and *The Hunger Games: Catching Fire* (2013, dir. Frances Lawrence), directed at young women but also pulling in their older sisters and mothers, constitute a notable exception, performing well at the box office, though overshadowed by the action adventure franchises geared toward young males. These teen series distinguish themselves from the chick flicks of the 1990s and first decade of the twenty-first century by offering heroines who are oblivious to the world of fashion, and feminine culture more generally, at least within the fantasy universe of the films. The actresses and actors, however, have very visible lives on the red carpet and through tabloids in which they both actively and passively support the fashion system.

This is not to say that Hollywood is ignoring women audiences – rather, producers emphasize "quality" television programming, such as the 2013 *Top of the Lake* (Screen Australia/BBC) created by the iconic woman director Jane Campion, recognizing the ways in which female viewers' leisure habits tie them more closely to the small screen. Women's tendency to remain within the home has also encouraged a culture of re-viewing, in which films from the past, including a much more substantial representation of melodramas than is found in current production practices, have been reclassified as chick flicks by various guides produced for the female audience.

The rise, fall, and reconfiguration of the chick flick, its simultaneous embrace and denial of feminism, in which nostalgia competes with raw ambition, testify to the complexities of contemporary culture's engagement with the terms of gender in a rapidly changing world.

SEE ALSO: Feminist Film Theory; Postfeminism

FURTHER READING

Ferriss, Suzanne, and Mallory Young, eds. 2008. *Chick Flicks: Contemporary Women at the Movies*. New York: Routledge.

Gwynne, Joel, and Nadine Muller, eds. 2013. *Postfeminism and Contemporary Hollywood Cinema*. New York: Palgrave Macmillan.

Radner, Hilary. 2011. *Neo-Feminist Cinema: Girly Films, Chick Flicks and Consumer Culture*. New York: Routledge.

Child Custody and the Father Right Principle

WENDY MICHAELS
University of Newcastle, Australia

Child custody refers to court orders that award physical possession of a child to a person who may or may not be the child's parent. It is distinguished from guardianship orders, which confer on a person or the state decision-making powers in respect of a child. Custody and guardianship orders originated in the English common law doctrine of *parens patriae* ("parent of the country") that granted power and authority to the state to protect persons, particularly children, who were legally unable to act on their own behalf. During the reign of Henry VIII (1509–1547) this "royal prerogative" passed to the newly established Court of Wards and Liveries and in 1600 was transferred by statute to Chancery. By the eighteenth century courts were acting as adjudicators in cases of interspousal and familial disputations over the custody of legal progeny.

Historically in Western cultures the family was conceptualized as a patriarchal institution with a patrilineal inheritance system that vested power and property ownership rights in the father, with the wife's legal identity subsumed under his, as *feme covert*. The common law father right principle that deemed the father's authority to be "natural" was central to this *pater familias* structure. The father right principle protected the father's ownership of his property, which included his wife and his legitimate (but not illegitimate) progeny. It also had the effect of enforcing his wife's obedience to him: if a marriage ended in separation or divorce the children remained the property of the father, and if a woman left her husband she left her children (James 2005). The Confirmation of Marriages Act 1660 reinforced this common law principle, and the influential eighteenth-century legal jurist Sir William Blackstone in his *Commentaries* (1765–1769) further upheld the father's natural right to his children.

At the same time, however, the authority of the principle began to be questioned through case law. In two separate judgments Lord Mansfield offered contesting interpretations of the principle's application in law. In *Rex v. Delaval* (1763) Lord Mansfield refused paternal custody of a minor, an 18-year-old girl, whom he emancipated, clarifying the principle by arguing the courts should make judgments on the basis of the circumstances of each individual case. In *Blissets Case* (1765) he went further, allowing a 6-year-old girl to remain with her mother after the father had abandoned the family. In this judgment Lord Mansfield advanced two rationales: first, the court should make a decision according to what would be best for the child, and second, that a father who abandoned his paternal duties forfeited his father right. Klaff (1982) notes these two rationales point toward two doctrines that came to be known as the child's best interests and the unfitness doctrines. However, Lord Mansfield's clarifications did not have an immediate effect on all subsequent cases. In *Rex v. DeManneville* (1804) the father was awarded custody of an 8-month-old daughter who was still being breastfed by the mother. Lord Ellenborough, adhering to the father right principle, argued that the father was lawfully entitled to possession of his daughter despite the mother having left him because of his cruelty. Similarly, in *Ex parte Skinner* (1824), the mother was refused custody of her 6-year-old daughter who had been given by the father to his mistress while he was in the debtor's prison.

Despite the persistence of the father right principle into the nineteenth century, concerns about the morality and efficacy of removing a young child from the mother were voiced beyond the courts. Vice Chancellor Sir Anthony Hart in 1827 stated there was nothing more harsh or cruel than such an action. The case *Rex v. Greenhill* (1836) gave further impetus to these concerns. The father had abandoned his wife and three daughters under the age of 6 to live with his mistress and the wife took her daughters back to her parents' home. When her husband sought to force her to return with them to the marital home, she refused. The court concluded it had no authority to deny the father custody and ruled the children be returned to him. In desperation the mother fled from the court's jurisdiction with her children.

The year 1836 saw further questioning of the authority of the father right principle and a new approach to seeking its removal. As liberal reform initiatives began to be implemented, momentum built outside the courts and the legislature for a statute to overturn the common law principle. Among the women agitators involved in this campaigning was the writer and social reformer Caroline Sheridan Norton, who had left her abusive husband after he denied her access to her sons. She penned a pamphlet (Norton 2013/1837) arguing against the father right principle which she sent to her parliamentary Whig friends, amongst whom was Thomas Talfourd MP. He had been counsel for the father in *Rex v. Greenhill* yet viewed that case as a denial of natural justice. Spurred on by Norton's campaign, he argued in parliament for legislative change. The passing of the Custody of Infants Act 1839 accorded Chancery discretionary power to order maternal custody of children up to the age of 7 years, a provision that was further extended in 1873 to children of 16 years. This statute disrupted the preeminence of the father right principle, marking a shift away from the assumption of the father as the natural and rightful guardian of his children to a new presumption that came to be known as the maternal preference or tender years doctrine.

This doctrine took root at a time of significant social developments and philosophical revolutions. Changing work conditions took men out of the home and relegated women to the domestic domain. Biological determinism cemented the ideology of separate sexual spheres with men constructed as providers for the family and women as homemakers.

Romantic philosophies that separated childhood from adulthood established the need for young children to be nurtured by the mother. The presumption of maternal custody of children of tender years was congruent with these changing situations and values. In the case of *Austin* (1865), Sir John Romilly argued that no other person could supply the place of the mother in caring for a child of tender years, a precept that was rearticulated in Australia more than a century later in *Epperson v. Dempney* as the "common knowledge" that mothers' human nature predisposed them to be natural carers of tender-age children.

The maternal preference doctrine was not a legal principle, as father right was, but an evidentiary presumption that did not alter a woman's legal rights. Moreover, it was limited to mothers who were innocent of marital fault and were thus able to demonstrate themselves to be fit and proper persons to be the child's custodian. Notwithstanding this shift to maternal preference, the demand for the mother (although not the father) to prove moral virtue continued. In *Re Besant, and Infant* (1878) Rev. F. Besant brought a case against his wife Annie Besant for the removal from her custody of their 8-year-old daughter whom he had previously abandoned. The court ruled the father's right to the child should be reinstated and it ordered the child be given up to the father on the grounds that the mother's reputation had been tainted by her advocacy of contraception, her admission of atheism, and her refusal to provide religious instruction for her daughter. Moreover, the judgment stated it was not in the young child's best interests to remain with a woman whose tarnished reputation prevented her from associating with respectable women.

In the United States of America during the nineteenth century, the principle that courts were empowered to subordinate proprietary parental interests in a child to a consideration of the child's best interests became entrenched in most jurisdictions. Associated with the child's best interests principle was the presumption of maternal custody for children of tender years. The term tender years was first introduced in an 1813 Pennsylvania case, *Commonwealth v. Addicks*. The father who had abandoned the mother and two daughters four years previously sought custody of his children, who were living with the mother and her second husband with whom she had also had a child. Although the mother had not been blameless of marital fault the court, emphasizing the tender age of the children and the preference for the mother to provide for their needs, awarded custody to her. This decision was later reversed on the basis of the mother's adultery, which resulted in the children being restored to the father. As in England, the compulsion for the mother to prove fitness countered maternal preference.

Australian jurisdictions were somewhat tardy in removing the father right principle and taking on board the tender years or maternal preference doctrine. In the most populous state, New South Wales, Section 5 of the Infants Custody and Settlements Act 1899 did permit a mother to make application to the Equity Court for custody of a child, although few women were in a financial position to do so and even those who did were not likely to succeed as prevailing social codes favored morally suspect fathers over morally upright mothers. This Act did, however, include the child's best interests principle, stating that this should be "paramount."

As in the 1836 Talfourd Act, it was campaigning by New South Wales women that prompted a shift away from the father right principle. Organizations such as the National Council of Women and the Feminist Club had been arguing for legislative change since the turn of the century. Their lobbying of parliamentarians had prompted John Francis Hughes, a member of the Legislative Council, to introduce a bill in 1903 that was rejected by the conservative non-elected Upper House. Their campaign was accelerated and expanded by a high-profile custody case in the New South Wales Equity Court in 1924. In *Ellis v. Ellis* the mother, Emélie (née Polini), an English-born actress, sought custody of her 2-year old daughter Patricia after her husband, Harold, had refused her access to the child. Justice Harvey, while acknowledging that he could not find any moral fault in the mother, nevertheless refused her application on the grounds of well-settled legal principles from which he argued that it was in the child's best interests for her to remain with the father. As Lake (1999) notes, the mother, in "pursuing her profession," had "forfeited her rights as a mother."

After the case, Polini made a public appeal in the press for women to ensure the laws were changed. The women's campaign strategies intensified with lobbying of parliamentarians, use of public forums and the press to publicize the issue, and the presentation to the justice minister of the Emélie Polini Petition with 25,000 signatures. In 1925 the campaign was given further impetus with the election to the New South Wales Legislative Assembly of the first woman member of parliament. Although Millicent Preston-Stanley, who had been one of the prominent campaigners, served only one term in the house (1925–1927), in 1926 she introduced a bill to amend the existing legislation. This bill, however, was not welcomed by the male parliamentarians and did not proceed beyond the first reading.

Outside the parliament, in 1932 Preston-Stanley employed a different strategy, staging the professional production of a play she had written based on the Ellis custody case and her parliamentary and campaigning experiences. *Whose Child?* was performed before a vice-regal opening night in Sydney's stylish Criterion Theatre on November 26, 1932. The didactic message was an argument that maternal preference should replace the father right principle since mothers were biologically the natural carers of young children. At the conclusion of the performance, Preston-Stanley read to the audience a note written by the minister of justice who was in the audience, which announced he would introduce a bill to provide for the mother's rights as depicted in the play (Michaels 2013). In October 1934 the Guardianship of Infants Act was placed on the statute books. While this Act removed the father right principle, it did not include maternal preference but positioned the child's welfare as the paramount consideration without specific guidelines for determining that welfare. As Funder (1991) notes, determining a child's best interests is problematic when no specific directions as to how those interests should be ascertained are provided.

During the twentieth century transformations in women's social, economic, and domestic roles and legal status saw further changes to child custody laws. Despite a resurgence of emphasis on the nuclear family in the aftermath of World War II, the social justice movements from the 1960s led to liberal law reforms in various fields. As women moved outside the home and into the workforce in greater numbers, the equity principle and emphasis on joint custody became more significant. In Australia, the Family Law Act 1975, which brought such matters under federal jurisdiction, removed matrimonial fault, abolished both the father right principle and the maternal preference doctrine, and instituted joint custody. Maintaining the child's best interests as the paramount consideration, it provided in Section 60CC 12 guidelines on which courts must base this determination.

Similarly, in the United States toward the end of the twentieth century, the presumption of maternal preference came under scrutiny in various states. In a 1976 New York case, *Watts v. Watts*, Judge Sybil Hart Kooper found that the presumption of maternal preference violated the right of the father to equal legal protection under the Fourteenth Amendment. Citing Margaret Mead, Judge Kooper argued that the fact of biological motherhood did not indicate capacity for mothering and that mothering was thereby gender neutral. The child's best interests were not served by the assumption of maternal preference (Klaff 1982). This judgment reflected the direction of gender debates in the late twentieth century. An upsurge of masculinist discourse emphasized the irrelevance of gender to the act of mothering and the importance of fatherhood in the life of the child. In Australia, despite studies that showed otherwise, some men's groups galvanized press and public support for their view of the discrimination against fathers supposedly occurring in custody cases. The resulting amendments to the Family Law Act in 1995 saw a clawing back of men's parenting authority through the principle of shared responsibility (James 2005). While this did not go as far as some men's groups had wished by reinstating full custody rights for fathers, it had the appearance of readjusting the perceived bias toward women of the maternal preference doctrine. In an attempt to neutralize emotionally charged situations surrounding custody applications, the 1995 Family Law Act also revised custody law language, replacing terms such as "guardianship" and "custody" with words such as "legal responsibility" and "parenting orders."

As Mason (1994) argues, the history of child custody reflects changing social attitudes toward gender and evolving conceptions of the family. Despite the shifts from father right to maternal preference to child's best interests to joint custody, courts tend to retain a conservative view of the nuclear family unit with parental authority invested in the father (Berns 1991). Views of mothering as a female activity tend to prevail to the extent that fathers are more likely to be awarded custody in cases where they are able to offer a stepmother or other female kin care for the child (Hasche 1989; Schaefer 2008). As James (2005) notes, despite the legislative changes, preserving the "marriage-based family as the cornerstone of society" remains paramount.

SEE ALSO: Fathers and Parenting Interventions; Feminist Movements in Historical and Comparative Perspective

REFERENCES

Berns, Sandra S. 1991. "Living under the Shadow of Rousseau: The Role of Gender Ideologies in Custody and Access Decisions." *Tasmanian Law Review*, 10: 233–255.

Blackstone, William. 1765–1769. *Commentaries on the Laws of England*, Book 1, Chapters 15 and 16. Accessed August 10, 2015, at http://www.lonang.com/exlibris/blackstone/

Funder, Kate. 1991. "Motherhood, Fatherhood: The Legal Balance." *Family Matters*, 30: 34–37.

Hasche, Annette. 1989. "Sex Discrimination in Child Custody Determinations." *American Journal of Family Law*, 218–235.

James, Colin. 2005. "Winners and Losers: The Father Factor in Australian Child Custody Law in the 20th Century." *ANZLH E-Journal*, 10: 207–238. Accessed August 10, 2015, at http://www.anzlhsejournal.auckland.ac.nz/pdfs_2005/James.pdf.

Klaff, Ramsay Laing. 1982. "The Tender Years Doctrine: A Defence." *California Law Review*, 70: 335–372.

Lake, Marilyn. 1999. *Getting Equal: The History of Australian Feminism*. Sydney: Allen and Unwin.

Mason, Mary Anne. 1994. *From Father's Property to Children's Rights: A History of Child Custody*. New York: Columbia University Press.

Michaels, Wendy. 2013. "The Final Factor: What Political Action Failed to Do." *Lilith*, 19: 18–31.

Norton, Caroline Sheridan. 2013. *Observations on the Natural Claims of a Mother to the Custody of Her Children as Affected by the Common Law Rights of the Father*. Cambridge: Cambridge University Press. First published 1837.

Schaefer, Tali. 2008. "Disposable Mothers: Paid In-Home Caretaking and the Regulation of Parenthood." *Yale Journal of Law and Feminism*, 19: 305–351.

FURTHER READING

Folberg, Jay. 1991. *Joint Custody and Shared Parenting*. New York: Guilford Press.

Kelly, Joan B. 1994. "The Determination of Child Custody." *The Future of Children*, 4: 121–142.

Smart, Carol, and Selma Sevenhuijeen. 1989. *Child Custody and the Politics of Gender*. New York: Routledge.

Child Labor in Comparative Perspective

C. NANA DERBY
Virginia State University, USA

Child labor is usually defined as illegal and often inhumane use of children's labor in economic activities. The concept signifies the negativity of deprivation, exploitation, hazards, and abuse, but children may also engage in acceptable work within the household and under the supervision of their own parents. This notwithstanding, the exploitation of children's labor is typically covert in some sectors and thus has the potential of thwarting efforts to determine its actual rate of incidence at any given time. The International Labour Organization (ILO) estimated there were about 250 million child laborers aged between 5 and 17 around the world in 2000. This dropped to 215 million in 2008, and by 2014, there were 168 million child laborers. From the 2008 estimates, 60 percent of children were engaged in agriculture, 15 percent worked in manufacturing in the informal sector, and 25 percent provided services. An estimated 53 percent of child workers were from Asia and the Pacific, 7 percent from Latin America, 10 percent from Europe and North America, and 30 percent from sub-Saharan Africa. One in four children under 18 years worked in sub-Saharan Africa. In Asia it was one in eight children, while in Latin America it was one in 10 (International Labour Organization 2010).

Child labor is a social construct that has, historically, been conceptualized variously through cultural practices and social institutions (Campbell, Miers, and Miller 2009). The nature of work, number of hours worked, and the extent of exploitation and hazards have, however, remained unchanged, spatially and historically. Prior to the twentieth century in parts of Europe, many poor children and orphans worked long hours – around 50 to 80 hours a week – in coal mines, construction, domestic servitude, and agriculture – earning merely 10–20 percent of the adult wage for doing the same thing. The demand for cheap labor, following the Industrial Revolution, intensified this exploitation of children's labor and they continued to work long hours in agriculture and manufacturing sectors, including glassmaking, textiles, and canneries. They were exposed to extreme hazards, such as heat, dust, sharp and heavy equipment, and chemicals that jeopardized their health, impeded their growth, and exposed them to serious or fatal injuries.

Some analysts locate frameworks of child labor exploitation in economic theories (Basu and Chau 2004), and fail to clearly evaluate, either qualitatively or quantitatively, the partial – and yet equally important – influence of culture, advocacy, and poor legislative practices. Such economic models seem fixated on poverty and address its positive correlation with child labor, arguing that extreme forms of poverty drive parents to send their children to work. From this assertion, it is deducible that where there is abundance or wealth, parents would have no reason to send their children to work. Conversely, Carol Ann Rogers and Kenneth A. Swinnerton (2005) hypothesized a negative correlation between poverty and child labor and illuminated this argument with its examination in parts of Asia. Their assessment focused on landownerships, agrarian systems, and household labor just as those extant economic models upon which they built their perspective. They perceived landownership as correlating directly with child labor because households with vast land for farming, although considered wealthy, relied extensively on the labor of their children. This latter model basically committed the same offense as other economistic perspectives because of the exclusion of other factors that created and sustained child labor, namely the state of economic systems, cultural practices such as processes of socialization, poor policies and unenforceable laws, and systems of extended family and the related culture of traditional fosterage.

Any disparities may be seen in terms of the cultural implications of the causes of child labor exploitation and governmental as well as unofficial responses to such abuses. Unlike other practices, however, the phenomenon of child labor is often given meaning within the international community in ways that somehow affect respective frameworks within individual countries. These frameworks either positively examine the functional roles of child labor or critically evaluate ways in which child labor constitutes abuse, erodes childhoods, and impedes growth and development in minors. This entry briefly defines child labor, outlines the weaknesses of some economic-based models of child labor exploitation, and provides alternative perspectives that compare the incidence of the problem in agrarian and non-agrarian systems while identifying the roles of culture in the problem.

Economic perspectives inadequately explain the factors that cause and sustain children's work or child labor exploitation. Forerunners of the perspectives on child labor defined it in terms of agrarian societies that they categorized as imperfect market economies in which landownership was based on inheritance rather than the markets. Additionally, agrarian farmers relied significantly on household labor, including that of children. The main precept of this model was a positive correlation between child labor and poverty, but in such societies wealth was defined on grounds of landownership, hence the hypothesis that as landownership expanded, the use of children's labor subsided (Rogers and Swinnerton 2005). Contrariwise, child labor exploitation within the household surged with expansions in landownerships and thus wealth. Following criticisms by authors such as Rogers and Swinnerton (2005), it could be concluded that child labor would be nonexistent in market economies where manufacturing and service provision dominated. The closest that this theory came to explaining this was in the assertion that parents sent their children off to work in factories in extreme poverty. Other flaws in this perspective related to the exclusion of non-agrarian economic systems, cultural practices, the significance and successes of advocacies, and the impact of laws aimed at the protection of children from exploitive labor.

Limited legislative instruments existed to protect children's rights until the twentieth century. Some of the earliest statutes were the English Factory Acts of 1802 and 1819, which failed to regulate children's work. Since the twentieth century, the adoption and ratification of international treaties on children's rights and protection have been prolific. In 1973, the ILO adopted the Minimum Age Convention (C138) and created the International Program on the Elimination of Child Labor in 1992. It adopted the Worst Forms of Child Labor Convention (C182) in 1999. In 1990, the United Nations (UN) adopted the Convention on the Rights of the Child.

The ILO illuminates the concept of child labor with its differentiation between negative and positive children's work. This definition encompasses both consensus and critical perspectives by framing "child labor" in relation to its negativity on one hand, and its potential as a functional component of society, on the other. From the consensus framework, this entry conceptualizes children's work as a positive social constituency, which derives from processes of socialization to which child labor, if appropriately framed, contributes. Through socialization, a society brings up its children and teaches them acceptable ways of behavior. The processes are partly enshrined in physical and social rites of passage. Physical rites of passage refer to the celebrations and practices associated with physiological changes in youth. Some extremely traditional cultures designate special ceremonies for such physiological changes. In parts of Africa, puberty rites such as the *dipo* of Ghana are examples of such rites. These mark a minor's entry into adulthood, and are determined solely on the basis of physical development. In the case of a female, the first menstrual period is usually considered a natural sign of entry into adulthood. In such traditional cultures, it is these signs that usually determine adulthood, not chronological age. Officially, however, one's chronological age takes precedence over all other practices in the determination of one's status as adult or minor.

Social rites of passage relate to teachings on cultural practices and expectations, part of which constitutes positive children's work if it does not pose any danger to the child's growth and development, does not harm them or deny them their childhood and social engagement, and accords them opportunities of learning skills that would be useful to them in adulthood. Furthermore, the number of hours worked should not interfere with their childhoods, right to formal education, play, and to living in a loving household.

The family is considered the primary agent of socialization because it is the child's first contact with society, which provides the platform for the various rites of passage. In extended family systems, other relatives besides the nuclear family play significant roles of socialization in a child's life, a practice that creates and sustains traditional fosterage that informally allows households to live with and care for non-biological children. Historically, relationships of traditional fosterage were customarily reciprocal because in return for care and education, the fostered child supported the household with labor by performing domestic chores and/or providing supplementary labor in farming, fishing, or carpentry. In some instances, the fosterage occurred for purposes of apprenticeship, in which case the child was sent to live with non-biological parents to learn a trade. This practice was meritorious if the child, depending on the age, was supported to go to school and to actually study while enrolled, or to learn a trade. With time, this practice became the means through which human traffickers recruited children for exploitation within the household and in the informal sector, trading, farming, and fishing. This was particularly the case in sub-Saharan Africa. This is where positive children's work, a major part of socialization, intercepts the negative and transitions into exploitive children's labor.

Negative children's work is exploitive and deprives the child of their childhood, their rights to formal education, personal development, health, and a loving home, and violates the minimum age laws of a nation. According to the ILO, exploitive child labor "is mentally, physically, socially or morally dangerous and harmful to children; and interferes with their schooling by depriving them of the opportunity to attend school, obliging them to leave school prematurely or requiring them to attempt to combine school attendance with excessively long and heavy work." The abuses of children's labor could be enslaving, discriminatory on grounds of gender, and may involve trafficking.

Through socialization, many cultures train their young members in gender-based roles and chores. Among several less traditional societies, such gender-biased chores seem to be dissipating, but this is contrary in other cultures where the exposure to gender role differentiations characterizes socialization in general. Girls learn the intricacies of femininity, and the exposure to specific forms of domestic chores dominates this. From a very early age, girls learn to cook, clean, and take care of children, and boys are nurtured for purposes of masculinity. In agricultural communities, while both girls and boys learn farming early in life, the latter may be required to complete more strenuous tasks – such as clearing thick and overgrown bushes in slash-and-burn farming – relative to what girls are assigned. In fishing communities, boys may be socialized to fish while girls learn traditional ways of preparing or processing fish for the market. Where child labor exploitation prevails, it may reflect these gender role expectations and practices that may be prevalent in the dominant culture.

Human trafficking is viewed as a component of child labor exploitation. Human trafficking is generally defined as "all acts involved in the recruitment, abduction, transport, harboring, transfer, sale or receipt of persons, within national or across international borders, through force, coercion, fraud or deception, to place persons in situations of slavery or slavery-like conditions, forced labor or services, such as forced prostitution or sexual services, domestic servitude, bonded sweatshop labor, or other debt bondage." In traditional fosterage, trafficking may occur through what is defined as non-formal and informal processes of recruitment, which may further be categorized into soft and hard trafficking respectively. Informal recruiters are seldom intermediaries between prospective child laborers and their employers and are neither registered nor regular, occasionally recruiting children for labor in other communities. The non-formal recruiter, although not formally established as an employment agent, regularly recruits children for labor, part of which tends to be exploitive and hazardous.

Both strategies of recruitment are not recognized legally, and they do not conform to employment statutes in their respective nations. The recruiters engage in practices that, while seeming acceptable and normal, may be deceptive or manipulative and lead to conditions of trafficking. Parents whose children are recruited this way may never suspect the dangers their children face and the traffickers' primary goal of child labor exploitation. When families approach relatively deprived households and offer to live with and take care of their young children, soft trafficking may be the consequence if the children work long hours, at times under hazardous conditions and at the peril of their education, self-esteem, and childhoods. Recruitment becomes hard trafficking when recruiters employ violent, abusive, and coercive strategies, such as drugging and kidnapping, to lure or force their victims to comply with their requests.

Traditional fosterage is predominant in sub-Saharan Africa. In some cases the middlemen, especially the non-formal recruiter, receive compensation for bringing the child to the employing household. In rare cases the parent may be given sums of money, which hardly qualifies as payment for the purchase of the child being recruited or trafficked. Parents simply want their children to migrate to the cities for better living conditions and opportunities in life. Debt bondage may occur in some cases, but it is rare in Africa. In parts of Asia, it is debt bondage, rather than traditional fosterage, that drives child labor exploitation. In this practice families employ their children's labor as collateral for loans, committing the children to work in some dangerous and extremely hazardous environments. What typically happens is that for loans of less than $200, children may lose their rights to education, uninterrupted childhood, and lives in loving households to move into factories where they would work long hours a day for several years because the creditors use dubious calculations to manipulate the duration of the loan. In cases where bonded children become invalid or deceased, the parents are required to send a replacement child.

Characteristically, cross-cultural gender role differentiations determine the modes and purposes of child trafficking. Children who find themselves in exploitive labor through trafficking or debt bondage may work within the household and in agriculture, manufacturing, and in the provision of services according to expectations of work-related masculinity and femininity. Many of them are enslaved in the sex industry. Most of the children illegally conscripted into the militia in war zones are boys. When rebels kidnap girls, they are typically used for sexual exploitation. For farming purposes, more boys than girls are exploited, and in domestic servitude, we observe a higher probability of girls than boys.

More girls suffer child domestic servitude than boys. This kind of child labor occurring within the household may go unnoticed, and for several reasons. Unless the child domestic servant is seen engaging in work outside the home during hours when they should be in school, researchers for a long time considered them as "free" children of the households in which they served. This was particularly the case in statistical studies that did not provide an opportunity for further probing to determine the statuses of the children, i.e., if they were biological or legal and non-working children of the household. In recent times, qualitative studies have provided in-depth assessments of children who work within the households, and while the findings may not be generalizable, the experiences that respondents share with researchers leave so much to be desired.

Child domestic servants are different from adult domestic workers. The latter are mature and knowledgeable enough to consent to employment agreements. They are able to negotiate working hours, frequency and form of remuneration, and other work-related incentives. Child domestic servants, on the other hand, are usually underage and cannot enter into any agreement when recruited to work in any field, and in domestic servitude they are compelled to work several hours without pay. Child servitude prevails primarily in developing nations around the world; nevertheless, this is observed to be evolving gradually among migrant communities in other cultures. The servants could be as young as 5 years old. They work several hours a day, between 10 and 20 hours. They may wake up very early in the morning, in some cases around 4 a.m.

Childcare, housekeeping, and petty trading are three main chores that child domestic servants perform. For childcare, they may supervise children, prepare them for daycare or school, and send them to and pick them up from school or daycare if there is no vehicle for that purpose. Other childcare responsibilities may include cleaning, feeding, and preparation of baby food. Housekeeping for domestic servants may entail cleaning, cooking, laundry, and running other related errands such as going to the corner store to get foodstuffs. For petty trading, child domestic servants walk several hours, hawking foodstuffs, water or convenience items, or simply keep corner stores for their "employers."

In some households, one domestic servant may combine all three categories of work. Even when a child performs only household chores as her main responsibility, the experience may still be exceptionally unpleasant, exploitive, and hazardous for the child, and it may impede her growth, erode her childhood, and prevent her from engaging in social activities. Some households that keep domestic servants also use verbal and physical abuse that is subjugating to brainwash them to remain in servitude; this strips them of their self-esteem. Besides working so many hours a day, unlike other children, the child domestic servant is abused emotionally and physically. These children are insulted, and in some cases they eat different food and are clothed differently from the other kids. In Jean-Robert Cadet's (1998) book narrating his experiences as a child domestic servant, he noted how he had to stand on a stone to peek through a hole in a door to watch the television, at times in a neighbor's house. In other instances Cadet observed, domestic servants had to bring stools from the kitchen to sit on in the back of the sitting room to watch television.

The child domestic servant normally does not receive remuneration commensurate with the work done. In Ghana, for instance, the child domestic sometimes agrees on a monthly wage, which can be paid at the end of the month, or accumulated and paid at the end of the contract period, usually two years. Alternatively, domestic servants may arrange to get paid in kind at the end of the contract period. Such in-kind payment includes apprentice training in hairdressing or dressmaking for female servants, or driving, carpentry, or masonry for boys. Unfortunately, at the end of the four-year-plus period of service, the impact of Ghana's inflation sometimes will have reduced the value of their salaries by about 50 percent or more. Employers may overlook the contract duration so that servants end up staying for at least four years, over 100 percent longer than the agreed period. If the servants feel they can no longer take the abuse, they find a way to leave, at times unannounced, which sometimes leads to forfeiture of the payments due them.

These instances of exploitation and segregation are not unique to child domestic servitude, but are observable characteristics of child labor exploitation in agriculture, manufacturing, and service sectors. In agriculture, children are seen primarily in fishing, quarrying, mining, and farming. In each of these sectors the exploited child works long hours and is exposed to hazards, some of which are fatal and/or capable of impeding their growth and development. They are exposed to sharp and heavy equipment and hazardous chemicals like pesticides and fertilizers, and are physically abused and deprived of basic rights including access to education, health, social activities, and nutrition. Along the borders of Côte d'Ivoire and Ghana, for example, physical abuse such as whipping left children who were trafficked and/or recruited into cocoa farming with very big sores and scars. In Egypt where child labor in agriculture exists primarily on cotton fields, children travel in overloaded trucks and sometimes are involved in fatal or dangerous accidents (Mikay 1997; Derby 2009). Along the Volta Lake of Ghana, trafficked children were forced to dive deep into the lake to release fishnets stuck in stones. Rescued child fishers interviewed by Derby (2010) indicated they witnessed the drowning of their young colleagues who could not make it out of the waters. Like their counterparts in other areas of abuse, children exploited in fishing had little or no playtime, slept four to six hours a night, worked long hours, ate very little, and were not compensated for the work done. Even though they worked in fishing, they had no protein in their meals, not even the fish they helped to catch; their diet comprised nothing more than carbohydrates. In quarrying, the children are exposed to similar hazards such as chemicals and dangerous dusts, long hours of work, lack of attention to their health, and poor nutrition.

The nature of child labor exploitation in any given nation corresponds with its main economic activities, although child domestic servitude occurs in several non-Western societies. Accordingly, in Asia, many of the abuses of children's labor occur in the manufacture of carpets, beads, beedi (cigarettes), matches, fireworks and explosives, glass, and brassware, and in mining (Burra 1995; Mikay 1997; Tucker and Ganesan 1997; Derby 2009). In parts of Africa, the phenomenon is relatively more prevalent in agriculture, i.e., in farming (cocoa in Côte d'Ivoire and Ghana, cotton in Egypt and Benin), and that is because the primary sector dominates African economies. In highly industrialized nations, child labor is significantly controlled, but it is more prevalent in the service sector, such as retail. In recent times, there have been extensive campaigns against child labor in sweat shops so that very little of it is seen in highly industrialized nations. In India and other Asian countries where manufacturing has been outsourced from other parts of the world, there are struggles to combat it. There have been calls to boycott carpets from parts of Asia and chocolates from parts of West Africa because of child labor exploitation.

Children are also exploited in sex slavery. Depending on which culture is being observed, children may be recruited into this through both soft and hard trafficking. In hard trafficking, children are trafficked across borders and forced to sleep with several men a day, at times without protection. Girls are coerced into prostitution by strangers or acquaintances that they may have just met. Some girls who suffer hard trafficking are tortured at several stages of their encounter, through their removal from their communities to their forced entry into prostitution. Documentaries abound on the exploitation of innocent children in pornography and prostitution (e.g., *The Day My God Died* (2003), directed by Andrew Levine, and *Sacrifice* (2007) by Ellen Bruno).

In recent times there have been numerous governmental and non-governmental efforts, both within the international community and at the local level, to address the labor exploitation not only of children, but of vulnerable women as well. Measures aim at the protection of children and the prevention of their recruitment into forced and hazardous labor. The identification and prosecution of perpetrators have also been foremost in efforts to fight child labor exploitation. In 2000, the US Department of State passed the Trafficking Victims Protection Act and followed that with the establishment of the Office to Monitor and Combat Trafficking in Persons. This office has been charged with the pursuit of global policies, partnerships, and practices that ensure that vulnerable women and children are protected, that trafficking in persons is prevented, and that the culprits are found and prosecuted. This is known as the 4P paradigm (partnership, protection, prevention, and prosecution).

Several international treaties that focus on child labor exploitation have also been adopted, as noted earlier. Prominent among them is ILO Convention No. 182 (C182) on the Worst Forms of Child Labor, which was adopted in 1999. Together with the UN Convention on the Rights of the Child, C182 has compelled signatory countries to promulgate laws requiring the protection of children from hazardous labor (International Labour Organization and Inter-Parliamentary Union 2002) and to promote their basic rights including the rights to grow up in loving homes, to enjoy their childhood and social activities, and to basic education. Many countries have implemented some form of free basic education, which, if effectively implemented, should keep children in school and reduce their engagement in exploitive labor. In some instances, however, there is resistance to the fight against child labor exploitation because of the denial of its existence or the harm it does to the child victims or survivors. In child domestic servitude, for instance, households refuse to admit it is abusive because of the illusion and deception that it is beneficial to the child servants.

SEE ALSO: Child Prostitution; Child Sexual Abuse and Trauma; Division of Labor, Domestic; Human Rights, International Laws and Policies on; Human Trafficking, Feminist Perspectives on; Sex Trafficking; Victimization

REFERENCES

Basu, Arnab K., and Nancy H. Chau. 2004. "Exploitation of Child Labor and the Dynamics of Debt Bondage." *Journal of Economic Growth*, 9(2): 209–238.

Burra, N. 1995. *Born to Work: Child Labour in India*. Delhi: Oxford University Press.

Cadet, Jean-Robert. 1998. *Restavec: From Haitian Slaver Child to Middle-Class American*. Austin: University of Texas Press.

Campbell, Gwyn, Suzanne Miers, and Joseph C. Miller, eds. 2009. *Children in Slavery through the Ages*. Athens: Ohio University Press.

Derby, C. Nana. 2009. *Contemporary Slavery: Researching Child Domestic Servitude*. Lanham: University Press of America.

Derby, C. Nana. 2010. "Enslavement and Human Trafficking: The Supple Swimmers of Fishing at Yeji, Ghana." In *Who Pays the Price? Foreign Workers, Society, Crime and the Law*, edited by Mally Shechory, Dan Soen, and Sarah Ben-David, 191–200. Hauppauge, NY: Nova.

International Labour Organization. 2010. *IPEC Action against Child Labor: Progress and Future Priorities*. Geneva: International Labour Organization.

International Labour Organization and Inter-Parliamentary Union. 2002. *Eliminating the Worst Forms of Child Labor: A Practical Guide to ILO Convention 182*. Geneva: International Labour Organization.

Mikay, E. 1997. "An Economic Essential?" *The Middle East*, 272: 38–40.

Rogers, Carol Ann, and Kenneth A. Swinnerton. 2005. A Theory of Exploitative Child Labor. Accessed June 24, 2015, at http://www.oep.oxfordjournals.org/content/60/1/20.abstract.

Tucker, Lee, and Arvind Ganesan. 1997. "The Small Hands of Slavery: India's Bonded Child Laborers and the World Bank." *Multinational Monitor*, 18(1–2): 17–19.

FURTHER READING

Derby, C. Nana. 2012. "Are the Barrels Empty? Are the Children any Safer? Child Domestic Labor and Servitude in Ghana." In *African Childhoods: Education, Development, Peacebuilding, and the Youngest Continent*, edited by Marisa O. Ensor, 10–32. New York: Palgrave Macmillan.

Hindman, Hugh D., ed. 2009. *The World of Child Labor: An Historical and Regional Survey*. Armonk: M. E. Sharpe.

Child Prostitution

CAROLINE NORMA
RMIT University, Australia

Prostitution is estimated to affect 600,000 children in the United States, plus another million in Asia. A total of 10 million children worldwide each year are understood to be sexually exploited, with girls the overwhelming victims. The sexual trading of children takes place in rich and poor countries, both online and in the streets, but disproportionately incorporates children from racially and economically oppressed groups. It takes forms including caste-based familial pimping of daughters, trading of children to sex tourists, and the prostitution of children through the commercial sex industry, including in pornography production. In the twenty-first century, men's prostitution of children is a problem of escalating proportions, and national governments are confounded by the size and scale of child protection systems needed to tackle the issue (Berelowitz et al. 2013). Cyber technologies have notably facilitated this escalation (Fredlund et al. 2013), and in the United States there have been significant campaigns against online advertising businesses generating revenues from the sexual trading of children (McGreal 2010).

International law on child prostitution is historically traceable to the work of feminists and abolitionists in the early twentieth century who campaigned against the trade, including through the League of Nations (Moschetti 2005). Today, child prostitution is addressed in the Optional Protocol to the Convention on the Rights of the Child on the Sale of Children, Child Prostitution and Child Pornography (2000). Prefacing this was the 1989 Convention on the Rights of the Child, and the appointment in 1990 of a Special Rapporteur on the sale of children, child prostitution, and child pornography. As early as 1974, the United Nations Commission on Human Rights established a working group on slavery that examined child prostitution, pornography, and trafficking. The working group promoted the development of a Programme of Action for the Prevention of the Sale of Children, Child Prostitution and Child Pornography, which was published in 1992. Following this, UNICEF sponsored three world conferences on child sexual exploitation in 1996 (Stockholm), 2001 (Yokohama), and 2008 (Rio de Janeiro). A Global Declaration and Agenda for Action was formally adopted by 122 governments after the Stockholm meeting. Since this time, the UK Office of the Children's Commissioner and the Women's Human Rights Commission of Korea (WHRCK) have been notably active among government agencies in research and policymaking on child prostitution. The UK Commissioner launched a policy framework for addressing child "commercial sexual exploitation" (CSE) in 2013, and for the last decade the WHRCK has administered shelters and support agencies assisting girls to escape the sex industry. In the United States, the issue of "domestic minor sex trafficking" (DMST) attracts increasing activist and research attention, and has generated a raft of policy and criminal justice initiatives in recent years (Williamson and Prior 2009; Kotrla 2010; Hakes 2011; Zabresky 2013). Internationally, the non-governmental End Child Prostitution, Child Pornography, and Trafficking of Children for Sexual Purposes (ECPAT) is active in research and advocacy on the issue.

Prostituting and pimping children is now criminalized in many countries, but age-of-consent laws, weak governance, beliefs about sexually transmitted diseases, bureaucratic corruption, commercial activity by organized crime, and euphemistic ideas like "compensated dating" and "survival sex" militate against legal implementation and enforcement. Child victims of prostitution also attract a significant degree of victim-blaming, and are sometimes themselves criminalized, including in the United States still today. Research on child prostitution mirrors this situation, and spans a continuum defined by the extent to which authors engage in "culpability attribution" (Menaker and Franklin 2013) in relation to victims.

Research attributing culpability for prostitution to child victims is theoretically animated by concepts like "agency" and "empowerment." When conceptualized weakly, these terms refer to children engaging in "survival sex." This view is articulated in terms of prostitution not necessarily extinguishing a child's "autonomy and agency"; rather, children, "just like adults," "trade sex as part of a survival strategy," and so are "social agents making choices between the bleak alternatives on offer to them" (O'Connell Davidson 2005). When conceptualized strongly, terms like "agency" refer to the proposition that prostituted children achieve financial and social status enhancement, and some commentators therefore advocate legalizing child prostitution on the basis that its criminalization obstructs children in "migrating" for "sex work." Nick Mai (2011) explains that "many migrant male minors and young adults are exerting a sense of agency and can empower themselves by selling sex."

Empirical research presents a challenge to the suggestion that prostitution empowers children. Health sequelae like "broken bones, bruises, reproductive complications, hepatitis, and STIs [sexually transmitted infections] … [and] psychological hardships including depression, PTSD [post-traumatic stress disorder], suicidal thoughts, self-mutilation, and strong feelings of guilt and shame" (Heilemann and Santhiveeran 2011) are the overwhelming observations of the literature. Family involvement in pimping (e.g., by sexually abusive male relatives) is identified as a factor exacerbating the harms of prostitution for children (Roe-Sepowitz n.d.), because of emotional and developmental dependency (Raphael 2004), and because of intensified circumstances of exploitation due to victims being unable to escape households (Gorkoff and Runner 2003). Similar exacerbations of harm occur when children are groomed to enter prostitution by individuals posing as boyfriends whom they trust; this phenomenon has been examined in depth for girls in the United States (Boxill and Richardson 2007) and Aboriginal girls in the United States and Canada (Sethi 2007; Mehrabadi et al. 2008; Farley et al. 2011; Greer 2013).

Factors making children vulnerable to prostitution include, broadly, a socially "low status and role" (Larsen 2011) as well as, individually, "lower educational attainment, drug and alcohol abuse, runaway behavior, having sex trade-involved friends, and involvement with child protection agencies" (Kidd, Liborio, and Coimbra Liborio 2011).

Among these factors, intra-familial sexual abuse (Clarke et al. 2012) and homelessness (Towe et al. 2009) are seen as two major background factors in the pimping and buying of children. Intra-familial sexual abuse is correlated with child prostitution in two ways. The first is pimping by sexual abusers (Raphael 2004), and the second is abuse victims fleeing households and becoming homeless and/or vulnerable to emotional predation by extra-familial parties (Wilson and Widom 2010; Holger-Ambrose et al. 2013). Homelessness is described as a precursor context to child prostitution in a wide range of ways, including vulnerability to blackmail in the form of shelter offered in return for prostitution, involvement in street gangs operating using funds from prostitution, exposure to drug trading, and peer grooming.

Poverty is a widely cited precursor of child prostitution, but researchers explain the nature of the correlation in different ways. For example, prostituted children "are often responsible for providing financial support (income remittances) to their families" (Willis and Levy 2002). Particularly in Asian countries, brokers entice poor families to take out loans against the trafficking of their daughters into urban sex industries (Truong 1990). Alternatively, in Laos, there is "stronger pressure on daughters than on sons to provide material support and care for their family," and so "[b]eing a prostitute secures the material support … whereas having a boyfriend might [not]" (Molland 2011). For African countries it is noted that girls moving to urban areas to escape child marriage or family violence are either unable to gain mainstream employment or there is a "failure of some employers to pay for work" (Gebre 2012). For children in rich countries the correlation is often described in terms of manipulation by business owners who transition indigent girls from "soft" exploitative entertainment activities into prostitution as well as pornography production (Wright Clayton, Krugman, and Simon 2013).

Much child prostitution research identifies poverty as a variable positively correlated with the problem while not explaining the nature of the correlation. A typical example is Simkhada's (2008) observation that "[m]any girls who become involved in sex work in Nepal do so because they are compelled by economic circumstances." Much of the literature takes as axiomatic the proposition that child prostitution exists because children need money, but Sara Dillon in 2008 critiqued confusion of socioeconomic risk factors making children vulnerable to predation by pimps and prostitution buyers and causal correlation. Dillon nominates male demand for the sexual exploitation of children as the solely correlating variable. Put simply, without sexual demand for children, child prostitution would not exist, regardless of economic need. Dillon urges clarified understanding of this correlation and a new direction for research.

Only limited comment has been made on the issue of male sexual demand for children, and why this demand appears to be growing (Raymond 2013). Sheila Jeffreys (2000) finds its cause in the "overall increase in the international sex industry," and argues that the phenomenon of men's prostitution of girls derives from widespread social acceptance of the prostitution of women. The fact that the average age of female entry into prostitution is found globally to fall below 18 years suggests prostitution is fundamentally a trade in girls. Melissa Farley (2007) suggests pimps and customers prefer underage victims for their vulnerability and malleability. Jonathan Todres (1999) adds that child prostitution has grown with the failure to prosecute US overseas sex tour operators, and Wells, Mitchell, and Ji (2012) suggest cyber technologies are furthering rates of child prostitution in the United States, and at younger ages.

A growing body of writing by adult survivors of child prostitution is likely to lead researchers to more seriously examine male sexuality in relation to the sexual exploitation of children. One survivor wrote in 2013 that, at age 15, she "always told the men who used me how old I was, because I found it had the effect of causing them to become very aroused, therefore getting them off quicker, therefore getting me out of there quicker" (Moran 2013). Why men are sexually aroused by children and are seeking them out for prostitution at escalating rates is a question only beginning to be addressed by researchers. The US-based Schapiro Group is at the forefront of quantitative inquiry into the problem, and published a major study of prostitution buyers in 2011 that found nearly half of the male research sample were willing to pay for sex with a young female even when they knew for sure she was an adolescent (Schapiro Group 2011).

SEE ALSO: Sex Tourism; Sex Trafficking

REFERENCES

Berelowitz, S., et al. 2013. *"If Only Someone Had Listened": The Office of the Children's Commissioner's Inquiry into Child Sexual Exploitation in Gangs and Groups Final Report*. London: Office of the Children's Commissioner.

Boxill, Nancy A., and Deborah J. Richardson. 2007. "Ending Sex Trafficking of Children in Atlanta." *Affilia: Journal of Women and Social Work*, 22(2): 138–149. DOI: 10.1177/0886109907299054.

Clarke, R. J., et al. 2012. "Age at Entry into Prostitution: Relationship to Drug Use, Race, Suicide, Education Level, Childhood Abuse, and Family Experiences." *Journal of Human Behavior in the Social Environment*, 22(3): 270–289.

Dillon, Sara. 2008. "What Human Rights Law Obscures: Global Sex Trafficking and the Demand for Children." *UCLA Women's Law Journal*, 17(1): 121–186.

Farley, Melissa. 2007. *Prostitution and Trafficking in Nevada: Making the Connections*. San Francisco: Prostitution Resource & Education.

Farley, Melissa, Sarah Deer, Guadalupe Lopez, Christine Stark, and Eileen Hudon. 2011. *Garden of Truth: The Prostitution and Trafficking of Native Women in Minnesota*. Minnesota Indian Women's Sexual Assault Coalition and Prostitution Research & Education. At http://www.cwis.org/fwj/61/prostitution_of_indigenous_women.htm.

Fredlund, Cecilia, Frida Svensson, Carl Göran Svedin, Gisela Priebe, and Marie Wadsby. 2013. "Adolescents' Lifetime Experience of Selling Sex: Development Over Five Years." *Journal of Child Sexual Abuse*, 22(3): 312–325. DOI: 10.1080/10538712.2013.743950.

Gebre, Ayalew. 2012. "Migration Patterns of Children Exposed to Sexual Exploitation in Selected Zones of Ethiopia." *Journal of Children's Services*, 7(4): 262–274. DOI: 10.1108/17466661211286481.

Gorkoff, Kelly, and Jane Runner. 2003. *Being Heard: The Experiences of Young Women in Prostitution*. Black Point, NS and Winnipeg: Fernwood Publishing and RESOLVE (Research and Education for Solutions to Violence and Abuse).

Greer, Benjamin Thomas. 2013. "Hiding Behind Tribal Sovereignty: Rooting Out Human Trafficking in Indian Country." *Journal of Gender, Race and Justice*, 16(2): 453–482.

Hakes, F. 2011. "Domestic Minor Sex Trafficking." *Trends in Organized Crime*, 14(2/3): 265–266.

Heilemann, Tammy, and Janaki Santhiveeran. 2011. "How Do Female Adolescents Cope and Survive the Hardships of Prostitution? A Content Analysis of Existing Literature." *Journal of Ethnic and Cultural Diversity in Social Work*, 20(1): 57–76. DOI: 10.1080/15313204.2011.545945.

Holger-Ambrose, Beth, et al. 2013. "The Illusions and Juxtapositions of Commercial Sexual Exploitation among Youth: Identifying Effective Street-Outreach Strategies." *Journal of Child Sexual Abuse*, 22(3): 326–340. DOI: 10.1080/10538712.2013.737443.

Jeffreys, Sheila. 2000. "Challenging the Child/Adult Distinction in Theory and Practice on Prostitution." *International Feminist Journal of Politics*, 2(3): 359–379. DOI: 10.1080/14616740050201940.

Kidd, S., R. Liborio, and S. Coimbra Liborio. 2011. "Sex Trade Involvement in São Paulo, Brazil and Toronto, Canada: Narratives of Social Exclusion and Fragmented Identities." *Youth & Society*, 43(3): 982–1009.

Kotrla, Kimberly. 2010. "Domestic Minor Sex Trafficking in the United States." *Social Work*, 55(2): 181–187.

Larsen, Joudo J. 2011. "The Trafficking of Children in the Asia-Pacific." *Trends and Issues in Crime and Criminal Justice*, 415: 1–6.

Mai, Nick. 2011. "Tampering with the Sex of 'Angels': Migrant Male Minors and Young Adults Selling Sex in the EU." *Journal of Ethnic and Migration Studies*, 37(8): 1237–1252. DOI: 10.1080/1369183X.2011.590927.

McGreal, Chris. 2010. "Craigslist is Hub for Child Prostitution, Allege Trafficked Women." *Guardian*, August 8. At http://www.theguardian.com/technology/2010/aug/08/craigslist-underage-prostitution-allegations.

Mehrabadi, A., et al. 2008. "The Cedar Project: A Comparison of HIV-Related Vulnerabilities amongst Young Aboriginal Women Surviving Drug Use and Sex Work in Two Canadian Cities." *International Journal of Drug Policy*, 19(2): 159–168.

Menaker, Tatyana, and Cortney Franklin. 2013. "Commercially Sexually Exploited Girls and Participant Perceptions of Blameworthiness: Examining the Effects of Victimization History and Race Disclosure." *Journal of Interpersonal Violence*, 28(10): 2024–2051. DOI: 10.1177/0886260512471078.

Molland, S. 2011. "The Trafficking of Scarce Elite Commodities: Social Change and Commodification of Virginity along the Mekong." *Asia Pacific Journal of Anthropology*, 12(2): 129–145.

Moran, Rachel. 2013. *Paid For: My Journey Through Prostitution*. North Melbourne: Spinifex Press.

Moschetti, Carole. 2005. *Conjugal Wrongs Don't Make Rights: International Feminist Activism, Child Marriage and Sexual Relativism*. Unpublished PhD thesis, University of Melbourne.

O'Connell Davidson, Julia. 2005. *Children in the Global Sex Trade*. Cambridge: Polity.

Raphael, Jody. 2004. *Listening to Olivia: Violence, Poverty and Prostitution*. Lebanon, NH: Northeastern University Press.

Raymond, Janice. 2013. *Not a Choice, Not a Job: Exposing the Myths about Prostitution and the Global Sex Trade*. North Melbourne: Spinifex Press.

Roe-Sepowitz, D. n.d. "Juvenile Entry into Prostitution." *Violence Against Women*, 18(5): 562–579.

Schapiro Group. 2011. *Men Who Buy Sex with Adolescent Girls: A Scientific Research Study*. Atlanta: Schapiro Group.

Sethi, Anupriya. 2007. "Domestic Sex Trafficking of Aboriginal Girls in Canada: Issues and Implications." *First Peoples Child and Family Review*, 3(3): 57–71.

Simkhada, Padam. 2008. "Life Histories and Survival Strategies Amongst Sexually Trafficked Girls in Nepal." *Children and Society*, 22(3): 235–248. DOI: 10.1111/j.1099-0860.2008.00154.x.

Todres, Jonathan. 1999. "Prosecuting Sex Tour Operators in US Courts in an Effort to Reduce the Sexual Exploitation of Children Globally." *Boston University Public Interest Law Journal*, 9: 1–23. At http://www.128.197.26.4/law/central/jd/organizations/journals/pilj/vol9no1/documents/9-1TodresArticle.pdf.

Towe, V., S. Ul Hasan, S. Zafar, and S. Sherman. 2009. "Street Life and Drug Risk Behaviors Associated with Exchanging Sex Among Male Street Children in Lahore, Pakistan." *Journal of Adolescent Health*, 44(3): 222–228.

Truong, Than. 1990. *Sex, Money and Morality: Prostitution and Tourism in Southeast Asia*. London: Zed Books.

Wells, M., K. Mitchell, and K. Ji. 2012. "Exploring the Role of the Internet in Juvenile Prostitution Cases Coming to the Attention of Law Enforcement." *Journal of Child Sexual Abuse*, 21(3): 327–342.

Williamson, C., and M. Prior. 2009. "Domestic Minor Sex Trafficking: A Network of Underground Players in the Midwest." *Journal of Child and Adolescent Trauma*, 2(1): 46–61. DOI: 10.1080/19361520802702191.

Willis, Brian, and Barry S. Levy. 2002. "Child Prostitution: Global Health Burden, Research Needs, and Interventions." *Lancet*, 359: 1417–1422.

Wilson, Helen W., and Cathy Spatz Widom. 2010. "The Role of Youth Problem Behaviors in the Path from Child Abuse and Neglect to Prostitution: A Prospective Examination." *Journal of Research on Adolescence*, 20(1): 210–236.

Wright Clayton, Ellen, Richard D. Krugman, and Patti Simon, eds. 2013. *Confronting Commercial Sexual Exploitation and Sex Trafficking of Minors in the United States*. Washington, DC: National Academies Press.

Zabresky, J. 2013. "Creating a Safe Harbor for Florida's Children: An Overview of Florida's Legislative Evolution in Domestic Minor Sex Trafficking." *Florida State University Law Review*, 40(2): 415–440.

Child Sex Offenders

DOYLE K. PRUITT
Keuka College, USA

CATHERINE N. DULMUS
University at Buffalo, USA

A juvenile sex offender is an individual under 18 years of age who engages in harmful or inappropriate sexual act(s). This may be contact (e.g., kissing, fondling, penetration) or non-contact (e.g., exposure to pornography, voyeurism) behavior. To be considered a sexual offense, the behavior must fall outside of established social and developmental norms, employ the use of coercion, threats, bribes, tricks, intimidation, or force, be void of consent, and/or cause physical or emotional harm to self or other. The behavior may be planned or opportunistic. Victims are often known to, and have an ongoing relationship with, the youthful offender (e.g., sibling, neighbor).

Of reported sexual assaults in the United States, 20 percent are attributed to youthful offenders. The majority are Caucasian, male, and between the ages of 15 and 17 years. The arrest rate of juveniles for sexual offenses peaked in 1991 and steadily declined by 63 percent over the following 10 years. This trend continues to this date. While less is known about juvenile sex offenders (JSO) in countries other than the United States, research findings point to similarities in demographic and offense characteristics.

The term sexual offender is inclusive of adults and juveniles. However, these two populations differ drastically not only from each other but also within the two groups. Juveniles who commit a sexual offense are demarcated into two primary categories, largely defined by age at offense. These are JSO and children with sexual behavior problems (CSBP).

Juvenile sex offenders are individuals 12 to 18 years old, but can extend up to 20 years in cases where a development delay is present. JSO sexual behavior may be sexually motivated or non-sexually motivated, for example, as a means to gain power and control or from a distorted understanding of healthy sexual relationships. Youths in this category who receive specialized treatment have sexual recidivism rates between 5 and 30 percent and non-sexual recidivism rates between 13 and 65 percent.

Children with sexual behavior problems are under 12 years old and engage in behaviors that involve sexual body parts (e.g., genitals, buttocks, breasts, anus) that are well outside developmental norms and societal limits. The behaviors may be initiated out of curiosity, to self-soothe or seek attention, or in imitation of behaviors observed or experienced as opposed to sexual gratification. Recidivism of sexual behaviors for this group when treatment is received ranges between 2 and 3 percent.

Over time individual, structural, and relational characteristics common to JSOs and CSBPs have been identified. It is important to note that not all youths possess each trait nor experience(d) all circumstances. The multitude combination of characteristics contributes to the complexity and heterogeneity of the population.

Individual characteristics common to child sex offenders include elevated rates of psychiatric diagnoses, a diagnosed learning disability, poor academic functioning, deficits in social competency, impaired conflict resolution skills, homo-negativity and gender stereotyping beliefs, hostile masculinity, social isolation, experience of being bullied, inadequate coping skills, affect dysregulation, impulsivity, and substance use (as compared with the general population). In addition, many of these youths have been exposed to severe domestic violence or been a victim of abuse or neglect.

Structural characteristics indicate that the majority of these youths are Caucasian and male. Most originate from families of middle to lower socioeconomic status. The family system tends to be mostly headed by a single parent (mother).

The relational characteristics pervasive to this population include family relationships that transgress healthy boundaries (enmeshed or disengaged), are rigid, involve frequent disruptions, and are inconsistent and difficult to navigate. Parents of JSOs tend to have elevated rates of psychiatric diagnoses, alcohol or illicit substance use, and involvement with the legal system. Perhaps because of this, parents tend to have insecure housing, struggle to maintain employment, and tend to be socially isolated. These stressors may contribute to the impaired parenting skills, negative and critical communication styles, and ultimately limited engagement with the child.

The traditional theoretical paradigm historically used to explain sexual offending is social learning theory. However, attachment theory has received increasing attention from researchers and practitioners in the field. Both theories are limited in their explanation of gender disparity among JSOs. When constructs of feminist perspectives, including gender norms, hostile sexism, rape myths, and hypermasculinity are considered, the discrepancy is better accounted for. Models developed to explain sexual offending have long been in existence with adults. These include Finkelhor's four factor model; the Marshall and Barbaree model; the Hall and Hirschman quadripartite model; and Ward and Seigert pathway model. More recently, Lane's sexual abuse cycle and the Rasmussen, Burton, and Christopherson trauma outcome process model seek to explain juvenile sexual offending as part of a cyclical process. Other typologies are based on the age of offender (adolescent or pre-adolescent) and victim or offense characteristics.

Regardless of theoretical framework, treatment of JSOs begins with a comprehensive assessment to determine level of risk for reoffending, factors contributing to the behavior, extent and severity of sexual offenses, support systems, and static and dynamic factors. There are three approaches to assessing risk: unstructured clinical judgment, empirically guided, and actuarial.

Actuarial tools are empirically validated measures designed to assess risk level. While several of these instruments currently exist for adult sex offenders, only the Juvenile Sexual Offense Recidivism Risk Assessment Tool-II (JSORRATII) is applicable to juveniles. Empirically guided approaches to assessment utilized structured checklists that inform a practitioner's determination of presumed risk. For juveniles, the most common instruments are the Juvenile Sex Offender Assessment Protocol-II (J-SOAP-II) and the Estimate of Risk of Adolescent Sexual Offense Recidivism (ERASOR). Unstructured clinical judgment is subjective and thus inconsistent and the least desirable approach.

The primary focus of any intervention implemented with this population has a preeminent focus on preventing future harm and delinquency. The means by which this is accomplished depends on the theoretical framework and treatment approach applied. Individual, family, and group treatments are ubiquitous modalities, as are a combination of psychoeducation and psychotherapy.

Historically, cognitive behavioral approaches, derived from treatments used with adult sex offenders, were implemented. Relapse prevention, cycles of abuse, and changing behaviors by aggressively confronting "denying" youths were employed. While cycles and other components common to adult sex offender treatment are no longer included in JSO treatment, the goal of ameliorating existing behavior patterns through the utilization of skills training, behavior modification, and relapse prevention strategies continues. Hence, cognitive behavioral therapy remains the most common form of treatment.

Psychoeducation is meant to promote the development of knowledge and behaviors in areas such as healthy relationships, social skills, and affect regulation (particularly anger management). Psychoeducation is a behaviorally based approach most often facilitated in a group format.

A holistic approach that explores precipitating factors contributing to the development of sexually harmful behavior and integrates family into the care of the youth has been increasingly used with JSOs. Examples include multi-systemic family therapy and psychotherapeutic interventions guided by attachment and social ecological theories. The underlying premise is a belief that by changing behaviors and addressing precipitating factors contributing to the development of sexually inappropriate behaviors, the probability that the sexually harmful behaviors would continue or resurface at future developmental stages and/or during stressful life events would dramatically decrease.

As a result of the exposure to pernicious systems and relationships, JSOs often develop distorted thought processes known as cognitive distortions. Coupled with defense mechanisms such as denial, minimization, and rationalization, cognitive distortions serve to protect the JSO from taking responsibility for the personal and external impact of their behavior. Empathy deficits and nescience of boundary violations further exacerbate behaviors and serve as key targets of any intervention.

SEE ALSO: Adolescent Pregnancy; Child Sexual Abuse and Trauma; Rape and Re-Victimization, Treatment of; Sexual Scripts; Sexual Subjectivity; Socialization and Sexuality

FURTHER READING

Association for the Treatment of Sexual Abusers. 2006. *Report of the Task Force on Children with Sexual Behavior Problems*, 1–34. Beaverton: ATSA.Center for Sex Offender Management. n.d. Accessed July 18, 2015 at www.csom.org.

Epperson, Douglas L., Christopher A. Ralston, David Fower, and John DeWitt. 2006. Juvenile Sexual Offense Recidivism Risk Assessment Tool-II (JSORRAT-II). Accessed July 18, 2015, at http://www.watsa.org/Resources/Documents/2.Epperson%20JSORRAT-II%20Scoring%20Guide.pdf.

O'Reilly, Gary, William L. Marshall, Alan Carr, and Richard C. Beckett. 2004. *The Handbook of Clinical Intervention with Young People who Sexually Abuse*. New York: Brunner-Routledge.

Prentky, Robert, and Sue Righthand. 2003. *Juvenile Sex Offender Assessment Protocol-II (J-SOAP-II) Manual*. Washington, DC: Department of Justice.

Puzzanchera, Charles. 2013. *Juvenile Offenders and Victims: National Report Series Bulletin*. Washington, DC: OJJDP.

Robertielloe, Gina, and Karen J. Terry. 2007. "Can We Profile Sex Offenders? A Review of Sex Offender Typologies." *Aggression and Violent Behavior*, 12: 508–518.

US Department of Justice. 2013. *Juvenile Arrests 2011. Juvenile Offenders and Victims: National Report Series*, December, 1–12. Washington, DC: OJJDP.

Worling, James R., and Tracey Curwen. 2001. *The Estimate of Risk of Adolescent Sexual Offense Recidivism Version 2.0: SAFE-T Program*. Toronto: SAFE-T Program.

Child Sexual Abuse and Trauma

SAM WARNER
Salford University, UK

Child sexual abuse affects a great many people around the world. The World Health Organization (2006) estimates that about 20 percent of women and 5–10 percent of men report being sexually abused as children, and every year about 150 million girls and 73 million boys under 18 years of age are raped or sexually assaulted. Exact figures are difficult to determine because child sexual abuse remains a taboo subject and many sex crimes go unreported, unheard, and unprosecuted. Additionally, prevalence figures are shaped by the breadth of the definition used. In general terms, child sexual abuse can be defined as any sexual activity involving a child that he or she does not understand, is not developmentally ready for, is unable to give informed consent to, and/or violates the laws and social mores of society. Sexual abuse may be perpetrated by adults and children who are, because of their age or developmental stage, in a position of power, trust, or responsibility over the victim. Sexual abuse may involve direct contact and/or indirect contact (via the Internet, for example). Most children who are victims of sexual violence are assaulted by someone they know and many are repeatedly assaulted. Most child sexual abusers are male (the proportion may be as high as 95 percent). As such, child sexual abuse is a highly gendered crime in which men predominate as offenders and, to a less extreme degree, girls predominate as victims. No genetic basis for sexual offending has been found. It is more relevant to consider how men and women are socialized into unequal relationships with sex and power. Assumptions about masculinized sexual aggression and feminized passivity and availability can be found not only in pornography, but also in science books, fairy tales, and popular culture, as well as in laws, edicts, and social institutions that preserve male privilege and male power over women and children. Men, in particular, are therefore invited to sexualize power and individual abusers can then draw on these widely available narratives to justify their actions to themselves and to silence and control the children they abuse.

Child sexual abuse therefore has a negative impact worldwide because it reinforces division, hierarchy, and inequality, and undermines the ability of individual victims to reach their full social and economic potential. This is because child sexual abuse can be deeply traumatic and can lead to immediate and long-term physical health problems and life-long mental health and social difficulties. The physical body has a great capacity for recovery, which means that in most cases there is no conclusive physical evidence of sexual abuse, although sometimes abuse does give rise to negative physical effects. These include genital and anal damage, sexually transmitted infections, pelvic inflammatory disease, gynecological problems, and other medically unexplained conditions. Physical ill-health can also result from unwanted pregnancies and repeated terminations, continually disrupted sleep, leaving abusive homes to live on the streets, declining or avoiding preventive health checks, self-injury, food problems, and misusing alcohol and drugs (Nelson and Hampson 2008).

Emotional trauma often persists longer than the physical effects of abuse. This is because sexual abuse is accompanied by psychosocial mechanisms of control that act to silence children and to dissuade potential protectors from asking questions and recognizing harm. As noted, this is a highly gendered activity that feminizes all victims.

Victims are thus groomed to "accommodate" (Summit 1983) the abuse through a process of coercive control that leaves victims feeling scared, threatened, powerless, ashamed, and sometimes confused by conflicting feelings of love. Dissociation plays a major role in enabling survivors to avoid focusing on the physical and emotional terror they endure. Dissociative coping strategies can generalize over time; in extreme cases, where abuse has been severe, enduring, and ubiquitous, this can lead to different aspects of the child and the child's memories being reconstructed as separate voices, visions, or different identities or parts within the same abused person. Dissociative coping strategies, coupled with active attempts not to notice, or think and talk about abuse, can result in patchy and fragmented memories of abuse thereafter. It is rare for children to be completely successful in repressing all traumatic memories. This is why the idea that completely lost memories of abuse can be recovered in therapy was challenged by Loftus (1993). This challenge led to the "memory wars" of the 1990s, which pitted feminist believers against sexual abuse deniers who argued that because some therapists implant *false* memories of child abuse in their (mainly female) clients' heads, all *recovered* memories of child sexual abuse are untrue. This is clearly not the case.

Commonly, abuse survivors are plagued by their traumatic memories and this can result in post-traumatic stress effects. These include intrusive and reoccurring thoughts and flashbacks, night terrors, reduced concentration, high anxiety, phobias and panic attacks, hyperarousal and avoidance of trauma triggers, hypervigilance, and reduced trust in others. These effects can leave victims feeling ashamed, depressed, angry, hopeless, and suicidal or, conversely, emotionally numb. Additionally, traumatic sexualization, experienced at any age, impacts on sexual desire and behavior. After about 7 years of age, identity feels more constant and stable (this relates to Kohlberg's reading of Piaget's developmental work on constancy; Kohlberg 1966). Early sexual abuse can therefore feel very much part of identity development. Talk about child sexual abuse can also be used to invalidate survivors' positive sexual choices and, in homophobic societies, boys in particular can feel particularly silenced in respect of talking about their abuse by men. At the same time, girls may be unable to articulate their abuse in societies and religious groups where female virginity is highly prized. Girls and boys therefore have sometimes shared, and sometimes contrasting, pressures and difficulties associated with disclosing child sexual abuse.

Because abuse victims have limited control over the external world, people frequently manage their unwanted feelings through harming their own bodies via self-injury. This is particularly the case for female victims who are primed in patriarchal societies (in which women and girls already have limited power) to turn their hurt inwards and self-harm. Conversely, male victims may be primed to turn their hurt outwards and hurt others. Both male and female victims therefore must resist and refuse gendered expectations that position girls as forever victims and boys as the next generation of offenders, otherwise these primary identifications (as victim or abuser) add another layer of social difficulty and psychological distress. Other forms of self-harm engaged in by survivors include abusing street or prescription drugs, alcohol, or food, or engaging in risky sexual behaviors. Sometimes abuse survivors avoid intimate relationships altogether.

Victims are increasingly treated with compassion, yet many societies deny or minimize the extent of abuse. In the West, second-wave feminists in the 1970s and 1980s can be credited with forcing child sexual abuse back onto the political agenda. They argued that, because most sex crime is perpetrated by men, there is a need to advocate for gender equality and a refusal of patriarchal power that otherwise, as noted, provides tacit permission for the control and exploitation of women and children. This rights-based approach has impacted the UN's policies against violence against women and children. It is enshrined in Human Rights legislation and is instrumental in current attempts to safeguard the interests of particularly vulnerable victims, such as those sexually abused and exploited in conflict situations, in and by gangs, and through prostitution. It also protects socially disenfranchised victims, such as those from ethnic minorities, street children, children from traveler communities, and children with disabilities.

There is increasing recognition that if *all* victims of sexual abuse are to be helped, then it is crucial to have strategic oversight and to operationalize care pathways in terms of both investigation and support at international, national, and local levels in the form of treaties, laws, policies, and frameworks for service delivery. There is increasing commitment to gender mainstreaming. That is, public bodies (including statutory services, private companies, non-governmental organizations, charities, and third sector providers) accept that it is crucial to address gender inequality if victims are to be fully supported. Inclusive services, therefore, must identify and address the gender-specific needs of sexual violence victims if they are to serve the whole community. Various countries around the world now provide integrated sexual assault referral services for children and adults. Such services are sometimes informed by a gender-mainstreaming perspective. They usually include an independent sexual violence advisor, who acts as an advocate and independent supporter who is available when a victim first discloses and helps that victim to navigate the criminal justice system and access appropriate and timely support (Department of Health 2009). Support may include psychopharmacology, which is used to manage unwanted "symptoms" of sexual abuse (e.g., depression, anxiety, psychosis). However, if clients are to be moved from victimhood, through survival and symptom management, and into recovery, it is generally accepted that talking therapies are more effective. Specifically, different forms of trauma-focused therapy are advocated. Unhelpful messages associated with past abuse are carefully challenged and revised, current stresses and worries are addressed, and clients are enabled to develop less harmful coping strategies.

Currently, there is interest in the use of "mindfulness" to manage negative thoughts and feelings associated with sexual abuse. Critics argue, however, that "acceptance" of negative thoughts and feelings undermines appropriate anger and leads to the dissipation of political will. There is also an emphasis on identifying those factors that increase or reduce victims' resilience to withstand childhood sexual abuse, and avoid further abuse and exploitation. Specifically, attachment theory is understood to provide relevant insights into how the general context of care is predictive of personal vulnerability and recovery. Future research should be directed towards illuminating these key issues and concerns.

SEE ALSO: Feminisms, First, Second, and Third Wave; Sexual Coercion

REFERENCES

Department of Health. 2009. *Revised National Service Guide: a Resource for Developing Sexual Assault Referral Centres*. London: Department of Health.

Kohlberg, Lawrence. (1966) "A Cognitive-Developmental Analysis of Children's Sex-Role Concepts and Attitudes." In *The Development of Sex Differences*, edited by Eleanor E. Maccoby, 82–173. Stanford: Stanford University Press.

Loftus, Elizabeth F. 1993. "The Reality of Repressed Memories." *American Psychologist*, 48: 518–537.

Nelson, Sarah, and Sue Hampson. 2008. *Working with Survivors of Childhood Sexual Abuse*, 2nd ed. Edinburgh: The Scottish Government.

Summit, Roland C. 1983. "The Child Sexual Abuse Accommodation Syndrome." *Child Abuse and Neglect*, 7: 177–193.

World Health Organization. 2006. *Preventing Child Maltreatment: a Guide to Taking Action and Generating Evidence*. Geneva: World Health Organization.

Children's Literature and Gender

ANNE BUBRISKI-McKENZIE
University of Central Florida, USA

STEPHANIE GONZALEZ-GUITTAR
Valdosta State University, USA

A popular agent of socialization in children's worlds is children's literature. In particular, children's literature can influence children's gender socialization. Gender socialization occurs in every society and culture throughout the world. Gender refers to the learned behaviors that often characterize one's sex. Gender is learned through cultural and social expectations and social interaction. Social science argues that gender is heavily influenced by one's interaction with the social environment and is more defined by the social environment and socialization than mere biology. Socialization occurs through social interaction with various social institutions, social structures, and interpersonal contact. Socialization shapes one's identity and sense of self while also teaching role expectations, norms, values, and behaviors of a given culture. Socialization is so powerful that most people internalize the process without question. Thus, through gender socialization, one learns what it means to be a "girl/woman" or "boy/man." One learns the societal expectations of being a girl/woman or boy/man.

Thus, children's books representing female and male characters help shape how children perceive their own and others' genders. Even though most children's literature is fiction, children's books are often central to children's first exposure to learning social morals and norms through numerous visual illustrations and storylines. Regardless of a children's book award status, children's books promote socially acceptable norms, values, and behaviors. Within these norms, values, and behaviors are messages of appropriate gender socialization. As sociologists assert, gender is socially constructed through multiple agents of socialization such as family, media, and peers. Children's books in many instances encompass all of these primary agents of socialization. Children's books are an aspect of media, read to young children often by their parents or other family members, and within school contexts, children's books tend to be explored among groups of children who engage in meaning-making dialogue and interaction about the book. Various studies argue that gender depiction in children's books impacts the gender socialization of children.

There is an array of children's literature available today. However, some suggest that award-winning books are cultural artifacts in American society, and therefore have significant influence within American culture. The Caldecott Award is one of the best known children's book honors. Books awarded this honor inevitably become significant cultural artifacts and are the most sought after children's books in schools and libraries. Caldecott books are also guaranteed substantial sales, notable recognition, and are considered the most influential books within children's literature (Clark, Lennon, and Morris 1993; Pescosolido, Grauerholz, and Milkie 1997). Furthermore, Pescosolido, Grauerholz, and Milkie (1997) deem that those who decide which books deserve the Caldecott award are in essence cultural gatekeepers. Therefore, it is not surprising that most research on gender representations in children's literature focuses on award-winning books, such as Caldecott books.

The topic of gender representations in children's books became particularly popular after the classic study by Weitzman et al. (1972) on gender role socialization in children's literature. This seminal publication researched Caldecott award winner and runner-up books, along with Newbery Award winners and Little Golden Books. The authors found that female and male characters were often stereotypically represented and male characters far outnumbered female characters in books across all samples. When the authors focused only on Caldecott books, they found that female characters were often represented as passive and playing indoors compared with male characters that were portrayed as active and adventurous and playing outdoors. The authors concluded that these patterned messages may teach children that "boys are more highly valued than girls" (Weitzman et al. 1972, 1125).

The classic study by Weitzman et al. (1972) sparked more research interest in gender representations in children's books. However, the research has produced two differing perspectives on how gender is represented within such books. Some research suggests that gender stereotypes and gender inequality represented within children's books decrease over time. Clark et al. (2003), for instance, found that the percentage of books with female characters increased dramatically from the 1960s to the 1990s. Furthermore, this study also found that gender stereotypes of characters in children's books also decreased from the 1960s to the 1990s. Others argue that this trend reflects the political, cultural, and educational changes throughout the twentieth century. As women gained more access and rights to education, labor force participation, and the political arena, there was also a cultural shift of greater value on women's rights and women's roles within the public sphere.

However, other researchers found that gender representations within children's books do not necessarily follow a linear path of more equality over time. Instead, some research suggests that gender representations within children's books may reflect the political climate of the era. Therefore, gender equality and gender stereotypes within children's books fluctuate depending on the political and social forces of the time. In fact, Grauerholz and Pescosolido (1989) found that the earlier and later decades of the twentieth century showed the most gender equality within main characters. However, when books featured only animals or adults, the proportion of male characters increased over time. Clark et al. (2003) also found fluctuations within gender representations in award-winning books. This study suggests that during the 1930s and 1950s there were more female characters represented within books compared with the 1940s and 1960s. However, according to this study, although female characters may have been more prevalent, they were also depicted in more stereotypical roles during the 1930s and 1950s compared with the 1940s and 1960s. It was concluded that this pattern of gender representations is "more likely to reflect local, temporal variations in gender norms than to express a long-term trend toward increasing the increasing visibility of female characters and decreasing gender stereotyping" (Clark et al. 2003, 446).

Hamilton et al. (2006) reported a study that updates these previous studies on gender images within children's literature. Similarly to the previous studies, Hamilton et al. (2006) analyzed Caldecott award winners. However, only 30 of the 200 books analyzed were Caldecott award winners and honor books; the remaining books included best-sellers from 1999 to 2001 by *The New York Times*, Amazon.com, and *Publishers Weekly*. The study's findings indicated that there were significantly more male title and main characters compared with females. Also, female characters tended to be portrayed in nurturing representations even more exclusively than in the 1980s and 1990s. Furthermore, gender stereotyping was also seen within the characters' occupations and female characters were more likely than male characters to have non-paid occupations. Hamilton et al. also suggested that subtle sexism is more likely to be found in newer books than overt sexism seen in older books. The study discusses a number of examples, such as a female character looking down at the ground while the male character is looking down on her as he escorts her to church. Thus, the authors conclude that "modern children's picture books continue to provide nightly reinforcement of the idea that boys and men are more interesting and important than are girls and women" (Hamilton et al. 2006, 764).

The large majority of research on gender representations within children's books specifically focuses on gender. However, focusing only on gender ignores the importance of how gender is also racialized. Clark, Lennon, and Morris (1993) carried out one of the very few studies that looks at the intersection of gender and race within children's books. Their comparison study of gender in a racial context within Caldecott and Coretta Scott King award and honor books indicated that gender illustrations and gender themes within Caldecott and King books differ drastically in the context of race. They found that gender depictions within King award and honor books aligned with black feminist perspectives whereas gender depictions within Caldecott award and honor books aligned with liberal feminist perspectives. Liberal feminism promotes women's autonomy and gender equality within the workforce, education, politics, and other spheres of public life historically dominated by men. The primary objectives of liberal feminism include gaining equal rights for women in all aspects of society based on the belief in equal human ability across the sexes. Black feminist perspective focuses on how women of color and entire communities of color often experience overlapping, intersecting inequalities based not only on one's gender, but also on one's race and class.

Over the past 40 years, research on gender representations within children's books has grown dramatically. Much of this research has focused on high-esteem books from the United States. However, it is plausible that there are many other types of popular books that are non-award winning that are also being read at high rates. Future studies should not only continue to examine award-winning books, but also include other types of popular children's books. The study by Grauerholz and Pescosolido (1989) did include popular books beyond award-winning books. Follow-up studies may consider replicating this study's methods to see if there have been major changes since the 1980s. Another future research possibility would be to consider how illustrations in book series have been updated over time with new editions of the same book. Identifying series of books and analyzing the illustrations would be helpful in seeing gender depiction trends over time.

In addition to examining books beyond award-winning stature, researching gender images within children's books worldwide should be expanded. Although there have been few studies that look at gender images within children's books in Western European countries, there is even less research on non-Western children's books. A global comparative analysis would provide a broader perspective on gender representations across cultures and countries. Future research could compare children's books in countries with greater gender equality than the United States to establish if there are differences in the gender representations within the books.

Furthermore, there is also a limited number of studies that have examined the intersection of race/ethnicity and gender. Clark, Lennon, and Morris (1993) carried out a foundational study that should be replicated in future studies. An intersectional approach to examining gender representations in children's books would provide a more comprehensive and inclusive analysis. Pescosolido, Grauerholz, and Milkie (1997) examined racial representations within children's literature and discovered some shocking findings. Throughout popular books published in the twentieth century, black characters were rarely main characters and often only peripheral characters. Black characters were also often portrayed in stereotypical ways. Furthermore, they found very few interracial representations, in which characters of different races interacted, within children's books. In fact, when examining only Caldecott Award winner books, they discovered that it was not until the 1990s that interracial themes were illustrated. Furthermore, even in the very few instances of interracial representations, black–white interactions within children's books "show a striking absence of mutuality – intimate, egalitarian relations central to the story line – throughout the entire period (1930s–1990s) and across the series" (Pescosolido et al. 1997, 455). Hence it would be informative to update research on both the gender and racial representations in children's literature, particularly examining how female and male characters of color are represented compared with each other and also with white female and male characters.

Lastly, research focusing on children's reactions to gender representations in children's books may provide some interesting findings through the eyes and perspectives of children. It would be interesting to know how children make meaning out of the gender representations within the books they read.

SEE ALSO: Children's Literature and Sexuality; Gender Identities and Socialization; Gender Stereotypes; Media and Gender Socialization

REFERENCES

Clark, Roger, Rachel Lennon, and Leana Morris. 1993. "Of Caldecotts and Kings: Gendered Images in Recent American Children's Books by Black and Non-Black Illustrators." *Gender and Society*, 7: 227–245.
Clark, Roger, Jessica Guilmain, Paul Khalil Saucier, and Jocelyn Tavarez. 2003. "Two Steps Forward, One Step Back: The Presence of Female Characters and Gender Stereotyping in Award-Winning Picture Books Between the 1930s and the 1960s." *Sex Roles*, 49: 439–449.
Grauerholz, Elizabeth, and Bernice A. Pescosolido. 1989. "Gender Representation in Children's Literature: 1900–1984." *Gender and Society*, 3: 113–125.
Hamilton, Mykol C., David Anderson, Michele Broaddus and Kate Young. 2006. "Gender Stereotyping and Under-representation of Female Characters in 200 Popular Children's Picture Books: A Twenty-first Century Update." *Sex Roles*, 55: 757–765.
Pescosolido, Bernice A., Elizabeth Grauerholz, and Melissa A. Milkie. 1997. "Culture and Conflict: The Portrayal of Blacks in U.S. Children's Picture Books Through the Mid-and Late-Twentieth Century." *American Sociological Review*, 62: 443–404.
Weitzman, Lenore J., Deborah Eifler, Elizabeth Hokada, and Catherine Ross. 1972. "Sex-Role Socialization in Picture Books for Preschool Children." *American Journal of Sociology*, 77: 1125–1150.

Children's Literature and Sexuality

KAY A. CHICK
Penn State Altoona, USA

Children's literature is an inclusive term to include books that are written for children from infancy through adolescence. The literature consists of picture books, chapter books, and graphic novels in genres such as nonfiction, realistic fiction, historical fiction, and poetry. Children's literature has a lasting impact on young people in a variety of ways. It teaches gender norms at a time when young children are forming their gender identity. Children's literature includes representations of both traditional and nontraditional families, as well as the multitude of gender stereotypes that are present in our society. In more recent years, children's books have served as a resource for teachers, parents, and caregivers who wish to introduce young people to diversity in gender and sexuality. Thus, books are now available that present characters who are gender nonconforming, gay, lesbian, and transgender.

Literature teaches gender norms (what is expected of males and females) and gender identity (whether children perceive themselves as male, female, both, or neither). Gender bias in books can be harmful to young people (Diekman and Murnen 2004) and gender inequalities and stereotypes are present in the subject matter, character portrayals, language, and illustrations in children's literature (Chick, Slekar, and Charles 2010; Chick and Corle 2012). Sexism in literature increases biased attitudes and behaviors (Schau and Scott 1984), enhances boys' feelings of entitlement and lowers girls' occupational ambitions and self-worth (Tognoli, Pullen, and Lieber 1994). The full impact of sexism may be more pronounced for children than for adults, as young children, especially, tend to believe what they read or what is read to them.

Stereotypes and gender inequities are present in children's literature in a variety of ways. There are significantly more males than females in the text and illustrations of children's books (Chick, Slekar, and Charles 2010; Chick and Corle 2012). Both male and female characters are represented and described in stereotypical ways. Female characters are often the helpers who frighten easily and need the assistance of male characters. Male characters are frequently portrayed as strong, brave, and willing to protect and save the female characters. In books with both male and female characters, females tend to consistently hold lower status jobs than males. Gender roles are often less rigid for females, with female characters demonstrating the ability to cross traditional gender boundaries more often than males (Chick, Slekar, and Charles 2010; Chick and Corle, 2012). The number of books published with strong female characters has increased dramatically in the last decade. Books such as *Old MacDonald had a Woodshop* (Shulman 2002) and *Girl Wonder: A Baseball Story in Nine Innings* (Hopkinson 2003) present females who demonstrate characteristics traditionally associated with the male gender role. Though fewer in number, there are also books available with sensitive male characters. Stories such as *The Knight who was Afraid of the Dark* (Shook Haven 1989) and *Even Firefighters Hug their Moms* (MacLean 2002) include male protagonists who demonstrate feminine attributes. Literature that presents male and female characters who do not conform to traditional gender roles helps children to understand the concept of multiple masculinities and femininities. Characters who portray multiple masculinities and femininities allow children to consider their own gender identity and learn about those who are gender nonconforming. This affords them the opportunity to become more accepting of those with gender differences as they rethink and challenge gender stereotypes.

Since the early 1990s children's books have also included characters who are gender variant, those who present as gay or lesbian. In the early years of these publications, gay characters were the parents or other adult characters in the stories. Gay-sensitive picture books help young children to develop an understanding of the differences that exist in family structure and an acceptance for all kinds of families. The issues, problems, and biases experienced by nontraditional families are often complex and confusing, even for adults. Picture books help to define the issues and translate them into experiences and language that young children can understand and identify with. Gay-themed literature also affords children of gay parents the opportunity to validate their experiences and see themselves and their families in the books they read. Books such as *And Tango Makes Three* (Richardson and Parnell 2005) and *The Harvey Milk Story* (Krakow 2001) help children to think about gay and lesbian characters from different perspectives *and* consider the consequences of prejudice.

It has only been in recent years that *children* were portrayed as gay, lesbian, or transgender in children's books. While it is very difficult to estimate accurately, gender specialists believe that 5–6 percent of children are gay, lesbian, or bisexual, and 1 in 500 children is transgender (Gender Spectrum 2013). The school experience, unfortunately, is typically less than supportive for children who are gender variant. While schools are places where respect for diversity is fostered, especially for children with disabilities, gender diversity is rarely valued. Children often find themselves in hostile environments where bullying and teasing from peers and adults is the norm. For example, transgender children and youth report that they hear derogatory and homophobic comments from peers and teachers. Students are frequently verbally and physically harassed and report that school personnel typically do not intervene when they observe the harassment (Gay, Lesbian and Straight Education Network 2009). It is clear that different demonstrations of masculinity and femininity are not equally respected in school settings and stereotypical views on gender and sexuality are deeply ingrained. Teachers and parents must have bias-free attitudes and the skills and resources to prevent bullying and harassment and allow children to be who they are.

Books such as *The Boy Who Cried Fabulous* (Newman 2004), *My Princess Boy* (Kilodavis 2010), *10,000 Dresses* (Ewert 2008), and *When Kathy is Keith* (Wong 2011) are books that teachers and parents can use to support the experiences and feelings of children who are gay, lesbian, or transgender. These stories go beyond traditional views of masculinity and femininity, incorporate characters who are believable and who face real problems, and help children challenge stereotypes and think beyond traditional gender identities. These books also allow boys and girls who are not drawn to the socially accepted traditional masculinity and femininity of our times to have a better chance of seeing themselves in the literature they read.

Although gender variance can be supported through reading and discussing children's books with gay, lesbian, and transgender characters, these characters are both rare and controversial. Children's book authors and publishers may be hesitant to publish books that will not be widely read.

In addition, censorship has become widely accepted, in part because conservative groups voice strong opposition to gay-themed books, and parents, teachers, and librarians tend toward self-censorship. Consequently, literature with gender-variant characters will not be found in many school libraries, especially at the elementary level. As a result, during the time when children are forming their gender identity, developing views on masculinity and femininity, and acquiring gender stereotypes, literature that supports diversity in gender and sexuality may not be available to them.

SEE ALSO: Gender, Definitions of; Gender and Development; Gender Identity, Theories of; Gender Variance; Masculinity and Femininity, Theories of

REFERENCES

Chick, Kay, and Stacey Corle. 2012. "A Gender Analysis of NCSS Notable Trade Books for the Intermediate Grades." *Social Studies Research and Practice*, 7(2): 1–13.

Chick, Kay, Timothy Slekar, and Eric Charles. 2010. "A Gender Analysis of NCSS Notable Picture Book Winners: 2006–2008." *Social Studies Research and Practice*, 5(3): 21–31.

Diekman, Amanda, and Sarah Murnen. 2004. "Learning to be Little Women and Little Men: The Inequitable Gender Equality of Nonsexist Children's Literature." *Sex Roles*, 50(5/6): 373.

Ewert, Marcus. 2008. *10,000 Dresses*. New York: Seven Stories Press.

Gay, Lesbian & Straight Education Network. 2009. "Harsh Realities: The Experiences of Transgender Youth in Our Nation's Schools." Accessed January 30, 2014, at: http://www.glsen.org.

Gender Spectrum. 2013. "Schools and Gender." Accessed January 30, 2014, at: http://genderspectrum.org/education/schools-gender.

Hopkinson, Deborah. 2003. *Girl Wonder: A Baseball Story in Nine Innings*. New York: Atheneum.

Kilodavis, Cheryl. 2010. *My Princess Boy*. New York: Aladdin.

Krakow, Kari. 2001. *The Harvey Milk Story*. Ridley Park, PA: Two Lives Publishing.
MacLean, Christine. 2002. *Even Firefighters Hug Their Moms*. New York: Dutton.
Newman, Lisa. 2004. *The Boy Who Cried Fabulous*. New York: Tricycle Press.
Richardson, Justin, and Peter Parnell. 2005. *And Tango Makes Three*. New York: Simon & Schuster.
Schau, C. G., and Scott, K. P. 1984. "Review of 21 Cause and Effect Studies." *Psychological Documents*, 76: 183–193.
Schulman, Lisa. 2002. *Old MacDonald Had a Woodshop*. New York: G. P. Putnam's Sons.
Shook Hazen, Barbara. 1989. *The Knight Who Was Afraid of the Dark*. New York: Puffin.
Tognoli, Jerome, Jane Pullen, and Judith Lieber. 1994. "The Privilege of Place: Domestic and Work Locations of Characters in Children's Books." *Children's Environments*, 11: 272–280.
Wong, Wallace. 2011. *When Kathy is Keith*. Bloomington, IN: Xlibris Corporation.

Christianity, Gender and Sexuality

JAMIE M. SOMMER
Stony Brook University, New York, USA

Christianity is a religion that claims over 2 billion followers (Central Intelligence Agency 2015). Over time, Christianity has had a major impact on the way people view gender and sexuality in many societies. Many of its teachings have been interpreted in different ways over time to either justify or condemn certain acts, marital unions, and genders. Recent developments in the study of ancient texts have imposed modern interpretations of gender and sexuality on the Bible, and therefore on Christianity. Most world religions have addressed moral issues concerning gender and sexuality; however, ethics derived from Christianity have been a major influence on gendering humans and reinforcing heterosexuality. Overall, Christianity has given the female gender and sexuality a negative connotation. Christianity has also imposed strict roles on the male gender over time and to different degrees. Ideas of science and Christianity have also influenced each other.

Over time, and with recent feminist, gender, and sociological studies, the meanings of gender and sexuality have transformed. It is helpful to go back to early Christianity to see how sexuality has been represented differently in the past. In early Christianity, the act of sex was only justifiable for the procreation of children. In early Christianity, it was not emphasized in comparison to the high appraisal of virginity and celibacy, as it is today. For example, Paul of Tarsus in 1 Corinthians thought that sex should not be of interest to Christians, but that within marriage it was permissible. In the thirteenth century, the Catholic Church recognized that baptized, consenting men and women could be married as a sacrament, as in a ceremony uniting man and woman before God. This led to sex being less taboo under the circumstance of the sacrament of marriage. However, sex was still viewed as an act for procreation only.

The Bible is the main religious text of Christianity. How the Bible is interpreted changes depending on the denomination of Christianity and the time period in question. Christians have used many biblical verses to discuss gender and sexuality. The verses cover topics including male homosexuality and bisexuality, transgender, polygyny, bestiality, incest, premarital sex, marriage, adultery, remarriage, and divorce. Many of these concepts did not exist at the time the Bible was written, nor when these passages were first interpreted, but scholars have applied contemporary understandings of gender and sexuality to these ancient verses. Because of this, translations of the Bible have been geared to specific worldviews or political agendas. Therefore, what these passages have come to mean today can be different for different groups, and does not necessarily represent how Christians from the past thought about these concepts, nor what contemporary Christians think. The meanings of verses have been socially and historically interpreted; verses change in wording, and therefore in meaning, depending on which version of the Bible is used. Modern Bible interpretations have also varied with the introduction of different scholars' understandings of gender, sex, and sexuality. Many social scientists have influenced Christian thinking, leading to some liberal Bible interpretation. Some social scientists who have had a great impact on Christianity's interpretation of gender and sexuality are Sigmund Freud, Michael Foucault, and Judith Butler.

Sigmund Freud was an Austrian neurologist, better known today as the father of psychoanalysis. He was born on May 6, 1856 and died September 23, 1939. Freud was a major influence in Western thought, and his work has infiltrated Christian sexuality and gender understanding in many ways. The work of Freud established that sexuality and gender happen almost simultaneously during the repression of the phallic stage. This is the stage of the Oedipus complex, where the child is said to have desire for their parent of a different gender and hatred for the other parent. The daughter sexualizes her father, while hating the mother, but then identifies with the mother. The son identifies with the father and sexualizes the mother, but knows he cannot have her because she is the father's. The son knows he must find someone like the mother. Freud said that homosexuality occurs when there is a problem with this process. Freud's work has influenced our cultural understandings of gender, sex, and sexuality, and his rhetoric has influenced Christian understanding. Freud was the first to see children as sexual and gendered beings, which contradicted Christian rhetoric. These developments in social science have drastically changed previously held Christian beliefs. An example is that in the traditional Christian view, sexuality has been focused strictly on procreation, limiting and demonizing other forms of sexual behavior, while Freud understands children to be sexual beings.

Another influence on Christianity's view of gender and sexuality is evident in the work of Michel Foucault in his three-volume *The History of Sexuality*. Michel Foucault was born on October 15, 1926 and died on June 25, 1984. Foucault's work has been integrated in the study of Christianity in various ways. He understood sex as determined by a historical context and the history that preceded it. His definitions of sex, gender, and sexuality are still used today. Sex is the biological difference between "male" and "female." Gender is constructed socially and culturally (as in roles, qualities, and expectations ascribed). Sexuality is who one is attracted to or oriented towards. Foucault's work staunchly contrasted with traditional Christian belief insofar as Christians interpret males and females to be products of God. Christianity has also viewed the roles of male and female as God's creation, and deviation from those roles as a sin.

Judith Butler reformed ideas of gender and sexuality with a feminist perspective. She was born on February 24, 1956. Her work has also brought new perspectives to Christian understandings. In her book, *Gender Trouble: Feminism and the Subversion of Identity* and *Bodies that Matter: On the Discursive Limits of "Sex,"* Butler claims that gender is a performance and our ideas of gender do not come from some innate biological genetics, but instead are socially constructed. In her work, she has advocated for lesbian, gay, bisexual, and transgender (LGBT) individuals. Butler has further advanced knowledge that pertains to gender, sex, and sexuality which contradicts traditional Christian beliefs.

With the introduction of these scholars and others, biblical interpretations have varied from liberal to conservative. Bible verses can be used to reestablish traditional Christian views, but as much of the language used to interpret the verses today was not established when the Bible was written, interpretations are subject to modern political and ideological views. To review these topics of gender and sexuality, the New International Version (NIV) is used here, as this is the version geared to an international audience.

Male homosexuality and bisexuality as a concept has been referenced in the NIV Bible in many different places: Leviticus 18:22; Romans 1:26–27; Corinthians 6:9–10; Timothy 1:8–11; Genesis 1 and 2; Genesis 19:1–13; and Jude 6–7. However, Leviticus 20:13 (NIV) has been most commonly cited: "If a man has sexual relations with a man as one does with a woman, both of them have done what is detestable. They are to be put to death; their blood will be on their own heads." This verse is commonly cited by anti-homosexuality groups from various religious denominations.

Another verse has been said to apply to what we call today "cross-dressing," or could be used to describe an individual who identifies as transgender. The verse is Deuteronomy 21:15–17 (NIV) which states: "A woman must not wear men's clothing, nor a man wear women's clothing, for the Lord your God detests anyone who does this." This verse has been applied to today's conceptions of gender, even though gendering of clothing has also changed over time.

Polygyny, bestiality, and incest are words used to describe and interpret specific Bible verses. Polygyny has been justified by some through an interpretation of Deuteronomy 21:15–17 (NIV), which states:

If a man has two wives, and he loves one but not the other, and both bear him sons but the firstborn is the son of the wife he does not love, when he wills his property to his sons, he must not give the rights of the firstborn to the son of the wife he loves in preference to his actual firstborn, the son of the wife he does not love. He must acknowledge the son of his unloved wife as the firstborn by giving him a double share of all he has. That son is the first sign of his father's strength. The right of the firstborn belongs to him.

This excerpt describes what can be understood today as polygyny as a commonplace act, but contemporary Christians treat it as an outdated practice that holds no relevance in society any more. This highlights how some Bible verses are often quoted to justify certain views, while others are ignored and considered outdated.

Other sections of the Bible have had the potential to demonize sexual acts. For example, Exodus 22:19 (NIV) has been interpreted to discourage what can be called bestiality. "Anyone who has sexual relations with an animal is to be put to death." The Bible had been quoted in this way to dissuade people from bestiality, and has been used to inform law. Passages in Leviticus 18:23 and 18:6–17 have been cited to dissuade people from enacting what we call today incest. Leviticus 18:17 (NIV) states, "Do not have sexual relations with both a woman and her daughter. Do not have sexual relations with either her son's daughter or her daughter's daughter; they are her close relatives. That is wickedness." These excerpts reflect how incest is understood today.

Other verses, such as Deuteronomy 22:13–21, Deuteronomy 22:28–29, and Exodus 22:16–17 have been said to apply to what we call premarital sex. Most are used to dissuade people from having premarital sex, and recommend violent punishment, especially for women. Others have been used to define and describe what type of marriage is permissible. These can be found in Deuteronomy

22:30 and Exodus 21:7–11. There are also many more verses that could be referencing what we call divorce (Deuteronomy 24:1–4), remarriage (Deuteronomy 25:5–10), and adultery (Deuteronomy 22:22–27, Leviticus 18:18, and Leviticus 20). Many of these verses recommend severe punishment of women, which has further perpetuated sexual double standards and sexism.

All of these translations and interpretations of translations have had many different meanings over time. For example, Corinthians 6:9 condemns fornication. To modern English speakers, this could mean a condemnation of voluntary sexual intercourse before marriage; to early Christians, it could have meant illegal sex, like incest or bestiality. Today, this verse could be used to condemn prostitution, pornography, and homosexuality.

After reviewing these verses, it is clear that they could be used to justify specific sex, gender, and sexuality viewpoints from the past and from today. People have used these verses and their interpretations to treat people of different sexes, sexualities, and genders differently. Some types of sexuality have not been given a negative connotation. For example, Pope John Paul II (1978–2005) taught that sexual intercourse between husband and wife was about redemption, and a form of worship. Pope Francis has been cited as saying that he is not one to judge homosexuality. His words have been taken to mean that, if a good Christian happens to be homosexual, there is no infraction in the eyes of God. Some have understood the Pope to be in "support" of homosexuality. However, it is unclear how this translates into the recent marriage debates as to whether homosexuals should be allowed to marry. Many Christians have argued that their doctrine suggests homosexuals are living in sin, but also that God intended marriage to be for a man and a woman for procreation purposes only. However, many Christians have also seen these arguments as false, and believe that homosexuals are not living in sin and also have the right to marry. Some Christian denominations, such as the Metropolitan Community Church and the Presbyterian Church, accept gays and lesbians and allow them to receive the sacrament of marriage. Others demonize homosexuals or believe some parts of these arguments and not others. Even so, these arguments have influenced policy and political debate on marriage as well as other issues that concern homosexuals.

SEE ALSO: Christianity and Homosexuality; Religious Fundamentalism; Same-Sex Marriage

REFERENCES

Central Intelligence Agency. 2015. "33.39% of 7.174 billion world population (under the section 'People and Society')." The World Factbook. Accessed August 11, 2015, at https://www.cia.gov/library/publications/the-world-factbook/geos/xx.html.

Foucault, Michel. 1978. *The History of Sexuality*, vol. 1. *An Introduction: The Will to Knowledge*. New York: Vintage.

The Holy Bible, New International Version, NIV Copyright 1973, 1978, 1984, 2011 by Biblica, Inc. Used by permission. All rights reserved worldwide.

FURTHER READING

Evans, John H., and Michael S. Evans. 2012. "Sociology and Christianity." In *The Blackwell Companion to Science and Christianity*, edited by J. B. Stump and Alan G. Padgett, 344–355. Chichester: Wiley-Blackwell.

Penner, Todd. 2015. *Women, Gender, and Sexuality in the New Testament and Early Christianity*. Oxford Bibliographies Online, Oxford University Press.

Wiesner, Merry E. 2000. *Christianity and Sexuality in the Early Modern World: Regulating Desire, Reforming Practice*. London: Routledge.

Christianity and Homosexuality

LISA ISHERWOOD
University of Winchester, UK

Christian history displays a tendency to equate the heretic, infidel, and witch with the sodomite. The sodomite was understood as the one who could threaten the social order by his/her "otherness," that is, his/her inability to conform to the norm that was white, male, Western, and heterosexual. Another term commonly associated with homosexual practice, buggery, also has its roots in this theory of non-conformity and heresy. It is a term that originated with the eleventh-century Bulgars, a Manichean Christian group who practiced non-procreative sex. They were declared heretical and a derivative of their name used to signal threats to medieval society. During the latter half of the twelfth century, Europe became conformist and it was not uncommon for orthodoxy in belief to be linked with certain sexual practices that were considered normal. It is of note that this threat to the social order should be portrayed in sexual terms, with the homosexual eventually being viewed as the ultimate threat and destroyer of civilized virtues. There seems to be an unconscious understanding that once those who rule society can control the physical, sexual expression of its citizens, then they can have a tightly governed and non-rebellious society. The perceived naturalness of certain bodily actions serves to regulate the social structure, which in turn literally comes to "embody" dominant values. The natural differences and roles of each sex take on symbolic boundary meaning, which was certainly the case in the medieval Christian world. The church has always understood that the body and the experiences we have through it are very powerful and so to this day attempts strict control.

The homosexual is the societal outlaw and to be feared. Bernadette Brooten (1996) makes the point that Paul's declarations against homosexuality were based on this same understanding. She claims that he realized homosexual, and particularly lesbian, love would set the social order on its head, based as it was on sexual hierarchy. People literally learned their place in society by the sexual role they were moulded into, and this was a largely heterosexual arrangement. Many biblical scholars, following Brooten's approach, have moved to this gendered reading of the Pauline texts and away from understanding them as sexually prohibitive.

The Hebrew Bible texts, particularly that of the destruction of Sodom (Genesis 19: 1–29), which have been used to outlaw homosexuality, have for many years been subject to alternate readings, with scholars pointing out that mistranslation plays a large part in how Christians have understood the text (Lings 2013). Countryman (1986) has drawn attention to the fact that underlying many of the morality declarations and customs in the Hebrew Bible was an understanding of purity and property that even Jesus appeared to challenge. In relation to homosexuality, the understanding at the time was that one partner would play the "female role," and this was considered against purity since it was a sin to mix two natures; a man had to be a "man" in all respects. Additionally, marriage came under the property laws of the time; it was inconceivable that a man could own a man of equal status, so unions akin to marriage were unthinkable. Countryman argues that the prohibitions in the Hebrew Bible and those carried through into the Christian scriptures are all based in these two concepts, which no longer apply in our times.

Some scholars working on the Christian scriptures and early Christian history, such as Mary Rose D'Angelo (1990), have examined the suggestion that there were women missionary partnerships in the early church. Her interest was aroused by a funerary relief depicting two women with right hands clasped in a common gesture of commitment. It is plain that others have seen it in this light also as the funerary relief has been defaced in order to make one partner look male. For D'Angelo, the existence of such a relief opened the possibility of women as committed partners during the early church period and made her wonder about the role and relationship of biblical women. Her work is extensive and she makes a case for the existence of same-sex couples in both the Hebrew Bible and the Christian scriptures, demonstrating that there is not an exclusive heterosexual picture or even a heterosexual expectation for those who lived religious lives. There have been a number of biblical scholars (Guest 2005) who have investigated the nature of relationships between people of the same sex in scripture, and their work has helped to develop a more gay-friendly starting point for some Christian theology and has helped to advance the creation of gay and lesbian hermeneutics.

The biblical work of Theodore Jennings (2003), a married Methodist biblical scholar, moves the debate forward and focuses on the negative power of binary opposites in debates about gender. Jennings proposes a gay-positive reading of scripture that does not assume the heterosexual orientation of characters in stories or the "normative" nature of marriage and family relations between people. However, the author is not concerned with establishing a gay identity for Jesus; rather, he wants to think outside that narrow box as well. He wants us to read in such a way as to liberate everyone, gay and straight, from the narrow confines of the dualistic binary opposites of male and female – binary opposites that do not necessarily lead to life in abundance and the full embrace of our rich and complex humanity. Jennings reexamined many texts that are central to the Christian gospel and paid special attention to the beloved disciple and the nude youth in the garden of Gethsemane who, Jennings argued, is a male prostitute. This is not to make the case that Jesus was gay, but rather to point out the flexible edges of what has been seen as a very tight group of disciples based on gender and purity. The readings that Jennings suggested are troubling to gender roles that underpin patriarchy, heterosexism, and masculinist understandings. It is far too simple to suggest that Jesus was gay, because that reading is a way of falling back into the binary opposites that it is suggested need to be overcome. However, we do see that Jesus had close and affectionate relationships with men (particularly the beloved disciple who is assumed to be young John) that would challenge standard masculinist understandings of gender. That is to say, the physical and emotional closeness exhibited to this particular disciple is beyond what would be normal within the society. There are only six verses in the Bible that read as opposed to homosexuality, and there is a large amount of gospel material that can be read as containing homoerotic elements.

As biblical scholarship moved on, so too did theology. Some contemporary theologians claim to create theology from their lived experience as gay and lesbian people. This move was enabled by liberation theology, which placed lived experience in relation with others as central in the creation of theology, thus destabilizing the notion that theology could be a purely abstract discipline. Carter Heyward (1989) made it quite plain that passion, and therefore sexual love, has a part to play in Christian lives. Basing her argument on Mark's gospel, she unpacked the concept of *dunamis*, which is the raw, erotic power with which we are born – the same power that Jesus was born with. It is a power that draws us to one another and the world and fuels our struggles for justice and right relation. She argued that sexual love, more than *agape*, fires our imaginations and our passion for justice. As a lesbian theologian, she followed this argument through by saying that to deny gay and lesbian people the right to this powerful love is to deny them full humanity. What makes her work important is that it is based on an interpretation of a gospel concept that appears to be inclusive of all sexualities and genders. It also develops what was to become known as sexual theology rather than theology of sex. The latter has been the way churches read scripture and then make declarations about sexuality, while the former values the sexual lives of believers as central to expanding their understanding of God.

During the 1980s and 1990s there was a marked shift from theologians attempting to show that gay and lesbian people could fit the rules and regulations of Christianity and that their humanity was the same as everyone else's, to a bold assertion that gay and lesbian experience could form the stuff of theological investigation. All aspects of gay and lesbian life were considered in order to reexamine theology and indeed to create new ways of understanding theology. It was also a time when declaring one's sexuality was still a matter to consider seriously and not to do rashly. Reflecting on this context, Michael Glaser (1998) argued that coming out had biblical and sacramental qualities to it. He argues it is biblical because it was an act of vulnerability not unlike the sacrificial offerings of ancient times that evoked God's presence and brought about reconciliation. Coming out could be viewed as a Christic act as it involves going against the spirit of the age as Jesus did; he loved even at times and in places where the laws of his day forbade such expression. Jesus' love was considered disordered, just as gay and lesbian love was thought of, because it was focused in the wrong place. It is the kind of loving that is urgent, risky, compassionate, and celebratory of life.

Many new images of Christ emerged from reflection on lived experience at the turn of the twenty-first century. For example, Althaus-Reid (1998) offered a very challenging image of Christ as Xena, warrior princess. A leather woman hanging on a cross, declaring love into eternity for the woman she loves, who is hanging next to her. This is a queer Christ indeed, one that challenges traditional images on many levels. She is not passive; she declares she would kill the Romans given a chance. She is in leather and she is a dyke and Althaus Reid suggests this makes her just as courageous and transgressive as Jesus of Nazareth was, if in a different way. This offers a dramatic clash of sexual and gender identities, but Althaus Reid argues it is as legitimate as the more passive images that had been offered from Latin America with peasants in pristine white garments hanging on crosses. This is not a Christ we can easily recognize, but it is one offered from certain realities of gay and lesbian culture, just as Latin American peasants had been offered previously.

As gay and lesbian theologians looked at the Christian tradition and placed it under scrutiny from their own lives, some ethical questions also came to light. Some gay and lesbian Christology imaged Jesus as friend and lover. By understanding friendship as central to gay and lesbian life, theologians and ethicists called into question the primary role of marriage in Christian life (Hunt 1991). It was argued that relationships based on friendship eliminate any notion of ownership and place emphasis on the equality to which they aspire. It also suggests that each person is calling out the very best from the other with loving challenge and tender support. Friendship in the West has rarely been equated with sex, and so some criticism has been leveled at this model, suggesting that it is a cosy way to legitimize same-sex relationships by removing the overt sexual element. It would be fairer to say that, in centralizing friendship, attention is being drawn to the fact that same-sex relationships can understand desire in a broad sense as the spur for justice and right relation. This understanding played a part in bringing to light the intrinsic inequalities of the sexes that Christian theologies of marriage were predicated upon. It also raised the issue for theology of gender, a topic previously ignored. Marvin Ellison (1996, 26) suggested that what was now possible to speak of was an ethic of sexual justice rather than sexual ethics being exclusively attached to marriage, as he suggests they had been within a Christian frame. An ethic of sexual justice challenges sex negativity, heterocentrism, and the eroticization of non-mutual relations, all of which he believes are alive and well in traditional theologies of marriage. Ellison commented, "heterosexual marriage is therefore far from being a free and voluntary choice; it is a political requirement for normative status in this culture" (Ellison 1996, 27). It acts as the glue for a hierarchical system that is based on ownership and lends itself to the generation of wealth. One of the most pressing aspects of this arrangement, for Ellison, is the power that is eroticized in patriarchal sexual relations. Ellison argued that Christian sex ethics have failed to address the issue of power precisely because they have always concentrated on marriage, a system that is based on power. While "compulsory coupling," as he calls marriage, may fit the dominant capitalist ethos, it does not lend itself to our full becoming as humans. It makes us dependent on one another for the fulfilment of our needs, limits our range and the importance that we place on friendship, and weakens our ties with the wider community.

While the churches remain slow in following the advances many societies have made regarding the humanity and social status of gay and lesbian people, many Christian theologians are still making strides in their work. With the opening up of questions concerning gender that the examination of marriage brought about, the narrow definitions involved in thinking about sexuality have been broadened and a wider range of experience placed under theological investigation. It is quite rare in the second decade of the twenty-first century to find works that simply address gay and lesbian theology; this has been expanded to include trans/sexual/gender, bisexual, intersex, and the term "queer," which has been reclaimed from a term of insult and shame to one of pride and inclusivity. Christian sexual theology has moved from apologetics for those considered to be sexual minorities to a confident questioning even of those considered sexually normal. This questioning has a political edge in that it critiques the type of society that Christian normative sexuality has underpinned. This has led to a call for heterosexuality to "come out," which means that heterosexuality, just like homosexuality, comes in many shades and identifications and that one solid norm should not be assumed. Nor should it be assumed that heterosexuality naturally underpins just and moral societies, as was once believed to be the case. The contribution of gay and lesbian experience to theology has been significant and it has opened the discipline for many further advances.

SEE ALSO: Christianity, Gender and Sexuality; Feminist Christology; Heteronormativity and Homonormativity; Heterosexism and Homophobia; Open and Affirming Religious Organizations; Religion and Homophobia

REFERENCES

Althaus-Reid, Marcella. 1998. "On Wearing Skirts Without Underwear: Indecent Theology Challenging the Liberation Theology of the Pueblo. Poor Women Contesting Christ." *Journal of Feminist Theology*, 19: 39–51.

Brooten, Bernadette. 1996. *Love Between Women: Early Christian Responses to Female Homoeroticism*. Chicago: University of Chicago Press.

Countryman, William. 1986. *Dirt, Greed and Sex*. London: SCM.

D'Angelo, Mary Rose. 1990. "Women Partners in the New Testament." *Journal of Feminist Studies in Religion*, 6: 65–86.

Ellison, Marvin. 1996. *Erotic Justice: A Liberating Ethic of Sexuality*. Louisville: Westminster John Knox Press.

Glaser, Michael. 1998. *Coming Out as Sacrament*. Louisville: Westminster John Knox Press.

Guest, Deryn. 2005. *When Deborah Meet Jael: Lesbian Biblical Hermeneutics*. London: SCM.

Heyward, Carter. 1989. *Touching Our Strength: The Erotic as Power and the Love of God*. New York: Harper Collins.

Hunt, Mary. 1991. *Fierce Tenderness*. New York: Crossroad Press.

Jennings, Theodore. 2003. *The Man Jesus Loved: Homoerotic Narratives from the New Testament*. Cleveland: Pilgrim Press.

Lings, K. Renato. 2013. *Lost in Translation: Homosexuality and the Bible*. New York: Trafford.

FURTHER READING

Althaus Reid, Marcella. 2000. *Indecent Theology: Theological Perversions in Sex, Gender and Politics*. London: Routledge.

Althaus Reid, Marcella. 2003. *The Queer God*. London: Routledge.

Althaus Reid, Marcella, and Lisa Isherwood. 2004. *The Sexual Theologian: Essays Sex, God and Politics*. London: T&T Clark.

Goss, Robert. 2002. *Queering Christ: Beyond Jesus Acted Up*. Ohio: Pilgrim Press.

Isherwood, Lisa, and Mark Jordan. 2012. *Dancing Theology in Fetish Boots: Essays in Honour of Marcella Althaus Reid*. London: SCM.

Jordan, Mark. 2000. *The Silence of Sodom: Homosexuality in Modern Catholicism*. Chicago: University of Chicago Press.

Loughlin, Gerard, ed. 2007. *Queer Theology: Rethinking the Western Body*. London: Blackwell Publishing.

Rambuss, Richard. 1998. *Closet Devotions*. Durham, NC: Duke University Press.

Stuart, Elizabeth. 1995. *Just Good Friends: Towards a Lesbian and Gay Theology of Relationship*. London: Mowbray.

Cisgender and Cissexual

PETER CAVA
Georgia State University, USA

The term *cissexual* is usually defined as "non-transsexual," and the term *cisgender* is usually defined as "non-transgender." *Cissexual* and *cisgender* disrupt the marked–unmarked relations between transsexuality and non-transsexuality and between transgender and non-transgender, relations in which non-transsexual, non-transgender womanhood is an unmarked norm for womanhood and non-transsexual, non-transgender manhood an unmarked norm for manhood.

The prefixes *cis-* and *trans-* are antonymic: roughly, *cis-* means "on this side of" and *trans-* means "to the other side of." The cis–trans distinction was introduced into sexology by Ernst Burchard in 1914. Burchard contrasted *Cisvestitismus* (a type of inclination to wear clothing associated with one's sex) with *Transvestitismus* (transvestism, or cross-dressing). *Cissexual* was coined by sexologist Volkmar Sigusch in 1991. *Cisgender* began circulating in online transgender discussion groups in the mid-1990s. Dana Leland Defosse and John Hollister used it in 1994, and Carl Buijs coined it independently in 1995. Biologist Julia Serano popularized *cissexual* and *cisgender* in 2007. *Cisgender* became increasingly widespread in gender and sexuality studies classrooms in 2008 and in peer-reviewed publications in 2009. Its deployment in gender and sexuality studies has come under intense critical scrutiny, particularly by A. Finn Enke (2012).

Cissexuality is usually conceptualized as the constitutive outside of transsexuality. By a traditional definition, a transsexual is a person with two characteristics: first, the person develops a gender identity (a sense of self as female, male, or otherwise) that is opposite of the sex at birth; second, the person aligns the majority of his or her primary and secondary sex characteristics with the gender identity through hormone replacement therapy and sex reassignment surgery (the latter now commonly called gender confirmation surgery).

More recently, the relation between these two characteristics has been destabilized by phenomena such as, first, no-hormone (no-ho) and non-operative (non-op) transsexuality and, second, genderqueerness. First, if a person with a transsexual gender identity is no-ho and non-op, then the person does not pursue and has not received hormone replacement therapy or gender confirmation surgery, because medical transition is too difficult to access (especially for someone who is underage, poor, racialized, or undocumented), too risky (especially in the absence of professional supervision), or otherwise undesirable. Second, a person may pursue or may have received hormone replacement therapy and gender confirmation surgery but have a non-binary gender identity (such as genderqueer) or no gender identity.

Today, a typical explanation of the distinction between transsexuality and cissexuality is as follows: a transsexual is a person with a gender identity that is opposite of the sex at birth, whereas a cissexual is a person with a gender identity that *matches* the sex at birth. This explanation is contested in at least four ways. First, if cissexuality is conceptualized as the constitutive outside of transsexuality, then this explanation effaces non-binary gender identities. Second, in contrast to the adjectival forms *transsexual person* and *cissexual person*, the noun forms *transsexual* and *cissexual* objectify people by defining them only by their transsexuality or cissexuality rather than also by their personhood. Third, the word *opposite* denies the possibility that femaleness and maleness are, or may be socially constructed as, analogues. And fourth, sex at birth is not a stable ground from which one can measure the distance to gender identity.

Common replacements for the phrase *sex at birth* include *sex, sex assignment, sex assignment at birth, gender assignment*, and *gender assignment at birth*. This variability suggests the extent to which sex is a contested category. Sex may be conceptualized from the perspective of essentialism or social constructionism. According to an essentialist perspective, femaleness or maleness is an essential property of the body. A social constructionist may emphasize the discursive assignment of sex (through language such as *clitoris, penis*, or *ambiguous genitalia*), the surgical assignment of sex (through genital surgery), or the administrative assignment of gender (through documentation such as a birth certificate). The discursive assignment may be female, male, or intersex; the discursive, surgical, and administrative assignments may or may not align normatively; and these assignments may or may not change over time. This myriad of possibilities raises complicated questions about the relation of cissexuality to embodiment.

Just as cissexuality is usually conceptualized as the constitutive outside of transsexuality, cisgender is usually conceptualized as the constitutive outside of transgender. Distinctions between transsexuality and transgender are predicated on distinctions among sex (which may be defined as biological femaleness, maleness, or intersexuality), gender (which may be defined as social femininity, masculinity, or androgyny), and sexuality (which may be defined as comprising erotic desires, erotic behaviors, and identities based on those desires and behaviors). In 1965, psychiatrist John F. Oliven used *transgenderism* as a preferred synonym for *transsexualism* to distinguish the desire to change gender from erotic desire. In 1969, transgender activist Virginia Prince coined the term *transgenderal*, explaining that whereas transsexuals change their sex (through medical intervention), transgenderals change their gender (through self-presentation). In the 1970s, alternative forms such as *trans-gender* became umbrella terms that designated a spectrum from transsexual people to cross-dressers. In the 1980s, trans- terms came to signify an even broader spectrum of "gender bending." In 1992, transgender activist Leslie Feinberg politicized *transgender*, describing "transgender liberation" as a movement to end the oppression of all who defy gender norms.

Usage of *cisgender* depends on that of *transgender*. If *transgender* is used as a preferred synonym for *transsexual*, then *cisgender* is used as one for *cissexual*. In contrast, if *transgender* is used as an umbrella term for gender non-normativity, then *cisgender* is used as one for gender normativity. The latter usage expands the purview of *cis-* from gender identity to gender expression and sex (insofar as sex is biological gender rather than discrete from gender).

As a term for gender normativity, *cisgender* is controversial when deployed in reference to people. The controversy centers on three issues. First, insofar as everyone deviates from, and is disciplined by, gender norms, *cisgender person* has an absent referent. To deny this absence is to efface the gender variance of, and the disciplinary power of gender norms for, non-transgender-identified people. Second, when individuals do not self-identify as cisgender, identifying them as such may disrespect their self-identities and right to self-definition. And third, in subcultural communities that center or value gender non-normativity, identifying individuals as cisgender may marginalize or denigrate them.

Alternative forms of *cissexual* and *cisgender* include *cis*, *cis-*, and *cisgendered*. *Cis* may serve as an abbreviation of *cissexual*, *cisgender*, or both. The hyphen in *cis-* signifies open-endedness, indicating that the user does not wish to foreclose possibilities for the word stem (possibilities such as *sex* and *gender*). *Cisgendered* – a past participial adjective, as in *cisgendered person* – implies that *cisgender* is a verb. That is, expressed in the active voice, someone or something cisgenders a person; expressed in the passive voice, the person is cisgendered (by someone or something); thus, a cisgendered person exists. If scholars continue to use the past participial adjectival form, then they may wish to identify, and theorize the nature of, the entity or process who/that cisgenders.

The cis family of concepts includes the cisgender gaze (a gaze that objectifies and misgenders transgender people), cisgenderism (an ideology that privileges cisgender), cisplaining (condescendingly explaining gender to transgender people), cisnormativity (the governance of cis norms), cissexism (an ideology that privileges cissexuality), cissexual assumption (the assumption that cissexual experiences of embodiment are universal (Serano 2007)), and cissexual gender entitlement (the belief that cissexual people are "the ultimate arbiters of which people are allowed to call themselves women or men" (Serano 2007, 166)).

The most generative cis-related concept is cis privilege. By a typical definition, cis privilege is the opportunity to improve one's life insofar as this opportunity is conferred on the basis of one's cis identity. Some interpret identity in such a definition as *self*-identity (one's psychological sense of self), whereas others interpret it as *public* identity (the visible representation of oneself by oneself or others). These interpretations implicate competing understandings of the nature and function of privilege, particularly at times when transsexual/transgender (trans) people "pass" as cis.

The concept of cis privilege was popularized by the "Cis Privilege Checklist" (Cedar 2008). This checklist details examples of cis privileged access to healthcare, identity documents, legal counsel, media representation, and public restrooms, as well as privileged expectations of privacy, recognition, respect, self-determination, support, and validation. Subsequent scholarship analyzes cis privilege in particular social contexts, such as gay male social spaces (Walls and Costello 2010) and airports (Shepherd and Sjoberg 2012).

The reality of cis privilege is denied by members of a radical feminist subculture sometimes known as trans-exclusionary radical feminism. Members of this subculture believe that gender privilege/oppression operates exclusively along the axis male/female: gender privilege is bestowed through raising some people as male, and gender oppression is imposed through raising others as female. From this perspective, *cisgender*'s raison d'être is as follows: trans people who were raised as male deny their privilege by claiming that they are oppressed as transgender, and they deny the oppression of women raised as female by claiming that these women are privileged as cisgender. This argument leads to the conclusion that *cisgender* obfuscates rather than names gender privilege.

Perhaps the most promising direction for future scholarship on cissexuality and cisgender is analysis of cis privilege from an intersectional perspective (one that acknowledges the distinct experiences produced by intersecting axes of privilege/oppression). Noting that gender normativity is always already mediated by race, nationality, class, and ability, Enke (2012) calls for interrogation of the mutual constitutivity of cis privilege and privilege along those other axes. Moreover, because some women who were assigned female at birth have developed a self-concept as victims of gender oppression, they resist the idea that they experience gender privilege, such as cis privilege; conversely, because of the same self-concept, some trans people resist the idea that they experience gender privilege, such as male or masculine privilege. Scholars may wish to illuminate a path out of this impasse by considering how gender itself comprises not a monolithic axis of privilege/oppression, but multiple intersecting axes, including cissexual/transsexual, cisgender/transgender, male/female, and masculine/feminine.

SEE ALSO: Feminism, Radical; Gender Bender; Genderqueer; Intersectionality; Intersexuality; Privilege; Sex Versus Gender Categorization; Transgender Movements in International Perspective; Transgender Movements in the United States; Transsexuality

REFERENCES

Cedar. 2008. "Cis Privilege Checklist: The Cisgender/Cissexual Privilege Checklist." *Taking Up Too Much Space: Trans Misogyny, Feminism, and Trans Activism*, July 10. Accessed July 24, 2015, at http://www.takesupspace.wordpress.com/cis-privilege-checklist.

Enke, A. Finn. 2012. "The Education of Little Cis: Cisgender and the Discipline of Opposing Bodies." In *Transfeminist Perspectives In and Beyond Transgender and Gender Studies*, edited by Anne Enke, 60–80. Philadelphia: Temple University Press.

Serano, Julia. 2007. *Whipping Girl: A Transsexual Woman on Sexism and the Scapegoating of Femininity*. Emeryville, CA: Seal Press.

Shepherd, Laura J., and Laura Sjoberg. 2012. "Trans-bodies in/of War(s): Cisprivilege and Contemporary Security Strategy." *Feminist Review*, 101: 5–23. DOI: 10.1057/fr.2011.53.

Walls, N. Eugene, and Kelly Costello. 2010. "'Head Ladies Center for Teacup Chain': Exploring Cisgender Privilege in a (Predominantly) Gay Male

Context." In *Explorations in Diversity: Examining Privilege and Oppression in a Multicultural Society*, 2nd ed., edited by Sharon K. Anderson and Valerie A. Middleton, 81–93. Belmont, CA: Brooks/Cole.

FURTHER READING

Boyd, Helen. 2009. "Jeez Louise This Whole Cisgender Thing." *en/Gender*, September 17. Accessed July 24, 2015, at http://www.myhusbandbetty.com/2009/09/17/jeez-louise-this-whole-cisgender-thing.

Cava, Peter. 2014. "Trans Liberation is for Everybody: Trans Allyship and the Trans Continuum." In *Trans Bodies, Trans Selves: A Resource for the Transgender Community*, edited by Laura Erickson-Schroth, 10. New York: Oxford University Press.

Deep Green Resistance. 2013. "The End of Gender: Revolution, Not Reform." YouTube, May 10. Accessed June 24, 2015, at http://www.youtube.com/watch?v=Ot8cBm0YmXo.

Lennon, Erica, and Brian J. Mistler. 2014. "Cisgenderism." *TSQ: Transgender Studies Quarterly*, 1(1–2): 63–64. DOI: 10.1215/23289252-2399623.

Schilt, Kristen, and Laurel Westbrook. 2009. "Doing Gender, Doing Heteronormativity: 'Gender Normals,' Transgender People, and the Social Maintenance of Heterosexuality." *Gender & Society*, 23(4): 440–464. DOI: 10.1177/089124320934003.

Shotwell, Alexis, and Trevor Sangrey. 2009. "Resisting Definition: Gendering through Interaction and Relational Selfhood." *Hypatia*, 24(3): 56–76. DOI: 10.1111/j.1527-2001.2009.01045.x.

Cisgenderism

Y. GAVRIEL ANSARA
University of Surrey, UK

ISRAEL BERGER
The University of Sydney, Australia

The term *cisgenderism* comes from the Latin prefix *cis-*, meaning "on the same side as," and *gender*, from the Latin *genus*, meaning "kind" or "type." The term *cisgenderism* was initially used interchangeably with the term *cisgender* to describe people who were "not transgender." More recently, however, the term cisgenderism has been used to describe the ideology that delegitimizes people's own understanding of their genders and bodies. Forms of cisgenderism that have been explored in research include pathologizing, which refers to constructing or treating people's genders, bodies, and experiences associated with their genders and bodies as disordered (e.g., "gender identity disorder," "gender dysphoria," and "disorders of sex development"), and misgendering, which misclassifies people's genders and bodies (e.g., describing a woman who was assigned as male as "a man" or describing someone who views their body as male as "a biological female").

In contrast to approaches that treat "cisgender" and "transgender" people as essentially distinct types of people, this newer cisgenderism framework is based on a critique of the "transgender/cisgender" gender binary as an essentializing form of cisgenderism. According to cisgenderism theory, the "transgender/cisgender" gender binary warrants critique, because the label "transgender" is often applied to people who self-identify simply as women or men rather than consider their "trans" experience their identity, and because this binary excludes a variety of people who cannot neatly be classified as "transgender" or "cisgender." Those excluded by this binary include, but are not limited to, people with intersex characteristics; women who would be classified as "cisgender" within this binary but who are misgendered as a result of stereotypically "male" facial and body hair associated with polycystic ovary syndrome; "cisgender" people who live in their assigned gender in everyday life but who engage in periodic or occasional "transgender" behavior such as expressing a drag persona in performance contexts or having gender fluidity that involves expressing another gender when socializing on weekends; people with non-binary genders in societies that recognize more than two valid genders; and people in societies that recognize changes of gender as culturally normative coming-of-age experiences (e.g., the Kaska society in parts of the Yukon territory and British Columbia, Canada, and the Bugis society of South Sulawesi, Indonesia).

Cisgenderism can describe systemic and individual acts that occur in a variety of cultural contexts, including those that are hostile or benevolent and those that are intentional or unintentional. Thus transphobia could be considered one form of hostile cisgenderism that is directed at people who either self-identify as or are perceived as "trans." Unlike the construct of "transphobia," however, the cisgenderism framework does not assume that all people who experience gender or body delegitimization necessarily constitute a distinct class of people (e.g., "trans people"). For example, many women who were raised as girls and who would not be classified as "trans" have reported experiences of being misgendered due to their minimal breast tissue or visible facial hair.

Y. Gavriel Ansara initiated the field of cisgenderism studies, which investigates distinct manifestations of delegitimizing ideology about bodies and genders across diverse cultural contexts. The cisgenderism framework is particularly informed by two social science approaches, critical disability studies and ethnocentrism studies. Cisgenderism shares with critical disability studies a critique of the external application of labels that the people to whom the labels are applied experience as stigmatizing or inaccurate. The cisgenderism framework also emphasizes the critique from ethnocentrism studies that categories that are developed in one particular cultural context cannot be categorically presumed to be applicable to another without evidence to that effect. For example, the colonial US and European notion of "trans" is based on the culturally relative assumptions that there are only two valid genders, that gender is determined by external genital appearance at birth, and that "trans" people go from one of two valid options to the other. This approach gives rise to forms of cisgenderism such as *coercive queering* (in which self-identified heterosexual people who have "trans" life experiences or intersex characteristics are conflated with lesbian, gay, bisexual, or queer individuals) and *retroactive misgendering* (in which people's pasts are described without their consent using language that invalidates their current gender self-identification).

Psychologists Y. Gavriel Ansara and Peter Hegarty published the first empirical research in the field of cisgenderism in a quantitative study that evaluated claims that views of children's genders were becoming more accepting and less pathologizing (Ansara and Hegarty 2012). The American Psychological Association recognized this research for the 2012 Transgender Research Award for making an original and significant contribution. Ansara and Hegarty assessed whether journal article records on children's genders and expression reflected or contrasted with the aims of the American Psychological Association's nondiscrimination statement on "transgender" and "gender variant" people by *misgendering*, which contradicts people's own understanding of their genders, and *pathologizing*, which constructs people's self-identified genders and expression as disordered. Although both were common, pathologizing was more frequent than misgendering in article records. Moreover, they found that cisgenderism has remained stable over time. They also found that articles on children's genders and expression had become more widely cited over time and that mental health professionals were more cisgenderist than authors in other professions.

Ansara and Hegarty (2012) found that the most highly cisgenderist research was authored by an *invisible college* centered around the most prolific author in the field, Kenneth J. Zucker. An invisible college is a term used by psychologists to describe a network of collaborating authors. Zowie Davy (2013) and Jake Pyne (2014) have explored how the invisible college linked by Zucker has been influential in promoting pathologizing and discriminatory approaches to people whose gender self-identifications, characteristics, or behaviors are problematized by these mental health professionals.

Mechanisms that are intended to promote responsive and community-informed treatment can often perpetuate cisgenderism in healthcare settings (Ansara, 2012). These include evidence-based medicine (EBM), consultation with community leaders, and feedback forms. EBM promotes the use of published research to make healthcare decisions, yet people who do not neatly fit their assigned gender or binary categories may be excluded from or misrepresented in research. Consultation often happens with community leaders or in focus groups, and both approaches are vulnerable to dominant people communicating views that may not represent the diverse needs of the population. Feedback forms often gather feedback on the behavior of individual staff while omitting questions about structural and policy aspects that affect people's care. In addition, people who have been treated particularly poorly may feel that their feedback will be ignored, even when these forms contain open-ended questions. It is essential to treat people's unsolicited feedback that systems are not meeting their needs as legitimate "evidence" and as input that can identify existing gaps to assist with the development of interventions to improve healthcare services. Active efforts to promote this kind of critical feedback must include a variety of disenfranchised individuals and not focus solely on the reports of community leaders.

Reducing cisgenderism in research and practice is one of the key aims of cisgenderism studies. Ansara and Hegarty (2013, 2014) have identified a number of research practices that can lead to misgendering: assuming gender based on given names, visual appearance, or culturally variable "clues"; conflating gender designations with physical attributes and assigned "sex" categories; assuming that people's self-identified gender should and does match their assigned gender category; failing to document how gender was determined by the authors; ignoring the existence of people with non-binary genders; misgendering people with non-binary genders by using binary pronouns and descriptors; and excluding all people who do not identify clearly as women or men as "outliers." By avoiding these practices, researchers, policy-makers, and other authors can help to reduce cisgenderism.

SEE ALSO: Gender-Based Violence; Gender Inequality and Gender Stratification; Gender Oppression; Gender Transgression; Gender Violence; Intersexuality; Strategic Essentialism; Transphobia

REFERENCES

Ansara, Y. Gavriel. 2012. "Cisgenderism in Medical Settings: How Collaborative Partnerships Can Challenge Structural Violence." In *Out of the Ordinary: LGBT Lives*, edited by Ian Rivers and Richard Ward, 102–122. Oxford: Cambridge Scholars Press.

Ansara, Y. Gavriel, and Peter Hegarty. 2012. "Cisgenderism in Psychology: Pathologising and Misgendering Children from 1999 to 2008." *Psychology and Sexuality*, 3(2): 137–160. DOI: 10.1080/19419899.2011.576696.

Ansara, Y. Gavriel, and Peter Hegarty. 2013. "Misgendering in English Language Contexts:

Applying Non-cisgenderist Methods to Feminist Research." *International Journal of Multiple Research Approaches*, 7(2): 160–177.

Ansara, Y. Gavriel, and Peter Hegarty. 2014. "Methodologies of Misgendering: Recommendations for Reducing Cisgenderism in Psychological Research." *Feminism & Psychology*, 24(2): 259–270.

Davy, Zowie. 2013. "The Construction of Gender Dysphoria at 'Classifying Sex: Debating DSM-5'." *Psychology of Women Section Review*, 15(2): 63–67.

Pyne, Jake. 2014. "The Governance of Gender Non-conforming Children: a Dangerous Enclosure."*Annual Review of Critical Psychology*, 11: 79–96.

FURTHER READING

Ansara, Y. Gavriel. 2010. "Beyond Cisgenderism: Counselling People with Non-Assigned Gender Identities." In *Counselling Ideologies: Queer Challenges to Heteronormativity*, edited by Lyndsey Moon, 167–200. Aldershot: Ashgate.

Blumer, Markie L. C., Y. Gavriel Ansara, and Courtney M. Watson. 2013. "Cisgenderism in Family Therapy: How Everyday Clinical Practices Can Delegitimize People's Gender Self-designations." *Journal of Family Psychotherapy*, 24(4): 267–285.

Civil Rights Law and Gender in the United States

MONIQUE N. RODRIGUEZ and LIA D. GUERRA
St. Mary's University, USA

The Civil Rights Act of 1964 prohibits discrimination based on race, color, religion, or sex. In the 1960s, Congress passed the law as part of the US civil rights legislation. Initially, the Civil Rights Act was challenging to include the word "sex" in the Fourteenth Amendment. Civil rights law varies from state to state, and also from country to country. As a result of the Fourteenth Amendment Equal Protection Clause and Title VII of the Civil Rights Act of 1964, the Equal Employment Opportunity Commission was created and moved to implement the law.

The final bill allowed for sex to be a consideration in equal employment opportunity and, since the passing of the Civil Rights Act in 1964, is referred to by the term gender. Gender is the state of being recognized as either male or female. Gender has been a topic for discussion for many aspects of civil rights. When discussing this topic it is automatically associated with discrimination against a certain gender in specific instances. The most general and prominent form of discrimination usually occurs against women. This type of discrimination has occurred in the workplace when women have been forced to give up occupations due to bearing children, receiving lower wages than men, or not being considered for the same positions as men because of their gender. Politically, women have also been discriminated against as in most countries women had to fight for their right to vote and have equal rights as their male counterparts. Although they may have political weight, that does not mean that women are equally represented amongst politicians.

Education has also been affected by gender and civil rights issues. Women have not always been able to attend school and receive an adequate education. Often, girls had to stay at home and take care of other children while their male counterparts attended school. As this has changed, we now see the discrepancy between males and females in higher education and academia. Although there are many women in high university positions there are not as many women publishing or presenting their work. There are many female academics but there is an underlying stigma that makes it more difficult for females to receive the same recognition. Socially, gender and civil rights law have come into conflict. Although laws can be created to reduce the amount of discrimination against a particular gender, society still has to allow the changes to take place in everyday life. This is the most difficult aspect of civil rights because society needs to adapt to the law and innovative thought. If society does not adapt to the civil rights efforts made to equalize the genders, then the laws are not able to serve their purpose.

Women have been discriminated against because of their gender in many ways. The right to have political power and have the same responsibilities as those of the opposite sex have been a struggle for women in many countries. The push for gender and civil rights in the Western world and most developed countries was initiated by the demand for racial equality. Gender equality was added to the social movement almost as an afterthought. Although decades have passed in the Western world since many of the gender civil rights movements, there is still a remnant of gender inequality. Employment equality, political equality, and social equality were some of the main areas targeted during the civil rights movement. However, moving into the twenty-first century we still see employment discrimination against women.

For most in the Western world, civil rights law and gender equality have been forced to meet at certain boundaries in the workplace and regarding political privileges. In contrast, in most underdeveloped or primarily theocratic countries, women cannot vote or even voice their personal opinions without censure. Women's rights are very limited and any efforts towards civil rights law to mend these issues could land individuals in prison. The people who live in these countries usually live with gender inequality and lack knowledge of the issues at hand. Gender-based social inequality is reinforced by their religion, therefore making it increasingly difficult to move towards civil rights.

Movement towards equality has been in place for some time in the United States but there appears to be a gap between legal equality and equality in social life. The notion that men and women are no different from one another simply does not fit in most cultures. Gender hierarchy organizes society and many argue that an Equal Rights Amendment is urgently needed, seeking a different way to approach gender equality and civil rights.

SEE ALSO: Customary Laws; Gender Redistributive Policies; History of Women's Rights in International and Comparative Perspective; Human Rights, International Laws and Policies on

FURTHER READING

Clark, Charles. 1991. *Sexual Harassment: Men and Women in Workplace Power Struggles*. Washington, DC: Congressional Quarterly.

Cornell University Law School. Legal Information Institute. 14th Amendment. Accessed August 9, 2015, at http://www.law.cornell.edu/constitution/amendmentxiv.

Hudson, David L. Jr. 2002. *The Fourteenth Amendment: Equal Protection Under the Law*. Berkeley Heights: Enslow.

National Archives. 2013. The Civil Rights Act of 1964 and the Equal Employment Opportunity Commission. Accessed August 9, 2015, at http://www.archives.gov/education/lessons/civil-rights-act/.

Class, Caste, and Gender

SMITA M. PATIL
Indira Gandhi National Open University, India

Class, caste, and gender intersect and structure the South Asian polity. Indian society has been caught in the politics of caste through its precolonial, colonial, and postcolonial periods. Caste, for B. R. Ambedkar, is "an enclosed class" (Ambedkar 1989, 15). It also maintains the division of labor and laborers in India. There are four distinct, hierarchical castes in India: the Brahmins (elites, or priestly class), Kshatriyas, Vaishyas, and Sudras, and an even lower caste, the dalits, or untouchables, also exists; the dalit caste has historically been the most oppressed. The castes are hierarchically ranked in terms of purity. Brahmins are considered the most "pure" caste, and the dalits the most "polluted." This strategy of classifying people on the basis of purity and pollution is deployed by the priestly class in order to maintain their power over the lower castes. Caste is a dominant form of mentality in India. Ambedkar argues that "caste is a notion; it is a state of mind. The destruction of caste does not mean the destruction of a physical barrier. It means a notional change" (Ambedkar 1989, 68). His classic idea of caste as a "notion of mind" is being replicated in the contemporary era in a new form.

Caste also determines gender relations. Scholars have observed that Indians are divided through the practice of caste-segregated marriage opportunities. The Brahmins acquired superior caste-based location and maintained caste by prohibiting inter-caste marriages and membership. Marriage between individuals from different castes is prohibited; thus, caste also determines sexuality.

Like caste, gender is subjected to the notions of purity and pollution. Brahmin males are the most pure, while dalit women are the most polluted. Caste-based norms that are prescribed for dalit women determine their sexuality. The ideology of caste has generated the stereotype that these women are women of lower character and morals. Sexual exploitation of dalit women is justified through the caste culture in India. Dalit women are forced to gratify the sexual interests of their upper caste male superiors.

Caste raises major issues related to gender and labor in India. It leads to the oppression of the majority of the landless dalit workers by the land-owning castes. The paths through which women of lower castes have to struggle against systematic caste oppression vary according to different contexts of the nation-state. Economic autonomy of dalit women has enabled them to organize politically and gain social protection via collective assertions. A small section of dalit entrepreneurs are reformulating the meanings of capitalism in the context of caste-based social mobility and accumulation of capital. Dalit capitalism is purported as a defense of capital against the exploitative caste system.

The history of the shifts in the Indian idea of capitalism has to be seen through the conflicting positions within the dalit intelligentsia and also dalit entrepreneurs on the question of capitalism. Ambedkar argued that capitalism and Brahmanism are the enemies of dalits (Teltumbde 2011, 11). It is criticized that the co-optation of Ambedkar by dalit capitalists in order to justify capitalism is problematic in this context. Socialism, for Ambedkar, appeals to the poor and not to the rich. The appropriation of capitalism by dalit entrepreneurs is contradictory to the majority of the poor, oppressed dalits in India. Impoverished dalits outnumber dalits who embrace the logic of capitalism. The larger economic and social inequities loom over the day-to-day life of dalits.

Nevertheless, it is argued that dalit females who own or manage business enterprises are freer than upper caste women. Still, dalit women have to confront the caste stigma related their entry into public spaces. Gopal Guru dismisses dalit capitalism as a "low-intensity spectacle" within the realm of caste, corporate sector, and state. In other words, dalit female's presence in business is overrated in the time of contemporary dalit feminist articulation; dalit women are excluded from knowledge production. Although there has been an increase in the representation of women in education, it has not increased their work participation.

The question of caste, class, and gender is being contested with the emergence of certain women leaders from the dalit community such as Mayavati, former Chief Minister of Uttar Pradesh. Her emergence as a leader is very much a part of the existing political system. It raises questions related to mainstream non-dalit perceptions about a highly socially mobile, dalit woman. Thus, the nuances of caste, class, and gender are reflected through discussions of her political career. It is argued that mainstream media calibrates their caste bias towards leaders such as Mayavati and projects her as autocratic and undemocratic in her dispositions with the people. For example, the statues and monuments that commemorate dalit historical figures, which were constructed during her term as Chief Minister of the state, were criticized as being part of corruption. In contrast, corruption by upper caste politicians in states such as Maharashtra was not publicized.

This is evidence that upper castes are reluctant to accept the social mobility of dalits. They consider socially mobile dalits as a challenge to their monopoly. Dalits have realized that upper castes are not sensitive to the atrocities perpetrated on dalit women in particular and dalits in general. The callous approach of upper castes toward the sexual exploitation of dalit women demonstrates this pathological societal character. In other words, such inhuman acts toward women in general and dalit women in particular are framed on the basis of the caste identities of rapists and victims.

Oppression of women is being operated through the interconnected nodes of class, caste, and gender. Sexual exploitation of plantation workers, according to Ravi Raman (2010), used to happen irrespective of the location of the women as slave laborers or indentured laborers. As a result, some women workers committed suicide as a revolt against such sexual exploitation. Women of northern Kerala were deployed for the sexual needs of European employees and forced to become concubines of the European planters.

Contemporary India is undergoing drastic political change that centers on the axis of class, caste, and gender. Hindu right-wing parties mobilize the middle- and lower-class women who live in the slums. For instance, the female activists of the Hindu right-wing movement in Maharashtra construct their identities by positioning "migrants" from south India, migrants from northern India, and Western women as "others." These others, for Hindutva forces, are projected as some alien characters that have the potential to challenge the labor and culture of Maharashtra. The ideology of caste and class works differently in the context of political agency that challenges the supremacy of caste-based Hindu religion and patriarchy. Anti-caste, middle-class women's organizations based on Dravidian ideology in Tamil Nadu have challenged the Brahmanic superiority without questioning the links between family and caste. For women who belong to lower classes, the aspirations related to their political articulations are also thwarted through the systematic conglomeration of patriarchal ideology that shrouds the lower-class men.

Women workers are governed through familial and masculine political spaces (Fernandes 1997). The broader dimensions of caste, class, and gender are being shaped through the changing economic ideologies and policy regimes. Macro-economic policies give advantage to capital markets and threaten small enterprises. The nature of work is being contained within the ideological forms of caste, class, and gender. It is also observed that domestic work produces divisions between women as employers and workers, which contains class, caste, and ethnicity. Male public space accelerates stigma of women laborers, and intersections of caste, ethnicity, and class in India structure domestic work. Upper- and middle-class/caste women hire women from the lower class and caste (Gothoskar 2013).

The retreat of the state from social security and the reformulation of a socially regulated neoliberal economy have aggravated the new form of Brahmanic articulation against affirmative action for the marginalized sections. The existing divisions among the women from different classes/castes are placated within the construction of women's rights and also a "quota within quota," which signifies the unequal representation driven through caste-gendered social forces. Contextual variations of caste and gender structure the contentions of women's reservation discourse (Menon 2009). The traditional values of caste, gender, and class in turn are being refashioned within neoliberal societal interests.

Norms based on caste, gender, and class reproduce new values that work according to the interests of capitalism. Respectable femininity operates within the global aspirations and family interests in post-liberalization India. It is argued that Indian women who are information technology professionals possess the symbolic capital of respectable femininity. This allows them to adopt global middle-class consumption behaviors, and has created "professional Indian womanhood" (Radhakrishnan 2009).

Social movements have been waging a struggle against the strict divisions of caste, class, and gender for decades. One of the first recorded challenges to the caste system came from B. R. Ambedkar, who burned the ancient Indian legal text *Manusmriti*, which defended the oppression of dalits and women, during a conference at Mahad in Maharashtra state in 1927. He exhorted dalit women to forge their solidarity with the liberating dalit assertions against caste and stressed the inevitable role of dalit women in the field of politics. Ambedkar challenged the patriarchy that exists within the dalit community and the brahmanic patriarchal values of Indian polity. This resulted in a major challenge to the dominant patriarchy in India. It is observed that privileged Brahmin women and the women who belong to the caste hierarchy oppressed dalit women. Ambedkar generated anti-caste political indoctrination among the dalit women and prompted dalit women to discard caste stigma-driven dress codes, ornaments, and occupations as a prelude to their emancipation. During a speech at Kamatipura Vasti, Bombay, in 1936, Ambedkar addressed sexually exploited dalit women and asked them to leave such stigmatizing forms of sexual labor that deny their self-dignity (Ambedkar 2002). He asked dalits to detach themselves from the Hindu religion, which rationalizes such menial labor, and embrace Buddhism, which is premised on gender equality and freedom from oppressive caste ideology.

Yet dalit women are still oppressed by non-dalit men, non-dalit women, and dalit men today; this constitutes a triple form of oppression. There is a conspicuous silence from the hegemonic feminist movements toward the category of caste within Indian feminism. Dalit woman activists from Nepal, such as Durga Sob, argue that mainstream feminist movements in Nepal have failed to address the issues related to dalit women.

The disparities that position women on the basis of caste, class, and gender are being articulated in parallel with academic interpretations of the category of labor. The interlinkages of caste, gender, and class have to be understood in the shifting context of the history of Indian labor. It is contested that the earlier historical accounts of labor are constructed within the modernist approach based on teleological ideas on industrialization and the formation of the modern industrial working class. Thus, there is a conceptual contestation of the idea of class with that of identities based on religion and ethnicity (Joshi 2008). Caste, class, and gender and their manifestations constitute destabilized growth in India.

SEE ALSO: Identity Politics

REFERENCES

Ambedkar, Bhimrao Ramji. 1989. "Castes in India, Their Mechanism, Genesis and Development." *Indian Antiquary*, 1917, 41 (May). In *Babasaheb Ambedkar Writings and Speeches (BAWS)*, edited by Vasant Moon, vol. 1. Bombay: Education Department, Government of Maharashtra.

Ambedkar, Bhimrao Ramji. 2002. *Babasaheb Ambedkar Writings and Speeches (BAWS)*, edited by Vasant Moon, Hari Narke, Ashok Gadghate, M. L. Kasare and N. G. Kamble, vol. 18, Part I (1920–1936): 548–551. Bombay: Education Department, Government of Maharashtra.

Fernandes, Leela. 1997. "Beyond Public Spaces and Private Spheres: Gender, Family, and Working Class Politics in India." *Feminist Studies*, 23(3): 525–547.

Gothoskar, Sujata. 2013. "The Plight of Domestic Workers: Confluence of Gender, Class and Caste Hierarchies." *Economic and Political Weekly*, 48(22): 63–75.

Joshi, Chitra. 2008. "Histories of Indian Labour: Predicaments and Possibilities." *History Compass*, 6(2): 439–454.

Menon, Nivedita. 2009. "Sexuality, Caste, Governmentality: Contests Over 'Gender' in India." *Feminist Review*, 91: 94–112.

Radhakrishnan, Smitha. 2009. "Professional Women, Good Families, Respectable Femininity and the Cultural Politics of 'New' India." *Qualitative Sociology*, 32: 195–212.

Raman, Ravi. 2010. *Global Capital and Peripheral Labour: The History and Political Economy of Plantation Workers in India*. Abingdon: Routledge.

Teltumbde, Anand. 2011. "Dalit Capitalism and Pseudo Elitism." *Economic and Political Weekly*, 46(10): 10–11.

FURTHER READING

Bedi, Tarini. 2006. "Feminist Theory and the Right-Wing: Shiv Sena Women Mobilize Mumbai." *Journal of International Women's Studies*, 7(4): 51–68.

Damodaran, Harish. 2008. *India's New Capitalists: Caste, Business and Industry in a Modern Nation*. Basingstoke: Palgrave Macmillan.

Das, Maitreyi Bordia, and Sonalde Desai. 2003. "Why are Educated Women Less Likely to be Employed in India? Testing Competing Hypothesis." *Social Protection Discussion Paper Series*. Washington, DC: World Bank.

Deshpande, Ashwini, and Smriti Sharma. 2013. "Entrepreneurship or Survival? Caste and Gender of Small Business in India." *Economic and Political Weekly*, 48(28): 38–49.

George, Glynis. 2002. "Four Makes Society: Women's Organization, Dravidian Nationalism and Women's Interpretation of Caste, Gender and Change in South India." *Contributions to Indian Sociology*, 36(3): 495–524.

Ghosh, Jayati. 1994. "Gender Concerns in Macro-Economic Policy", *Economic and Political Weekly*, 29(18): WS2–WS4.

Guru, Gopal. 1995. "Dalit Women Talk Differently." *Economic and Political Weekly*, 30(41–42): 2548–2550.

Guru, Gopal. 2012. " Rise of the 'Dalit Millionaire.' A Low Intensity Spectacle." *Economic and Political Weekly*, 47(50): 41–49.

Hyam, Ronald. 1990. *Empire and Sexuality: British Experience*. Manchester: Manchester University Press.

Patil, Smita M. 2013. "Revitalising Dalit Feminism: Towards Reflexive, Anti-caste Agency of Mang and Mahar Women in Maharashtra." *Economic and Political Weekly*, 48(18): 37–43.

Pattenden, Jonathan. 2011. "Social Protection and Class Relations: Evidence from Scheduled Caste's Women's Associations in Rural South India." *Development and Change*, 42(2): 469–498.

Prasad, Chandrabhan, and Milind Kamble. 2013. "Manifesto to End Caste: Push Capitalism and Industrialisation to Eradicate this Pernicious System." *The Times of India*, January 23, 2013. Accessed February 1, 2013, at http://articles.timesofindia.indiatimes.com/2013-01-23/edit-page/36485155_1_dalit-youth-upper-castes-caste-system.

Rao, Deepa, Randall Horton, and R. Raghuram. 2012. "Gender Inequality and Structural Violence Among Depressed Women in South India." *Social Psychiatry and Psychiatric Epidemiology*, 47: 1967–1975..

Rege, Sharmila. 1988. "Dalit Women Talk Differently: A Critique of 'Difference' and Towards a Dalit Feminist Standpoint." *Journal of Vikas Adhyayan Kendra*, 6(2): 5–23.

Sahni, Rohini, and V. Kalyan Shankar. 2012. "Girls' Higher Education in India on the Road to Inclusiveness: On Track but Heading Where?" *Higher Education*, 63: 237–256.

Sob, Durga. 1977. "Dalit Women within Oppression," *Studies in Nepali History and Society*, 2(2): 348–353.

Tamang, Seira. 2009. "The Politics of Conflict and Difference or the Difference of Conflict in Politics: The Women's Movement in Nepal." *Feminist Review*, 91: 61–80.

Teltumbde, Anand. 2008. *Khairlanji: A Strange and Bitter Crop*. New Delhi: Navayana Publishers.

Teltumbde, Anand. 2010. "Mayavati's Mega Service to the Nation." *Economic and Political Weekly*, 45(15): 12–14.

Teltumbde, Anand. 2013."Delhi Gang Rape Case: Some Uncomfortable Questions." *Economic and Political Weekly*, 48(6): 10–11.

Climate Change and Gender

EDWARD F. HUDSPETH
Henderson State University, Arkadelphia, USA

Hypotheses about climate change as well as research concerning it have existed for nearly two centuries. In the early nineteenth century, much of what was written about climate change was theoretical in nature (Sherwood 2011), but over the last half of a century theoretical concepts have become definable research topics. Key to contemporary climate change research is global warming and its precipitory factor, greenhouse gas emission. Global warming inevitably follows increased greenhouse gas emission, which often requires the use of more natural resources to offset changing climates, the impact of changing rainfall, altered growing seasons, and food production. This pattern becomes cyclical, as greater assets are needed to offset shortfalls, all leading to a greater impact on the environment and humankind.

At first glance, climate and gender may seem unrelated; however, upon closer inspection, it is evident that the two are intricately connected. This relationship is one of dependence as well as impact affecting all individuals, regardless of gender. Be that as it may, some individuals, specifically those in developing countries, are affected at a much broader level than those in advanced societies. Depending on their country or geographic region of the world, many individuals lack the capacity to prepare for and cope with the impact of climate change. This may be more pronounced among the poor and in women (Djoudi and Brochhaus 2011). Denton (2000), when writing about the human dimension of climate change, notes that much of what has been written is theoretical and descriptive in nature, thus lacking the level of empirical validation of the cause–effect research that garners the attention of those solely seeking quantitative proof. As a result, research concerning the full extent of the impact of climate change on gender does not receive the funding that other concerns do. Nevertheless, the impact of climate change can be seen on all aspects of the quality of life of vulnerable populations. Vulnerability takes many forms; however, women often experience more types of vulnerability and are thus impacted more by climate change. To illustrate, an example, which is often discussed in organizational reports and journal articles, is the impact of temperature changes and rainfall amounts on agricultural productivity which in turn affects food security and ultimately health and lifespan.

The interrelated phenomena of greenhouse gas emissions and global warming have detrimental effects on farming, ranching, fishing, food and water security, health, energy assets, and migration. The impact of these phenomena is also greater for women than men. Women in all societies tend to be more vulnerable to or disadvantaged by climate change.

In agrarian societies, as growing seasons shift, individuals have to expend more resources in order to sustain productivity; the same is true when land is over-farmed and the soil becomes depleted of the nutrients necessary to sustain healthy, productive plant life for food for individuals or livestock. When it is not possible to maintain minimal productivity, because resources have been depleted, individuals are faced with the decision to migrate or remain with the hope that things will improve. The outcome is uncertain: remaining means having less and facing starvation and waning health, but migration entails a period of re-establishment prior to potential productivity. According to Carr and Thompson (2014), within many regions of the world, agrarian as well as ranching or fishing dependence can be particularly difficult for women. In these regions, climate change has an impact (productivity) that is compounded by the fact that women tend to have less access to land, fewer financial resources to purchase land or the legal right to own land, thus making them dependent and more vulnerable.

Climate change can also exacerbate water shortages and affect a family's or community's ability to irrigate crops. Water shortage leads to dehydration, which impacts health and an individual's ability to work. In many societies or communities, women have the responsibility of gathering water. So if a community's water supply is low, women must travel farther to collect water, thus needing to spend more time on this task, leaving less time for other tasks. Whether the impact of climate change directly affects productivity or affects water supply, which impacts crop and livestock growth, the outcome is food insecurity as well as financial instability. Also, climate change, via rising sea levels, changes in water temperature and currents, and sea life habitats, can affect communities that rely on fishing. Potable water supplies become scarce as fresh water, in low-lying areas, becomes contaminated by seawater seepage.

Water shortages can lead to unsanitary conditions, whether this is due to cleanliness or reliance on fewer water supplies. When a community has many water supplies, contamination of one by parasites may have minimal effects on health and well-being. However, when the water supply is limited, parasite infestation can greatly debilitate an already suffering community and lead to various disease-related conditions. Without good health individuals become less productive. To complicate this matter, women tend to be family caregivers for their children as well as extended family members, so when children or other family members are ill, women have less time for other responsibilities. As part of a real or perceived societal belief, women often take on caregiving responsibilities while knowing that their time is already in short supply. Women also frequently underreport their own health problems in order to attempt to maintain their diverse responsibilities. Health and health disparities are often more prominent in women because of a lack of resources and an inability to access healthcare.

Health is also affected by climate change. Lack of food leads to malnutrition, potential starvation, and an increased vulnerability to disease. In an attempt to maintain food security and financial stability, there may be a push to grow different crops that are more hardy, which results in a food source change and ultimately dietary change. Dietary changes affect immune systems and the hardiness of a plant or animal does not guarantee that either is of equal nutritional value to the traditional crops and livestock of a region.

Climate change can also have a dramatic effect on the availability of energy resources. As natural resources such as wood for cooking and heat become scarce, people have to spend more time in search of wood in order to survive. Deforestation and droughts hasten the depletion of fuel sources. The more time spent in search of fuel, the less time there is for other responsibilities. As with water collection, women are often responsible for wood collection, thus making them more vulnerable.

Another aspect of climate change is migration. Migration is often a necessity when an area lacks the natural resources necessary for sustainability or when the environment has been depleted of resources. Climate change may have a role in preventing a region from recovering after a natural disaster, or climate change may simply lead to the devastation of a once fertile region. However, migration may not be possible if an individual lacks the resources to migrate. Chindarkar (2012) notes that women may be the least likely and financially capable of migration, and thus this adds to their vulnerability to the effects of climate change. Chindarkar (2012, 4) describes the vulnerability components of climate-induced migration as: (1) exposure; (2) sensitivity; and (3) adaptive capacity. Indicators of exposure are chronic variability and environmental disaster frequency. Indicators of sensitivity are water, land, food, economics, and perceptions. Indicators of adaptive capacity are education, health, livelihood diversification, safety nets and social safeguards, and technological capacity. Therefore, possession of these adaptive capacities, reduced sensitivity, and lower exposure results in less vulnerability but the lack of adaptive capacities, greater sensitivity, and greater exposure results in greater vulnerability, often the case in women.

Gender differences have also been reported based on how women perceive climate change compared with how it is perceived by men. McCright (2010), when discussing the outcome from 8 years of Gallup poll data, noted that women have a greater scientific knowledge about climate change than men, yet women consistently underestimate their knowledge about climate change when compared with men. McCright (2010) also reported that women express slightly greater concern about climate change when compared with the concern about climate change reported by men.

An individual's ability to cope with climate change is determined by individual adaptation factors such as gender, socioeconomic status, education, health, and ability to access resources or a combination of these factors (Chindarkar 2012). The interactional effects of varying levels (low levels equate to less adaptability) of these factors compounds the impact of climate change. Adaptation can be defined simply as an individual or community's ability to reduce vulnerabilities to climate change. Hunter and David (2009, 2) describe a sustainable livelihood framework which includes assets such as human capital, financial capital, physical capital, social capital, and natural capital. These assets are impacted by individual, familial, and/or communal vulnerabilities. To be adaptive, individuals must attain these assets to reduce vulnerabilities and reach a level of sustainability.

Most research reports note that in order for the impact of climate change to be lessened there must be a movement toward global sustainability. Sustainability is not an easy task, especially in those who experience multiple vulnerabilities (i.e., the poor and women).

SEE ALSO: Environment and Gender; Gender Difference Research; Health Disparities

REFERENCES

Carr, Edward R., and Mary C. Thompson. 2014. "Gender and Climate Change Adaptation in Agrarian Settings: Current Thinking, New Directions, and Research Frontiers." *Geography Compass*, 8(3): 182–197. DOI: 10.1111/gec3.12121.

Chindarkar, Namrata. 2012. "Gender and Climate Change-Induced Migration: Proposing a Framework for Analysis." *Environmental Research Letters*, 7: 1–7. DOI: 10.1088/1748-9326/7/2/025601.

Denton, Fatma. 2000. "Gendered Impacts of Climate Change: A Human Security Dimension." *ENERGIA News*, 3(3): 13–14.

Djoudi, Houria, and Maria Brockhaus. 2011. "Is Adaptation to Climate Change Gender Neutral? Lessons from Communities Dependent on Livestock and Forests in Northern Mali." *International Forestry Review*, 13(2): 123–135. DOI: 10.1505/146554811797406606.

Hunter, Lori M., and Emmanuel David. 2009. "Climate Change and Migration: Considering the Gender Dimensions." Working Paper of the Institute of Behavioral Science, Population Program, University of Colorado, Boulder. Accessed August 7, 2015, at http://www.colorado.edu/ibs/pubs/pop/pop2009-0013.pdf.

McCright, Aaron M. 2010. "The Effects of Gender on Climate Change Knowledge and Concern in the American Public." *Population and Environment*, 32: 66–87. DOI: 10.1007/s11111-010-0113-1.

Sherwood, Steven. 2011. "Science Controversies Past and Present." *Physics Today*, 64(10): 39–44.

FURTHER READING

Aboud, Georgina. 2011. *Gender and Climate Change: Supporting Resources Collection*. Bridge: Institute of Development Studies.

Lambrou, Yianna, and Grazia Piana. 2006. "Gender: The Missing Component of the Response to Climate Change." Food and Agriculture Organization of the United Nations (FAO). Accessed August 7, 2015, at http://www.fao.org/docrep/010/i0170e/i0170e00.htm.

United Nations. 2009. "Women, Gender Equality, and Climate Change." UN Women Watch, Fact Sheet. Accessed August 7, 2015, at http://www.un.org/womenwatch/feature/climate_change/downloads/Women_and_Climate_Change_Factsheet.pdf.

United Nations. 2014. "United Nations Framework Convention on Climate Change (UNFCCC) Decisions and Conclusions: Existing Mandates and Entry Points for Gender Equality." Accessed August 7, 2015, at http://unfccc.int/gender_and_climate_change/items/7516.php.

United Nations Population Fund (UNFPA). 2009. *State of World Population* 2009. *Facing a Changing World: Women, Population, and Climate*. New York: UNFPA.

World Health Organization. 2015. "Gender, Climate Change, and Health." Accessed August 7, 2015, at http://www.who.int/globalchange/GenderClimateChangeHealthfinal.pdf.

Clinical Trials and Experimental Science, Bias Against Women in

SUE V. ROSSER
San Francisco State University, USA

Questions about the degree to which concepts of sex and gender influence science and engineering or are deemed appropriate subjects for scientific research and technological manipulation emerge at several levels. Gayle Rubin (1975) described the sex and gender system, distinguishing the biology of sex from the cultural and social construction of gender and revealing the male-centered social processes and practices that constrain and control women's lives. Rubin articulated the connection between biological sex and the social construction of masculinity and femininity that resulted in superiority being attached to what was labeled masculine and discrimination against what was defined as feminine across various societies. Rubin's articulation of the operation of the sex/gender system in a variety of contexts within a society and across societies provoked questions about unequal treatment based on sex/gender in all arenas, including science and technology.

Science may constitute an androcentric province in part because men create science and technology that reflect masculine approaches, interests, and views of the world. This can result partly from science being populated mostly by men. Evelyn Fox Keller (1985) has explored whether the dearth of individuals of one sex has led to the construction of a gendered science.

In the behavioral sciences, investigations of possible sources of bias resulted from the difficulties of studying complex, changing interactions among living beings. For example, the gender, race, class, and even the presence of a researcher during an interview have been shown to influence the responses of the interviewee. Different societies at particular historical periods have also used varying biological and genetic data as determinants for the social construction of gender and race.

Helen Longino (1990) has explored the extent to which methods employed by scientists can be objective (in the sense of not being related to individual values) and can lead to repeatable, verifiable results. These same methods are socially constructed and may contribute to hypotheses or theories that conform to institutions that are not objective and to current ideologies about gender, race, and class. Scientists may calculate rocket trajectories and produce bombs that efficiently destroy living beings without raising the ethical questions of whether the money and effort for this research to support the military could be better spent on other research questions.

Critics reveal that the scientific research undertaken in the United States reflects the societal bias toward the powerful, who are overwhelmingly white, middle or upper class, and male. Given the high costs of sophisticated equipment, maintenance of laboratory animals and facilities, and salaries for qualified technicians and researchers, little behavioral or biomedical research is undertaken without governmental or foundation support. In the United States, the choice of problems for study in medical research is substantially determined by a national agenda that defines what is worthy of study – that is, worth funding. Members of Congress and the individuals in the theoretical and decision-making positions within the medical and scientific establishments that set priorities and allocate funds for research do not exemplify the demographics of the US population. This lack of diversity may allow unintentional, undetected flaws to bias the research in terms of problem choice and approaches to study. Some have pointed out that scarce resources have been diverted away from public health research that could prevent diseases and redirected toward the multibillion-dollar Human Genome Project and personalized medicine. This is one example of placing the interests of the powerful above those of the general public, since gene therapy and designer genes are likely to benefit fewer, wealthier people.

Unintentional bias may be reflected in at least four stages of application of the scientific method: (1) exclusion of females as experimental and design subjects; (2) choice and definition of problems to be studied; (3) methods and approaches used in data gathering; and (4) theories and conclusions drawn from the data.

EXCLUSION OF FEMALES
AS EXPERIMENTAL AND DESIGN
SUBJECTS

Cardiovascular diseases provide an example of the many diseases that occur in both sexes, but from which women were excluded until androcentric bias was revealed in the studies. Research protocols for large-scale studies of cardiovascular diseases failed to assess sex differences. Women were excluded from clinical trials of all drugs in the United States because of fear of litigation resulting from possible damaging effects on fetuses. Exclusion of women from clinical drug trials was so pervasive that a meta-analysis published in September 1992 in the *Journal of the American Medical Association* that surveyed the literature from 1960 to 1991 on clinical trials of medications used to treat acute myocardial infarction found that women had been included in less than 20 percent and the elderly in less than 40 percent of those studies (Gurwitz, Col, and Avorn 1992).

Dominance of men in engineering and the creative design sectors may result in similar bias, especially design and user bias. The air bag fiasco in the US auto industry provides an excellent example of gender bias reflected in design: female engineers on the design team might have prevented the fiasco, recognizing that a bag that implicitly used the larger male body as a norm would be flawed when applied to smaller individuals, killing rather than protecting children and small women. The Clayman Institute for Gender Research at Stanford University, through its Gendered Innovations project, seeks to bring attention to the need for changes in both technology and policy to fit the needs and requirements of women, such as a different seatbelt design for pregnant women and an obligation that the new design be tested on appropriate subjects (pregnant women) before wearing the belt is required by law.

CHOICE AND DEFINITION OF PROBLEMS

A study by Zucker and Beery (2011) found that many articles across all science and medical fields failed to report subject sex at all, while two thirds that included both males and females failed to analyze the data by sex. Some subjects that concern women receive less funding and study.

Excessive focus on male research subjects and definition of cardiovascular diseases as male led to under-diagnosis and under-treatment of those diseases in women. A study in Massachusetts and Maryland (Ayanian and Epstein 1991) demonstrated that women were significantly less likely than men to undergo coronary angioplasty, angiography, or surgery when admitted to the hospital with a diagnosis of myocardial infarction, angina, chronic ischemic heart disease, or chest pain. A similar study (Steingart et al. 1991) revealed that women had angina before myocardial infarction as frequently as and with more debilitating effects than men, yet women were referred for cardiac catheterization only half as often.

In contrast, osteoporosis has been defined traditionally as a disease of postmenopausal white women, since the lifetime incidence of osteoporotic fracture is higher, the average age of onset is earlier, and the fraction of hip fracture in women is more than double that in men. More recent data (Amin 2010) revealed that osteoporosis-related hip fractures result in worse outcomes, including mortality, for men and black women. Studies are currently underway on several continents using male and female reference populations of different races and ethnicities to determine the appropriate cut-off score for diagnosis for both men and non-white women.

Male engineers often create technologies that are useful from a male perspective but fail to address important issues for women users. In addition, the military origins of the development and funding of much technology make its civilian application less useful. Men who design technology for the home frequently focus on issues such as regulation and control of centralized functions rather than those that are more important to women users such as housework.

Scandinavian researchers (Gunnarsson and Trojer 1994) suggested that the creation and protection of human life should be the point of departure for technological development for women. Some of the inventions most useful for women's daily lives, such as Nystatin to prevent yeast infections, the folding crib, pull-down stations for baby changing, and disposable diapers, were invented by women, suggesting that gender of inventor may influence choice of problem to solve.

METHODS AND APPROACHES USED IN DATA GATHERING

Using the white, middle-aged, heterosexual male as the "basic experimental subject" not only ignores the fact that females may respond differently to the variable tested; it also may lead to less accurate models even for many men. For example, the standard dosage of certain medications is inappropriate not only for many women and the elderly, but also for most East Asian men, because of their smaller body size and weight. Recognizing that the bone mineral density (BMD) reference values for white US men proved inappropriate for white Danish men led researchers to new approaches to gather data on secondary contributors to osteoporosis and bone disorders, including exercise level, diet, body composition, tobacco use, and alcohol, in individuals of different sexes, races, and ethnicities in different countries.

Although much research related to HIV microbicides occurs in developed countries, possible future users of such products are in sub-Saharan Africa, where the prevalence of HIV infection is about six times higher than the world average and where 68 percent of HIV infections and 72 percent of HIV-related deaths occur. These HIV microbicides provide ways for women to have more control over HIV protection when they live in cultures where women may have less power to say no to sex or cannot rely on their partners to use condoms. Because gels being developed as microbicides and contraceptives also act as lubricants, they may not be acceptable for women to use in areas where dry sex practices are prevalent, such as rural parts of Zambia. Interdisciplinary collaborations and involving women in developing the research approaches will be needed to find effective means for HIV prevention that are also culturally acceptable.

Science and engineering research typically draws a line between technology developers and technology users. In contrast, participatory research involves the community stakeholders who use the technology in the methods for data gathering and developing the technology. The United Nations has found that in most countries women, who statistically spend significantly more time acquiring water than men, are the primary stakeholders in the water and sanitation sectors and are the primary providers of water for domestic consumption. In Tanzania, a non-governmental organization (NGO) backed by the Swiss Agency for Development and Cooperation used more local women in choosing locations for water wells, resulting in fewer wells that dried up because of the women's knowledge of the relationship between soil conditions and well productivity.

THEORIES AND CONCLUSIONS DRAWN FROM THE DATA

Theories and conclusions drawn from medical research data may be inappropriately extended beyond the population studied, articulated incorrectly, or applied inappropriately to other populations. Often this extension reinforces bias and oppression.

When lesbians are lumped together with heterosexual women in studies of the incidence or cause of sexually transmitted diseases or other gynecological problems from which they are exempt or for which they are at low risk because they do not engage in heterosexual intercourse, this leads to inappropriate conclusions for both lesbians and non-lesbians. Defining results from such studies generally as research on "women's health issues" rather than on "health issues for women engaging in heterosexual sex" leads the general population and some healthcare workers to think that lesbians are at risk for diseases that they are unlikely to contract, while obscuring the true risk behavior for women engaging in heterosexual sex.

Concluding from research data that only one possible design can result may reflect bias and limit exploration of other possible data interpretations. The policy decision by US Secretary of Defense Les Aspin to increase the percentage of women pilots uncovered the gender bias in cockpit design that excluded only 10 percent of male recruits by dimensions as opposed to 70 percent of women recruits. The officers initially assumed that the technology reflected the best or only design possible and that the goal for the percentage of women pilots would have to be lowered and/or the number of tall women recruits would have to be increased. That initial reaction, representing the viewpoint of men, changed when political conditions reinforced the policy goal. A new cockpit design emerged that reduced the minimum sitting height from 34 to 32.8 inches, thus increasing the percentage of eligible women (Weber 1997).

Frequently, designing products or technology for the needs of a particular group viewed as the "other" yields a resulting design or product better for the "norm" as well. For example, the curb cuts designed for wheelchairs also facilitate crossing the street for people with strollers, suitcases on wheels, and other wheeled devices. Raising the question of gender with regard to clinical trials and experimental science results in removing bias to make the subject population more inclusive, broadening the choice of problems and methods of approach. It also ensures application of results to appropriate populations and may expand the theories and conclusions drawn from the data beyond the intended subgroup to benefit the population as a whole.

SEE ALSO: Disability Rights Movement; Feminist Objectivity; Gender Bias in Research; Gender Difference Research; Strong Objectivity; Women's Health Movement in the United States

REFERENCES

Amin, Shreyasee. 2010. "Epidemiology for Fractures." In *Osteoporosis in Men: The Effects of Gender on Skeletal Health*, edited by Eric S. Orwoll, John P. Bilezikian, and Dirk Vanderschueren, 2nd ed., 351–361. London: Elsevier.

Ayanian, John Z., and Arnold M. Epstein. 1991. "Differences in the Use of Procedures between Women and Men Hospitalized for Coronary Heart Disease." *New England Journal of Medicine*, 325: 221–225.

Gunnarsson, Ewa, and Lena Trojer, eds. 1994. *Feminist Voices on Gender, Technology and Ethics*. Luleå, Sweden: University of Technology Centre for Women's Studies.

Gurwitz, Jerry H., Nananda F. Col, and Jerry Avorn. 1992. "The Exclusion of the Elderly and Women from Clinical Trials in Acute Myocardial Infarction." *Journal of the American Medical Association*, 268(8): 1417–1422.

Keller, Evelyn Fox. 1985. *Reflections on Gender and Science*. New Haven: Yale University Press.

Longino, Helen. 1990. *Science as Social Knowledge: Values and Objectivity in Scientific Inquiry*. Princeton: Princeton University Press.

Rubin, Gayle. 1975. "The Traffic in Women: Notes on the 'Political Economy' of Sex." In *Toward an Anthropology of Women*, edited by Rayna Reiter. New York: Monthly Review Press.

Steingart, R. M. et al. 1991. "Sex Differences in the Management of Coronary Artery Disease:

Survival and Ventricular Enlargement Investigator." *New England Journal of Medicine*, 321: 129–135.

Weber, Rachel. 1997. "Manufacturing Gender in Commercial and Military Cockpit Design." *Science, Technology and Human Values*, 22: 235–253.

Zucker, Irving, and Annaliese K. Beery. 2011. "Sex Bias in Neuroscience and Biomedical Research." *Neuroscience and Biobehavioral Reviews*, 35(3): 565.

Clitoridectomy, Female Genital Cutting Practices, and Law

LISA WADE
Occidental College, USA

The phrase female genital cutting (FGC) refers to a set of controversial practices that involve varying degrees of physical alteration to women's genitals. A wide range of practices is included under the label and the reasons communities provide for the cutting also vary, as do the conditions under which they occur. While beliefs about the harmful psychological and physical consequences of the practices are widespread, research documenting these relationships is new and supports only some of the claims of harm. Nevertheless, there is widespread consensus among global powers that the practices should end, making FGC a flashpoint for the theoretical and practical difficulties involved in transnational politics. Efforts to end the practice of FGC in long-practicing communities have been only marginally successful, while immigrants to Western countries tend to voluntarily abandon the practices. Both the practices and opposition to them remain controversial.

The World Health Organization (WHO) estimates that about 140 million girls and women alive today have undergone FGC (WHO 2015). The term is typically used only to refer to genital cutting practices that occur outside of Western contexts – especially Africa, but also sometimes Asia and the Middle East – and among emigrants from those regions. WHO divides the procedures into four categories: clitoridectomy (removal of the clitoral foreskin or part of the clitoris); excision (clitoridectomy plus trimming of the labia minora); infibulation (a fusing of the anterior vulva, sometimes accompanied by clitoridectomy or excision); and a catch-all category that includes all other forms of genital cutting for non-medical purposes (including scarring, pricking, piercing, cauterizing, and scraping of the genitals).

The stated purpose for the cutting varies by ethnic group and has changed over time. Most communities identify it as a coming of age ritual. Religious obligation, aesthetics, feminization of the body, control of women's sexuality, and tradition are sometimes cited as reasons for continuing the practice.

At times the procedures occur in sanitary conditions; other times the conditions are quite dangerous. Access to safe surgical procedures and the training and skill of the practitioner vary as well. Some procedures are performed by poorly trained practitioners, while an increasing number are performed in hospitals and health clinics by medical professionals; many are somewhere inbetween these two poles.

RESEARCH ON HARM

It is routinely stated that FGC is responsible for a wide range of negative health consequences, including psychological trauma (e.g., fear, pain, post-traumatic stress), acute harm (e.g., hemorrhage, shock, infection, death), long-term damage (e.g., lesions, scars, cysts, fistula, urinary retention or incontinence), reproductive complications (e.g., infertility, labor and delivery problems, fetal distress or death), and sexual dysfunction (e.g., lack of arousal, pain during intercourse, anorgasmia).

Research aiming to confirm these assertions is rather recent. Carla Obermeyer (2005) performed a systematic review of the literature on the incidence of negative health consequences. She found statistically significant relationships between FGC and some types of infections but not others, suggestive but not conclusive evidence for problems related to anatomical damage, and mixed evidence for increased levels of obstetric and gynecological problems. She concludes that it is unlikely that research will confirm an increased risk of all of the commonly cited health complications for every variation of genital cutting. That said, most existing studies involve populations that have not undergone infibulation, and increased medicalization of these procedures may be contributing to lower rates of complications.

Obermeyer also considered negative consequences for sexual function and pleasure, cautiously concluding that there was not sufficient evidence for any negative effect. A more recent review concludes the opposite (Berg and Denison 2012). Qualitative research on sexual pleasure suggests that, insofar as genital cutting harms sexual response, it does not do so inevitably or to the same degree for all women (e.g., Dopico in Hernlund and Shell-Duncan 2007). Women who have undergone clitoridectomy or excision, for example, often report a robust sexual appetite and are able to accurately describe the experience of orgasm. Scholars who have themselves undergone genital cutting are among those who contest claims that FGC is always damaging to women's sexuality. Fuambai Ahmadu chose to undergo excision as an adult and argues that women do not necessarily experience a reduction in their ability to enjoy sex (in Shell-Duncan and Hernlund 2000). She observes that the clitoris resides mostly within the body, so all clitoridectomies involve amputation, but not removal of the organ, perhaps leaving the physiological capacity for orgasm. Any measure of sexual dysfunction in women with genital cutting must be considered alongside the significant number of Western and non-Western women who, despite unaltered genitalia, also report problems defined as sexual dysfunction.

No systematic evaluation of the literature on psychological trauma has been conducted. The emotional impact on individuals is probably strongly related to the degree of coercion, nature of the cutting, extent to which they experienced pain and complications, the meaning they assign to the procedure, and the circumstances of their lives. Johansen (2002) offers some insight into these dynamics. She interviewed Somali immigrants to Norway about the pain they experienced during infibulation. They overwhelmingly agreed that the pain was extraordinary, making an indelible mark upon their body and psyche that was with them always, above and beyond later deinfibulation and the health complications they suffered. A silence around the practice in Somalia left many confused about why they had to endure something so agonizing. Meanwhile, immigration had changed many women's perceptions of the necessity of their suffering, shifting their view of the pain in turn.

In contrast, Ahmadu, discussed above, wrote that her own experience was "excruciating," but that the "positive aspects have been much more profound" (in Shell-Duncan and Hernlund 2000, 306). For her, excision was the entrance into a secret society of women who exercise significant power in their communities. Her cohort's shared experience marked them as equals and positioned them in a hierarchy of women who controlled important rights and responsibilities. From her perspective, the ceremony was not an enactment of women's oppression, it was a "celebration of women's preeminent roles in history and society." The ways in which women process the experience of genital cutting are likely varied and complex.

POLITICS AND DISCOURSE

Though it often goes unacknowledged, opposition to FGC within practicing communities long preceded Western involvement (Abusharaf 2006). In almost every country where genital cutting occurs, there is a long history of contention. As Gruenbaum (2001, 32–33) wrote in her influential ethnography: "The women and men of the societies in which circumcision is now practiced are arguing this issue out for themselves … and their ideas are as diverse and varied as the political discourse on women's issues is anywhere."

The modern Western-originated transnational impetus to end the practices began in 1979 when feminist activist Fran Hosken coined the phrase "female genital mutilation" in *The Hosken Report*. Western feminists mobilized by Hosken pressed the United Nations (UN) to start a campaign against the practices. Efforts to facilitate ending FGC found a home in WHO and eradication arguments emphasized the harmful physical effects of the practices. By the 1990s, it became clear that this frame was encouraging medicalization instead of abandonment. By this time, both feminist politics and the human rights frame had gained legitimacy and the campaign refocused, centering opposition on the idea that FGC was violence against women and an effort to control women's sexuality.

Lisa Wade has traced the emergence and trajectory of American discourse about FGC in both the news media and academia (Wade 2011, 2012). Coverage was rare until the publication of *Possessing the Secret of Joy* in 1992. The novel, by the Pulitzer Prize-winning author Alice Walker, tells the story of a woman who suffers devastating physical and psychological harm as a result of genital cutting. Widely discussed in the book review sections of the nation's most high-profile newspapers, the book is responsible for the initiation of American interest in the practices outside of feminist circles. Not only did it attract the interest of readers, but it also inspired powerful media actors to make reporting on FGC a personal priority. These columnists and reporters made a habit of visiting and revisiting the practices. News articles and editorials increased in frequency throughout the early 1990s and peaked in 1996, offering a previously uninformed American public a narrative about the practices. The framing of FGC as an example of cultural barbarism can be traced to the mass media and, within these circles, it has been resistant to change.

Western feminist academics began writing about FGC in earnest in the early 1980s and the conversation quickly became acrimonious. In the early years, most academic engagement with the practices took the form of anthropological ethnographies or eradication-oriented arguments against them. Scholars who brought an aggressively condemnatory approach were quickly balanced by those who opposed the practices but were more cautious in attributing negative characteristics to practicing people and their cultures. By the early 1990s, the academic discourse about FGC had been swept into a larger conversation among feminist scholars about the possibility of "global sisterhood" and the relative benefits and compatibility of multiculturalism and feminism, now known as the postcolonial turn.

The postcolonial critique of Western engagement with FGC was levied broadly at activists, journalists, and scholars (see James and Robertson 2002; Nnaemeka 2005). Critics argued that Western engagement with the practices fed into a larger, culturally imperialist discourse about African backwardness as contrasted with a supposedly rational and civilized West. Specifically, scholars argued that (1) the word "mutilation" was offensive to supporters of the practices and counterproductive for abandonment efforts; (2) the practice was described as "African," though it occurred in only parts of the African continent and elsewhere in the world; (3) the most extensive form of cutting was often falsely used to represent the whole range of practices, even though it accounted for about 15 percent; (4) descriptions of the procedures were sensationalistic, feeding a Western voyeurism for titillating and shocking stories out of Africa; (5) practicing communities were portrayed as primitive and either infantilized or demonized; and (6) there was a failure to also consider female genital cosmetic procedures and male circumcision in the West and elsewhere. In academia, these critiques powerfully shifted the discourse. By the mid-1990s, the majority of published scholarship either adopted or acknowledged the postcolonial critique. Largely in response, many academics choose to call the practices "cutting" instead of "mutilation."

EFFORTS TO END FGC

Despite contentious politics, widely divergent interest groups agree that reducing the incidence of and harm caused by FGC should be a global priority. Elizabeth Boyle's (2002) sweeping analysis of the global spread of formal laws criminalizing FGC showed that both cultural and economic transnational pressure was instrumental in globalizing an anti-FGC agenda, at least in principle. Anti-FGC laws spread during the 1990s and today even countries in which the practices remain common have laws against them. Anti-FGC laws, both in Africa and the West, have been largely unenforced; they have translated into prosecutions only very rarely, except in France. Instead of functioning to penalize individuals who arrange, perform, or facilitate genital cutting, these laws have served a largely symbolic function.

Boyle and Corl (2010) review the strategy of criminalization and its impact in both non-traditionally practicing and traditionally practicing communities. There is some evidence that laws against FGC in non-practicing countries are bad for immigrants and efforts to end the practices. Since the laws simultaneously affirm the dominant global culture and condemn the cultures that have traditionally practiced FGC, they often have the effect of reminding immigrants and refugees that they are not wholly embraced by their host societies. This may discourage them from turning to medical authorities or the police, even if they are inclined to do so. Laws against FGC have also encouraged some families to have their daughters undergo the procedures at younger ages when they are easier to control and less likely to have been exposed to anti-FGC messages. Immigrants may also underreport to legal authorities and on surveys for fear of prosecution and the removal of children from their parents. Laws in non-practicing countries, then, may inhibit the reduction of FGC by making it difficult for immigrants to be open about what is going on in their communities.

Laws, however, may not be essential. Abandonment of the practice may be typical among immigrants to non-practicing societies. Outside of a handful of anecdotal accounts, there is little evidence that daughters of immigrants routinely undergo genital cutting. Studies on populations in Sweden, Australia, the United Kingdom, and Seattle and Minnesota in the United States have found very little evidence that girls commonly, or even infrequently, undergo procedures. They also find a willingness to abandon the practices among parents. These rather rapid cultural changes may be related to fear of prosecution under the law, but are more likely the result of a real desire among migrants to fit into their new societies, a lessening of the pressures and incentives to go through with cutting, and mothers' deep and personal familiarity with the short- and long-term pain that accompanies the practices.

In long-practicing regions, attitudes toward FGC are less positive than they were before the transnational mobilization to end the practices. There is evidence that some communities are turning to less extensive versions of cutting (e.g., moving from infibulation to excision) or adopting entirely symbolic rituals (e.g., Hernlund in Shell-Duncan and Hernlund 2000). In almost all countries for which we have data, rates of FGC have gone down, but only slightly (in parts of Mali and one part of Tanzania, rates have gone up).

Laws, however, have probably played even less of a role in the marginal decline of FGC outside of Western contexts except, perhaps, in communities where FGC is actively contested. The most effective interventions have been village development projects that have no agenda regarding cutting, especially when they are centrally concerned with the lives of women. When women in a community have the power to do so, they often autonomously decide to abandon FGC. Tostan, a development project initiated in Senegal, is a standout example (Tostan 2015).

MEDICALIZATION

An alternative to encouraging the wholesale abandonment of FGC is medicalization, the movement of procedures into hospitals and clinics (see Shell-Duncan, Obiero, and Muruli in Shell-Duncan and Hernlund 2000). Medicalization is defended on two grounds. First, when allowed for adults who opt into the procedure voluntarily, it may be a culturally sensitive alternative to zero-tolerance approaches that simply condemn all procedures and their supporters. This approach is consistent with critics who point to the fact that genital cutting procedures occur in Western societies but, because they are either familiar or medicalized, it is difficult for Westerners to see them as similar to what we call "female genital cutting." These include intersex surgeries, transsexual surgeries, cosmetic surgeries on the vulva, and male circumcision (which is also sometimes performed by non-medically trained staff as a religious ritual).

The second defense of medicalization involves the claim that it will significantly reduce the harm associated with FGC. Though there has been no research on the impact of medicalization, it could arguably reduce some of the psychological trauma, especially the pain and incidence of post-traumatic stress, and the likelihood of acute consequences, hemorrhage, shock, infection, and death. This harm reduction approach, also in contrast to zero tolerance, is a primary strategy of protecting public health in other arenas and some argue that it is equally viable here.

While the benefits and costs of medicalization are strongly contested, the fact of medicalization is not. Genital cutting in clinics and hospitals occurs in many countries with long-practicing communities. There have been efforts to introduce modified genital cutting practices for immigrants to Western countries as well. Individuals in the United States, Italy, and the Netherlands have all proposed modified, medicalized genital cutting procedures for immigrants. In all cases, the proposals have been roundly criticized and efforts to initiate the procedures terminated. As recently as 2010, the American Academy of Pediatrics released a statement endorsing a "ritual nick" as a harm reduction measure. One month later, in response to outcry from feminist and transnational organizations, the Academy revoked its recommendation.

SEE ALSO: Body Politics; Female Genital Cutting; Feminism, Postcolonial; Feminist Activism; Human Rights, International Laws and Policies on; Male Circumcision

REFERENCES

Abusharaf, Rogaia Mustafa. 2006. *Female Circumcision*. Philadelphia: University of Pennsylvania Press.

Berg, Rigmor, and Eva Denison. 2012. "Does Female Genital Mutilation/Cutting (FGM/C) Affect Women's Sexual Functioning? A Systematic Review of the Sexual Consequences of FGM/C." *Sexuality Research and Social Policy*, 9(1): 41–56.

Boyle, Elizabeth. 2002. *Female Genital Cutting: Cultural Conflict in the Global Community*. Baltimore: Johns Hopkins University Press.

Boyle, Elizabeth, and Amelia Corl. 2010. "Law and Culture in a Global Context: Interventions to Eradicate Female Genital Cutting." *Annual Review of Law and Social Science*, 6: 195–215.

Gruenbaum, Ellen. 2001. *The Female Circumcision Controversy: An Anthropological Perspective*. Philadelphia: University of Pennsylvania Press.

Hernlund, Ylva, and Bettina Shell-Duncan, eds. 2007. *Transcultural Bodies: Female Genital Cutting in Global Context*. New Brunswick: Rutgers University Press.

James, Stanlie, and Claire Robertson, eds. 2002. *Genital Cutting and Transnational Sisterhood: Disputing U.S. Polemics*. Chicago: University of Illinois Press.

Johansen, R. Elise. 2002. "Pain as a Counterpoint to Culture: Toward an Analysis of Pain Associated with Infibulation among Somali Immigrants in Norway." *Medical Anthropology Quarterly*, 16(3): 312–340.

Nnaemeka, Obioma, ed. 2005. *Female Circumcision and the Politics of Knowledge: African Women in Imperialist Discourses*. Westport, CT: Praeger.

Obermeyer, Carla Makhlouf. 2005. "The Consequences of Female Circumcision for Health and Sexuality: An Update on the Evidence." *Culture, Health and Sexuality*, 7(5): 443–461.

Shell-Duncan, Bettina, and Ylva Hernlund. 2000. *Female "Circumcision" in Africa: Culture, Controversy, and Change*. Boulder, CO: Lynne Rienner.

Tostan: Dignity for All. 2015. "The Tostan Model." Accessed August 10, 2015, at http://www.tostan.org/.

Wade, Lisa. 2011. "Journalism, Advocacy, and the Social Construction of Consensus." *Media, Culture & Society*, 33(8): 1166–1184.

Wade, Lisa. 2012. "Learning from 'Female Genital Mutilation': Lessons from 30 Years of Academic Discourse." *Ethnicities*, 12(1): 26–49.

World Health Organization (WHO). 2015. "Female Genital Mutilation." Accessed August 10, 2015, at http://www.who.int/mediacentre/factsheets/fs241/en/.

Cognitive Critical and Cultural Theory

CHRISTA KNELLWOLF KING
Sultan Qaboos University, Oman, and University of Queensland, Australia

Exciting developments in critical and cultural theory are currently emerging in response to the neuroscientific change of direction during the 1990s, which occasioned a revised understanding of brain and mind. The disciplinary area that can broadly be called cognitive studies, or cognitive critical and cultural theory, is opening up valuable perspectives on the processes by which the mind registers information and records it in retrievable fashion, and by doing so collects what is known as experience (Solms and Turnbull 2002). In principle, the new ideas about the architecture of the mind provide new tools for challenging gender stereotypes. However, the empirical methods employed by brain research have also been used to confirm heavily disputed ideas about the supposedly natural characteristics and propensities of men and women, and have therefore been severely criticized by feminist scholars (Falmagne 2000; Schmitz 2014).

Applications of the new theories in psychological and sociological research are giving rise to a new understanding of the rationale of human behavior and social interactions. For example, empirical research is revising established views about the complex social interactions that can make people adopt certain behavior. A vibrant new area of analysis concentrates on the neural processes of motivation (Ferguson 2000; French 2001), which, in their turn, demand a revised understanding of the cultural conditioning of education, upbringing, and socialization. However, empirical research has the tendency to essentialize. This means that it documents culturally evolved patterns of behavior as if they were biologically given facts (Koppensteiner and Grammer 2011).

The aura of objectivity that clings to the methodologies of the natural sciences favors mechanistic and deterministic models, especially if their explanations reduce the extraordinary complexity of the topic. However, there is no doubt that neuroscientific approaches are triggering dramatic reorientations in the humanities and social sciences concerning the possibilities of relating experience that is represented in the minds of people to experience that is represented in the form of literature and culture.

The neurosciences have provided new impetus to the development of critical theories (Stockwell 2007; Zunshine 2010), which in their turn inspire new approaches to interpretation. For scholars in the humanities, it is a fascinating challenge to speculate, for example, about the implications of Antonio Damasio's claim that "the self" should be understood as a process rather than an "object" (Damasio 2010, 8). Such a model pushes the power of our imagination to its limits. However, it also confirms the premises of cultural theories which describe identity as a process that continues for the entire duration of a person's life.

Ever since Simone de Beauvoir stated that "One is not born, but rather becomes, a woman," it has been accepted that gender roles are called into existence by cultural practices. Interrogating and applying the scientific arguments in the humanities and social sciences, cognitive theories can offer new explanations of how and why established practices have an extraordinary capacity to reproduce themselves.

Neuroscientific research has revealed that the mind not only retrieves the entirety of information that has been collected in the course of an individual's life but also that it establishes mental databases. The concepts "schema," "frame," and "script" were coined in order to describe how the mind develops certain patterns for storing information so that it is available as a point of reference at a later stage. In the 1970s, Reuven Tsur was one of the first scholars to apply cognitive models to the interpretation of literature and culture (Tsur 1992; Stockwell 2002).

Empirical research has shown that the mind organizes information in a manner that permits new information to be compared continuously against similar types of information. In other words, the responses to any concrete situation are modeled on similar experiences that were collected in the past (Semino and Culpeper 2002). Precisely because these organizing principles encourage the repetition of types of behavior that were used in the past, it is extremely difficult to adjust established habits of making sense of the world. Stuart Hall addresses this observation when he argues that practices are always grounded in previous practices (Hall 1997). An example to illustrate this is that people (men and women) who have been physically, sexually, and/or emotionally abused in the past have an almost uncanny tendency to enter into a relationship with a similarly abusive partner in the future. Given that practices also include practices of interpretation, we gain a new perspective on why the habits of interpretation that are brought to bear on particular representations are such seminal instruments for the creation of cultures of consent, for example, about the understanding of gender roles.

THEORIES AND HISTORIES OF EMOTION

A further major development in the humanities and social sciences concerns the emphasis on studying the history and the social significance of representations of emotion. Studies of emotion have traditionally played a major role in feminist critiques of experience and its representation. Feminist approaches to literature and culture have always had to grapple with deeply rooted stereotypes concerning women's supposedly natural proclivity towards emotionality while reserving rationality as a prerogative of the male gender. According to a populist weighting, rationality was valued while the emotions were discredited. It was in fact frequently argued that women were inferior precisely because they were supposed to be less capable of controlling their emotions than men. The belief in a gendered distribution of the modalities for the expression of emotion survived all feminist efforts to describe gendered behavior as the result of the cultural conditioning of upbringing and socialization.

The recent upsurge of interest in studying emotion has also been motivated by neuroscientific conclusions that emotion is inseparable from cognition. Furthermore, far from accepting that emotions are irrational eruptions of a confused mind, empirical studies have described them as responses that make sense in a particular context (Griffiths 1997, 9): for example, responding angrily when somebody interrupts a presentation is a perfectly rational means of minimizing future interruptions.

Neuroscientific studies have also shown that the emotion–cognition nexus is necessarily embodied, hence giving rise to "embodied cognition" (Borghi and Cimatti 2010) as another new subdiscipline.

Antonio Damasio (1995) and Joseph LeDoux (1998), the brain researchers who spearheaded a new account of the impossibility of describing cognition and emotion as separate phenomena, proposed that "emotion" and "feeling" should be used to differentiate between the physical experience of an emotion and its expression in a culturally defined signifying code (or language). In literary studies, some critics have tried to differentiate between "emotions" and "affects." However, since it is impossible to register a "pure" emotion (that is, an emotion that has not been mediated by cultural traditions of describing physical experience), the three terms "emotion," "feeling," and "affect" are used largely synonymously.

The question of why there is a powerful compulsion to repeat patterns of behavior was addressed by Sigmund Freud in the early twentieth century. A new approach to the conundrum of why even overtly self-destructive forms of behavior are repeated is provided by a more recent strand of psychological analysis that is inspired by the neurosciences: emotion regulation (Gross 2007). Studies of the force of social pressure on the formation of emotions are based on the assumption that the way we feel about ourselves and our environment is the result of life-long habits of socialization.

Upbringing and socialization do not only inculcate standards of behavior. Even more importantly, they enforce "emotional regimes," that is, they dictate what are considered to be appropriate emotions. For example, children are taught that it is appropriate to be sad when somebody dies, regardless of whether they liked the deceased person or not. They are also taught to establish certain feelings about themselves: their potential capacities for success, their ideas about entitlements to privileges and financial rewards, and also their understanding of happiness. Sara Ahmed has studied the significance of socially sanctioned stories of success for the development of male and female individuals' conception of an ideal future (Ahmed 2010). The force of success stories – or by contrast, the force of cautionary tales – lies in the emotions associated by the narrative with the outcome of the behavior described by them. This is an immensely complex area where much future research is still needed. Emotion regulation is a new area of interest in psychology whose ramifications on the formation of personality traits and identity (and their representation in literature and culture) is only starting to be recognized.

The work by Paul Ekman (1997) has overturned another popular belief about the emotions. He has shown that far from being private experiences, emotions express themselves physically and are used, like a language, to communicate how we feel about issues and people. Emotions are social phenomena because they invite the participants of a communicative situation to read them, or rather, to deduce the messages expressed by them. Emotions are displayed in a whole range of non-verbal media: facial expressions, postures and gestures, tone of voice.

That the emotions are described as profoundly social instruments (Griffiths 1997) is raising a number of questions about the ways and means by which social norms and even identities might be defined by processes of emotion regulation. Recent studies in empirical psychology have demonstrated that human interactions are underpinned by incessant attempts to figure out the emotional responses of an interlocutor to the messages which are communicated and the person who participates in an act of communication. In light of this research it seems that the tendency toward repetition (of positive and negative patterns of behavior) is occasioned by the feedback loops by which an individual's emotions related to the self and its place in a social community are being defined and confirmed over a lifetime.

MIND READING AND THEORIES OF READING

The recognition of the profound importance of social exchanges, and feedback loops, by which the participants of face-to-face communications seek to evaluate the attitudes toward themselves and what they are saying, has given rise to a further influential subdiscipline in cognitive studies: mind reading, or theory of mind.

Mind reading is the practice of ascribing a state of mind to others in order to be prepared for their responses. For instance, by calculating the likelihood of whether an interlocutor might respond with physical aggression, we are preparing ourselves to act without losing any time. This means that hypotheses are formed on the basis of reading facial expressions, gestures, tone of voice, the constellation of circumstances, and so on. This is a skill without which humans cannot function effectively in social environments (Turner 1994).

Mind reading is a useful tool for explaining and negotiating the complex web of social interrelations of ordinary life, and it also offers a new perspective on the human relationships which are portrayed in literary and cultural works. Studies of how people attribute motives and emotional states to others is an immensely useful tool for explaining the "social dialogue" that is taking place, for example, in the portrayals of gender relations in Hollywood films. It can also offer a new perspective on the function played by literature and culture in the consolidation (and interrogation) of established beliefs, for example, about the motives and desires of male and female characters interpreted as representatives of male and female gender categories.

Important research questions evolving in this context concern the development of new approaches to studying the reception and "uses" of literature (Felski 2008). Rather than concentrating on the meanings of a literary work, new research directions discuss literature as an act of communication – involving writers, readers, publishers, funding, and educational institutions. Yet another area of interest in the field of cognitive studies is therefore devoted to studying the mental processes involved in reading and making sense of the messages embraced by literature, advertising, film, and visual culture (Gerrig 1993; Herman 2003; Miall 2003). Emphasis on the way in which literature functions (rather than its formal aspects and meanings) is currently opening up a new understanding of how literature establishes shared experience, and both challenges and proposes socially defined standards and values.

SEE ALSO: Cognitive Sex Differences, Debates on; Domestic Violence in the United States; Emotion Work; Emotional Abuse of Women; Essentialism; Feminist Theories of Experience; Gender as a Practice; Gender, Definitions of; Gender Role Ideology; Gender Schema Theory; Gender Stereotypes; Gender-Based Violence; Language and Gender; Neuroscience, Brain Research, and Gender; Neuroscience, Brain Research, and Sexuality; Representation

REFERENCES

Ahmed, Sara, 2010. *The Promise of Happiness*. Durham, NC: Duke University Press.

Borghi, Anna M., and Felice Cimatti. 2010. "Embodied Cognition and Beyond: Acting and Sensing the Body." *Neuropsychologia*, 48: 763–773.

Damasio, Antonio. 1995. *Descartes' Error: Emotion, Reason and the Human Brain*. London: Picador.

Damasio, Antonio. 2010. *Self Comes to Mind: Constructing the Conscious Brain*. London: Vintage Books.

Ekman, Paul, ed. 1997. *What the Face Reveals: Basic and Applied Studies of Spontaneous Expressions Using the Facial Action Coding System*. New York: Oxford University Press.

Falmagne, Rachel Joffe. 2000. "Deconstructing Cognitive Psychology: A Feminist Critical Opening." *Theory and Psychology*, 10(2): 277–282.

Felski, Rita. 2008. *The Uses of Literature*. Oxford: Blackwell.

Ferguson, Eva Dreikurs. 2000. *Motivation: A Biosocial and Cognitive Integration of Motivation and Emotion*. New York: Oxford University Press.

French, Jeffrey A., ed. 2001. *Evolutionary Psychology and Motivation*. Lincoln: University of Nebraska Press.

Gerrig, Richard. 1993. *Experiencing Narrative Worlds: On the Psychological Activities of Reading*. New Haven: Yale University Press.

Griffiths, Paul E. 1997. *What Emotions Really Are: The Problem of Psychological Categories*. Chicago: University of Chicago Press.

Gross, James J., ed. 2007. *Handbook of Emotion Regulation*. New York: Guilford.

Hall, Stuart. 1997. "Representation, Meaning and Language." In *Representation: Cultural Representations and Signifying Practices*, edited by Stuart Hall, 15–74. London: Sage.

Herman, David, ed. 2003. *Narrative Theory and the Cognitive Sciences*. Stanford: CSLI.

Koppensteiner, Markus, and Karl Grammer. 2011. "Body Movements of Male and Female Speakers and Their Influence on Perceptions of Personality." *Personality and Individual Differences*, 51(6): 743–747.

LeDoux, Joseph. 1998. *The Emotional Brain*. New York: Simon and Schuster.

Miall, David S. 2005. "Beyond Interpretation: The Cognitive Significance of Reading." In *Cognition and Literary Interpretation in Practice*, edited by Harri Veivo, Bo Petterson, and Merja Polvinen, 129–156. Helsinki: Helsinki University Press.

Schmitz, Sigrid, ed. 2014. *Gendered Neurocultures: Feminist and Queer Perspectives on Current Brain Discourses*. Vienna: Zaglossus.

Semino, Elena, and Jonathan Culpeper, eds. 2002. *Cognitive Stylistics: Language and Cognition in Text Analysis*. Amsterdam: John Benjamins.
Solms, Mark, and Oliver Turnbull. 2002. *The Brain and the Inner World: An Introduction to the Neuroscience of Subjective Experience*. London: Karnac Books.
Stockwell, Peter. 2002. *Cognitive Poetics: An Introduction*. London: Routledge.
Stockwell, Peter. 2007. "Cognitive Poetics and Literary Theory." *Journal of Literary Theory*, 1(1): 135–152.
Turner, Mark. 1994. *Reading Minds: The Study of English in the Age of Cognitive Science*. Princeton: Princeton University Press.
Tsur, Reuven. 1992. *Toward a Theory of Cognitive Poetics*. Amsterdam: Elsevier.
Zunshine, Lisa, ed. 2010. *Introduction to Cognitive Cultural Studies*. Baltimore: Johns Hopkins University Press.

FURTHER READING

Bluhm, Robyn, Anne Jaap Jacobson, and Heidi Lene Maibom, eds. 2012. *Neurofeminism: Issues at the Intersection of Feminist Theory and Cognitive Science*. London: Palgrave Macmillan.
Easterlin, Nancy. 2012. *A Biocultural Approach to Literary Theory and Interpretation*. Baltimore: Johns Hopkins University Press.
Hogan, Patrick Colm. 2011a. *What Literature Teaches Us About Emotion*. Cambridge: Cambridge University Press.
Hogan, Patrick Colm, ed. 2011b. *The Cambridge Encyclopedia of the Language Sciences*. Cambridge: Cambridge University Press.
Johnson, Mark. 1987. *The Body in the Mind: The Bodily Basis of Meaning, Imagination, and Reading*. Chicago: University of Chicago Press.
Opdahl, Keith. 2002. *Emotion as Meaning: The Literary Case for How We Imagine*. Lewisburg: Bucknell University Press.
Rose, Nikolas, and Joelle M. Abi-Rached. 2013. *Neuro: The New Brain Science and the Management of the Mind*. Princeton: Princeton University Press.
Stockwell, Peter. 2009. *Texture: A Cognitive Aesthetics of Reading*. Edinburgh: Edinburgh University Press.
Wilson, Elizabeth A. 1998. *Neural Geographies: Feminism and the Microstructure of Cognition*. London: Routledge.

Cognitive Sex Differences, Debates on

EMILY K. CLARKE and JANET HYDE
University of Wisconsin–Madison, USA

Mathematical, verbal, and spatial abilities are three domains that have been stereotyped as showing gender differences, with males outperforming females in mathematical and spatial skills and females outperforming males in verbal skills. This entry reviews contemporary scientific evidence on whether there are gender differences in these three domains. Although for decades the prevailing thought was that males outperformed females in math, this is no longer the case. Over the past 30 years the gender gap has narrowed to the point where females have reached parity with males in math performance. Regardless of the narrowing gender gap, males disproportionately dominate in math-intensive STEM (science, technology, engineering, and medicine) fields. The female advantage in verbal ability is small. A male advantage in spatial performance, particularly in mental rotation, has been implicated in male STEM dominance. Newer research, however, has suggested that spatial skills, especially mental rotation, can be trained to the point of greatly reducing the gender spatial gap.

MATHEMATICAL PERFORMANCE

Prior to 1990, the majority of studies showed clear gender differences in math performance at all grade levels. Meta-analysis is very relevant in this area of research; it is a statistical method that allows the researcher to combine results from all previous studies of a given question. Meta-analysis can evaluate what the direction of the difference is (males scoring higher or females scoring higher) and how large the gender difference is (large, medium, small, or no difference). A 1990 meta-analysis of existing North American research indicated that males outperformed females, but only by a small amount (Hyde, Fennema, and Lamon 1990). The most up-to-date evidence is a 2010 meta-analysis, which found that there are no longer any gender differences in math performance in the United States, although this is not true in every nation (Lindberg et al. 2010).

The content and presentation of math tests play a role in the magnitude of gender differences. Some studies find that males show slightly superior performance in problem-solving and geometry tasks, whereas females tend to show slightly superior performance in computation tasks. Regardless of content, multiple choice math tests favor males, whereas short answer and open-ended math tests favor females.

Gender differences are also present in personal and societal attitudes regarding math ability. Mathematics is stereotyped as a male domain. Males report a higher math self-concept (more confidence in their math ability) than females do, and females report more math anxiety than males.

Gender differences in math performance have also been studied internationally. The results show that some nations have a larger gender gap, whereas some nations have none at all. Across nations, measures of nations' gender inequality correlate significantly with the magnitude of gender differences in math achievement (Else-Quest, Hyde, and Linn 2010). That is, nations that have more gender inequality at a societal level also tend to have large gender gaps in math performance, and nations with more gender equality tend to have no gender gap.

Researchers have found that there is an implicit, or non-conscious, association between "math" and "male" as measured by reaction times. Data across many nations indicate that nations in which people have stronger implicit associations between "male" and "math" also tend to have larger gender differences in math performance (Nosek et al. 2009).

Males tend to dominate upper-level STEM fields, such as physics and engineering. One potential explanation for this is the greater male variability hypothesis. It states that males are more variable (show greater variance from the mean) than females for traits such as intelligence. This means that there would be an excess of males at the top of the ability distribution, but also an excess of males at the bottom. Males do represent a higher proportion of performance at the 99th percentile of math skill – 67 percent of 99th percentile performers are males, whereas 33 percent are females (Hyde et al. 2008). However, cultural factors may be at work in creating the pool of highly talented male mathematicians. For example, parents and teachers may be more likely to notice and cultivate exceptional math talent in boys compared with girls.

VERBAL ABILITY

Contrary to stereotypes, a meta-analysis found that the gender difference in verbal skills, although it favors females, is small when averaged over all types of verbal performance (Reilly 2012). The size of the female advantage varies by the subjects tested. Overall, females outperform males in both reading and writing performance. Females have small advantages in general verbal ability, anagram solving, verbal fluency, and reading comprehension. Males have advantages in retrieval of picture names, retrieval of definitions, and analysis of relationships among words.

SPATIAL ABILITY

The gender difference in spatial ability, with males outperforming females, is larger than the differences in math performance and verbal ability. It is moderate in magnitude and observed cross-culturally (Voyer, Voyer, and Bryden 1995). There are multiple types of spatial ability, tapped by different types of tests. The largest gender difference, moderate in magnitude, is found on mental rotation tests, which measure the ability to rotate a two- or three-dimensional figure rapidly and accurately.

The gender difference in mental rotation can depend on the administration of the test. Tests that award no penalties for guessing tend to show a stronger gender difference favoring males. Individual testing also favors males, and tests with short time limits favor males.

Although the gender differences in spatial skills seem fairly robust, there is also evidence that spatial ability can be trained (Uttal et al. 2013). Training methods such as video gaming, instructional courses, and specific practice can improve spatial skills substantially. It is possible for these training effects to endure over time with robust methods. Despite the evidence that spatial skills can improve with training and practice, a spatial curriculum is rarely found in schools. Such curricula could have a major impact on closing the gender gap in spatial performance.

SEE ALSO: Women in Science

REFERENCES

Else-Quest, Nicole M., Janet S. Hyde, and Marcia C. Linn. 2010. "Cross-National Patterns of Gender Differences in Mathematics: A Meta-Analysis." *Psychological Bulletin*, 136: 103–127. DOI: 10.1037/a0018053.

Hyde, Janet S., Elizabeth Fennema, and Susan J. Lamon. 1990. "Gender Differences in Mathematics Performance: A Meta-Analysis." *Psychological Bulletin*, 107: 139–155. DOI: 10.1037/0033-2909.107.2.139.

Hyde, Janet S., Sara M. Lindberg, Marcia C. Linn, Amy B. Ellis, and Caroline C. Williams. 2008. "Gender Similarities Characterize Math Performance." *Science*, 321: 494–495. DOI: 10.1126/science.1160364.

Lindberg, Sara M., Janet S. Hyde, Jenni Petersen, and Marcia C. Linn. 2010. "New Trends in Gender and Mathematics Performance: A Meta-Analysis." *Psychological Bulletin*, 136: 1123–1135. DOI: 10.1037/a0021276.

Nosek, Brian A., et al. 2009. "National Differences in Gender-Science Stereotypes Predict National Sex Differences in Science and Math Achievement." *Proceedings of the National Academy of Sciences of the United States of America*, 106: 10593–10597. DOI: 10.1073/pnas.0809921106.

Reilly, David. 2012. "Gender, Culture, and Sex-Typed Cognitive Abilities." *PLoS ONE*, 7(7): e399040. DOI: 10.1371/journal.pone.0039904.

Uttal, David H., et al. 2013. "The Malleability of Spatial Skills: A Meta-Analysis of Training Studies." *Psychological Bulletin*, 139: 352–402. DOI: 10.1037/a0028446.

Voyer, Daniel, Susan Voyer, and Philip M. Bryden. 1995. "Magnitude of Sex Differences in Spatial Abilities: A Meta-Analysis and Consideration of Critical Variables." *Psychological Bulletin*, 117: 250–270. DOI: 10.1037/0033-2909.117.2.250.

FURTHER READING

Gerson, Helena B. P., Sheryl A. Sorby, Anne Wysocki, and Beverly J. Baartmans. 2001. "The Development and Assessment of Multimedia Software for Improving 3-D Visualization Skills." *Computer Applications in Engineering Education*, 9: 105–113. DOI: 10.1002/cae.1012.

Maeda, Yukiko, and So Yoon Yoon. 2013. "A Meta-Analysis on Gender Differences in Mental Rotation Ability Measured by the Purdue Spatial Visualization Tests: Visualization of Rotations (PSVT:R)." *Educational Psychology Review*, 25: 69–94. DOI: 10.1007/s10648-012-9215-x.

Cohabitation and *Ekageikama* in the Kandyan Kingdom (Sri Lanka)

KALINGA TUDOR SILVA
University of Peradeniya, Sri Lanka

Cohabitation refers to a living arrangement where an unmarried couple lives together in a socially accepted long-term relationship inclusive of sexual intimacy. There were several patterns of heterosexual cohabitation in the Kandyan Kingdom (1463–1815). *Ekageikama* (literally, eating together in the same house) involved a polyandrous union where two or more male siblings lived with a common wife who was married to one of them, usually the oldest one, but had consensual sexual alliances with one or more of his male siblings without necessarily going through any kind of formalization of such alliances. In addition to this form of adelphic/fraternal polyandry, there were also some instances of polygyny, monogamous cohabitations, and extramarital cohabitations usually of a hypergamous nature, where a higher-caste man had a lower-caste woman as his mistress.

Of the various forms of cohabitation in the Kandyan Kingdom, adelphic polyandry (*ekageikama*) received wider attention as it was considered an important feature of the Kandyan kinship system, which was of a bilateral character (Pieris 1956; Tambiah 1965, 1966; Hiatt 1980). In the Kandyan Kingdom polyandry was rather uncommon, and where it was found it was usually of the adelphic type. Having surveyed areas under the former Kandyan Kingdom, Lawrie (1899), for instance, noted that polyandry was the exception rather than the rule. In adelphic polyandry the relationship among the co-husbands, between them and the common wife, as well as between the children born to such unions and their multiple parents was determined according to kinship norms and customary sanctions. For instance, Niti Niganduwa, a treatise on Kandyan customary laws, not only recognized such cohabitations but also specified laws of inheritance applicable to such unions. The children would address one of the cohabiting male siblings, usually the person to whom their mother was formally married, as their father and his brothers as *mahappa* (father's older brother) or *kudappa* (father's younger brother), in keeping with the classificatory kinship terminology in Kandyan society. Sexual relations among partners were typically consensual with none of the co-husbands having a sexual monopoly over the common wife. The symbolic display of the loincloth worn by the man over the door in the room where one of the brothers slept with the woman symbolized possible sexual intimacy between them on a given night (Modder 1898). Tambiah (1965) noted that male siblings involved in a polyandrous relationship in Kandyan society were typically not adjacent but distant in the birth order, with a corresponding age gap among them. It was not uncommon for younger male siblings in a polyandrous union to break away from it and set up a separate monogamous union with another woman once they reached the marriageable age.

From a structural functional perspective adelphic polyandry was considered a social adaptation to prevailing circumstances in the Kandyan Kingdom. The Kandyan feudal order involved a service tenure system (*rajakariya*) under which the peasantry held land subject to mandatory provision of certain services to the state in the form of participation in either periodic military service or corvee labor needed for the upkeep of public works (Pieris 1956). This, in turn, often meant that one of the adult males in a household was away from home for some months each year. Under these circumstances adelphic polyandry enabled the households to better cope with the demands of the state on the one hand, and the need for a male caretaker and regular farm hands at the household level on the other. A similar pattern was involved in labor organization in chena (swidden) cultivation where one of the male household members needed to be away from home for some months of the year protecting crops against wild animals. More importantly adelphic polyandry prevented fragmentation of landholdings among male heirs in a family if they each contracted a separate monogamous marriage. This was particularly important in the hilly Kandyan Kingdom where farmland was scarce and the prevailing bilateral inheritance pattern had a natural tendency to subdivide property when it was transmitted from one generation to the next. Customary Kandyan marriage practices, including cross-cousin marriage and polyandry, served to conserve ancestral property within closely knit kinship networks. Literature from other polyandrous societies in South Asia (e.g., Tibetans in Nepal) suggests that adelphic polyandry also served to contain population growth and overcome demographic imbalances caused by the scarcity of females, which in turn resulted from higher female mortality and the female infanticide practiced in those societies (Goldstein 1976). How far this explanation had any relevance to the Kandyan society is not clear from the available data.

How various forms of cohabitation in Kandyan society affected the status and agency of women requires further research. In *ekageikama* the consent of the woman was reportedly required for sexual union with any male siblings of the original husband (Panabokke 1898). How far she was able to exercise her choice in mate selection cannot be determined from the available literature. Of the two customary forms of marriage in Kandyan society, the virilocal (*deega*) marriage, where property transmission as well as control over female labor and female sexuality were vested in the male line, was more common. On the other hand, uxorilocal (*binna*) marriage strengthened the hands of the wife both in terms of property rights and household decision-making in general.

Traditional forms of cohabitation in Kandyan society gradually declined due to the impact of colonialism and processes of modernization and Westernization, including legal reform. Legislation introduced by the British Raj in 1859 made monogamy the only legally sanctioned form of marriage in British Ceylon. This, in turn, led to the gradual disappearance of all traditional forms of cohabitation, including polyandry, in Sri Lankan society in general.

SEE ALSO: Polygamy, Polygyny, and Polyandry

REFERENCES

Goldstein, Melvyn C. 1976. "Fraternal Polyandry and Fertility in a High Himalayan Valley in Northwest Nepal." *Human Ecology*, 4(3): 223–233.

Hiatt, L. R. 1980. "Polyandry in Sri Lanka: A Test Case for Parental Investment Theory." *Man, n.s.* 15(4): 583–602.

Lawrie, A. C. 1899. "The Custom of Polyandry as Practiced in Ceylon." In *Papers of the Custom of Polyandry as Practiced in Ceylon*. Manchester: University of Manchester (Foreign and Commonwealth Office Collection).

Modder, F. H. 1898. "The Custom of Polyandry in Kurunagala District." In *Papers of the Custom of Polyandry as Practiced in Ceylon*. Manchester: University of Manchester (Foreign and Commonwealth Office Collection).

Panabokke, T. B. 1898. "The Custom of Polyandry in Matale District." In *Papers of the Custom of Polyandry as Practiced in Ceylon*. Manchester: University of Manchester (Foreign and Commonwealth Office Collection).

Pieris, Ralph. 1956. *Sinhalese Social Organization*. Colombo: University of Ceylon Press.

Tambiah, S. J. 1965. "Kinship Fact and Fiction in Relation to the Kandyan Sinhalese." *Journal of the Royal Anthropological Institute of Great Britain and Ireland*, 95(2): 131–173.

Tambiah, S. J. 1966. "Polyandry in Ceylon." In *Caste and Kin in Nepal, India and Ceylon*, edited by C. von Fuhrer-Haimendorf, 264–358. London: Asia Publishing House.

Colonialism and Gender

NARIN HASSAN
Georgia Institute of Technology, USA

Studies of European imperialism constitute a large body of interdisciplinary scholarship encompassing the fields of history, literature, anthropology, political science, and psychology. Within this scholarship, analyzing the intersections of gender and colonialism has become critical to understanding the dynamics and long-term impact of imperial rule. Especially within the past four decades, studies of gender have formed a large area of research within broader analyses of European empires. While reading gender is recognized as critical in the study of colonialism, it is not a unified or static category. There were multiple notions of gender over the various historical stages of colonialism, and gender intersected with categories such as race, sexuality, and class which were also at work within imperial realms. Further, meanings of gender were shaped, challenged, and re-articulated through colonial encounters.

Colonialism impacted the power structures of native locations and influenced the dynamics and relationships of colonized cultures, but it also functioned in fluid and distinct ways during various moments of history and within specific geographic regions. In the eighteenth and nineteenth centuries, colonial exchanges influenced and shaped notions of sexuality and identity and consolidated ideas about what it meant to be civilized and modern. Colonialism, as a system of power and domination, reflected patriarchal and oppressive systems, and as such motivated questions and movements towards gender equality. Thus, the relationship of gender and colonialism was forged in an interconnected way.

The relationship between colonialism and gender can be analyzed through a number of key points. First, the spaces of colonial expansion and moments of encounter within them can be read as gendered. In early histories of exploration for example, the act of discovery is often established in masculine terms of penetration while land and territories are described in feminized ways. Second, a range of colonial representations, such as literary texts and visual images, reveal the gendered ways that native peoples are described. For example, stereotypes such as images of submissive and secluded women dominated nineteenth-century travel narratives, historical documents, and fiction. At the same time, notions of "dangerous" dark men emerged in both textual and visual representations. During points of conflict, such as the Indian Rebellion in 1857 for example (a key moment of upheaval and native resistance in India), colonial fictions, historical documents, and visual representations emphasized the figure of the rebellious and threatening native man and the vulnerability of English women and families.

Another key area of study moves beyond representation to analyze the activities and interactions of Europeans with natives within colonial spaces. Gender is particularly useful in this area of analysis, because the increased inclusion of women and families shifted the structures of communities and produced new opportunities for contact with native peoples. Thus, the study of Western women (and increased settlement of families) traveling and living within imperial spaces and their relationship to native peoples and cultures forms a key area of study. Colonial texts often highlighted the rituals and practices of native women and depicted them as upholding native customs, while asserting an idealized image of Western womanhood. The relationship of European women to their native counterparts reveals the ways that both parties negotiated identity within the colonial context. In the nineteenth century, women abroad interacted with natives, participated in colonial activities, and produced narratives that helped to shape notions of colonial cultures and create their own agency. By the end of the nineteenth century, increasing numbers of texts by native subjects revealed their responses to the colonial experience. Recent criticism in colonial studies considers not only the narratives and representations of Europeans abroad, but also of natives. By the late nineteenth century, the movement of peoples included large numbers of colonial subjects who traveled West either for pleasure or as immigrants to Europe and the United States. Indeed, the breadth of literature and criticism that now falls under the categories "commonwealth," "postcolonial," or "anglophone" represents these movements and underscores the broad ways that colonial histories continue to shape current notions of ethnic, racial, and gendered identities.

POINTS OF ENCOUNTER: GENDER, DISCOVERY, AND COLONIAL CONTACT

Historically, various episodes of encounter reveal how colonial expansion and conquest was viewed in gendered terms. Narratives and depictions of conquest established discovery and travel as masculine ventures, and the cultures and spaces of empire were typically portrayed as a male domain of exploration – one that shaped notions of European civilized masculinity and power. On the other hand, colonized spaces and the people within them were often represented as feminized, vulnerable, and primitive. While the gendering of colonial spaces clearly revealed ways that European masculinity was shaped and upheld as an ideal, it also produced specific representations of native women. Harems and other secluded women's spaces, for example, were often represented as exotic and sexualized spaces of male fantasy. Further, women and the native traditions they were imagined to uphold and share with families represented the "uncivilized" nature of these geographic spaces.

Mary Louise Pratt (1992), in her reading of travel and colonial expansion, has shown that early expeditions to discover foreign lands in the seventeenth and early eighteenth centuries created what she terms "planetary consciousness" through which European powers, intrigued by the allure and potential of foreign lands, expanded their explorative impulse and competed to mark and name new territories. Pratt traces the various means through which such "planetary consciousness" was achieved and discusses how the culture of print, along with the expansion of major national expeditions, increased European influence and presence around the globe. Pratt notes the relevance of emerging scientific fields such as natural history in the colonizing process, examining how Carl Linnaeus's monumental encyclopedia, *System of Nature* (1735), sought to name and categorize all the plants of the globe and establish Latin as an intellectual language. Linnaeus created a system of understanding plant parts through the binary of male and female sexual parts.

At this moment in history, travel was largely a male enterprise, and such voyages and territorial "discoveries" became opportunities to assert European masculine power and authority. However, what often interested travelers, scientists, and explorers were the cultures of foreign lands and the role of women within them. Darwin's *Voyage of the Beagle* (1839) is a good example. While much of his travelogue traces the distinctive qualities of flora and fauna in foreign locales, Darwin also associates the landscape with cultural notions of difference. In his account of Tierra Del Fuego he describes domestic activities of women and children, their nomadic lifestyle, and the wild qualities of the environment to highlight his sense of the primitivism of both the landscape and the people. Thus, in what Pratt terms "contact zones" of colonial travel, new representations of peoples, cultures, and geographies established notions of difference and consolidated perceptions of domesticity and gender.

As Anne McKlintock has carefully argued, even in earlier periods of history, representations of land and exploration took a gendered turn, establishing the act of travel and conquest as male and "newly discovered" lands as female. Describing how women function as "boundary markers" of empire, McKlintock writes:

> As European men crossed the dangerous thresholds of their known worlds, they ritualistically feminized borders and boundaries. Female figures were planted like fetishes at the ambiguous points of contact, at the borders and orifices of the contest zone … explorers called unknown lands "virgin" territory. Philosophers veiled "Truth" as female, then fantasized about drawing back the veil. In myriad ways, women served as mediating and threshold figures by means of which men oriented themselves in space, as agents of power and agents of knowledge. (McKlintock 1995, 24)

McKlintock highlights the erotic qualities of imperial conquest, using the term "pornotropics" to reveal how, as early as the Renaissance period, colonial scenes created gendered notions of discovery and penetration. Such scenes and moments of imperial expansion and discovery shaped not only a sense of femininity within the margins, but also established and shaped notions of modern masculinity in relation to colonial expansion. Reinforcing McKlintock's argument, Ania Loomba (2005, 128) notes that "from the beginning of the colonial period, till its end (and beyond) female bodies symbolize the conquered land."

Thus, from early moments of European discovery, colonial spaces were gendered and, in turn, shaped the construction of masculine and feminine identity. By the beginning of the nineteenth century, in the age of both imperial and industrial expansion, colonial experiences were narrated, visualized, and understood at a much wider scale. New technologies and improvements in printing allowed large numbers of texts – fiction, travel journals, travel guides, scientific reports, and historical documents – to be distributed widely, and newspapers documented the various political and economic shifts that took place through colonial expansion. Transportation and communication innovations, such as the development of more elaborate railway systems, faster trains and steamships, and the emergence of the transatlantic cable in the 1860s (which made New York and London centers of the "new" and "modern" world) also created a more interconnected sense of the globe and the possibilities of travel. Improved transportation encouraged trade and a new global economy where the commodities and specimens of empire came home – establishing specifically gendered categories of "civilized" and "primitive" behaviors. Colonial commodities such as tea, sugar, spices, shawls, and other consumer goods helped to shape notions of middle-class identity and femininity within Europe and the United States.

Beyond the goods that filtered through new marketplaces and homes, foreign plants, animals, and even people became popular highlights of nineteenth-century zoos, exhibitions, and performances. Native women became the spectacles and specimens of colonial encounter at the dawn of the nineteenth century as the culture of "freak shows" and circuses began to evolve. One of the most notable examples is the case of Saartjie Baartman, a South African woman from the Khoikhoi tribe. Baartman, more popularly known as the "Hottentot Venus," was brought to Europe as a specimen of her tribe and then displayed in Paris and London as a spectacle of entertainment, simply because her physical features were considered unusual for European viewers and different from white women. Baartman was examined by some of the "great scientists" of the nineteenth century including Georges Cuvier and Étienne Geoffroy St. Hilaire, who were intrigued by what they thought were her distinctive body parts. Baartman thus stood for notions of "African femininity" and through her body both popular and scientific interests attempted to capture and evidence some sense of essential differences between European and African people. The case of the "Hottentot Venus" reveals the widening impact of colonialism during this period, and the fascination with African women such as Baartman who then stood for their culture as a whole. Baartman was represented as a stark contrast to the ideals of modesty and femininity to which middle-class European women were asked to conform.

The case of Saartjie Baartman foregrounds the ways that the emergence of science and scientific disciplines intersected with colonialism and gender to construct specific notions of European femininity in relation to "other" African women. After Baartman's death, her body was the object of scientific analysis by French scientists including Georges Cuvier and Henry Blainville. As Anne Fausto-Sterling, Sander Gilman, and other critics have argued, these nineteenth-century scientists focused upon locating racial difference through their observation, with the goal to secure inherent "primitivism" in African bodies and establish a hierarchy of races. Later in the nineteenth century, events such as the Great Exhibition of 1851 and other "world's fairs" became locations to display cultural differences and establish superiority based on race and industrial expansion. Exhibitions, fairs, circuses, and zoos created artificial and exotic "colonial" environments and exposed viewers to the peoples, animals, plants, and cultures of foreign spaces, establishing distinct differences among regions and peoples.

GENDER AND TRAVEL: COLONIAL CONTACT AND REPRESENTATION

Nineteenth-century industrialization fostered colonial expansion and produced a faster paced and expanding culture of "work" in which women were asked to function as the domestic ideal or, to use Coventry Patmore's term, "the angel in the house." Scholars have used the term "separate spheres" to describe the gendered ways that middle-class women were increasingly relegated to the domestic sphere in the nineteenth century while men engaged in public activities. However, the nineteenth century and its innovations in transportation and technology also gave more women the opportunity to travel and engage in colonial realms, thus challenging the rigidity of this nineteenth-century public and private dichotomy. Foreign travel could be a liberating experience as it allowed women to escape gendered constraints at home and establish themselves as adventurers abroad. The act of travel gave women increased mobility and the opportunity to redefine themselves and locate their relationship to political and economic forces of expanding empires. While on the one hand, women travelers held the burden of representing Western femininity and cultural norms, on the other, they established relationships with natives and to native spaces that were often inaccessible to men. Prior to the nineteenth century, it was primarily privileged and wealthy women travelers who had the opportunity to travel and then record the experience in writing. Figures such as Elizabeth Craven and Lady Mary Wortley Montagu traveled and recorded their experiences as early as the eighteenth century. Lady Mary Wortley Montagu, who lived in Constantinople as wife of the British Ambassador and produced letters documenting her travels from 1716 to 1718, established the female traveler as a distinctive and authoritative figure – one who could visit female private spaces such as harems and baths, and forge friendships with native women in ways not open to European men. In her letters, Lady Mary describes her close engagement with native women and shows an interest in their native rituals. For example, Lady Mary observes their practice of "variolation" against smallpox and performs the procedure herself. Her letters were popular with readers and established private women's spaces as sites rich with material for narrative description.

As the nineteenth century progressed, travel became a more common experience for women from a broader range of classes, and the female travel narrative became one of the most popular textual forms. By the mid-nineteenth century, travel narratives from colonial regions included extensive descriptions of Egypt from figures such as Hester Stanhope, Lucie Duff Gordon, and Florence Nightingale, representations of other areas of the Middle East such as Palestine and Syria from Isabel Burton, accounts of West Africa from Mary Kingsley, and numerous records of life in India from Catherine Elwood, Fanny Parks, Mary Carpenter, and many others. Some women, such as Flora Annie Steel, produced travel narratives as well as novels and household guides that depicted life for European women in colonial spaces.

Drawing upon the early fascination with private domestic spaces and rituals surrounding marriage, motherhood, and childrearing, nineteenth-century travel accounts continued to shape notions of native women and the cultures and customs of colonial spaces. While early nineteenth-century travelers such as Emma Roberts and Fanny Parks highlighted exotic scenes such as native weddings and performances by Indian dancers ("nautch girls," as they were known), their accounts also titillated readers with enticing objects of consumption, such as shawls, jewels, and silk fabrics. Such commodities became fashionable for European women at home as they became more common in marketplaces, and also were described in popular novels of the period. Travel narratives and other literary texts highlighted the ways that middle- and upper-class women could exhibit the empire's wealth and sustain the circulatory nature of imperial objects.

Women's travel accounts quickly became popular, because they highlighted the spaces most private, but also most enticing, to Western readers. Well-known figures such as Harriet Martineau produced travel accounts, but their depictions also served as a way of keeping colonial order in place. For Martineau, "the hareem" in Egypt was a site of disorder and disease – unlike women writers who described their desire to see and experience the pleasures of harem spaces, Martineau "dreads" her visit as she would visiting a dentist. She describes the lack of air and outdoor exercise of Egyptian women as contributing to their unhealthy pallor, and encourages readers to witness the harem as a site of primitive and unhealthy disorder in need of repair. Other mid- to late Victorian women travelers such as Mary Carpenter and Florence Nightingale produced narratives that outlined the need for better schools and support systems for women and children, but in the process also emphasized the ways that native systems could be reorganized through colonial rule.

By the end of the nineteenth century, colonial spaces became a way for women to participate in and build professional authority in a way unavailable to them at home. The most obvious example is in the case of the health professions. By the final decades of the nineteenth century, a number of women doctors traveled overseas to pursue medical degrees and practice medicine. Edith Pechey-Phipson had a successful medical practice in India as did Mary Scharlieb, who was inspired to study medicine after hearing about how Indian women avoided male doctors and how "purdah" (seclusion) made it difficult for men to access female spaces to provide medical care. Both of these women are considered pioneering women doctors who pursued their degrees during a time when women were still fighting for access to medical education and struggled with recognition for their efforts and abilities in scientific realms. Colonial spaces were integral in establishing the careers of women doctors and became a field in which they could practice. In turn, women doctors became particularly influential in shaping notions of native practices and spaces. While these late nineteenth-century women doctors were able to gain medical experience abroad and use this to make arguments for the need for "lady doctors," one of the earliest female practitioners abroad was "Dr. James Barry" who disguised herself as a man in the early nineteenth century and managed to work as an army doctor traveling through various regions before the discovery, at her death, that she was a woman.

Whether women writers were sympathetic to the conditions of their native counterparts or critical of their cultures (indeed, often women vascillated between these points in their depictions), the act of travel functioned as a form of liberation. Many of these accounts revealed the freedoms European women enjoyed through their travels, and the crucial role they had in shaping the breadth of the colonial experience.

TEXTUAL REPRESENTATIONS AND DISCOURSES

Literary texts of the nineteenth century reveal the ways that colonialism influenced and shaped notions of gender at home and the ways that the "metropole" and colonies were interconnected. By the middle of the nineteenth century, Britain emerged as the imperial superpower, with control over lands on every continent. Hence, the term "the sun never sets on the British Empire" described the breadth of the British imperial domain. The British East India Company had been operating for several centuries as an economic influence, but by the beginning of the Victorian period it and other British operations had expanded around the globe. Industrial and technological innovations, improvements in printing technologies, photography, and eventually film technology allowed the imperial project to flourish and be recognized on a much wider scale. The colonial expansion of this period coincided with the rise of the novel as a popular textual form and the birth of mass media in multiple forms. Newspapers, medical guides, travel narratives, gardening magazines, and numerous periodicals and journals flooded the marketplace and created ways of knowing and shaping ideas of the self and nation.

Classic adventure novels such as Haggard's *King Solomon's Mines* (1885) produced scenes of Africa and other locales, while travel narratives continued to educate and entice readers to explore and imagine exotic spaces. Some of the most popular fictional texts of this period were written by women whose work was circulated more broadly not just at home but within imperial spaces. Mid-century texts such as Emily Brontë's *Wuthering Heights* (1847) and Charlotte Brontë's *Jane Eyre* (1847), written on the moors of England, represented the domestic pursuits of English characters, but alluded to the relationship of Britain to its colonies quite directly. For example, in *Wuthering Heights* Heathcliff is repeatedly exoticized and described in terms of a dangerous and foreign masculinity. Rochester, the master of Thrushcross Grange and love interest of Jane Eyre, is similarly described as "dark" and "gruff" and his fortune comes from his family's investment in West Indian plantations. Within this novel, Jane's English femininity is repeatedly contrasted with Rochester's hidden wife Bertha, the West Indian woman confined to the attic as a "madwoman" and represented as mentally ill and animalistic. Sandra Gilbert and Susan Gubar have artfully argued in their groundbreaking *Madwoman in the Attic* that Bertha stands as Jane's double. Other critics, such as Gayatri Spivak, suggest that she also represents the silenced voice of the native woman and the implication of British women within colonial efforts, as Jane's independence and the yearning for freedom contrasts with Bertha's imprisonment, and the closure of the novel – Jane's marriage to Rochester – can only occur after Bertha's death.

Other nineteenth-century texts reveal the ways that colonialism redefined European culture and domestic life. A range of nineteenth-century novels depict the influx of new goods within the European marketplace, and focus specifically upon ways that women fashioned the goods of empire. Shawls, curry, and other consumer items such as tea and sugar became staples of European households, and women became the consumers of such goods. Nineteenth-century paintings and novels represented tea and the rituals of tea making as part of the female domain, and so female middle-class respectability was shaped through a relationship to colonial culture and goods. English novels such as Anthony Trollope's *The Eustace Diamonds* (1871) and Wilkie Collins' *The Moonstone* (1868) based their plots on exotic diamonds gifted to female characters, while numerous other texts highlighted the influx of goods within European homes.

While novels had a role in representing the exotic goods of empire, as well as the interrelatedness of colonies to home – texts such as *Mansfield Park, Jane Eyre,* and *Wuthering Heights* show how European wealth depended on colonial transactions – other kinds of media forms also participated in the construction of gendered and racial notions of difference. By the middle of the nineteenth century, an explosion of "orientalist" paintings by visual artists such as Ingres, Gérôme, and Delacroix were inspired by colonial spaces and built upon representations available in print. The French artist Ingres turned to the letters of Lady Mary Wortley Montagu for inspiration in his famous painting *Le Bain Turk* (The Turkish Bath). The detail of Lady Mary's account allowed this French artist to depict a scene within a women's bath in Turkey with great detail and realism. Other artists such as Gérôme and Delacroix in France and John Frederick Lewis in Britain created images of women's harems and private spaces that once again reflected notions of Eastern women's passivity and cultural difference. By the late nineteenth century, photographs and postcards that constructed images of North African women created similar depictions of native spaces and rituals. As Malek Alloula has shown in his reading of French postcards in Algeria, these images were constructed to create an imaginary notion of Algerian culture; in fact, many of the models within the photographs were French women.

Clearly, particular stereotypes of colonial spaces were repeatedly established through the various representational forms of this period. However, as more women traveled and indeed lived in the colonies these spaces became reshaped in the image of European domesticity. As Ann Stoler (1994) has carefully argued using the example of Dutch colonies, women "made empire respectable" by bringing European norms, foods, and expectations to colonial spaces. As Stoler and others have shown, the increased entry of European women to colonial realms resulted in a shift in the social and cultural dynamics of these spaces. While European men may have initially been encouraged to have relationships with native women (to forge deeper alliances within these spaces and gain greater access to them), the inclusion of European women created a culture in which natives and Europeans became more greatly divided. The creation of "compounds" dedicated to European families, the establishment of schools and other institutions for expatriates, and even the increased number of single women abroad such as governesses, adventurers, and women seeking professional advancement abroad resulted in micro-societies that echoed domestic spaces within Europe.

In late nineteenth century and fin de siècle India, a range of texts reflect the figure of the English "memsahib" and the role of families overseas in the colonial enterprise. English novels such as Frances Hodgson Burnett *The Secret Garden* (1911) and Flora Annie Steel's *On the Face of the Waters* (1896) described English family life abroad and depicted the figure of the Englishwoman in colonial settings. Manuals for women and families such as Edward Tilt's *Health for Women in British India* (1875) guided women about ways to stay healthy and adjust to their new colonial environments. Such texts also established particular notions of European womanhood, encouraging women to recognize how to maintain the health of their families and educate children on their journeys. Finally, the publication of cookbooks and household guides such as Flora Annie Steel and Grace Gardiner's *The Complete English Housekeeper and Cook* (1909) prescribed ways for European women to interact with servants and natives, design households, and create menus within colonial environments, further emphasizing the critical and increased role of women within the empire and the interrelatedness of colonial spaces to the metropole. As they note in the introductory pages of their manual, running a household could be compared to managing imperial possessions: "an Indian household can no more be governed peacefully, without dignity and prestige, than an Indian Empire" (Steel and Gardiner 1909, 9). Recent critics such as Ann Stoler, Mary Procida, and Durba Ghosh have traced the impact of European families within colonial spaces, illuminating the ways that the management of bodies and homes was intricately related to the organization of empire and its structures.

CRITICAL MOVEMENTS: FEMINIST AND POSTCOLONIAL INTERVENTIONS

In his groundbreaking text, *Orientalism*, Edward Said (1978) argues that colonized lands and peoples were often depicted in a unified and static way – the "orient" as both a space and an idea was constructed through the imaginary of the "occident" that created powerful and stereotypical notions of "other" lands and peoples. Imperial rhetoric focused upon the presumed laziness and disorganization of natives, and the dominant images of Eastern spaces represented the exotic, dangerous, or lascivious qualities of native people and their customs, frequently establishing these foreign lands as feminized spaces open to "discovery" by European male explorers and reform by settlers. While Said has been criticized for the binary sense in which he defines the "orient" and "occident" and the fact that his reading largely ignores gender, his theories helped to shape the field of postcolonial theory. Said's reading of Orientalism was influenced by the critical work of Gramsci, Foucault, and other theorists who were studying notions of power and institutional structure within societies. At the same time, the field of feminist theory was evolving, with critical work being produced in multiple disciplines.

A range of critical work on colonialism and gender emerged in the early 1980s and has continued to evolve. The publication of groundbreaking works, such as Sandra Gilbert and Susan Gubar's *The Madwoman in the Attic*, which impacted the study of gender in literary studies, and Joan Scott's *Gender: A Useful Category of Historical Analysis* (1986), which asked readers the rethink the role of gender in history and consider gender as a useful category of analysis, helped to shape and influence academic work engaging with the relationship of colonial modernity to identity and to gender politics. The publication of such feminist criticism alongside key texts in postcolonial studies focused upon questions of gender, such as Gayatri Spivak's "Can the Subaltern Speak" (1988), and Chandra Talpade Mohanty's "Under Western Eyes: Feminist Scholarship and Colonial Discourses" (1984) inspired the development of new areas of scholarship examining the intersections of postcolonial and feminist theory.

While postcolonial feminism became an area of study within critical theory during the 1980s and 1990s, analysis of Orientalism and travel were also notable areas of interdisciplinary academic growth. One of the earliest texts to examine gender in relation to theories and concepts of Orientalism is Rana Kabbani's *Europe's Myths of Orient* (1986). Like Edward Said, Kabbani describes how the "occident" shapes images of the "orient," although Kabbani focuses more closely upon representations of women, and specifically of the harem. Other contributions to this area of study include Reina Lewis's *Gendering Orientalism: Race, Femininity, and Representation* (1996) and Lisa Lowe's *Critical Terrains: French and British Orientalisms* (1991) which examine the relationship of women to Orientalism and travel. Both authors expand the boundaries of Orientalism by analyzing a range of works and analyzing shifting terms of race and gender. Lewis also considers how women writers and artists participated within the Orientalist gaze, sometimes challenging and sometimes reinforcing dominant representations.

Along with research focusing on Orientalism and the representation of women, some of the earliest work in the area of colonialism and gender carefully unearthed archival materials to show the presence and activities of European women in colonies. For example, texts such as Dea Birkett's *Spinsters Abroad* (1989) recovered the work of women travelers overseas, providing analysis of the ways that journeys provided European women with the freedom to escape limitations that may have been set for them at home. Other readings of travel writing such as Billie Melman's book, *Women's Orients: English Women and the Middle East 1718–1918* (1992), outlined the range of activities that women engaged in abroad and the ways in which their texts were increasingly popular and authoritative. While a surge of material on travel writing, and specifically on the white woman traveler, emerged in the mid-1980s from authors including Indira Ghose, Sara Mills, and Alison Blunt, tourism also became an area of study for many scholars. Cynthia Enloe's *Bananas, Beaches, and Bases: Making*

Feminist Sense of International Politics (1989) examined the culture of tourism in relation to gender, while Malek Alloula's *The Colonial Harem* and Sarah Graham-Brown's *Images of Women* (1988) revealed how visual images such as paintings, photographs, and postcards from the nineteenth century exoticized native cultures. Important critical collections such as Nupur Chaudhuri and Margaret Strobel's *Western Women and Imperialism* (1992) highlighted the multiple ways that Western women engaged in colonial realms and began to ask enduring questions about what roles women had in colonies to examine how they were marginal or central to establishing colonial rule.

While these early studies were groundbreaking in the ways that they documented the work of white women in colonies and their range of experiences, other critical work in the 1990s began to consider the interconnectedness of colonial spaces and the relationship of colonies to the metropole. A key text in this area is Antoinette Burton's *Burdens of History* (1994). In this study, Burton provides a reading of women's activities in colonial realms, but also considers how colonial activities help to shape feminist movements at home. Burton traces the intersection of colonial activities with cultures and communities within Europe and with the emergence of British feminism. Building upon an analysis of the gendered exchanges of colonialism, Burton's later work, such as *At the Heart of Empire* (1998), considers travel and colonialism in a more circular way, tracing the narratives and experiences of native Indian women who traveled to Europe and their contact and collaboration with Europeans. Recent work by Antoinette Burton, Tony Ballantyne, and Catherine Hall continues to consider the mobility and circularity of nineteenth-century colonialism and the continued impact of empires on contemporary culture and globalization.

Critical work in the past 20 years has also increasingly analyzed sexuality within colonial realms. Ronald Hyam's *Empire and Sexuality* (1990) is one of the earliest studies of imperial sexuality which benefits from the work of feminist critics, but focuses on the nature and regularity of sexual contact for European men in colonies. Responding to this work, feminist historians such as Philippa Levine and Ann Stoler show the centrality of sexuality within colonial structures and the impact of sexual controls and the regulation of bodies on both native and European cultures. Both scholars argue that issues surrounding the body and sexuality are integral to the politics of imperial cultures. Philippa Levine's scholarship has been vast, and much of it focuses specifically on prostitution and the impact of the Contagious Diseases Acts upon colonial institutions, while Stoler, building upon Foucault's work on sexuality, considers the relevance of intimacy, sexuality, and family to the overall structures of colonialism.

Scholarship on sexuality and gender is not limited to the category of "women" or to heterosexual configurations. Mrinalini Sinha's, *Colonial Masculinity: The "Manly Englishman" and the "Effeminate Bengali"* (1995) is an important work that considers constructions of masculinity and the relationship of masculinity to nationalist politics and movements. Indeed, nationalism and gender is a crucial area of study for postcolonial scholars. Groundbreaking research such as Lata Mani's *Contentious Traditions: The Debate on Sati in Colonial India* (1998) analyzes how native practices became central within colonial discourses and politics. Mani traces how sati or widow burning in India was a topic that produced dialogues and debates from British administrators, Indian nationalists, and a range of players in imperial

India, but ultimately silenced native women in the process. The debates surrounding sati established native women as symbols of native custom and tradition. Other critics such as Partha Chatterjee, Sangeeta Ray, Nancy Paxton, and Veena Das have analyzed the relationship of nationalism to colonialism and gender, tracing the ways that nineteenth- and twentieth-century nationalist movements realigned gender configurations in colonial spaces.

A range of twentieth- and twenty-first-century critical theory in the areas of feminism and postcolonial studies analyzes the complex relationship of colonialism and gender both within a historical context and in relation to contemporary globalization. Literary production in the areas of "postcolonial" or "commonwealth" literatures also analyzes this relationship and how it endures in the twenty-first century. Tsitsi Dangarembga's novel *Nervous Conditions* traces girlhood, familial rites, and educational reform in Rhodesia to describe the enduring impact of colonialism on twentieth-century African cultures. Assia Djeber considers the impact of colonial history on Algerian culture, and specifically on North African women, in her memoir, *Fantasia,* and South Asian writers Bapsi Sidhwa, Jhumpa Lahiri, and Sara Suleri reveal the enduring ways that colonialism impacts contemporary tensions between gender, immigration, and nation.

SEE ALSO: Colonialism and Sexuality; Feminism, Nineteenth-Century United States; Feminism, Postcolonial; Postcolonialism, Theoretical and Critical Perspectives on; Women Travelers

REFERENCES

Burton, Antoinette. 1994. *Burdens of History: British Feminists, Indian Women, and Imperial Culture 1865–1915.* Chapel Hill: University of North Carolina Press.

Chaudhuri, Nupur, and Margaret Strobel. 1992. *Western Women and Imperialism: Complicity and Resistance.* Bloomington: Indiana University Press.

Lewis, Reina. 1995. *Gendering Orientalism: Race, Femininity, and Representation.* New York: Routledge.

Loomba, Ania. 2005. *Colonialism/Postcolonialism: A New Critical Idiom.* London and New York: Routledge.

McClintock, Anne. 1995. *Imperial Leather: Race, Gender, and Sexuality in the Colonial Contest.* New York: Routledge.

Melman, Billie. 1992. *Women's Orients: English Women and the Middle East 1718–1918.* Ann Arbor: University of Michigan Press.

Pratt, Mary Louise. 1992. *Imperial Eyes: Travel Writing and Transculturation.* New York: Routledge.

Sinha, Mrinalini. 1995. *Colonial Masculinity: The "Manly Englishman" and the "Effeminate Bengali" in the Late Nineteenth Century.* Manchester: Manchester University Press.

Spivak, Gayatri. 1988. "Can the Subaltern Speak?" *Marxism and the Interpretation of Culture,* edited by Cary Nelson and Lawrence Grossberg, 271–313. Urbana: University of Illinois Press.

Steel, Flora Annie, and Grace Gardiner. 1909. *The Complete Indian Housekeeper and Cook: Giving the Duties of Mistress and Servants, the General Management of the House and Practical Recipes for Cooking in all its Branches.* London: William Heinemann. First published 1888.

Stoler, Ann. 1994. *Race and the Education of Desire: Foucault's History of Sexuality and the Colonial Order of Things.* Durham: Duke University Press.

FURTHER READING

Burton, Antoinette, ed. 1999. *Gender, Sexuality and Colonial Modernities.* London and New York: Routledge.

Ghosh, Durba. 2008. *Sex and the Family in Colonial India: The Making of Empire.* Cambridge: Cambridge University Press.

Hall, Catherine. 2006. *At Home with the Empire: Metropolitan Culture and the Imperial World.* Cambridge: Cambridge University Press.

Levine, Philippa, ed. 2004. *Gender and Empire.* Oxford: Oxford University Press.

Paxton, Nancy. 1999. *Writing under the Raj: Gender, Race, and Rape in the British Colonial Imagination*. Rutgers University Press.

Colonialism and Sexuality

CHRISTELLE TARAUD and MIRIAM PENSACK
Université Paris I/Panthéon-Sorbonne, France

By no means an anecdotal or peripheral element within the political establishment of colonialism, sexuality is, to the contrary, a central issue in colonial Africa, Asia, and Oceania as early as the beginning of the nineteenth century. From the role of Europeans within the colonial context to the presence of sexual diversity (mixed couples, sexual relations between men, prostitution) and the question of virility, colonial administrations, whether French, British, Belgian, Dutch, German, Italian, or Portuguese, have all theorized and tested certain mechanisms of sexual supervision and regulation.

Primarily considered symbolic of a state of civilization, the sexuality of "the indigenous" is often presented as "primitive," "bestial," and "dangerous." Yet, many Europeans either had or dreamed of having sexual relations with the colonized woman. Colonized women of Moorish, North African (*moukères*), Tonkinese, and Indochinese descent, as well as the African "negress" and the *Mousso*, not only fed the imagination of colonizers, as seen in a number of pseudo-scientific works such as Doctor Jacobus's famous *The Art of Love in the Colonies*, published in France in 1893, but also informed the daily life of many white men. Thus Ernest Feydeau, author and native of Algiers, wrote in 1862, "The French arrived in Algiers starving for Moorish women," reiterating the fact that Europeans perceived the colonies as a "sexual Eden" where all sexual relations were possible. This voracious hunger was generally sated by the indigenous population, given that the presence of European women in the majority of colonial empires remained relatively rare until the end of the interwar period. In Algeria, for example, at the beginning of the military conquest of 1833, we find 336 European women and 1,000 European men; in 1839, the figure stood at 383 women; and in 1842, the number again increased to 474. Nevertheless, during certain epochs and within certain colonial configurations, any European female presence was simply forbidden. Thus, in the Dutch East Indies, marriage between the colonizers and white women was prohibited, with the exception of high officials in the Dutch East India Company. This policy was upheld for at least the first 10 years of Dutch presence in the colony. The colonized woman, conceptualized as the "other" in female form, was therefore a structural element in the pursuit of sexual equilibrium from the very establishment of colonial society.

Nevertheless, the increasingly significant arrival of European women at the beginning of the twentieth century often modified the internal equilibrium of mixed couples and families (Stoler 2002). From this moment onward, a number of indigenous women who, up until that point, had maintained the "official" role of wife, saw themselves relegated to the status of concubine at best, or prostitute at worst. The European wife therefore reinforced her social status in terms of both legality (insofar as wives' marital status was officially recognized by the laws of the respective countries) and superiority (as actors of the sexual colonial order that they incarnated). These new dispositions not only marginalized and stigmatized mixed practices and sexual and/or conjugal interrelations that had hitherto been perfectly socially integrated, but also created problems regarding the filiation of mixed-race children in almost every colonial empire. Thus, in the regions of eastern Africa under colonial Italian fascism, mixed marriage was strictly forbidden by the statutory order of November 17, 1938, whose goal was to "defend the Italian race" and to avoid the births of numerous mixed-race children who might sully the "Italian bloodline."

Furthermore, by the end of the nineteenth century, the indigenous women who did engage in mixed sexual and/or conjugal relations were increasingly and systematically considered as objects, something given, shared, and therefore "denigrated," and were henceforth stigmatized by both the colonizers and the colonized. Of course, this stigmatization varied depending on the epoch, the context, and the level of permissiveness with which a given society addressed the question of mixed sexual practices and reproduction. The category of "housewife," which is to say, a country's definition of housewife according to sexual, reproductive, and domestic practices, was better perceived in certain parts of sub-Saharan Africa, Asia, and Oceania. Yet, in other regions of a given empire, sexual "mixing" could be relegated to the marginalized practice of prostitution, as was the case most notably for the French Maghreb, where a system of regulation was established similar to the one found in mainland France (Taraud 2012). Among its main objectives, this regulation aimed to establish a sex market that was both financially profitable and morally acceptable according to the sexual and racial colonial order, as well as for the greater colonial society. So functioned a sort of tacit accord between men on both sides of the colonial frontier: certain women would be "sacrificed" to "venal" sexual mixing (mixed marriage being popularly condemned) in order to preserve the majority. From military campaign brothels (*les bordels militaires de campagne*) to allotted neighborhoods (Bousbir in Casablanca, Abdallah Gueche in Tunis), from houses of tolerance to slaughterhouses, these women, whether indigenous or European, became symbols of the constructed line between "venal" sexual mixing and the stigma of prostitution.

As racial hierarchy would oblige, any white woman engaging in sexual and/or conjugal relations with an indigenous person was *de facto* suspected of possessing questionable morals, and of being "perverse" and "pathological." In almost all colonial empires, the incontrovertible condemnation of unions between white women and "native" men persisted in the case of prostitution: colonial administrations sometimes attempted to establish, with little success, denominational and/or racial segregation pertaining to sexual relations. Thus, an ideological boundary very clearly marked the "sharing of women." This similarly created the concept of the virile and superior white male, whose hegemony was expressed most notably in his "right of coitus" with all women, including of course the women of the vanquished and the dominated. Colonial domination went so far as to impose itself *into* the bodies of women, rendering sexual relations with the indigenous a central issue.

Along with these already complex relationships between men and women, sexual relations strictly between men were by no means any less problematic. From the first half of the nineteenth century, in all colonizing countries, an idea developed that regarded colonization as the "fabric" from which real men were made, and as a space for virile and national regeneration (Taraud 2011). Indeed, theorists of colonial conquest agree that colonial expansion became *essential* to Europe, and that Europeans were engaged in a manifestation of social Darwinism – a sort of "fight for survival," "struggle for life," from which the strongest would "naturally" emerge. As an aspect of virility, colonization indicated the necessary hardening of supposedly "castrated" and/or "effeminate" men, even within Europe itself. This demanded that such virility be regenerated outside of the colonizing country. Civil or semi-civil societies, but also penitential societies, therefore determined the bases of relations between men, which necessarily manifested – on the battlefield, in the bathhouse, at work, at school, in the café, and in the brothel – according to a mode of virility. Hierarchies, social spaces, and approaches to the indigenous were all constructed upon a normalized and hegemonic masculinity, from which deviation was an assured failure, and which bestowed a number of privileges upon the dominating male.

One of the components of colonial policy and its resulting practices was to delegitimize any notion of genuine manhood within the colonized population, particularly on the grounds of sexuality. Considered either as inveterate "sodomites" or as uncontrollable "sexual predators," the colonized were systematically stigmatized based on an appreciation of their morals. As proof of the "brutal" and "primitive" character of this "sexual predator," nineteenth- and twentieth-century authors often placed an emphasis on the morphology of his genitalia. For example, we encounter frequent commentary on the hypertrophy of the Arab man's penis. This particular anatomic characteristic, presumed and generalized within the Maghreb as well as sub-Saharan Africa, rendered the indigenous within the colonial world a man of "monstrous member," which, through the period's rationale of cause and effect, moralized him as "abnormal," "abhorrent," and "primitive." For instance, authors who discuss the excessive sensuality of the Arab world, particularly the existence of harems and polygamy, permit themselves to do so because of their own "superior" morals. This hyper-genitalization is mobilized still further by the forceful critique of perverse sexual practices – zoophilia, necrophilia, and sodomy – as well as those practices directed toward women – violence and, of course, rape. As for pederastic relations, in regions such as the Maghreb and French Indochina for example, they are presented as a frequent indigenous practice (Aldrich 2002; Massad 2007). The indigenous pederast is often considered "passive," which clearly differentiates him from the "sexual predator," who is always "active," even when sexually engaged with men. He is, of course, also deemed effeminate. This effeminate quality, as a threat to colonial morality and virility, underlines the precariousness and fragility of heterosexual male identity in the colonies. The European who yielded to indigenous pederasty became "morally unkempt," thereby undermining the prestige of his "race" and the honor of his country. This further disturbed the practice and principle of distance (between whites and the indigenous population) that constituted the colonial order. However, such a challenge to the colonial order might posit a reversal of this stigma: the effeminate "native" "contaminates" the French or the European and, to a certain extent, in "taking possession of him," jeopardizes the very institution of French colonization. Despite this potential reversal, the generally accepted order maintained an appraisal of indigenous sexuality as either too virile or insufficiently virile. This is yet again a convenient means of delegitimizing the normalcy of the indigenous male population. Indigenous men therefore find themselves excluded from the legitimate virility that symbolized a sort of "sexual civilization" still in construction at the end of the nineteenth century. Within this structure, in the sexual as well as other domains, the indigenous are consigned to the "bestiality" and "perversity" of their practices and to the "savagery" and "primitivism" of their morals.

SEE ALSO: Colonialism and Gender; Masculinities; Sexualities

REFERENCES

Aldrich, Robert. 2002. *Colonialism and Homosexuality*. New York: Routledge.
Feydeau, Ernest. 1862. *Alger*. Paris: Michel Lévy Frères.
Massad, Joseph A. 2007. *Desiring Arabs*. Chicago: University of Chicago Press.
Stoler, Ann Laura. 2002. *Carnal Knowledge and Imperial Power: Race and the Intimate in Colonial Rule*. Berkeley: University of California Press.
Taraud, Christelle. 2011. "La virilité en situation coloniale." In *Histoire de la virilité*, edited by Alain Corbin, Jean-Jacques Courtine, and Georges Vigarello, vol. 2, 331–347. Paris: Le Seuil.
Taraud, Christelle. 2012. "Amour interdit." *Prostitution, marginalité et colonialisme: Maghreb 1830–1962*. Paris: Petite Bibliothèque Payot.

FURTHER READING

Clancy-Smith, Julia, and Frances Gouda, eds. 1998. *Domesticating the Empire: Race, Gender and Family Life in French and Dutch Colonialism*. Charlottesville: University Press of Virginia.
Taraud, Christelle. 2009. *La prostitution coloniale: Algérie, Tunisie, Maroc, 1830–1962*. Paris: Payot. First published 2003.

Comfort Women

DIANE KHOLOS WYSOCKI
University of Nebraska at Kearney, USA

During World War II, it is believed that 200,000 women were forced into prostitution by the Japanese military (Edwards 2013; Kuki 2013). The women were called "comfort women," "juugun ianfu," or "sanitary public toilets" (Mendoza 2003). They were beaten, raped, and held prisoner under the direct control and mandate of the Japanese military. Typically, comfort women were taken from their homes in Korea, Japan, Indonesia, China, the Philippines, and the Netherlands.

The colonization of Korea by Japan lasted until August 15, 1945, when Japan was defeated and the Pacific War ended. In that last stage of the colonization, between 1937 and 1945, Korea was used by the Japanese to supply food and other war materials and Koreans were forced to provide all types of material for the Japanese military. During this time, Korean laborers were forced to go to Japan and other Asian countries. This included 200,000 unmarried women between the ages of 12 and 40, who were sent to Japan as the "women's voluntary service corps" (Min 2003).

The first state-sanctioned comfort stations for the Japanese army were established in 1932. Following the invasion of Nanking in 1937, troops increased their looting, rape, and murder of civilians. Rape was widespread, with large numbers of women and girls of all ages raped and then murdered in just a few weeks (Edwards 2013).

Most comfort women were Korean. They were moved from rural areas by bus or train and then placed on large ships to be taken to their final destinations. Once they arrived at a comfort station, typically they were raped by an officer. It was a Japanese belief that having sex with a virgin would protect the officer from death or injury. The young women or girls were raped over and over again and describe pain, bleeding, and beatings. Officers said this was to toughen them up before they went to work in the comfort stations.

According to Maria Rosa Henson, who was only 16 when she was taken from her home, a typical day began "at two in the afternoon, the soldiers came. My work began, and I lay down as one by one the soldiers raped me. At six p.m., we rested for a while and ate dinner. Often I was hungry because our rations were so small. After thirty minutes, I lay down on the bed again to be raped for the next three or four hours. Every day, anywhere from ten to over twenty soldiers raped me" (Henson 1996, 64).

Based on the interviews of 19 surviving Korean former comfort women Min (2003) found that power, gender, and class were major contributing factors in the victimization of sexual slaves. Min stated that:

> Korean comfort women basically differed from other groups of Korean Pacific War victims because they suffered far more brutality and humiliation. Furthermore, as victims of sexual violence, they have had to live with shame and humiliation throughout their lives … Moreover, sexual double standards and related practices associated with the patriarchal ideology in Korea played a key role in preventing the former Korean sexual slaves from maintaining normal family lives and in keeping them silent for half a century. Thus, gender hierarchy and patriarchal customs in Japan intersected with the imperial war in the establishment of the military "comfort" system, while the experiences of Korean victims with sexual slavery interplayed with patriarchal customs in Korea to keep them silent for half a century. (Min 2003, 947)

According to Azuma Shiro, a former Japanese soldier:

> At first we said some kinky words like *pikankan*. *Pi* means hip. *Kankan* means look. *Pikankan* means let's see a woman open up her legs. Chinese women didn't wear underpants. Instead they wore trousers tied with a string. There was no belt. We pulled the string, the buttocks were exposed. … After a while we would take turns raping them. It would be alright if we only raped them … But we always stabbed and killed them. Because dead bodies don't talk. (Choy 1997)

This issue of the comfort women came to light in the early 1990s. Until this time, the Japanese government claimed they had no involvement in these comfort stations, but stated the women knowingly chose to provide sex in exchange for money (Mendoza 2003). However, the testimonials of many former comfort women state that they were kidnapped, forcibly drafted, or even deceived into service with the promise of legitimate work as cooks or laundrywomen (Mendoza 2003). The first woman to testify in front of the Japanese government was a Korean woman named Hak-sun Kim. Then other women such as Yi Yongsu and Mun Okju began speaking out about their abductions and requirement to provide sexual services to 30 or more soldiers a day (Pilzer 2014). Finally, on January 13, 1992, Japan issued a apology and on August 4, 1993, the Japanese government publicly released the results of an inquiry confirming that the Japanese military were involved in the establishment and operation of comfort stations. With only 63 registered comfort women remaining in South Korea in 2012, the pressure on Japan to accept legal responsibility and apologize to the victims is very important (Kuki 2013).

SEE ALSO: Militarism and Gender-Based Violence; Militarism and Sex Industries; Prostitution/Sex Work; Sexual Assault/Sexual Violence; Sexual Slavery; Sexual Violence and the Military

REFERENCES

Choy, C. 1997. *In the Name of the Empire*. New York: Filmakers Library: 50 minutes.
Edwards, Wallace. 2013. *Comfort Women: A History of Japanese Forced Prostitution During the Second World War*. Absolute Crime Books.
Henson, Maria Rosa. 1996. *Comfort Woman: Slave of Destiny*. Manila: Philippine Center for Investigative Journalism.
Kuki, S. 2013. "The Burden of History: The Issue of 'Comfort Women' and What Japan Must Do to Move Forward." *Journal of International Affairs*, 67(1): 245–256.
Medoza, K.R. 2003. "Freeing the 'Slaves of Destiny': The Lolas of the Filipino Comfort Women Movement." *Cultural Dynamics*, 15: 247–266.
Min, P.G. 2003. "Korean 'Comfort Women': The Intersection of Colonial Power, Gender and Class." *Gender and Society*, 17(6): 938–957.

Pilzer, Joshua D. 2014. "Music and Dance in the Japanese Military 'Comfort Women' System: A Case Study in the Performing Arts, War, and Sexual Violence." *Women and Music*, 18: 1–23.

Coming Out

RINA ARYA
University of Wolverhampton, UK

The phrase "to come out" was first used to describe a debutante's coming-out party. It was a social ritual that concerned white, upper middle-class women of a certain age in the United States making their grand entrance into social circles. The act traditionally involved descending the staircase in a formal gown, and marked the acceptance of a woman into high society. Although this was the original use of the phraseology, it is now used more commonly within the context of gender and sexuality studies to refer to the self-unveiling of a subject who is gay, lesbian, or bisexual, and it has become a key concept in the sociology of sexualities and in gay and lesbian studies. It can be used more loosely to denote the unveiling of sexualities that differ from heterosexual normativity.

Particularly in the United Kingdom and the United States of America, coming out involves the social and public act of acknowledging one's sexual orientation (or sexual preferences) to people in one's life including family, friends, employers, and others. This implies a prior and initial awareness of one's own sexual identity that then subsequently becomes shared with others, often in a particular order decided by the individual. The action of coming out is not a singular event but an ongoing process that happens throughout one's life and involves an awareness of needing to be upfront and authentic about one's identity. It may be done explicitly by actually stating that one is gay, for instance, or implicitly by talking about aspects that would indicate one's sexual preference. The revealing of sexuality does not need to be done in a uniform or linear way and involves a spectrum of choices about how much to disclose, to which people, and in what contexts. One of the pivotal shifts in thinking about sexual difference in critical theory, following the writings of thinkers such as Michel Foucault and Eve Kosofsky Sedgwick, is the focus on the identity and *not* the act of homosexual difference. Coming out entails a reconciliation of identity where sexuality is one part – but not the whole – of one's personhood. Gilbert Herdt (1992) analyzes coming out in terms of a ritualistic process (as a rite of passage) that constitutes a process of re-socialization, where different values and notions are embraced and gayness is constructed as a valid cultural identity.

The legalization of homosexuality in the United Kingdom and the United States led to a growing number of autobiographical "coming out" narratives about the personal testimony of what it meant to come out, which included accounts about coming to terms with desire and sexuality. Many narratives work toward the moment of realization or awareness of one's sexuality as being life changing, with the subsequent revealing of one's true identity as being fraught and accompanied by conflicting emotions of feeling liberated and yet opening oneself up to shame and hurt. Evocative accounts include Alice Walker's *The Color Purple* (1982) and Jeanette Winterson's *Oranges Are Not the Only Fruit* (1985).

The imperative to come out has been and remains more fraught in the case of certain groups and communities, and the implication is that heterosexism exerts different pressures on different cultural groups. In the case of black and ethnic minority homosexual subjects in the United Kingdom or the United States, for example, conflicting priorities of identity politics means that they are not necessarily able to come out as readily as members of other groups. While they may want to express their sexual otherness, they are also allied to their other markers of difference, namely their race and/or ethnicity, and do not want to disrupt their community links. This means that they are at risk from homophobia from their racial communities and potential racism from heterosexual and homosexual communities. The recognition of their dual oppression and conflicting loyalties has an impact on choices about whether or not to come out.

Although the concept of coming out is steeped in Western ideology, it is important to recognize the phenomenon transnationally, especially because the manifestations take different forms by employing different metaphors and attitudes. In some cases the phrase "coming out" is used either in English or in translation, where the term may have become indigenized. In other cases other metaphors are used, such as "unfurling the cape" in the Philippines or "opening to the gay/lesbian world" in Indonesia. Unlike in most parts of the West, where coming out is a form of activism that involves taking pride and acknowledging one's status, in other cultures such as in East Asia and South Asia coming out involves further ramifications and often risks shame and dishonor. Particularly in countries where the decriminalization of homosexuality has only occurred in the very recent past, activism of any kind creates visibility, which has the potential to bring about violence. This is the case in the regions that formerly comprised the USSR (Union of Soviet Socialist Republics). In some cultures, coming out refers to acknowledging one's sexual orientation only to a queer community, often on gay websites, with no assumption of also doing so to family or employers. A distinction is made between the public realm (work), where the emphasis is placed on one's identity as a worker, and the private. In some cultures, such as China, the act of coming out to one's elders is not regarded as respectful due to the cultural expectations and attitudes of the older generations, and strategies have evolved to accommodate lesbians and gays within the community that convey the different kinship systems that are at work (see Chou 2000). Although in parts of the West coming out was regarded as presenting a challenge to heterosexism or homophobic practices, being gay in other cultural contexts does not necessarily relieve individuals of the expectations placed on them by their families and the wider communities, especially with regard to the prospect of heterosexual marriage and procreation.

The act of coming out is of personal and also political significance. On a personal level it can signify a need to be true to oneself as well as to brave external judgment. Politically, it represents the importance of acknowledging the need to convey difference as a collective action, which in lesbian and gay history occurred during the Stonewall Rebellion that stemmed from the uprising on June 27, 1969, when members of the gay bar The Stonewall Inn (often shortened to Stonewall) refused to be moved by the police and staged a riot. This marked the beginning of civil rights action for gays and lesbians and was central to the gay liberation movements of the 1960s and 1970s. In a non-Western context, coming out as gay was regarded as an expression of embracing certain constructions of modernity, and concomitantly represented resistance towards constraining governmental regulation, as in the case of China in the post-Mao reform era.

A concept that is allied to coming out is that of the closet. By acknowledging and declaring one's sexuality, one is coming out of the closet, which refers to a social and psychological space of regulation that encompasses manifold emotions and ideas about secrecy, discretion, privacy, and invisibility. The closet was a safety net for gays and lesbians from reprisals both before the legalization of homosexuality and also following it. The closet indicated the extent of repression that those in it experienced and is "a shaping presence" (Sedgwick 2008, 68). Being in the closet was a metaphor for someone who had not announced or declared his/her sexuality while being out was synonymous with the process of coming out.

Coming out is a multilayered concept that has individual and collective significance. At its core is a desire to disclose one's identity in life. Self-identifying as gay, for instance, is thought to be a way of embracing one's whole identity and of empowering oneself as well as others in a similar situation. The greater equality and awareness of gay rights that now exist and the "normalization" of homosexuality means that in many quarters coming out is less of an issue. However, without the initiative to come out in the later decades of the twentieth century, liberationist politics such as gay pride events and the cultivation of gay and lesbian critical theory, including queer theory, would not have progressed to the extent it has. It is fair to conclude that coming out is a process that is essential to the discourse of sexualities.

SEE ALSO: Epistemology of the Closet; Gay and Lesbian Pride Day; Lesbian and Gay Movements; Queer Theory; Sexual Identity and Orientation

REFERENCES

Chou, Wah-shan. 2000. *Tongzhi: Politics of Same-Sex Eroticism in Chinese Societies*. New York: Haworth Press.

Herdt, Gilbert. 1992. "'Coming Out' as a Rite of Passage: A Chicago Study." In *Gay Culture in America: Essays from the Field*, edited by Gilbert Herdt, 29–67. Boston: Beacon Press.

Sedgwick, Eve Kosofsky. 2008. *Epistemology of the Closet*, updated with a new preface. Berkeley: University of California Press. First published 1990.

FURTHER READING

Weeks, Jeffrey. 1977. *Coming Out: Homosexual Politics in Britain, from the Nineteenth Century to the Present*. London: Quartet.

Commitment Ceremonies

ELLEN LEWIN
University of Iowa, USA

Commitment ceremonies are rituals that mark the union of same-sex couples. The term developed to describe observances devised where legal marriage and other forms of official recognition for same-sex couples were not available. Those who chose this term felt that they had to find an alternative to the term "wedding," which they felt only designated the celebration of legally recognized marriage. In practice, however, many couples and those who attended these ritual events tended to call them weddings, finding that term simpler and more descriptive. Other terms were also sometimes used, such as "holy union," that label being common in LGBT-positive religious contexts where ceremonies might be performed, such as the Metropolitan Community Church (MCC).

Calling a ritual a commitment ceremony has many possible meanings. It might highlight the extra-legal nature of the occasion, marking the fact that the couple is barred from achieving a legal marriage, and perhaps emphasizing the need for legal redress. But it also sometimes signals a couple's rejection of the symbols of conventional marriage by expressing a preference for an alternative form of union, one that the couple believes to be different from, or perhaps superior to, legal marriage. When the term is used in this way, it may convey a critique of legal marriage as an institution mired in a history of exploitation (by men over women) and, in any case, fragile in current US and Western European contexts.

Commitment ceremonies may use religious symbols and ritual practices or may be entirely secular in content. Use of religious imagery or content and location in a house of worship with a member of the clergy officiating may be preferred by couples who are strongly attached to a particular religious tradition or members of a congregation. In such cases, the notion that God is endorsing the relationship can be an important source of authorization for the couple. A religious ceremony may also be chosen to put family members at ease. But in many other cases, religious content seems to be desired because such ritual practices seem to convey the authenticity of a union to all who might question its legitimacy. As Ellen Lewin showed in *Recognizing Ourselves* (1998), a ceremony conducted in a house of worship by a clerical authority *looks* more like a real wedding than one conducted in a secular manner, a concern that highlights the performative significance of the ritual.

Similarly, couples may deploy some other symbols associated with weddings in their commitment ceremonies. Couples typically choose to wear clothing associated with weddings, such as tuxedos (for gay men and some lesbians) and white dresses (for some lesbians), or variations on such attire, such as matching or color-coordinated outfits. Most couples mark their union with rings, and the form of these may designate some aspect of the union they wish to emphasize; for example, the femme in a gender-variant lesbian couple may wear a diamond engagement ring in addition to a wedding band while her spouse wears only a wedding band. Other aspects of ceremonies also recall weddings that celebrants have attended or ritual elements they may admire or that indicate public approval. For Jewish couples, these may include such elements as the Jewish marriage contract (the *ketubah*, possibly requiring expensive calligraphy and artwork), a wedding canopy (*chuppah*), or the ritual smashing of a wine glass at the end of the ceremony. Other symbols used in ceremonies include the unity candle (two candles used to light a single one to mark the shift from two individuals to a couple), jumping the broom (a ritual developed by slaves to mark unions that could not be legally sanctioned), and a variety of ritual elements drawn from Native American, Buddhist, and other traditions to which the couple may or may not have a direct connection. In some cases, couples may devise symbolic mechanisms that convey their views of their union, such as highlighting symbolic expressions associated with their race or ethnicity (e.g., a Jewish *chuppah* made of kente cloth for a couple who are Jewish and African American). Some celebrants create ritual language that draws on historical research, with frequent attention to the work of historian John Boswell on same-sex unions in premodern Europe (1994), or use various how-to volumes and memoirs that have come out over the years, such as Ayers and Brown's *The Essential Guide to Lesbian and Gay Weddings* (1994) on the esthetics and social strategies involved in planning a ceremony, and Hertz and Doskow's *Making It Legal* (2014) for guidance on legal issues.

While some commitment ceremonies may be very small, private affairs, many couples choose to elaborate them in various ways, drawing on the repertoire of wedding imagery in staging the events. Ceremonies may be followed by catered receptions featuring food and alcohol, live music, and other celebratory elements, or, bespeaking a different esthetic, they may be low-cost events with food produced potluck style. Couples may expect to receive presents, and many register for gifts to avoid receiving items they cannot use. Receipt of linens, dishes, silver, and crystal serve to legitimate the union, as do decisions by families to bestow family heirlooms on couples having a commitment ceremony. The cost of most commitment ceremonies is borne by the couple, with occasional contributions by families.

Guest lists for commitment ceremonies tend to expand beyond the boundaries of LGBT communities, with invitations going to the couple's families, friends, neighbors, co-workers, and others in their widest networks. The presence of multiple generations is preferred, as well, as that indicates a community affirmation of the couple's union. But when families and others who are not members of the LGBT community fail to support the ceremony or perhaps even to attend, couples may experience deep feelings of rejection that may have long-term consequences for their relationships with their families. It is so common for family members to fail to appear at commitment ceremonies that when such relatives do make an appearance, they may be overwhelmed by the enthusiastic response to their presence by the couple and other guests.

SEE ALSO: Same-Sex Marriage

REFERENCES

Ayers, Tessa, and Paul Brown. 1994. *The Essential Guide to Lesbian and Gay Weddings*. San Francisco: Harper.

Boswell, John. 1994. *Same-Sex Unions in Premodern Europe*. New York: Villard Books.

Hertz, Frederick and Emily Doskow. 2014. *Making It Legal: A Guide to Same-Sex Marriage, Domestic Partnerships & Civil Unions*. Berkeley, CA: Nolo Press.

Lewin, Ellen. 1998. *Recognizing Ourselves: Ceremonies of Lesbian and Gay Commitment*. New York: Columbia University Press.

FURTHER READING

Badgett, M. V. Lee. 2010. *When Gay People Get Married: What Happens When Societies Legalize Same-Sex Marriage*. New York: New York University Press.

Ball, Carlos A. 2014. *Same-Sex Marriage and Children: A Tale of History, Social Science, and Law*. Oxford: Oxford University Press.

Bernstein, Mary, and Verta Taylor. 2013. *The Marrying Kind?: Debating Same-Sex Marriage within the Lesbian and Gay Movement*. Minneapolis: University of Minnesota Press.

Butler, Becky. 1990. *Ceremonies of the Heart: Celebrating Lesbian Unions*. Berkeley, CA: Seal Press.

Chauncey, George. 2005. *Why Marriage: The History Shaping Today's Debate over Gay Equality*. New York: Basic Books.

Hull, Kathleen E. 2006. *Same-Sex Marriage: The Cultural Politics of Love and Law*. Cambridge: Cambridge University Press.

Jordan, Mark. 2005. *Blessing Same-Sex Unions: The Perils of Queer Romance and the Confusions of Christian Marriage*. Chicago: University of Chicago Press.

Savage, Dan. 2006. *The Commitment: Love, Sex, Marriage, and My Family*. New York: Plume Publishing.

Communism in Eastern Europe

KATJA M. GUENTHER
University of California, Riverside, USA

Communist Eastern Europe presents a rich terrain for examining the relationships between state, society, and gender. Scholars from a range of disciplines, including anthropology, history, political science, and sociology, have examined gendered relations and structures of gender inequality in the region. Part of the fascination with communist gender relations stems from their marked differences from the US and Western European experiences. Unlike in capitalist democracies, where feminists struggled to win rights for women, the state largely initiated social policies that benefited women in communist states. Still, women and men in communist Eastern Europe hardly enjoyed gender equality; rather, they experienced a diverse and often contradictory range of approaches to the organization of gender.

Any discussion of gender in communist Eastern Europe must begin with recognition of the diversity of this region and the variation across time and place in state development and gender politics. The communist era in Eastern Europe began with the Bolshevik revolution in Russia in 1917 and the subsequent founding of the Union of Soviet Socialist Republics (USSR or Soviet Union, comprised of Armenia, Azerbaijan, Belarus, Estonia, Georgia, Kazakhstan, Kirgizstan, Latvia, Lithuania, Moldovia, Russia, Tajikistan, Turkmenistan, Ukraine, and Uzbekistan) in 1922. The reach of communism expanded substantially at the conclusion of World War II as the Red Army liberated Eastern Europe from the Nazis. Thus, while Eastern European communism began in the Soviet Union, it moved westward after World War II. Soviet communism ultimately extended to seven nations outside of the USSR – Albania, Bulgaria, Czechoslovakia, East Germany, Hungary, Poland, and Romania – following the war.

The communist era ended with the collapse of the last socialist state in Eastern Europe in December 1989 (the USSR dissolved in 1991, but was democratizing already prior to dissolution).

As a theoretical ideal developed by Karl Marx, communism is a system of economic and political organization in which there is no private property and where the state, currency, and class inequality do not exist. In Eastern Europe, this ideal form of communism remained a goal, but was not achieved, so that many argue that the region can more accurately be described as having practiced socialism, the stage of development that precedes and ideally leads to communism. In keeping with current practice, the terms are used interchangeably here. To accomplish communism, states in Eastern Europe took control over and collectivized the means of production, including industry, agriculture, and mining. Private ownership of land, factories, mines, and other assets was abolished. State centralization ensured ideological cohesion among leaders and the concentration of power in the hands of a small political elite (in some cases, largely in the hands of a sole dictator). State socialism also involved high levels of state repression of the citizenry, including incarceration of dissidents and the widespread use of spying on the general population.

While Western narratives of communism tended to focus on the repressive elements of such a system, communist societies also offered citizens safety and security. Communist states centered on an ideology of collectivism, and every member of society was expected to contribute to the social and economic good to the best of their ability, and in exchange would benefit from having their basic needs met throughout the life course. In such societies, class inequalities were markedly reduced relative to such inequalities in capitalist democracies. While the overall standard of living was lower than in capitalist Western Europe, citizens of communist nations had high levels of personal security.

Each of the Soviet states and its satellite nations enacted communism differently, and each state encountered differences in local attitudes and expectations of gender. The Soviet bloc and its allied states in Eastern Europe encompassed an immense amount of diversity, including differences in resources, ethnicity, religion, landscape, urbanization, culture, pre-communist political structures, and ideology. Furthermore, like all societies, communist societies also were far from static; the Soviet Union, for instance, experienced severe repression under the leadership of Joseph Stalin, and later liberalization under Mikhail Gorbachev. Thus, it is not possible to speak of communism as monolithic; instead, communism must be understood as operating with a multiplicity of forms and interacting with other social systems in different ways across geographic boundaries and across time.

To this end, the social organization of gender under communism varied significantly across Eastern Europe and across time. One important constant across communist Eastern Europe was an emphasis on women's roles as workers. All communist states encouraged women's labor force participation, and women were often pressed into employment outside of the home. Women's employment was grounded in at least two logics. First, World War II had devastating impacts on the populations of most European nations, and women's labor was needed to rebuild and to grow economically. Bringing women into the workforce was one relatively easy way to increase economic activity and redevelopment after the war. Second, communist ideology often invoked the idea of a gender-neutral worker, and women were understood as being a central part of the project of building a communist state and society. To this end, the state constructed women as worker-citizens who, alongside men, had an important role to play in building and maintaining communist society.

Communist policies thus promoted women's labor force participation. In fact, in many socialist states, *not* working was no longer an option for women. East Germany soon became the global leader in women's labor force participation with upwards of 90 percent of women of working age studying or working, a pattern that was typical across communist Eastern Europe. Although many women followed gendered career paths, entering into occupations such as childcare and nursing, the state also encouraged women's participation in workplaces involving hard physical labor or technical skills. In rural areas, women worked alongside men in agricultural collectives, often engaged in physically strenuous work that also involved knowledge of agricultural science. The state pushed girls and women to obtain higher education in fields that had long been men's domain only, such as engineering and chemistry, and the rates of women's participation in science, technology, engineering, and medicine (STEM) exceeded those in Western Europe by wide margins. Although women continued to be underrepresented at the highest levels of management, the state forced the breakdown of barriers that had historically prevented them from entering most of these occupations.

Still, women and men had different life experiences and were constrained by gendered norms and policies under communism. Pressure on women to work outside of the home did not translate into equality within the workplace or the home. At work, supervisors disfavored women for leadership roles because they continued to view women's primary allegiance to the home, and feared women would be less productive and/or less committed workers because of the demands of their families on their time. At home, women were disproportionately responsible for domestic work, including childcare and the time-consuming acquisition of tightly rationed goods. While in many socialist states mothering work was supported by state policy – such as generous maternity leave and days off each month for women to take children to appointments and meet other domestic responsibilities – mothering continued to be gender-specific labor. Further, the gendered nature of family-friendly policies ensured that women, rather than men, were constructed as workers with other obligations that interfered with their workplace contributions. Given the emphasis on women as caregivers in communist Eastern Europe, it is no surprise that labor market sectors that involved caregiving work, such as nursing, day-care provision, and elementary school teaching, continued to be viewed as feminine. Thus, while women entered into men-dominated occupations in much higher proportions than in Western Europe, men did not likewise enter into women-dominated fields, which continued to be viewed as uniquely appropriate for women.

Women's bodies were also subject to state control in different and sometimes competing ways. Even as the state celebrated women's workplace contributions and sought to encourage their full participation in communist society, women had minimal state protection from gender-based violence, and rape and battering were widespread with limited legal or social remedies. In spite of failing to protect women from gender-based violence, socialist governments wanted to encourage reproduction as a strategy for population growth following the devastating losses of World War II, and took varying approaches to achieving this. In many socialist states, birth control and abortion were relatively accessible, intended to give women control over their reproduction and empower them to choose when and how to start families. The USSR was the first European nation to legalize abortion in 1920, but Joseph Stalin banned the practice again in 1936 out of concern about population growth, instead promoting a set of policies intended to make it easier for single women to have children. Following his death, abortion was legalized again in 1955 in the USSR, and the USSR had one of the highest abortion rates in the world in the 1960s when it was seen as an acceptable form of birth control; some analyses suggest that there were more abortions performed than live births in the Soviet Union in the late 1950s and 1960s.

Although the trend in the Soviet and allied states was toward accessible birth control and abortion, in Romania, communist head of state Nicolae Ceaușescu made divorce almost impossible to obtain and banned abortion and access to birth control (at least through official means) in 1967. These pro-natalist policies were substantial departures from state policy in Romania prior to 1967, where divorce and abortion had been quite accessible. To promote family formation and childrearing, the Romanian state even went so far as to fine people over the age of 25 who were childfree. While reproductive rights and family policies under Ceaușescu's rule are examples of extremes in many respects, they point to the variation that existed within communist Eastern Europe.

Many communist states deemphasized marriage as a necessary element of family life; rates of births to unwed mothers were far higher in communist Eastern Europe than in capitalist democratic Western Europe, and divorce was also easy for men or women to obtain in most communist countries. Women's and men's ability to form families outside of marriage was an effort by socialist states to undermine ties to family and to make the primary bond to the nation. While single motherhood was indeed common in communist Eastern Europe, and divorce also very common, the family continued to be a sanctuary from the intrusion of the state, and thus was never eroded as a major system of social organization in the way some communist leaders had hoped.

Variation in gender policy and practice also occurred over time. In Hungary, for example, how the state defined which of its citizens warranted state assistance – a definitional process deeply entwined with gender – shifted roughly every 20 years. In Romania, women's right to control their reproductive capacities was eroded as the state became more repressive. In the Soviet Union, women's rights were enshrined in the Constitution in the late 1970s with additional legal protections added in the 1980s, suggesting an expansion of women's rights and greater state acknowledgment of the need to regulate gender discrimination, especially in the workplace.

Political power largely remained with men in communist states. Party leaders were overwhelmingly men, and women were often encouraged to focus their energies on the women's leagues of the party. None of the communist states ever had a woman ruler, nor routine participation by women in the top ranks of the party. Thus, although communist states supported the breakdown of many occupational barriers, access to political power remained a privilege only men could enjoy.

Gender relations in communist Eastern Europe also intersected with chronic housing shortages that existed in most urban areas. Following World War II, many fledgling socialist states began aggressive programs of building housing for workers, most often in mid-rise apartment buildings. Still, the rate of housing construction did not keep up with the rate of urbanization, and housing shortages remained acute. In Russia, each family was promised an allocation of five square meters per member, but many families received smaller allotments. Many families lived in communal apartments in which between two and seven families cohabited, each with a single private room and with access to a shared kitchen and living room. Adults often continued to cohabit with their parents, or lived in barrack-style housing for unmarried people. Most housing lacked amenities taken for granted in Western Europe, such as laundry facilities and private bathrooms and kitchens. In these conditions, privacy was rare, and divorced couples often continued to live with each other after divorce due to a lack of other options. The lack of privacy seems to have contributed to an openness about sexuality and other human behaviors, while also providing the state with opportunities for surveillance as apartment-mates in communal apartments would routinely spy on one another. Some suggest that this type of communal living also encouraged changes in romantic/sexual partners.

Like other gendered aspects of life under communism, sexual norms varied across place and time. In Russia, for example, Vladimir Lenin decriminalized homosexuality in 1917, but Joseph Stalin re-criminalized it in 1933 in a ban that lasted 60 years and imposed severe criminal penalties on those caught engaging in same-sex sex acts such that those even suspected of being gay could be sent to a gulag, the infamous forced labor camps. Homosexual subcultures persisted, particularly in cities, but the risks of being gay or lesbian or engaging in same-sex sex acts were great, and those suspected of homosexuality faced criminal penalties and/or efforts at conversion therapy and other psychiatric treatments. Homosexuality was socially constructed as a form of bourgeois self-indulgence, and as a threat to the moral fiber and reproductive capacity of the nation. However, state policies toward gays and lesbians also varied across time and place; in many socialist states, homosexuality was largely invisible and omitted from public discourse, while at least four socialist states decriminalized homosexuality in the 1960s, and East Germany had an active and visible gay and lesbian subculture in the 1970s and 1980s.

SEE ALSO: Communism in Russia; Gender and History of Revolutions in Eastern and Central Europe; Gender, Politics, and the State in Central and Eastern Europe

FURTHER READING

Ashwin, Sarah, ed. 2000. *Gender, State and Society in Soviet and Post-Soviet Russia*. New York: Routledge.

Edmondson, Linda, ed. 2008. *Women and Society in Russia and the Soviet Union*. Cambridge: Cambridge University Press.

Harsch, Donna. 2008. *Revenge of the Domestic: Women, the Family, and Communism in the*

German Democratic Republic. Princeton, NJ: Princeton University Press.

Lenin, Vladimir Il'ich. 1969. *The Emancipation of Women.* New York: International Publishers.

Penn, Shana, and Jill Massino, eds. 2009. *Gender Politics and Everyday Life in State Socialist Eastern and Central Europe.* New York: Palgrave Macmillan.

Stella, Francesca. 2014. *Lesbian Lives in Soviet and Post-Soviet Russia.* Basingstoke, UK: Palgrave Macmillan.

Communism in Russia

LAURIE ESSIG
Middlebury College, Vermont, USA

With the Communist Revolution in Russia in 1917, gender and sexuality were revolutionized. In terms of gender roles, many Bolsheviks believed in the liberation of women from the domestic sphere. The 1918 Family Code created legal equality for women, established no-fault divorce, and created equal rights for all children whether born to wed or unwed parents.

Many Bolsheviks at the time relied on Friedrich Engel's (1902) formulation, in *The Origin of the Family, Private Property and the State,* that private property and the transmission of that property from father to son represented the "world historical defeat of the female sex." Thus, the 1918 Code took property out of marriage relations completely.

The Bolsheviks quickly set up a *Zhenotdel* (Women's Committee) under the leadership of Alexandra Kollentai. In her 1920 essay, "Communism and the Family," Kollentai wrote:

> There is no escaping the fact: the old type of family has had its day. The family is withering away not because it is being forcibly destroyed by the state, but because the family is ceasing to be a necessity. (Kollentai 1980)

In the same way that women were freed from traditional patriarchal family forms, sexual minorities were also granted an unprecedented amount of freedom under the Bolsheviks. Laws against sodomy (*muzhelozhestvo*) were abolished in the 1922 code and in the early years there was a lack of state interest in same-sex relationships.

These initially revolutionary stances toward traditional sex and gender roles disappeared after Joseph Stalin came to power. Although women continued to enter the workforce in large numbers, in Stalinist Russia there was a reinvigoration of women's roles as mothers and wives. This made women responsible for (free) domestic labor as well as paid labor, a typical double-burdening of women under patriarchal industrialization. This created a paradoxical position for women in Communist Russia, one in which they were entering industry in unprecedented numbers, but also entering into lower paid jobs and continuing to provide free labor at home.

For sexual minorities, Stalinism rebranded homosexuality not just as a bourgeois illness, but a foreign one as well. As Maksim Gorky put it in a speech in 1933, "eliminate homosexuality and you'll make fascism disappear." In 1934, sodomy was recriminalized and medical experts continued to describe non-heterosexual practices as pathological. This set the stage for what would become Soviet attitudes toward sexual minorities. Women who desired other women were often labeled as mentally ill and put into psychiatric institutions. There they were treated with psychiatric drugs and electric shock therapy. Men were subject to Article 121.1, which could result in imprisonment.

By the time the Communist regime began to lose its hold in Russia, these more traditional attitudes toward women and sexual minorities were firmly in place. When Mikhael Gorbachev began to import consumer goods under his program of "perestroika," the first three goods to be imported were pantyhose, cosmetics, and high heels. Yet this was at a time when Soviet women had no access to reliable birth control other than abortion and did not even have sanitary napkins or tampons.

When the anti-sodomy law was finally overturned in Russia in 1993, the Soviet attitude that homosexuality was a foreign perversion did not disappear. It was exactly this formulation that was used in the recent debates around "homosexual propaganda" and the passage of a 2013 federal law banning "the propaganda of non-traditional sexual relationships."

Despite the persistence of sexism and homophobia, both feminism and queer rights activists found space in late Soviet Russia. Under the direction of Olga Lipovskaya, the feminist journal *Women's Reader* was published and a network of feminist activists formed. Gay and lesbian rights groups such as Treugolnik and Krylia demanded the de-criminalization of sodomy and an end to diagnosing same-sex desire as mental illness.

Despite the promise of liberation contained in the early Communist Revolution, the continued oppression of women and sexual minorities in Soviet Russia and the contemporary resurgence of patriarchal nationalism have left behind a contradictory history of gender and sexuality, one of extreme optimism and brave activism coupled with continued state oppression of both women and sexual minorities.

SEE ALSO: Communism in Eastern Europe; Communism and Gender in China; Communism and Gender in the United States; Feminisms, Marxist and Socialist; Women's and Feminist Activism in Russia, Ukraine, and Eurasia

REFERENCES

Engels, Friedrich. 1902. *The Origin of the Family, Private Property and the State*, translated by Ernest Untermann. Chicago: Charles H. Kerr & Co.

Kollentai, Alexandra. 1980. *The Selected Writings of Alexandra Kollentai*, translated by Alix Holt. New York: W.W. Norton & Company.

FURTHER READING

Attword, Lynne. 1999. *Creating the New Soviet Woman: Women's Magazines as Engineers of Female Identity, 1922–53*. New York: Palgrave Macmillian.

Essig, Laurie. 1999. *Queer in Russia: A Story of Sex, Self and the Other*. Durham: Duke University Press.

Goldman, Wendy. 1993. *Women, the State and Revolution: Soviet Family Policy, 1917–1936*. New York: Cambridge University Press.

Goldman, Wendy. 2002. *Women at the Gates: Gender and Industry in Stalin's Russia*. Cambridge: Cambridge University Press.

Healey, Dan. 2001. *Homosexual Desire in Revolutionary Russia*. Chicago: University of Chicago Press.

Lapidus, Gail Warshofsky. 1978. *Women in Soviet Society: Equality, Development and Social Change*. Berkeley: University of California Press.

Stites, Richard. 1978. *The Women's Liberation Movement in Russia: Feminism, Nihilism, and Bolshevism, 1860–1930*. Princeton: Princeton University Press.

Wood, Elizabeth A. 1997. *The Baba and the Comrade: Gender and Politics in Revolutionary Russia*. Bloomington: Indiana University Press.

Communism and Gender in China[1]

WANG ZHENG
University of Michigan, USA

As depicted in most scholarship on socialist China, the socialist state appeared as a paradoxically "women-friendly" patriarchal

[1] Adapted with permission from Wang Zheng. *Finding Women in the State: Feminism and Revolution of Culture in the Early People's Republic of China (1949–1964)*. University of California Press. In press.

party-state that sporadically promoted gender equality. An adequate understanding of Chinese communism has to integrate knowledge of socialist state feminists who fought on multiple fronts as Communist Party members towards an egalitarian vision of a socialist modern China premised on *nannü pingdeng* (男女平等) – equality between men and women.

The concentration of revolutionary women and men from diverse backgrounds in a political party formed amidst the cross-currents of feminism, socialism, Marxism, nationalism, liberalism, and anarchism in the early twentieth century and shaped by decades of military combat, political strife, and violent suppressions by their enemies, including imperialist colonizers, Japanese fascists, and the Nationalist government, necessarily constituted extremely complex historical legacies and messy interpersonal networks. Passionate revolutionary women and men with firm convictions, though diverse visions of a modern socialist China, shaped the complicated dynamics and multifaceted struggles in the Chinese Communist Party's highly volatile and historically contingent experiment of establishing a socialist state.

WOMEN AND CHINESE COMMUNISM

In the course of the Communist Revolution before it won state power in 1949, tens of thousands of women from diverse social backgrounds joined the Chinese Communist Party (CCP). The first cohort joined the CCP in the 1920s. Most early Communist women were urban-based educated feminists of the May Fourth generation, and some were women factory workers active in the CCP-led workers' movement. Many in this cohort died either in the Nationalist Party's hunt-down of Communists after the break-up of the first United Front between the CCP and the Nationalist Party (1924–1927) or in the subsequent military battles. The survivors of this cohort served in various official posts at the national level in the early People's Republic of China (PRC). Two CCP women from this cohort, Cai Chang (康克清) and Deng Yingchao (邓颖超), became founders and leaders of the All-China Women's Federation, a women's rights organization established in 1949.

The second cohort was mainly comprised of rural women who joined the Communist Revolution when the CCP established its rural military bases after the break-up of the first United Front. CCP membership swelled from over 40,000 in 1928 to over 300,000 in 1934. Many rural women were involved in guerrilla warfare and the Soviet-style local government in the CCP bases in southern and central China. After the CCP's military defeat by Nationalist Party (GMD) forces in 1934, however, only 10 percent of the Communist troops survived the brutal ordeal of the two-year-long retreat and relocation, which Mao Zedong later named "the Long March." Among the Communist women who survived the Long March and reached the CCP's new bases in the northwest, several rural women guerrilla leaders from the second cohort rose to leadership at the national level, including Kang Keqing (康克清), who became the vice chair of the All-China Women's Federation in 1957, and the chair from 1978 to 1988 (Young 2001).

The third cohort joined the CCP in the war of resistance against Japan's invasion, especially after the Marco Polo Bridge Incident in 1937 when Japanese troops attacked China proper. Patriotic zeal for national salvation as well as dislocation caused by the war drove hundreds and thousands of urban students and young professionals to the CCP bases established in peripheral rural areas after the Long March. A desolate rural town in the northwest, Yan'an, became the CCP headquarters during the resistance war period, attracting many left-oriented urbanites. The party membership expanded dramatically from about 40,000 in 1937 to over 800,000 in 1940. In this cohort, some urban celebrities, such as Chen Bo'er and Shen Zijiu, took on leading official posts in various branches of the central government of the early PRC. In most cases, educated women in the third cohort became officials at provincial or municipal levels, and rural women with little education staffed the county governments or held lower level posts in the early PRC.

The fourth cohort joined the CCP during the civil war between the CCP and the GMD in the late 1940s, after Japan's surrender. This cohort was more diverse, including urban young students, factory workers, professionals, and rural women in the old CCP base areas and newly occupied regions. Many in this cohort staffed the new socialist state's local governments, as well as women's federations at the urban district, street, rural county, or township level. By the time of the CCP's victory in 1949, its membership had expanded to 4.49 million, of whom 11.9 percent were women. Integrating these 530,000 CCP women in our understanding of socialist China is a crucial step towards engendering the Chinese revolution, an agenda proposed by the late historian Christina K. Gilmartin (1995) in her work on radical women of the CCP in the 1920s, which has remained largely unfulfilled.

Women who joined the CCP out of conviction expressed their conscious rejection of a conventional life for women of their time. By 1949, given that 90 percent of Chinese women were still illiterate, educated women were predominantly from families with some degree of social privilege. Their choice to risk their lives by joining an embattled political force, either to pursue an idealistic dream or to escape from predicaments in their personal life, or both, indicates the presence of a clear political consciousness and commitment, as well as strong will and inclination for action.

FEMINISM AND CHINESE COMMUNISM

Feminism was one of the many ideologies embraced by educated Chinese in their pursuit of modernity and rejection of an ancient dynastic system since the turn of the twentieth century. Just as the imagination of a modern China has never been singular, feminism has also been understood in diverse ways that, nevertheless, express a shared concern with gendered social arrangements. At the turn of the twentieth century, anarchist, socialist, liberal, evolutionary, eugenic, and nationalist positions shaped various feminist articulations. In their proposals for changing gender hierarchy rooted in ancient Chinese philosophy and gender norms based on Confucian ideals of gender differentiation and segregation, feminists expressed different imaginings of a better future: a more humane society that centered on social justice and equality, a modern society that allowed individuals to break away from the constraints of Confucian social norms embedded in kinship relations as well as the control of an imperial polity, and/or a stronger nation that turned China from being the prey of imperialist powers into a sovereign state. Regardless of their diverse political positions, reformers, revolutionaries, professionals, and educated women and men from elite social backgrounds who embraced various versions of feminism agreed on the necessity of changing gender practices in transforming their ancient civilization, which had fallen into deep crisis in a time of imperialist and colonialist expansion. The confluence of diverse and often contradictory ideas and practices rapidly made a neologism a key phrase in twentieth-century China: "equality between men and women" (男女平等), a Chinese rendition of the English phrase "sexual equality" that had been circulating globally since the late nineteenth century. Signifying a conscious rejection of the foundation of Confucian social order prescribing *nannü* (men and women) distinction, 男女有别 and *nannü youbie* (differentiation between men and women), 男女平等 *nannü pingdeng* (equality between men and women) became a badge of modernity adopted by social groups and political parties that attempted to assert a progressive identity. A powerful promotion of and identification with feminism transformed the subjectivities of a small group of educated Chinese women and men to various degrees in the early part of the twentieth century.

Amidst the rapidly shifting political and cultural cross-currents in China, informed by global socialist and feminist movements, the CCP endorsed "equality between men and women" in its platform from its inception in 1921. In fact, its founders, such as Chen Duxiu (陈独秀) and Li Dazhao (李大钊), had been among the most vocal advocates of feminism in the New Culture Movement before they turned their attention to organizing a Marxist party. The birth of the New Culture Movement was marked by Chen Duxiu's publication of *The New Youth* magazine in 1915, which rapidly became a rallying point for cultural radicals aiming to transform the dominant Confucian morality and cultural practices in order to modernize China. Gender hierarchy and differentiation were highlighted as the quintessential symbol of the backwardness of Confucian culture – defined as "feudalist" – in much of the New Culture intellectuals' critiques. Feminism was enthusiastically embraced as a powerful weapon to combat "feudalism" that had dominated China for millennia.

The small circle of cultural radicals rapidly expanded its social and intellectual influence after May 4, 1919, when college and secondary school students spearheaded a nationwide patriotic movement. Ignited by the treaty signed by world powers at the Versailles Conference which transferred all of Germany's rights in Shandong Province to Japan after World War I, the May Fourth Movement, with passionately anti-imperialist male and female students as major constituents, became a powerful vehicle that carried the New Culture's advocacy of anti-feudalism, including the promotion of feminism, into mainstream urban society. The confluence of the New Culture and May Fourth movements (1915–1925) sprouted an organized feminist movement that peaked in 1922, and many May Fourth feminists later had important roles in China's political, social, and cultural transformations. From the two cohorts – the older New Culturalists and younger May Fourth Movement participants – emerged a small group of men and women, disillusioned with the Western liberal but imperialist powers, who formed the Communist Party to pursue a socialist modernity modeled after the newly founded Soviet Union.

Fighting for female constituencies through feminist organizations in the early 1920s, leading feminists in the CCP defined feminists who did not embrace the Communist Revolution as Western, bourgeois, and narrow feminists, turning the word "feminism" 女权主义 *nüquanzhuyi* into a negative one in the CCP's discourse. Nevertheless, feminists in the CCP inherited and revised May Fourth feminist agendas of women's liberation in the course of the Communist Revolution. Replacing the discredited word 女权 *nüquan*, which carried multiple meanings including women's rights, women's power, and feminism, the term 妇女权利 *funü quanli* (women's rights) gained unchallenged legitimacy in the CCP, and CCP members' activities centering on promoting *funü quanli* and mobilizing women for the Communist Revolution, named "women-work" 妇女工作 *funü gongzuo*, was institutionalized in the CCP since the early 1920s. Managed by a women's department or a women-work committee in various periods, women-work was a major platform for CCP feminists engaged in pursuing gendered social justice and equality as well as an important branch of the CCP specialized in mobilizing women's participation in the Communist Revolution.

The CCP feminists' firm identification with the party's ultimate goal had complex consequences. Most significantly, the victory of the CCP enabled them to wield the socialist state power to materialize their feminist dreams. The numbers and power of Chinese socialist state feminists of the early PRC were arguably unprecedented in feminist histories of the world, as a consequence of a historically specific Communist Revolution in the world's most populous nation. The first National Women's Congress, organized by the CCP feminists in March 1949, was the first national conference of any social groups convened in anticipation of a transfer of political power to plan for action in a socialist China. It resolved to set up a national women's organization, All-China Democratic Women's Federation (ACDWF; its name was changed to All-China Women's Federation in 1957, hence ACWF), an umbrella organization that horizontally united all pro-CCP women's organizations, and an official institution that vertically reached all women down to the rural villages and urban neighborhoods nationwide. State feminists made this major move when the top CCP leaders were preoccupied with the political takeover and military maneuvers to drive the remaining Nationalist Party forces down to the south.

Two months after the founding of the PRC, one of the first international conferences of the new socialist China was convened in Beijing on December 10, 1949. The All-Asian Women's Congress, attended by 197 representatives from 23 countries, was organized by the ACDWF in its new role as a member of the Women's International Democratic Federation (WIDF). Hosting an international conference on women before the PRC established any diplomatic relationship with any nation except for the Soviet Union indicated the CCP leadership's full support for this initiative. The event not only demonstrated state feminists' conscious efforts to merge the women's movement in the PRC with socialist women's movements globally, it also revealed the crucial role the ACDWF played in the new socialist state's efforts to establish international connections.

ROLE OF THE CHINESE COMMUNIST STATE IN RESTRUCTURING GENDER RELATIONS

In late September 1948, before the CCP headquarters moved to Beijing, the Central Committee of Women-Work was assigned a task, to draft a marriage law for the new socialist China. Chairing a group of six CCP feminists of the first three cohorts, Deng Yingchao provided a strong leadership in drafting a feminist law, the first law passed in the PRC. A central debate concerned the freedom to divorce. Some CCP women officials supported restrictions on divorce in order to deter male CCP officials from replacing their old wives with young, urban, educated women. Deng Yingchao insisted on removing restrictions on the ground that the law should prioritize the interest of the vast majority of women, that is, rural women. Poor rural women who were sold to men or endured an abusive marital life needed a divorce law that could assist their escape from their predicament.

The 1950 Marriage Law stipulated women's autonomy in marriage and divorce, as well as equal rights. The radical feminist law is a quintessential case of how CCP feminists used state power to dismantle an ancient marriage institution based on parental authority to arrange marriages for children, as well as many customary marriage practices that were against women's will, and treated women as property of men. The ACDWF, coordinating support from multiple branches of different levels of government, turned the promulgation and enforcement of the Marriage Law into a powerful mass campaign promoting women's equal rights and personal freedom, ideas they inherited from May Fourth feminism. The May Fourth agenda of anti-feudalism in the expression of women's equal rights and independent personhood was most widely circulated among the vast population in this period to the extent that the Chinese term "feudalism" (封建主义) has become a gender-inflected key word encompassing everything we today call sexism: masculinism, patriarchy, male chauvinism, and/or misogyny. "Equality between men and women" and "women's liberation," popularized via state-owned media and cultural production, became household slogans intimately connecting gender equality with the authority of the new socialist state. The feminist law promulgated with socialist state power effectively transformed not only the marriage institution, but also gendered cultural practices and discourses.

MASCULINISM AND PATRIARCHY IN CHINESE COMMUNISM

Feminist CCP members have existed in a contradictory political environment. Ideologically, the party's platform has endorsed a feminist pursuit of gender equality and upholds "equality between men and women" as the law of the land. The Constitution of the PRC grants legitimacy for feminist expressions and actions in the official system. Institutionally, however, the various administrative levels of the CCP's leadership have always been predominantly occupied by men, many of whose subjectivities seem to have been shaped by a pervasive patriarchal culture rather than fundamentally transformed by feminist and socialist principles of eliminating all hierarchies. In practice, the presumptions and power dynamics of male supremacy could overrule the ideological and legal legitimacy of feminist actions. A masculinist in a position of authority could easily tell a woman official who proposed action on behalf of women's interests that he also believed in the importance of this issue, but more important and larger issues deserved the government's resources and energy. The ACWF, after all, was organized as a party-led mass organization rather than an executive branch of the government, although everyone in the Women's Federation is also on the government payroll. The distribution of power between this gender-based mass organization and the government was a contested matter in the new socialist state. The subsequent institutional marginalization of Women's Federation officials has conditioned the routine experiences of feminists in the CCP that women-work was of lesser value, except for those moments when some item on the Party Central's agenda required that women be mobilized or attention be paid to gender equality.

A major erasure of state feminists arose in the production of historical knowledge of socialism since the late 1970s, when the CCP began to depart from the socialist course after Mao's death in 1976. In Chinese intellectuals' concerted critique of the CCP's crimes under Mao Zedong's dictatorship, the socialist period was mainly described through condemnations of the ills of that era, and Mao became synonymous with socialism. This antisocialist discourse is both grossly reductive and openly masculinist. In postsocialist intellectuals' efforts to dismantle both the CCP's authoritarian rule and socialist egalitarian values and practices, the mainstream gender ideology and practices of the socialist period that promoted equality between men and women were characterized as the Maoist state's imposition of gender sameness, a crime of the CCP that distorted women's natural femininity and masculinized them. Restoring gender differentiation was promoted by both of the urban elite's conflicting proposals: embracing a Western capitalist modernity symbolized by sexualized and commoditized women in advertisements; or reviving a Confucian tradition by retrieving "Oriental women's traditional virtues." Rearranging gender practices became a prominent theme in elite proposals to undo socialist modernity. The vehemence with which these ideas were advocated was strikingly similar to their forebears' passionate agitation for change in gender practices at the turn of the twentieth century, though pointing towards a reverse direction in their imagining of a gendered future. As many scholars have observed, this initiative constituted an open and powerful backlash against the gender policies of the socialist period.

At the Fourth UN Conference on Women hosted by the Chinese government in 1995, China's then-president, Jiang Zemin, gave a welcome speech that did not attract much public attention. The following year, on March 8, International Women's Day, the *China Women's News* published by the ACWF reprinted Jiang's speech. It chose one sentence to stand as the title, "Equality between Men and Women is the Fundamental State Policy in Promoting Social Development in Our Country," and framed it as a new official decree from the CCP's top leadership. Reporters from the newspaper interviewed heads of provincial governments and ministers of various branches of the central government asking what concrete measures they had taken to implement this "fundamental state policy." By continuously publishing interviews in which officials felt obliged to say something about equality between men and women, the state feminists created an illusion that a political campaign to advance this policy was going on. Although this strategy encountered resistance when some male officials insisted on seeing the official decree announcing this "fundamental state policy," state feminists forged ahead, disguising their own initiative as if it were merely an effort to implement existing principles. Equality between men and women as the fundamental state policy was finally written into the Law of Protecting the Rights and Interests of Women in 2005, and it appeared in the Work Report of the CCP 18th Congress in 2012.

The ACWF embodied a dilemma emerged since the early days of the CCP: the institutionalized women-work in the CCP, a prominent progressive stance superior to those political parties or forces that totally exclude or ignore women, was turned into a marginalized enclave of feminists within the political system. State feminists had to fight for political and material resources as well as recognition of women's interests and rights from an internally structured disadvantaged position. The tactic of self-effacing public representation of the ACWF's work similarly emerged in CCP feminists' long experience of operating in a male-dominated party that often created a perilous political environment for feminists.

Historically, the label of "narrow bourgeois feminism" was used as a political club to beat down those outspoken CCP feminists who insisted on the priority of women's interests or raised a critical voice against male chauvinism in the CCP. In this historical context, camouflaging their feminist agenda with legitimate, seemingly ungendered party slogans and attributing their own accomplishments to the "wise leadership of the Party" were, and still are, the hallmark of their public statements. Not only did this maneuver claim legitimacy for their actions by appealing to the authority of the party, it also publicly acknowledged their role as dutiful subordinates to the Party Central, or to the various administrative levels of the Party Committees, which were the immediate supervisors of the women's federations. In sum, a women's organization that aimed to transform the gender hierarchy nevertheless staged a gendered performance in accordance with prevailing gender norms that extolled the womanly virtues of modesty, hard work, self-effacement, self-sacrifice, and a lack of desire for power and fame. Acting in accordance with this gender script could most effectively ease the possible irritation or even resentment of male authorities. By glossing over their struggles behind the scenes, this self-effacing rhetoric ensured that these dynamic women leaders were, and remained, unknown to the public. Receding into the shadows, socialist state feminists contributed to the myth of a monolithic patriarchal party-state that sporadically showed benevolence to women.

In many political storms after the founding of the PRC, state feminists were sometimes the targets of deliberate suppression or the inadvertent casualties of power struggles. Even when they were not affected personally, their feminist agenda would often be brushed aside by imperatives from the Party Central. Achieving women's liberation in an actual socialist state proved to be far more complicated than what was conceptualized in theory.

Though never in the center of the political power of the CCP, the first generation of state feminists simultaneously enjoyed tremendous institutional and informal power gained from their seniority in the party and suffered from deep entanglement in the political system. Their empowerment as state feminists came at a price: serious constraints resulted from their being an integral part of the CCP, whose male-dominated leadership's embrace of gender equality was often conditional and instrumental and whose preoccupations could be detrimental to women's interests.

Postsocialist Chinese intellectuals' condemnation of Mao's dictatorship consolidated a lingering Cold War paradigm of a "totalitarian Communist party-state" in the field of Chinese studies in the United States. By ignoring fissures, contradictions, gaps, and conflicts inherently embedded in the socialist state formation, and by assuming the impossibility of expressions of feminist agency in the male-dominated power structure, a masculinist fixation on power struggles among top male leaders in high politics has effectively worked to erase feminist contentions in the socialist state. At the same time, feminist criticism of a centralized socialist patriarchal state has also become a blindfold that prevents us from seeing subversive women in the state and from exploring theoretical implications of gender transformations and feminist possibilities generated in the process of building it. As a result, the gendered internal workings of the "party-state" remain unexplained, inside feminist agitators are unknown, and conventional assumptions persist.

SEE ALSO: Feminism, Chinese; Gender, Politics, and the State in East Asia; Women's and Feminist Activism in East Asia

REFERENCES

Gilmartin, Christina K. 1995. *Engendering the Chinese Revolution: Radical Women, Communist Politics, and Mass Movements in the 1920s.* Berkeley: University of California Press.

Young, Helen Praeger. 2001. *Choosing Revolution: Chinese Women Soldiers in the Long March.* Urbana: University of Illinois Press.

FURTHER READING

Chuanhui, Huang. 2004. *Tianxia Hunyin: Gongheguo Sanbu Hunyinfa Jishi* [天下婚姻:共和国三部婚姻法纪事] *(Marriage Under the Heaven: Three Marriage Laws of the PRC)*. Shanghai: Wenhui Press.

Davin, Delia. 1976. *Woman-Work: Women and the Party in Revolutionary China*. Oxford: Oxford University Press.

Feng, Jin. 1993. *Deng Yingchao Zhuan* [邓颖超传] *(A Biography of Deng Yingchao)*. Beijing: People's Press.

Qiong, Luo. 2007. "Xinzhongguo diyibu hunyinfa qicao qianhou" [新中国第一部婚姻法起草前后] ("Drafting the First Marriage Law of the New China"). In *Kangzheng, Jiefang, Pingdeng-Luo Qiong Wenji* [抗争 解放 平等—罗琼文集] *(Resistance, Emancipation, Equality: An Anthology by Luo Qiong)*, 427–428. Beijing: Chinese Women's Press.

Yongqiang, Duan. 2000. *Luo Qiong Fangtan lu* [罗琼访谈录] *(Interviews with Luo Qiong)*. Beijing: Chinese Women's Press.

Zheng, Wang. 1995. *Women in the Chinese Enlightenment: Oral and Textual Histories*. Berkeley: University of California Press.

Communism and Gender in the United States

ELIZABETH MAYNARD
McGill University, Canada

The post-World War II period in the United States is an acutely useful example in understanding how political systems both inform and are informed by constructions of gender. As the fear of communism, or the "Red Scare," reached histrionic levels, so too did the terms of the postwar "crisis of masculinity." The political and popular rhetoric of postwar America was infused with language that blurred the borders between gender, sexuality, and political affiliation, often explicitly stating a correlation between communist and non-normative gender identity and sexuality. This entry traces the ways in which the political rhetoric of the late 1940s and 1950s responded to the external threats of fascism and communism by shoring up "commonsense" constructions of gender – specifically the hard, resilient, individualistic masculinity of America that helped to win World War II, and was vital to the success of the nation in the postwar period. As this construction of gender proved to be less self-evident than previously believed, the paranoid fear about the insidious infiltration of communism mirrored the terms of the corrupting forces of deviant gender and sexual identity.

The construction of the normative masculine subject in the postwar period was white, Christian, middle class, and heterosexual (May 1988; Gilbert 2005). He served as the nucleus for the middle-class family, the unit upon which the United States' economic prosperity was built. These components were necessarily interrelated parts of the constructed subjectivity that underpinned the postwar "dominant fiction," which can be defined as a contingent and constructed ideological reality (Silverman 1992). The dominant fiction, sustained by ideological beliefs, must appear as completely natural and obvious in order to be believed.

Arthur Schlesinger's *The Vital Center: The Politics of Freedom* is understood as a seminal text in the development of the gendered political discourse of the postwar era (Schlesinger 1949). Its project was to recover and redefine liberalism and push it toward the center. For Schlesinger, the liberals of the Depression era put too much stock in utopian fantasies, while the horrors of World War II and the solidification of Stalin's totalitarian regime only proved the fallibility, and indeed the potential evil, of humans. Schlesinger articulated the contemporary problems of America as primarily psychological. In this "age of anxiety," freedom had become a burden for the modern individual, which resulted in the allure of surrendering to totalitarianism. Schlesinger's text is infused with language that invokes the valuated gender binary. As James Gilbert points out, the terms masculine and feminine carried "inherent implications of positive and negative" in the postwar era: when Schlesinger mourns the feminization of the liberal, he is implying that a previous "vital" subject position has become soft, weak, and vulnerable to totalitarian thought (Gilbert 2005, 66). Indeed, Schlesinger made a point of averring his anti-Communist stance in masculinist terms while criticizing leftist intellectuals of the 1930s who refrained from getting involved in the "real" political world, that is, serving in the military (Cuordileone 2005).

The infamous 1948 Kinsey Report, officially entitled *Sexual Behavior in the Human Male*, revealed the tenuousness of the "commonsense" assumptions about gender and sexuality upon which texts such as Schlessinger's relied (Kinsey et al. 1948). Despite being a dense, scientific text, nearly one quarter of a million copies were sold in the first few months of publication; within 10 days of its release, the publisher ordered a sixth printing for a total of 185,000 copies in print. It seeped into popular culture, inspiring not only articles and interviews, but also cartoons and songs. It elicited a flurry of conversations about sex, but the most immediate impact was the "homosexual panic" and juridical construction of the categories "homosexual" and "lesbian." The report made evident the gap between the "truth" of a subject's sexuality and their visibility. It suggested, strongly, that sexual identities were far more fluid than previously believed: 50 percent of men admitted to having been aroused by members of the same sex, 37 percent to having a post-adolescent homosexual encounter that brought them to orgasm, and 4 percent to being solely homosexual. According to Kinsey, only very few people were "purely" homosexual or heterosexual, and most people existed somewhere in the middle on the spectrum of attraction. It was this newly discovered flexibility of categories believed to be static, certain, and defining that was most shocking. Not only did the Kinsey Report reveal that *far* more American people were participating in homosexual acts than had previously been thought, but gender, thought to be inextricably intertwined with sexuality, now appeared perhaps not quite as binary as commonsense literature of the dominant fiction suggested.

Widely influential literary critic Lionel Trilling responded to the surprising popularity of the report in a 1948 article entitled "Sex and Science: The Kinsey Report," first published in *Partisan Review* (Trilling 1948). He presciently makes note of the growing influence of sociology and in his opening paragraph simultaneously lauds the report for making raw data available to the public while arguing that it makes use of a façade of science and objectivity ultimately to further an agenda of sexual permissiveness. While the outrage of some of the report's more rabid critics focused on the lack of condemnation on the commonness of practices such as premarital sex, oral sex, anal sex, and homosexuality, Trilling argues that the text did not display sufficient objectivity, that it actually supports the "naturalness" and by extension "normality" of homosexuality (Trilling 1948, 232). Ironically, contemporary sociological texts promoted "commonsense" knowledge, that is, they rely on the "naturalness" of masculine codes of behavior, to support their arguments about the American man. That Kinsey's findings *defied* these naturalized expectations is why Trilling finds fault with its objectivity. Trilling's loudest complaint, however, is that Kinsey and the report focus only on the physical aspect of sexual behavior and do not make sufficient allowance for the inner lives of individuals, suppressing the "connection between the sexual life and the psychic structure" (Trilling 1948, 232). Trilling disputed the attempt to de-pathologize homosexuality through the claim that it was a purely physical act that was actually much more prevalent than previously believed, and doubled the stakes by suggesting that the report was suppressing the more broadly popular psychoanalytic model in favor of a Marxist reading of emotions and the inner life as merely a "superstructure" of physical conditions.

Trilling was one of the many intellectuals who tried to distance themselves from their left-wing politics of the 1930s in the period during and after World War II. Film theorist and queer historian Robert Corber argues that Trilling's rebuttal of the findings of the Kinsey Report was an attempt to shift critical focus from Jewish intellectuals who had sympathies for the communist movement prior to World War II – like himself – toward homosexuals who were also and already perceived as a threat to national security (Corber 1996, 39). While the report argued that homosexual behavior was rooted in the physical, the presiding wisdom on homosexuality understood it as a psychological pathology. While the so-called "well-adjusted" men who performed homosexual acts might have appeared mentally healthy to Kinsey and his interviewers, Trilling argues that they simply did not have the evidence of their inner lives and could *not* prove that homosexuality was not a developmental disorder. And so, by arguing that Kinsey neglected psychoanalysis in favor of an essentially Marxist model, Trilling writes off the statistical findings of the report that suggested that homosexuality was far more prevalent than previously believed and could not be easily detected by the physical features, while also implying that the report was complicit in the project of the communist and homosexual infiltration of the American government.

Indeed, it was this potential ubiquity of an indiscernible homosexuality that led in large part to the panic over homosexuals in the government and daily life. In 1950, a State Department official disclosed to the Senate Appropriations Committee that the Department had dismissed employees on charges of homosexuality (Corber 1996, 61). Ironically, this led to the accusation that the government was tolerating homosexual employees, and also raised the question of how the government could employ thousands of "sexual deviates" without knowing it. An ensuing investigation by the Senate Appropriations Committee refuted the notion that male homosexuals were effete and female homosexuals were masculine (Corber 1996, 63). This indecipherability of sexuality led to a panic of attempts at identification, most notoriously in the witch-hunt tactics of Senator Joseph McCarthy – indeed, homosexuals were perceived to be as much of a threat to national security as communists. In order to circumvent the apparent normalcy (with respect to gender presentation) of homosexuals, the Committee subscribed to a psychologically pathologizing model of same-sex eroticism that argued that homosexuals were emotionally unstable and were vulnerable to the "blandishments of the foreign espionage agent," the presiding wisdom of the time, and that which Kinsey worked hard to disprove statistically and which Trilling loudly defended. In this model, homosexuals who appeared normatively masculine or feminine were thought to be even *more* unbalanced because of their apparent normalcy – pointing to the accepted correlation between sexuality and masculinity or femininity. Indeed both scholarly and popular writers saw psychological instability – often in psychosexual terms – as the primary explanation for the appeal of communism.

Kinsey's attempt to articulate the flexibility of sexuality and the notion that sex is an act that one performs and does not necessarily constitute or even inform other parts (i.e., one's masculinity or femininity) of one's expressed identity resulted in a backlash, the main element of which was a culture of suspicion. As the Kinsey Report imperiled the stability of the masculine construct's basis of heterosexuality, attempts to articulate and perform masculinity according to the dominant fiction became ever more pronounced. Robert Corber succinctly describes this play of identity through the concept of "the enemy within." Initially used to refer to the threat of communism infiltrating the American government and security structures, Corber suggested that the phrase also applied to subjects who disrupted the "American way of life" (i.e., the family unit of the dominant fiction), most notably homosexuals. However, because homosexuality was constructed as a medical neurosis, Corber argues that the "enemy within" might also be constituted by an individual's psyche, which might betray him at any moment (Corber 1996, 99).

The intense fear and paranoia about the Communist threat of the postwar period resulted in increasing vigilance of gender expression, evident in the postwar flurry of texts concerned with gender, sexuality, and their social and political implications. In this cross-section of sources, it is possible to pick out the tenuous relationships between these mutually constitutive categories. An ideal masculine subject was the head of the family unit, which was the basis for postwar economic prosperity. As both the muddying findings of the Kinsey Report and the unforeseen government purges of suspected homosexual employees proved, appearances were not sufficient criteria to determine the adequacy of American citizens. And so the inner life of the subject became increasingly vulnerable to judgment. Indeed, one of the main reasons cited by the government's dismissal of queer employees was that their "unstable" sexuality might be used to blackmail them into divulging information to communist spies (Corber 1996, 8, 63). The constructed pathology of non-normative gender and sexuality was perceived as a fertile environment for the parallel pathology of communist ideology; for example, male subjects who did not exhibit the strength and individuality demanded by figures such as Schlesinger were understood as weak and susceptible to the groupthink and collectivist ethic of communism. Furthermore, homosexuality was seen as a blackmailable offense. Citizens should be wary of the "enemy within" their psyche. Only if they were "impeccable" in their sexuality and gender expression were they invulnerable to the machinations of the imagined communist blackmailer. Ironically, it was the juridical construction of homosexuality as a pathology that would have made this blackmail possible.

SEE ALSO: Gender Stereotypes

REFERENCES

Corber, Robert J. 1996. *In the Name of National Security: Hitchcock, Homophobia, and the Political Construction of Gender in Postwar America*. Durham, NC: Duke University Press.

Cuordileone, Kyle A. 2005. *Manhood and American Political Culture in the Cold War*. New York: Routledge.

Gilbert, James. 2005. *Men in the Middle: Searching for Masculinity in the 1950s*. Chicago: University of Chicago Press.

Kinsey, Alfred, Clyde Eugene Martin, and Wardell Baxter Pomeroy. 1948. *Sexual Behavior in the Human Male*. Philadelphia: Saunders.

May, Elaine. 1988. *Homeward Bound: American Families in the Cold War Era.* New York: Basic Books.

Schlesinger, Arthur M., Jr. 1949. *The Vital Center: The Politics of Freedom.* Boston: Houghton Mifflin. Reprinted 1998, New Brunswick: Transaction Publishers.

Silverman, Kaja. 1992. *Male Subjectivity at the Margins.* New York: Routledge.

Trilling, Lionel. 1948. "Sex and Science: The Kinsey Report." Reprinted 2008 in *The Liberal Imagination: Essays on Literature and Society,* 223–242. New York: New York Review Books.

FURTHER READING

Attwood, William, George B. Leonard, Jr., J. Robert Moskin, and Robert Osborn. 1958. *The Decline of the American Male.* New York: Random House.

Butler, Judith. 1988. "Performative Acts and Gender Constitution: An Essay in Phenomenology and Feminist Theory." *Theater Journal,* 40(4): 519–531.

Corber, Robert. 1997. *Homosexuality in Cold War America: Resistance and the Crisis of Masculinity.* Durham, NC: Duke University Press.

Ehrenreich, Barbara. 1983. *The Hearts of Men: American Dreams and the Flight from Commitment.* London: Pluto.

Halberstam, David. 1993. *The Fifties.* New York: Random House.

Jones, Amelia. 1998. "The 'Pollockian Performative' and the Revision of the Modernist Subject." In *Body Art/Performing the Subject,* 53–102. Minneapolis: University of Minnesota Press.

Riesman, David. 2001. *The Lonely Crowd: A Study of the Changing American Character.* New Haven: Yale University Press. First published 1950.

Schlesinger, Arthur M., Jr. 2008. "The Crisis of American Masculinity." Reprinted in *The Politics of Hope and the Bitter Heritage: American Liberalism in the 1960s,* 292–311. Princeton: Princeton University Press. First published 1958.

Seltzer, Charles C. 1945. "The Relationship Between the Masculine Component and Personality." *American Journal of Physical Anthropology,* 3(1): 33–47.

Whyte, William H. 2013. *The Organization Man.* Philadelphia: University of Pennsylvania Press. First published 1956.

Community and Grassroots Activism

KAREN B. HANNA
University of California, Santa Barbara, USA

Community and grassroots activism refers to the ways that everyday people organize and advocate for their daily needs, such as better healthcare, housing, disability access, and community control of schools, and against injustice in their communities, like police violence and environmental racism. At the forefront of community and grassroots activism are women and other marginalized people whose activism "grows out of the concrete, immediate, everyday experience of struggles around issues of survival" (Krauss 1998, 129).

Feminist scholars describe community and grassroots activism as existing in multiple interrelated ways. Karen Sacks (1988), for example, argues that "centerpeople," or those who mobilize existing workplace social networks, are key actors in network formation and consciousness shaping. They differ from spokesmen, who serve as official or unofficial representatives who speak to the media and before large groups of people. Building on Sacks's work, Dolores Delgado Bernal (1998) recognizes five dimensions of grassroots leadership: acting as spokespeople, networking, helping others develop political consciousness, organizing meetings, events, and activities, and holding office. While traditional studies of community activism focus on men who take the lead as spokespeople and "charismatic leaders," Bernal and Sacks recognize contributions of women that often go unrecognized yet are fundamental to understanding community and grassroots activism. Scholars recognize that the tendency for women to adopt nontraditional leadership roles is not inherent to them as women but instead reflects socially constructed factors, such as class, cultural values, social expectations, and the sexual division of labor, all of which are shaped by patriarchy.

Given that community and grassroots activism involves confronting daily injustices in one's own neighborhood, a cornerstone of this work is that of mothers. Many mothers advocate for their right to secure the survival of their families and raise their children safe from violence. For example, La Asociación Madres de Plaza de Mayo marched in front of the presidential palace in Buenos Aires each Thursday from 1977 to 2006. These mothers fought for the Argentinian government's recognition of their children's torture and murder by the military dictatorship which lasted from 1976 to 1983. Feminist scholars of community activism have expanded traditional definitions of motherhood to encompass not only advocacy for the welfare of one's own biological children but also the protection of one's community and culture. Nancy Naples refers to this concept as "activist mothering" (1998). Naples' work complements the ideas of Patricia Hill Collins (1991) who describes the role of many African American women as their communities' "othermothers." Collins describes othermothers as sisters, aunts, neighbors, grandmothers, cousins, and other women who hold families together, build community institutions, and teach ethics of care and service to others. Othermothers facilitate religious, neighborhood, and friendship networks that strengthen community mobilization and activism.

Recognizing community and grassroots activism as blurring the lines between the private and public spheres challenges the traditional approaches of Saul Alinsky. Some refer to Saul Alinsky as the father of US-based community organizing, as he was arguably the first person to document a theory of organizing that could be replicated. Anti-racist and feminist organizers and scholars have critiqued the Alinsky model, leading to the formation of alternative networks for people of color, queer people, and women, including the Center for Third World Organizing (CTWO) and the National Organizers Alliance (NOA) (Sen 2003). Regardless of the critiques, many community organizations continue to adapt Alinsky's basic concepts to match their theories for change and the needs of their communities. Community organizing is comprised of multiple components, which differ according to an organization's methods and theories. These include base-building, political education, leadership development, networking, campaigns, advocacy, and fundraising. Many organizations also conduct research.

Feminist evaluations of community and grassroots activism require recognition of non-traditional forms of community and grassroots activism led by women, people of color, indigenous communities, queer and trans* people, and the chronically ill and disabled. For example, Rinku Sen's research (2003) on community organizing addresses unnatural separations between the public and private spheres, highlighting domestic violence and women's health activism in the United States that encourages women to work together in the private sphere before they publicly tackle these issues. She also documents studies of women activists who focus on the process of building nurturing and compassionate relationships and learning opportunities rather than strictly focusing on policy initiatives.

Likewise, ecofeminists call for a radical shift away from profit, militarism, violence, and domination, in the interests of both women and men. Ecofeminists view making peace with the earth a survival imperative and seek leadership from indigenous people who have maintained this sensibility and women of the Global South who live and work in close proximity to the land. Mies and Shiva (1993) underscore the activism of women like those of the Chipko movement in India for explicitly merging the ecological and feminist movements, resisting the exploitation of the natural forest. Haunani-Kay Trask (2003) too emphasizes the centrality of self-determination for Native peoples in their struggles to protect cultural identity, land base, self-government, and regional security. The Audre Lorde Project in New York City emerged from the need to address multiple issues impacting LGBTST (lesbian, gay, bisexual, two spirit, trans and gender non-conforming) people of color communities, such as homelessness, prison reform, AIDS and HIV activism, and immigration activism. Finally, chronically ill and disabled queer activists of color have reclaimed the terms "sick," "mad," and "crippled" as they work to dismantle racism, homophobia, ableism, patriarchy, and other forms of oppression. In these ways, community and grassroots activists have challenged traditional single-issue forms of activism by adopting intersectional approaches to social justice.

Scholars illustrate how global capitalism, structural adjustment programs, and international institutions have significantly impacted women's lives and their involvement in community and grassroots activism (Desai 2002). Neoliberal state policies, the globalization of transnational corporations, and the creation of structural adjustment programs have led to a "feminization of labor" and increased employment of women of color and Third World women in low-wage service and informal sector jobs all over the world. While women's unpaid labor at home has increased as public funding for health, education, and other social services has declined due to austerity measures in some countries, immigrant women and women of color are increasingly hired to do domestic labor for middle- and upper-class women for wages below poverty level. At the same time, many of these immigrant women work without benefits or protection from abuse and exploitation from their employers.

Yet, just as global economic processes foment gender, racial, and class inequalities, they have also led to the creation of transnational resistance spaces across the world. These spaces make important connections between local grassroots struggles, international organizations, and global politics. Manisha Desai describes the multiple ways in which women have responded to globalization as "scattered resistance" (2002, 17). For example, she cites how women in maquiladoras along the US and Mexico border engage in work stoppages for cultural celebrations and use religious and other traditional practices to organize workers. Marina Karides' research (2002) about Trinidad's National Union of Domestic Employers (NUDE), a registered trade union of Trinidad and Tobago, illustrates how domestic and low-wage workers link their struggles to existing United Nations policy initiatives and the International Wages for Housework campaign to generate international support for their work. Additionally, Jan Boontinand's work (2005) in the Mekong region shows how community members and women in local brothels collaborate with the non-governmental organization Global Alliance Against Traffic in Women to investigate and end trafficking in Cambodia and Vietnam.

The development of technology and social networking has led to the growth of a critical global consciousness, with many community activist groups making links with movements all over the world in seeking global change. Digital technologies have enabled the delivery of local information and community concerns to global audiences, catalyzing social movements. Activists use them to organize, communicate, and raise global awareness in the face of what they believe to be state repression and Internet censorship. Examples of Internet activists include Esraa Abdel Fattah, known as "Facebook girl" for her role in launching Egypt's April 6 Movement, Libya's Danya Bashir, and Bahrain's Zainab and Maryam al-Khawaja, whose Twitter accounts have received international recognition (Radsch and Khamis 2013).

Some critics of digital activism argue that it is less effective than activism in the streets. They believe it separates people from one another and that online petitions are unlikely to persuade those in power to change. Furthermore, critics reason that digital activism furthers class divisions, as only those with access to the Internet and computers can participate. Yet, digital activism and blogging are crucial ways that sick and disabled people participate in community and grassroots activism vis-à-vis social media.

In addition to traditional activist methods of protests, boycotts, demonstrations, marches, rallies, press releases, and petitions, activists utilize a variety of creative methods to educate the public about issues they care about. They include teach-ins, community research projects, educational workshops, courses, forums, art, and radio shows. For example, the only transgender rights organization in Africa, Gender DynamiX, participates in local radio talk shows to promote transgender awareness (Gender DynamiX 2013).

Community-based art also raises political consciousness and brings people together. It includes music, such as folk, queercore (an offshoot of punk that challenges society's disapproval of LGBTQ communities and promotes queer pride) punk rock, hip hop, graffiti, filmmaking, photography, theater, movement and dance, print and mural making, literature, poetry, spoken word, and other types of writing, performance, and visual art. The use of art can lead to transformative outcomes. For instance, public protests by community members and media documentation by Iranti-org, a queer human rights visual media organization, led to the arrest of the perpetrator of a "corrective rape" and murder of a local lesbian woman in South Africa in 2013. Activists also use art to uplift their communities, promote political ideas, and create social change. Ladyfest, a volunteer-run, community-based, not-for-profit global arts and music festival for feminist and women artists, features a combination of bands, musical groups, performance artists, authors, spoken word and visual artists, films, lectures, art exhibitions, and workshops. Since 2000, it has been held in cities all over the world, including Amsterdam, Auckland, Sao Paulo, Johannesburg, Melbourne, Tallinn, and Jakarta (Chidgey, Reitsamer, and Zobl 2009).

Although community and grassroots activism is rooted in community members' local everyday concerns, activists gain strength by working in solidarity with people beyond their immediate geographic areas. By linking their movements, activists have expanded local causes into national and global social movements.

SEE ALSO: Activist Mothering; Anti-Globalization Movements; Anti-Poverty Activism; Anti-Racist and Civil Rights Movements; Arab Spring Movements; Community Other Mothers; Disability Rights Movement; Ecofeminism; Lesbian and Gay Movements; Transgender Movements in the United States

REFERENCES

Bernal, Dolores Delgado. 1998. "Grassroots Leadership Reconceptualized: Chicana Oral Histories and the 1968 East Los Angeles Blowouts." *Frontiers*, 19: 113–142.

Boontinand, Jan. 2005. "Feminist Participatory Action Research in the Mekong Region." In *Trafficking and Prostitution Reconsidered: New*

Perspectives on Migration, Sex Work, and Human Rights, edited by Kamala Kempadoo. Boulder, CO: Paradigm Publishers.

Chidgey, Red, Rosa Reitsamer, and Elke Zobl. 2009. "Ladyfest: Material Histories of Everyday Feminist Art Production." *n. paradoxa* 24: 5–12.

Collins, Patricia Hill. 1991. "The Meaning of Motherhood in Black Culture." In *The Black Family: Essays and Studies*, edited by Robert Staples. Belmont, CA: Wadsworth.

Desai, Manisha. 2002. "Transnational Solidarity: Women's Agency, Structural Adjustment, and Globalization." In *Women's Activism and Globalization: Linking Local Struggles and Transnational Politics*, edited by Nancy A. Naples and Manisha Desai. New York: Routledge.

Gender DynamiX. 2013. Gender DynamiX's Annual Report. Accessed September 20, 2014. www.genderdynamix.org.za/wp-content/uploads/2012/10/pol-492-essay.pdf.

Karides, Marina. 2002. "Linking Local Efforts with Global Struggle: Trinidad's National Union of Domestic Employees." In *Women's Activism and Globalization: Linking Local Struggles and Transnational Politics*, edited by Nancy A. Naples and Manisha Desai. New York: Routledge.

Krauss, Celine. 1998. "Challenging Power: Toxic Waste Protests and the Politicization of White, Working Class Women." In *Community Activism and Feminist Politics: Organizing Across Race, Class, and Gender*, edited by Nancy A. Naples. New York: Routledge.

Mies, Maria, and Vandana Shiva. 1993. *Ecofeminism*. London: Zed Books.

Naples, Nancy. 1998. *Grassroots Warriors: Activist Mothering, Community Work, and the War on Poverty*. New York: Routledge.

Radsch, Courtney C., and Sahar Khamis. 2013. "In Their Own Voice: Technologically Mediated Empowerment and Transformation Among Young Arab Women." *Feminist Media Studies*, 13(5): 881–891.

Sacks, Karen. 1988. "Gender and Grassroots Leadership." In *Women and the Politics of Empowerment*, edited by Ann Bookman and Sandra Morgen, 77–94. Philadelphia: Temple University Press.

Sen, Rinku. 2003. *Stir It Up: Lessons in Community Organizing and Activism*. San Francisco: Jossey-Bass.

Trask, Haunani-Kay. 2003. "Self-Determination for Pacific Island Women: The Case of Hawai'i." In *Sing, Whisper, Shout, Pray! Feminist Visions of a Just World*, edited by M. Jacqui Alexander, 138–150. Canada: Edgework Books.

FURTHER READING

Naples, Nancy A., and Manisha Desai, eds. 2002. *Women's Activism and Globalization: Linking Local Struggles and Transnational Politics*. New York: Routledge.

Community Other Mothers

DANIELLE DOCKA-FILIPEK
Otterbein University, USA

Patricia Hill Collins defines "othermothers" as "women who assist bloodmothers by sharing mothering responsibilities," and represents the practice as a defining characteristic of black communities (Collins 1990, 119). Most literally, "othermothering" refers to the practice of grandmothers, sisters, aunts, cousins, or other women assuming responsibility for the care and development of children, through practices ranging from temporary childcare to more long-term care or adoption (Stack 1974; Collins 1990). More broadly, "othermothering" refers to "mothering" that extends beyond parent–child relationships to include care for the broader community via forms of activism that take up collective responsibility for nurturance, advocacy, and justice on the behalf of others (Gilkes 1980, 1982; Naples 1992). Vital knowledge imparted by othermothers ranges from the repertoire of skills necessary for navigating and surviving oppressive structures to practices and strategies designed to challenge, reject, transform, and transcend those structures.

Othermothering, broadly conceived, is a practice with radical and transformative potential. Collins posits that the practice of othermothering stems from the vital recognition that "vesting one person with full responsibility for mothering a child may not be wise or possible" (Collins 1990, 119). Feminist theorist bell hooks suggests that othermothering is especially revolutionary, as "it takes place in opposition to the idea that parents, especially mothers, should be the only childrearers. ... It cannot happen ... if parents regard children as their 'property,' their possession" (hooks 1984, 144). Naples (1992) argues that an examination of low-income women's community work provides a direct challenge to narrow conceptualizations of mothering that would otherwise hinge on biological and legal definitions, suggesting that race, gender, and class mediate and construct social understandings of mothering. The concept of othermothering therefore serves as a challenge to frameworks that posit the atomized nuclear family as the most "functional" of all family forms, presenting an alternative to normative structures that otherwise exclude "familial" bonds outside of orthodox forms.

Historically, othermothering is sometimes read both as a continuation of values and practices derived from precolonial African cultural traditions, and also a functional adaptation to the pressures imposed by racism and sexism (Sudarkasa 1996). Historian Robin D. G. Kelley (1998), however, rejects the impulse to read unique African American practices as unidimensional "coping responses" developed in rote response to oppressive structures, and instead argues for an analytic framework that emphasizes and honors the creativity and agency that characterizes complex social actors and their family relationships. Additionally, Collins (1990) takes issue with the romanticization of the strengths of minority women, arguing that such frameworks reinscribe problematic stereotypes, and also neglect to theorize fully the impacts of contemporary, interlocking sources of marginalization.

Overall, the development of the concept of "othermothering" should be read in juxtaposition to scholarly and popular understandings of the "culture of poverty." A good amount of the early scholarship on othermothering serves as a response to "tangle of pathology" narratives, perhaps most memorably articulated in Senator Daniel Patrick Moynihan's policy report *The Negro Family: The Case for National Action* (Moynihan 1965). In this landmark work, Moynihan names a number of contemporary social problems often associated with African American families (such as disproportionate levels of poverty, teenage and out-of-wedlock childbearing, poor educational outcomes, and juvenile and adult law enforcement encounters) as attributable to the "unnatural" dominance of black women, "emasculated" and therefore absent black father figures, and a resulting lack of moral foundation and discipline for black children. A good amount of the literature on the American "underclass" further echoes these understandings, either explicitly or implicitly (Wilson 1987; Anderson 1990).

Criticism of Moynihan's analysis, and criticism of the application of "culture of poverty" understandings to minority families more generally, take issue with the positing of black family "disorganization" as the origin of causation for contemporary urban ills, arguing that such frameworks mistake symptoms for root causes. More specifically, critics lodge that complex, non-normative, and otherwise "strong" family forms had been reduced, caricatured, and distorted, which served to reestablish racial hierarchy and obscured the true sources of hardship for black family life: racism, deindustrialization, the dismantling of the welfare state, defunding of the public sector, and gendered criminalization processes (Logan 1999). Early scholars in this tradition sought to provide more accurate portrayals of the conditions under which bloodmothers and othermothers nurture their children and their communities.

Notable among these powerful responses is Ladner's *Tomorrow's Tomorrow: The Black Woman*, which examines the meaning of black womanhood through the eyes of teenaged girls residing in and around public housing in Saint Louis (Ladner 1971). The main contributions of Ladner's work include the articulation of a conceptual framework that seeks to forward concepts, definitions, and analyses from the standpoint of a black perspective to avoid ethnocentric comparisons of elements of black culture to a middle-class, white ideal. Ladner refers to this process of reformulation as "decolonization:" "… the refusal to allow the oppressor to define the problems and solutions of the Oppressed" (Ladner 1971, 272). Regarding the black family more specifically, Ladner critiques the cultural arrogance of the "moral–immoral dichotomy," suggesting that because black communities are governed with a distinct moral code, no child can be defined as "illegitimate," as all have inherent and recognized worth that mitigates degradation and stigmatization.

Stack's pioneering ethnographic work *All Our Kin* examines the kin structures and survival strategies prevalent among one neighborhood-based network of urban, low-income, African American families in a Midwestern city (Stack 1974). Stack's fieldwork uncovered that urban black families were far from "disintegrated," in that the extended families she researched exhibited a high level of dense, cooperative interconnections which served both to nurture and to support children and share vital resources. Primary among Stack's contributions is the concept of "fictive kin" – community members who are not related by blood, marriage, or formal adoption, yet nevertheless acknowledge familial relationships, and therefore play vital roles in childrearing and overall community cohesion.

More recently, Sarkisian and Gerstel (2012) refer to approaches highlighting the strengths of minority families as constituting a "super-organization" argument, which works to highlight the positive outcomes associated with reliance on extended networks beyond that of the traditional nuclear family. The hallmark of such an approach amounts to a repudiation of the tendency to refer to nuclear families as "intact" and non-nuclear families as "broken." Therefore, the practice of othermothering in particular, and the extended networks for exchange of resources and caring within minority families in general, are both interpreted as evidence of the superior strength of minority family forms. Lempert's insight that some black men may serve as "other fathers" via deep involvement in parenting children other than their own is especially relevant (Lempert 1999).

Sarkisian and Gerstel (2012) ultimately offer that minority families are "disorganized" only if definitions of family are narrowly confined to nuclear structures. When extended family structures are examined, "a different picture emerges" that highlights the persistence and resilience of family bonds, in addition to the necessity for considering the impact of socioeconomic structures on family forms and practices (Sarkisian and Gerstel 2012, 23). Significantly, however, they also caution against a romanticizing impulse that might otherwise minimize the very real pressures, barriers, and destructive contemporary forces that confront poor and minority families, and mothers in particular.

SEE ALSO: Activist Mothering; Black Feminist Thought; Extended Families; Fictive Kin; Household Livelihood Strategies; Kinship; Matriarchy

REFERENCES

Anderson, Elijah. 1990. *Code of the Street: Decency, Violence, and the Moral Life of the Inner City*. New York: Norton.

Collins, Patricia Hill. 1990. *Black Feminist Thought: Knowledge, Consciousness, and the Politics of Empowerment*. New York: Routledge.

Gilkes, Cheryl Townsend. 1980. "'Holding Back the Ocean with a Broom:' Black Women and Community Work." In *The Black Woman*, edited by La Francis Rodgers-Rose, 217–231. Beverly Hills: Sage.

Gilkes, Cheryl Townsend. 1982. "Successful Rebellious Professionals: The Black Woman's Professional Identity and Community Commitment." *Psychology of Women Quarterly*, 6(3): 289–311.

hooks, bell. 1984. *From Margin to Center*. Boston: South End Press.

Kelley, Robin D. G. 1998. *Yo Mama's Disfunktional: Fighting the Culture Wars in Urban America*. Boston, MA: Beacon Press.

Ladner, Joyce. 1971. *Tomorrow's Tomorrow: The Black Woman*. New York: Doubleday Press.

Lempert, Lora Bex. 1999. "Other Fathers: An Alternative Perspective on Black Community Caring." In *The Black Family: Essays and Studies*, edited by Robert Staples, 189–201. Belmont: Wadsworth.

Logan, Enid. 1999. "The Wrong Race, Committing Crime, Doing Drugs, and Maladjusted for Motherhood: The Nation's Fury over 'Crack Babies.'" *Social Justice*, 26(1): 115–138.

Moynihan, Daniel Patrick. 1965. *The Negro Family: The Case for National Action*. Washington, DC: Office of Planning and Research, United States Department of Labor.

Naples, Nancy. 1992. "Activist Mothering: Cross-generational Continuity in the Community Work of Women from Low-income Urban Neighborhoods." *Gender and Society*, 6(3): 441–463.

Sarkisian, Natalia, and Naomi Gerstel. 2012. *Nuclear Family Values, Extended Family Lives: The Power of Race, Class, and Gender*. New York: Routledge.

Stack, Carol. 1974. *All Our Kin*. New York: Basic Books.

Sudarkasa, Niara. 1996. *The Strength of Our Mothers: African & African American Women and Families: Essays and Speeches*. Trenton: Africa World Press.

Wilson, William Julius. 1987. *The Truly Disadvantaged: The Inner City, the Underclass, and Public Policy*. Chicago: University of Chicago Press.

Comparable Worth/ Work of Equal Value

JUDITH A. McDONALD and
ROBERT J. THORNTON
Lehigh University, USA

Most women in most professions and countries earn less than their male counterparts. These gender pay gaps affect women of all ages, races, and educational backgrounds; and they are due in large part to occupational segregation, women working in female-dominated fields characterized by lower-status and lower-paying jobs, rather than men and women being paid differently for the same job (England 2005, 382; OECD 2012). There are different perspectives, however, as to why occupational segregation and the associated pay gaps exist. Sociologists tend to believe that these gaps reflect cultural biases or society valuing female-dominated professions less than male-dominated professions, whereas economists tend to believe they can be largely explained by human-capital factors (e.g., education, training, and experience) and also by women's choices and tastes. Understanding why these gender pay gaps exist and what to do about them is difficult. If they reflect men's and women's choices rather than discrimination, then perhaps there is no need for government policies to close the gaps. However, if discrimination exists then government intervention may make sense, and dealing with these gaps is important not simply for the women themselves, but also for the broader public-policy issues of equity and fairness, poverty reduction, and economic growth.

Beginning in the mid-1980s, comparable worth emerged in the United States as a way to deal with a gender pay gap that had persisted despite several decades of anti-discrimination legislation. Although the Equal Pay Act of 1963 had prohibited employers from paying women less than men for the *same* jobs, comparable worth proposed that equal pay be required for jobs that, although dissimilar, could be shown to be of *comparable worth* using job-evaluation methods based on factors such as working conditions, knowledge and skills, effort, and responsibility. About two dozen states in the United States have set up comparable-worth (or "pay-equity") programs that affect the pay of some state employees. However, the US private sector has not adopted comparable-worth principles in its pay practices. Comparable worth is an attempt to value traditionally female occupations at their "true worth" using gender-neutral, unbiased job-evaluation systems because, according to Steinberg (1990, 456), women's work has been systematically undervalued precisely because it was being done by women. According to this reasoning, the gender pay gap cannot be explained away by suggesting that men are more likely to be in higher-paying skilled jobs or ones that require more education. For example, despite their being more skilled and better educated, licensed practical nurses in Ontario, who are 90 percent female, have median earnings of only $38,261, whereas the comparable figure for cable television service and maintenance technicians, who are 97 percent male, is $51,030 (Equal Pay Coalition).

Evans and Nelson (1989, 165) point out that comparable worth, by raising "fundamental ideological issues" – challenging the way in which society values the work of women and minorities – has provoked vehement opposition. Opponents have been troubled by comparable-worth's use of job-evaluation techniques not only because these techniques can be sensitive to the choice of factors and weights, but also because relying on them means larger bureaucracies with burdensome tasks (i.e., studying the wage gap at regular intervals and adjusting the pay scale appropriately). In addition, it is argued that market-based definitions of value (i.e., labor-market supply and demand conditions) are ignored, leading to possible resource misallocation. Proponents of comparable worth counter that occupational segregation necessitates the use of such methods to compare different jobs and also that job-evaluation techniques have been successfully used for many decades. However, even proponents admit that comparable worth, at least as it has been implemented so far, may be flawed. For example, Acker (1989, 5) note that "gender inequalities seem to be so deeply embedded in social structures and processes that they are recreated even as we try to eliminate them."

For full-time, year-round workers in 2013, the ratio of women's to men's median annual earnings in the United States was 78.3; however, clearly not all of the 21.7 percent pay differential reflects employer discrimination. When factors such as hours of work, experience, occupation, and other human-capital factors are taken into account, the gap shrinks. Although Goldin (2014, 4) claims that the human-capital part of the gender wage gap has been "squeezed out" because women have increased their "productivity-enhancing characteristics," other researchers still disagree over just how much of this gap can be attributed to human-capital and other factors, and how much may be due to discrimination. Among the plausible additional explanations for the gap are the possibility of gender differences in psychological and psychosocial attributes and preferences that make some types of occupations more attractive to men or women. In such cases, there is the possibility that, as Goldin states

(2014, 4), wage differences between men and women mostly reflect how firms "reward individuals who differ in their desire for various amenities." There is also some evidence that women are more risk averse than men, which may lead women to choose occupations with more stable, but lower, earnings. Furthermore, there exist social (or gender identity) norms concerning what types of work are more appropriate for men and for women. Attitudes towards negotiations and competition have also been shown to differ in men and women. Stereotyping or cultural norms may also help to perpetuate the gender wage gap. As Bertrand (2011) notes, the last 10 years have seen a growing literature on the importance of these factors in explaining gender differences in labor-market outcomes.

Although comparable worth has had only limited success in the US private sector, comparable-worth mandates have succeeded in certain other countries, most notably Australia, where in 2012 more than 200,000 women in the "social and community services sector" received pay raises based on comparable-worth principles. In the European Union, claims for "equal pay for work of equal value" have been common and are covered by equal-pay legislation. In fact, Article 119 of the 1957 Treaty of Rome required that each member state should "ensure and subsequently maintain the application of the principle that men and women should receive equal pay for equal work," where "equal work" was interpreted broadly to mean "work of equal value." It should be noted, however, that the manner in which member states have adopted comparable-worth policies has varied. As for assessment of the effects of such policies, the evidence is mixed, with most studies showing that their effects have been modest, at best. For example, Ontario introduced the most comprehensive pay-equity legislation in North America, if not the world, in January 1988. The female–male pay gap in Ontario subsequently fell from 35.6 percent in 1988 to 23.3 percent in 2011; however, despite its broad coverage and pro-active nature, there is no indication that the Act materially affected the gender pay gap (McDonald and Thornton 2015). Perhaps Ontario's law did not do a better job of reducing the pay gap because without employment-equity legislation ("affirmative action," repealed in 1995) and equal access to the workplace (e.g., affordable, available childcare), women have continued to face systemic, discriminatory barriers to accessing full-time, higher-paying male-dominated jobs. With the growing body of evidence that equal-pay laws alone do not seem to work well, governments might be well advised to put their efforts toward tackling the gender segregation that exists, both in occupations and in workers' attitudes toward, and in preparation for, the job market. The gender wage gap is a product of many different phenomena; therefore, fixing it is likely to require a multi-pronged approach.

SEE ALSO: Gender Stereotypes; Occupational Segregation

REFERENCES

Acker, Joan. 1989. *Doing Comparable Worth: Gender, Class, and Pay Equity*. Philadelphia: Temple University Press.

Bertrand, Marianne. 2011. "New Perspectives on Gender." In *Handbook of Labor Economics*, edited by David Card and Orley Ashenfelter, vol. 4B, 1544–1590. Amsterdam: North-Holland.

England, Paula. 2005. "Emerging Theories of Care Work." *Annual Review of Sociology*, 31: 381–399.

Evans, Sara M., and Barbara J. Nelson. 1989. *Wage Justice*. Chicago: University of Chicago Press.

Goldin, Claudia. 2014. "A Grand Gender Convergence: Its Last Chapter." *American Economic Review*, 104(4): 1–30.

McDonald, Judith A., and Robert J. Thornton. 2015. "'Coercive Cooperation'? Ontario's Pay Equity Act of 1988 and the Gender Pay Gap." *Contemporary Economic Policy*, 33(4): 606–618.

OECD. 2012. *Closing the Gender Gap: Act Now*. Paris: OECD Publishing. Accessed January 13, 2015, at http://dx.doi.org/10.1787/9789264179370-en.

Steinberg, Ronnie J. 1990. "Social Construction of Skill: Gender, Power, and Comparable Worth." *Work and Occupations*, 17(4): 449–482.

Complementary and Alternative Medicine

YAEL KESHET

Western Galilee Academic College, Israel

Women figure prominently in engagement with complementary and alternative medicine (CAM), mindfulness, and holistic spiritual practices. Such engagement appears to self-empower women and serve as an emancipating alternative; however, the extent of gendered social change is limited.

CAM is an umbrella term used to denote a group of diverse medical modalities, which include the use of natural products (such as herbs, vitamins, minerals, and probiotics); mind–body practices (such as healing touch, hypnotherapy, and mindfulness meditation); body and movement therapies (such as massage and Feldenkrais Method); modalities that derive from long-established and traditional Eastern systems of healthcare (such as Ayurvedic medicine and traditional Chinese medicine); and modalities of Western origin (such as naturopathy, homeopathy, and anthroposophical medicine).

Most CAM modalities share certain metaphysical orientations (Andrews, Evans, and McAlister 2013). Examples include vitalism, which believes in living energies and forces that are distinct from scientific energies (Keshet 2011); naturalism, which believes in "laws of nature" and in the benefits of a natural life; humanism, which is proposed as the essence of patient–practitioner relationships and personalized healthcare; and holism, which promotes the idea that the totality of interconnected systems is greater than the sum of their parts – that the body and mind form a unified system that is part of broader social and cosmic systems. To a large extent, CAM's metaphysical positions overlap with the New Age and holistic spirituality movement, which has also become very popular in Western societies.

CAM does not conform to the knowledge, norms, and practices of mainstream biomedicine and is not generally considered to be part of conventional biomedicine in Western countries. When used instead of conventional treatments it is termed "alternative medicine." Currently CAM is used primarily to complement conventional biomedical care, and in such cases it is termed "complementary medicine." CAM's popularity in Western countries has led to the integration of certain CAM modalities into conventional healthcare organizations, and the result is thus termed "integrative medicine." Scholars have questioned whether this process is truly integrative or is rather an indication of co-optation or commodification (Singer and Fisher 2007; Baer and Coulter 2008).

Women are more likely than men to use CAM. This has been established in diverse surveys conducted both in the United Kingdom and the United States, as well as in other countries (Eardly et al. 2012; Frass et al. 2012). Women were also found to have a greater propensity toward New Age and holistic spirituality (Houtman and Aupers 2007). Both as users and as practitioners in the labor market, women engage extensively with CAM specifically, and with the holistic milieu in general (Keshet and Simchai 2014).

Several explanations of the prominence of women in CAM and mindfulness practices have been offered. First, women's greater use of CAM is attributed to their traditional family roles, which demand significant involvement in care and nurturing, which in turn leads them to be more "health conscious" than men and to seek help also from orthodox healthcare professionals. Second, CAM patient–practitioner relationships may be more attractive to women. The practice of conventional medicine has been branded by feminist health activists, as well as others, as a site for the production and maintenance of social power. CAM practitioners are generally more committed to non-hierarchical and egalitarian relationships, which potentially modify power asymmetries and become a key element in patients' empowerment (Nissen 2011). Third, CAM's fundamental principle of encouraging "inner healing" further reinforces the empowerment of the patient. Fourth, holistic spiritualities offer ways of negotiating contemporary dilemmas of selfhood. The discourse of well-being and of authentic, unique, and responsible subjectivity places the self at the center, thus providing an alternative to traditional notions of other-directed caring femininity (Sointu 2011). Holistic spirituality is frequently used as a means of identity construction, whereby women's perceived traditional role of caring for the material and emotional well-being of others is turned into a career that affords them considerable autonomy, self-direction, and a measure of economic reward. And fifth, women who were trained in CAM reported that they envisioned themselves as pioneers in promoting a more equitable, community-oriented, and compassionate system of medicine (Flesch 2010).

Although CAM practice appears to empower women (Nissen 2011), some evidence suggests that it reproduces conventional female roles and reinforces the existing gendered order. More women than men choose careers in CAM and CAM education because of constraints that do not necessarily apply to men. Among these are insufficient financial resources and societal support to pursue more extensive medical training and enter demanding occupations, particularly within Western medicine (Flesch 2010). Furthermore, analysis of the ways in which CAM use is interpreted by women and men reveals that women tend to reproduce traditional gendered identities. Men frame their CAM use in terms of science and rationality, while simultaneously distancing themselves from CAM's feminine-encoded components, such as emotions. Women frame their CAM use as a quest for self-reinvention that largely reflects and reproduces conventional femininity (Brenton and Elliott 2013).

The field of CAM and holistic spirituality lacks political support, legitimacy, and a solid institutional base, and is easily aligned with the private sphere of familial care that is already historically associated with women. It allows women to take up part-time employment and hence creates economic and social dependence, since they become reliant on their male partner's income. Moreover, the empowering impact of CAM is largely restricted to Western women who enjoy a high income and a high level of education. While these women can use CAM in addition to biomedicine, women from ethnic minorities, as well as populations living in poverty in developing countries, tend to use cheap indigenous traditional medicine rather than biomedicine. When imported to the West, these same modalities are termed CAM. One example is the prevalent view of female family members in Indian society's patriarchal structures as being of less "value" to the family. As a result, women who contract cancer are frequently denied expensive biomedical treatment because of the financial constraint, and are forced to rely on traditional medicine alone (Broom, Doron, and Tovey 2009).

Thus, CAM and holistic spirituality practices, as an alternative that extends beyond the medicine of the body, are constructed as empowering to women. Yet the empowerment that women experience is construed as a form of personal empowerment that stems from power-from-within (Rowlands 1995). "Power-from-within" is a form of personal power that comprises the subjective sense of power in the minds of people and focuses on the sense of self: self-confidence, self-esteem, and self-respect (Wong 2003). This type of power is not directed toward resistance. CAM and holistic spirituality practices are generally shifted to the margins, while patriarchal notions of femininity are preserved and encouraged (Keshet and Simchai 2014).

SEE ALSO: Alternative Medicine and Therapies; Empowerment; Woman-Centeredness

REFERENCES

Andrews, Gavin J., Joshua Evans, and Seraphina McAlister. 2013. "'Creating the Right Therapy Vibe': Relational Performances in Holistic Medicine." *Social Science and Medicine*, 83: 99–109.

Baer, Hans A., and Ian Coulter. 2008. "Introduction – Taking Stock of Integrative Medicine: Broadening Biomedicine or Co-option of Complementary and Alternative Medicine?" *Health Sociology Review*, 17(4): 331–341.

Brenton, Joslyn, and Sinikka Elliott. 2013. "Undoing Gender? The Case of Complementary and Alternative Medicine." *Sociology of Health and Illness*, 36(1): 91–107.

Broom, Alex, Assa Doron, and Philip Tovey. 2009. "The Inequalities of Medical Pluralism: Hierarchies of Health, the Politics of Tradition and the Economies of Care in Indian Oncology." *Social Science and Medicine*, 69: 698–706.

Eardley, S., et al. 2012. "A Systematic Literature Review of Complementary and Alternative Medicine Prevalence in EU." *Forsch Komplementmed*, 19(suppl. 2): 18–28.

Flesch, Hannah. 2010. "Balancing Act: Women and the Study of Complementary and Alternative Medicine." *Complementary Therapies in Clinical Practice*, 16(1): 20–25.

Frass, M., et al. 2012. "Use and Acceptance of Complementary and Alternative Medicine among the General Population and Medical Personnel: A Systematic Review." *The Ochsner Journal*, 12: 45–56.

Houtman, Dick, and Stef Aupers. 2007. "The Spiritual Revolution and the New Age Gender Puzzle: The Sacralisation of the Self in Late Modernity (1980–2000)." *Journal for the Scientific Study of Religion*, 46(3): 305–320.

Keshet, Yael. 2011. "Energy Medicine and Hybrid Knowledge Construction: The Formation of New Cultural-Epistemological Rules of Discourse." *Cultural Sociology*, 5(4): 501–518.

Keshet, Yael, and Dalit Simchai. 2014. "The 'Gender Puzzle' of Alternative Medicine and Holistic Spirituality: A Literature Review." *Social Science and Medicine*, 113: 77–86.

Nissen, Nina. 2011. "Challenging Perspectives: Women, Complementary and Alternative Medicine, and Social Change." *Interface*, 3(2): 187–212.

Rowlands, Jo. 1995. "Empowerment Examined." *Development in Practice*, 5(2): 101–107.

Singer, Judy, and Kath Fisher. 2007. "The Impact of Co-option on Herbalism: A Bifurcation in Epistemology and Practice." *Health Sociology Review*, 16(1): 18–26.

Sointu, Eeva. 2011. "Detraditionalisation, Gender and Alternative and Complementary Medicines." *Sociology of Health and Illness*, 33(3): 356–371.

Wong, Kwok-Fu. 2003. "Empowerment as a Panacea for Poverty – Old Wine in New Bottles? Reflections on the World Bank's Conception of Power." *Progress in Development Studies*, 3(4): 307–322.

FURTHER READING

Barker, Kristin K. 2014. "Mindfulness Meditation: Do-it-Yourself Medicalization of Every Moment." *Social Science and Medicine*, 106: 168–176.

Ben-Arye, E., et al. 2009. "Complementary Medicine in the Primary Care Setting: Results of a Survey of Gender and Cultural Patterns in Israel." *Gender Medicine*, 6(2): 384–397.

Cameron, Mary. 2010. "Feminization and Marginalization? Women Ayurvedic Doctors and Modernizing Health Care in Nepal." *Medical Anthropology Quarterly*, 24(1): 42–63.

Flesch, Hannah. 2007. "Silent Voices: Women, Complementary Medicine, and the Co-option of Change." *Complementary Therapies in Clinical Practice*, 13: 166–173.

Foltz, Tanke G. 2000. "Women's Spirituality Research: Doing Feminism." *Sociology of Religion*, 61(4): 409–418.

Nissen, Nina. 2010. "Practitioners of Western Herbal Medicine and their Practice in the UK: Beginning to Sketch the Profession." *Complementary Therapies in Clinical Practice*, 16: 181–186.

Nissen, Nina. 2013. "Women's Bodies and Women's Lives in Western Herbal Medicine in the UK." *Medical Anthropology*, 32(1): 75–91.

Sointu, Eeva, and Linda Woodhead. 2008. "Spirituality, Gender, and Expressive Selfhood." *Journal for the Scientific Study of Religion*, 47(2): 259–276.

Taylor, Scott. 2010. "Gendering in the Holistic Milieu: A Critical Realist Analysis of Homeopathic Work." *Gender, Work & Organization*, 17(4): 454–474.

Upchurch, Dawn M., and Laura M. Chyu. 2005. "Use of Complementary and Alternative Medicine among American Women." *Women's Health Issues*, 15: 5–13.

Upchurch, Dawn M., and Bethany K. Wexler Rainisch. 2012. "A Sociobehavioral Model of Use of Complementary and Alternative Medicine Providers, Products, and Practices: Findings from the 2007 National Health Interview Survey." *Journal of Evidence-Based Complementary and Alternative Medicine*, 18(2): 100–107.

Woodhead, Linda. 2010. "Why So Many Women in Holistic Spirituality?" In *The Sociology of Spirituality*, edited by Kieran Flanagan and Peter C. Jupp, 115–126. Aldershot: Ashgate.

Compulsory Heterosexuality

MIMI SCHIPPERS
Tulane University, USA

Compulsory heterosexuality refers to a social system that institutionalizes heterosexuality as the only legitimate way for individuals to form emotionally intimate, sexual, and kinship bonds. As a social system, compulsory heterosexuality includes a network of beliefs, rituals, customs, norms, and codified rules or laws that systematically compel individuals to form intimate bonds with one person of the other gender.

The idea of compulsory heterosexuality is attributed to Adrienne Rich, a radical lesbian feminist writing in the 1970s and early 1980s. In her essay "Compulsory Heterosexuality and Lesbian Existence" (1980), Rich had two main goals. The first was to critique feminist scholarship for its erasure of lesbians. The second was to develop a theoretical explanation for why women go against their "nature" and political interests to form exploitive and oppressive bonds with men.

Offering a critique of women's psychology and feminist theories of kinship that were paradigmatic at the time, Rich argued that these theories presume heterosexuality as a given, as if women's emotional and erotic bonds with men were natural, inevitable, and therefore not in need of explanation. Adopting a psychoanalytic approach to gender identity development, Rich suggested that bonds with the mother make men's *and* women's sexual orientation one that is naturally directed toward women. Given the natural and initial bonds between mother and daughter, Rich argued, there must be an overwhelming social force that drives women away from each other and toward men. That force is compulsory heterosexuality.

In her essay, Rich offered a taxonomy of the institutionalized ways in which women are compelled or forced to form bonds with and serve men, including: (1) denying women their own sexuality; (2) forcing male sexuality on women; (3) exploiting and controlling women's productive and reproductive labor to benefit men; (4) controlling and robbing women of their children; (5) confining women physically; (6) using women as objects in male transactions; (7) cramping women's creativity; (8) withholding large areas of knowledge and culture from women.

Within this context, women become "male identified" to the extent that they focus their attention on men rather than women and care more about and attend to men's interests, needs, and accomplishments rather than women's. Here, Rich argued, is the historical and political importance of compulsory heterosexuality. Heterosexuality, as an institutionalized set of arrangements that compel women to identify with men instead of women, ensures that women do not form emotional, erotic, or political bonds with each other. Building on Karl Marx's notion of false consciousness, Rich argued that compulsory heterosexuality instills a form of false consciousness in women so they spend their time and energy in ways that benefit individual men and men as a group while undermining their own emotional, physical, and political interests for and as women. Compulsory heterosexuality, then, is the main mechanism by which men are guaranteed and systematically benefit from unencumbered access to women's bodies, labor, children, and emotional investment and, as such, is the main impediment to feminist consciousness in women.

If heterosexuality is culturally and socially forced on women to serve men's interests and maintain women's subordination, Rich argued, then efforts to resist compulsory heterosexuality become an important feminist practice. In this way, the concept of compulsory heterosexuality was central to the development of what is referred to as cultural or lesbian separatist feminism. However, it is important to note that, in this essay, Rich's emphasis was on compulsory heterosexuality as an institution, not individual women's erotic desire. Resistance to compulsory heterosexuality would mean not necessarily having sex with women, but instead becoming woman-identified.

According to Rich, the definition of lesbian as a sexual identity is yet another arm of compulsory heterosexuality and is meant to erase the emotional and political bonds that women are naturally prone to develop with one another. Rich argued that, in the context of patriarchy and compulsory heterosexuality, lesbian is a political identity that signifies woman identification, not a sexual identity. She offers the "lesbian continuum" as a term signifying variations in degree and quality of women's bonds with each other. A lesbian, then, is not necessarily a woman who is sexually attracted to or intimately involved with women; a lesbian is a person who is committed to feminist struggle. In this formulation, because women who are sexually intimate with other women are not bonded or devoted to men, sexual lesbians are, by definition, feminists.

While the idea of compulsory heterosexuality is foundational to and continues to shape subsequent feminist and queer theory (see below), Rich's notion of a political lesbian was controversial and has been critiqued for glossing the effects of heterosexism in lesbian women's and gay men's lives, for denying the importance of sex and the erotic in women's, especially lesbian women's lives, for dismissing heterosexual women's desire and lived experience as false consciousness, and for denying the necessity of political bonds between women and men of the same class and race/ethnicity to fight class oppression and white supremacy.

Despite these critiques of Rich's theory, compulsory heterosexuality was a central and foundational concept in the development of contemporary feminist and queer theory. Though her use of psychoanalytic theory to claim a "natural" feminine sexual orientation was criticized and superseded by a constructionist theory of sexuality, the notion that sexuality is institutionalized as a system of beliefs, practices, and rules outside of the realm of sex and reproduction was a radical shift in theory and research on gender and sexuality. Rich's theory of compulsory heterosexuality was also one of the first theories to place attention on heterosexuality rather than discrimination against lesbian and gay individuals and communities. This focus on heterosexuality as an institution rather than a sexual identity resonated with postmodern critiques of identity and poststructural methods of deconstruction and is foundational in queer theorists' interest in the social construction of heterosexuality and the privileges conferred through heteronormativity.

SEE ALSO: Feminism, Cultural; Heteronormativity and Homonormativity; Lesbian and Womyn's Separatism

REFERENCE

Rich, Adrienne. 1980. "Compulsory Heterosexuality and Lesbian Existence." *Signs*, 5(4): 631–660.

Consciousness-Raising

MICHELLE SAN PEDRO
University of Connecticut, Storrs, USA

Consciousness-raising involves increasing one's awareness of social conditions that sustain injustice. In this continual process, individuals make sense of their role within oppressive structures. For example, privileged groups of people use power to sustain their self-interests. This privileged group defines reality for all; it is considered "the way things are." The privileged create prescribed norms, which appear normal or fixed to disadvantaged groups. Disadvantaged groups, on the other hand, do not typically recognize their own exploitation. The disadvantaged groups internalize these norms and fear changing them. Disadvantaged groups must become aware of their situation, or the limits of the social context in which they exist. This dynamic process is called consciousness-raising. Individuals become aware of the circumstances of their situation. Consciousness-raising serves as a foundation for activism, experiential learning, and feminist pedagogy.

The concept of false consciousness, which is used to justify oppression and exclude others, is important to feminist thought. In a class-based hierarchy, Marxist scholars assert that subordinate workers collectively understand oppression with a false consciousness. Social mechanisms and institutions create distortions in the way the subordinate class perceives reality. Workers perceive the existence of social classes as natural and legitimate. This false consciousness conceals the realities of their exploitation. It controls the workers and reproduces power relations. The failure to recognize constraints on choices preserves discriminatory practices and masks the social forces of oppression. Without the framework of false consciousness, the workers, composed of the majority, would overthrow the dominant class of capitalists. By understanding their role in the social relations of oppression, the subordinate class can change social order through revolution (Pines 1993).

Various historical practices contributed to consciousness-raising in class-based societies. During the Chinese Revolution, peasants "spoke bitterness" to express anger and sorrow to landlords about widespread starvation. Speaking bitterness provided a political empowerment tool for peasants to advocate for land redistribution (Naples and Bojar 2002, 10). Consciousness-raising is situated in the circumstances of daily life. Critical theorist Paulo Freire developed a consciousness-raising approach when teaching sugar-cane workers to read. At this time, literacy was a prerequisite to vote in presidential elections in Brazil. Freire and other teachers invited workers to examine photographs and drawings of ordinary life in the villages. The sugar-cane workers sought liberation and challenged oppressive conditions (Freire 1970). Consciousness-raising connects abstract knowledge and social activism. Consciousness-raising is known as an emancipatory method. When disadvantaged groups become conscious of their actions, they move toward liberation, or realization of their full potential. Disadvantaged groups no longer view social conditions as static. Through reflection and dialogue, they become aware of obstacles and work toward transformation (Freire 1970). Consciousness-raising may not bring imminent change. This protracted process undergoes constant negotiation within and between individuals and groups. Consciousness-raising is a self-reflexive practice that can lead to collective social action. The transformation of structural inequalities requires long-term commitment to an ideological struggle.

The emancipatory nature of consciousness-raising is relevant to the second wave of the women's movement in the United States. In the 1960s and 1970s, writing and reading were political acts. Women gathered throughout the country to express individual experiences as mothers and wives in favor of a new collective identity. Inspired by the Civil Rights Movement, women identified patriarchy as a source of oppression and proposed strategies of resistance in consciousness-raising groups. They reflected on the patriarchal false consciousness which they learned from childhood. The entry of women into the workforce and access to contraception also transformed the way in which women thought of bodies and relationships. Although fragmented at times with debate, the political vision of feminism merged public and private spheres. Through consciousness-raising techniques, individuals were mobilized by the social, cultural, economic, and political oppression of women.

The unity of theory and practice in consciousness-raising is also relevant in the classroom. Education involves the practice of freedom (hooks 1994). The classroom is a public space in which students create meaning, integrate personal experience with theory, and enact change in daily life. Students gain a more complex understanding of the world and social justice. The cultivation of consciousness generates political agency; students emerge with greater confidence to challenge existing beliefs and assumptions. With critical inquiry into the gendered system of relations, politics of power, and systematic oppression, students imagine alternative social possibilities. In this learning process, the teacher should not impose values or reproduce oppressive structures. Education is a value-laden, impartial process. Both the teacher and student critique social relations embedded in society and question their role in resisting or sustaining them. In their respective positions in society, teachers and students alike grasp the constraints and potential for change. This interdependent relationship allows individuals to move toward liberation without becoming oppressors of those subordinate to them (Freire 1970).

SEE ALSO: Anti-Poverty Activism; Community and Grassroots Activism; Empowerment

REFERENCES

Freire, Paulo. 1970. *Pedagogy of the Oppressed*, trans. Myra Bergman Ramos. New York: Continuum.
hooks, bell. 1994. *Teaching to Transgress: Education as the Practice of Freedom*. New York: Routledge.
Naples, Nancy A., and Karen Bojar, eds. 2002. *Teaching Feminist Activism: Strategies from the Field*. New York: Routledge.
Pines, Christopher. 1993. *Ideology and False Consciousness: Marx and His Historical Progenitors*. Albany: State University of New York Press.

FURTHER READING

Giroux, Henry. 1997. *A Pedagogy and Politics of Hope: Theory, Culture, and Schooling*. Boulder: Westview Press.
Mcintosh, Peggy. 1983. "Interactive Phases of the Curricular and Personal Re-Vision: A Feminist Perspective." Center for Research on Women, Working Paper No. 124. Wellesley: Wellesley College.
Sarachild, Kathie. 1978. "Consciousness-Raising: A Radical Weapon." In *Feminist Revolution*, 144–150. New York: Random House.
Schniedewind, Nancy. 1993. "Teaching Feminist Process in the 1990s." *Women's Studies Quarterly*, 21(3/4): 17–30.
Weiler, Kathleen. 1991. "Freire and a Feminist Pedagogy of Difference." *Harvard Educational Review*, 61(4): 449–474.

Contraception and Contraceptives

ROBYN LEE
Brock University, Canada

Contraception, also known as birth control or fertility control, consists of methods or devices used to prevent pregnancy. Contraceptives are forms of contraception. Some, but not all, forms of contraception also provide protection against STIs (sexually transmitted infections). Access to contraception and adequate information on how to use it is a critical part of women's health and equality. The ability to choose if and when to become pregnant is a major cornerstone of women's freedom and autonomy. Contraception is crucial to women's health, because of the health risks associated with pregnancy and because some contraceptives also protect against STIs. Use of contraception can prevent closely spaced and ill-timed pregnancies and births, which contribute to high infant and maternal mortality rates. Contraception also increases the economic autonomy and financial security of women in allowing them to plan and avoid pregnancies. Restrictions against access to contraception therefore constitute gender discrimination.

Coercion in the use of contraception and forced sterilization are important issues, particularly for women of color, poor women, and women with disabilities. Women with disabilities often face significant barriers in gaining access to contraceptives and receiving accurate knowledge about their contraceptive options due to discriminatory beliefs about their sexuality and fitness as parents. In addition, contraception is an important issue for trans and gender-non-conforming individuals, who may also become pregnant.

There has historically been heavy opposition to contraception on moral and religious grounds. Debates over contraception have been linked to abortion and opponents of contraception often view it as a form of abortion. For example, the contemporary controversy over emergency contraception (the morning after pill) was the consequence of it being considered a form of abortion. Legal and practical obstructions to accessing contraception have been framed as issues of morality, with support for contraception viewed as condoning extramarital sex and promiscuity. For example, in the United Kingdom until 1974 the birth control pill was restricted to married women who had children, and the pill became legal for married women in the United States beginning in 1965, but legal access was not extended to single women until 1972. The widespread acceptance of contraception required a major reorientation of sexual values.

Sexual and reproductive rights are protected in various internationally recognized principles of human rights relating to health and self-determination. The Convention on the Elimination of All Forms of Discrimination against Women (CEDAW), adopted in 1979 by the United Nations General Assembly (United Nations General Assembly 1979), protects access to contraception and family planning, along with the right to information and education concerning sexual health, family planning, and reproductive services (CEDAW, Articles 12 and 14b).

Contraception was illegal in many places, including Canada and the United States, from the late nineteenth century onwards. The struggle for access to safe, legal contraception began in the nineteenth century and increased in the twentieth century. The birth control movements in Canada and the United States made great strides in disseminating information about contraception and opening clinics providing contraception (Liu and Fisher 2002; Engelman 2011). Contraception was legalized in 1965 in the United States, in 1969 in Canada, and in 1967 in France. Contraception has become increasingly available worldwide since then, with Ireland legalizing contraception in 1980 and Argentina in 1985.

Despite widespread legalization, barriers to accessing contraception persist. These include cost, parental consent requirements, requirements for prescriptions rather than over-the-counter availability, differential prescription practices depending on race and socioeconomic status, and conscientious objection among prescribers and healthcare professional service providers. When barriers to contraception are combined with restrictions on access to abortions, reproductive choice is seriously impaired.

There are substantial global inequalities in access to contraception. Unmet need is highest in the poorest countries, particularly in Sub-Saharan Africa and Southern Asia (UNFPA and Guttmacher Institute 2014). Many vulnerable individuals still have unmet needs for contraception, particularly adolescents, the poor, those living in rural areas and urban slums, people living with HIV, and internally displaced people (WHO 2014). In developing countries, 225 million women have an unmet need for contraception, with unmet need highest for women in the poorest households, those with less education, and those living in rural areas (UNFPA and Guttmacher Institute 2014).

Population control was an early incentive to promote contraception. The neo-Malthusians, following after Thomas Malthus (1766–1834), argued for contraception in order to prevent overpopulation. Concern for population control continues to drive contraception use; for instance, China's one-child policy led to one of the highest rates of contraception use in the world. How the loosening of the policy in November 2015 will affect use of contraceptives remains to be seen.

Support for contraception has historically been linked to eugenics, the concern with increasing the purity and fitness of the population, as defined in terms of race, class, and absence of disability. Eugenics programs attempted to remove from society unwanted or undesirable characteristics that were thought to be hereditary, and operated in a larger context of colonial racism and xenophobia. Early proponents of contraception such as Margaret Sanger, leader in the American birth control movement and pivotal in the development of the birth control pill, openly professed eugenicist views. Although for many women access to contraception has been emblematic of reproductive freedom, contraception has produced troubling injustice for some groups of women.

Women have been subject to coerced contraception based on race and socioeconomic status. Sexual sterilization was carried out without consent on women of color and aboriginal women, poor women, women with mental and physical disabilities, and women suspected of being criminally deviant or promiscuous. Many US states had compulsory sterilization laws, and even after the laws were repealed doctors routinely sterilized poor, racialized, teenaged, and disabled women without consent (Roberts 1997). In Canada, forced sterilization was legal in Alberta until 1972 (Grekul et al., 2004), and an organization widely referred to as the Eugenics Board carried out mass sterilizations, particularly of Aboriginal and Métis women (Caulfield and Robertson, 1996). In the 1990s, attempts were made to encourage welfare recipients to receive the Norplant implant in exchange for financial incentives. Women were offered the implants as an alternative to jail terms, particularly racialized women and women on welfare, and the implants were heavily promoted to teenage girls in predominantly black schools in the United States (Roberts 1997).

Organizations of women of color have responded to historical oppression in the use of contraception by forming the movement for reproductive justice. While recognizing the importance of ensuring access to contraception and abortion, they called for a broader analysis of the racial, economic, cultural, and structural constraints on women's reproductive choices.

Contraception has been used for thousands of years, but modern forms of effective contraceptives became available beginning in the late nineteenth century and gained widespread acceptance and use in the twentieth century, with new forms of contraception continuing to be developed today. Patterns of use differ significantly internationally and many contraceptive methods are available. Factors influencing the choice of method include availability, cost, reversibility, ease of use, cultural preferences, privacy, side-effects, and medical risks. Debates continue over the side-effects of different forms of contraception.

Permanent forms of contraception include tubal blockage, tubal ligation, and vasectomy. In a tubal ligation, the fallopian tubes are cut and tied, or blocked. This cuts off the sperm's access to the egg, preventing fertilization. A vasectomy involves cutting the tubes that carry sperm from the testes to the penis. Both methods of sterilization are considered permanent and irreversible, although in a very small percentage of cases an individual undergoing vasectomy reversal may become fertile again.

Temporary contraceptives may be hormonal, non-hormonal, and natural. Hormonal contraceptives include the oral contraceptive pill (also known as the birth control pill), the contraceptive patch, the vaginal contraceptive ring, the contraceptive injection, and the intrauterine device (IUD). Hormonal contraceptives mimic the hormones regulating ovulation and menstruation: both estrogen and progestin, or progestin alone. They work by suppressing ovulation, thickening the cervical mucus, preventing sperm from getting through, changing the lining of the uterus, making implantation of a fertilized egg less likely, and reducing sperm access to the fallopian tubes, where eggs are fertilized.

The oral contraceptive pill or birth control pill must be taken daily, in the correct order, and on time. The contraceptive patch is worn on the skin of the lower abdomen, buttocks, or upper body (but not on the breasts). It releases the hormones progestin and estrogen into the bloodstream. A new patch is worn each week for 3 weeks, with no patch worn in the fourth week. The vaginal contraceptive ring is placed inside the vagina and releases the hormones progestin and estrogen. The ring is worn for 3 weeks, taken out for the fourth week, than replaced with a new ring. Hormonal contraception can also be taken in the form of injections once every 3 months. The intrauterine device (IUD) is a small, T-shaped device that can be fitted into the uterus by a doctor and is effective for up to 5 years, after which it must be replaced.

Non-hormonal contraceptives include the male condom and female condom, diaphragm, cervical cap, copper intrauterine device (copper IUD), spermicide, and contraceptive sponge. Male condoms are unrolled onto an erect penis prior to intercourse and prevent sperm from reaching the female reproductive tract. Latex condoms, the most common type, also help prevent HIV and other STIs, as do the newer synthetic condoms. Condoms made from lambskin help prevent pregnancy, but may not provide protection against STIs, including HIV. Female condoms line the vagina and are inserted before intercourse. They are thin, soft pouches made of polyurethane plastic (they can be used by people allergic to latex) with flexible rings at either end. One ring is used to insert the condom, and the other remains outside, covering external genitalia.

The diaphragm and cervical cap are barrier methods placed inside the vagina to cover the cervix and block sperm from entering. The diaphragm is shaped like a shallow cup. The diaphragm is a shallow, dome-shaped latex cup. The cervical cap is a smaller, thimble-shaped cup. They fit over the cervix in the vagina, blocking the opening to the uterus. These methods should always be used along with a spermicide.

Spermicides are chemicals that inactivate or kill sperm. They are available as creams, gels, aerosols, dissolvable films, and vaginal suppositories or tablets. Some condoms are coated with spermicide for extra protection. Contraceptive sponges contain spermicide. A sponge is placed at the cervix where the spermicide kills any sperm attempting to enter. The sponge provides 12-hour protection. The copper IUD is effective for up to 10 years. Copper affects the lining of the uterus so as to prevent implantation; it also changes the chemistry in the uterus and kills sperm.

Emergency contraception is taken after unprotected intercourse. There are two types of oral contraceptive pills (also known as morning after pills): progestin-only pills (Plan B) and combined estrogen and progestin pills (Yuzpe Regimen). The morning after pills are more effective the sooner after unprotected intercourse they are taken, but can be taken up to 5 days after. The copper IUD can also be used as emergency contraception.

Natural birth control methods include the fertility awareness method (FAM), the temperature method, the rhythm or calendar method, and the lactational amenorrhea method (LAM), in addition to withdrawal and abstinence. The sympto-thermal method, also known as the FAM, involves a woman observing, charting, and interpreting her waking temperature (basal body temperature) and cervical mucus to determine when she is fertile and when she is not fertile. In the temperature method, a woman takes her waking temperature to identify a rise in temperature, indicating that ovulation has passed. Elevated waking temperature for 3 days in a row is considered confirmation of the post-ovulatory, less fertile phase.

The rhythm (calendar) method predicts fertile periods using calculations based on the length of past cycles rather than daily observations of fertility signs and is consequently a much less effective birth control method.

The lactational amenorrhea method (LAM) relies on the fact that lactation interferes with ovulation and causes amenorrhea (lack of menstruation). The method relies on three measures of a woman's fertility: the return of her menstrual period, her patterns of breastfeeding, and the time postpartum. In the withdrawal method, the penis must be completely removed from the vagina before ejaculation. This is an unreliable method of birth control, since some sperm can be released before ejaculation. Sexual abstinence can mean choosing to abstain from different levels of sexual activity.

The effectiveness of contraception depends on how well it is used. Effectiveness rates are divided into use effectiveness – how well a birth control method works in typical use, taking into consideration human error and other non-ideal factors, and theoretical effectiveness – how well a birth control method works when it is used correctly and all other conditions are ideal. Multiple forms of contraception are sometimes used together, either in order to increase effectiveness in preventing pregnancy or to provide protection against STIs along with pregnancy prevention.

SEE ALSO: Abortion, Legal Status in Global Perspective on; Birth Control, History and Politics of; Fertility Rates; Health Disparities; Pro-Choice Movement in the United States; Reproductive Health; Reproductive Justice and Reproductive Rights in the United States; Sexually Transmitted Infections; Sterilization

REFERENCES

Caulfield, Timothy, and Gerald Robertson. 1996 "Genetic Policies in Alberta: From the Systematic to the Systemic." *Alberta Law Review*, 35(1): 59–80.

Engelman, Peter C. 2011. *A History of the Birth Control Movement in America*. Santa Barbara: Praeger.

Grekul, Jana, Arvey Krahn, and Dave Odynak. 2004. "Sterilizing the 'Feeble-minded': Eugenics in Alberta, Canada, 1929–1972." *Journal of Historical Sociology*, 17(4): 358–384.

Liu, Kimberly E., and William A. Fisher. 2002. "Canadian Physicians' Role in Contraception from the 19th Century to Now." *Journal of Obstetrics and Gynaecology Canada*, 24(3): 239–244.

Roberts, Dorothy E. 1997. *Killing the Black Body: Race, Reproduction, and the Meaning of Liberty*. New York: Vintage Books.

UNFPA and Guttmacher Institute. 2014. "*Adding It Up: The Costs and Benefits of Investing in Sexual and Reproductive Health*." New York: United Nations Population Fund (UNFPA).

WHO. 2014. *Ensuring Human Rights in the Provision of Contraceptive Information and Services: Guidance and Recommendations*. Geneva: World Health Organization.

United Nations General Assembly. 1979. *Convention on the Elimination of All Forms of Discrimination against Women (CEDAW)*. New York: United Nations General Assembly.

FURTHER READING

McLeod, Carolyn. 2010. "Harm or Mere Inconvenience? Denying Women Emergency Contraception." *Hypatia*, 25(1): 11–30. DOI: 10.1111/j.1527-2001.2009.01082.x.

Sistersong: Women of Color Reproductive Justice Collective. 2015. Accessed September 7, 2015, at http://www.sistersong.net/.

Convention on the Elimination of All Forms of Discrimination against Women (CEDAW)

WADE M. COLE
University of Utah, USA

The Convention on the Elimination of All Forms of Discrimination against Women (CEDAW), adopted by the United Nations (UN) General Assembly in 1979, is one of 10 core UN human rights instruments. Often described as a bill of rights for women, CEDAW's 30 articles enshrine a series of civil, political, economic, and social rights for women. Among other things, the Convention recognizes the full equality of women and men under the law and proscribes discrimination against women in education, employment, political participation, healthcare, and economic life. CEDAW recognizes the right of women to vote and to stand for elected office; to receive equal pay for equal work; to own and dispose of property; to obtain loans, mortgages, and other forms of credit independently of husbands or male relatives; to enter into or dissolve marriage freely and with full consent; and to exercise equal parental rights. State parties are obligated, among other things, to provide equal educational opportunities, paid maternity leave, and access to family planning services, and to suppress prostitution and the trafficking of women.

The foundations of CEDAW trace to 1946, when the Commission on the Status of Women (CSW) was established under the auspices of the UN Economic and Social Council with a mandate to promote women's political, economic, civil, social, and educational rights. Over the next 15 years, the CSW adopted several conventions on women's rights, including the Convention on the Political Rights of Women (1953), the Convention on the Nationality of Married Women (1957), and the Convention on Consent to Marriage, Minimum Age for Marriage and Registration of Marriages (1962). CSW also worked with the International Labour Organization (ILO) on a convention guaranteeing equal pay for equal work (1951) and joined forces with UNESCO to promote women's literacy and equal access to education.

In 1963, the General Assembly directed CSW to consolidate these disparate standards into a single document, the Declaration on the Elimination of Discrimination against Women. The Declaration, adopted in 1967, called on states to eliminate discrimination against women in public education, employment, and criminal punishment; to extend full electoral rights and equality with respect to marriage and divorce to women; and to combat prostitution and the exploitation of women. The Declaration, however, was a purely aspirational document; its provisions were not legally binding on countries.

Over the next decade CSW set to work on a treaty that would create stronger legal obligations. The worldwide diffusion of women's rights movements during the 1970s, together with a thaw in tensions between the Soviet Union and the United States, produced conditions favorable to this enterprise. The United Nations declared 1975 to be the International Women's Year, during which the World Conference on Women, attended by representatives from 133 governments, convened in Mexico City. Conference participants adopted a plan of action for drafting a legally binding convention on women's rights. After three years of deliberations, CEDAW was adopted in 1979 by a vote of 130 to 0, with 10 abstentions. It entered into force in 1981.

Support for CEDAW, at least nominally, is widespread. Nearly 97 percent of the world's countries – from Switzerland and the United Kingdom to Saudi Arabia and the United Arab Emirates – are party to the Convention; only a handful of states, including Iran, Somalia, Sudan, and the United States, have not ratified it. The decision to ratify CEDAW is shaped by both national and global factors (Wotipka and Ramirez 2008). Ratification rates are higher in democratic and communist countries, but they are lower in Islamic nations. The propensity to ratify also increases as the number of parties regionally and globally increases, in countries with greater linkages to women's non-governmental organizations (NGOs), and during UN women's rights conferences.

Despite high levels of rhetorical commitment, CEDAW is one of the most heavily reserved human rights treaties (Neumayer 2007). Reservations, which function as line-item vetoes, purport to render specified treaty provisions non-binding while leaving the remainder intact. Roughly one third of all ratifications to CEDAW have been entered with reservations; predominantly Muslim countries are especially prone to modify their commitments in this manner. Not all reservations, however, enervate treaty effects; in non-Islamic societies, reservations seem to improve CEDAW's effectiveness, perhaps because countries that take the care to enter reservations also take their obligations seriously (Cole 2012).

Article 17 of CEDAW established the Committee on the Elimination of Discrimination against Women, a body of independent experts charged with monitoring implementation of the Convention. State parties submit regular reports to this Committee, detailing the measures they have taken to implement CEDAW. Countries that ratify an optional protocol, adopted in 1999, acknowledge the Committee's competence to receive complaints from individuals alleging violation of their treaty-protected rights. Although 104 countries have ratified this protocol, to date only 24 complaints have been submitted. State parties have been found in violation of CEDAW in half of these complaints (Bayefsky 2012). The Committee also issues general recommendations that draw attention to and clarify countries' obligations under CEDAW. The Committee has adopted 29 recommendations, including one (No. 28) that forbids discrimination on the basis of sexual orientation and gender identity.

Research examining the effects of CEDAW on countries' practices is still in its infancy. In their statistical analysis of 180 countries, Gray, Kittilson, and Sandholtz (2006) concluded that women in countries that have ratified CEDAW enjoyed higher literacy rates, greater participation in the economy, and more representation in parliament than did their counterparts in non-ratifying countries. A similar analysis by Simmons (2009) found that CEDAW membership was associated with greater access to primary and secondary education for girls, increased government support for contraceptive access, and a larger share of women in public employment. More recently, Cole (2013) showed that CEDAW ratification improved political rights for women, but it had no discernible effect on women's economic and social rights; he surmised that economic and social rights may be resistant to change due to resource constraints and cultural opposition in many countries. These preliminary findings, while instructive, leave much room for additional discovery, discussion, and debate going forward.

SEE ALSO: Declaration of the Rights of Women; Human Rights, International Laws and Policies on; Human Rights and Gender; UN Decade for Women; Universal Human Rights; Women's Movements: Modern International Movements; Women's Worlds Conference

REFERENCES

Bayefsky, A. F. 2012. "Jurisprudence: CEDAW." Accessed August 11, 2015, at http://www.bayefsky.com/docs.php/area/jurisprudence/node/3/treaty/cedaw/opt/0.

Cole, Wade M. 2012. "Human Rights as Myth and Ceremony? Reevaluating the Effectiveness of Human Rights Treaties, 1981–2007." *American Journal of Sociology*, 117(4): 1131–1171.

Cole, Wade M. 2013. "Government Respect for Gendered Rights: The Effect of the Convention on the Elimination of Discrimination against Women on Women's Rights Outcomes, 1981–2004." *International Studies Quarterly*, 57(2): 233–249.

Gray, Mark M., Miki Caul Kittilson, and Wayne Sandholtz. 2006. "Women and Globalization: A

Study of 180 Countries, 1975–2000." *International Organization*, 60: 293–333.
Neumayer, Eric. 2007. "Qualified Ratification: Explaining Reservations to International Human Rights Treaties." *Journal of Legal Studies*, 36: 397–429.
Simmons, Beth A. 2009. *Mobilizing for Human Rights: International Law and Domestic Enforcement*. New York: Cambridge University Press.
Wotipka, Christine Min, and Francisco O. Ramirez. 2008. "World Society and Human Rights: An Event History Analysis of the Convention on the Elimination of All Forms of Discrimination against Women." In *The Global Diffusion of Markets and Democracy*, edited by Beth A. Simmons, Frank Dobbin, and Geoffrey Garrett. Cambridge: Cambridge University Press.

Cosmetic Surgery in the United States

DAVID FREDERICK, REYN YOSHIURA, and TERRI SCOTT
Chapman University, USA

Cosmetic surgery has existed for thousands of years in one form or another and body modification more generally is common across the world. Surgical techniques to reshape or repair noses were practiced by ancient Greeks, Europeans, and Indians long before the development of modern medical procedures. Breast implants made of paraffin, beeswax, and vegetable oil were used to enlarge breasts in the nineteenth and early twentieth centuries. It was not until the advent of anesthesia, however, that cosmetic surgery became more common. In the United States and Europe, World War I sparked the further development of cosmetic surgery practices because thousands of soldiers desired plastic surgery, particularly for facial injuries resulting from gunshot wounds.

Cosmetic surgery has become one common way in which appearance is modified in industrialized countries, and many men and women are interested in pursuing cosmetic surgery. In a study of over 60,000 adults, 71 percent of women and 40 percent of men expressed some level of interest in cosmetic surgery (Frederick, Lever, and Peplau 2007). Participants were asked: "If you could afford it, would you consider getting cosmetic surgery or liposuction to improve your looks or body?" Overall, the percentage of women and men responding in each category were: "Not interested" (29% vs. 60%), "Maybe" (23% vs. 17%), "Cosmetic surgery only" (15% vs. 9%), "Liposuction only" (13% vs. 7%), and "Both cosmetic surgery and liposuction" (20% vs. 6%).

These gender differences in interest in cosmetic surgery are reflected in the actual rates of cosmetic surgery. The American Society of Plastic Surgeons tracks national data in the United States each year (American Society of Plastic Surgeons 2014). In 2013, there were 1.6 million cosmetic surgeries, 13.4 million cosmetic procedures, and 5.7 million reconstructive procedures. The vast majority of cosmetic surgeries and procedures were performed on women (91%). The sex difference in interest in cosmetic surgery is often explained by the fact that men's attractiveness is defined more heavily by traits not easily modified by cosmetic surgery (e.g., muscularity and athletic ability) compared with women (e.g., cues of youth such as smooth skin). There is a small to moderate difference between men and women in body dissatisfaction and in how much importance they place on their appearance (Frederick, Peplau, and Lever 2006). Finally, there may be more stigma associated with pursuing cosmetic surgery for men than for women.

The top five most common cosmetic surgeries in 2013 for women (American Society of Plastic Surgeons 2014) were breast augmentation (290,224), eyelid surgery (185,243), liposuction (179,259), nose reshaping (163,662), and facelift (120,621). Men pursued a similar set of cosmetic surgeries: nose reshaping (57,391), eyelid surgery (30,398), liposuction (23,558), breast reduction (22,939), and facelift (12,669). The top cosmetic procedures for women were injection of botulinum toxin (e.g., Botox) (5.9 million), soft tissue fillers (2.1 million), chemical peels (1.1 million), and laser hair removal (0.9 million). The top cosmetic procedures for men were Botox (385,358), laser hair removal (190,548), microdermabrasion (178,410), soft tissue fillers (95,361), and chemical peel (94,625).

Breast augmentation is designed to enlarge a naturally small breast, restore breast size following breastfeeding or weight loss, or increase symmetry in breast sizes when a woman's breasts are naturally different sizes. Incisions are typically made underneath the breast, in the armpit area, or under the areolas, and a breast implant is inserted. Breast implants are made of sacks filled with saline (sterile salt water) or silicone. Breast augmentation differs from breast lift surgery, which raises and firms the breast by removing excess skin and tightening the surrounding breast tissue. Liposuction removes fat deposits and recontours the body shape. It can be performed on many areas of the body (stomach, thighs, buttocks, chest, ankles, etc.). Small incisions are made in the body, a thin hollow tube is inserted to loosen fat, and then this dislodged fat is vacuumed out.

Cosmetic surgeries designed to alter the appearance of genitals have recently garnered attention. Labiaplasty refers to reducing the length of the labia minora (e.g., the "lips" of the vulva). This can be to reduce irritation and pain or for cosmetic reasons. The skin is trimmed or removed with scissors or scalpels and then resewn. Phalloplasty refers to augmentation of the penis. This can be done by inserting fat tissue from other parts of the body or by cutting the suspensory ligaments of the penis, increasing the size and length of the flaccid penis, but the procedure has little impact on erect length.

There are also ethnic differences in cosmetic surgery rates, and possibly ethnic differences in motivations for seeking specific types of surgery. The ethnic breakdown of people who sought cosmetic surgery is similar to the general population, although non-Hispanic whites are slightly overrepresented: non-Hispanic White (70%), Hispanic (11%), African American (8%), Asian American (7%), Other (5%).

Recently, attention has been paid to the practice of "ethnic cosmetic surgery." Ethnic cosmetic surgery has the effect of modifying traits that are stereotypically associated with their ethnic group. One concern raised regarding these surgeries is that some ethnic minorities in the United States are seeking these surgeries because these ethnic facial features are devalued relative to the white ideals prevalent in the media. Motivations for pursuing these surgeries are not well researched, and different women may seek these surgeries for different reasons, both in the United States and elsewhere. Based on a series of interviews, Kaw (1993) raised the concern that Asian American women were seeking blepharoplasty (eyelid surgery) for this reason. In 2011, however, China and Japan were in the top five countries in terms of number of blepharoplasty procedures (International Society of Aesthetic Plastic Surgery 2012). The popularity of this procedure may not be due solely to exposure to Western media, but rather to culture-specific beauty ideals, or because women with relatively larger eyes are more attractive in multiple cultures, possibly because they are perceived to be younger (Jones 1995).

People are motivated to pursue cosmetic surgery for many reasons. Generally speaking, people who seek cosmetic surgery do not differ in overall body satisfaction from people who do not seek this surgery. Instead, they typically have higher dissatisfaction with the specific aspect of the body they are seeking surgery for. The exception to this is that people desiring liposuction tend to have lower body satisfaction, presumably because body fat distribution affects the majority of the body and thus has a bigger impact on overall evaluation of one's appearance (Frederick, Lever, and Peplau 2007). Generally speaking, research finds that body satisfaction does improve after cosmetic surgery, particularly satisfaction with the aspect of the body receiving surgery, but there have been few carefully conducted studies that use validated measures of body image as well as matched control groups (van Soest et al. 2011).

There is a slightly higher rate of body dysmorphic disorder among cosmetic surgery patients than in the general population. Body dysmorphic disorder is characterized by a preoccupation with an imagined or slight defect in appearance. Estimates range from 1–5 percent in the general population but 6–15 percent in cosmetic surgery patients (Aouizerate et al. 2003). Other factors increasing interest in cosmetic surgery include higher household income, higher weight, older age, having children, lower educational status, greater acceptance of media images of beauty, greater importance attached to one's appearance, friends or family who have undergone procedures, and history of being teased about one's appearance.

SEE ALSO: Eating Disorders and Disordered Eating; Feminist Theories of the Body; Footbinding; Self-Esteem; Sex Reassignment Surgery; Sexual Objectification; Skin Lightening/Bleaching

REFERENCES

American Society of Plastic Surgeons. 2014. 2014 Plastic Surgery Procedures. Accessed March 13, 2015, at http://www.plasticsurgery.org/news/plastic-surgery-statistics/2014-statistics.html.

Aouizerate B., et al. 2003. "Body Dysmorphic Disorder in a Sample of Cosmetic Surgery Applicants." *European Psychiatry*, 18: 365–368. DOI: 10.1016/j.eurpsy.2003.02.001.

Frederick, David A., Janet Lever, and Letitia Anne Peplau. 2007. "Interest in Cosmetic Surgery and Body Image: Views of Men and Women across the Lifespan." *Plastic & Reconstructive Surgery*, 120: 1407–1415. DOI: 10.1097/01.prs.0000279375.26157.64.

Frederick, David A., Letitia Anne Peplau, and Janet Lever. 2006. "The Swimsuit Issue: Correlates of Body Image in a Sample of 52,677 Heterosexual Adults." *Body Image*, 4: 413–419.

International Society of Aesthetic Plastic Surgery. 2012. ISAPS Statistics. Accessed March 13, 2015, at http://www.isaps.org/Media/Default/global-statistics/ISAPS-Results-Procedures-2011.pdf.

Jones, Doug. 1995. "Sexual Selection, Physical Attractiveness, and Facial Neoteny: Cross-Cultural Evidence and Implications." *Current Anthropology*, 36: 723–745.

Kaw, Eugenia. 1993. "Medicalization of Racial Features: Asian American Women and Cosmetic Surgery." *Medical Anthropology Quarterly*, 7: 74–79.

Soest, Timann von, et al. 2011. "Psychosocial Changes after Cosmetic Surgery: A 5-year Follow-Up Study." *Plastic & Reconstructive Surgery*, 128: 765–772. DOI: 10.1097/PRS.0B013e31822213f0.

FURTHER READING

International Society of Aesthetic Plastic Surgery. 2014. ISAPS Statistics. Accessed March 13, 2015, at http://www.isaps.org/blog/isaps-statistics.

Courtly Love

JOHN W. ELLIS-ETCHISON
Rice University, USA

Courtly love is a highly circumscribed code of conduct first established and adumbrated in the works of troubadour poets in the courts of late eleventh-century southern France, namely that of Duke William IX, to reflect on and direct the construction of the love relationship between the long-suffering noble, and often male, aspirant and an aloof aristocratic, and often female, paramour. Relying on an amalgamated language of feudalism and noblesse oblige to convey a sense of intrinsic disparity in the power dynamics between the lovers, courtly love embodies an intriguing tension between erotics and spirituality, desire and attainment. Having long recognized this complicated interplay and trajectory, critics regularly hone in on the contours of courtly love's incongruent and perhaps contradictory aims and objects; dogmatically paradoxical, courtly love may be understood as a category of affection that embraces piety and prurience, passion and reason, as well as the quotidian and the numinous in nearly equal measure (Newman 1968).

Though first conceptualized in the courts of medieval Aquitaine, Provence, Champagne, and Burgundy, and codified shortly thereafter by works like Andreas Capellanus's *De Amore*, or as it is commonly known in English, *The Art of Courtly Love*, the actual term "courtly love," or "amour courtois," is an anachronistic neologism attributed to Gaston Paris in an article from 1883. In medieval parlance, the concept was known by many designations, including "amour honestus," or honest love, and "fin amor," or refined love. Such florid terminology helps to encapsulate courtly love as an amorous epistemology posited on a notion of chivalrous, idealized affection that ostensibly ennobles and purifies the characters of those participating in it. However, such lofty and overblown notions of courtly love belie that its enactment relies almost exclusively on clandestine, extramarital encounters between members of the upper strata of courtly society. Thus, courtly love's execution reveals its stark moral ambivalence, marking it as love's gray area where noble ambitions commingle with base drives.

Such a complicated construction of love pays homage to numerous sources, especially classical depictions of desire and affection. Ovid's *Ars Amatoria*, or *The Art of Love*, for instance, represents the lover in pursuit of the beloved as in thrall to his or her desirous emotions. Not only is the lover audibly emotive, sighing and even crying, this figure is physically affected by his or her passions, becoming sleepless and wasting away, sometimes even dying as a consequence of this quest for love. Scholars debate the distinction between this Ovidian standard and courtly love, parsing out that where the medieval conception departs from the classical concerns the aims of their respective loves: the Ovidian lover seeks carnal pleasure, whereas the courtly lover reveres the object of his affection to the point of apotheosis. Some critics have noted that in the medieval construction of courtly love, the beloved feminine object is almost heretically elevated to the status of the divine in a way that problematizes the lines between the object that evokes such desires and the feelings that this object is intended to inspire. For these researchers, courtly love is actually the mystical eroto-theological assemblage that heralded occidental interest in fervent, transcendent love and divine, ecstatic adoration (de Rougemont 1940).

While depictions of normative gender roles within this tradition seem rigidly demarcated, merely reifying as natural masculine activity and feminine passivity, the overt sexualization and objectification of the feminine, and the ascendancy of patriarchal dominion, this is not a foregone conclusion. Scholars continue to debate the ways in which courtly love sounds the depths of gender and sexuality, calling into question, reversing, and undermining hidebound constructions of masculine authority through the enactment of feminine autonomy. In the traditional courtly love narrative, romance begins with surreptitious eye contact between the lover and the beloved, followed by distant worship of the latter by the former, which shortly thereafter provokes his protestations and impassioned declarations of devotion. The beloved demurely rebuffs these overtures, which only fuels the lover's ardor, causing him to redouble his commitments. Falling into prone lovesickness, the exhausted lover somehow negotiates valorous acts that ultimately win the beloved's heart and secure the consummation of their illicit love, which perpetuates an endless series of adventures involving dissimulation and misdirection in the name of this selfsame forbidden love. The fetishistic interest this tradition places on the idolized female has led some feminist scholars to critique courtly love's exaltation of the feminine as nothing more than a male conceit, a ploy to mete out power in exchange for narrowly defining virtuous femininity, ultimately alienating and disempowering women (Millett 1970).

Nonetheless, other scholars locate puissance in this elevation of the feminine, observing an element of subversive empowerment in courtly love's treatment of gender, sex, and sexuality. They maintain that courtly love centers around feminine liberation, contending that the lover's unwavering devotion to his beloved mistress instills within her a kind of supreme authority within their relationship and an unqualified ability to shape and direct his actions, especially to noble and upright ends. Even still, critics debate whether this relationship constitutes real empowerment or merely artifice. Recently, some have begun to draw connections between the tenets of courtly love and modern peripheral sexual acts, especially the master and slave relationship that is part and parcel of sadomasochism (Schultz 2006). The lover's public rejection and humiliation at the hands of the cold beloved invigorates and whets his appetite, mirroring the slave's erotic debasement and subjugation at the hands of the master in the world of bondage and domination. It is important, nevertheless, to recognize that others are quick to assert how these similarities are too facile to adequately elucidate courtly love further.

SEE ALSO: Gender Role Ideology; Sado-masochism, Domination, and Submission; Sexualities

REFERENCES

De Rougemont, Denis. 1940. *Love in the Western World*. Princeton: Princeton University Press.
Millett, Kate. 1970. *Sexual Politics*. New York: Doubleday.
Newman, Francis X. 1968. *The Meaning of Courtly Love*. Albany: SUNY Press.
Schultz, James A. 2006. *Courtly Love, the Love of Courtliness, and the History of Sexuality*. Chicago: University of Chicago Press.

Creation Stories

GILA STOPLER

College of Law and Business, Israel

The biblical story of Adam and Eve is one of the most powerful myths of Western civilization and has defined the relationships between men and women for generations and until this very day. According to the story, told in the book of Genesis (Genesis 2:18), after creating Adam from the dust of the earth, God decided to create a helpmate for him. He put Adam to sleep and from his rib created his helpmate, which Adam named Woman. After Woman ate from the Tree of Knowledge and seduced Adam into eating as well, they were banished from paradise and Adam renamed the woman Eve, for she was to be the mother of all. The creation of Eve from Adam's rib has been interpreted for thousands of years to denote the God-given inferiority of woman

(Lerner 1986). An additional justification for women's inferiority, especially in the Christian tradition, is found in Eve's responsibility for the fall of Adam, which was interpreted as the responsibility of all women for the advent of evil in the world (Radford Ruether 1993). Woman's punishment for the fall is comprised of her eternal subjugation to her husband, the restriction of her sexuality strictly for purposes of procreation within the conjugal relationship, and the pain of childbearing (Genesis 3:16). In Christian thought, woman's role as a submissive wife and mother is not only her punishment but also her only means of salvation (Timothy 2:12–15).

Contrary to the centrality of the Adam and Eve myth in the Judeo-Christian tradition, the alternative story of creation, which is hinted at in the book of Genesis – the story of the creation of Adam and Lilith – has been paid very little attention throughout the ages. The book of Genesis contains two contradictory versions of the creation story. One is the Adam and Eve story, while the second, which appears in the first chapter of Genesis, ahead of the Adam and Eve story, tells a very different story of the creation of man and woman (Genesis 1:27–29). According to the second creation story, which was written several centuries after the first (Lerner 1986), man and woman were created simultaneously, as one. "God created man in his own image. In God's image he created him; male and female he created them" (Genesis 1:27). This verse is the basis for the egalitarian story of creation of Adam and Lilith. According to the story, God created the first human double with two faces and then sawed it in the middle, separating the first human into two completely equal human beings: male, Adam, and female, Lilith. Soon, however, Adam and Lilith quarreled and when Lilith left Adam, refusing to return, God created Eve, his second wife, making sure of the success of the match by creating her out of Adam's rib and making her his subordinate.

The egalitarian myth of the creation of Adam and Lilith has been largely suppressed and forgotten, only to be resurrected in modern times by the occasional feminist. To the extent that Lilith's image as Adam's first wife continued to exist throughout the ages, it served as a patriarchal creation to demonstrate the dangerous consequences of women's aspirations to equality. For example, according to the Alphabet of Ben Sira, the first "official" compilation of the myth of the creation of Lilith, God formed Lilith just as he formed Adam, only instead of using pure dust he used filth and sediment, and consequently, "from Adam's union with this demoness sprang innumerable demons that still plague mankind" (Rivlin 1998). Despite its reference to Adam and Lilith's union, which is responsible for the introduction of demons into the world, the Alphabet continues to say that Adam and Lilith could not find peace together because of her refusal to lie beneath him during intercourse, and that after Adam tried to force his will on her, Lilith uttered the magic name of God and left him. Thus, a woman's aspiration to equality both produces eternal evil and destines her to loneliness and misery. The demonization of Lilith has served as a powerful tool in the hands of the patriarchal social order. Kamir (2001) argues that the image of Lilith as the she-devil was created with the rise of the new male-oriented Sumerian, Babylonian, and later, Hebrew monotheists in order to suppress the powerful image of the ancient Sumerian Great Goddess. The all-powerful female Goddess was slashed into two distinct feminine images: the Goddess's life-giving, motherly traits were transmuted to Eve, the domesticated and powerless feminine figure, while the Goddess's wisdom, sexuality, strength, and intimate connection with death were vilified and demonized and bestowed upon

Lilith, the bloodthirsty she-devil. Through this cultural maneuver, evident within Western culture to this day, women were taught to regard Eve, the domesticated female, as their role model, and to fear Lilith, the she-devil, as their mortal enemy (Kamir 2001).

While Lilith fails to appear officially in Christianity, in the Middle Ages she was sometimes portrayed as the snake who seduces Eve into eating from the Tree of Knowledge (Witcombe 2000). In this role Lilith represents Eve's free sexuality, which is responsible for the fall and which should never again be allowed to raise its head. Within Christianity, the demonic seductress Lilith was transformed from a mythical creature to an internal flaw in every woman (Kamir 2001). In her internal fight against the devilish Lilith within her, each woman is called upon to struggle against everything that Lilith represents, namely women's equality, free sexuality, and independent strength and wisdom.

SEE ALSO: Gender Equality; Patriarchy

REFERENCES

Kamir, Orit. 2001. *Every Breath You Take: Stalking Narratives and the Law*. Ann Arbor: University of Michigan Press.
Lerner, Gerda. 1986. *The Creation of Patriarchy*. New York: Oxford University Press.
Radford Ruether, Rosemary. 1993. *Sexism and God-Talk: Toward a Feminist Theology*. Boston: Beacon Press.
Rivlin, Lilly. 1998. "Lilith." In *Which Lilith?: Feminist Writers Re-Create the World's First Woman*, edited by Enid Dame, 4–14. New York: Jason Aronson Inc.
Withcombe, Christopher L. C. E. 2000. "Eve and the Identity of Women," Ch. 7. Accessed April 22, 2014, at http://witcombe.sbc.edu/eve-women/7evelilith.html.

Criminal Justice System and Sexuality in the United States

VANESSA R. PANFIL
Old Dominion University, Virginia, USA

AIMEE WODDA
University of Illinois at Chicago, USA

The criminal justice system has traditionally attempted to regulate sexuality by deeming certain acts and desires as deviant, illegal, or both. Sexuality can be associated with reproductive capacities and functions, but it also refers to behaviors, desires, attractions, orientations, emotions, attachments, pleasures, risk-taking, intimacy, and spirituality. While sexuality does retain certain biological elements (e.g., the physical sensation of desire and attraction), it too is socially constructed; human sexuality is shaped by social forces and societal constructs. Although sexuality is historically, socially, and culturally contingent (Foucault 1978), the criminal justice system has often taken legal action upon those whose behaviors stray outside the boundaries of private, heteronormative, conjugal relations.

As a mechanism of control, the criminal justice system, increasingly referred to as a crimino-legal complex, involves not only criminal justice personnel and scholars, but also politicians and even ordinary citizens. A specific division of the crimino-legal system, often referred to as the juvenile justice system, may deal with individuals who have not yet reached the age of majority. Both criminal and juvenile justice systems are comprised of police, courts, and corrections, and are guided by law. Thus, following the establishment of legal measures and the enforcement of such measures by agents of the state (such as police), someone accused of violating the law (or even societal norms) is likely to be processed by the criminal justice system in the form of courts, and may be incarcerated in correctional facilities. In light of the relationship between human sexuality and its control, whether by law, agents of the state, courts, and/or corrections, an evaluation of the history and current status of such efforts is warranted.

SEXUALITY REGULATED BY LAW

Historically, sexual activity and its possible outcomes have been governed by law, with lawful or ethical behavior often determined by religious or spiritual morality. Laws are culturally relative in that they have differed across time and space, and there are few universals regarding criminalized sexuality. In the contemporary United States, the law and the crimino-legal system are sex negative. Sex negativity regards sex as a "dangerous, destructive, negative force" and overburdens sex acts with significance they do not deserve (Rubin 2012, 146). Theorist Gayle Rubin uses a "charmed circle" graphic to illustrate the sex hierarchy that results from sex negativity. In this circle, only certain acts fall under the umbrella of "good, normal, natural, blessed sexuality" (Rubin 2012, 152). In order to qualify as good, normal, and natural, an act may occur only in private between two heterosexual and married cisgender (cisgender is a relatively recent term intended to denote persons comfortable performing the gender that normatively aligns with the sex they were assigned at birth) individuals from the same generation who are monogamous, and engage primarily in procreative/penetrative "vanilla" sex using only their bodies and no other tools or fantasy generating images. Any other act or identity category belongs to the "outer limits" occupied by "bad, abnormal, unnatural, damned sexuality" (Rubin 2010, 152). Variations that lie in this outer zone include, but are not limited to: sex between people of the same sex and/or gender; sex between unmarried persons; promiscuity; non-procreative sex; commercial sex; sex alone or in groups; casual sex; cross-generational sex; sex in public; sex using pornography and/or with objects; and sadomasochistic sex (Rubin 2010, 152). Many acts that lie outside the "charmed circle" are also illegal (e.g., public sex, commercial sex, some cross-generational sex).

Societal reaction has varied widely in its response to the variety of sexual behaviors and sexualities sometimes considered outside the morality of the dominant culture. For example, although modern Western cultures place extreme stigma and expend social control efforts on sex offenders, particularly those who commit offenses against children, cross-generational sex has not been discouraged in all contexts. For example, in Ancient Greek society, an adult male citizen's sexual partners could be male or female, as long as they were younger, submissive, and in a lower social position than the free male; cross-generational sex was fairly uncontroversial (Halperin 1989). Contemporary age of consent laws (which dictate how old partners must be before they can freely consent to sexual activity), however, sometimes differ depending on the gender of the partner, with typically higher ages of consent for same-sex partners (Majd, Marksamer, and Reyes 2009).

Lawbreaking activities where there are clear victims (e.g., someone did not consent or was injured) are more universally criminalized, though enforcement is not uniform. One example of this uneven enforcement can be found in historical stereotypes of black women's alleged sexually aggressive and predatory nature that was used to account for miscegenation that actually originated from the rape of slaves by their masters, whereas black men's alleged insatiable sexual appetite for white women was used to create trumped-up rape charges to justify lynchings and punish successful blacks. These "jezebel" and "black rapist" myths persist today, as evidenced by the disparity in sentencing for black men who rape white women versus white men who rape black women; black women's representation in women-in-prison films as predators; and black women's profiling as sex workers, among other examples (Mogul, Ritchie, and Whitlock 2011). In addition, although gay and lesbian people were persecuted during World War II by the Nazi party because they allegedly threatened the "moral fiber" of German youth and adults and were "anti-community minded," certain gay Nazi leaders and beloved gay entertainers were not targeted for execution or work camps (Plant 1986). These examples illustrate how the group in power can influence which "crimes" are prioritized, especially depending on who commits them, and how certain statuses are codified by law.

North American colonizers' motives for criminalizing and punishing certain behaviors related to gender and sexuality were an integral part of colonization, genocide, and enslavement (Mogul et al. 2011, 1). Casting indigenous populations as "morally perverse" and as "polluted with sexual sin" was taken as justification to physically punish or kill them. Instituting rigid gender hierarchies also helped facilitate the relationship between colonizer and colonized. Colonial legacies influenced sodomy laws in the United States and globally and continue to do so today, even though laws against consensual sodomy in the United States have been struck down by the Supreme Court. Policing of gender and sexuality from the 1500s to 1900s went far beyond sodomy laws, often outside of any legal framework; furthermore, it was often tied to race, class, nationality, and other factors, with poor people of color (and/or colonial subjects) even being executed, while upper-class white people were given numerous chances to reform. Furthermore, sodomy has been codified in a number of ways, including oral or anal sex among same- or opposite-sex partners, as well as sex acts that were forcible, cross-generational, or inter-species. Although sodomy laws are often thought to be exclusively associated with gay and lesbian populations, same-sex consensual sex acts comprised a minority of sodomy prosecutions until the very recent past (Mogul et al. 2011).

After previously upholding sodomy laws in *Bowers v. Hardwick* (1986), the Supreme Court of the United States struck down all remaining sodomy laws in the United States with *Lawrence v. Texas* (2003). The court's reasons for their decision rested on the fact that the question before them was not actually about a sex act, but about people's freedom in their lives and private homes, inherent in their Constitutional right to liberty under the Due Process Clause. The Court also noted that sodomy as consensual same-sex sexual activity had not necessarily been banned throughout history; the ban was quite recent and was only found in a few states. Furthermore, many states and countries had already dismantled their sodomy laws by the time of the 2003 decision.

In some cases regulation occurs freshly, as when lawmakers criminalize an act or behavior that was previously unregulated. In the United States, abortion became illegal by the end of the nineteenth century due to various cultural fears. Specifically, it was linked to a concern about declining birth rates of Anglo-Saxon women compared with women who were immigrants, non-white, and/or of lower socioeconomic status, as well as a negative reaction to women's changing roles in the legal and labor spheres. Although *Roe v. Wade* (1973) legalized abortion in the United States, efforts to define the fetus as a child or person persist, and the availability and affordability of legal abortion in many states is precarious. Under laws that attempt to defend the "personage" of a fetus, actions such as drug use while pregnant can be considered child abuse or neglect, and drug use can qualify someone as an unfit parent. Additionally, evidence suggests that women of color may be selectively screened for drug use during pregnancy, as well as selectively punished for such crimes depending on the drug they used or their other life circumstances (see, for example, Paltrow 2004). Additionally, in the United States, there has been a history of forced sterilization of women, particularly those who are poor, mentally ill, intellectually disabled, imprisoned, and those who have been regarded as "promiscuous." *Buck v. Bell* (1927), an infamous Supreme Court case which has never been formally overturned, allowed the forced sterilization of women who were considered "unfit" under the reasoning that compulsory sterilization of "feeble-minded" persons did not violate the Due Process Clause of the Fourteenth Amendment, and, furthermore, compulsory sterilization benefited the "health of" the state.

Another manner in which the state has attempted to regulate the sexuality of its citizens is through the establishment of obscenity laws, where underlying sex negativity is disguised as concern for safety and morality. A historical example of this type of regulation can be found in the Comstock Law of 1873 which attempted to halt the transmission of all materials deemed obscene or pornographic through the US mail, including birth control devices, sex toys, erotic literature, abortifacients, and information about birth control and abortion. A contemporary example of censorship can be found in pornography restrictions in the United Kingdom proposed by the British Board of Film Censors' (BBFC) Audiovisual Media Services Regulations 2014 amendment, which aims to restrict content in on-demand Internet-based videos on the grounds that particular acts are "not acceptable." Censored acts include a variety of consensual bondage, discipline, sadism, and masochism (BDSM) practices (e.g., erotic, consensual domination and submission), certain fetishes including urophilia and role playing, and also acts that have been characterized as "taking aim at female pleasure" that include female ejaculation, fisting, and face-sitting (Hooton 2014). Fisting and face-sitting have been characterized by the BBFC as "potentially life-threatening" and, in response, sex-positive free speech communities staged demonstrations outside parliament where they simulated sex acts to protest the censorship.

Sex work (or prostitution) is an exchange of some form of sexual contact for remuneration (e.g., money, food, clothing, shelter, jewelry) which has been variously criminalized, regulated, celebrated, and tolerated across the globe and across time. At various moments across history, prostitutes have been considered sacred, commonplace, evil, necessary, as "fallen women," and as lawbreakers. Even in times and places where commercial sex is illegal, policing and enforcement of laws regulating the sale of sex have been unevenly applied to individuals. The regulation of sex is heavily influenced by class, race, heteronormativity, and the rift between public and private spaces. Other inconsistencies are inherent in the regulation of commercial sex: for example, while certain individuals may be forced or coerced into selling sex, others participate of their own free will. Further, although the stereotypical person who sells sex is a woman, about half of the individuals who sell sex are male. Research has not adequately captured the numbers of transgender individuals who sell sex (Weitzer 2005).

The most stringent regulation of commercial sex occurs at the street level and is aimed at policing young, poor persons of color who sell sex. One example of this type of intense policing of "deviant" populations can be found in the practice of arresting transgender women in New York City for carrying condoms, using the rationale that possessing more than two or three condoms on your person is an indicator that the person is a sex worker. This phenomenon is aligned with the over-policing of youth for minor sexual offenses (e.g., sexting, which is regarded by the law as "distributing child pornography"), and exists alongside assumptions that young persons do not fully comprehend the ramifications of sexual activity while simultaneously punishing them with the full force of law (Eraker 2010).

SEXUALITY ON TRIAL

Although individuals have faced legal trials for their sexual conduct for hundreds of years, issues of sexual identity also come into play. In the modern period, research suggests that the majority of gay and lesbian litigants in civil and criminal courts have experienced negative incidents in court based on their sexual orientation. These incidents include homophobic remarks and "jokes," derogatory terms, ridicule, offensive gestures, or being discredited because they were perceived to be gay or lesbian. Furthermore, because legal personnel may not be informed about gay and lesbian peoples' lived realities and may not understand how to counteract negative stereotypes about their clients, queer people arguably receive subpar representation, particularly in criminal cases (Mogul et al. 2011).

Criminal archetypes of queer people are harmful for the lesbian, gay, bisexual, transgender, and questioning (LGBTQ) community at large, as these archetypes place undue emphasis on the sexuality and/or gender non-conformity of an alleged killer, while failing to rely upon a heterosexual killer's sexuality as providing an explanation for a crime (Mogul et al. 2011). For example, in contrast to gay male serial killers, male heterosexual serial killers' behavior is never interpreted in ways that are attributed to depravity intrinsic to heterosexuality, nor as pathological by virtue of their heterosexuality, despite the brutality that these serial killers also inflict upon their victims. The "sexually degraded predator" archetype takes numerous forms which are discussed elsewhere in this entry, including the "male child molester," the "gay prison rapist," and the "sexually aggressive black lesbian," among others. Because of concerns about gay peoples' alleged predatory and promiscuous nature, gay men were often targeted for police sweeps of various sexual crimes, including child molestation, public sex, and even consensual sodomy, including instances where there was no proof of such crimes. Because gay men were believed to be predisposed to commit sexual offenses, judges and juries easily believed that gay men committed any sexual offense they were accused of. More generally, queer criminal archetypes reflect several main themes, including beliefs that gay and lesbian people are mentally unstable, dangerous, deceptive, depraved, and driven to violence as a result of such natures, which are allegedly inherent to queer sexual desire (Mogul et al. 2011).

Farr's (2000) research on lesbians on death row is illustrative of these themes. Women are much less likely to commit murders that qualify for the death penalty, such as those that are premeditated, or that are in the course of or to cover up another felony. Women are most likely to kill their romantic partners, typically for an affective (emotional) or defensive motive. Female murderers are also less likely to have prior felony convictions for violent crimes and to be involved in criminal subcultures than male murderers. Capital murders committed by women are more similar to non-capital murders committed by women than to capital murders committed by men. Since their murders would not normally qualify them for a capital sentence, Farr argues that factors such as gender non-conformity in appearance or demeanor, engaging in typically "masculine" crimes, and perceived or actual lesbianism can tip the scales and contribute to female murderers being sentenced to the death penalty.

In addition to negative perceptions about queer criminal archetypes, Farr (2000) notes that depictions of lesbians contribute to punitive ideas. Lesbians are "easily stereotyped" as "man-haters," but also "male wannabes"; such perceptions are facilitated by ongoing cultural images of "lesbian evil" and as vampires, specifically. Past medical and criminological representations such as those compiled by Lombroso helped establish lesbians as abnormal women who had inverted their gender expectations, and there was an assumed linkage between lesbianism and deviance/criminality. Early criminologists attempted to sort individuals according to mostly biological, but also behavioral categories. Potentially criminal "types" included lesbians (referred to as "inverts," "tribades," and "Sapphists"), gay men (referred to as "homosexuals," "perverts," and "pederasts"), and women who suffered from an "excess of sexuality." These women were mostly thought to be lesbians, but women thought to be heterosexual were also included in this category (Lombroso and Ferrero 2004). These early criminologists also conflated gender and sexuality; for example, lesbian women were often thought to possess an excess of masculinity, and gay men were often linked with an excess of femininity, hence, the term "invert" had more to do with gender non-conforming appearance and behaviors than sexual conduct. Extant literature suggests women who are viewed as "manly" or who have committed "masculine" offenses (such as murder and other violent crimes) are sentenced more harshly than feminine women, perhaps because they are no longer seen as being entitled to chivalry or paternalism that has historically characterized the treatment of girls and women in the criminal and juvenile justice systems. Because the norms of femininity that they have violated are typically those of white, middle-class femininity, other social statuses may also intersect with masculine gender presentation in order to create negative biases against defendants (Farr 2000).

Scholars of the death penalty have argued that it is necessary for prosecutors to defeminize and dehumanize a female defendant in order to convince the jury she deserves the death penalty. Victor Streib, as quoted in Farr (2000, 53), states, "The more 'manly' her sexuality, her dress, and her demeanor … the more easily the jury may forget that she is a woman." And indeed, although the five self-identified lesbians on death row at the time of Farr's research had aggravating circumstances in their cases that could warrant the death penalty, their sexuality or gender presentation was used against them during their trials. For several women, their murders of men or boys were framed not situationally, but as a result of their hatred of men, which was allegedly connected to their lesbianism. Mogul et al. (2011) provide additional details on these and related cases. For example, Wanda Jean Allen shot and killed her lover who tried to leave her in front of a police station; during the trial, prosecutors emphasized Allen's controlling, violent, and masculine behavior within the relationship, and highlighted her previous manslaughter conviction. Aileen Wournos, a sex worker who admitted to killing seven "johns" (clients) in Florida, was portrayed in the media as a mannish, man-hating lesbian. Headlines about Wournos read "Lethal lesbian hooker" and "Rampage of the Bull-Dyke Man-Eater!" (Farr 2000).

Such perceptions of lesbian, gay, bisexual, and queer people as allegedly predatory or depraved can even extend to ideas about LGBQ victims. LGBQ victims may be devalued, their cases not taken seriously, or agents of the state may deem that their victimization was deserved or appropriate (Mogul et al. 2011). In addition, some defendants have successfully utilized the "gay panic" defense as to why they perpetrated violence against a gay person. Claims of "gay panic" are typically presented within the context of an existing criminal law defense, such as temporary insanity, provocation, or self-defense. Specifically, defendants advancing this defense claim that a gay man "made an unwanted sexual advance that caused the defendant to panic, lose self-control, and respond with fatal violence" (Lee 2013, 817). The logic that defendants want the court to believe is that same-sex sexual activity is so offensive to a heterosexual male that he is justified in punishing the alleged instigator with violence. Although the gay panic defense has led to the acquittal of some defendants, it is more likely unsuccessful. An offshoot of this defense is the trans* panic defense where a defendant attempts to absolve his culpability for assaulting or killing a transgender person by claiming he was "tricked" into romantic and/or sexual activity with someone who had not revealed their "true" gender. That is, the defendant essentially claims that if a potential romantic partner does not reveal the sex they were assigned at birth, then the defendant feels he was deceived and engaged in "gay" sexual activity he would not have consented to otherwise – a mistaken conflation whose explanation is beyond the scope of this entry (but see Wodda and Panfil, 2015). In summary, victims who do not conform to society's expectations for sexual identity and/or gender presentation can face challenges in gaining justice.

Expectations for sexual assault victims' sexual propriety also exist, but rape shield statutes prevent defendants from introducing evidence about an alleged victim's past sexual conduct or reputation in court. As part of their criminal defense strategy, defendants may be able to present evidence pertaining to a personal sexual relationship with their accuser, but not general character-based claims about the accuser's willingness to consent to sexual conduct. Such laws help to prevent public re-traumatization of sexual assault victims, as well as focus on the particular characteristics of the incident and whether consent was given or not. Before the passage of rape shield laws, reputational "evidence" could be used to conclude that if a person consented to sex with other individuals, then that person likely consented to sex with the defendant. In these ways, victims were held to standards of purity and morality regarding their past sexual behavior instead of being limited to the facts of the case at hand. Rape shield laws exist primarily in Anglo-American legal worlds, continue to face legal challenges on constitutional grounds, and simultaneously endure critique from feminist legal scholars regarding existing loopholes in such laws (Roman 2011).

These phenomena indicate a preoccupation with sexual morality, which has a long history in the United States. The progressive era (1890–1920) was an era rooted in goals of humanitarianism, but had repressive results for young women. Progressivism was part of a larger cultural reaction to revitalize Victorian sexual morality, including calls for sexual moderation and purity, and punishment for girls and women who subverted those goals. Victorian images of women fashioned them as the "gatekeepers of sexual virtue." Girls, especially poor and immigrant girls, received harsher treatment than boys for the relatively minor offense of "immorality." The offenses that girls were arrested for were typically sexual in nature, such as "using obscene language," "strutting about in a lascivious manner," or going to dance-houses. These behaviors were taken as indicators of current or future sexual behavior. Girls were not tried for criminal offenses as often as boys were (as they typically committed status offenses and other non-serious offenses), but went to reformatories more often (Schlossman and Wallach 1978).

In progressive era court proceedings, judges made moral judgments when they admonished a girl to become a "good woman"; these comments reflected the values of the time. Girls who rebuffed these ideals or whose parents did not control them were sent away; their mothers were seen as responsible for girls' misbehavior for not giving them proper instruction in how to be good women, wives, and mothers. Physical tests and intense questioning determined whether or not a young woman was a virgin and, if she was not, whether she was morally repulsed by her prior sexual behaviors. Those who were virgins or disgusted with their behavior were seen as capable of reformation (Schlossman and Wallach 1978). Pasko (2010) notes that although coerced and/or incestuous acts were often present in girls' sexual histories, these were not deemed to be mitigating factors.

Targeting girls' sexuality played on long-term cultural fears, including the devolution of sexual purity. Girls targeted for reformation were primarily poor and/or immigrant girls, who were already targeted for eugenicist policies. Eugenicist policies sought to institutionalize and/or sterilize "dangerous classes" of people to prevent them from "breeding," as eugenicists thought it was unsafe for "feeble-minded" (low IQ) girls to procreate. Immigrant girls were also seen as particularly vulnerable to male attention. Theories of adolescence also came into play; the dominant thinking was that girls matured faster than boys and were less malleable, so sexually precocious girls gave up claims to childhood/innocence (Schlossman and Wallach 1978). There also existed the perception that girls could not repair their reputations or "start over" like boys, and of course, all of this existed against a backdrop of women's status in society being lower than that of men.

Although the Juvenile Justice and Delinquency Prevent Act of 1974 led to the diversion and deinstitutionalization of status offenders, the juvenile justice system has continued to incarcerate girls for wayward sexuality, but indirectly. Young people cannot be arrested for "immorality," but probation violations and higher risk assessment scores can result in detention. Girls may have their probation violated for staying out past curfew, or "running away" to see a romantic interest, which are viewed as making choices that are sexually unhealthy. In order to guard against unwanted pregnancies that can result from girls' sexual activities (including prostitution) while on furlough from a correctional institution, facilities can mandate birth control. These examples suggest a continued interest in controlling young women's sexuality through legal statutes and court intervention; problematic sexual behavior committed by boys has received some similar attention through legal efforts to define non-consensual sexual "experimentation" as sexual violence and to identify and treat juvenile sexual predators. However, both girls and boys can be adjudicated for such offenses, while boys historically have not been adjudicated for status offenses that were sexual in nature (Pasko 2010).

SEXUALITY AND CORRECTIONS

The very terms "corrections" and "reformatories" suggest that a period of incarceration should bring about positive change, and such concerns have been on the minds of correctional officials. Regarding girls in the progressive era, while in reformatories, girls were isolated from boys and men and kept until "marriageable age," typically 16.

They were instructed solely in domestic skills, which were thought to be helpful in attracting eligible male mates who would marry them. At the very least, this training provided marketable job skills. It also kept girls busy while in reformatories and thus easier to control. Furthermore, it was regarded as part of a larger rehabilitative goal: "According to correctional administrators, a girl's delinquency alone revealed that she had not learned to revere domestic pursuits" (Schlossman and Wallach 1978, 77). Boys were not kept for a comparable length of time or for comparable reasons – there was no emphasis on them learning how to be good husbands and fathers. Reformatories upheld social purity goals by preventing girls from getting or spreading venereal disease, acting as temptation for boys/men, being "recruited" for prostitution, and punishing them for expressing an interest in sex.

Although girls and women with "wayward sexuality" were deemed to be in need of judicial and correctional intervention, the mere existence of individuals in facilities who did not conform to sexual or gender expectations was seen as a challenge to the penal system. Estelle Freedman's (1996) historical research on the "prison lesbian" is illustrative. By the 1920s, almost every state had a separate women's reformatory, because officials were initially concerned with discouraging inmates from illegal heterosexual acts, as well as preventing pregnancy and sexual violence against women. Most inmates in these facilities came from working-class and/or immigrant backgrounds, and most had been sentenced for "crimes against public order" or "crimes against chastity," such as public drunkenness, vagrancy, or prostitution. Soon, attention turned to prison "homosexuality," but it was racialized: African American women (though there were comparatively few of them) were seen as aggressive, masculine, and hypersexual, and therefore attractive to white, feminine inmates seeking relationships and male attention while inside. Prison officials feared that upon their release, white women would continue the same-sex relationship and neglect their "racial duty" of reproducing. These fears underlined efforts towards race segregation in prison. Negative perceptions of black women contributed to this targeted intervention. The prison lesbian seemed to substantiate the prevailing medical notion that homosexuality was a result of gender "inversion." The label of "lesbian" denied gender privileges such as chivalry and paternalism from black women because it implied their maleness and a lack of feminine virtue. In correctional officers' minds, black women's alleged aggression and sexual deviance were linked; both were assumed to be due to their willingness to engage in "male" behaviors (see also Kunzel 2008). However, black women were not diagnosed with sexual psychopathy: because they were assumed to be sexually insatiable and naturally promiscuous, it would not be "abnormal" for them to engage in these sorts of behaviors (Freedman 1996).

Freedman (1996) also places these concerns and policies in historical context. From the 1920s to the 1940s, administrators of women's prisons were unwilling to discuss "the problem of homosexuality" partially because it was embarrassing and they thought it would reflect poorly on them as administrators. Additionally, they all worked closely with other women and did not want to be swept up into the scandal. Finally, some of them were involved romantically with other women and either did not want to be exposed, or to punish inmates for similar behaviors. Willingness to acknowledge it during the 1940s was due in part to increased prostitution arrests, overcrowding, and concerns about women's sexual deviance related to the war. By the 1950s, administrators' concerns were linked to Cold War fears, and the aggressive prison lesbian entered popular culture in pulp novels and women-in-prison films. Such sources demonized working-class women, who now spread "moral contagion"; Freedman notes that an increased concern with the prison lesbian was also likely linked to a growing white, working-class lesbian bar culture. There were concerns about "true" homosexuals and those who would become "addicted" to such behavior; "true" homosexuals or "hard core" lesbians were transferred to jails that did not provide programs. "Hard core" lesbians were women who continued their same-sex relationships outside of prison, indicating that their homosexuality was *not* a result of deprivation in prison. And interestingly, the courts were more committed to punishing women's homosexuality than the prisons were, and handed down contradictory punishments such as sentencing a woman to an additional 2 years' incarceration in the reformatory for a same-sex sexual relationship she had in that reformatory.

During this time period, similar concerns existed in girls' facilities, specifically regarding same-sex sexual behavior and the issues it posed for control of inmates, girls' emotional states, and to girls' treatment issues. Ford (1929) argued that deprivation was a leading cause of institutional homosexuality, but also suggested same-sex sexual behavior could be a symptom of sexual disturbance, as many of the girls were incarcerated for sexual indiscretions; keeping girls busy could curb these behaviors. Halleck and Hersko (1962) felt that girls' "homosexual behavior" in institutions was very self-destructive, but suggested deprivation, promiscuity, or peer pressure were its causes, instead of outright sexual perversion. They also believed that girls engaged in same-sex sexual behavior in institutions because of a mistrust of men due to sexual abuse, a failure to identify with femininity due to bad mothering, and non-satisfying sexual and emotional relationships in general. They insisted that staff must convince girls that this behavior would not be tolerated, but in such a way that girls did not engage in this behavior in order to get back at staff, nor would the girls think that staff would be prejudiced against them. Even some residential facility staff in the contemporary era express doubt that same-sex attraction while in facilities is a matter of identity, and instead suppose it is a way for girls to manipulate and control staff and other inmates (Pasko 2010).

In an interesting contrast to the deprivation hypothesis, Propper (1978) found that the rates of same-sex sexual behavior were highest in one of the co-educational facilities in her sample. Propper theorized that, because co-ed institutions have very strict rules about physical contact between sexes in order to prevent unwanted pregnancies, girls' contact with other girls was not as policed. She found no support for the "deprivation theory," which suggests various deprivations lead to same-sex sexual behavior. Instead, Propper found support for the "importation theory," which suggests that same-sex sexual orientation is brought into the facility with the girl, because the best predictor of same-sex sexual behavior while incarcerated is previous homosexuality (Propper 1978, 270). When this variable was eliminated from the model, no other variable predicted homosexual behavior. Furthermore, about one fourth of girls who had prior same-sex sexual experience abstained from it while incarcerated. Mogul et al. (2011) suggest that such a preoccupation with preventing "situational homosexuality" in institutions is related to fears that heterosexuality is itself unstable or fragile.

In the modern period, gay, lesbian, and bisexual youth continue to face difficult interactions with justice system actors or staff in facilities who challenge their sexual identities or behavior as a treatment issue – that is, young people's gayness, bisexuality, or lesbianism is seen as being related to their delinquent behavior and targeted for intervention. Majd, Marksamer, and Reyes (2009) note LGBT youth may be overcharged with sex offenses (in cases where the age of consent differs for same- or opposite-sex partners, for example), receive unnecessary sex offender treatment for normal and age-appropriate sexual activity, or even be forced to undergo "reparative" therapy that attempts to "cure" their sexual orientation. They may be hospitalized for their same-sex desire, or face inappropriate or coercive attempts to change their sexual orientation. Pasko (2010) found that young women's LBQ identities are pathologized particularly when such identities are assumed to be the result of sexual victimization; young women's histories of abuse were seen as contributing to problematic sexuality more generally, and their victimization may not have been addressed properly in treatment with juvenile justice practitioners. Even practitioners who doubted that self-identified LBQ young women in facilities would identify that way on the outside articulated the difficulty in not having specific programming or treatment groups for identity issues.

Regarding sexual activity within correctional institutions, all ban inmate–staff and inmate–inmate sexual relationships, and some go so far as to restrict personal pleasure via masturbation, whether an inmate touches their own body or utilizes objects. Inmates' agentic consensual sexuality and intimate relations (even with oneself in the form of masturbation) are generally seen as punishable because they interfere with the rights and sensibilities of those engaged in surveillance (Kunzel 2008).

As for consensual relationships and sexual behavior among inmates, such consensual interactions in facilities were documented as early as the 1800s, despite efforts to prevent them. Mogul et al. (2011) note several complicated factors that exist for inmate sexuality. Sexual activity with fellow inmates can result in various punishments, including solitary confinement, loss of earned "good time" (credit towards release date), and reduced eligibility for parole. Non-sexual but affectionate conduct, such as hugging or hand-holding, can be seen as sexual when committed by inmates who self-identify as lesbians or gay men (Kunzel 2008). Affection between same-sex inmates and visitors is sometimes penalized, when among straight couples or non-romantically involved people it raises no issue whatsoever. In these ways, assumptions about LGBQ people as hypersexual results in yet additional negative consequences for those who are incarcerated. But among all inmates, Mogul et al. (2011, 95) state, "This wholesale denial of any and all sexual desire, agency, and identity is, in turn, an essentially queer experience."

In addition to consensual sexual activity in facilities, inmate coercion into sexual activity has also been a concern of justice system actors, though until recently it was viewed as an inevitable (and perhaps even appropriate) aspect of confinement. Research findings regarding the proportion of general population inmates who have experienced sexual assault or coercion can differ depending on the definitions, study methodology, and sampling strategy utilized, and thus vary from less than 5 percent to nearly 30 percent. Among a large sample of inmates in 10 different prisons, about one fifth of both male and female inmates reported experiencing sexual coercion. Men were overwhelmingly more likely to be victimized by another man, whereas women were about equally as likely to be victimized by a man or a woman. Men were much more likely to be victimized by fellow inmates than staff, whereas women were about equally as likely to be victimized by staff or fellow inmates. Finally, gay, lesbian, and bisexual inmates were more likely to report experiencing sexual coercion than heterosexual inmates (Struckman-Johnson and Struckman-Johnson 2006; see also Jenness et al. 2007).

Mogul et al. (2011) argue that referring to male inmate-on-inmate sexual violence as "homosexual rape" is based on irrational fears about gay men's predatory natures and is fairly inaccurate – that the crime is overwhelmingly committed by heterosexually identified, cisgender men. However, gay/bisexual, effeminate, or otherwise gender non-conforming male inmates are more likely to be *victims* of such violence. Furthermore, research with transgender inmates in men's prisons suggests that their risk of experiencing sexual assault is 13 times higher than randomly selected inmates (Jenness et al. 2007). The physical and sexual abuse faced by gay, bisexual, and transgender inmates in men's prisons includes beatings and being forced to perform "wifely duties," such as sex acts and domestic chores. For those who force other inmates into these behaviors, such violence serves as a way to establish masculinity in the prison culture. For those who are victimized, reporting violence can be ignored by correctional officers or seen as deserved, or even worse, it can cause someone to be labeled as a snitch, resulting in further victimization. Inmates can request protective custody, but they may be placed in solitary confinement, which is often used as a punishment. Inmates in solitary are only allowed one hour outside of their cell per day, no physical contact with relatives, and other restrictions depending on the institution. Mogul et al. (2011) suggest that administrative segregation can actually result in more violence to inmates, especially violence perpetrated by staff, because fewer people can witness staff misconduct in segregated prison wings.

Although there have been a number of stories in the US media regarding allegedly consensual relationships between correctional officers and inmates, it is arguable that inmates are fundamentally unable to freely give consent in these circumstances due to the unequal power dynamic. On this note, some inmates may engage in a form of survival sex with staff, meaning that they trade sexual activity for tangible items such as commissary privileges or as insurance against disciplinary action (Mogul et al. 2011).

Concerted efforts to combat sexual abuse in confinement have been in place at the federal level since the 2003 passage of the Prison Rape Elimination Act (PREA). The PREA guidelines include provisions for the prevention, reporting, and investigation of sexual abuse through mechanisms such as: staff and inmate training and education; inmate screening (for risk of sexual victimization and/or abusiveness); zero tolerance policies; housing decisions; medical care; disciplinary actions; data collection; and audits. Standards for achieving these goals include preventing cross-gender viewing and searches of inmates by staff, and informing inmates of the policies and reporting procedures upon entering a facility. Although this ruling applies to all facilities in the United States, some locales and institutions are still non-compliant or are working towards full compliance. The PREA standards are meant to prevent all forms of sexual abuse and harassment, whether between inmates or between inmates and staff (National PREA Resource Center 2015).

SEE ALSO: Age of Consent in Historical and International Perspective; Colonialism and Sexuality; Eugenics, Historical and Ethical Aspects of; Heterosexism and Homophobia; Lesbian Stereotypes in the United States; Nazi Persecution of Homosexuals; Prostitution/Sex Work; Regulation of Queer Sexualities; Reproductive Justice and Reproductive Rights in the United States; Sexual Orientation and the Law; Sexual Regulation and Social Control; Sexualities; Stigma; Transphobia

REFERENCES

Eraker, Elizabeth C. 2010. "Stemming Sexting: Sensible Legal Approaches to Teenagers' Exchange of Self-Produced Pornography." *Berkeley Technology Law Journal*, 25: 555–596. Accessed August 14, 2015, at http://scholarship.law.berkeley.edu/cgi/viewcontent.cgi?article=1837&context=btlj.

Farr, Kathryn Ann. 2000. "Defeminizing and Dehumanizing Female Murderers: Depictions of Lesbians on Death Row." *Women and Criminal Justice*, 11: 49–66.

Ford, Charles A. 1929. "Homosexual Practices of Institutionalized Females." *Journal of Abnormal and Social Psychology*, 23: 442–448.

Foucault, Michel. 1978. *The History of Sexuality*, vol. 1. New York: Pantheon.

Freedman, Estelle B. 1996. "The Prison Lesbian: Race, Class, and the Construction of the Aggressive Female Homosexual, 1915–1965." *Feminist Studies*, 22: 397–423.

Halleck, Seymour L., and Marvin Hersko. 1962. "Homosexual Behavior in a Correctional Institution for Adolescent Girls." *American Journal of Orthopsychiatry*, 32: 911–917.

Halperin, David M. 1989. "Sex Before Sexuality: Pederasty, Politics, and Power in Classical Athens." In *Hidden from History: Reclaiming the Gay and Lesbian Past*, edited by Martin Baume Duberman, Martha Vicinus, and George Chauncey, 37–53. New York: NAL Books.

Hooton, Christopher. 2014. "A Long List of Sex Acts Just Got Banned in UK Porn." *The Independent*, December 2. Accessed August 14, 2015, at http://www.independent.co.uk/news/uk/a-long-list-of-sex-acts-just-got-banned-in-uk-porn-9897174.html.

Jenness, Valerie, Cheryl L. Maxson, Kristy N. Matsuda, and Jennifer Macy Sumner. 2007. *Violence in California Correctional Facilities: An Empirical Examination of Sexual Assault*. Irvine: Center for Evidence-Based Corrections.

Kunzel, Regina G. 2008. *Criminal Intimacy: Prison and the Uneven History of Modern American Sexuality*. Chicago: University of Chicago Press.

Lee, Cynthia. 2013. "Masculinity on Trial: Gay Panic in the Criminal Courtroom." *Southwestern Law Review*, 42: 817–831.

Lombroso, Cesare, and Guglielmo Ferrero. 2004. *Criminal Woman, the Prostitute, and the Normal Woman*, translated by Nicole Hahn Rafter and Mary Gibson. Durham: Duke University Press. First published 1895.

Majd, Katayoon, Jody Marksamer, and Carolyn Reyes. 2009. *Hidden Injustice: Lesbian, Gay, Bisexual, and Transgender Youth in Juvenile Courts*. San Francisco: Legal Services for Children, National Juvenile Defender Center, and National Center for Lesbian Rights.

Mogul, Joey L., Andrea J. Ritchie, and Kay Whitlock. 2011. *Queer (In)Justice: The Criminalization of LGBT People in the United States*. Boston: Beacon Press.

National PREA Resource Center. 2015. "PREA Essentials." Accessed August 14, 2015, at http://www.prearesourcecenter.org/training-technical-assistance/prea-essentials.

Paltrow, Lynn M. 2004. "The War on Drugs and the War on Abortion." In *The Criminal Justice System and Women: Offenders, Prisoners, Victims, and Workers*, 3rd ed., edited by Barbara Raffel Price and Natalie J. Sokoloff, 165–184. New York: McGraw-Hill.

Pasko, Lisa. 2010. "Damaged Daughters: The History of Girls' Sexuality and the Juvenile Justice System." *Journal of Criminal Law and Criminology*, 100: 1099–1130. DOI: 0091-4169/10/10003-1099.

Plant, Richard. 1986. *The Pink Triangle: The Nazi War against Homosexuals*. New York: Holt.

Propper, Alice M. 1978. "Lesbianism in Female and Coed Correctional Institutions." *Journal of Homosexuality*, 3: 265–274.

Roman, Denise. 2011. "Under the Rape Shield: A Historical and Comparative Perspective on the Rape Shield Laws." *Working Papers in Feminist Research*. Los Angeles: UCLA Center for the Study of Women. Accessed August 14, 2015, at https://escholarship.org/uc/item/0w62h4dp.

Rubin, Gayle. 2012. "Thinking Sex: Notes for a Radical Theory of the Politics of Sexuality." In *Deviations: A Gayle Rubin Reader*, 137–181. Durham: Duke University Press. First published 1984.

Schlossman, Steven, and Stephanie Wallach. 1978. "The Crime of Precocious Sexuality: Female Juvenile Delinquency in the Progressive Era." *Harvard Educational Review*, 48: 65–94.

Struckman-Johnson, Cindy, and David Struckman-Johnson. 2006. "A Comparison of Sexual Coercion Experiences Reported by

Men and Women in Prison." *Journal of Interpersonal Violence*, 21: 1591–1615. DOI: 10.1177/ 0886260506294240.

Weitzer, Ronald. 2005. "New Directions in Research on Prostitution." *Crime, Law and Social Change*, 43: 211–235. DOI: 10.1007/ s10611-005-1735-6

Wodda, Aimee, and Vanessa R. Panfil. 2015. "'Don't Talk to Me about Deception': The Necessary Erosion of the Trans* Panic Defense." *Albany Law Review*, 78: 927–971. Accessed August 14, 2015, at http://www. albanylawreview.org/Articles/Vol78_3/78.3. 0927%20Wodda%20and%20Panfil.PDF.

Critical Race Theory[1]

NICOLA ROLLOCK
University of Birmingham, UK

ADRIENNE D. DIXSON
University of Illinois, Urbana-Champaign, USA

Critical Race Theory (CRT) is a body of scholarship steeped in radical activism that seeks to explore and challenge the prevalence of racial inequality in society. Central to CRT is the understanding that race and racism are the products of social thought and power relations. Racism is understood to operate through structures and assumptions that appear entirely normal and unremarkable to most people in society. Scholars of CRT therefore work to challenge and expose dominant narratives of race that permit and legitimize the existence of racism.

---

[1] A shorter version of this article was published by the British Educational Research Association (BERA). I am grateful to BERA for permission to produce extracts from that resource: Rollock, N. and Gillborn, D. 2011. *Critical Race Theory (CRT)*, British Educational Research Association online resource. Accessed August 19, 2015, at https://www.bera.ac.uk/wp-content/uploads/2014/03/Critical-Race-Theory-CRT-.pdf.

HISTORY

The historical context in which CRT emerged is pivotal to understanding its development and ambitions as an intellectual and political movement. CRT has its foundations in the 1970s "leftist legal movement" (Ladson-Billings 1998, 10). Critical legal studies (CLS) which saw a small group of academics seek to challenge traditional liberal approaches to legal ideology with a view to better conceptualizing how structural inequalities, in terms of class, were perpetuated and maintained in US society. While initially identifying with the language and goals of CLS, many scholars of color (including Derrick Bell, Kimberlé Crenshaw, Richard Delgado, Cheryl Harris, and Patricia Williams), argued that it failed to engage meaningfully with the realities of racism by reductively positioning it as an aspect of class-based discrimination. Therefore CRT emerged, in part, in response to the limitations of CLS and ultimately moved into the field of education in the mid-1990s (Ladson-Billings and Tate 1995; Dixson and Rousseau 2006). Scholars, involved in the development of CRT, describe the process:

> Critical Race Theory sought to stage a simultaneous encounter with the exhausted vision of reformist civil rights scholarship … and the emergent critique of left legal scholarship. … [CRT's] engagement with the discourse of civil rights' reform stemmed directly from our lived experience as students and teachers in the nation's law schools. We both saw and suffered the concrete consequences that followed from liberal legal thinkers' failure to address the constrictive role that racial ideology plays in the composition and culture of American institutions. (Crenshaw et al. 1995, xix)

There is no single position statement that defines CRT. The approach continues to undergo revision and refinement in response to the scholarship and experiences of CRT theorists in different countries, with different specialisms and in relation to new developments in legal doctrine and policy discourse. However, CRT scholars share two key principles: first, they acknowledge that race and racism are socially constructed; and, second, they *proactively* work to name and challenge the systems that continue to subjugate people of color.

NORMALCY AND PERMANENCE OF RACISM

Central to CRT is that racism is normal, not aberrant, in wider society:

> Because racism is an ingrained feature of our landscape, it looks ordinary and natural to persons in the culture. Formal equal opportunity – rules and laws that insist on treating Blacks and Whites (for example) alike – can thus remedy only the more extreme and shocking forms of injustice, the ones that do stand out. It can do little about the business-as-usual forms of racism that people of color confront every day. (Delgado and Stefancic 2000, xvi)

CRT scholars emphasize that racism does not only exist in crude explicit forms, but operates in a sociopolitical context where it is becoming more embedded and increasingly nuanced. Racism is fluid; it changes form depending on the context and presence or interaction of other inequalities.

INTERSECTIONALITY

Intersectionality concerns the examination of "multiple grounds of identity when considering how the social world is constructed" (Crenshaw 1991, 1245). The term originated in the work of African American scholar Kimberlé Crenshaw, who was one of the early proponents of CRT. A black feminist perspective which attends to the intersection of race and gender has been central in the history and development of CRT. Legal scholars such as Patricia J. Williams, Regina Austin, Dorothy Roberts, and Cheryl L. Harris along with Crenshaw have led the way in foregrounding the experiences of women of color:

> Black women are sometimes excluded from feminist theory and antiracist policy discourse because both are predicated on a discrete set of experiences that often does not accurately reflect the interaction of race and gender. These problems of exclusion cannot be solved simply by including Black women within an already established analytical structure. Because the intersectional experience is greater than the sum of racism and sexism, any analysis that does not take intersectionality into account cannot sufficiently address the particular manner in which Black women are subordinated. (Crenshaw 1989, 58)

Intersectionality emphasizes fluidity and the importance of taking account of different locales, situations, spaces, times, dispositions, and subjectivities when seeking to understand particular interactions and identities. It recognizes that different dimensions of identity cannot necessarily be separated out into discrete strands.

Related to intersectionality is the concept of "differential racialization" (Delgado and Stefancic 2001, 8) which is concerned with the way in which dominant society racializes and gives focus to different minoritized groups at different times to suit hegemonic arguments of racial superiority and inferiority. An example of differential racialization in UK education debates positions Chinese and Indian students as both aberrant and unique, "model minorities," in juxtaposition to their less successful black and white peers (Gillborn 2008, 146).

Intersectionality has become something of a "buzzword" in academia (Davis 2008) with many misinterpretations and overcomplications of its use. However, Richard Delgado, one of the founders of CRT, has warned against using the framework to such an

VOICES AND EXPERIENCES OF PEOPLE OF COLOR

CRT recognizes and foregrounds the experiential knowledge of people of color in analyzing and deconstructing racism. One of the ways in which this is carried out is via the tool of counternarrative. Counternarratives are accounts that speak back to the dominant status quo and center marginalized voices:

> The stories or narratives told by the ingroup [dominant group] remind it of its identity in relation to outgroups, and provide it with a form of shared reality in which its own superior position is seen as natural. The stories of the outgroups aim to subvert that reality. (Delgado 2000, 60)

These accounts can be semi-autobiographical or fictional in nature and often comprise composite characters (that is, sourced from a range of experiences or actors), drawn from real life, in order to reveal the everyday nature of racism (Rollock 2012).

Counternarrative has the potential to act as a persuasive and transformative tool to challenge liberal racist ideology. The approach has been taken up by a number of prominent CRT theorists but Derrick Bell's scholarship is the most well-known and influential. Bell uses chronicles (metaphorical tales) as a powerful and compelling means of critically examining and revealing racial and legal injustices (see Bell 1980, 1992, 2009).

Counternarrative is not simply storytelling about race. As a process, counternarrative works to center the experiences of people of color, deconstruct whiteness and add constructively and explicitly to the racial justice project. There is a particular imperative for white scholars seeking to employ counternarrative to be mindful of these principles or risk repositioning whiteness as the norm.

WHITENESS AND WHITE SUPREMACY

Revealing and deconstructing whiteness is central to the CRT agenda and to advancing racial justice. Whiteness has been described as a form of power and privilege that remains unseen and which allows the acts, behaviors, and views of whites to retain an unquestioned normalcy and apparent moral neutrality within debates on race and in society generally.

It is important to distinguish between whiteness as "a racial discourse" and the "category 'white people' [which] represents a socially constructed identity, usually based on skin color" (Leonardo 2009, 169). White people are the primary beneficiaries of whiteness. Whiteness enables whites to proceed in everyday practice without recognizing or being conscious of their own racial positioning or, crucially, how they continue to benefit from whiteness.

There is an important distinction to be made between white supremacy, white privilege, and whiteness. It has been argued that the notion of white privilege fails to attend sufficiently the full extent of power, domination, and subjugation of others that is central to whiteness. Whiteness can be more accurately understood as practices, beliefs, and behaviors that serve to maintain white supremacy. Racism serves to reinforce and advance white supremacy, helping to maintain a status quo that while disproportionate or inequitable to racial minorities allows whites to retain their positions of power.

Whiteness takes little if any account of the experiences of racially minoritized groups. Instead, acts of whiteness serve to marginalize, subjugate, and "other" the experiences of people of color. One way in which this occurs is through acts of racial microaggressions (Pierce 1970). These are slight but persistent daily reoccurrences that serve to remind people of color that they are perceived and positioned as inferior, odd, less trustworthy, and less intelligent than whites. These occurrences often take the form of subtle but pervasive acts of dismissal through acts, comments, looks, snubs, gestures, and tone of voice that leads to frustration, racial battle fatigue, and stress for people of color.

INTEREST CONVERGENCE

White people have little incentive to work to eradicate racism as it serves to support white domination. However, there are times when greater race equality operates in the perceived interests of white people, and this notion of "interest convergence" helps to explain how advances can be achieved: "the interest of blacks in achieving racial equality will be accommodated only when it converges with the interests of whites" (Bell 1980, 523). An analysis of past victories in the struggle for race equality confirms Bell's analysis:

> [A]dvances for blacks always coincided with changing economic conditions and the self-interest of elite whites. Sympathy, mercy, and evolving standards of social decency and conscience amounted to little, if anything. (Delgado and Stefancic 2001, 18)

Bell has analyzed civil rights legislation and demonstrated the modes through which interest convergence operates. The concept has been examined by other critical race theorists in relation to landmark cases and policies that ostensibly advance the interests of race equality but where in reality there is little long-lasting change or improvement in life chances for racially minoritized groups.

IMPORTANT POINTS OF NOTE

CRT is often denigrated by people working with alternative perspectives who view the emphasis on race and racism as misguided or even threatening. Such attacks often rest on a lack of understanding and oversimplification of the approach. There are some key points to note:

1. White supremacy as used by critical race theorists does not merely refer to extremist or far right groups (such as the Ku Klux Klan or, in the United Kingdom, the English Defence League). Through the lens of CRT, white supremacy pertains explicitly to the power and privileges that tend to benefit white people and normalizes particular behaviors, ways of being, and speech, among other phenomena and characteristics, as being positively, constructively, and productively "white."
2. CRT does not assume that all white people are racist. There are many white allies involved in the fight for racial justice. However, unless engaged in a proactive, critically reflective engagement, and deconstruction of whiteness, whites will continue to benefit from whiteness and thus enable processes and procedures that subjugate people of color.
3. CRT does not assume that all whites benefit equally from whiteness. An intersectional framework lends acknowledgment to the fact that class variations among the white population equates to differences in the distribution of power. However, CRT provides scope to acknowledge the different historic and contemporary readings, meanings and treatment afforded to different racialized groups because of the color of their skin.
4. Like other academic theories, CRT does not attempt to explain *all* injustices. CRT continues to evolve and scholars

around the world (e.g., Europe, South America, Australia, and Africa) engage critically with it in ways that speak to the particular context or experiences of specific marginalized groups. Critical race feminism (CRF), for example, is a form of scholarship based on the intersection between CRT and black feminism/womanism (Hill Collins 1996). It emerged at the end of the twentieth century to emphasize the legal concerns of those who are women, racially minoritized, and often poor. CRF emphasizes the diversity of voices of women of color and highlights how their experiences are shaped by race, class, and gender discrimination within a patriarchal, oppressive system. CRF foregrounds practices that both analyze and combat gender and racial oppression. In so doing it highlights how the perspectives and experiences of females of color vary from their male and white female counterparts and how equity and liberty might be reached for women of color. DisCrit (disability critical race studies) scholars working in disability studies have paired an analysis of issues such as disproportionality and Othering as they intersect with race. Those interested in a critical examination of the experiences of Latina/o communities have drawn on CRT (LatCrit) to enhance their analyses, and similar work continues with scholars interested in race and sexual orientation (QueerCrit).

SEE ALSO: Affirmative Action; Black Feminist Thought; Intersectionality; Outsider Within; Tokenism

REFERENCES

Bell, Derrick. 1980. "Brown vs Board of Education and the Interest Convergence Dilemma." *Harvard Law Review*, 98: 518–533.

Bell, Derrick. 1992. *Faces at the Bottom of the Well: The Permanence of Racism*. New York: Basic Books.

Bell, Derrick. 2009. "Who's Afraid of Critical Race Theory?" In *Foundations of Critical Race Theory in Education*, edited by E. Taylor, D. Gillborn, and G. Ladson-Billings, 37–50. New York: Routledge.

Crenshaw, Kimberlé. 1989. *Demarginalising the Intersection of Race and Sex: A Black Feminist Critique of Antidiscrimination Doctrine, Feminist Theory and Antiracist Politics*, 139–168. University of Chicago Legal Forum.

Crenshaw, Kimberlé. 1991. "Mapping the Margins: Intersectionality, Identity Politics, and Violence against Women of Color." *Stanford Law Review*, 43(6): 1241–1299.

Crenshaw, Kimberlé, N. Gotanda, G. Peller, and K. Thomas, eds. 1995. *Critical Race Theory: The Key Writings that Formed the Movement*. New York: New Press.

Davis, K. 2008. "Intersectionality as Buzzword: A Sociology of Science Perspective on What Makes Feminist Theory Successful." *Feminist Theory*, 9(1): 67–85.

Delgado, Richard. 2000. "Storytelling for Oppositionists and Others: A Plea for Narrative." In *Critical Race Theory: The Cutting Edge*, 2nd ed., edited by Richard Delgado and J. Stefancic. Philadelphia: Temple University Press.

Delgado, Richard. 2011. "Rodrigo's Reconsideration: Intersectionality and the Future of Critical Race Theory." *Iowa Law Review*, 96: 1247–1288.

Delgado, Richard, and J. Stefancic, eds. 2000. *Critical Race Theory: The Cutting Edge*, 2nd ed. Philadelphia: Temple University Press.

Delgado, Richard, and J. Stefancic. 2001. *Critical Race Theory: An Introduction*. New York: New York University Press.

Dixson, Adrienne, and Rousseau, C.K., eds. 2006. *Critical Race Theory in Education: All God's Children Got a Song*. New York: Routledge.

Gillborn, D. 2008. *Racism and Education: Coincidence or Conspiracy?* London: Routledge.

Hill-Collins, P. 1996. "What's In a Name? Womanism, Black Feminism and Beyond." *Black Scholar*, 26(1): 9–17.

Ladson-Billings, Gloria. 1998. "Just What is Critical Race Theory and What's It Doing in a Nice Field Like Education?" *International Journal of Qualitative Studies in Education*, 11(1): 7–24.

Ladson-Billings, Gloria, and W. Tate. 1995. "Towards a Critical Race Theory of Education." *Teachers College Record*, 97(1): 47–68.
Leonardo, Z. 2009. *Race, Whiteness, and Education*. New York: Routledge.
Pierce, C. 1970. "Offensive Mechanisms." In *The Black Seventies*, edited by F. Barbour, 265–282. Boston: Porter Sargent.
Rollock, Nicola. 2012. "Unspoken Rules of Engagement: Navigating Racial Microaggressions in the Academic Terrain." *International Journal of Qualitative Studies in Education*, 25(5): 517–532.

Cross-Cultural Gender Roles

COURTNEY C. C. HEARD HARVEY
South University, USA

The term gender role may be defined as "culturally prescribed behaviors and traits that dictate how males and females should act" (Muehlenhard and Peterson 2011). Reference to the word *culturally* in this definition magnifies the diverse perspectives regarding gender roles for men and women based on influences such as geographical location, ethnicity, nationality, religion, and more. An exploration of cross-cultural gender roles to include a discussion of specific cultures internationally would be beyond the scope of this entry, particularly given the attention that must be given to within-group differences. However, what should be highlighted are those social processes that can shape the development of gender role perspectives cross-culturally.

Kimberlé Crenshaw is credited with the development of the term intersectionality. Critical race theorists have used the term to describe the interconnectedness of status variables such as race, gender, or class to contextualize politics, power, and oppression (Crenshaw 1991). Intersectionality may be used to contextualize the development of a gender identity, of which gender roles are a facet (Heard and Ricard 2013). For many ethnic cultures of people, the development and conveyance of gender roles are rooted in marginality and oppressive conditions that have for some cultures led to behaviors and traits that depart from the stereotypical standards of the dominant culture (Davenport and Yurich 1991).

Intersectionality is a concept indicative of the fact that people are continually navigating layered identities that are shaped by experiences. Moore-Thomas indicated that gender identity development, which encompasses awareness and acceptance of gender roles, is not a linear process and is shaped by "biological, psychological, and social experiences" (2010, 43). The intersection of race and gender identities can be significant, depending on the degree to which one identifies with a race of people, and one's perception of the treatment afforded members of the group. For instance, some authors suggest that males and females are exposed to stereotypical roles for men and women at an early age. For men, some of these stereotypical roles may include being assertive, independent, and physically strong, being the primary financial contributor in a family, and restricting emotions such as sadness and fear (Moore-Thomas 2010). Many authors have indicated that these stereotypical roles for men conform to puritanical, white, middle-class values and may not be applicable cross-culturally. For instance, Heard (2013) conducted a study assessing sex-role egalitarian attitudes and gender role socialization experiences of African Americans. African American men voiced roles similar to their white male counterparts to include being a provider, protector, and fulfilling maintenance-based chores. The African American men in this study were largely middle class, formally educated, and endorsed a spiritual and/or religious affiliation. There is potentially a dissonance for many African American men, as authors have written about the disparity in employment, income, educational attainment, and marital status of this population compared with their white male counterparts. The impact of institutionalized racism and discrimination has largely affected the ability of many African American men to achieve or adopt some of the stereotypical gender roles perceived for men. Thus, the manifestation of gender roles for some members of this population may be different from men of other cultures.

Gender role socialization for men and women may be influenced by a number of channels to include family, society, media, religious principles, and politics. Religion offers a powerful example of external influences on perceptions of gender roles. For instance, religions such as Catholicism may reinforce the church's position on roles for men and women through the use of biblical scriptures, church documents, and religious imagery (Arredondo 2004). These traits and roles may not be applicable to most men or women. However, these images inundate media outlets and may unconsciously influence the perceptions of roles men and women should adopt. For instance, relating to the intersectionality of ethnicity, religion, and gender roles, roles for Mexican American men and women have been widely discussed. Mexican American men are often portrayed as being the dominant figure in the family and are characterized as strong, protectors of family, and providers. In the absence of equal opportunities to engage in activities that promote evolvement into these roles, many authors discuss *machismo*. This term represents a set of behaviors considered culturally relevant to Mexican American males to include physical strength, sexual attractiveness, and demanding respect (Fragoso and Kashubeck 2000). Mexican American women have been characterized as caregivers, nurturers, and submissive to husband and family. *Marianismo* is the feminine equivalent to *machismo* and represents a set of behaviors that characterize the ideal woman as passive and nurturing (Villegas, Lemanski, and Valdéz 2010).

It is highly relevant to consider within-group differences when discussing cross-cultural gender roles, as many authors have suggested that variables such as acculturation, experiences with racism, educational attainment, and socioeconomic status can significantly impact the roles men and women assume and their manifestation. Additionally, as explored by King and King (1993), conceptualizing roles for men and women is a multifaceted task, and perceptions of appropriate behaviors for men and women may differ when looking at factors such as marriage, occupation, education, equality, and more. For instance, Perrone-McGovern and colleagues (2014) conducted a review of the literature assessing culture, gender, and socioeconomic status as influences on work and family roles. These authors reported that much of the existing literature examining work–family interface has covered the United States and may not be generalizable to international populations. When researching German and American women's perception of their ability to balance work and family roles, it was discovered that German women reported greater work–family conflict than their American counterparts (Perrone-McGovern et al. 2014). This result may have been influenced by German cultural attitudes related to working mothers, and the fact that Americans were found to have greater sex-role egalitarian attitudes than their German counterparts.

There have been cross-cultural comparisons of gender role portrayals in Chinese, Indian, and American media outlets. Results have indicated that commercials in Chinese and American cultures depict men in more occupational and recreational roles and women in domestic roles. Similar to American, Latino, and Chinese cultures, the stereotypical primary role of Indian men is to provide financially, and for Indian women to display virtuousness, honor family ties, and support their husbands (Khairullah and Khairullah 2009).

The culture-specific gender roles discussed throughout this work are largely stereotypical and in no way meant to be representative of all men and women who endorse these ethnic cultural groups, though they may depict some individuals. Global economic expansion continues to alter the roles men and women cross-culturally endorse, particularly in areas related to marriage, occupation, parenting, and education, which are modified to suit the needs of individuals and families. Thus, it is pertinent to the assessment of cross-cultural gender roles that the evaluation of role expectations encompasses a multidimensional assessment. It may be beneficial to also evaluate alternative constructs in conjunction to gender role attitudes such as gender equality and social desirability. In addition, considering variables of influence such as within- and between-group differences, geographical culture, socioeconomic status, education, marital status, and occupation may provide a more in-depth impression of gender roles cross-culturally.

SEE ALSO: Division of Labor, Domestic; Division of Labor, Gender; Gender as Institution; Gender Belief System/Gender Ideology; Intersectionality

REFERENCES

Arredondo, Patricia. 2004. "Psychotherapy with Chicanas." In *The Handbook of Chicana/o Psychology and Mental Health*, edited by Roberto J. Velasquez, Leticia M. Arellano, and Brian W. McNeill, 231–249. Mahwah, NJ: Lawrence Erlbaum Associates.

Crenshaw, Kimberlé. 1991. "Mapping the Margins: Intersectionality, Identity Politics, and Violence against Women of Color." *Stanford Law Review*, 43(6): 1241–1299.

Davenport, Donna S., and John M. Yurich. 1991. "Multicultural Gender Issues." *Journal of Counseling and Development*, 70: 64–71.

Fragoso, Jose M., and Susan Kashubeck. 2000. "Machismo, Gender Role Conflict, and Mental Health in Mexican American Men." *Psychology of Men and Masculinity*, 1(2): 87–97.

Heard, Courtney. 2013. *Sex-Role Egalitarian Attitudes and Gender Role Socialization Experiences of African American Men and Women: A Mixed Methods Paradigm*. Doctoral dissertation. Accessed August 19, 2015, at http://gradworks.umi.com/35/87/3587931.html.

Heard, C., and Ricard, R. J. 2013. "Contextualizing the Concept of Intersectionality: Layered Identities of African American Women and Gay Men in the Black Church." Manuscript submitted for publication.

Khairullah, Durriya H. Z., and Zahid Y. Khairullah. 2009. "Cross-Cultural Analysis of Gender Roles: Indian and U.S. Advertisements." *Asia Pacific Journal of Marketing and Logistics*, 21(1): 58–75. DOI: 10.1108/13555850910926245.

King, Lynda A., and Daniel W. King. 1993. *Sex-Role Egalitarianism Scale: Technical Manual*. Port Huron, MI: SIGMA Assessment Systems, Inc.

Moore-Thomas, Cheryl. 2010. "Cultural Identity Development." In *Developing Multicultural Counseling Competence: A Systems Approach*, edited by Danica G. Hays and Bradley T. Erford, 32–52. Upper Saddle River, NJ: Pearson.

Muehlenhard, Charlene L., and Zoe D. Peterson. 2011. "Distinguishing Between *Sex* and *Gender*: History, Current Conceptualizations, and Implications." *Sex Roles*, 64: 791–803. DOI: 10.1007/s11199-011-9932-5.

Perrone-McGovern, Kristin M., Stephen L. Wright, Desiree S. Howell, and Emily L. Barnum. 2014. "Contextual Influences on Work and Family Roles: Gender, Culture, and Socio-Economic Factors." *Career Development Quarterly*, 62: 21–28. DOI: 10.1002/j.2161-0045.2014.00067.x.

Villegas, Jorge, Jennifer Lemanski, and Carlos Valdéz. 2010. "*Marianismo* and *Machismo*: The Portrayal of Females in Mexican TV

Commercials." *Journal of International Consumer Marketing*, 22: 327–346. DOI: 10.1080/08961530.2010.505884.

FURTHER READING

Harris, Allen C. 1996. "African American and Anglo-American Gender Identities: An Empirical Study." *Journal of Black Psychology*, 22(2): 182–194.

Kane, Emily W. 2000. "Racial and Ethnic Variations in Gender-Related Attitudes." *Annual Review of Sociology*, 26: 419–439.

Powers, Rebecca S., et al. 2003. "Regional Differences in Gender-Role Attitudes: Variations by Gender and Race." *Gender Issues*, 21(2): 40–54.

Shaw, Thomas M. 2010. *Reclaiming and Reconstructing Our Lady of Guadalupe: A Symbol of Transformation and Empowerment for Latina/Chicana Lesbians*. Doctoral dissertation. Available from ProQuest Dissertations and Theses database.

Cross-Dressing

VICTORIA FLANAGAN
Macquarie University, Australia

Cross-dressing linguistically marks a very simple act – the transgression of cultural boundaries related to the wearing of various articles of gender-specific clothing. Cross-dressing behavior is associated with both *transvestism* and *transsexualism*, although the relative neutrality of the term "cross-dressing" elides the significant distinctions between these two practices. Examples of what might be characterized in accordance with the contemporary frameworks of transvestism and transsexualism – and also the broader category of *transgender* – have been practiced and well documented in a range of societies and cultures since the beginning of recorded history. Sabrina Ramet remarks that "Many societies in the past institutionalised procedures for permanent or temporary gender reversal or gender change" (1996, xvii). However, the problem with applying modern terminology to age-old cultural practices is that it is not always transferable or applicable. This is very much the case when discussing historical gender-bending practices that were socially acceptable and practiced openly, unlike transvestite and transsexual behaviors, which have traditionally been subject to social stigmatization and medical and state interference in Western society. The histories of transvestism and transsexualism are therefore largely entwined within the broader cultural history of cross-dressing, as differences between the two are a product of twentieth-century medical discourses (Flanagan 2008, 3).

Cross-dressing has enjoyed a somewhat complex (and often paradoxical) relationship with Western legal institutions, due to the correlation of transgressive gender behavior with immorality and social deviance. This can be explicitly linked to the biblical prohibition against cross-dressing: "The woman shall not wear that which pertaineth unto a man, neither shall a man put on a woman's garment: for all that do so are abomination unto the LORD thy God." (Deuteronomy 22: 5, King James Bible). In spite of this condemnation, several female Catholic saints are known to have cross-dressed in order to bring themselves closer to (a masculine) God, such as Athanasia of Antioch and Pelagia. The most celebrated case of religious-inspired cross-dressing is that of Joan of Arc, a woman who inspired pious devotion in her followers and whose legend has taken on mythic proportions in contemporary retellings. Joan's refusal to abandon her masculine costume was one of the grounds upon which she was tried and executed by the Inquisition in 1431 (Garber 1993, 216; Warner 2000, 5). Marjorie Garber's characterization of Joan of Arc's cross-dressing as behavior that overtly contravened both class and gender structures effectively illustrates why she was perceived as a dangerous figure.

Joan of Arc's cross-dressing was conducted very publicly and thereby constituted a particular political and social threat, but female cross-dressers in later centuries would enjoy much more success (in that they were never "outed" or, if discovered, were able to escape with little or no punishment). In the sixteenth, seventeenth and eighteenth centuries, Dekker and van de Pol identify what they call a "flourishing tradition of female cross-dressing" (1989, 99). This was due to a variety of social transformations in Europe which allowed women to escape the domestic sphere by "dressing like and passing as men" (Bullough and Bullough 1993, 94). Our knowledge of these women and the lives they led while cross-dressed as men is generally the product of court transcripts, the result of trials that were held when the cross-dressed woman's biological sex was discovered. Dekker and van de Pol cite a number of case histories that provide evidence of judicial/official leniency extended to such women. They argue that a number of "women who had successful careers as sailors and soldiers and who had resumed respectable lives as women met with praise and reward. Successful female soldiers or sailors were sometimes even granted exceptional favours from monarchs ..." (101). Cross-dressing was thus perceived as a form of feminist advocacy, enabling women to prove that they were capable of performing similar roles to men.

The cross-dresser's ability to destabilize normative categories of gender and sexuality has proved to be effective for modern theorists of gender. The figure of the cross-dresser features prominently in Judith Butler's significant treatise, *Gender Trouble: Feminism and the Subversion of Identity* (1990), as an illustration of how gender is performatively constituted through the "stylized repetition of acts" that approximate rather than express a stable and fixed gender identity (1999, 197). Drag performances, according to Butler, epitomize the disjunction that exists between sex and gender because they are contingent upon a distinction between the physical body of the performer and the feminine subject position that is being performed (1999, 175).

Within Western popular culture, however, cross-dressing is often associated with physical and visual comedy. A variety of filmmakers since the 1950s have sought to capitalize on audiences' appetites for the comic effect of a man (struggling) to wear a dress, creating an established history of male-to-female cross-dressing in Western cinema. Films within this tradition, which include *Some Like It Hot* (1959), *Tootsie* (1982), *Nuns on the Run* (1990), and *White Chicks* (2004), feature male protagonists who cross-dress out of necessity rather than desire, and whose heterosexualized cross-dressing is constructed as harmless fun. These popular representations of male-to-female cross-dressing rarely delve into issues such as motivation, eroticism, social stigmatization and vilification, connections to homosexuality or the challenge to constructed gender identity that cross-dressing presents. Films such as *Outrageous!* (1977), *Kiss of the Spider Woman* (1985), and *Torch Song Trilogy* (1988) gradually pushed sympathetic male cross-dressing characters into the view of mainstream cinema audiences, while more recent films such as *All About My Mother* (1999) and *Boys Don't Cry* (1999) feature cross-dressing characters whose transgendered identities are centralized within the plot and compassionately constructed. The ideological development of cinematic representations of cross-dressing is symptomatic of broader cultural change in relation to transgressive gender and sexual behavior. To this end, the term "cross-dressing" has become anachronistic. It has been replaced by the more politicized concept of "transgender," which refers to all people who exhibit non-normative gender and sexual identities and is often associated with the right of such subjects to seek legal and social reform.

SEE ALSO: Trans Identities, Psychological Perspectives; Transsexuality; Transvestitism

REFERENCES

Bullough, Vern, and Bonnie Bullough. 1993. *Cross-Dressing, Sex, and Gender*. Philadelphia: University of Pennsylvania Press.

Butler, Judith. 1999 [1990]. *Gender Trouble: Feminism and the Subversion of Identity*. New York: Routledge.

Dekker, Rudolf M., and Lotte C. van de Pol. 1989. *The Tradition of Female Transvestism in Early Modern Europe*. New York: St Martin's Press.

Flanagan, Victoria. *Into the Closet: Cross-Dressing and the Gendered Body in Children's Literature and Film*. New York and Abingdon: Routledge, 2008.

Garber, Marjorie. 1993 [1992]. *Vested Interests: Cross-Dressing and Cultural Anxiety*. London: Penguin.

Ramet, Sabrina Petra, ed. 1996. *Gender Reversals and Gender Cultures: Anthropological and Historical Perspectives*. New York: Routledge.

Warner, Marina. 2000 [1981]. *Joan of Arc: The Image of Female Heroism*. California: University of California Press.

Cult of Domesticity

KATHLEEN CONNELLAN
University of South Australia, Australia

The cult of domesticity is a belief in the process of homemaking and nurturing. Cult is a term that emanates from group religious affiliation, power, practice, and worship. Domesticity stems from the Latin root *domus* (home or dwelling), thereby locating domesticity within a designated space where a familial group resides. In the histories of religion and myth, the Greek deity Hestia is known as the goddess of the hearth and home; in ancient Rome this is the goddess Vesta.

While the above etymological origin relates to the English language and the mythological reference is Western, the connotations of cult as worshipping and domesticity as located in the home stretch across cultures. Cult worship predates written history especially in relation to fertility, but domesticity is a more recent concept. The combination of domesticity and cult results in shared attributes of ritual, sacrifice, control, and caring. Central to this is the mother figure who takes on the roles of childrearing and nurturing, homemaking, cooking, and cleaning. Historically this matriarchal role was endorsed by the male-hunter/female-gatherer dichotomy and the biological argument that the woman is the childbearer (McClintock 1995). A division of gender roles in the domestic arena became entrenched in both rural and urban settings through societal norms, family expectations, and also visual representations such as the seventeenth-century Flemish domestic interior paintings.

With the advent of industrialization and the shift from predominantly agrarian economies there was a growth of middle classes. These changes diluted previous extended domestic family arrangements and the associated community support experienced in village life. Domesticity changed with the times and, depending on the affluence of the family, domestic servants, new furniture, and decorations were acquired. Domestic respectability was an important social marker that rested on the interior and exterior presentation of the home, which was regarded as the responsibility of the woman but a reflection of the man's wealth (Oakley 1974). Manuals and domestic science/home economics courses for maintaining a home were introduced to educate young women into their role as homemaker, wife, and mother. The language of the manuals such as *Mrs Beeton's Book of Household Management* emphasized the domestic duty of the woman, with minute details from stain removal techniques, to cooking for all occasions, to medicating minor ailments, to making ends meet financially. Women made their own jams, preserves, and breads in addition to sewing and knitting for their family (Beeton and Humble 2000). The gendered arrangement was premised upon heteronormative sexual relationships. Indoor domestic work was assigned to women and outdoor domestic tasks generally to men. Most homes in colonized countries acquired local domestic servants at low cost, thus emulating the domestic arrangement of upper middle classes elsewhere in the world but adding race to the gendered aspect of domestic work. Domesticity and the civilizing project of colonialism encouraged the home to be a site of moral learning associated with cleanliness and order. The importance of keeping a neat and clean home was supported by fears of dirt and contagion and fed by Christian beliefs in purity that upheld the cult of domesticity (McClintock 1995). Colonial policies on domesticity also extended beyond the home, providing training for an "evolved" class who paralleled "white civilized" society (Hunt 1990).

World Wars I and II were a major catalyst for the production of domestic appliances because factories developed unprecedented efficiencies learned from weapons and vehicle manufacturing. The postwar "domestic appliance revolution" and the introduction of electricity in homes resulted first in the domestic refrigerator for cooling and freezing food. Other significant electrical domestic appliances in the postwar period included vacuum cleaners, washing machines, and food mixers. This period also marked the advent of the "nuclear family" as a "new locus of socialization" with family planning measures (Hunt 1990). The size of families varied greatly across cultures but the cult of domesticity in the mid- to late twentieth century was emphasized in visual culture and the media by homemaking magazines such as *Women's Weekly* with advertorial advice. Such advice was not restricted to the English-language press and was taken up in colonized countries, for example *Die Huisgenoot* in South Africa. The ideal home was also promoted further through modernist design also known as Good Design, with the advent of the first Design Council in Great Britain. Women who had previously worked in positions vacated by men during the war whilst also maintaining the home were encouraged to return home with the novel assistance of domestic appliances and utility furniture that was easy to clean (Sparke 1995). The domestic appliances were also promoted as "labor-saving devices," encouraging women to purchase them to have more time of their own. Ann Oakley (1974) exposed the myth of the domestic appliance revolution in Britain and showed that women ended up doing even more housework as a result of appliances. Apart from the capitalist premise for selling new products, what the domestic appliance revolution did was emphasize the role of women in creating a comfortable nest for her family. As a result domestic work became devalued because it was not paid for outside of the home. This cult of domesticity was supported by masculinized views of motherhood but was questioned by feminist scholarship throughout the twentieth century in different waves. For example, postwar developmental analysis failed to look at the development of women outside of the domestic sphere, perpetuating the home as the "natural" place for women to develop (Rogers 1980).

Despite critiques, the home and its cult of domesticity remain lodged in twenty-first-century societies; however, domestic gender stereotypes are shifting alongside revised sexualities. The public domain remains a hectic sphere of social, economic, and professional pressures and the home as haven offers an escape into a private domain where domestic order and comfort are idealized and performed across sexualities (Carrington 1999). Shifting personal identities are also enacted and displayed through architectural and interior design improvements and the consumption and collection of home possessions (Miller 2001). The growth of memory studies is stimulating additional interest in domestic family histories and the increased personal value of family heirlooms in a revered cult of domesticity.

SEE ALSO: Colonialism and Gender; Division of Labor, Domestic; Fertility Rates; Heteronormativity and Homonormativity; Matriarchy; Media and Gender Socialization; Work–Family Balance

REFERENCES

Beeton, Isabel, and Nicola Humble. 2000. *Mrs Beeton's Book of Household Management*, abridged ed. Oxford: Oxford World Classics.

Carrington, Christopher. 1999. *No Place Like Home: Relationships and Family Life amongst Lesbians and Gay Men*. Chicago: University of Chicago Press.

Hunt, Nancy R. 1990. "Domesticity and Colonialism in Belgium Africa: Usumbura's Foyer Social, 1946–1960." *Signs*, 15(3): 447–474.

McClintock, Anne. 1995. *Imperial Leather: Race, Gender and Sexuality in the Colonial Context*. New York: Routledge.

Miller, Daniel, ed. 2001. *Home Possessions: Material Culture Behind Closed Doors*. Oxford: Berg.

Oakley, Ann. 1974. *Housewife*. London: Allen Lane.

Rogers, Barbara. 1980. *The Domestication of Women: Discrimination in Developing Societies*. London: Tavistock.

Sparke, Penny. 1995. *As Long as it's Pink: The Sexual Politics of Taste*. London: Pandora.

FURTHER READING

Connellan, Kathleen. 2007. "White Skins, White Surfaces: The Politics of Domesticity in South African Domestic Interiors 1920–1950." In *Taking Up the Challenge: Critical Race and Whiteness Studies in a Postcolonising Nation*, edited by Damien W. Riggs, 248–259. Adelaide: Crawford House.

Cook, Matt. 2014. *Queer Domesticities: Homosexuality and Home Life in Twentieth-Century London*. London: Palgrave Macmillan.

Gillis, Stacy, and Joanne Hollows. 2009. *Feminism, Domesticity and Popular Culture*. New York: Routledge.

Rybczynski, Witold. 1987. *Home: A Short History of an Idea*. New York: Penguin.

Shove, Elizabeth. 2003. *Comfort, Cleanliness and Convenience: The Social Organization of Normality*. Oxford: Berg.

Welter, Barbara. 1966. "The Cult of True Womanhood: 1820–1860." *American Quarterly*, 18(2): 151–174.

Curriculum Transformation

LESLIE REBECCA BLOOM
Roosevelt University, Chicago, USA

There is a global educational transformation movement to foster gender and sexuality curricula to improve the academic and schooling experiences of girls and LGBTQ students. Both part of and distinct from queer, feminist, and social justice movements, this movement seeks to transform school climates and academic content and, in doing so, promote large-scale alteration of the status quo in schools regarding the persistent and pervasive discrimination against girls and LGBTQ youth.

The term curriculum, which comes from the Latin root *currere* – to run, or a racecourse – is used to refer to educational ideologies, documents, and processes. Ideologies underpin all curriculum documents and processes. As with any ideologic formations, there are dominant ideologies that influence schooling at national and local levels.

Dominant ideologies of curricula tend to be homophobic, misogynist, and patriarchal; they are also cisexist. Cisexism refers to the discrimination against those whose individual self-perceptions of their gender, their bodies, and their personal identities do not match the sex they were assigned at birth (Serrano 2007). Gender and sexuality curricula ideologies are non-dominant. They are typically rights-based, grounded in the belief that girls and LGBTQ youth have the right to learn in schools that are safe, supportive, inclusive, respectful, and nurturing.

Curriculum processes are shaped by ideologies about what, why, and how the curriculum is taught and by those who have the power to have their interests served. Processes include the systematic organization of schools and districts, the pedagogic strategies and student–teacher relationships that frame everyday learning, and the construction of the school climate or culture as a learning environment. Most importantly, curriculum processes ask us to question if the purpose of schooling is to reproduce or to transform society. With regard to gender and sexuality curricula processes, the purpose of schooling is to transform society through education. Gender and sexuality curricula challenge the normative androcentric, homophobic, and capitalist structures of schooling that permeate educational content, pedagogy, and climate. Transformation would be achieved when school processes are universally grounded on the belief that girls and LGBTQ youth have the right to learn in an inclusive environment where they freely and openly express their sexualities, sexual orientations, and gender identities intellectually and socially without fear of judgment, discrimination, bullying, or reprisal.

Curriculum documents align with ideology and processes. Documents include programs of study or sequences of courses, lesson plans and course syllabuses, materials for content areas, and expected learning experiences and outcomes for students based on a set of skills and content to be mastered. Curriculum documents for gender and sexuality curricula integrate resources, materials, and knowledge about and by girls/women and LGBTQ people across all disciplines. The intellectual contributions, histories, and knowledge of women and LGBTQ people are included on a par with other curriculum content. Curricula address how both LGBTQ people and women and girls have been historically and persistently denied basic social, civil, political, and economic rights through formal legislation and policies and through cultural and social practices. Finally, curriculum documents promote reflection, analysis, and discussion about discrimination, rights, equity, and individual and community responsibility.

The need for a movement to promote transformative gender and sexuality curricula is made manifest by two key socioeducational circumstances. First, school climates globally are often characterized by physical and emotional abuse and violence against girls and LGBTQ youth. This widespread violation of human rights persists in every country in the world and in all socioeconomic groups (United Nations Entity on Gender Equality 2013). Girls and LGBTQ students are harassed, bullied, abused, and threatened in schools and girls may be forced or coerced to have sex with male teachers for grades. Girls are raped on school grounds or on the journey to and from school. Compulsive heterosexuality and hegemonic masculinity are normative, fostering, and maintaining acquiescence to violence against girls and

LGBTQ youth (Klein 2012). Teachers and administrators often perpetuate and contribute to damaging school climates rather than challenge or eliminate them. Girls are the victims of violence simply for attending school and others are denied schooling by being forced into prostitution, child labor, and child marriages. Sexual and gender-based violence constitutes one of the major reasons why some girls and LGBTQ students do not complete K-12 schooling. Cyberbullying is also a problem worldwide (Gottfried 2011). Cyberbullying has the power to humiliate and abuse girls and LGBTQ students, often resulting in school failure, depression, and suicide (Cyberbullying Research Center 2013).

Second, neoliberal control over public education results in capitalist and patriarchal educational ideologies and policies (Kumashiro 2008). Under neoliberalism, economic growth and knowledge as a commodity are valued over public education as a right and common good for all youth. State control of mandated content for standardized curricula increases corporate access to profit-making through privatized schools and for-profit educational companies. Standardized curricula contribute to the erasure of the sexual and gender diversities of humans, allowing ignorance, misunderstandings, stereotyping, and violence to flourish.

Schools are not on the frontline of teaching about and ensuring gender and sexuality equity; however, there are global policies that indicate increasing awareness of the need to address gender and sexuality in schools and society. For example, in response to the lack of attention to sexuality issues in the Universal Declaration of Human Rights, the Yogyakarta Principles provide a universal guide to applying international human rights law to violations experienced by LGBTQ people to ensure the universal reach of human rights protection. Such principles can be used to inform school curricula and disciplinary policies. In the United States, at both the state and federal levels, there have been efforts to include gender and sexuality education in curricula and to overtly address school violence through revised disciplinary codes, student handbooks, and the inclusion of restorative justice over punishment. Research on gender and sexuality education is extensive and accessible (Blackburn et al. 2010; Meiners and Quinn 2012) and curriculum materials are widely available from not-for-profit organizations and research centers at universities (Future of Sex Education 2012; GLSEN 2013). Also in the United States, legislation for a Student Non-Discrimination Act was introduced to Congress, although it has little chance of being passed. Globally, there are numerous non-governmental organizations and community-based organizations fighting for new school and social policies, LGBTQ and women's rights, and transformational curricula for gender and sexuality education.

SEE ALSO: Bullying; Capitalist Patriarchy; Gender Equity in Education in the United States; Gender-Based Violence; NGOs and Grassroots Organizing; Sexism; Sexual Rights; Yogyakarta Principles

REFERENCES

Blackburn, Molly V., Caroline T. Clark, Lauren M. Kenney, and Jill M. Smith, eds. 2010. *Acting Out!: Combating Homophobia Through Teacher Activism*. New York: Teachers College Press.

Cyberbullying Research Center. 2013. Accessed July 15, 2015, at http://www.cyberbullying.us/publications.

Future of Sex Education. 2012. "National Sexuality Education Standards: Core Content and Skills, K-12. A Special Publication of the Journal of School Health." Accessed July 15, 2015, at http://www.futureofsexed.org/.

Gay, Lesbian and Straight Education Network (GLSEN). 2013. *Inclusion and Respect: GLSEN Resources for Educators*. Accessed July 15, 2015, at http://glsen.org/educate/resources.

Gottfried, Keren. 2011. "Cyberbullying: Citizens in 24 Countries Assess Bullying via Information Technology for a Total Global Perspective." Accessed July 15, 2015, at http://www.ipsos-na.com/download/pr.aspx?id=14179.

Klein, Jessie. 2012. *The Bully Society: School Shootings and the Crisis of Bullying in America's Schools*. New York: New York University Press.

Kumashiro, Kevin K. 2008. *The Seduction of Common Sense: How the Right has Framed the Debate on America's Schools*. New York: Teachers College Press.

Meiners, Erica R., and Therese Quinn, eds. 2012. *Sexualities in Education*. New York: Peter Lang.

Serano, Julia. 2007. *Whipping Girl: A Transsexual Woman on Sexism and the Scapegoating of Femininity*. New York: Seal Press.

United Nations Entity on Gender Equality and the Empowerment of Women. 2013. "Breaking the Silence on Violence against Indigenous Girls, Adolescents and Young Women: A Call to Action Based on an Overview of Existing Evidence from Africa, Asia Pacific and Latin America." Accessed July 15, 2015, at http://www.unfpa.org/sites/default/files/resource-pdf/VAIWG_FINAL.pdf.

FURTHER READING

Gay, Straight Alliance Network. Accessed July 15, 2015, at http://www.gsanetwork.org/resources/research-reports/national-research.

Customary Laws

PETER ØREBECH
UIT Arctic University of Norway, Norway

Customary laws – defined as bottom-up, popularly established rules based on cultural norms and Blackstonian prerequisites (see below) – qualify as legal rules in most industrialized countries. Customary laws are drawn from practices among trades, tribes, or local municipalities, established either from popular acknowledgment *inter partes* or by the competent courts. The democratic principle that reserves the art of lawmaking to the national assembly does not hinder customary law from playing a vital role in civil as well as common law countries. To the contrary, legislators often refer directly to custom and usage in codifying customary law, as is the case in South Africa and Namibia (d'Engelbronner-Kolff, Hinz, and Sindano 1998), where most family law and law of wills and succession refer to tribal or traditional courts.

In Western countries arbitrational courts like mediation boards play a role in family disputes, paternity, and child custody cases. In Norway, gender discrimination may often find a solution in the Equal Status Council. Often these instances draw upon equity law, that is, extra-legal norms. In such cases the distinction between legal and extra-legal principles is insignificant. Disputants seeking a resolution by referring a case to the dispute settlement body ask for a verdict, not a *non liquet* (no applicable law) in return (Judge Huber 1928). Since systems of law do not recognize loopholes (Judge Higgins 1996), customary laws are appropriate.

Not all normative structures qualify as customary laws. In industrialized countries, what have been the qualifying criteria for the transformation of informal practice into "the law of the land"? In civil law countries (Germany, France, Switzerland) top-down codifications (e.g., Germany's Bürgerliches Gesetzbuch) are the basic instruments of the law. Some countries, like Sweden, have explicitly banned ancient customs. At the end of the nineteenth century Sweden prescribed that all customs that failed to be recognized by the parliament (*Riksdagen*) should be terminated. Denmark and Norway found other solutions. Here newly adopted legal codes (Christian V's Norwegian and Danish Codes respectively) failed to impede customary laws. This was also the case in most Anglo-Saxon countries. In dispute settlements common and customary laws are not inferior to codifications.

Customary law differs from common law. Common law is the law produced from top-down principles by the King's (Queen's) courts in Great Britain. On the other hand, customary laws are recognized through popular acceptance and, thus, become the law of the land. If long-term successful practices have more or less tacitly become the accepted social norm, then the normativity of the popular practices ("Die normative Kraft des Faktischen") is fulfilled (Jellinek 1959/1914). In this transition from extra-legal to legal norms, the courts play a vital role.

According to Blackstone (1871), Anglo-American law acknowledges customs as law if seven prerequisites are satisfied: (1) antiquity; (2) non-concurring use; (3) no verbal disagreement; (4) reasonableness; (5) certainty; (6) uniformity; and (7) consistency. Danish and Norwegian case law differs from Anglo-American customary law on one point: "since ancient times" (*usus longaevis*) departs from the Blackstone prerequisite that a particular custom must trace its origin from the reign of Richard Lionheart (1189) or before. According to Norwegian case law, the ancient criterion is satisfied by a century-old practice that is followed by many (*opinio juris necessitatis*) without the knowledge of any contradictory norm.

In general, popular norms qualify as law if they result from a common belief that a rule of law, and not just a social norm (ethical or moral), is being followed, that the usage is reasonable and so ancient that the oldest living people know of nothing else, and that the practice is related to continuous usage (i.e., is consistent and regular).

A theoretical position in civil law countries has been that customary laws are valid *praeter legem* (before formally acknowledged by the court) only if not *contra legem* (breaching the positive law) (Vinding Kruse 1943): customary laws may not contradict the codified law. Consequently, a practice that qualifies as a fact may only take on normative, legal status in cases in which a legal loophole exists and thus moves from *praeter legem* to *infra legem* (a valid, legal norm).

However, this is not always the case. Constitutional practices may become legal principles, resulting in constitutional amendments. One illustration is the Swedish procedure for transferring sovereignty to the European Union (EU) without a qualified majority vote, in direct opposition to the Swedish constitution (2009). Another is the introduction of the principle of parliamentary rule in Norway (1884). International law recognizes new practice as law, for example the Truman proclamation regarding jurisdiction over resources of the outer continental shelf (1945). This "instant customary law" was established regardless of failing (in theory) to fulfill the prerequisites. Thus, a *contra legem* limitation for validating customary laws is not absolute.

The Huber–Higgins position is shared by most judges in the Western hemisphere and presupposes a well-defined system of customary laws and general principles of law. As legal courts cannot refuse to take a case due to lack of written law, codes, or statutes, legal disputes call for solutions ruled by general principles of law or customary laws, which fill in the legal loopholes. This opens the door for legal norms established from the bottom up. Consequently, courts "shall not conclude by a 'non liquet,' but shall in any event decide" the case (Judge Huber 1928). The judge's role is "to resolve … why the application of one norm rather than another is to be preferred in the particular case. As these norms indubitably exist, and the difficulties that face the Court relate to their application, there can be no question of judicial legislation" (Judge Higgins 1996).

To achieve a settlement in cases in which loopholes in the law exist, a judge seeks normative structures that go beyond codifications, statutes, and other written rules. Long-followed practices that constitute popular customs occasionally find their way into these open spaces in the legal landscape. However, if popular practices or custom lack reasonableness, even long-term usage will fail to gain court approval.

SEE ALSO: Civil Rights Law and Gender in the United States; Convention on the Elimination of All Forms of Discrimination against Women (CEDAW); Democracy and Democratization; Governance and Gender; Human Rights, International Laws and Policies on

REFERENCES

Blackstone, William. 1871. *Commentaries on the Laws of England*. Chicago: Callaghan.
d'Engelbronner-Kollf, F. M., Manfred O. Hinz, and J. L. Sindano, eds. 1998. *Traditional Authority and Democracy in Southern Africa*. Windhoek: New Namibia Books.
Higgins, Rosalyn. 1996. *Legality of the Threat or Use of Nuclear Weapons*. Advisory opinion of the International Court of Justice.
Huber, Max. 1928. Island of Palmas Case. *Permanent Court of Arbitration (PCA)*.
Jellinek, Georg. 1959. *Allgemeine Staatslehre*. Darmstadt: Wissenschaftliche Buchgesellschaft. First published 1914.
Vinding Kruse, Frederik. 1943. *Retskildelæren I* [Legal sources]. Copenhagen: Nyt Nordisk.

FURTHER READING

Austin, John. 1869. *Lectures on Jurisprudence*, vol. 1, edited by Robert Campbell. London: John Murray.
Clanchy, Michael T. 2012. *From Memory to Written Record*. Hoboken: John Wiley & Sons.
Ørebech, Peter. 2013. "Western Scandinavia: Exit Bürgerliches Gesetzbuch – the Resurrection of Customary Laws." *Texas International Law Journal*, 48(3): 406–433.
Ørebech, Peter, and Fred Bosselman. 2005. *The Role of Customary Law in Sustainable Development*. New York: Cambridge University Press.

Sumner Maine, Henry. 1876. *Village-Communities in the East and West, New York*. Whitefish, MO: Kessinger Publishing.
Sumner Maine, Henry. 1885. *Popular Government*. London: John Murray.
Sumner Maine, Henry. 1886. *Dissertations on Early Law and Custom*. New York: Henry Holt.

Cyber Intimacies

PANTEÁ FARVID
Auckland University of Technology, New Zealand

Cyber intimacies is a rather nebulous term that refers to sexual or otherwise intimate relationships that are initiated or maintained via computer-mediated communication (CMC). Breaking down the term helps us to narrow down what cyber intimacies typically relate to. "Cyber" refers to the online world known as "cyberspace," where computer software produces a virtual reality (Whitty 2003), and intimacy refers to romantic, sexual, or close personal relationships (Santore 2011) that involve the process of physical and personal disclosure (Jamieson 1998). Identified as part of the globalization process, which involves the expansion of information and communication technology (ICT), cyber intimacies are in many ways (re)shaping how we seek and do "connectedness." Although there is uneven access to this technology worldwide (Valentine 2006), CMC allows many individuals a low-cost, round-the-clock, and anonymous mode of contact. The academic literature related to cyber intimacies has largely focused on how people use the Internet to maintain already established relationships when there is a geographic separation, how new relationships are formed via the Internet, and how the Internet is used for erotic purposes or contact. The main focus of this research has been examination of online dating and cybersex.

ALREADY ESTABLISHED RELATIONSHIPS

Certain trends associated with globalization (e.g., increasing rates of transnational migration, fluid employment placement) means that friends, families, and romantic partners increasingly find themselves separated from each other geographically. This separation can be temporary, for short periods of time, long term, or permanent. CMC allows individuals with preexisting intimate ties new ways of maintaining contact. In this context, face-to-face video calling via webcam (e.g., Skype), instant messaging (e.g., MSN Messenger), social media (e.g., Facebook), and email become useful tools for maintaining intimacy. This process has been termed *living together apart* (Valentine 2006; Couch and Liamputtong 2008) and allows the maintenance of closeness during separation, although not replacing or making up for *in-person* communication, touch, or contact.

MEETING NEW PEOPLE

Not long after its inception, the Internet rapidly became a site where individuals could meet *new* people with whom they would not normally come into contact, in person, during their daily routine. These connections often center around particular interests or hobbies (e.g., book clubs), provide space for "specialist" sites linked to specific sexual practices (e.g., BDSM (bondage, dominance/submission, and sadomaschism)), minority ethnic groups or sexual communities (e.g., lesbian, gay, bisexual, transgender, or queer (LGBTQ)), and allow individuals to search for romantic or sexual partners (rather than leaving it to chance social encounters) (Cooper 1998; Hardey 2004). *Online dating*,

for example, is a burgeoning industry where people can search for dating or sexual partners, longer-term relationships, and "love." The online dating platform came into use during the mid-1990s and has largely replaced personal ads in newspapers in the search for intimate connections. Unlike newspaper advertisements, online dating websites allow more space for detailed profiles, where individuals can represent who they are and what they are looking for in a sexual or romantic partner, through a process of selective information sharing (Toma, Hancock, and Ellison 2008). The characteristics that individuals can stipulate include: sexual orientation, age, height, weight, hair color, eye color, occupation, education level, income, marital status, geographic location, personality type, hobbies/interests, and future goals (Whitty and Gavin 2001). The process of online dating involves constructing the "ideal" profile (via self-reflection on who you are and what you are looking for), reading others' profiles, exchanging messages/information, and building rapport via mutual self-disclosure. This mutual self-disclosure online often leads to face-to-face meetings, which determine whether a connection that was instigated online will continue offline (Davis et al. 2006; Valentine 2006; Zakelj 2011). Although initiated and maintained online, once an online dating relationship is established, it moves offline and takes on the characteristics of typical dyadic or monogamous relationships.

Online dating is sometimes likened, historically, to telegraph use in the nineteenth century for facilitating romantic courtship. This is evidenced nicely in the novel *Wired Love: A Romance of Dots and Dashes*, Cheever Thayer (2013). Contemporary online dating has moved far beyond a one-on-one communication and has widened the net for individuals searching for sexual or romantic partners (Dawn and Farvid 2012) by providing a smorgasbord of (ostensibly) available singles to choose from. A marketplace metaphor appears to operate on these sites, where one is marketing "the self" and buying "the other" under the rhetoric of "choice" (Heino, Ellison, and Gibbs 2010). The process of "choosing" who to contact and meet offline involves a filtering or screening system where individuals can ignore/delete undesirable profiles or flag/contact individuals with desirable profiles (Hardey 2004). The anonymity that online dating provides also means that individuals can choose to ignore contact initiated by members in whom they feel they are not interested (whereas in a face-to-face meeting, if someone initiates contact in pursuit of a date, for example, there is a requirement for an on-the-spot response). The *nature* of online contact involves asynchronous communication via textual conversations. Unlike a face-to-face synchronous conversation, asynchronous contact allows individuals to *really* think about how to construct a response (and communicate with a number of individuals simultaneously) (Döring 2002). CMC via online dating is typically more expressive and hyperpersonal than offline communication. The sense of online anonymity may provide space for more disclosure and involve an "acceleration of intimacy" (Mills 1998; Padgett 2007). Hence the norms of developing intimacy appear to be different in online relationships (where it is faster) from offline relationships (where it is slower) (Zakelj 2011).

Rates of online dating use appear to be around 10–15 percent of the Western population, meaning that online dating is neither a niche market, nor has it taken over as the means for meeting romantic and sexual partners (Döring 2002; Finkel et al. 2012). A country where online dating is quite popular is the United States. Here, out of 54 million single individuals, 40 million report having used online dating (Hefner and Kahn 2014), with 22 percent of the population having met their partner online (Rosenfeld and Thomas 2012). As well as providing a useful tool for meeting new people, online dating has been identified as presenting a spectrum of risks. The main risks of online dating are deception (the most common being individuals who lie about their relationship status), fraud, the social stigma (although decreasing) that is attached to online dating (e.g., it is seen as a last resort or for otherwise socially inept individuals), and sexual and physical safety (Buchanan and Whitty 2013). Physical safety is an arena that is gendered and mainly associated with women's online dating practices (Kreager et al. 2014; Hayden and Farvid forthcoming).

CYBERSEX

Sex that occurs *online*, without the proximity of bodies, is typically defined as *cybersex* (Whitty 2003). The Internet not only provides erotic material for consumption (e.g., online pornography), but also allows individuals to connect with others for erotic play, sexual communication, masturbation, cyberflirting, role playing, fantasy enactment, and offline sex (Valentine 2006; Ashford 2009). Cybersex involves chatting over video or text, via webcams and fast broadband, whilst one or both parties engage in some form of auto-stimulation. Such contact can also be pursued offline when individuals meet specifically for engaging in some form of sexual contact (Wakeford 2000). Cybersex can occur between already established partners or strangers who have met in an online forum. Such "virtual sex" opens up extra computer-mediated erotic possibilities but can carry some risks. The risks of cybersex are physical/sexual safety when meeting strangers offline, or developing compulsive cybersex behavior (Daneback, Cooper, and Månsson 2005).

Advocates of CMC note that it reduces social boundaries, connects people, and facilitates intimacies, whilst critics caution that CMC is dangerous and can be shallow and impersonal (Jerin and Dolinsky 2001). Whatever shape cyber intimacies take, the practice is altering the way many instigate and engage in connectedness.

SEE ALSO: Cybersex; Information Technology; Internet and Gender; Internet Sex; Intimacy and Sexual Relationships; Sexualities

REFERENCES

Ashford, Chris. 2009. "Queer Theory, Cyber-Ethnographies and Researching Online Sex Environments." *Information and Communications Technology Law*, 18(3): 297–314. DOI: 10.1080/13600830903424734.

Buchanan, Tom, and Monica T. Whitty. 2013. "The Online Dating Romance Scam: Causes and Consequences of Victimhood." *Psychology, Crime and Law*, 20(3): 261–283. DOI: 10.1080/1068316X.2013.772180.

Cooper, Alvin. 1998. "Sexuality and the Internet: Surfing into the New Millennium." *CyberPsychology and Behavior*, 1: 187–193.

Couch, Danielle, and Pranee Liamputtong. 2008. "Online Dating and Mating: The Use of the Internet to Meet Sexual Partners." *Qualitative Health Research*, 18(2): 268–279. DOI: 10.1177/1049732307312832.

Daneback, K., A. Cooper, and S. A. Månsson. 2005. "An Internet Study of Cybersex Participants." *Archives of Sexual Behavior*, 34: 321–328.

Davis, Mark, Graham Hart, Graham Bolding, Lorraine Sherr, and Jonathan Elford. 2006. "E-dating, Identity and HIV Prevention: Theorizing Sexualities, Risk and Network Society." *Sociology of Health and Illness*, 28(4): 457–478. DOI: 10.1111/j.14679566.2006.00501.x.

Dawn, David, and Panteá Farvid. 2012. "'Trawling for a Girlfriend': Heterosexual Men's Experiences of Online Dating in Aotearoa New Zealand." In *The 10th Dangerous Consumptions Colloquium*. Auckland, New Zealand.

Döring, Nicola. 2002. "Studying Online-Love and Cyber-Romance." In *Online Social Sciences*, edited by Bernard Batinic, Ulf-Dietrich Reips, and Michael Bosnjak. Seattle: Hogrefe & Huber.

Finkel, Eli J., Paul W. Eastwick, Benjamin R. Karney, Harry T. Reis, and Susan Sprecher. 2012. "Online Dating: A Critical Analysis from the Perspective of Psychological Science." *Psychological Science in the Public Interest*, 13(1): 3–66. DOI: 10.1177/1529100612436522.

Hardey, Michael. 2004. "Mediated Relationships." *Information, Communication and Society*, 7(2): 207–222. DOI: 10.1080/1369118042000232657.

Hayden, Katie, and Panteá Farvid. Forthcoming. "'It's Like Conventional Dating on Steroids': Heterosexual Women's Experiences of Online Dating."

Hefner, Veronica, and Julie Kahn. 2014. "An Experiment Investigating the Links among Online Dating Profile Attractiveness, Ideal Endorsement, and Romantic Media." *Computers in Human Behavior*, 37: 9–17. DOI: 10.1016/j.chb.2014.04.022.

Heino, Rebecca D., Nicole B. Ellison, and Jennifer L. Gibbs. 2010. "Relationshopping: Investigating the Market Metaphor in Online Dating." *Journal of Social and Personal Relationships*, 27(4): 427–447. DOI: 10.1177/0265407510361614.

Jamieson, Lynn. 1998. *Intimacy: Personal Relationships in Modern Societies*. Cambridge: Polity.

Jerin, Robert, and Beverly Dolinsky. 2001. "You've Got Mail! You Don't Want It: Cyber-Victimization and On-Line Dating." *Journal of Criminal Justice and Popular Culture*, 9(1): 15–21.

Kreager, Derek A., Shannon E. Cavanagh, John Yen, and Mo Yu. 2014. "'Where Have all the Good Men Gone?' Gendered Interactions in Online Dating." *Journal of Marriage and Family*, 76(2): 387–410. DOI: 10.1111/jomf.12072.

Mills, Russell. 1998. "Cyber: Sexual Chat on the Internet." *Journal of Popular Culture*, 32(3): 31–46. DOI: 10.1111/j.0022-3840.1998.3203_31.x.

Padgett, Paige M. 2007. "Personal Safety and Sexual Safety for Women using Online Personal Ads." *Sexuality Research and Social Policy*, 4(2): 27–37. DOI: 10.1525/srsp.2007.4.2.27.

Rosenfeld, Michael J., and Reuben J. Thomas. 2012. "Searching for a Mate: The Rise of the Internet as a Social Intermediary." *American Sociological Review*, 77(4): 523–547. DOI: 10.1177/0003122412448050.

Santore, Daniel. 2011. "Gender and the Organization of Heterosexual Intimacy." In *Introducing the New Sexualities Studies*, edited by Steven Seidman, Nancy Fischer, and Chet Meeks. London: Routledge.

Thayer Ella C. 2013. *Wired Love: A Romance of Dots and Dashes*. London: Sovereign. First published 1880.

Toma, Catalina L., Jeffrey T. Hancock, and Nicole B. Ellison. 2008. "Separating Fact from Fiction: An Examination of Deceptive Self-Presentation in Online Dating Profiles." *Personality and Social Psychology Bulletin*, 34: 1023–1036.

Valentine, Gill. 2006. "Globalizing Intimacy: The Role of Information and Communication Technologies in Maintaining and Creating Relationships." *Women's Studies Quarterly*, 34(1/2): 365–393. DOI: 10.2307/40004765.

Wakeford, Nina. 2000. "Cyberqueer." In *The Cybercultures Reader*, edited by David Bell and Barbara M. Kennedy. London: Routledge.

Whitty, Monica T. 2003. "Cyber-Flirting: Playing at Love on the Internet." *Theory & Psychology*, 13(3): 339–357. DOI: 10.1177/0959354303013003003.

Whitty, Monica T., and J. K. Gavin. 2001. "Age/Sex/Location: Uncovering the Social Cues in the Development of Online Relationships." *CyberPsychology & Behavior*, 4(5): 623–630.

Zakelj, Tjasa. 2011. "Intimacy in the Context of Internet Dating." *Annales: Series Historia et Sociologia*, 21(1): 187–196.

FURTHER READING

Romm-Livermore, Celia, and Kristina Setzekorn, eds. 2009. *Social Networking Communities and E-dating Services: Concepts and Implications*. Hershey, PA: Information Science Books.

Cybersex

R. E. DAVIS
College of the Mainland, Texas, USA

Cybersex is the use of computer technologies to access, interact, and utilize erotic or sexual material, spaces, or situations creating sexual stimulation transmitted by computer. Cybersex can take place through the use of programs or data on a user's computer, but cybersex has more recently become framed as an online activity. This can include accessing erotic pictures and photographs, videos and films, stories and text, role-playing games, social media, audio, video games, multi-user video game interfaces, and other content online. It also includes accessing mediated content that is partially user generated, either in real time or across time.

Cybersex can take place with an inactive, computer-mediated object such as erotic video. It can also take place with an active partner, either known or unknown to the user. The element of anonymity in cybersex can add to the sexual stimulation and allow users to explore parts of their sexuality that they would be too nervous or embarrassed to experience in their non-mediated experience.

The term cybersex first appears in the early 1990s as a way of representing both the material and process of engaging with sexual material on the emergent Internet and on home computers. Cybersex is a portmanteau of cyberspace and sex. The terms cybersex and cyberspace entered popular consciousness at roughly the same time, as emergent computer technologies and their impact were moving from an arena of scientific specialty to home and popular use. Early forms of cybersex included messaging with others over bulletin board systems (BBS), sexual adventure games, and downloadable pictures. As BBS were launched, some boards became specific sites of exchanging sexual material such as stories, erotic adventures, and games. As the Internet became more prevalent, cybersex became a topic of concern for the general public. Current cybersex forms include those that utilize higher bandwidth such as video chat and voice over Internet protocol (VoIP).

Cybersex – or computer-mediated sex – has been a topic in science fiction, often accompanying fears of losing humanity to technology. Woody Allen's 1973 film, *Sleeper*, was one of the first iterations of technology and sex appearing in popular culture. The film included machines like the Orgasmatron which replaced erotic human encounters. With the rise of mediated erotic content, many writers predicted that virtual reality sex would soon replace physical erotic encounters, similar to what happens in the film, where a large closet-like device and an orb replace physical sexuality. While this has not occurred as quickly as some futurists have predicted, the development and theorizing on teledildonics has increased the interaction between the body and machine as a means of sexual stimulation and erotic gratification.

Lisa Palac was one of the first writers to explore cybersex with the publication of *Future Sex*, a magazine that cataloged the ways that sexuality and the erotic were being delivered and utilized online and through computers. *Future Sex* recorded early web spaces, BBS, and programs that provided erotic content and experiences. The magazine was one of the first efforts to normalize accessing erotic content through computer mediation. The rise of cybersex allowed some users with traditionally stigmatized sexualities to grow and interact as communities, explore the diversity of sexuality, and share acceptance. Cyberqueer arose as a term to describe the growth of queer interaction and exploration in cyberspace. This form of mediated sexuality also grew during the height of the HIV/AIDS scare, prompting some to praise cybersex as a safe alternative (Maxwell 1996).

The literature on cybersex, individuals who engage in cybersex, and sexuality scholars struggle with the concept of mediation in the erotic. The central question becomes whether cybersex constitutes an equal or similar gravitas to actual physical sexuality, or something different. This distinction becomes important with the rise of the concept of affairs online (Attwood 2009).

The rise of Internet communication technologies, video technology, and cybersex was accompanied with writing containing a sense of moral panic. Early writing on cybersex focused on the way that sexually explicit materials could enter the home unintentionally and how live sex was being replaced with electronic forms. The term cybersex addiction was created to express the utilization of sexual material online as a replacement for intimate human contact. How much use constituted addiction became a point of debate that continues. Often, the discussion on cybersex addiction focuses on the replacement of *meaningful* sexual contact transposed against the *meaninglessness* of sexual activity with strangers online (Delmonico 1997). Discussion of cybersex addiction often focuses on the destructive nature of loss of intimate human relationships to cybernetic connections. Discussions also center on pornographic addiction, children, and infidelity.

While cybersex as a term is still in use, because of the ubiquity of the Internet and computer-mediated communication, specialized terms for accessing erotic content and engaging with partners online have arisen, thus reducing its popularity. Terms like sexting have been created to describe particular forms of computer-mediated erotic stimulation.

SEE ALSO: Cyber Intimacies; Internet Sex; Pornography, Feminist Legal and Political Debates on; Sexual Addiction

REFERENCES

Allen, Woody. 1973. *Sleeper*. 89 Minutes. USA.
Attwood, Feona, ed. 2009. *Mainstreaming Sex: The Sexualization of Western Culture*. London: I.B. Tauris.

Delmonico, David. 1997. "Cybersex: High Tech Sex Addiction." *Sexual Addiction and Compulsivity*, 4(2): 159–166.

Maxwell, Kenneth. 1996. *A Sexual Odyssey: From Forbidden Fruit to Cybersex*. New York: Plenium Press.

FURTHER READING

Bone, James. 1993. "Virtually Better than the Real Thing." *The Times*, February 11.

Cava, Marco. 1993. "Turned on by Technology in the World of Cybersex." *USA Today*, August 30.

Garreau, Joel. 1993. "Bawdy Bytes: The Growing World of Cybersex." *The Washington Post*, November 29, A1.

Morton, Donald. 1995. "Birth of the Cyberqueer." *PMLA*, 110(3): 369–381.

Smith, Vivian. 1993. "The Word is Out." *The Globe and Mail*, December 30.

Waskul, Dennis, ed. 2004. *Net.Sexxx*, edited by Steve Jones. Digital Formation. New York: Peter Lang.

Cyborg Manifesto

JACOB W. GLAZIER
University of West Georgia, USA

"A Manifesto for Cyborgs: Science, Technology, and Socialist Feminism for the 1980s" or more colloquially known as the "Cyborg Manifesto" was an invited article written by Donna Haraway for the *Socialist Review* published in 1985. The piece was in response to socialist feminism in the United States in the 1980s after the rise of conservatism and the election of Ronald Reagan as President of the United States. In the article, Haraway presents what she calls an ironic political myth that counters the dangers of theorizing femininity, or any entity for that matter, through the philosophical understanding of essentialism, which holds entities to be static. This loosely categorizes Haraway's project as fitting under the auspices of third-wave feminism. Yet, the Manifesto's breadth is much wider, casting a net that gathers together disparate disciplines such as science studies, postmodernism, critical theory, biology, and linguistics.

The essentialism that the Manifesto is set in relief against comes from the first- and second-wave feminists (and, undoubtedly, the larger patriarchal narrative reigning during the time of its writing) who often articulated the necessary conditions that demarcate the female as categorically distinct, usually from its dialectical antimony male. Haraway, on the contrary, rejected this view that sought to define the conditions of womanhood, which, in turn, positioned the woman-as-other, and, instead, she advocated for embracing the metaphor of a cyborg as a way beyond these essentialist discourses, as a way of co-inhabiting the very discourses that marked the female through otherness.

Importantly, for Haraway, metaphor does not connote a kind of removed abstraction from the literality of everyday language because meaning and materiality are intertwined with each other. That is to say that the kinds of metaphors at play in the reigning discourse of the times literally configure the materiality of the world and, as a result, that which constitutes the human being. Nevertheless, Haraway is opposed to any conception of the "human being" as an enclosed, individual self; thus, her conception of the cyborg figure takes the place of the self or human being because it more accurately invokes the radical enmeshment humans have with not only machines, but also with other entities in the world like animals. This philosophical position Haraway begins to call, approximately a decade after the publication of the Manifesto, metaphorical realism or cyborg surrealism – both of which constitute a kind of Janus head (Haraway 1997).

The cyborg, in fact, best embodies this position insofar as it amalgamates human and machine with the aim of inhabiting this intersection to subvert a politics of identity. That is, the cyborg remains committed to identities that are partial, strategic, and situated. The illusion of an imaginary wholeness or an essentialized self, which had been the crux of humanistic, patriarchal, and even Marxist conceptions of personhood, for Haraway and the cyborg, is a veiled form of imperialism insofar as it opens up the subject to various alignments of power such as those of patriarchy, heterosexism, classism, racism, and colonialism – the very alignments the cyborg sutures and thwarts. Lack of the whole, critically, does not imply an ahistoricity whereby the cyborg arises from nothing. Rather, Haraway argues, the situated identities that the cyborg seeks to exploit and co-inhabit actually become invigorated and radically historicized insofar as they are set in motion by the cyborg's ability to induce proliferation.

In line with the anti-holism of the cyborg project, Haraway takes aim at various origin myths that have promulgated culture and technoscience. These include Christian genesis and salvation stories as well as the psychoanalytic Oedipal myth that has featured so predominantly in the development of twentieth-century theorizing in the humanities and social sciences (Haraway 1997). Contradistinctive to these narratives, the cyborg, Haraway asserts, is the illegitimate offspring of militarism, patriarchal capitalism, and state socialism thereby giving it an ancestry that arises not from the Garden (of Eden) formed of mud and dirt, but from the world of hyper-technology, strategic corporatism, and the informatics of domination.

The irony in this conception should not be lost; namely, that the "birth" of the cyborg is not so much a birth in the conventional sense as it is a creation and regeneration since, as Haraway argues, metaphors of reproductive birth mask a politics of holism (Haraway 1991). These kinds of metaphors show up in the discourse of heterosexism and patriarchy wherein they recapitulate a form of biological essentialism. Being a cybernetic organism, the cyborg, while certainly biological in a sense, is, nonetheless, just as much a machine that can be reconfigured and recoded to the politics of any situation.

Such a recoding marks the cyborg as the entity, which wields signification as its most sacred and infiltrative technology. That is, cyborg writing is masterful at swerving between and among tropes and metaphors, generating a never ending deferral of possible descriptions, and, above all, subverting any entrenched master narrative or the belief in the ability to construct a meta-language. The position for a clear and complete symbolic system that describes reality as objectively given is impossible, according to Haraway, and, in fact, should be viewed with the utmost skepticism and suspicion since it favors a certain channeling of power at the expense of others (Haraway 1991).

The Manifesto has had considerable influence in the years since its publication; most notably, in the fields of feminism, science studies, and critical theory. It may also be viewed as an important precursor to the development of queer theory and posthumanism in the 1990s for its rejection of gender and sexual categories and its approbation of polymorphous sexuality. Some scholars, however, have criticized it on the grounds that it puts forth a level of theorizing that is far removed from lived experience. Namely, the vast majority of people simply are not cyborgs; a criticism which Haraway is somewhat ready to cede insofar as the Manifesto is meant to be read ironically, as a kind of joke (Haraway 2003).

SEE ALSO: Essentialism; Feminism and Postmodernism; Feminisms, First, Second, and Third Wave; Identity Politics

REFERENCES

Haraway, Donna J. 1985. "A Manifesto for Cyborgs: Science, Technology, and Socialist Feminism for the 1980s." *Socialist Review*, 15(2): 65–107.

Haraway, Donna J. 1991. *Simians, Cyborgs, and Women: The Reinvention of Nature*. New York: Routledge.

Haraway, Donna J. 1997. *Modest_Witness@Second_Millennium.FemaleMan© Meets_OncoMouse™: Feminism and Technoscience*. New York: Routledge.

Haraway, Donna J. 2003. *The Companion Species Manifesto: Dogs, People, and Significant Otherness*. Chicago: Prickly Paradigm Press.

D

Daoism

VICTORIA CASS
Johns Hopkins University, USA

Daoism has been singled out for the richness of its female imagery, first articulated in the ancient texts of the *Laozi* and the *Zhuangzi*. Some have argued that the elliptical references to the yin force – the feminine – encodes a symbolism that exalts the female force of yin as equal to the force of yang – the masculine. Although there is indeed merit in this assertion, the picture is more complex. In its many manifestations over its 2,000-year history from its early articulation in the fourth century BCE to contemporary Daoist practices in China, Taiwan, Southeast Asia, and beyond, Daoism has seen multiple characterizations of feminine and masculine identities and of feminine and masculine sexuality. Indeed, Daoism is a rich source on views of female fertility and male potency, as well as on the erotic and the physical in men and women. The human body, gender, and sexuality have all figured importantly in Daoist discourse for over 2,000 years.

In Daoist practice as articulated in the *Daozang* – the Daoist archive of sacred texts – both men and women can achieve transcendence. "The adept's activities were believed to transform [the] body into something fragrant and radiant, perfect and permanent, like metal or stone that would never decay and would in the end ascend to heaven" (Cahill 2003, 253–254). Within the discipline of transforming the self – both mind and body – variations occur based on male and female physiology. In order to obtain immortality, women are instructed in methods of repressing or eliminating the menstrual processes, referred to as "slaying the red dragon." Men have similar demands required by the discipline; they are instructed to practice repressed emission, that is, to copulate without completing emission. Both processes are regarded as equal sources of pollution as they drain the adept of his or her life force, or "qi." Nor is the theory of repressed emission limited to esoteric practice. It is widespread in medical literatures, and is commonly articulated in popular venues. In erotic novels as well as in novels of the romantic or of domestic life, death by excessive emission – and the consequent exhausting of the yang life force – is a common occurrence.

A number of texts from the early medieval period (not all of them extant) address the practices of sexual intercourse in the context of Daoist theories of cosmic alliances. In the so-called texts of the bedchamber (*fangzhong xing*) unknown Daoist writers interpreted

The Wiley Blackwell Encyclopedia of Gender and Sexuality Studies, First Edition. Edited by Nancy A. Naples.
© 2016 John Wiley & Sons, Ltd. Published 2016 by John Wiley & Sons, Ltd.

human sexuality. In the *Su Nü jing* (*Plain Girl Classic*), the acts of sexual intercourse are allied with the cosmic forces of yin and yang, which meet and intermingle as opposing and equal forces. Several of these "bedchamber" texts addressed fertility, offering times of day, days of the month, and so on, that align the acts of marriage with the cosmic forces of yin and yang and the five elements. The *Su Nü fang* (*The Bedchamber of the Plain Girl*), the *Xuan Nü jing* (*The Classic of the Dark Girl*), and the *Xuan Nü fangzhong jing* (*Within the Bedchamber of the Dark Girl*) provide times appropriate for marriages and sexual intercourse as determined by cosmic alignments.

Daoism, in addition to allying sexual processes with the Dao, also takes special interest in the metaphors of embryonic development. The practices of inner alchemy (*neidan*), as articulated especially by the Shangqing (Highest Clarity) sect, privilege the body as the locus for the process of achieving transcendence. For *neidan* practices, the body is configured as a vessel that holds a sacred embryo; the adept – male or female – controls an inward alchemical pregnancy to achieve transcendence. However, the appropriation of pregnancy imagery does not imply that the actual processes of childbearing were "granted any special prestige in medieval Daoism. On the contrary, giving birth was regarded as an obstacle to religious goals" (Cahill 2003, 271).

Overall, the symmetry of the male and female influence in Daoism provides a narrative of the divine that does not privilege male over female. The Queen Mother of the West (Xi Wang Mu) is worshipped by the devout of both sexes. The paths to transcendence are equally available to men and women. This mirroring of male and female and lack of gender distinction yield important social consequences. "Daoist female deities and saints provided women with devotional foci and models for their spiritual lives," and "provided examples of female agency... Along with nuns, priestesses and laywomen there were prominent female Daoist saints, hermits and wonderworkers" (Cahill 2006, 10). Even the lower levels of feminine society have had an embracing religious narrative: the great deity of the Daoist pantheon, the Queen Mother of the West, was a patron saint to female musicians, high-level courtesans, and prostitutes.

Daoist iconography provides a narrative of the divine for the most troublesome element in society. The female rebels and female political outcasts have had divine Daoist exemplars – tracing their skills to the Dark Girl or to the Primal Woman of the Nine Heavens – and have practiced "magic arts" of Daoism. They in turn have influenced popular gender roles for women. These magicians of the battlefield are richly archived in multiple sources: in vernacular and classical fiction, in vernacular storytelling productions, and theater. It was commonly said in such tales, "When approaching women in battle be especially careful; they control magic arts" (Cass 1999, 65). Nor was this dismissed as vulgar entertainment. Brigades of such divinely inspired women (and men) operated in the countryside and in the cities. Most famously, the brigade of fighters called the Red Lanterns – with a mélange of Daoist and Buddhist arts – fought in the Boxer Rebellion in the last days of the Qing dynasty (1644–1911). The state took the narrative of Daoist magic arts seriously, as these forms of religious practice could sanction millenarian rebellion. Thus, a disengaged population that was difficult to monitor could yet find religious sanction and survive in the context of economic privation and political disorder. The divine and human exemplars of magician warriors offered, to women and men alike, a seductive counter-tradition antithetical to the pervasive narrative of the imperium.

SEE ALSO: Buddhism; Yin-Yang

REFERENCES

Cahill, Suzanne. 2003. "Discipline and Transformation: Body and Practice in the Lives of Daoist Holy Women of Tang China." In *Women and Confucian Cultures in Premodern China, Korea, and Japan*, edited by Dorothy Ko, JaHyun Kim Haboush, and Joan R. Piggott. Berkeley: University of California Press.

Cahill, Suzanne. 2006. *Divine Traces of the Daoist Sisterhood*. Magdalena, NM: Three Pines Press.

Cass, Victoria. 1999. *Dangerous Women: Warriors, Grannies, and Geishas of the Ming*. Lanham, MD: Rowman & Littlefield.

FURTHER READING

Despeaux, Catherine, and Livia Kohn. 2003. *Women in Daoism*. Magdalena, NM: Three Pines Press.

Declaration of the Rights of Women

R. CASEY DAVIS
Independent scholar

In 1791, French playwright Olympe de Gouges wrote the Declaration of the Rights of Women. At the time, the tumultuous waves of the French Revolution, which began in 1788, were still rippling through the country. De Gouges' tract was modeled on the Declaration of the Rights of Man, published in 1789.

Olympe de Gouges' writing career began in the 1780s. Along with plays, de Gouges also wrote novels and articles for newspapers and journals at the time. In the heady days of revolution and change, many of her articles addressed subjects such as divorce, which were still taboo even in revolutionary France. Being passionate about feminism as well as abolitionism, her writings were always politically charged, and advocated for equality.

De Gouges used the frustration she felt towards the new revolutionary government to ignite her writing. She believed that the spirit of the revolution had been lost in the bureaucracy of the newly formed revolutionary government. Suffragists' fervent hopes of universal suffrage and equality had not come to fruition.

De Gouges wrote the Declaration of the Rights of Women in direct response to this frustration. The document openly challenged the government, calling for the newly installed revolutionary government to formally acknowledge the rights of women in France.

This simple challenge dared to overturn centuries of social, political, and economic thinking in France. In the document, de Gouges demands that the inherent inferiority assigned to women in the Declaration of the Rights of Man be removed.

The second half of the Declaration of the Rights of Women is an actual contract to be drawn up between a man and a woman. This social contract was based on the political philosophy of Jean-Jacques Rousseau, which de Gouges argued should replace the ecclesiastical marriage vows used by the Roman Catholic and Protestant Churches in France.

The structure of both these revolutionary documents was based on the Declaration of Independence, drafted by the Continental Congress in the American colonies. This may be due in part to the close ties that the nascent United States had with France.

Never before had anyone, let alone a woman, demanded official recognition of equality between men and women. Unlike later suffragist movements in Europe and the United States, de Gouges led the charge against centuries-old assumptions regarding marriage in particular, and women in general.

De Gouges believed this document would provide protection against the inherent hypocrisy and oppression that was ingrained in society at that time. She also believed that the Declaration of the Rights of Women would pave the way for greater equality among men and women in general.

Providing women with the right to divorce their husbands as well as engage in extramarital affairs with impunity immediately established social equality between the sexes. However, this bold move was not the only part of the Declaration of the Rights of Women that affected this massive paradigm shift.

In the final two paragraphs of the document, de Gouges calls also for economic responsibility and equality between women and men. In France, both before and after the revolution, women were the property of their fathers until given away in marriage. If a woman was widowed, none of her late husband's estate would be passed to her unless it was officially decreed in a legal will.

The same held true for the daughters of deceased fathers. If they had not already been betrothed to a man, a penniless future awaited them. Even if the mother survived, neither would receive any money to live on, unless expressly stated in a legal last will of the husband/father.

Along with this provision, the Declaration of the Rights of Women called for a law to financially protect women who had been deceived by the false promises of suitors and spouses. Under the proposed law, the newly established revolutionary government was asked to make these men either respect their obligations, or pay an indemnity equal to their financial wealth at the time.

In the final paragraph of the Declaration of the Rights of Women, de Gouges claims that by granting women equality with men in the eyes of the law, men would be held legally responsible for their sexual follies.

In her document, de Gouges proposes that these changes would strengthen the nation as well as the French government, specifically the king. As the French Revolution spiraled into a greater frenzy, de Gouges' writings grew more inflammatory. In June 1793, she was arrested by the revolutionary government for sedition and treason, and held for months without legal counsel. She was finally sentenced to be executed, and in November 1793, de Gouges was guillotined.

SEE ALSO: Gender Equality; Gender, Politics, and the State: Overview

FURTHER READING

Blanc, Olivier. 2003. *Marie-Olympe de Gouges* [in French]. Paris: Editions René Viénet.

Mousset, Sophie. 2007. *Women's Rights and the French Revolution: A Biography of Olympe de Gouges*. New Brunswick/London, UK: Transaction Publishers.

Vanpée, Janie. 1999. "Performing Justice: The Trials of Olympe de Gouges." *Theatre Journal*, 51(1): 47–65.

Declaration of Sentiments

R. CASEY DAVIS
Independent Scholar

At the Seneca Falls Convention in New York in 1848, 68 women and 32 men signed the Declaration of Sentiments. The document's structure and content were modeled after the Declaration of Independence. A total of 100 attendees signed out of the 300 individuals present. The low number of signatories is directly related to the controversial nature of the document. The most influential male signatory was Frederick Douglass, one of the few male abolitionists who understood the meaning of universal suffrage.

The Declaration of Sentiments was largely written by noted suffragist and abolitionist Elizabeth Cady Stanton. She wrote the first draft of the Declaration on a three-legged tea table. The table, now a national relic, was symbolic of the seemingly quaint sphere of women's influence in American culture at the time. A precarious piece of drawing room furniture being used to compose such a momentous document regarding women's rights, including suffrage, was a statement in itself.

While the Quakers did not play an official role in the organization and administering of the Seneca Falls Convention, many Quakers were involved, particularly Lucretia Mott. Mott worked with Cady Stanton in arranging the sessions, as well as contributing her opinions to the Declaration. Mott was a gifted orator, leading discussions and giving speeches that directly influenced the content and tone of the document. Like the earlier Declaration of Independence, the Declaration of Sentiments is divided into three major sections.

The first section extols the natural rights and equality of women. Like Jefferson and the Declaration of Independence, Cady Stanton called upon the major Enlightenment philosophers such as Jean-Jacques Rousseau and John Locke. In her version, Cady Stanton argued that women were endowed with the same natural rights that were given to men by their creator. In fact, Cady Stanton borrowed many of the phrases that Jefferson used in drafting the first part of the Declaration of Independence, thus providing a solid theological, philosophical, and political foundation from which to proceed.

Though drawing on major European philosophers, the Declaration of Sentiment challenged liberal, Enlightenment ideas and ideals in both their depth, content, and breadth. Just as white, property-owning males had argued for the expression of their natural rights against despotic and tyrannical monarchs, so too did the women at Seneca Falls. The women and a few men at the Convention saw the old aristocratic patriarchy, which had guided American society for so long, as tired and expired. The masterful move of utilizing the same reasoning for universal suffrage and equality as the Founding Fathers had used in declaring America's independence provided little room for argument against the women's grievances. Building on the idea of natural and inalienable rights, the signatories of the Declaration of Sentiments utilized Enlightenment ideals to further their cause and reach their goal of equality.

The true weight of the document is contained firmly in the middle section, the largest and longest of the document, which sets out the grievances against male domination of US society. Just as Jefferson had done in the similar section of the Declaration of Independence, Cady Stanton lists the most important legal and social issues and lays bare the complaints that had been discussed and voted on by the majority at the Convention. These address particular legal and social issues, for example, the right of mothers to gain custody of their children after a divorce, the right of women to sue for divorce, the right to own real estate, the right to work outside the home, as well as the right to pursue an education equal to that of men.

This section added extra fuel to the fire ignited by the first section. This middle section is both the figurative and literal heart of the document. The short paragraphs, some only a single sentence, outline the grievances in plain and direct language.

The grievances each start with the masculine pronoun "He." In doing this, Cady Stanton not only directly addresses the patriarchy ensconced in American society, but also their individual male family members and relatives. The "He" is both universal and personal; it is addressing all men, regardless of their opinions of women's suffrage and equality.

Moving on from this succinct list of grievances, the document transitions to a current point of view. The third and final portion of the Declaration of Sentiments is an interesting adjustment in the course of the argument. Again, similar to the Declaration of Independence, this section of the document gives a precise evaluation of the situation of women at the time of composition and the shared vision of progress towards equality. In this final section, Cady Stanton presents not only a possibility, but also future expectations, as envisaged by the signatories of the document.

Here, Cady Stanton calls for progress to bring gender relations, in every arena, to a natural state, namely, one of equality. This is powerfully presented by the request to grant United States citizenship to all women in the country. Cady Stanton posits that this will lead to political and legal equality between men and women, the first step in the continuing struggle for equality.

Even though 100 attendees signed the document, it proved too controversial at the time for widespread, positive reception. However, women's equality groups and suffragists continued to meet annually to discuss and refine the issues laid out in the document. The only time these meetings were interrupted was during the Civil War. They resumed, with fewer attendees, after the cessation of hostilities. At that point, the focus was more on equality for freed African American males than on women's rights. Suffrage for Caucasian women was secondary to this effort after the bloody conflict that ended slavery.

Of the historical contexts to keep in mind while women were struggling for political, legal, economic, and social equality with men were issues such as Prohibition. Yet, it was not until the early twentieth century that women were legally given the right to vote at the federal level. The other grievances set out in the Declaration of Sentiment would gradually be addressed during the ensuing decades.

SEE ALSO: Declaration of the Rights of Women; Gender Equality; Women's Political Representation

FURTHER READING

Faulkner, Carol. 2011. *Lucretia Mott's Heresy: Abolition and Women's Rights in Nineteenth-Century America*. Philadelphia: University of Pennsylvania Press.

Mani, Bonnie G. 2007. *Women, Power, and Political Change*. Lanham: Lexington Books.

Wellman, Judith. 2004. *The Road to Seneca Falls: Elizabeth Cady Stanton and the First Women's Rights Convention*. Champaign: University of Illinois Press.

Deep Ecology

LESLIE W. O'RYAN
Western Illinois University, USA

JAKE W. GLAZIER
University of West Georgia, USA

Deep ecology can be regarded as analogous to ecofeminism in many regards; however, major philosophical differences exist between the two. Deep ecology emerged as an environmental movement in the early 1970s primarily by Arne Naess, a Norwegian philosopher and environmentalist, prompted by his exposure to the environmental movement and Rachel Carson's book, *Silent Spring* (1962). Naess introduced the term "deep ecology" in an article, "The Shallow and the Deep, Long-Range Ecology Movement" that he presented at the 1972 Third World Future Research Conference (Naess 1973). It was at this time that Naess called for a rethinking of the environmental movement from a "shallow" anthropocentric concentration that focused on environmental reform, to a "deep" or substantial cultural reorientation that questioned fundamental Western assumptions about the separation of humans from the rest of nature.

Deep ecologists believe that humans have no more inherent value than any other organism and should not be elevated above other creatures based on special selection by a supreme being. Instead, they believe that the science of ecology has provided evidence for the interrelatedness of all life. Along with Bill Devall, George Sessions, and Warwick Fox, Naess understood deep ecology from the perspective of interdependence. While Naess conceptualized deep ecology from an ecocentric perspective, Devall and Sessions, in their 1985 book, *Deep Ecology*, focused more on the science, philosophy, spirituality, and ethical considerations of deep ecology. Drawing from spiritual sources such as Buddhism, Native American spirituality, Taoism, and Jainism, the movement also gained inspiration from philosophers, scientists, and environmentalists such as Henry David Thoreau, John Muir, Aldo Leopold, Baruch Spinoza, Martin Heidegger, and Paul Shepard.

Adherents of deep ecology hold the Western industrial worldview responsible for ecologically destructive behaviors. Deep ecology challenges forms of domination, destruction, and oppression that encourage consumption, materialism, and a separation between humans and nature. As a result, it is founded on eight major principles created by Arne Naess and George Sessions. These eight principles are:

1. All life has value in itself, independent of its usefulness to humans.
2. Richness and diversity contribute to life's well-being.
3. Humans have no right to reduce this richness and diversity except to satisfy vital needs in a responsible way.
4. Human impact on the world is excessive and is rapidly getting worse.
5. Human lifestyles and population are key elements of this impact.
6. The diversity of life can flourish only with reduced human impact.
7. Basic ideological, political, economic, and technological structures must change.
8. Those who accept the foregoing points have an obligation to peacefully and democratically implement change.

Some ecofeminists such as Karen Warren (Sessions 1991) suggest that, while ecofeminism shares many of the same ideologies as deep ecology, it differs in that ecofeminists have challenged deep ecology's underlying philosophies on a number of topics. Ecofeminists have critiqued deep ecologists for falling short in their emphasis on anthropocentrism, believing the problem lies in androcentrism – man-centeredness.

Ecofeminists claim that deep ecology's lack of attention to gender issues has disregarded important social justice concerns that surround patriarchal and hierarchical structures of domination that associate nature with femininity and as a result devalue and oppress it. Ecofeminists have challenged deep ecologists to adopt a more inclusive model that resists the temptation to draw upon an androcentric perspective and adapt a more biocentric view of nature that recognizes the historical connections of domination found in phallogocentrism as well as imperialistic, racist, and classist structures and practices. While ecofeminists such as Ariel Salleh believe that deep ecology follows a number of correct assumptions, it still needs to recognize a theory of labor and embodied materialism, which positions it at the intersection of humanity and nature.

In comparison to "mainstream environmentalism," the deep ecology movement is viewed by some as controversial because of its views surrounding human overpopulation, economic development, and conservation, which some consider to be "anti-human," a factor that deep ecologists argue is simply not true. Social ecologists have expressed concern about the danger of deep ecology's call to "return to nature" that may regress to a collective authoritarianism. Deep ecologists maintain that their efforts are directed towards developing self-determination and self-awareness that will promote global awareness of a life-sustaining path of conscious evolution allowing for what Devall termed, "Earth wisdom – the dance of unity of plants, animals, humans and the earth."

SEE ALSO: Ecofeminism; Environment and Gender; Mother Nature

REFERENCES

Carson, Rachel. 1962. *Silent Spring*. Boston: Houghton Mifflin.
Næss, A. 1973. "The Shallow and the Deep, Long-Range Ecology Movement." *Inquiry*, 16, 95–100.
Sessions, Robert. 1991. "Deep Ecology Versus Ecofeminism: Healthy Differences or Incompatible Philosophies?" *Hypatia*, 6(1): 9.

FURTHER READING

Devall, Bill. 1991. "Deep Ecology and Radical Environmentalism." *Society and Natural Resources*, 4(3): 247–258.
Devall, Bill, and George Sessions. 1985. *Deep Ecology: Living as if Nature Mattered*. Salt Lake City: Peregrine Smith Books.
Diehm, Christian. 2002. "Arne Naess, Val Plumwood, and Deep Ecological Subjectivity." *Ethics & The Environment*, 7(1), 24.
Drengson, Alan, and Bill Devall, eds. 2008. *Ecology of Wisdom: Writings by Arne Naess*. Berkeley, CA: Counterpoint.
Fox, Warwick. 1990. *Towards a Transpersonal Ecology*. New York: SUNY Press.
Fox, Warwick. 2006. *A Theory of General Ethics: Human Relationships, Nature, and the Built Environment*. Cambridge, MA: MIT Press.
Henning, Daniel H. 2002. *Buddhism and Deep Ecology*. Bloomington: 1st Books Library.
Katz, Eric, Andrew Light, and David Rothenberg, eds. 2000. *Beneath the Surface: Critical Essays in the Philosophy of Deep Ecology*. Boston: MIT Press.
Salleh, Ariel. 2000. "In Defense of Deep Ecology: An Ecofeminist Response to a Liberal Critique." In *Beneath the Surface: Critical Essays in the Philosophy of Deep Ecology*, edited by Eric Katz, Andrew Light, and David Rothenberg, 107–124. Cambridge, MA: Massachusetts Institute of Technology.
Sessions, George, ed. 1995. *Deep Ecology for the Twenty-First Century*. Boston: Shambhala.

Democracy and Democratization

VALENTINE M. MOGHADAM
Northeastern University, USA

Studies of democracy certainly predate the proliferating scholarship of the 1990s and afterwards, but Samuel Huntington's 1991 book on the "three waves of democratization," along with political change in various parts of the world, launched debates and discussions that continue to this day and have expanded since the 2011 Arab Spring. The early writings of Seymour Martin Lipset, Gabriel Almond, and Ronald Dahl have been followed by analyses on the part of scholars such as Adam Przeworski, Philippe Schmitter and Terry Karl, Ronald Inglehart and Christian Welzel, and Larry Diamond of the roots of democracy movements, the sequencing of democratic transitions, and the necessary conditions for effective democracy (Schmitter and Karl 1991; Przeworski et al. 2000; Welzel 2006; Welzel and Inglehart 2008).

Feminist scholars have provided a gender lens that raises questions about the nature and timing of democracy. Sociologist Pamela Paxton has compared official figures on the emergence of democracy with dates of women's suffrage and asked, for example, whether the United States could be accurately called a democracy in the 1800s and early 1900s when half the population could not vote (Paxton and Hughes 2007). Today, feminist social scientists argue that a polity is not fully democratic when there is no adequate representation of women.

International organizations agree. Goal 3 of the world community's Millennium Development Goals includes the narrowing of the gender gap in political representation.

Feminist scholars also have contributed to the literature on democratic transitions, and they have taken part in the broad discussion of definitions, meanings, and understandings of democracy, of the different historical and contemporary models of democracy, of democracy's "deficits," and of alternative visions. In particular, feminist scholars have sought to examine democracy's possibilities and its risks for women's rights, the role of women's mobilizations within pro-democracy movements, and prospects for successful, women-friendly democratic transitions and consolidation.

ENGENDERING DEMOCRATIC TRANSITIONS

Feminists began to examine democratization in the aftermath of the transitions in Eastern Europe and the former Soviet Union, and early studies compared transitions there and in Latin America. These include the pioneering 1994 study by Georgina Waylen (Waylen 1994), works by Jane Jaquette and Sharon Wolchik comparing Latin America and Eastern Europe, Sonia Alvarez on Brazil, Graciela Di Marco on Argentina, and Lisa Baldez's comparative examination of Poland, East Germany, Brazil, and Chile. This was followed by research on South Africa and Northern Ireland, and also South Korea, the Philippines, Indonesia, and Turkey, with contributions by Yesim Arat, Jocelyn Viterna and Kathleen Fallon, and Pamela Paxton and Melanie Hughes. A number of studies also have examined the role of women in, and the gender dynamics of, the earlier "third-wave" democratic transitions of Portugal, Greece, and Spain. Studies examined the participation of women in pro-democracy or anti-dictatorship movements, the gendered outcomes of democratic transitions, elections, and the new state policies, and women's mobilizations for women's rights.

For Lisa Baldez, women mobilize on the basis of their gender identity as a result of "three significant causes": (1) resources (specifically, preexisting formal or informal networks), (2) the way issues are framed (and here, international connections with global feminism are crucial), and (3) the exclusion of women from the agenda-setting process within the opposition, which affords them an opportunity to unite in a broad coalition on the basis of their shared identity (Baldez 2003). Peaks of protest consolidate women's political clout. They attract the attention of (primarily) male political actors, who seek to harness women's capacity to mobilize for their own electoral goals. In countries as diverse as Argentina, Korea, Spain, and South Africa, women saw popular demands for democracy as an opportunity to press for the democratization of everyday life and the extension of women's rights. Baldez examines this argument with regard to three countries in which women mobilized during democratic transition (Brazil, Chile, and East Germany) and one in which women did not (Poland). The women's movements that emerged in Chile and Brazil were two of the largest and most vibrant in Latin America; they joined human rights groups, feminist organizations, and shanty-town groups organized around issues of economic subsistence. In East Germany, the movement included women's peace organizations, lesbian collectives, radical feminists, socialists, and neighborhood groups. In contrast, the level of autonomous organizing among Polish women remained miniscule.

Positive outcomes for women include the new constitution of post-apartheid South Africa, which stipulated its commitment to gender equality; Nelson Mandela's inaugural speech called for the construction of a "non-racist, non-sexist" democracy; and a new institution was formed to realize these goals – the South African Commission on Gender Equality. In 1990, post-transition Argentina was the first country to institute a quota for women's parliamentary representation, raising women's participation significantly and consistently since then, and launching what has come to be known as "the quota revolution."

Yet not all transitions have seen women mobilizing as women, and not all transitions to democracy have been accompanied by policies and programs in favor of women's full citizenship and gender equality. In many countries of Eastern Europe, women were not elected to the first democratic parliaments, and a pervasive discourse tying women to family roles emerged in Poland, Hungary, and Russia. Thus democratic transitions and elections, like revolutions, hold risks for women and minorities in particular. Whether gendered outcomes are positive or negative for women's rights has much to do with preexisting institutional, normative, and organizing factors, and also with the ideology of the pro-democracy movements.

Drawing on various feminist studies, Moghadam (2013) has identified key factors and forces that may explain gendered outcomes, which she has classified as endogenous, or internal, and exogenous, or external and international. The principal endogenous factors are preexisting gender roles; women's legal status and social positions prior to the revolutionary outbreak or democratic transition; the institutional legacy of the authoritarian regime; the degree of women's mobilizations; the number and visibility of women's networks, organizations, and other institutions; the nature of the transition and of the political parties and movements involved in the transition; and the ideology, values, and norms of the new state and its capacity and will for rights-based development. The relevant exogenous factors – which may work to the advantage of women's rights or against them – are international linkages with transnational advocacy networks, multilateral organizations, and global media; women's rights norm diffusion; and wars, invasions, and occupations. Applying this framework to the Middle East and North Africa, Moghadam notes that neither elections nor a parliamentary quota have brought about women's equality in Afghanistan, Iraq, or Palestine, due principally to the conservative nature of the governments in place and to societal reaction to wars, invasions, and occupations waged by the United States, United Kingdom, and Israel.

The feminist literature has contributed significantly to our understanding of the gendered nature of democracy and democratic transitions, but it is important to step back and consider the factors that contribute to the emergence of democracy movements. These factors – elaborated in the wider and more mainstream political science literature – have implications for gendered outcomes and prospects for women-friendly democratic consolidation.

In this wider literature, there remains a debate about the relative weight and hierarchy of socioeconomic development as the major structural driver of pro-democracy movements and consolidation, which largely draws on the early work of Seymour Martin Lipset, versus the role of cultural values and norms as indicated by the early works by Gabriel Almond and Sidney Verba. Questions that have been posed include the following. Is economic development a prerequisite/causal factor, or is its impact to make democracies endure, once they have been established through other means? This is the position of Adam Przeworski and colleagues. Or do pro-democracy movements and their consolidation *presuppose* a democratic culture, with citizens demonstrating and practicing "emancipative" or "self-expression values"? This is the position of Ronald Inglehart, Christian Welzel, and their colleagues, who also argue that there is no strong relationship between democracy and another cultural construct, namely overt support for democracy (as, for example, indicated on surveys).

The main contours of the debate are summarized here; for ease of exposition, and also because of the author's contention that external or international forces and factors play a key role, both the cultural and socioeconomic prerequisites for pro-democracy movements and their success are grouped under "endogenous" or internal factors and forces. The main features identified by various scholars are socioeconomic development; wealth; capitalism; an educated population; a large middle class; civil society; civic culture; human empowerment and the emergence of emancipative values; a homogeneous population; "modernizing bourgeoisie" (Moore 1996); and "modernizing women" (Moghadam 2013). Exogenous variables that influence democratization via forces that work globally and within a region include diffusion processes that may come about via various institutions (intergovernmental organizations, non-governmental organizations, other international linkages, or the media), and foreign intervention or involvement, whether through diplomacy, occupation, or post-conflict activities. The endogenous and exogenous factors and forces generate or otherwise influence grievances, political opportunities, the capacity of protest or movement leaders to frame grievances and aspirations in a way that resonates with fellow citizens or broader publics, mobilizing capacities, and the ability to build and sustain new democratic institutions.

Applying both feminist and mainstream frameworks toward an analysis of the divergent outcomes of the Arab Spring, Moghadam (2013) highlights the advantages that Tunisia had in terms of socioeconomic and institutional development, cultural and normative changes, a vibrant civil society that included well-organized feminist groups with links to the large trade union and human rights groups, and the absence of external interference in its political processes. What model of democracy Tunisia would adopt, however, would depend on the balance of sociopolitical forces in the political process.

Political scientists have defined democracy in various ways and presented different models. A common minimalist definition is one that reduces democracy to the circulation of political power though regular elections, or electoral democracy. The participation and rights of citizens are also included in a somewhat broader definition, and these typically refer to citizen participation through the vote and in "interest groups." Others have sought more substantive or expansive definitions and understanding, sometimes differentiating liberal, radical, and socialist models of democracy.

Schmitter and Karl (1991) cite Joseph Schumpeter: "Modern political democracy is a system of governance in which rulers are held accountable for their actions in the public realm by citizens and acting indirectly through the competition of their elected representatives." Here control over government decisions about the polity is constitutionally vested in elected officials. Elected officials are chosen in frequent and fairly conducted elections in which coercion is comparatively uncommon. All adults have the right to vote in the election of officials (an exception may include the incarcerated and others) at local and national levels and to run for elective offices in government. Citizens have a right to express themselves on political matters without the danger of punishment and to seek out varied sources of information.

Citizens also have the right to form relatively independent associations or organizations, including independent political parties and interest groups. Popularly elected officials must be able to exercise their constitutional powers without being subjected to overriding opposition from unelected officials; this usually refers to the military but should also be extended to refer to the corporate sector. A democratic polity must be self-governing and it must be able to act independently of constraints imposed by some other overarching political system. Schmitter and Karl (1991) point out that this definition implies a non-interventionist state: it guarantees citizen participation and rights – called "equal opportunities" in the liberal model – without necessarily providing the material means for citizens to enjoy those rights in a more or less equal manner. They also point out that democracies are not necessarily economically more efficient or administratively more efficient.

Historically, paths to democracy have differed and, as Barrington Moore showed, there were varied and divergent paths in the Western world, which evolved slowly and gradually (Moore 1966). For example, in the United States, democracy was enjoyed first by property-owning white males, then extended to all men, and finally to women. In the southern states, blacks remained disenfranchised until well into the second half of the twentieth century, when the civil rights movement and the Civil Rights Act of 1964 ended the Jim Crow laws that prevented American blacks from exercising political rights of citizenship. By that time, most of the world's women had received formal political rights, that is, the right to vote and stand for elections. However, women remained a small proportion of those who enjoyed the benefits of democracy, notably political participation and representation. Moreover, despite political rights, the gap between formal equality (as written in laws) and substantive equality (as enjoyed in practice and expressed in participation and representation) has been large for certain segments of the population, and especially large for women. This is why many feminists demand changes and reforms to expand women's public presence. These include institutional and social reforms such as childcare centers, paid maternity leave and paternity leave, and political reforms such as constitutional or political party quotas. Such reforms are needed to "level the playing field," allow women to catch up to men, and compensate for past marginalization and exclusion. As advocates have noted, women need to be at least a large minority to have an impact. Research and advocacy alike suggest that a benchmark of at least 30 percent is needed before women can make a difference in a legislative body. Research also has found that, in general, the presence of left parties and a proportional representation system are positively related to women's participation in the political system.

In this regard, the *gender* of democracy matters for several reasons. First, as Anne Phillips has explained, women have interests, experiences, values, and expertise that are different from those of men, due principally to their social positions (Phillips 1991, 1995). Thus women should be represented by women. Second, if the "core of democracy" is about the regular redistribution of power through elections, then attention must be paid to the feminist argument that gender is itself a site and source of power, functioning to privilege men over women, and to privilege masculine traits, roles, and values over feminine equivalents in most social domains, as has been argued by Catherine MacKinnon, R. W. Connell, Judith Lorber, and Ruth Lister (Lister 2003), among others. Here power is understood not as an individual trait but in structural terms as deriving from and inhering in social relationships. Third, women's participation and rights are "good" for democracy. There is evidence that women, more precisely employed women, have different political preferences from men, with a tendency to vote in a more leftward direction, in particular supporting public services, with implications for the nature of contemporary welfare states. In other words, with the increase in employed women around the world, social democracy may have a newly emerging champion in working women, as Sylvia Walby has argued. Finally, a high rate of women's political participation and representation may enhance the quality of democracy; that is, a plausible connection may be made between the sustained presence of a "critical mass" of women in political decision-making and the establishment of stable and peaceful societies. If the Nordic model of high rates of women's participation and rights correlates with peaceful, prosperous, and stable societies, could the expansion of women's participation and rights in the Middle East and North Africa also lead the way to stability, security, and welfare in the region, not to mention effective democratic governance? In the United States, if more women were involved as decision-makers in government and in the corporate sector, could the wide income gaps, social inequalities, and oligarchic tendency identified as America's democratic deficits be avoided?

SEE ALSO: Arab Spring Movements; Feminist Theories of the Welfare State; Political Participation in Western Democracies; Women in Development

REFERENCES

Baldez, Lisa. 2003. "Women's Movements and Democratic Transition in Chile, Brazil, East Germany, and Poland." *Comparative Politics*, 35(3): 253–272.

Lister, Ruth. 2003. *Citizenship: Feminist Perspectives*, 2nd ed. London: Macmillan.

Moghadam, Valentine M. 2013. "What is Democracy? Promises and Perils of the Arab Spring." *Current Sociology*, 61(4): 393–408.

Moore, Barrington. 1966. *Social Origins of Dictatorship and Democracy*. Boston: Beacon Press.

Paxton, Pamela, and Melanie Hughes. 2007. *Women, Politics and Power*. Thousand Oaks: Pine Forge Publishers.

Phillips, Anne. 1991. *Engendering Democracy*. University Park: University of Pennsylvania Press.

Phillips, Anne. 1995. *The Politics of Presence: the Political Representation of Gender, Ethnicity and Race*. Oxford: Clarendon Press.

Przeworski, Adam, Michael E. Alvarez, José Antonio Cheibub, and Fernando Limongi. 2000. *Democracy and Development: Political Institutions and Well-Being in the World, 1950–1990*. Cambridge: Cambridge University Press.

Schmitter, Philippe C., and Terry Lynne Karl. 1991. "What Democracy Is … And Is Not." *Journal of Democracy*, 2(3): 75–88.

Waylen, Georgina. 2007. *Engendering Transitions: Women's Mobilizations, Institutions, and Gender Outcomes*. London: Oxford University Press.

Welzel, Christian. 2006. "Democratization as an Emancipative Process." *European Journal of Political Research*, 45: 871–896.

Welzel, Christian, and Ronald Inglehart. 2008. "The Role of Ordinary People in Democratization." *Journal of Democracy*, 19: 126–140.

FURTHER READING

Eschle, Catherine. 2000. *Global Democracy, Social Movements, and Feminism*. Boulder: Westview Press.

Hadenius, Axel, and Jan Teorell. 2005. "Cultural and Economic Prerequisites of Democracy: Reassessing Recent Evidence." *Studies in Comparative International Development*, 39(4): 87–106.

Depression

MICHELLE N. LAFRANCE
St. Thomas University, Canada

Sadness and distress are expectable parts of the human experience and these have been understood and managed in various ways across culture, time, and place (Marecek 2006). Currently in the West, intense periods of sadness are typically labeled as "depression," understood in terms of biomedical illness, and managed with antidepressant medication or psychotherapy. This approach persists despite a lack of evidence that depression is caused by individual pathology and psychiatry's failure to explain how antidepressants "work" other than as placebos (Gardner 2003; Moncrieff and Kirsch 2005).

While the term depression is used colloquially to refer to everything from passing low mood to profound despair, according to the American Psychiatric Association (APA 2013), a diagnosis of depression (formally, "Major Depressive Disorder") requires the experience of five or more of the following "symptoms" over a minimum of a two-week period: depressed mood, loss of interest or pleasure (at least one of these first two symptoms must be present), significant change in weight or appetite, sleep disturbances, psychomotor agitation or retardation, fatigue or loss of energy, feelings of worthlessness or inappropriate guilt, diminished ability to think or concentrate, and suicidal ideation. This diagnosis is one of the most common mental disorders and considered to be a leading cause of disability worldwide (World Health Organization 2008). While depression is relatively common in the general population, certain groups have been identified to be at particular risk. For example, in the West, women have been found to experience depression at a rate two to three times higher than men (Marecek 2006; Ussher 2010; APA 2013). Similarly, high rates of depression are found among racial minority groups (Kirmayer, Brass, and Tait 2000; Plant and Sachs-Ericsson 2004), as well as individuals who are lesbian, gay, bisexual, transgendered, or queer (LGBTQ) (Meyer 2003; King et al. 2008).

The psy disciplines, primarily responsible for treating depression, are dominated by two central ways of understanding. In the first approach, depression is considered a biomedical illness of the brain, produced, for example, by neurochemical dysregulation, functional abnormalities, or genetic inheritance. Within this framework, treatment is focused on the prescription of antidepressant medication. In the second approach, depression is thought to be a product of dysfunctional psychological processes such as maladaptive thinking patterns. Cognitive behavioral therapy (CBT) is a primary approach to treating depression, and its aim is to restructure patients' thoughts and beliefs such that they are more rational and useful. In practice, these two approaches overlap significantly, and a combination of medication and psychotherapy is often recommended.

In contrast to mainstream formulations, feminist and critical scholars regard the individualized notion of "depression" as a cultural category, outlining the ways in which distress is differentially experienced and expressed across historical and cultural locations (Marecek 2006). In doing so, they highlight the social and political context of people's lives including the finding that social injustice reliably predicts depressive experiences (Belle and Doucet 2003). Elevated rates of depression among certain groups are not regarded as indications of individual pathology but of oppression. For instance, poverty, lower social status, childhood sexual abuse, and family violence are all "depressing" experiences that are also significantly more likely to be experienced by women than men (Belle and Doucet 2003). Furthermore, dominant discourses of femininity and the taken-for-granted aspects of women's everyday lives, such as care work and domestic labor, have been elaborated as central to their experiences of depression (Stoppard 2000; Lafrance 2009). Higher rates of depression among black and

Hispanic Americans than white Americans have been accounted for by disproportionate negative experiences including discrimination, inequity, and poverty (Belle and Doucet 2003; Plant and Sachs-Ericsson 2004). Similarly, scholars have pointed to the poisonous effects of colonization, cultural discontinuity, and oppression in accounting for the elevated rates of depression and suicide in some Aboriginal communities (Kirmayer, Brass, and Tait 2000). Rather than look to individualist explanations for heightened risk of depression among LGBTQ individuals, a wealth of research points to the central roles of stigma, prejudice, discrimination, violence, harassment, and family rejection (e.g., Meyer 2003). Thus, it is not one's gender, race, or sexuality that necessarily predicts depression, but the interpersonal, social, and political location in which these intersecting facets of identity are experienced. Not surprisingly, when people are discriminated against, "othered," victimized, and oppressed, they experience distress.

Accordingly, feminist and critical scholars have advocated for the importance of deconstructing the overlapping powers of patriarchy, heterosexism, sexism, and racism. Rather than pathologize people's pain as individual dysfunction and assist them to adapt to oppression, they have pointed to the urgent need for social and political reform. Feminist and critical approaches to intervention aim to support individuals in distress while at the same time mobilizing for social change through, for example, the adoption of anti-poverty efforts, pay equity, national childcare, legalization of gay marriage, and significant reductions in discrimination, violence, bullying, and hate crimes.

SEE ALSO: *Diagnostic and Statistical Manual of Mental Disorders* (DSM), Feminist Critiques of; Feminist Psychotherapy; Psychological Theory, Research, Methodology, and Feminist Critiques

REFERENCES

American Psychiatric Association (APA). 2013. *Diagnostic and Statistical Manual of Mental Disorders*, 5th ed. Washington, DC: American Psychiatric Association.

Belle, Deborah, and Joanne Doucet. 2003. "Poverty, Inequality, and Discrimination as Sources of Depression among US Women." *Psychology of Women Quarterly*, 27: 101–113.

Gardner, Paula. 2003. "Distorted Packaging: Marketing Depression as Illness, Drugs as Cure." *Journal of Medical Humanities*, 24(1–2): 105–130.

King, Michael, Joanna Semlyen, Sharon See Tai, Helen Killaspy, David Osborn, Dmitri Popelyuk, and Irwin Nazareth. 2008. "A Systematic Review of Mental Disorders, Suicide, and Deliberate Self Harm in Lesbian, Gay and Bisexual People." *BMC Psychiatry*, 8: 70. DOI: 10.1186/1471-244X-8-70.

Kirmayer, Laurence, Gregory Brass, and Caroline Tait. 2000. "The Mental Health of Aboriginal Peoples: Transformations of Identity and Community." *Canadian Journal of Psychiatry*, 45: 607–616.

Lafrance, Michelle. 2009. *Women and Depression: Recovery and Resistance*. London: Routledge.

Marecek, Jeanne. 2006. "Social Suffering, Gender, and Women's Depression." In *Women and Depression: A Handbook for the Social, Behavioral and Biomedical Sciences*, edited by Corey Keyes and Sherryl Goodman, 283–308. Cambridge: Cambridge University Press.

Meyer, Ilan. 2003. "Prejudice, Social Stress, and Mental Health in Lesbian, Gay, and Bisexual Populations: Conceptual Issues and Research Evidence." *Psychological Bulletin*, 129(5): 674–697. DOI: 10.1037/0033-2909.129.5.674.

Moncrieff, Joanna, and Irving Kirsch. 2005. "Efficacy of Antidepressants in Adults." *British Medical Journal*, 331: 155–157.

Plant, Ashby, and Natalie Sachs-Ericsson. 2004. "Racial and Ethnic Differences in Depression: The Roles of Social Support and Meeting Basic Needs." *Journal of Consulting and Clinical Psychology*, 72(1): 41–52. DOI: 10.1037/0022-006X.72.1.41.

Stoppard, Janet. 2000. *Understanding Depression: Feminist Social Constructionist Approaches*. London: Routledge.

Ussher, Jane. 2010. "Are We Medicalizing Women's Misery? A Critical Review of Women's Higher Rates of Reported Depression." *Feminism & Psychology*, 20(1): 9–35.

World Health Organization (WHO). 2008. *The Global Burden of Disease 2004 Update*. Geneva: World Health Organization.

Desexualization

PATTI GIUFFRE
Texas State University, USA

COURTNEY CAVINESS
University of California, Davis, USA

Desexualization is the process by which sexuality is extracted from an identity (or presentation of self), interaction, setting, or discourse. Application of the term is contextual, and its meaning varies based on who does the desexualizing, who (or what behavior) is desexualized, and why the desexualization occurs. Individuals can desexualize themselves through how they dress or behave. Cultures, governments, and workplaces can desexualize via laws, policies, and norms. This entry describes the meanings and consequences of desexualization in three areas of research: workplaces, rape, and sex education.

There are several debates about desexualization in workplaces. Concerns over sexual harassment litigation prompted employers in the United States to attempt to desexualize workplaces. In the early 1990s, Anita Hill accused Supreme Court nominee, Clarence Thomas, of sexual harassment while they were both employed at the Equal Employment Opportunity Commission. This case contributed to a media frenzy in which commentators lamented that workers could not even joke in the workplace anymore, and that women were overly sensitive. Employers grew concerned about an increase in litigation and, consequently, many passed strict policies in their businesses. In some workplaces, workers were not permitted to touch each other or tell sexual jokes. To desexualize meant to remove all forms of sexuality and decrease possibilities of sexual harassment.

Scholars have criticized such efforts to desexualize the workplace. Schultz (2003) and Williams (1998) argue that the emphasis should not be on removing sexuality from workplaces, but instead on eradicating harassment that is exploitative. Commentators outside the United States have also been perplexed by efforts to desexualize workplaces. European onlookers have wondered what the fuss is about. Saguy's (2003) research compares how sexual harassment is understood differently in French and American contexts. By French cultural standards, sexuality is a natural part of life, and thus removing it from interactions is impossible.

Workers themselves may wish to remove sexual undertones from their interactions. Dellinger (2002) found that some women editors of men's pornographic magazines, for example, desexualize their presentation of self to avoid sexism, sexual harassment, or allegations that they use their sexuality to move up the career ladder. Desexualization in this context is gendered: Men wear business attire, but not to desexualize their appearance or avoid harassment.

Some workers must attempt to desexualize their interactions with customers, clients, patients, or students. For example, healthcare providers desexualize their interactions with patients to assure the patients that they are examining them for medical reasons only. Giuffre and Williams (2000) found that doctors and nurses were careful about what they said during physical examinations of patients. Men and women differed in how they desexualized examinations. In some cases, men had a chaperone present for their own comfort, while women had chaperones in the examining room to protect themselves from male patients' harassment.

Attempts to desexualize workplace interactions have more negative consequences for groups stereotyped as overtly sexual, and have the impact of bolstering heteronormativity. Gay and lesbian workers may never be desexualized, and may in fact be "hypersexualized." Williams, Giuffre, and Dellinger (2009) find that gay and lesbian workers downplay their sexual identities and relationships at work to be accepted or promoted, or to discourage prejudice and discrimination. Calhoun (1993) writes that to desexualize is to erase and make invisible non-heterosexual sexual identities.

Debates about desexualization have also been explored in the context of rape. Feminists have debated whether rape is a crime of violence, sex and sexuality, or power. Brownmiller (1975), for example, desexualized rape to highlight the violence and power of it. She argued that rape and sex are not the same because rape involves dominance, power, and lack of consent. Cahill (2000) is concerned about the consequences of desexualizing rape because doing so reinforces a sexual hierarchy that violently maintains men's dominance over women. Thus, to remove sex from our understanding of rape obscures the influence rape (and the fear of rape) has on how women dress and behave every day.

Finally, research on sex education highlights how some parents desexualize their own teenagers. Elliott (2012) finds that American parents prefer to think of their own children as pure, asexual, and naïve. In contrast, Schalet (2011) finds that Dutch parents see adolescent sexuality as natural. Parents in the Netherlands do not try to desexualize their children, but instead encourage open discussions about sexuality.

There are many consequences of desexualization. Desexualization can be used to erase, ignore, or deemphasize sexuality. In some contexts, it may help employees function in their workplaces. Yet, desexualization varies along gender lines, and can have deleterious consequences for groups who are stereotyped as hypersexual. Future research should examine how experiences of, and expectations for, desexualization might differ by race, sexual orientation, gender, and class.

SEE ALSO: Gender Neutral; Hostile Work Environment in the United States; Rape Culture; Sexual Assault/Sexual Violence; Sexual Minorities; Sexualities

REFERENCES

Brownmiller, Susan. 1975. *Against Our Will: Men, Women, and Rape.* New York: Simon and Schuster.

Cahill, Ann J. 2000. "Foucault, Rape, and the Construction of the Feminine Body." *Hypatia*, 15(1): 43–63.

Calhoun, Cheshire. 1993. "Denaturalizing and Desexualizing Lesbian and Gay Identity." *Virginia Law Review*, 17(7): 1859–1875.

Dellinger, Kirsten. 2002. "Wearing Gender and Sexuality 'on Your Sleeve': Dress Norms and the Importance of Occupational and Organizational Culture at Work." *Gender Issues*, 20(1): 3–25.

Elliott, Sinikka. 2012. *Not My Kid: What Parents Believe about the Sex Lives of Their Teenagers.* New York: New York University Press.

Giuffre, Patti A., and Christine L. Williams. 2000. "'Not Just Bodies': Strategies for Desexualizing the Physical Examination of Patients." *Gender & Society*, 14: 457–482.

Saguy, Abigail. 2003. *What is Sexual Harassment?: From Capitol Hill to the Sorbonne.* Berkeley: University of California Press.

Schalet, Amy. 2011. *Not Under My Roof: Parents, Teens, and the Culture of Sex.* Chicago: University of Chicago Press.

Schultz, Vicki. 2003. "The Sanitized Workplace." *The Yale Law Journal*, 112: 2061–2193.

Williams, Christine L. 1998. "Sexual Harassment in Organizations: A Critique of Current Research and Policy." *Sexuality & Culture*, 1: 19–43.

Williams, Christine, Patti Giuffre, and Kirsten Dellinger. 2009. "The Gay-Friendly Closet." *Sexuality Research and Social Policy*, 6: 29–45.

FURTHER READING

Crouch, Margaret A. 2001. *Thinking about Sexual Harassment: A Guide for the Perplexed*. New York: Oxford University Press.

Fields, Jessica. 2008. *Risky Lessons: Sex Education and Social Inequality*. New Brunswick, NJ: Rutgers University Press.

Rumens, Nick, and Deborah Kerfoot. 2009. "Gay Men at Work: (Re) Constructing the Self as Professional." *Human Relations*, 62: 763–786.

Zippel, Kathrin. 2006. *The Politics of Sexual Harassment: A Comparative Study of the United States, the European Union and Germany*. Cambridge: Cambridge University Press.

Diagnostic and Statistical Manual of Mental Disorders (DSM), Feminist Critiques of

EMILY E. WHEELER and ELENA KOSTERINA
University of Massachusetts Boston, USA

LISA COSGROVE
University of Massachusetts Boston and Harvard University, USA

The *Diagnostic and Statistical Manual of Mental Disorders* (DSM), the mental health diagnostic manual published by the American Psychiatric Association, is now the reigning standard of US psychiatric nosology. Because of its congruence with the *International Classification of Diseases and Related Health Problems* (ICD), the diagnostic system developed by the World Health Organization and used by over two dozen countries, the DSM has a profound international impact as well. It is frequently referred to as the "bible" of psychiatry; it is the most widely used diagnostic system in the mental health fields in the United States and plays a central role in health and disability claims and in forensic settings. This manual is also integral in sustaining the multibillion dollar psychopharmacology drug market and is used in clinical trials around the world. Each successive edition of the DSM (the first in 1952, the second in 1968, the third in 1980, the fourth in 1994, and the fifth in 2013) has marked the expansion of mental disorders and clinical entities. Historically, women have been overrepresented in many diagnostic categories, rendering the DSM a steady subject of feminist criticism. Early critiques addressed issues of gender bias that arose from the psychoanalytic approach of the DSM's first two editions, such as labeling as pathological traits that are considered more traditionally feminine.

Feminists have also offered compelling critiques of specific diagnoses such as depression, late luteal phase dysphoric disorder, female sexual dysfunction, and histrionic, dependent, and borderline personality disorders. However, feminist scholars have contributed most uniquely to an analysis of the biopsychiatric discourse that has grounded the DSM since the publication of the third edition. (For salient examples from this body of literature, see Ussher 1992; Hare-Mustin and Marecek 1997; Tiefer 2004; Cosgrove and Wheeler 2013.) These authors have questioned the DSM's claims of value neutrality and its biological reductionism. Biological reductionism refers to the attempt to reduce explanations of distress to biological processes, locating the cause and cure of emotional distress within the body of the individual and not in relational and contextual realms.

More recently, feminists have analyzed and challenged the pharmaceutical industry's role in expanding diagnostic boundaries. These critiques have focused on the ways in which the DSM has played handmaiden to industry because of its "diagnosis by checklist" approach. Additionally, scholars have cautioned that industry relationships on the part of DSM panel members (i.e., individuals charged with decision-making responsibility for the inclusion of new diagnoses) create subtle but powerful pro-pharma ways of thinking and reinforce the hegemony of the medical model. Organized psychiatry's financial dependence on industry is a major factor in the commercialization of the DSM, which marginalizes feminist and other critical approaches to understanding emotional distress. From this view, the needs of certain stakeholders (e.g., the pharmaceutical industry) are privileged over others (e.g., patients) in terms of how experience is understood and how distress is conceptualized and treated.

One example of a DSM diagnosis that has captured the attention of feminists in this way is premenstrual dysphoric disorder. The American Psychiatric Association (APA) maintains that the mood-related distress in women that is captured by this diagnosis is caused by variations in hormones as a result of the menstrual cycle. Researchers have noted the lack of empirical evidence for the validity of this diagnosis as a distinct "mental disorder" and have shown that this biological conceptualization of women's distress serves commercial interests. For example, Caplan (2004) described how Eli Lilly was able to extend its patent and sustain its multibillion dollar profits for its antidepressant Prozac by repackaging it as Sarafem, a treatment approved for premenstrual dysphoric disorder more than a decade before it became an official diagnosis in the DSM's fifth edition.

Despite the lack of biological markers for any DSM disorders, the APA adopts a neurobiological framework. As a result, the larger sociopolitical context is ignored and women's experiences are pathologized – refashioned as mental disorders requiring treatment. In turn this positions practitioners and researchers in the "expert" role, determining normality and failing to fully appreciate the diversity and individuality of lived experiences of those who receive diagnoses. For example, the DSM diagnosis of agoraphobia shows how the biopsychiatric discourse and disease model gloss gendered power dynamics and fail to consider the hostile social environment as a contributor to women's fear of or anxiety about public places. Similarly, many feminist authors have noted the DSM's blindness to abusive environments as a primary cause of somatization, or expression of psychological distress in the form of physical symptoms, in women.

The absence of a genuine multicultural perspective and the concomitant failure of the DSM's authors to acknowledge the limited international applicability of many of its categories also have been a focus of concern. Non-Western feminist critiques of the DSM have addressed the lack of applicability of particular diagnostic categories such as eating disorders (e.g., Katzman and Lee 1997). Researchers and clinicians have argued that the manual has incorporated a Western or, even more narrowly, a US-centric, white, middle-class cultural understanding of mental health and illness. Critics have emphasized the lack of attention to experiences of women of color, women of various ethnic backgrounds, and lack of sensitivity to intersections of cultural and gendered experiences in DSM diagnoses (Eriksen and Kress 2005). Although each revision of the DSM is marketed as having a greater multicultural focus and international sensitivity, the APA neither acknowledges the cultural boundedness of many of its diagnoses nor presents adequate guidance for practitioners on how to use this system with diverse clientele.

Criticism of the DSM nosology within feminist psychology has increased with the publication of the fifth edition, and concerns about the lack of reliability and validity of many DSM diagnoses have also been voiced in the news media and by chairs of its earlier editions. In response to their critical analyses of the existing system, feminists have proposed alternative diagnostic categories and classification and assessment systems (e.g., Brown and Ballou 1992). These alternative conceptualizations and modifications draw upon feminist theories, with increased attention to contexts and to clients' experiences and perspectives.

SEE ALSO: Eating Disorders and Disordered Eating; Feminism and Psychoanalysis; Feminist Psychotherapy; Feminist Studies of Science; Feminist Theories of Experience; Feminist Theories of the Body; Gender Bias in Research; Masculinity and Femininity, Theories of; Medicine and Medicalization; Psychological Theory, Research, Methodology, and Feminist Critiques

REFERENCES

Brown, Laura S., and Mary Ballou, eds. 1992. *Personality and Psychopathology: Feminist Reappraisals*. New York: Guilford Press.

Caplan, Paula. 2004. "The Debate about PMDD and Sarafem: Suggestions for Therapists." *Women & Therapy*, 27: 55–67. DOI: 10.1300/J015v27n03_05.

Cosgrove, Lisa, and Emily E. Wheeler. 2013. "Industry's Colonization of Psychiatry: Ethical and Practical Implications of Financial Conflicts of Interest in the *DSM-V*." *Feminism & Psychology*, 23(1): 93–106. DOI: 10.1177/0959353512467972.

Eriksen, Karen, and Victoria E. Kress. 2005. *Beyond the DSM Story: Ethical Quandaries, Challenges and Best Practices*. Thousand Oaks: Sage.

Hare-Mustin, Rachel T., and Jeanne Marecek. 1997. "Abnormal and Clinical Psychology: The Politics of Madness." In *Critical Psychology: An Introduction*, edited by Dennis R. Fox and Isaac Prilleltensky, 104–120. Thousand Oaks: Sage.

Katzman, Melanie A., and Sing Lee. 1997. "Beyond Body Image: The Integration of Feminist and Transcultural Theories in the Understanding of Self Starvation." *International Journal of Eating Disorders*, 22(4): 385–394. DOI: 10.1002/(SICI)1098-108X(199712)22:4<385::AID-EAT3>3.0.CO;2-I.

Tiefer, Lenore. 2004. *Sex is not a Natural Act, and Other Essays*, 2nd ed. Boulder: Westview Press.

Ussher, Jane M. 1992. *Women's Madness: Misogyny or Mental Illness?* Amherst: University of Massachusetts Press.

FURTHER READING

Caplan, Paula J., and Lisa Cosgrove, eds. 2004. *Bias in Psychiatric Diagnosis*. Lanham, MD: Jason Aronson.

Hirshbein, L. D. 2006. "Science, Gender, and the Emergence of Depression in American Psychiatry, 1952–1980." *Journal of the History of Medicine and Allied Sciences*, 61(2): 187–216.

Marecek, Jeanne, and Nicola Gavey, eds. 2013. "*DSM*-5 and Beyond: A Critical Engagement with Psychodiagnosis" (Special Issue). *Feminism & Psychology*, 23(1).

Dieting

ALYSSA J. MATTEUCCI
University of Pennsylvania, USA
MICHAEL LOWE
Drexel University, Philadelphia, USA

An upsurge in dieting in Western countries was spurred by a historical shift in the idealization of thinness and the emergence of the obesity epidemic that occurred in the last quarter of the twentieth century (Popkin and Doak 1998). Since the 1960s, Americans began experiencing steady weight gains, culminating in what we now know as the "obesity epidemic." This development spawned investigations on how to better manage this increase in body mass, and, more specifically, the environmental and genetic factors that contributed to the etiology of obesity (Popkin and Doak 1998). As more and more people experienced increases in weight, substantial weight control strategies (such as dieting) became commonplace. Additionally, Western societal preference for a thin physique produced a corresponding preoccupation with dieting. The extent of this fixation is such that it may now be accurate to regard dieting as normative in some cultures (Polivy and Herman 1987). Factors central to the development of dieting behavior include sociocultural influences and developmental processes (Birch and Fisher 1997). These variables affect those of different gender and sexual orientations in diverse ways and these differences can be instrumental in the formation of dieting behavior (Connor, Johnson, and Grogan 2004). For example, mood factors have an active and influential role in determining which types of food women consume (Steptoe, Pollard, and Wardle 1995) and due to societal norms, the gay male subculture is particularly associated with greater appearance emphasis (Connor, Johnson, and Grogan 2004).

The impact of the shift in idealized shape was exemplified by the pervasiveness of dieting among women, specifically. The thin ideal is nearly impossible to attain healthily and contributes to the high levels of dissatisfaction, fueling desires to diet to lose weight. From early childhood, girls learn from various agents of socialization that appearance, more specifically thinness, is a primary way of obtaining and maintaining self-esteem and sexual appeal (Friedan 1963). Emphasis on the thin ideal continues through adolescence and into adulthood. Women are confronted with key transitional periods (i.e., puberty, pregnancy) that are associated with weight gain (Peat, Peyerl, and Muehlenkamp 2008). These periods have been found to leave women at increased risk for the development of body image concerns and dieting efforts.

Local mass media messages, the entertainment industry, and the Internet act as some of the strongest transmitters of the pressure to conform to the thin ideal of feminine beauty, especially among middle-class and affluent communities. As the preference for the thin physique became more entrenched, the media promulgated information on how to achieve a lean body type, mainly by means of weight-reducing diets. Between 1960 and 1980, the number of diet articles in women's magazines increased dramatically in the United States, and have been accused of leading the charge in disseminating the thin ideal. Conforming to new societal norms, *Playboy* centerfolds and Miss America contestants became increasingly thinner during this time period, reinforcing that thinness is a critical component of attractiveness (Silverstein et al. 1986). Exposure to media body ideals have contributed to the belief that women are uniquely subject to experiences where the female body is treated as an object valued for its use to others, otherwise known as self-objectification. Many studies have found associations between self-objectification and the inclination to change body weight (Calogero, Tantleff-Dunn, and Thompson 2010). An intersectional approach reveals that not all women are affected in the same way. For example, compared with elderly white women in the United States, elderly black women were found to feel less guilty about overeating, be less likely to diet, far more likely to be satisfied with their weight, and far more likely to consider themselves attractive (Stevens, Kumanyika, and Keil 1994).

Although an extensive amount of research has been conducted in heterosexual female samples, much less work has been conducted on dieting in male and homosexual populations. Aside from Keys et al.'s (1950) famous dieting study with "normal" weight men, few studies could be located examining dieting in male samples. It has been suggested that the primary reason why males may develop preoccupation with their bodies is due to societal pressure to achieve muscularity. The research that has been conducted on homosexuality and dieting suggests that gender is a more salient factor in influencing dieting than sexual orientation, with both lesbians and heterosexual women reporting greater frequency of dieting than gay or heterosexual men (Connor, Johnson, and Grogan 2004). Lesbians and heterosexual women are influenced by cultural pressures to be thin, but these pressures may be greater for heterosexual women (Connor, Johnson, and Grogan 2004). Gay men, compared with heterosexual men, are more likely to be weight conscious.

Scholarship on non-Western populations reveal many of the same patterns around dieting that emerge in Western contexts. The 1990s saw a large increase in dieting behaviors among high school girls in Israel, similar to those reported in Western countries (Neumark-Sztainer 1995), and the same trend towards young women desiring to be thin emerged in Kuwait (Kabir, Zafar, and Waslien 2013). Globalization has led to an increase in influence from Western corporations, which have spread the "never too thin" body ideal to non-Western societies (Talukdar 2012). However, a cross-cultural study found that although Korean women were less satisfied with their bodies, US women were more likely to diet (Jung and Lee 2006).

It is likely that dieting behaviors will vary between individuals across cultural contexts, and that gender and sexual orientation will have a role in that relationship; however, additional research is warranted to fully understand these relationships.

SEE ALSO: Body Politics; Eating Disorders and Disordered Eating

REFERENCES

Birch, Leann L., and Jennifer O. Fisher. 1997. "Development of Eating Behaviors Among Children and Adolescents." *Pediatrics*, 101: 539–549.

Calogero, Rachel, Stacey Tantleff-Dunn, and Kevin Thompson. 2010. *Self-objectification in Women: Causes, Consequences, and Counteractions*. Washington, DC: American Psychological Association.

Connor, Mark, Charlotte Johnson, and Sarah Grogan. 2004. "Gender, Sexuality, Body Image, and Eating Behaviors." *Journal of Health Psychology*, 9: 505. DOI: 10.1177/1359105304044034.

Friedan, Betty. 1963. *The Feminine Mystique*. New York: W.W. Norton.

Jung, Jaehee, and Seung-Hee Lee. 2006. "Cross-Cultural Comparisons of Appearance Self-Schema, Body Image, Self-Esteem, and Dieting Behavior Between Korean and U.S. Women." *Family and Consumer Sciences Research Journal*, 34(4): 350–365. DOI: 10.1177/1077727X06286419.

Kabir, Yearul, Tasleem Zafar, and Carol Waslien. 2013. "Relationship Between Perceived Body Image and Recorded Body Mass Index Among Kuwaiti Female University Students." *Women and Health*, 53(7): 693–706. DOI: 10.1080/03630242.2013.831017.

Keys, Ancel, Josef Brozek, Austin Henschel, Olaf Mickelsen, and Henry Longstreet Taylor. 1950. *The Biology of Human Starvation*, 2 vols. Minneapolis: University of Minnesota Press.

Neumark-Sztainer, Dianne. 1995. "Weight Concerns and Dieting Behaviors Among High School Girls in Israel." *Journal of Adolescent Health*, 16(1): 53–59. DOI: 10.1016/1054-139X(94)00046-H.

Peat, Christine, Naomi Peyerl, and Jennifer Muehlenkamp. 2008. "Body Image and Eating Disorders in Older Adults: A Review." *Journal of General Psychology*, 135: 343–358. DOI: 10.3200/GENP.135.4.343-358.

Polivy, Janet, and Peter C. Herman. 1987. "Diagnosis and Treatment of Normal Eating." *Journal of Consulting Psychology*, 55: 635–644.

Popkin, Barry M., and Colleen M. Doak. 1998. "The Obesity Epidemic is a Worldwide Phenomenon." *Nutrition Reviews*, 56: 106–114.

Silverstein, Brett, Lauren Perdue, Barbara Peterson, and Eileen Kelly. 1986. "The Role of the Mass Media in Promoting a Thin Standard of Bodily Attractiveness for Women." *Sex Roles*, 14: 519–532.

Steptoe, Andrew, Tessa M. Pollard, and Jane Wardle. 1995. "Development of a Measure of the Motives Underlying the Selection of Food:

The Food Choice Questionnaire." *Appetite*, 25: 267–284.
Stevens, June, Shiriki K. Kumanyika, and Julian E. Keil. 1994. "Attitudes Toward Body Size and Dieting: Differences between Elderly Black and White Women." *American Journal of Public Health*, 84(8): 1322–1325.
Talukdar, Jaita. 2012. "Thin But Not Skinny: Women Negotiating the 'Never Too Thin' Body Ideal in Urban India." *Women's Studies International Forum*, 35(2): 109–119. DOI: 10.1016/j.wsif.2012.03.002.

FURTHER READING

Calogero, Rachel M., and Kevin J. Thompson. 2010. "Gender and Body Image." In *Handbook of Gender Research in Psychology*, edited by Joan C. Chrisler and Donald R. McCreary, 153–184. New York: Springer.

Digital Divide

B. PAIGE MILLER
University of Wisconsin–River Falls, USA

CLAIRE M. NORRIS
Xavier University of Louisiana, USA

The digital divide, a term first coined in the latter part of the twentieth century, is a multidimensional concept used to describe the socially unequal access to and use of information and communication technology (ICT) in terms of both infrastructure and literacy (Selwyn 2004). While the question of what constitutes ICT is often overlooked, the term generally encompasses computers, the Internet, email, and increasingly mobile phones, digital broadcast technologies, and high-speed web connections. Because digital inequalities tend to reflect socioeconomic, demographic, and spatial inequalities, they have the potential to both reproduce existing social, political, and economic divides and create new ones. For this reason, digital divides are seen as important by academics and policymakers alike, not because access to and use of technology is inherently beneficial, but because closing them possesses a number of broader implications.

The digital divide is typically assessed along three dimensions: (1) access to and use of technology; (2) perceived skills/abilities and motivation/willingness to use a particular technology; and (3) ability to use a technology in a way that might be socially, economically, or politically empowering.

Early research on the digital divide concerned itself primarily with the first dimension and examined adoption of new technologies, primarily computers and the Internet, along a simple dichotomy of access versus non-access, adopters versus non-adopters. Based on this characterization of the spread of computers and the Internet, empirical evidence indicated that early on women, members of racial minority groups, older individuals, those from poorer socio-economic backgrounds, and those living in rural or low-income areas were less likely to be online.

Around the turn of the twenty-first century, digital divide research began to focus more on the latter two dimensions for a number of reasons. First, over the last approximately 10 years, access to ICTs, at least on some measures, increased dramatically. To take just one example, within the United States the gender gap in access to the Internet has largely disappeared. While men may, on average, be earlier adopters of ICTs, women now report approximately equal access to the Internet and both are equally likely to identify as users of the technology (Chen and Wellman 2004). Although this is particularly true in more industrialized countries, there have also been significant increases in low-income areas as well.

Second, the original conception of the digital divide had a number of weaknesses; chief among them is the notion that the divide can be defined as a simple dichotomy of the technological haves and the technological have-nots. From this perspective, it is assumed that once women and other "marginalized" groups gain equal access to online information and communication tools, economic independence, political empowerment, and active social engagement will naturally follow. Empirical and theoretical accounts, however, have highlighted the need to avoid linear and normatively grounded discussions of the relationship between technologies and a variety of economic, political, and social outcomes. The ability to *use* access in a way that is beneficial, in other words, does not follow naturally from simply having an Internet connection or a smartphone. Instead, those with low skill, low motivation, and few resources to use a technology are unlikely to define themselves as having access in the first place or to benefit from use. While the percentage of men and women reporting access to a variety of ICTs may be approximately equal, women also tend to perceive themselves as less skilled users and they tend to possess less positive attitudes toward the Internet and computers than men, a finding that emerges in the United States and Britain as well as China.

As such, it is important to distinguish not only between access to and use of ICT, but also between use of ICT and *meaningful* use of ICT, with the latter measure consisting of various arenas of social participation including: production activity (activity that is economically valued), social activity (interacting and communicating with family and friends), political activity (collective efforts to improve one's environment), consumption activity (purchasing of goods and/or services), savings activity (pensions, entitlements, or income savings), and recreational activity. When the arenas of participation are examined, women tend to use the Internet more for social and consumption activities, while men tend to participate more in online political and recreational activities. Given these issues, a more accurate depiction of the digital divide is of a technological continuum ranging from those with no access, low skill, and little motivation to those who are the most frequent, intense, and skilled users. Because of the variability between these two extremes, assessments of the "digital divide" have moved to examining quality of access, the variability and breadth of use, technological skills, and consequences of use. The digital divide, in other words, is now conceived less as a dichotomy and more in terms of gradations of inclusion, which are mapped along the intersections of gender, race/ethnicity, age, education, socioeconomic class, and geography, i.e., rural versus urban and industrialized versus low-income countries.

While explanations for why these inequalities exist are varied, some of the most fruitful areas of analysis stem from the social construction of technology (SCOT) perspective. Broadly, this perspective argues that, far from being neutral tools, technologies are a product of the culture and social context in which they are developed and used. Individuals whose cultural, political, and economic orientations resemble those of a particular ICT are better equipped to use, and benefit from, that innovation. As such, the social inequalities and power relationships that exist at any given moment or in any given space shape, and are shaped by, access to and uses of ICT. To the extent that men and women are socialized differently and unequally, offline gender roles, responsibilities, and opportunities influence online behavior and any corresponding benefits.

While disentangling the factors shaping the digital divide has proven to be challenging, some of the richest areas of research are those highlighting the socially embedded nature of technology and the way technology is both shaped by social processes – economic, racial, and gendered – and also shapes those processes. Moving forward, it is critical to keep such factors at the core of the theoretical and empirical questions asked. Indeed, technologies can come to embody different values through social action or alternative uses, but understanding what shapes this process is limited by overly deterministic conceptualizations of the relationship between technology and a variety of social outcomes.

SEE ALSO: Feminist Design in Computing; Information Technology; Internet and Gender

REFERENCES

Chen, Wenhong, and Barry Wellman. 2004. "The Global Digital Divide: Within and Between Countries." *IT & Society*, 1: 18–25.

Selwyn, Neil. 2004. "Reconsidering Political and Popular Understandings of the Digital Divide." *New Media & Society*, 6: 341–362. DOI: 10.1177/1461444804042519.

FURTHER READING

Tsatsou, Panayiota. 2011. "Digital Divides Revisited: What is New About Divides and their Research?" *Media Culture Society*, 33: 317–331. DOI: 10.1177/0163443710393865.

Digital Media and Gender

AKANE KANAI
Monash University, Melbourne, Australia

AMY DOBSON
University of Queensland, Australia

The study of gender and digital media encompasses interdisciplinary scholarship that seeks to understand gendered engagements with digital media, how digital media spaces become gendered, and how gendered practices change through digital media. The construction of gendered identities, and play and experimentation with gender identities in digital media spaces, was the focus of some key early research in this area. Inspired by the work of Erving Goffman, much scholarship on gender and digital or "new" media has focused on symbolic interactionist accounts of how gender is presented. Youth, women, and girls in the West have been a major focus of research in gender and digital media, while older femininities, masculinities, gender diversity, and accounts of the interaction between race, globalization, and gender remain under-researched areas.

The second wave of feminist activism in the 1970s brought much attention to representations of women in Western broadcast media, and how gender representation contributed to sexual inequalities. Feminist scholars documented how women were represented in limited roles in broadcast media, as housewives, mothers, and sex objects. Further, women have historically been positioned as consumers of media, rather than producers. With increasingly widespread availability of the Internet and the growth of digital media technologies, many girls and women are now able to produce and distribute media themselves more easily. Scholars have thus reconsidered approaches to gender and media that characterize women as typically marginalized by and in media representations, and have looked towards digital media as a source of empowerment through media representations, practices, social connection, and activism.

Scholars have also considered the ways in which gender itself, as a performative construct produced via embodied social interactions, can be challenged in spaces of digital interaction (Turkle 1995; Haraway 2000). But feminist scholars remain cautious about the claim that gender as an embodied experience can be meaningfully "overcome" or disrupted via digital communication (Herring and Stoerger 2014). Herring and Stoerger (2014) note there are differences between men's and women's normative forms of computer-mediated communication which have remained stable over the last 20 years.

However, postcolonial scholars suggest that simply concentrating on "women's" engagement masks other forms of identity and oppression, based on reproduction of Global North and South power dynamics online (Gajjala, Zhang, and Dako-Gyeke 2010). Many feminist scholars remain cautious about the extent to which digital technologies have driven women's empowerment globally. While mobility and social transformation are often associated in popular conceptions of the Internet, research indicates that mobile digital technologies can reproduce existing gendered practices. For example, Lim and Soon (2010) note that mobile technologies in South Korea and China provide mothers with tools to extend and intensify mothering practices of monitoring, scheduling, and caring. In a media landscape where the lines between media producers and consumers have been blurred, and interactivity and participation is encouraged in users as a corporate profit strategy, scholars have argued for renewed, nuanced understandings of power, coercion, cultural influence, and exploitation in digital media cultures. The importance of understanding diversity among users has also been noted, and a growing number of analyses consider how race, class, sexuality, and geographic location, along with gender, impact access to and experience of using digital media (O'Riordan and Phillips 2007; Nakamura 2008; Gajjala, Zhang, and Dako-Gyeke 2010).

Early American studies on multi-user domains (MUDs) and object-oriented multi-user domains (MOOs) were among the first to explore gender identity in digital media cultures. These social chatroom-type spaces mainly operated on the basis of anonymity, and were not openly accessible, but usually dominated by middle-class educated men with significant levels of technical knowledge.

Accordingly, these spaces occupied a certain subcultural status. Such sites were popular in the 1990s, when use of the Internet was not yet mainstreamed. Exemplified by the work of Sherry Turkle (1995), scholars explored the possibilities of anonymous, textual interaction for free and fluid identity performance and experimentation. While Turkle's work was subsequently critiqued as overly stressing the voluntary nature of identity, Turkle's vision reflected dominant social ideas about the possibilities of digital communication via the types of popular online forums in this period. Relatedly, Donna Haraway (2000) considered the potential freedoms of the computer as a prosthetic device to eradicate gender, human/animal, and human/machine distinctions through a combined machine/cyborg identity.

Since the 1990s, the Internet has become an everyday tool for wider sections of the population in developed nations and is also growing in accessibility in many developing nations. Accordingly, research investigating gendered Internet use spans a range of online environments and activities such as homepage creation, web design, blogging, vlogging, webcam culture, instant messaging, games, forums, as well as social network sites (SNSs). SNSs, in particular, exemplify how Internet use has expanded to become an everyday social practice often attached to offline social identities. In contrast to the primarily male spaces of MUDs and MOOs of the 1990s, SNSs are widely used among young people and teenagers with regular access to the Internet, and it appears that women and girls are an active demographic of users. Thus, research into SNSs has particularly centered on youth, and often girls', practices.

Scholarship on girls' digital media use has foregrounded the potential of the Internet as a safe space for girls and young women to express themselves creatively, sometimes in ways that experiment with or resist gendered identities and feminine norms. Much of this research counteracts popular media panics which position the Internet as dangerous for girls, in line with broader narratives of danger for women inhabiting public spaces. Research has pointed to the possibilities of blogging, vlogging, and SNSs as media practices that allow girls and young women to express themselves freely, and suggests that via digital media girls can share experiences and learn from each other in ways that might not be possible in offline social interaction.

However, with the growth of social media, a notable shift has occurred from conceiving digital media as spaces of potential gender exploration and freedom, to spaces where identity, including gender, is more tightly regulated and policed. Scholars increasingly contest a neat distinction between the online and offline realms and, accordingly, have raised concerns about how gender and sexual identity is increasingly *fixed* via more "anonymous" digital media use. In this move to the quotidian integration of social media into people's lives, conventions have developed around social media infrastructures that tie bodies, images of bodies, and offline identities and social networks to online social media profiles. Facebook, one of the most popular and widely used SNSs, is one example which calls for the consistent, unified and coherent self to be presented to a wide audience of friends, peers, colleagues, family, and sometimes strangers. Only one profile is permitted per user, meaning that multiple offline social contexts are "collapsed" into one online. This has been experienced as coercive, with many transgender and gender-queer Facebook users shutting down their profiles in response to Facebook's "real name only" policy in 2014, and Facebook subsequently issuing an apology. The impact of "context collapse" on individuals with non-heteronormative gender and sexual identities is increasingly a topic of concern.

Some scholars have suggested that social media infrastructures set up intense and persistent forms of surveillance, both by peers and by unknown Internet audiences, including companies seeking to track consumer data. Banet-Weiser (2012), for example, suggests that social media creates a context where users are encouraged to work continually on the presentation of self for others. In personal SNS profiles, blogs, and platforms like Twitter and YouTube, women's digital identities are observed as increasingly *branded*, and often sexualized and gender normative, as such self-branding is thought to generate both social and material capital for girls and women (Banet-Weiser 2012). This is also reflected in the growth of commercial lifestyle blogs run by women, where a mixture of the personal and the commercial is blogged for an income. This is far from an exclusively Western phenomenon, with digital blogging agencies originating in Singapore expanding across Asia and into Australia and the United Kingdom to capitalize on this gendered market of bloggers and blog audiences.

Social media has been subject to feminist critique, whereby it is argued that women's bodies are increasingly judged, regulated, and evaluated in relation to gendered norms of appearance and behavior. Scholarship on femininity and social media suggests the constant management of contradictory narratives of femininity, where girls and women are encouraged to engage in both self-sexualization and self-promotion, and simultaneously derided for being narcissistic or attention-seeking (Dobson 2015). Self-exposure is often a condition of participation in social media, but is also highly regulated via peers and wider Internet audiences. Scholars and prominent feminist bloggers and vloggers have additionally documented gendered harassment and violence online, which constricts women's ability to be full participating members of digital networked publics. Incidents in 2014 where well-known feminist personalities, including gaming critic Anita Sarkeesian, had their address and contact details posted on public digital forums, highlighted feminist concerns about privacy breaches and women's subsequent vulnerability to violence. Despite increasing gender equity in terms of the overall numbers of Internet and digital media users, many online spaces remain male-dominated spaces, where female users are harassed or marginalized (Herring and Stoerger 2014).

Work on men's practices of contemporary masculinity in online spaces analyzes how a process of navigation and balancing of contradictions is required in the maintenance of masculinity. Research indicates that online spaces may in some respects allow men to practice masculinity in more flexible, diverse ways. But although hegemonic masculinity might be disavowed by men, femininity and homosexuality or queer sexualities are still positioned in opposition, and inferior, to hegemonic masculinity.

A turn towards more anonymous social media use, similar to the aforementioned MUDs and MOOs popular in the 1990s, may be one reaction to the pressures of "context collapse" on popular social media platforms. Research suggests there is renewed interest in anonymous and pseudonymous connection with others, in ways that decenter the importance of branded, normative gender performance common on popular social network sites. For example, burgeoning research on Tumblr suggests potential moves towards user anonymity. Fink and Miller (2014) propose that Tumblr has fostered cultural exchange for queer and transgender people through its norms of anonymity and in allowing freedom for highly customizable and personalized design. Differing from "first wave blogging" in its practices of individual authorship, they suggest that the ability to "reblog" (republish other users' blog posts on one's own blog) blends accessibility *and* obscurity for users, providing a space oriented in opposition to dominant discourses of gender and sexuality.

Studies of gender and digital media have traditionally focused on feminist concerns with the possibilities of girls and women gaining access to new technologies, being able to represent themselves rather than being represented, and resisting and disrupting norms of femininity. Digital identity has undergone changes in how it has been understood by scholars, from a means of potential gender empowerment, to a source of gender regulation within new digital media infrastructures. As is shown through the shifts in the brief history of gender and digital media scholarship, work in this field promises to respond to changing configurations of gendered practices and digital media technologies.

SEE ALSO: Cyber Intimacies; Cybersex; Gendered Innovations in Science, Health, and Technology; Media and Gender Socialization; Queer Theory; Technosexuality

REFERENCES

Banet-Weiser, Sarah. 2012. *Authentic TM: The Politics of Ambivalence in a Brand Culture*. New York: New York University Press.

Dobson, Amy Shields. 2015. *Postfeminist Digital Cultures: Social Media and the Politics of Self-Representation*. New York: Palgrave.

Fink, Marty, and Quinn Miller. 2014. "Trans Media Moments: Tumblr, 2011–2013." *Television & New Media*, 15(7): 611–626. DOI: 10.1177/1527476413505002.

Gajjala, Radhika, Yahui Zhang, and Phyllis Dako-Gyeke. 2010. "Lexicons of Women's Empowerment Online." *Feminist Media Studies*, 10(1): 69–86. DOI: 10.1080/14680770903457139.

Haraway, D. 2000. "A Manifesto for Cyborgs." In *The Cybercultures Reader*, edited by David Bell and Barbara M. Kennedy, 291–324. Abingdon: Routledge. First published 1991.

Herring, S. C., and S. Stoerger. 2014. "Gender and (A)nonymity in Computer-Mediated Communication." In *The Handbook of Language, Gender, and Sexuality*, 2nd ed., edited by S. Ehrlich, M.

Meyerhoff, and J. Holmes, 567–586. Chichester: John Wiley & Sons.

Lim, Sun Sun, and Carol Soon. 2010. "The Influence of Social and Cultural Factors on Mothers' Domestication of Household ICTs: Experiences of Chinese and Korean Women." *Telematics and Informatics*, 27(3): 205–216. DOI: 10.1016/j.tele.2009.07.001.

Nakamura, Lisa. 2008. *Digitizing Race: Visual Cultures of the Internet*. Minneapolis: University of Minnesota Press.

O'Riordan, Kate, and David J. Phillips, eds. 2007. *Queer Online: Media Technology and Sexuality*. New York: Peter Lang.

Turkle, Sherry. 1995. *Life on the Screen: Identity in the Age of the Internet*. New York: Simon & Schuster.

Disability Rights Movement

ELIZA CHANDLER
Ryerson University, Toronto, Canada

Comprising around 15 percent of the world's population, disabled people are the largest minority group in the world. Though typically thought of as a medical problem in need of a cure, disabled people are important global citizens. The disability rights movement (DRM), which emerged globally in the latter half of the twentieth century, is dedicated to asserting that disability rights are human rights and that disabled people are meaningfully included in all aspects of civic and social life. The DRM focuses on legal and legislative changes directed at dismantling inaccessibility and ableism – discrimination of disabled people – as well as bolstering public awareness of disability identity, community, and culture.

Throughout the 1800s and early 1900s, disabled people were displayed in freak shows throughout the Westernized world and colonized territories and used as entertainment in royal courts and private homes. At the same time, disabled people were banned from public spaces through legislation such as the "ugly laws" in the United States and the United Kingdom's poor laws. The most widespread practice of the segregation of disabled people was institutionalization, a practice in which disabled people were sent to live and die in institutions.

De-institutionalization occurred throughout the world between the 1950s and 1970s sparked by a number of factors: growing awareness of the unfit conditions of institutions; neoliberal economic policies which decreased funding to public institutions; and emerging resistance from disabled people from within the institutions. The return of wounded World War II veterans to Canada, the United States, and the United Kingdom was recognized as a turning point for advancing the rights of disabled people as it prompted the development of disability advocacy groups, such as WarAmps, and a significant increase in federal funding dedicated to disabled people through support rehabilitation programs and workplace reintegration programs. However, these programs targeted wounded soldiers rather than all disabled people and operated within a charitable framework, promoting the understanding that disability was shameful and needed to be fixed, an understanding that the DRM was determinedly working against.

Emerging in the 1960s, the DRM, in line with other civil rights movements of the time – such as the women's movement, the black liberation movement, and the queer movement – mobilized activist groups of disabled people and their allies to challenge the social attitudes and systemic barriers that perpetuated their oppression. After de-institutionalization, disabled people were integrated into a physically inaccessible social environment built up during industrialization without disabled people in mind. Because of this, the DRM took accessibility as their key concern asserting that, more than being simply unfortunate, inaccessible public spaces (e.g., schools/universities, government buildings, and public transit) violate the civil rights of disabled people.

Full inclusion of disabled people is a long way from being realized, although the DRM has achieved some significant legislative wins. On December 9, 1975, the United Nations (UN) drafted the Declaration on the Rights of Disabled Persons outlining legislation that would secure the advancement and protection of disabled people internationally. The UN named 1981 the Year of Disabled Persons (UN Enable 2008), which was followed by the Decade of Disabled Persons, 1981–1991. This year and the decade that followed increased public awareness of disability issues and supported organizations formed and led by disabled people by bringing an unprecedented level of public and political support for disabled people internationally. In 1982, the International Day of Person's with Disabilities was established by the World Programme of Action concerning Disabled Persons and adopted by the UN General Assembly and is celebrated annually on December 3. In 1982, Canada amended the Canadian Charter of Rights and Freedoms to include the protection of the rights of people with disabilities, making Canada the first country to include disability rights in its constitution. Canada is still only one of 36 countries whose constitution protects disability rights. Ensuring that disabled people have equal protection under the law, the Convention on the Rights of People with Disabilities (CRPD) was adopted in 2007. However, as of 2015, the CRPD has only been ratified in 151 countries.

When the North American DRM was emerging in the 1980s, the built environment was largely inaccessible and the only public conversation about disability was happening in charities and telethons wherein disability was represented as a problem in need of a cure. Therefore it was necessary for the movement to focus on shifting the public's understanding of the location of the "problem" of disability from disabled bodies to inaccessible social spaces. However, as the DRM developed, so did feminist critiques of the way such a focus on the inaccessibility depoliticized personal experiences of disability by neglecting embodied (e.g., gendered, racialized, queer) experiences, following the formative feminist adage that the personal is political. These necessary critiques emerged from feminist, queer, and anti-racist disability activists in the late 1990s and early 2000s through what we now recognize as a disability justice perspective. While acknowledging the importance of dismantling inaccessibility, the disability justice perspective submits that by decentering the body in order to disrupt the understanding that the disabled body is "in need of fixing," early DRM efforts effectively elided the multiplicitous and intersectional ways that disability is experienced. As activist Mia Mingus (2012) writes, "we cannot let the liberation of disabled people be boiled down to logistics."

One of feminist and queer disability activisms's greatest contributions to the DRM was to return a focus to the embodied ways of experiencing disability and the multiple and intersectional ways disabled people are oppressed, suggesting that justice for disabled people requires more than an accessible built environment. Some of the issues that feminist disability activists have worked with the DRM to address include: the right to make informed decisions about one's healthcare, particularly reproductive healthcare; the right to be recognized as a parent by society, in healthcare, and under the law; the right to accessible women's shelters and transitional housing; combating violence against women and trans people with disabilities. These are issues,

issues beyond accessibility, that are integral to achieving justice for disabled people.

SEE ALSO: Eugenics, Historical and Ethical Aspects of; Identity Politics; Medicine and Medicalization; Normalization; Politics of Representation; Social Identity; Universal Human Rights

REFERENCES

Mingus, Mia. 2012. "Leaving Evidence." Accessed August 11, 2015, at http://leavingevidence.wordpress.com/.
United Nations Enable. 2008. "International Year of Disabled Persons." Accessed August 11, 2015, at http://www.un.org/esa/socdev/enable/disiydp.htm.

FURTHER READING

Brownworth, Victoria, and Susan Raffo, eds. 1999. *Restricted Access: Lesbians on Disability*. Seattle: Seal Press.
Clare, Eli. 1999. *Exile and Pride: Disability, Queerness, and Liberation*. Cambridge, MA: South End Press.
Davis, Lennard J. 1995. *Enforcing Normalcy: Disability, Deafness, and the Body*. New York: Verso.
Department of Public Information. 2006. "Conventions on the Rights of Persons with Disabilities." Accessed August 11, 2015, at http://www.un.org/disabilities/convention/questions.shtml#five.
Erevelles, Nirmala. 2011. *Disability and Difference in Global Contexts: Enabling a Transformative Body Politic*. New York: Palgrave Macmillan.
Kafer, Alison. 2013. *Feminist, Queer, Crip*. Bloomington: Indiana University Press.
McRuer, Robert. 2006. *Crip Theory: Cultural Signs of Queerness and Disability*. New York: New York University Press.
Ministry of Economic Development, Employment and Infrastructure. 2015. "About the Accessibility for Ontarians with Disabilities Act." Accessed August 11, 2015, at http://www.mcss.gov.on.ca/en/mcss/programs/accessibility/understanding_accessibility/aoda.aspx.
Morris, Jenny. 1996. *Encounters with Strangers: Feminism and Disability*. London: Women's Press.

Oliver, Michael. 1990. *The Politics of Disablement*. London: Macmillan.
Shakespeare, Tom. 2011. *Word Report on Disability*. World Heath Organization. Accessed August 11, 2015, at http://www.who.int/disabilities/world_report/2011/report.pdf.
United Nations Enable. 2008. "Promoting the Rights of Persons with Disabilities." Accessed August 11, 2015, at http://www.un.org/disabilities/.
United States Department of Justice Civil Rights Division. 2014. "Information and Technical Assistance on the Americans with Disabilities Act." Accessed August 11, 2015, at www.ada.gov.

Discourse and Gender

ANN WEATHERALL
Victoria University of Wellington, New Zealand

The topic discourse and gender emerged and further developed gender and language studies, which arose with the women's movement in the 1970s. Early feminist language research had two primary concerns: the ways gender inequality was reflected in language and how the speech of women and men was different. The issues presuppose a simple representation relationship between language, thought, and society where gender identity and sexism are straightforwardly reflected in language structures and use. Questions of difference rest on essentialist ideas about the nature of gender – that gender identity is something stable and enduring and that it underpins and reveals itself in speech. These initial assumptions still underlie a lot of sound gender and language research. However, they have also been called into question by contemporary ideas associated with constructionism and poststructural theories of meaning. Language's more pivotal, powerful, and dynamic role in the gendered organization of social life and meaning-making is captured by the term discourse, which opens up new and exciting avenues of research.

Constructionist and poststructural ideas inspired a discursive turn in gender and language studies. Discursive work continues an earlier interest in the relationships between gender, language, and power but greatly expands its scope. Key issues such as gender identities, parenting, sexual violence, and workplace discrimination can all be examined from a discursive approach. Different media (e.g., advertising, books, magazines, and movies) can be examined for the ways they draw upon gender as a broad meaning system in their communications. Some discursive studies investigate how broad areas of life (e.g., science, religion) are variously described or constructed in gendered ways. Others, such as those using conversation analysis, examine the ways gender becomes explicitly visible in recorded instances of everyday interactions in institutional (e.g., courtrooms, telephone helplines) and mundane (e.g., mealtime, children's playgrounds) contexts.

One meaning of the term discourse is language in use. However, it is also used in the theories of social constructionism and poststructuralism to acknowledge the pervasive relationships between knowledge and power. In this second sense, discourse is deeply implicated in both the production of gendered and sexualized identities and the regulation of them. For example, discourses of motherhood as a natural and inevitable part of being a woman support widespread access to medical services for infertility. Motherhood can also be construed using a neoliberal discourse of individual choice. Women who choose to be childfree are marginalized in a society where motherhood is so closely bound to femininity. The notion of motherhood as choice can justify a lack of affirmative action to support equal employment opportunities for women in their careers. In sum, the mandate of motherhood is a pervasive discourse that produces and shapes women's identities.

Poststructural theories posit that discourse produces what counts as knowledge, which is at the heart of its power. Used in a poststructural sense, discourse makes the gendered organization of social life seem effortless and not constructed at all. Judith Butler's landmark work *Gender Trouble* (1990) described how cultural meaning systems and everyday practices (such as gender assignment of infants before or at birth) effectively routinize and reproduce sex differentiation and heterosexuality in a way that seems natural and inevitable. Butler overturned conventional thinking about the relationships between sex and gender – elevating the social and cultural or discursive realm over a biological one as producing pervasively binary understandings of sex and gender, nature and nurture. She also recognized non-normative or marginalized genders and sexualities for their potential to expose gender and sexuality as products of discourses.

Judith Butler's work inspired new lines of inquiry in gender and discourse. The topic of sexuality has come to the fore partly because sexual identity has primarily been organized around gender categories (i.e., same-sex or opposite-sex attraction). The notion of heteronormativity has been coined to refer to the pervasiveness and dominance of opposite-sex attraction and desire. Gender and language research has been criticized for the ways it assumes heterosexuality. As a result, language issues for lesbians and gay men have been largely ignored. Notions of discourse as power and knowledge are key in queer linguistics, a newly emergent field which addresses the historical heterosexist bias in gender and language research. A queer approach importantly highlights and examines the sexual identities and desires of those who fall outside culturally dominant gender and sexuality categories. The notion of performativity is important in studies of gender, sexuality, and discourse. It captures the idea that a person's gender and sexual identity is something that is done – a performance – rather than an essential aspect of their being. People who successfully pass as a gender that is different from their sexed body highlight the performative nature of identity.

Another area that has arisen from the discursive turn is the study of men and masculinities – a topic long absent in gender and language studies. Studies of men and masculinities show that multiple versions of masculinity exist. The research also highlights that masculine identities are changing with the social world. The notion of hegemonic masculinity has developed as a way of theorizing how traditional gender stereotypes persist alongside new masculine identities that are more feminine and/or sympathetic to women (e.g., new men, ubersexuals, metrosexuals). Hegemonic masculinities are elements of gender discourses that create social contexts that naturalize men's dominance as normal. Physical strength, aggression, non-emotionality, and hyper-heterosexuality are characteristics associated with hegemonic masculinity.

Many studies have identified a male sex drive discourse which underpins, justifies, and naturalizes cultural practices that subjugate women such as rape, prostitution, and pornography. It has been identified as part of a cultural scaffolding of rape (Gavey 2005). The male sex drive discourse supports rape myths. For example, the idea that scantily clad women invite sexual advances presumes men have a predatory and uncontrollable sexuality. A male sex drive discourse is also a compelling and pervasive explanation for prostitution – men need sex and perhaps the only way they can get it is by paying for it. Women are objectified and rendered sexually passive by the male sex drive discourse, which is proving hard to challenge. The emergence of new, more active feminine identities such as girl power and web grrls is an ongoing area of research that points to shifts in gender discourses. Feminist commentators point to new femininities as being progressive insofar as they produce an active and desiring subject. However, new feminine identities are often also hypersexualized.

The discursive turn in gender and language studies has necessitated the development of new qualitative methodologies. Discourse analysis is an umbrella term for a broad range of research techniques that examine language in use. Feminist forms of discourse analysis share a concern with how gendered patterns of power and privilege operate in texts and talk. One dimension that has traditionally distinguished the type of discourse-analytic approach used is whether the data examined are written, visual, or spoken. However, the development of new communication technologies and social media blurs that distinction. Even with spoken language the level of analysis can differ from an examination of the micro or small details of talk, to an investigation into the broader meaning systems that position people as gendered subjects and justify a gendered status quo. Feminist discourse analysis, feminist critical discourse analysis, feminist poststructuralist discourse analysis, and feminist conversation analysis are some of the different types of approaches that examine discourse and gender.

One of the earliest feminist discourse-analytic studies that examined how broad discourses produce and justify gender-based inequality was Wetherell, Stiven, and Potter's (1987) analysis of the ways British university students talked about equal employment opportunities (EEO) for women. They identified two contradictory themes or practical or culturally normative ways of describing EEO. On the one hand, participants suggested it was up to individuals to show that they had the knowledge, experience, and skills worthy of employment. On the other, there were practical considerations (e.g., lack of adequate childcare) making the employment of women a problem. The contradictory notions of individualism and pragmatism were mobilized by speakers in ways that simultaneously allowed them to endorse the concept of EEO *and* to deny that a general bias against women in employment existed.

The subtle rhetorical management of talk about inequality in ways that endorse egalitarianism and non-action has been dubbed a "new sexism." This concept highlights a shift in how gender bias operates from explicit and overt forms of prejudice and discrimination to more complex and often covert practices. Contradiction can be at the heart of new sexism. For example, the notion of girl power has emerged from feminism. Girl power celebrates an active, youthful version of femininity. It is a postfeminist feminine identity. However, it is also a highly sexualized identity that is commodified. The objectification and sexualization of women is sexist but that sexism is occluded by the emergence of a postfeminist feminine identity. Postfeminism is now a new discursive context that itself requires a feminist analysis, which is a newly emerging area in gender and language studies.

Cultural and media studies have become an important arena for discursive research on gender, not least of all because of the explosion of social media. Research investigates how people produce their gender and sexual identity in an online environment and in virtual worlds. A quite different analytic focus is taken by studies of gender and interaction, where questions about how gender is reproduced are examined at a micro level of structures that organize mundane talk. Feminist conversation analysis is a new and distinctive research approach that examines how gender and sexuality norms are seen in the structures that organize conversation (Speer and Stokoe 2011). In gender and language studies, conversation analysis has been controversial. Its analytic mentality requires that gender and/or sexuality be examined only when they are explicitly and observably visible in talk. Although somewhat restrictive in its scope compared with more macro forms of discourse analysis, its rigorous grounding in actual practices produces compelling insights.

A conversation-analytic study of sexual refusals illustrates the important contribution the approach makes to the feminist language research. Kitzinger and Frith (1999) show two recurrent patterns in the structures of response turns to invitations. In talk, an invitation is typically accepted quickly and straightforwardly. That is, a turn of talk that accepts an invitation comes with no delay after the turn making the offer or the invitation. The accepting turn is also quite short – just a few words, such as saying "that would be great." However, if the response is rejecting the offer or invitation the structure of the responsive turn is more complex. A turn of talk that rejects an invitation is regularly started after a short delay. Its content also tends to be more complex. There is typically a short silence before the response is begun – the responding turn is delayed and the talk often is produced with perturbations and hesitation. The turn is also longer in a refusal than an acceptance. It regularly contains an explanation for the refusal. Another element that is typical of a refusal is some kind of palliative that compliments the person inviting – for example, saying *that is awfully sweet of you to ask*. Kitzinger and Frith (1999) used the conversation-analytic findings on the ways refusals are done in talk to question communication training that advises "just saying no" to invitations, including sexual advances. They suggest that communication training that advises women how to say no to sex, for example, ought to be grounded in studies of actual talk – not in common sense about effective communication.

A challenge for gender and language studies that focus on language in use is to analyze gender in ways that avoid the kinds of essentialist and binary ways of thinking that support gender-based inequality. Feminist conversation analysis justifies its focus by only examining gender and sexuality when it is observably and explicitly relevant to the people whose talk is being examined. In other forms of interactional research a focus on how women speak is justified because of gendered stratification in the contexts examined. Documenting the kinds of language behaviors or communication strategies women use to succeed in areas of social life still dominated by men (e.g., in politics and business) importantly contributes to the study of gender and discourse. For example, Holmes (2006) found that women leaders working in areas traditionally occupied by men were skillful communicators, often using humor in the practice of their authority.

Feminism is as important in the study of gender and discourse as it was in the study of gender and language. It remains a critical perspective in a social world that has seen a marked increase in the commodification and marketization of sexual and gender identities. It also plays an important role in highlighting women's disadvantage on a global scale. An ongoing challenge for studies of gender and discourse is to appreciate the diversity and dynamism of gender and sexuality. Some gendered discourses challenge the legitimacy and continuing relevance of feminism. A feminist backlash was evident in the men's rights movement that constructed a world where social change had gone too far, leading to women's privilege and men's disadvantage. Postfeminism is a relatively new concept that has emerged and implies that gender equality has been achieved. It is likely that gender and discourse research will increasingly have to consider the power of postfeminism to erase enduring global patterns of gender inequality.

SEE ALSO: Heteronormativity and Homonormativity; Language and Gender; Non-Sexist Language Use; Sexism in Language

REFERENCES

Butler, Judith. 1990. *Gender Trouble: Feminism and the Subversion of Identity.* London: Routledge.

Gavey, Nicola. 2005. *Just Sex? The Cultural Scaffolding of Rape.* London: Routledge.

Holmes, Janet. 2006. *Gendered Talk at Work: Constructing Gender Identity Through Workplace Discourse.* Oxford: Blackwell.

Kitzinger, Celia, and Hannah Frith. 1999. "Just Say No? The Use of Conversation Analysis in Developing a Feminist Perspective on Sexual Refusal." *Discourse and Society,* 10(3): 293–316.

Speer, Susan A., and Elizabeth Stokoe. 2011. *Conversation and Gender.* New York: Cambridge University Press.

Wetherell, Margaret, Hilda Stiven, and Jonathan Potter. 1987. "Unequal Egalitarianism: A Preliminary Study of Discourse and Employment Opportunities." *British Journal of Social Psychology,* 26: 59–71.

FURTHER READING

Baker, Paul. 2008. *Sexed Texts: Language, Gender and Sexuality.* London: Equinox.

Baxter, Judith. 2003. *Positioning Gender in Discourse: A Feminist Methodology.* Basingstoke: Palgrave Macmillan.

Cameron, Deborah, and Don Kulick. 2003. *Language and Sexuality.* Cambridge: Cambridge University Press.

Gill, Rosalind. 2007. *Gender and the Media.* Cambridge: Polity.

Discursive Theories of Gender

LAURA DEANE
Flinders University of South Australia, Australia

The term "discursive theories of gender" refers to the ways that gender is culturally constructed in, and enacted by, discourse.

The understanding that gender is performed according to dominant (and subordinated) discourses of masculinity and femininity that circulate in culture, rather than deriving from an essence internal to the body, is central to poststructuralist theorizing. Poststructuralist theory has no singular definition, but is understood to respond to Ferdinand de Saussure's theory of structural linguistics, and to encompass a range of theoretical approaches, from deconstruction and post-Lacanian psychoanalysis to Foucauldian understandings of the role of discourse, knowledge, and institutional power in producing subjects.

The poststructuralist notion of subjectivity derives from Michel Foucault's conceptualization of the subject as shaped by, subjected to, and enmeshed in a complex flow of power relations, which takes the form of discursive formations and disciplinary practices (Foucault 1995/1975). Discourse, in this instance, refers to the language acts associated with disciplinary institutions such as schools, prisons, psychiatric hospitals, or the military, the episteme (bodies of knowledge) informing their values, rules, and practices, and the ideologies underpinning their procedures. Discourses (such as criminology or psychiatry) both authorize and legitimize the practices of these institutions or systems, using dividing practices (such as mad/sane or doctor/patient) to determine categories of normalcy and deviance. These institutions enact disciplinary power insofar as they regulate the bodies and minds of the student, the prisoner, the mentally ill, or the soldier, producing the "docile bodies" that will serve the interests of the state (Foucault 1995). In this way, power acts as a form of subjection. However, for Foucault, power does not simply comprise coercion or repression (power *over*), but also produces resistance (power *to*). This hinges on a particular linguistic usage. There are many words for "power" in French, but the noun *le pouvoir* also denotes the ability or authority of individuals or public institutions to exercise power and influence. This derives from the French verb *pouvoir*, which translates as the modal verb "can," but also means "to have the ability to." This includes the ability to willingly submit to or resist power. Power is therefore productive, as resistance is one of its effects.

These concepts have been influential in the field of gender studies, which has interrogated the role of discursive power in producing or engendering gendered subjects. Gender refers to the cultural construction of masculinities and femininities, and is distinct from biological sex. The introduction of the sex/gender distinction is credited to French feminist phenomenologist Simone de Beauvoir, who in *The Second Sex* famously argued: "One is not born but *becomes* a woman" (1988, 295). Beauvoir argues that patriarchal structures of oppression accord men positions as universal human subjects, while women are relegated to the secondary status of inessential and inferior Other. While the Other is conceptualized as inessential, the power differential between men and women is rationalized as the product of a biological essence that results in women being perceived as "naturally" or biologically weaker. This rests on the mind/body opposition in Western thought, which associates men with mind, reason, and rationality, while constructing women as "somehow *more* biological, *more* corporeal, and *more* natural than men" (Grosz 1994, 14; emphasis in original). Cultural constructions of gender are therefore framed by notions of "sex." As the deconstructionist approach makes clear, these constructions take place in language, so that the term "woman" comes to be defined against "man" as that-which-it-is-not. As Grosz points out, this dichotomous thinking "ranks the two polarized terms, so that one becomes the privileged term and the other its suppressed, subordinated, negative counterpart" (1994, 3). As feminist theory has developed into the discipline of gender studies from the mid-1980s onwards, there has been a shift away from women as the object of feminist critical inquiry to a focus on cultural constructions of masculinity and femininity, understandings of gender as a learned and social artifact, and to the discursive production and reproduction of gender relations as social and ideological relations of power. Therefore the female body, and the ideological constructions of femininity dominant in particular temporal and cultural contexts, have become sites for critical debate in the intellectual and political project of feminist struggle.

A key development in the poststructuralist theorizing of gender has been the recognition that constructions of the female body are not "natural" products of the difference between the sexes but of the meanings of these differences, and of how they have come to bear these meanings (Grosz 1994, 107). Poststructuralist feminists argue that because language preexists the subject, the subject is not an independent entity, but rather a product of its own location within the sociolinguistic system (Weedon 1997, 42–70). Poststructuralist feminism therefore deals with systems of knowledge and representation as systems of meaning-making, interrogating the meanings ascribed to the female body in disciplines such as philosophy, psychiatry, medicine, history, politics, and the arts. Poststructuralists further argue that these systems of knowledge production act as discursive formations in that they mobilize a cultural politics of gender, but conceal their ideological origins, in such a way that patriarchal myths of femininity are reconfigured as "natural" facts, serving to normalize patriarchal regimes of oppression. The French feminists Luce Irigaray, Julia Kristeva, and Hélène Cixous have been influential in this development. While these theorists have to some extent been influenced by the construction of the female body as the Other in Lacanian psychoanalysis, they have attempted to denaturalize the persistent myths of femininity that circulate in Western culture. Irigaray argues that "any theory of the subject has always been appropriated by the 'masculine'," resulting in the female body being constructed "as an object: of representation, of discourse, of desire" (1985a, 133). As a result, constructions of femininity in philosophy and psychoanalysis are "phallocentric," mythical ideals of gender that originate in the male Imaginary. Similarly, Kristeva (1986) contends that "femininity" is collapsed into the term maternity and, in turn, into the category of Virgin Mother within Western Judeo-Christian traditions, locking women into an impossible situation of having to take up a male-defined femininity that is unattainable. Cixous (1980, 95) argues that "Woman has always functioned 'within' man's discourse, a signifier referring always to the opposing signifier." French feminist approaches suggest ways that this feminine Other could be reconstituted. Irigaray (1985b) proposes that women need to create their own models of femininity to replace these patriarchal constructions. Cixous (1976, 880) champions *écriture féminine* as a disruptive force to contest patriarchal constructions of femininity, exhorting women writers to write the body. Kristeva (1982) offers a sustained critique of the corporeal and cultural inscriptions that imprint the female body with abjection to justify women's positioning as cultural "outsiders" in patriarchal cultures. Although French feminism has been met with critical opposition in the United States, with critics such as Judith Butler (1990), Diana Fuss (1989), and Naomi Schor (1994) arguing they reproduce essentialist conceptions of the female body, these approaches have led to productive understandings of how sexual difference is configured in discourse.

Sexual difference refers to the meanings assigned to anatomical differences in male and female sexual organs, and to the cultural construction of these as signs and signifiers of gender. Poststructuralist feminists recognize that the body is "always already sexually coded" and that "the social and psychical significance of sexual differences are [sic] signified to it long before the Oedipus complex" (Grosz 1995, 36). That is, the body is inscribed from the outside, and is accorded certain meanings based on its biological "maleness" or "femaleness." Kristeva situates the biological body as framed by social systems that give meanings to biology, while Irigaray and Cixous argue that the female body constitutes systems of meaning: "On one hand it is a signifying and signified body; on the other, it is an object of systems of social coercion, legal inscription, and sexual and economic exchange" (Grosz 1994, 18). For poststructuralists, then, there is no "real" body that exists outside of historical and cultural representations. Rather, the sexed body is a textual body produced by and within representation, as preexisting cultural scripts and fictions of gender both constitute it and determine its meanings (Grosz 1994, x). Accordingly, the body:

> becomes a text, a system of signs to be deciphered, read, and read into. While social law is incarnate, "corporealized," correlatively, bodies are textualized, "read" by others as *expressive* of a subject's interior ... Bodies speak, without necessarily talking, because they become coded with and as signs. They speak social codes. They become intextuated, narrativized; simultaneously, social codes, laws, norms, and ideals become incarnated. (Grosz 1995, 34–35)

In reconfiguring the body as a semiotic process and a signifying practice, poststructuralist feminists have opened up the intersections between body, nature, and culture to show how the body is articulated by and articulates the discourses, codes, and laws of gender that construct it.

The rethinking of gender has developed from Judith Butler's theorizing in this area. For Butler, gender is a theater for the production of culturally sanctioned styles of "femininity" that provide cultural scripts or templates for women as gendered subjects to follow. Butler argues that gender is performative, comprising a set of repeated "acts" performed in line with a preexisting social "script" that has always already been "rehearsed" (1997b, 410). Accordingly, gender is not hard-wired to the brains and minds of human subjects, but rather is rewritten through repetitive daily postures, practices, styles, and even costumes. These constitute bodily performances that not only consolidate into a gender over time, but also correspond to prevailing ideas about what femininity or masculinity is (1997b, 406). Thus, doing gender comprises both a semiotic performance and a signifying practice that results in a more or less stable gender being discursively assigned to a particular body (1990, 184). Gendered subjects are "authors" of their gender, but are so "entranced" by their productions that they cannot see them for the fictions and illusions that they are (1997b, 405). For Butler, gender is therefore "tenuous," because it is sustained by a "compelling illusion" that only gives the "*appearance of substance*" (1997b, 402, 405; Butler's emphasis). Butler's idea that gender is a set of representational practices that are primarily performative has contributed to the notion that gender is not simply inscribed upon bodies, but that the body writes itself into those dominant models of gender that already circulate within the culture.

While Butler and Grosz both draw on Foucault's conceptualization of subjectivity, they also point out that Foucault tends to reduce the body to a *tabula rasa* upon which discourses of power and gender are written (Grosz 1994, 156), or to situate it as precultural and presignification (Butler 1990, 165–166). However, the notion that subjectivity is also a form of subjection to powerful preexisting discourses has been exceedingly useful in the contemporary theorizing of gender and sexuality. As Foucauldian understandings of power are not reducible to regimes of coercion to which bodies are violently subjected, but rather comprise the proliferation of ideologies into which the human body is interpellated (Louis Althusser, 1918–1990), gender has been rethought as a discursive construction and a naturalizing "trick." Because gender discourses preexist and saturate the human body, conforming to them appears "normal" and "natural," so that doing gender relies upon both the internalized reception and acceptance of, and externalized compliance with, dominant gender ideologies. These are both hidden and so widely institutionalized and normalized that they conceal their ideological origins. Therefore, the processes by which people seem to willingly consent to or agree to take up normative modes of masculinity or femininity that allow them to be read as either men or women comprise forms of hegemony, or domination that appears to take place by consent (Antonio Gramsci, 1891–1937). Accordingly, gender comprises a set of regulatory norms and disciplinary practices that people both internalize and embody, while the "micro-physics of power" to which they are subjected remain largely invisible (Foucault 1995, 30). For Butler, then, gender is disciplinary: it is a set of rules to which a "culturally intelligible subject" is subordinated, as punishments and penalties apply to people who refuse to "do" their gender in accordance with these powerful cultural scripts and templates (1990, 178). There is of course both power and agency in refusing to "do" one's gender in accordance with such rigid discursive regimes, but also a price to be paid for locating oneself as resistant to and outside the dominant discourse. As a result, discourses of gender and heterosexuality constitute "normative and normalizing" ideals to which the body is subjected (1997a, 90).

Contemporary theorizing in feminism, gender studies, masculinity studies, queer theory, and postcolonial theory has mobilized these understandings to argue that because subjects are the products of discourses, ideologies, and institutional practices, gender, "race," and sexuality are normalizing and regulatory discursive constructions.

SEE ALSO: Essentialism; Feminism, French; Feminism, Poststructural; Gender Identity, Theories of; Gender Role Ideology; Patriarchy; Queer Theory

REFERENCES

Beauvoir, Simone de. 1988. *The Second Sex*, trans. E. M. Parshley. London: Pan Books. First published 1949.

Butler, Judith. 1990. *Gender Trouble: Feminism and the Subversion of Identity*. New York: Routledge.

Butler, Judith. 1997a. *The Psychic Life of Power: Theories in Subjection*. Stanford: Stanford University Press.

Butler, Judith. 1997b. "Performative Acts and Gender Constitution: An Essay in Phenomenology and Feminist Theory." In *Writing on the Body: Female Embodiment and Feminist Theory*, edited by Katie Conboy, Nadia Medina, and Sarah Stanbury, 401–417. New York: Columbia University Press.

Cixous, Hélène. 1976. "The Laugh of the Medusa." *Signs*, 1(4): 875–893.

Cixous, Hélène. 1980. "Sorties." In *New French Feminisms: An Anthology*, edited by Elaine Marks and Isabelle de Courtivron, 90–98. Amherst: University of Massachusetts Press.

Foucault, Michel. 1995. *Discipline and Punish: The Birth of the Prison*, trans. Alan Sheridan. New York: Vintage Books. First published 1975.

Fuss, Diana. 1989. *Essentially Speaking: Feminism, Nature and Difference*. New York: Routledge.

Grosz, Elizabeth. 1994. *Volatile Bodies: Towards a Corporeal Feminism*. St. Leonards, NSW: Allen and Unwin.

Grosz, Elizabeth. 1995. *Space, Time, and Perversion: The Politics of Bodies*. St. Leonards, NSW: Allen and Unwin.
Irigaray, Luce. 1985a. *Speculum of the Other Woman*, trans. Gillian C. Gill. Ithaca: Cornell University Press.
Irigaray, Luce. 1985b. *This Sex Which Is Not One*, trans. Catherine Porter with Carolyn Burke. Ithaca: Cornell University Press.
Kristeva, Julia. 1982. *Powers of Horror: An Essay on Abjection*, trans. Leon S. Roudiez. New York: Columbia University Press.
Kristeva, Julia. 1986. "Stabat Mater." In *The Female Body in Western Culture: Contemporary Perspectives*, edited by Susan Rubin Suleiman, 99–118. Cambridge, MA: Harvard University Press.
Schor, Naomi. 1994. "This Essentialism Which is Not One." In *Engaging With Irigaray*, edited by Carolyn Burke, Naomi Schor, and Margaret Whitford. New York: Columbia University Press.
Weedon, Chris. 1997. *Feminist Practice and Poststructuralist Theory*, 2nd ed. Oxford: Blackwell.

Disease Symptoms, Gender Differences in

LAKSHMEN SENANAYAKE
Colombo, Sri Lanka

It is well known that biological differences between men and women lead to differentials in symptoms, prevalence, and health outcomes of certain diseases, such as systemic lupus erythematosus and multiple sclerosis (Ngo, Styne, and McCombe 2014). In such situations, a range of genetic, hormonal, and other biological factors influence men and women differently. However, it is only rarely that biology acts alone to determine health impacts. Gender interacts with other social markers like class and race and exacerbates some of the biological vulnerabilities that result in such differences.

Gender, which is a social construct, becomes an important determinant of awareness of symptoms, delays in seeking care leading to complications, negative impact on quality of life, and the final outcome of the disease for both men and women. It is well known that one's gender also has important implications in terms of decision-making, access to resources and services, engagement in risk behaviors, and environmental exposures which in turn affects one's health (Viasoff 2007).

The influence gender has on health is illustrated when the global burden of blindness is considered. This is unequally distributed between the two sexes, with women comprising nearly 62 percent of the total blind population (World Health Organization 2002a). This cannot be explained by biological differences alone, and is due to gender-determined factors such as limited access to a health facility for surgery as women need to be accompanied by someone, often a male, and the perceived value of undergoing costly surgery for women within the family hierarchy, especially if availability of resources is limited.

Gender stereotyping leads to the view that women are "frail" and likely to be ill and men are "rugged and tough" and likely to be well (Travis, Meltzer, and Howerton 2010). Such notions have an impact on the symptoms, health-seeking behavior, and responses from care providers which in turn leads to differentials in the outcomes of disease. Gender norms in most countries lead to a readiness for women to divulge their symptoms and they are not likely to be culturally sanctioned for doing so. In contrast, stereotyping leads to the reluctance of men to admit to having symptoms and to maintain a pose of "bravado" as they fear they would be admitting to a flaw in their masculinity. Even when they present with symptoms, they are likely to underscore their significance, often "jokingly" mentioning them rather than complaining.

Men and women differ in the way they perceive health, being vigilant about illnesses, and in beliefs about the efficacy of healthcare interventions. In this regard, men tend to hold riskier beliefs and engage in more high risk behaviors than women do (Travis, Meltzer, and Howerton 2010). This attitude of "invincibility" among men contributes to a "carefree" approach which leads to delay in diagnosis and treatment.

Travis, Meltzer, and Howerton (2010), in their study on diabetes in the United States, found that long-term complications such as peripheral artery disease were 40 percent higher, ulcerations and inflammation 60 percent higher, and neuropathy rates 23 percent higher among men than women. One of the factors for this difference is a delay in making the decision to seek care, perceiving the initial symptoms as "trivial."

Based on global averages women tend to have longer life expectancy than men within the same socioeconomic circumstances (World Health Organization (WHO) 2014). Despite their greater longevity, in most communities women report more morbidity than men and are more likely to visit the doctor. The explanation for this apparent paradox lies in the complex relationship between biological and social influences in the determination of human health and illness (WHO 1998). Such health inequalities between men and women are likely to reflect biological sex and gender differences and the interplay within this complex relationship. In most countries there are differences in the legal, social, and economic rights between men and women leading to gender inequality which is reflected in their health indicators.

Globally, road traffic accidents are one of the leading causes of deaths among those aged 15–44 years. Due to injuries caused by these accidents, almost three times (2.7) as many males as females die, accounting for the largest sex differentials in mortality rates from unintentional injury (WHO 2002b). Injury and fatality rates for males are higher for every category of road traffic injury. A similar preponderance of fatalities is seen among male pedestrians who meet with road traffic accidents in several industrialized countries, with the United States recording 70 percent of male victims (WHO 2002b). Gender stereotypical behavior of "being brave enough to take risks" is a probable explanation for this finding.

When one considers the common noncommunicable diseases, cardiovascular disease is the leading cause of mortality in women. In fact, cardiovascular disease occurs in one third of women worldwide, but affects men and women differently (Pilote et al. 2007). Women develop symptoms and a heart attack 10 years later than men do and they do not fare as well thereafter, as they tend to develop more frequent complications after the attack and due to therapeutic interventions. While some of these differences may be attributed to hormonal and functional differences on a biological basis, all findings cannot be explained in this manner. Symptoms perceived by women are often non-specific, such as breathlessness and fatigue, in contrast to men who more often complain of chest pain. Health professionals tend to carry out stress testing and coronary angiography less often in women and use less proven medications in women they believe to have angina because coronary heart disease is usually considered a "male problem." Some of the medical interventions may affect men and women differently. Miller and Best (2011) state that statin therapy in established coronary disease reduces global cardiovascular risk in women to the same degree as in men, but the absolute benefit in women who do not have established coronary disease (prophylactic use) is small, in contrast to a clearly beneficial effect in men.

Mental illness is a significant global health burden and gender is a critical determinant of mental health and mental illness. Women receive more care for mental health issues in primary healthcare settings than men but this difference is less marked when specialist psychiatrist services are considered. Never married and separated/divorced men have higher overall admission rates to mental health facilities than women of the same marital status. In contrast, married women have higher admission rates than married men (WHO 2015).

As Afifi (2007) states, during adolescence girls have a higher prevalence of depression and eating disorders, and engage more in suicidal ideation and suicidal attempts than boys, who are more prone to high risk behavior and suicide. Eating disorders including anorexia nervosa and bulimia nervosa are common in women. The female to male ratio has been recorded as 4.2 : 1 for anorexia nervosa (full syndrome) and 11.4 : 1 for bulimia nervosa (full syndrome) (Tetyana 2012). However, the disparity is less marked, but is persistent, for partial syndrome. A high variability of prevalence found across different cultures suggests that gender has a substantial role in the etiology of eating disorders.

The strikingly higher prevalence of migraine in females than males is well known, with female to male ratios ranging from 2 : 1 to 3 : 1 (Buse et al. 2013). A large survey showed that differences were observed in symptoms, headache-related disability, and healthcare resource utilization for headache (Buse et al. 2013). While some of the differences could be due to biological factors such as cyclical hormonal changes, the finding of this survey that females with migraine were less likely than males to be using preventive pharmacologic treatment for headache is likely to be gender related.

Women have been commonly portrayed in literature as prone to hysteria. Women often suffer from pain associated with menstruation and childbirth, which are considered as biological functions and women are expected to bear them with grace. This gender attitude often leads to women being undertreated by their caregivers for their pain as it is "normal/natural" to have pain in such situations. Women with chronic pain are more likely to be considered to have a psychosomatic cause and are more likely to be referred for psychiatric help than men in a similar situation.

Beyond the biological differences in susceptibility to HIV infection, there are many gender-based issues related to sexual behavior, social attitudes, and vulnerabilities related to decision-making in the use of safe sex, which should be considered in providing care. Gender inequalities and harmful gender stereotyping continue to contribute to HIV-related vulnerability, an example being the finding that women who have experienced intimate partner violence are 50 percent more likely to be living with HIV (UNIAIDS 2013).

For healthcare providers, overlooking gender-based differences or being gender blind may have drastic consequences for their patients. Gender does have a significant role in shaping the interphase between provider and patient, both in terms of the quality of care given by the provider, and the quality of care received as perceived by the patient.

Complying with or transgressing gender norms in an insensitive manner impacts the provider – patient relationship, and can lead to a very negative outcome for the patient. Some patients may avoid seeking care at specific facilities because of the gender of the healthcare workers or if the healthcare workers are judgmental on the basis of gender norms.

Govender and Penn-Kekana (2007) state that, particularly in the developing world, doctors tend to stereotype women as "shy," "hesitant," with "limited knowledge in healthcare seeking matters," and often "not following their doctor's prescription." By comparison, men were described as "daring and open" and "willing to follow directions."

Doctors are more likely to diagnose depression in women than men, even when they have similar scores on standardized measures of depression or present with identical symptoms, with the chances of diagnosing depression increasing with each visit (Govender and Penn-Kekana 2007). Gender stereotyping regarding proneness to emotional problems in women and alcohol problems in men appear to reinforce social stigma and constrain help-seeking as well as care provision.

Although the medical information provided is similar for male and female doctors, female physicians often engage in significantly more active discussion, positive talk, psychosocial counseling, psychosocial questioning, and emotionally focused talk, and spend longer with clients than their male counterparts (Govender and Penn-Kekana 2007).

In developing countries, especially in highly patriarchal societies, gender concordance between provider and patient is important because of sociocultural and/or religious norms and practices which not only demarcate gender roles, but also restrict social and physical contact between men and women. In contrast, the selection of a physician by a patient in a developed country mostly depends on factors other than the gender of the provider. In addition, gender consciousness among care providers will minimize the gender discrimination that may take place during the provision of care.

It is clear that for many diseases affecting men and women, gender has a profound and consistent impact on symptoms, diagnosis, management, patient compliance, and satisfaction, which needs to be recognized and responded to appropriately.

SEE ALSO: Cardiac Disease and Gender; Eating Disorders and Disordered Eating; Gender Bias; Gender Difference Research; Gender Mainstreaming; Gender Stereotypes

REFERENCES

Afifi, M. 2007. "Gender Differences in Mental Health." *Singapore Medical Journal*, 48(5): 385.

Buse, Dawn C., et al. 2013. "Sex Differences in the Prevalence, Symptoms, and Associated Features of Migraine, Probable Migraine and Other Severe Headache: Results of the American Migraine Prevalence and Prevention (AMPP) Study." *Headache*, 53(8): 1278–1299.

Govender, Veloshnee, and Loveday Penn-Kekana. 2007. "Gender Biases and Discrimination: A Review of Health Care Interpersonal Interactions." Background paper prepared for the Women and Gender Equity Knowledge Network of the WHO Commission on Social Determinants of Health. Accessed July 23, 2015, at http://www.who.int/social_determinants/resources/gender_biases_and_discrimination_wgkn_2007.pdf.

Miller, Virginia M., and Patricia J.M. Best. 2011. "Implications for Reproductive Medicine: Sex Differences in Cardiovascular Disease." *Sexuality, Reproduction and Menopause*, 9(3): 21–28.

Ngo, S.T., F.J. Styne, and P.A. McCombe. 2014. "Gender Differences in Autoimmune Disease." *Frontiers in Neuroendocrinology*, 35(3): 347–369.

Pilote, Louise, et al. 2007. "A Comprehensive View of Sex-Specific Issues Related to Cardiovascular Disease." *Canadian Medical Association Journal*, 176(9): S1–S44.

Tetyana. 2012. "Eating Disorders: Do Men and Women Differ?" *Science of Eating Disorders*. Accessed July 23, 2015, at http://www.scienceofeds.org/2012/07/03/eating-disorders-men-women-differ/.

Travis, Cheryl Brown, Andrea L. Meltzer, and Dawn M. Howerton. 2010. "Gender and Health Care Utilization." In *Handbook of Gender Research in Psychology*, edited by Joan C. Chrisler and Donald R. McCreary, 517–540. New York: Springer.

UNIAIDS. 2013. "Global Report: UNAIDS Report on the Global AIDS Epidemic 2013." Accessed July 23, 2015, at http://www.unaids.org/en/media/unaids/contentassets/documents/epidemiology/2013/gr2013/UNAIDS_Global_Report_2013_en.pdf.

Viasoff, Carrol. 2007. "Gender Differences in Determinants and Consequences of Health and Illness." *Journal of Health Population and Nutrition*, 25(1): 47–81.

World Health Organization. 1998. "Gender and Health: A Technical Paper." Accessed July 23, 2015, at http://www.who.int/docstore/gender-and-health/pages/WHO%20-%20Gender%20and%20Health%20Technical%20Paper.htm.

World Health Organization. 2002a. "Gender and Health, Gender and Blindness." Accessed July 23, 2015, at http://whqlibdoc.who.int/gender/2002/a85574.pdf.

World Health Organization. 2002b. "Gender and Road Traffic Accidents." Accessed July 23, 2015, at http://whqlibdoc.who.int/gender/2002/a85576.pdf?ua=1.

World Health Organization. 2014. "News Release: World Health Statistics 2014: Large Gains in Life Expectancy." Accessed July 23, 2015, at http://www.who.int/mediacentre/news/releases/2014/world-health-statistics-2014/en/.

World Health Organization. 2015. "Mental Health, Gender and Women's Health, Gender Disparities and Mental Health." Accessed July 23, 2015, at www.who.int/mental_health/prevention/genderwomen/en/.

Division of Labor, Domestic

ORIEL SULLIVAN
University of Oxford, UK

The division of domestic labor refers to the division of unpaid household work and care between household or family members. It forms part of and is related to the wider domestic division of labor, which describes the division of paid and family work between household members (e.g., Becker 1965; Berk 1985). It is therefore a key area of research for scholars of gender and family within the disciplines of both sociology and economics. Reference is most often made to the division of domestic labor between heterosexual spouses; however, its application is wider than that, for example in the division of domestic labor within same-sex couples. In recognition of the importance of distinguishing between housework and care, which exhibit different dynamics, gender and family scholars prefer to refer to the division of domestic labor and care.

Two important sociological perspectives emerging from this area of research are the resource theory of marital power (Blood and Wolfe 1960) and "doing gender" (West and Zimmerman 1987). Empirical analyses of the effect of relative spousal resources on marital power have focused on the performance of housework as an undesirable task reflecting the unequal gender distribution of power (Brines 1994). The "doing gender" perspective, whereby men and women enact gender-appropriate behaviors in an interactive context, identified housework as a central locus of the doing of gender due to the strong normative identification of the core housework tasks as "feminine."

The origin of research into the division of domestic labor can be traced to the second wave of feminism in the 1960s and 1970s. Feminist sociologists started to look within the "black box" of the family, revealing the hidden burden of "women's work" within the home (Oakley 1974). Indeed, feminist Marxists have argued that capitalism is predicated on this reservoir of unrecognized reproductive labor (Federici 2004). The growing awareness of the contribution of unpaid domestic work to national economies has meant that the valuation of unpaid work and care within the home is now in many countries a feature of national accounting.

Research into the division of domestic labor and care over the past half century in all areas of the world has shown that women still do the vast majority of family work and care in heterosexual couples, and that, despite some changes in the direction of greater gender equality, this pattern persists even in the face of increasing female employment. The finding that this imbalance holds even in dual-earner households led researchers to refer to employed women's "double burden," created by doing a "second shift" of unpaid work (Hochschild 1989).

A succession of decade reviews (e.g., Coltrane 2000; Bianchi et al. 2012) outlines the main features and trends of the division of domestic labor in Western countries. Individual-level factors affecting it are: educational level (in general, the higher the level of women's education the less housework they do, while the opposite is true for men; on the other hand there is a strong positive relationship between childcare and educational level for both men and women); gender ideology (on average, the greater an individual's belief that men and women should share career and family responsibilities equally, the more equal is their division of domestic labor and care); the absolute and relative resources of spouses (in general, the higher the absolute and relative resources of one spouse, the less housework they do), and the sexuality of the couple (lesbian women have been shown to be the most equal in their division of domestic work, ahead of gay men and heterosexual couples). At the macro-level the institutional context is highly influential (Kan, Sullivan, and Gershuny 2011). National contexts in which female empowerment is greater and in which political structures advocate gender equity tend to favor egalitarian allocations of household labor. In particular policies relating to parental leave and flexible working arrangements have been shown to lead to a more equal division of domestic labor and care (Treas and Drobnic 2010).

Trends in the time spent by men and women in unpaid family work and care in all countries for which data are available show a slow convergence by gender. In the case of housework this has largely been caused by long-term declines in the time that women spend doing housework, accompanied by some increases in the time spent by men. For childcare, trends are generally strongly positive in direction for both men and women. Whether these trends are likely to deliver domestic gender equality in the future is a topic of much current debate. Recent research has referred to a "stalled revolution," whereby the decline in women's housework leveled off around the turn of the twenty-first century, while men's housework increased only slowly. Other authors have taken a more optimistic view over the long term (Sullivan 2006). However, the consensus of opinion is that the future division of domestic labor and care depends both on men being able to embrace forms of work and care that have traditionally been conceived as "feminine," and on committed institutional support of the equal division of unpaid family work and care.

SEE ALSO: Division of Labor, Gender; Gender Equality

REFERENCES

Becker, Gary S. 1965. "A Theory of the Allocation of Time." *Economic Journal*, 75: 493–517.

Berk, Sarah F. 1985. *The Gender Factory: The Apportionment of Work in American Households*. New York: Plenum.

Bianchi, Suzanne M., Liana C. Sayer, Melissa A. Milkie, and John P. Robinson. 2012. "Housework: Who Did, Does or Will Do It, and How Much Does it Matter?" *Social Forces*, 91: 55–63.

Blood, Robert O., and Donald M. Wolfe. 1960. *Husbands and Wives: The Dynamics of Married Living*. New York: Free Press.

Brines, Julie. 1994. "Economic Dependency, Gender, and the Division of Labor at Home." *American Journal of Sociology*, 100: 652–688.

Coltrane, Scott. 2000. "Research on Household Labor: Modeling and Measuring the Social Embeddedness of Routine Family Work." *Journal of Marriage and the Family*, 62: 1208–1233.

Federici, Silvia. 2004. *Caliban and the Witch: Women, the Body and Primitive Accumulation*. Brooklyn: Autonomedia.

Hochschild, Arlie R. 1989. *The Second Shift: Working Parents and the Revolution at Home.* Berkeley: University of California Press.

Kan, Man Yee, Oriel Sullivan, and Jonathan Gershuny. 2011. "Gender Convergence in Domestic Work: Discerning the Effect of Interactional and Institutional Barriers from Large-Scale Data." *Sociology*, 45: 234–251.

Oakley, Ann. 1974. *The Sociology of Housework.* London: Martin Robinson.

Sullivan, Oriel. 2006. *Changing Gender Relations, Changing Families: Tracing the Pace of Change.* New York: Rowman & Littlefield.

Treas, Judith, and Sonia Drobnic. 2010. *Dividing the Domestic: Men, Women, and Household Work in Cross-National Perspective.* Palo Alto: Stanford University Press.

West, Candace, and Don H. Zimmerman. 1987. "Doing Gender." *Gender & Society*, 1: 125–151.

Division of Labor, Gender

DRUCILLA K. BARKER
University of South Carolina, USA

The sexual division of labor has been a characteristic of societies throughout history. What constituted men's work and women's work differed from society to society depending on location, social class, and traditions. For example, in sub-Saharan Africa, before the invention of the plow, hoe farming was women's work. In Medieval Europe and the British Isles, peasant women participated in farm work along with men but cooking, milking cows, feeding the fowl, and so on, were women's work. Today we speak not of the sexual division of labor but the gender division of labor. The differences today between men's work and women's work refer not only to the biological sex of the people doing the work, but also to the social status and gender coding of the work. For example, physicians are coded masculine while nurses are coded feminine. Physicians enjoy a higher social status and higher compensation. This gender and status coding is the case for nearly all occupations. The first part of this entry examines the anthropological literature on foraging societies and shows that explanations of the sexual division of labor in pre-industrial societies still hold sway in contemporary societies. The second part of the entry examines the gender division of labor in contemporary societies, and the third section concludes with a discussion of the new global division of labor.

SEXUAL DIVISION OF LABOR IN HUNTER-GATHERER SOCIETIES

Anthropologists have shown that the division of labor by sex is a universal property of hunter-gatherer, or small-scale, foraging societies. Men hunted large game while women were responsible for foraging and childrearing. Early explanations of this division were based on kinship, physiology, and psychology (Brown 1970). One early explanation posited that the sexual division of labor was necessary to make men and women mutually dependent on one another and ensure heterosexual marriage, which was the basis for kinship. Interdependence arises not so much from sex differences as from cultural taboos that ensure differences (Lévi-Strauss 1956). Others argued it naturally emerged due to physical differences between women and men and women's reproductive capacities (Murdock 1949). Psychology played a role as well in that it was thought that women had the capacity for dull, monotonous work while men had the capacity for short spurts of energy followed by periods of relaxation (Mead 1949).

That women sometimes became successful hunters and men gatherers means that the universal tendency to divide subsistence labor by sex is not solely the result of innate physical or psychological differences between the sexes (Kuhn and Stiner 2006). A more rigorous explanation can be made in terms of the relationship between women's economic activities and their childrearing responsibilities. Keeping children alive was their top priority. Hunting is an inherently dangerous activity requiring hazardous travel and intense concentration. Infants require nursing and toddlers and young children require watching, even if sporadically. Thus women are best suited for work that is easily interrupted and easily resumed, does not place the child in danger, and does not require traveling long distances from home (Brown 1970). The work done by women, however, was skill intensive, physically demanding, time consuming, and crucial to the survival of their societies (Kuhn and Stiner 2006).

The anthropological investigation of the sexual division of labor debunks explanations based on assumptions that women are physically unfit to engage in strenuous tasks and are psychologically better suited for monotonous work. The core of the feminist explanation is that women bear the primary responsibility for childrearing. This made sense in a time when women's lifespans were relatively short and nursing infants required the presence of their mothers. Neither of these things is true today. Nonetheless, many of the assumptions about women's work and men's work today have their origins in debates about the division of labor in foraging societies. Rearing children is still primarily the responsibility of women, and men who step in to take on the childrearing activities are the exception rather than the rule. Childrearing remains women's work. Thus if women want to engage in occupations that are not compatible with childrearing, they must make substitute arrangements through relatives, childcare centers, nannies, and older siblings. Although forager societies did not have childcare centers or professional nannies, there is ample ethnographic evidence that women did find other substitute arrangements for childcare. They relied on older children, elderly adults, and reciprocal agreements among women (Brown 1970).

Arguing that the sexual division of labor is necessary to ensure sexual difference in order to make men and women mutually dependent on one another and result in heterosexual marriage, which was the basis for kinship, is still found in conservative justifications for the male breadwinner, female caretaker model of the family today. For foraging societies, whose social order is structured by kinship, gift giving creates reciprocal social bonds and relationships. Marriage is the most basic form of gift giving and women are the most valuable of gifts because the relationship formed is not only based on reciprocity but also on kinship (Mauss 2000/1954). This is, however, a partial representation of the ways that kinship systems work. While men and women may be different, these are not mutually exclusive categories. They are more similar to each other than they are to any other animal species. The argument also requires heterosexual unions and the suppression of same-sex desire, an assumption not supported by the ethnographic evidence (Rubin 1975). Similarly, many contemporary models of the gender division of labor, both feminist and non-feminist, assume that heterosexual unions are the norm, an assumption that again is not supported by the evidence (Bergeron 2009).

Many contemporary explanations for the gender division of labor recycle outdated assumptions about the appropriate social roles for women and men. Lifespans are far longer and women no longer spend the bulk of their time caring for children. Yet, childrearing is still advanced as a justification and an explanation for their small numbers in any number of high status occupations. The nuclear family based on the marriage between a man and a woman is no longer the norm. Single parent families, one-person households, and cohabiting couples are the fastest growing household types (Sorrentino 1990). Same-sex marriage is becoming more and more common and the social exclusion of LGBT people is fast disappearing. So why do scholars and policy makers hold to clearly outdated and deeply gendered explanations? The social changes engendered by the Industrial Revolution are part of the answer.

THE GENDER DIVISION OF LABOR AND THE INDUSTRIAL REVOLUTION

Prior to the Industrial Revolution, with the shift from small-scale home production into large-scale, mass production factories, families were mainly self-sufficient. They produced the bulk of the goods they needed for subsistence. What they could not produce themselves they purchased from artisanal producers in fairs and small markets. The sexual division of labor was prevalent, and as in foraging societies, women generally performed the tasks that were commensurate with their childrearing obligations. Everyone, except the landed nobility who lived off the rents of their tenants, worked.

In Britain the enclosure movement drove peasants from their farms into cities to work in factories and mines. The factory system of production also created two new social classes: the workers who depended on their wages for survival and the bourgeoisie who owned the factories and mines. Bourgeoisie families were able to distinguish themselves from workers (and show their similarity to the nobility) by systematically withdrawing the labor of women and children from the industrial workplace. While the entrepreneurial men of this era engaged in the cutthroat competition of early capitalism, women in this class were expected to become housewives, properly occupied with duties that were increasingly seen as natural to their sex – homemaking and mothering. Running a household required servants from the lower class to do the cooking, cleaning, and washing. This arrangement reflected the aspirations of the bourgeoisie to emulate the nobility who had survived for centuries without working and ushered in a new division of labor based on class as well as gender.

The social status of a family was enhanced by stay at home wives. While this was only possible for a relatively small number of families, the ideology that women's work was not really work was pervasive and reinforced the gender division of labor. Women were not workers: they were wives, mothers, and daughters living in patriarchal households and hence needed wages only for incidentals (Pujol 1998). Today the gender division of labor in the household is reflected in the paid labor force where it is referred to as occupational segregation. Dental hygienists, elementary schoolteachers, clerical workers, secretaries, and receptionists are still most likely to be women. Dentists, judges, police officers, firefighters, and electricians are still most likely to be men. Occupational segregation reflects social stereotypes about women's roles and abilities: women are naturally caring and nurturing, are followers rather than leaders, have less physical strength than men, and are not as good at math and science (Barker and Feiner 2004). Thus women are clustered into occupations that are less prestigious and poorly paid (Bergmann 2005/1986).

One explanation for this is that women choose these occupations because they are compatible with their household responsibilities and do not require large commitments of time and money. This explanation is reminiscent of explaining the sexual division of labor in terms of kinship, physiology, and psychology. In this case, the question must be asked: why do women choose women's work? One answer is that they expect the returns to their waged labor to be less than that of their male partners so they specialize in domestic labor (Becker 1981). This is, however, a circular argument. Their earnings are less because they choose to specialize in household labor; they choose to specialize in household labor because they expect their earning to be less.

Just as in foraging societies, women's occupational choices today are constrained by their childrearing responsibilities. It is well established that women's earnings are dramatically decreased when they have children (Budig and England 2001). The gender division of labor is not, however, the inevitable result of motherhood. Women's occupational opportunities open up when they are able to find adequate childcare or live in countries with a strong commitment to gender equality. Moreover, in industrialized societies only relatively small portions of women's lives are taken up by childbirth and childcare. Nor do all women choose to be mothers or be in heterosexual unions. Labor market discrimination and cultural norms about women's roles play a much larger role. The gender division of labor privileges one group, in this case men, over another, in this case women. The gender division of labor is, however, not a simple binary. Work is also divided by race, class, citizenship, and nation. Work that is poorly paid, low status, or hazardous is done by economically and culturally marginalized groups.

GENDER AND THE NEW GLOBAL DIVISION OF LABOR

Just as the Industrial Revolution engendered a change in the gender division of labor, so did globalization, a process of loosening national barriers to trade and finance and integrating countries, markets, and cultures. Globalization is made possible by digital technologies that make global communications instantaneous, improvements in transportation that decrease costs, and neoliberal policies that deregulate the flows of people, financial capital, and goods and services. These factors have contributed to two significant changes in the gender division of labor: a shift of manufacturing from developed countries in the Global North to developing countries in the Global South and a change in the gender and class division of domestic labor.

The deregulation of financial capital played a significant part in causing these changes. During the 1970s, countries in the Global South incurred large debt obligations to the financial sectors of the Global North in order to finance development projects. However, these investments rarely paid off, and by the 1980s the Global South found itself deeply mired in bad debt. Structural adjustment policies (SAPs), imposed by the transnational policy makers such as the International Monetary Fund, were seen as the solution to evading default. SAPs demanded timely debt service that in turn required indebted countries to attract foreign capital in order to do so (Barker and Feiner 2004). This was done in two ways: by the remittances from women's migration to work in transnational domestic labor markets and the foreign capital earned by establishing export processing zones to sew clothes, assemble electronics, and make toys (Peterson and Runyan 2010).

Women's labor force participation rates in the industrialized countries have increased substantially in the post-World War II period. In 1950 about one in three women participated in the labor force in the United States. By 1998 this had risen to three in every five women of working age in the labor force. An important factor explaining this upward trend is the change in female labor force participation over women's life cycles, particularly the sustained labor force participation of women during their childbearing years (US Bureau of Labor Statistics 2000). This increased the demand for domestic workers to provide domestic labor. Women's cross-border migration, both legal and illegal, played an important role in increasing the supply, creating a new division of domestic labor based on gender, race, class, and nationality (Ehrenreich and Hochschild 2003).

Nearly instantaneous communications, lower transportation costs, flexible production schedules, and the deregulation of global finance have allowed transnational corporations in the developed world to shift labor-intensive production processes from the industrialized countries in the Global North to the low-wage, developing countries in the Global South. Corporations carry out the research and development needed to design the products in the Global North, while the actual manufacturing, which is the relatively labor-intensive part, is subcontracted out to factories in countries where wages are low, unions are either weak or non-existent, and environmental regulations are lax. Generally these small- to medium-size factories are not owned and managed by the transnational corporation but rather by local entrepreneurs. They require significant pools of workers willing to work for low wages at monotonous, often hazardous, tasks. A willingness to work for low wages at jobs that do not require extensive training and carry little opportunity for advancement are characteristics associated with women workers (Standing 1999). Women now comprise more than one third of the manufacturing labor force in developing countries and nearly a half in some Asian countries (Barrientos, Kabeer, and Hossain 2004).

Women's attractiveness to transnational capital stems from their subordinate gender status, and the perception that women in the developing world are docile, passive, and easily subject to the discipline required by factory work. The perception that women in the Global South are docile reflects their extremely limited options for earning income rather than any intrinsic gender traits (Pearson 1998). Moreover, globalization entails a conversion of all labor to the conditions of female labor: jobs that are more insecure, more flexible, and even more poorly paid. The proportion of jobs requiring craft skills acquired through apprenticeship has declined, labor market regulations have been eroded, and unionized, full-time, stable jobs are disappearing (Standing 1999). On a global scale work continues to be segregated by gender, race, class, and nationality. The women and men who hold good jobs – whether workers in information technologies or as executives and managers in traditional industries – are well compensated for their labor, while other, poorly paid workers – male as well as female – assemble products and provide services necessary for the daily functioning of highly paid workers. This is the new global division of labor.

SEE ALSO: Comparable Worth/Work of Equal Value; Division of Labor, Domestic; Dual Labor Market; Feminization of Labor

REFERENCES

Barker, Drucilla K., and Susan Feiner. 2004. *Liberating Economics: Feminist Perspectives on Families, Work, and Globalization*. Ann Arbor: University of Michigan Press.

Barrientos, Stephanie, Naila Kabeer, and Naomi Hossain. 2004. "The Gender Dimensions of the Globalization of Production," Working Paper No. 17, 204–221. New York: Metropolitan Books.

Becker, Gary S. 1981. *A Treatise on the Family*, vol. 113. Cambridge, MA: Harvard University Press.

Bergeron, Suzanne. 2009. "An Interpretive Analytics to Move Caring Labor off the Straight Path." *Frontiers: A Journal of Women Studies*, 30(1): 55–64.

Bergmann, Barbara. 2005. *The Economic Emergence of Women*, 2nd ed. New York: Palgrave Macmillan. Originally published 1986.

Brown, Judith K. 1970. "A Note on the Division of Labor by Sex." *American Anthropologist*, 72(5): 1073–1078.

Budig, Michelle J., and Paula England. 2001. "The Wage Penalty for Motherhood." *American Sociological Review*, 66(2): 204–225.

Ehrenreich, Barbara, and Arlie Russell Hochschild. 2003. *Global Woman: Nannies, Maids, and Sex Workers in the New Economy*. New York: Metropolitan Books.

Kuhn, Steven L., and Mary C. Stiner. 2006. "What's a Mother to Do? The Division of Labor Among Neanderthals and Modern Humans in Eurasia." *Current Anthropology*, 47(6): 953–980.

Lévi-Strauss, Claude. 1956. "The Family." In *Man, Culture, and Society*, edited by Harry Lionel Shapiro, 261–285. New York: Oxford University Press.

Mauss, Marcel. 2000. *The Gift*. London: Routledge. First published 1954.

Mead, Margaret. 1949. *Male and Female: A Study of the Sexes in a Changing World*. New York: William Morrow.

Murdock, George Peter. 1949. *Social Structure*. New York: Macmillan.

Pearson, Ruth. 1998. "'Nimble Fingers' Revisited: Reflections on Women and Third World Industrialization in the Late Twentieth Century." In *Feminist Visions of Development: Gender Analysis and Policy*, edited by C. Jackson and R. Pearson, 171–188. London: Routledge.

Peterson V. S., and A. S. Runyan. 2010. *Global Gender Issues in the New Millennium*. Boulder: Westview Press.

Pujol, Michelle. 1998. *Feminism and Anti-Feminism in Early Economic Thought*. Aldershot: Edward Elgar.

Rubin, Gail. 1975. "The Traffic in Women." In *Toward an Anthropology of Women*, edited by Rayna R. Reiter, 157–210. London: Monthly Review Press.

Sorrentino, Constance. 1990. "The Changing Family in International Perspective." *Monthly Labor Review*, 113.

Standing, Guy. 1999. "Global Feminization through Flexible Labor: A Theme Revisited." *World Development*, 27(3): 538–602.

US Bureau of Labor Statistics. 2000. Changes in Women's Labor Force Participation in the 20th Century. Accessed July 23, 2014, at http://www.bls.gov/opub/ted/2000/feb/wk3/art03.htm.

Documentary Film and Gender

DOMITILLA OLIVIERI
Utrecht University, The Netherlands

The relation between documentary films and images and concerns about gender issues is a multilayered one, and as complex as the very debate about how to define what a documentary film is. Speaking about gender and documentary means engaging with questions of aesthetics and politics, of social movements and of power imbalances, of the politics of representation, of the relation between reality and language, truth and objectivity, facts and fiction, of processes of signification and their effects on social reality and lived experiences.

Documentary is a contested term, a "fuzzy concept" (Nichols 2001, 21), a genre with a canon and a history but without a fixed set of techniques or, for some, maybe even a concept that should be abandoned or at least radically redefined. Talking about documentary means reflecting on concepts such as fiction and non-fiction, objectivity and subjectivity, actuality, truth claims, factuality, realism, and authenticity. Accordingly, there are many multifaceted and, at times, contradictory explanations of the term "documentary," but they all revolve around the problem of referentiality (Gaines and Renov 1999, 5) as the specific kind of relation between the documentary sign and its referent, that is: reality, the social world. The complexity of the matter leads to the impossibility of providing a conclusive definition of documentary. Yet, never before have terms traditionally associated with the documentary genre been so often uttered as it has in the last 20 years, in the most diverse contexts and across new and old technologies – "factual filming forms" (Cowie 2011, 16) are gaining popularity and audiences.

Gender is engaged in documentary films, or more broadly, in "factual filming forms" (which include also other non-fictional formats, short videos, TV items, genres, or media that mix fictional and documentary techniques, etc.) with a minimum of five levels. The most straightforward level is that of the content, which refers to what a documentary is about, its subject matter; when taking this aspect into account it is possible to refer to all documentary films that address themes such as gender roles, sexuality, family, and kinship. The identity and "location" of the filmmaker is a second level to consider when looking at how documentary engages gender and vice versa. Whether the filmmaker is a man or a woman, of what age, nationality, and sexual orientation, and from whatever geopolitical, social, and ethnic background, it can be said to carry significance for how a documentary is made. At stake here are, for example, matters of access to certain spaces and events and the kinds of relations established between filming and filmed subjects.

However important and necessary, considering these as the only dimensions of how gender is engaged in documentary representations – that is, focusing only on the subject matter of a documentary or on the gendered position of the filmmaker – runs the risk of underplaying the specificity of the medium and of the genre. Hence, other levels are to be taken into account. Third, how these films are received and by whom is where matters of reception, specific audiences, communities, and social movements are of relevance. The fourth level concerns the macro dimension of how economical changes, technological developments, and geopolitical relations affect the production and distribution of documentaries. Fifth, the broader dimension of how documentary representations work and what they do can be taken into account. This entails focusing on the relation between politics and aesthetics.

These last levels of documentary films – their reception, production and distribution, and politics and aesthetics – affect and are affected by issues of gender and other differences. Feminist goals, the struggles and claims of various political groups, and matters of visibility for marginal communities and marked subjectivities are of importance here. Some of these concerns have been studied from different angles and within different disciplines. However, the two areas of scholarship most directly engaged with this issue are that of gender and feminist studies and of documentary studies. These two interdisciplinary fields have seen alternate moments of reciprocal interest and mutual myopia.

Feminism and gender studies have been greatly concerned with the politics and ethics of images, and of representation more broadly across disciplines. In the decades between the 1960s and the 1980s, the relation between feminism(s) and documentary film was officially established, and interrupted soon thereafter. As filming technology became cheaper and more widely available, documentary films about and for women were produced for informational, propaganda, or political purposes. However, it was only with the so-called "realist debate" that the relation between documentary and feminism entered into the theoretical and academic realm, and was subsequently acknowledged and critically analyzed.

The years between the late 1970s and the late 1990s witnessed a gap between theoretical investigations and documentary film practice (Waldman and Walker 1999, 8–11). Activists and filmmakers kept on producing documentaries that circulated in small political circles. In the meantime, feminist film scholars "forgot" the documentary form and focused their attention on mainstream or fiction films with particular emphasis given to the iconic representation of women in Hollywood movies, the star system, and the "male gaze" within these film and issues of spectatorship and identification. Exceptions to this approach are texts written during these years by scholars such as Annette Kuhn, Julia Lesage, and Jane Gaines. They presented important contributions for feminist film scholarship and, in particular, for documentary film studies, but their voices at the time remained somewhat marginal in the field of feminist film theory. They argued either in favor of the use of realist techniques for the purpose of clarity and political efficacy, or for a new kind of documentary that would at the same time use and challenge traditional documentary forms and the realist aesthetic.

It is only since the late 1990s that feminist critiques and reflections on documentary forms have found a new impetus. In 1999, the first and only anthology of older and newer essays specifically on feminism and documentary was published (Waldman and Walker 1999).

One of the reasons for this relative absence of scholarly reflections on the relation between gender and documentary, in the 1980s and 1990s, can be found in the approach that eminent feminist scholars developed in the 1970s. The debate can be roughly summarized as the "realist debate." Despite the name, only one perspective of the debate has been widely circulated, the "anti-realist" side, and consequently became greatly influential. Characteristic of the "anti-realist" stand in the realist debate was a distrust of realistic cinematic strategies. It followed the structuralist, semiological criticism that signifying practices are complicit with and produced by hegemonic ideologies of gender, and that they are "all we can ever 'know'" (Kaplan 1983, 130). This is the assumption that there is no knowable "reality" outside signifying practices. From here, feminist film theorists such as Claire Johnston inferred that the cinema *vérité* style – understood as the preferred style of documentary – was dangerous for feminists, since it used a realist aesthetic embedded in the capitalist and patriarchal representations of reality. Accordingly she argued that "any revolutionary must challenge the depiction of reality" (Johnston 1976/1973). This kind of critique focused the attention on the "language," the aesthetics of such films, in terms of how representational strategies could shape subject positions, and reproduce power inequalities and gendered oppressions.

The consequences of these discussions are long lived. An example of argument in favor of realism, and against this anti-realist position, is the one elaborated by Alexandra Juhasz in her 1999 article. She engages with the "realist debate" and specifically with Kaplan's article "The Realist Debate in the Feminist Film." In this article, Kaplan states that "realism, as a style, is unable to change consciousness because it does not depart from the forms that embody the old consciousness" (Kaplan 1983, 131). Juhasz strongly challenges the assumption that all 1970s realist feminist documentaries were "naive;" thus, she criticizes the theory according to which realism is seen as intrinsically complicit with patriarchy, and hence masking the production of meaning. She reclaims the importance of making feminist realist films, stressing the accessibility and positive political value of such films.

Beyond these two positions – those against realism and those in favor of it in the service of feminist politics – other perspectives on gender and documentary address the links between documentary films, as tools for hegemonic "scientific" knowledge production, and notions of objectivity and truth claims. One example of such an approach is that expressed by, among others, postcolonial feminist scholar and filmmaker Trinh T. Minh-ha. Her contribution is twofold.

She provides further insights on the relation between gender and documentary, especially concerning processes of othering in ethnographic films. It should, in fact, be noted that in particular anthropological and ethnographic documentaries have always been implicated in constructing images and imaginaries about the Other. Additionally, in various articles, Trinh (1988, 1993) claims that revealing the artifice in documentary becomes crucial in order to uncover and address the risks inherent to a rigid and hegemonic distinction of fact and fiction, reality and mediation. This approach also helps problematizing and overcoming the normative notions that link documentary film to universal claims of objectivity, factuality, and truth.

Despite their different angles of critique, these three perspectives on gender and documentary, broadly speaking, all point at the interrelation between documentary as a genre and a set of aesthetics, gender norms, sexualized and racialized hegemonic discourse, and (gendered) power dynamics, and the relation between subjectivity, reality, and representation.

Since the late 1990s there has been a flourishing of important publications that explicitly or implicitly connect feminist theory, concerns with the representation of identities and differences, and the complexities of documentary forms. In this sense, the innovations in the field of documentary film, and their implications, have been addressed by prominent scholars such as Jane Gaines, Bill Nichols, Michael Renov, and Brian Winston. Film theorists who instead explicitly move within feminist studies, although addressing broader questions of identification, experience, and corporeality in the moving image culture at large, or in digital or intercultural cinema, are also considering the specific issues raised by factual filming forms and questions of referentiality, indexicality, or authenticity (see, for example, the latest texts of Vivian Sobchack, Laura Marks, and Laura Mulvey).

Other recent and contemporary trends of scholarship in this field include but are not limited to: works that engage with the question of emotions and desire, such as Cowie (2011) and Smaill (2010), putting on the agenda also the relation between psychoanalysis and documentary; approaches that focus on genres that blur the boundaries between factual and fictional filming forms, such as Juhasz and Lerner (2006); and studies that deal with the relation between documentary and subjectivity, such as Renov (2004) and Lebow (2012).

In particular, some of the critical insights into gender and sexuality developed within feminist theory and gender studies have found great resonance in the works produced in what has become one of the main catalysts of what is now known as documentary studies: the conferences and publications of the community and critical platform of the visible evidence (e.g., see Gaines and Renov 1999).

Finally, technological developments in the field of cinema and audiovisual technologies have brought to the fore other documentary forms, such as collaborative documentary or online documentary, and new possibilities of recording in contexts of war and conflicts, such as mobile phone recording, online platform sharing, and so on. These new devices and media that enable and stimulate the use of documentary strategies presents new sets of claims and implications, and are therefore a new arena where gender and documentary, identity and representation, referentiality and mediation, and aesthetics and politics are being mobilized and critically studied.

SEE ALSO: Discourse and Gender; Feminist Activism; Feminist Film Theory; Language and Gender; Representation; Visual Culture

REFERENCES

Cowie, Elizabeth. 2011. *Recording Reality, Desiring the Real*. Minneapolis: University of Minnesota Press.

Gaines, Jane, and Michael Renov, eds. 1999. *Collecting Visible Evidence*. Minneapolis: University of Minnesota Press.

Johnston, Claire. 1976. "Women's Cinema as Counter-Cinema." In *Movies and Methods*, edited by Bill Nichols. Berkeley: University of California Press. First published 1973.

Juhasz, Alexandra. 1999. "They Said We Were Trying to Show Reality." In *Collecting Visible Evidence*, edited by J. Gaines and M. Renov. Minneapolis: University of Minnesota Press.

Juhasz, Alexandra, and Jesse Lerner, eds. 2006. *F is for Phony: Fake Documentary and Truth's Undoing*. Minneapolis: University of Minnesota Press.

Kaplan, E. Ann. 1983. *Women and Film: Both Sides of the Camera*. New York: Methuen.

Lebow, Alisa, ed. (2012) *The Cinema of Me: The Self and Subjectivity in First Person Documentary*. New York: Columbia University Press.

Nichols, Bill. 2001. *Introduction to Documentary*. Bloomington: Indiana University Press.

Renov, Michael. 2004. *The Subject of Documentary*. Minneapolis: University of Minnesota Press.

Smaill, Belinda. 2010. *The Documentary: Politics, Emotion, Culture*. New York: Palgrave Macmillan.

Trinh, T. Minh-ha. 1988. "Not You/Like You: Post-Colonial Women and the Interlocking Questions of Identity and Difference." *Inscriptions*, 3–4.

Trinh, T. Minh-ha. 1993. "The Totalizing Quest of Meaning." In *Theorizing Documentary*, edited by M. Renov. New York: Routledge.

Waldman, Diane, and Janet Walker, eds. 1999. *Feminism and Documentary*. Minneapolis: University of Minnesota Press.

FURTHER READING

Winston, Brian (2000) *Lies, Damn Lies and Documentaries*. London: British Film Institute.

Domestic Technology

JAN PAUL HEISIG
WZB Berlin Social Science Center, Germany

It is not difficult to give an example of a domestic technology. When asked for one, most people readily mention appliances such as washing machines, dishwashers, or vacuum cleaners. Providing a general definition of "domestic technology" turns out to be a more challenging task. Previous research illustrates that it can be fruitful to define domestic technologies broadly as any technology used in domestic production. Here, "domestic production" refers to the everyday processes wherein members of private households expend (unpaid) labor to produce goods – meals, cleanliness, or childcare – for direct consumption and enjoyment by themselves and other household members. Prototypical household appliances such as washing machines, whose primary function is to facilitate the provision of clean clothes, clearly meet this definition. At the same time, it is general enough to accommodate technologies that are not usually considered as domestic yet may play a crucial role in the process of household production: access to a car or the Internet can dramatically influence how households do their shopping. Basic utilities such as electricity, water supply, and plumbing that are nowadays taken for granted in advanced economies likewise play a key role in the execution of many domestic tasks.

Regardless of definitional details, there is no doubt that domestic technologies have advanced and diffused enormously over the past one or two centuries. In wealthy economies access to reliable public utilities has been practically universal for many decades and the vast majority of households now possess a large set of domestic appliances. This development has been studied from various angles. For example, feminist work in science and technology studies has analyzed the paradoxical situation that the users of domestic technology are predominantly female, whereas its designers are predominantly male (e.g., Wajcman 1991). The most prominent research question, however, has been if – and why or why not – advances in domestic technology have freed women from domestic demands, leaving them more time for paid work and leisure. The implications for men's time use have received far less attention, if only because women have long carried the lion's share of unpaid domestic work across the world.

In a series of influential contributions, Joann Vanek (e.g., 1978) reported that the housework time of US housewives did not decrease between the mid-1920s and the mid-1960s, a period characterized by massive proliferation of key domestic technologies such as the washing machine. A common interpretation of her findings is that productivity gains from technological innovation were primarily used to meet more demanding housekeeping standards (e.g., cleaner homes and clothes) rather than to reduce domestic work time. That there was some such increase in housekeeping ideals is indeed uncontroversial. What is more contested is the assertion that the productivity gains from technology diffusion were entirely consumed by this increase and had practically no effect on women's housework time.

First, later research found that the housework time of American homemakers did decrease more noticeably after the mid-1960s. Second, it is important to acknowledge the often overlooked fact that Vanek's finding of near-constant housework time refers to homemakers only. As is well known, the labor force participation of women in the United States and in many other countries increased markedly during the twentieth century. Several recent studies suggest that the proliferation of domestic technology was an important factor behind this trend (e.g., Coen-Pirani, León, and Lugauer 2010). Another possibility why homemakers' average housework time did not decline more strongly during the first half of the twentieth century is that the benefits of domestic technologies were partly offset by declining employment of domestic servants in middle- and upper-class households (Gershuny 2000). Class differences are also emphasized in a recent cross-national study which finds that differences in women's housework time by level of income are less pronounced in economically more developed countries where even low-income households have access to domestic technologies (Heisig 2011). A few studies have directly compared households with and without a given appliance such as a washing machine (e.g., Bittman, Rice, and Wajcman 2004). Most of these studies fail to find marked negative effects of appliance ownership on women's housework time, which some read as further evidence that domestic technologies do not reduce the domestic workload. Other authors question this interpretation, arguing that unobserved differences (e.g., in clothing needs or cleanliness standards) render direct comparisons between owners and non-owners problematic (e.g., Heisig 2011).

On the whole, available evidence suggests that the diffusion of domestic technologies has been used both to fulfill higher housekeeping standards and to reduce women's domestic (and increase their paid) work time. That said, the effects of individual technologies may sometimes be more ambiguous than this global summary suggests. This is illustrated by Cowan's (1983) classic study of domestic production in the United States during the nineteenth and twentieth centuries, which also underlines the benefits of construing domestic technologies broadly. Cowan shows how some technological innovations increased rather than reduced unpaid work time by making "self-servicing" more attractive: for example, growing access to automobiles and public transport induced households to substitute (women's) unpaid shopping time for delivery services. Various examples in her study also illustrate the importance of basic utilities such as electricity or water supply. Not only are these utilities indispensable prerequisites for using appliances such as washing machines, they also relieve households of the need to engage in time-intensive activities such as carrying and pumping water. Relatedly, a recent study suggests that access to basic utilities can have important consequences for women's time use in today's developing countries: Dinkelman (2011) finds substantial positive effects of rural electrification on female employment in South Africa which at least partly seem to operate via changes in household production.

SEE ALSO: Division of Labor, Gender; Gender Inequality and Gender Stratification

REFERENCES

Bittman, Michael, James Mahmud Rice, and Judy Wajcman. 2004. "Appliances and Their Impact: The Ownership of Domestic Technology and Time Spent on Household Work." *British Journal of Sociology*, 55(3): 401–423.

Coen-Pirani, Daniele, Alexis León, and Steven Lugauer. 2010. "The Effect of Household Appliances on Female Labor Force Participation: Evidence from Microdata." *Labour Economics*, 17(3): 503–513.

Cowan, Ruth S. 1983. *More Work for Mother: The Ironies of Household Technology from the Open Hearth to the Microwave*. New York: Basic Books.

Dinkelman, Taryn. 2011. "The Effects of Rural Electrification on Employment: New Evidence from South Africa." *American Economic Review*, 101(7): 3078–3108.

Gershuny, Jonathan. 2000. *Changing Times: Work and Leisure in Postindustrial Society*. Oxford: Oxford University Press.

Heisig, Jan Paul. 2011. "Who Does More Housework: Rich or Poor?" *American Sociological Review*, 76(1): 74–99.

Vanek, Joann. 1978. "Household Technology and Social Status: Rising Living Standards and Status and Residence Differences in Housework." *Technology and Culture*, 19(3): 361–375.

Wajcman, Judy. 1991. *Feminism Confronts Technology*. Cambridge: Polity.

Domestic Violence in the United States

KEITH KLOSTERMANN
Medaille College, USA

Between 2003 and 2012, domestic violence (DV) accounted for 21 percent of all violent victimizations (US Department of Justice 2014). This type of abuse can appear in several forms including physical, sexual, emotional, psychological, or economic (Catalano 2007). Domestic violence includes rape, sexual assault, robbery, and aggravated and simple assault committed by intimate partners, immediate family members, or other relatives (US Department of Justice 2014). Individuals affected by DV encompass all cultures, ethnicities, and socioeconomic backgrounds, and victims can be women, men, children, and the elderly, (Catalano 2007). The act determines the crime, but the relationship between the victim and perpetrator determine whether the interaction is domestic. Each state dictates the laws regarding domestic violence and so the determining variables can vary from state to state. However, for many states, domestic includes people who are married, unmarried, and living together, cohabitating same-sex partners, roommates, and family members (Catalano 2007). Past or present boyfriends or girlfriends (7.8 percent) currently commit the greatest percentage of all violent victimizations compared to spouses (4.7 percent) and ex-spouses (2.0 percent) (US Department of Justice 2014). Immediate family members (parents, children, and siblings) account for

4.3 percent of all violent victimizations, while other relatives account for 2.4 percent (US Department of Justice 2014). The costs of domestic violence are systemic, impacting not only the family, but society as a whole (National Center for Injury Prevention and Control 2003). Because of the complexity of this issue, addressing and understanding the dynamics of domestic violence has multiple challenges and perspectives.

Men and women engage in overall comparable levels of abuse and control such as diminishing the partner's self-esteem, isolation, and jealousy, using children and economic abuse; however, men engage in higher levels of sexual coercion and can more easily intimidate physically (Coker et al. 2002). Between 2003 and 2012, 65 percent of serious violent crimes against females were committed by someone the victim knew compared to 35 percent by a stranger (US Department of Justice 2014). In contrast, serious violent crime against men were more likely to be committed by a stranger (55 percent) rather than someone the victim knew (34 percent) (US Department of Justice 2014). Results from the 2014 Special Report collected by the US Department of Justice indicated that 37 percent of serious domestic violence incidents involved a female victim compared to 10 percent of crimes where men were victimized. Also, both men and women were more likely to experience violence by an intimate partner rather than a family member or other relative (US Department of Justice 2014).

Physical abuse is defined as hitting, slapping, shoving, grabbing, pinching, biting, hair-pulling, and can include denying medical care or forcing alcohol and/or drug use (Catalano 2007). Severe, repeated violence occurs in 1 in 14 marriages with an average of 35 incidents before the victimization is reported (Avis 1992). Many times, physical assaults are not reported. Recent longitudinal data suggested that only 55 percent of domestic violence incidents were reported to the police (US Department of Justice 2014). Intimate partner abuse is the leading cause of injury and death for women, and the most dangerous time is when the woman decides to leave the abusive relationship (Bragg 2003). In the United States, during the year 2000, 1,247 women and 440 men were killed by an intimate partner. These numbers account for 30 percent and 5 percent of the murders of women and men respectively (Bragg 2003). On average this is more than three women and one man a day being murdered by their partners (Catalano 2007). The average health-related costs of intimate partner violence exceeds $5.8 billion a year and nearly $4.1 billion are for direct medical and mental health care services; $1.8 billion are for the indirect costs of lost productivity or wages (National Center for Injury Prevention and Control 2003).

Factors such as alcohol and drug use, a family history of violence, and abuse toward animals are shown to increase the likelihood that someone will be a perpetrator of DV (Catalano 2007). Fifty percent of men who assaulted their wives also abused their children. Annually, it is estimated 3.3 to 10 million children are at risk for witnessing or being exposed to domestic violence, increasing the likelihood for emotional, psychological, and behavioral problems (Bragg 2003). Children who experience domestic violence are also more likely to continue the cycle of violence or be revictimized as adults in the future (Bragg 2003). In addition, those who abuse their partners are more likely to abuse their children. Reviews of child protective cases in multiple states in the United States identified domestic violence in approximately 41 to 43 percent of cases that ended in critical injury or the death of a child (Bragg 2003).

Sexual abuse is the coercing or attempting to coerce any sexual contact or behavior without consent (Catalano 2007). It can include but is not limited to marital rape, attacks on sexual parts of the body, forcing sex, or treating one in a sexually demeaning way (US Department of Justice 2014). Approximately one in five female high school students reported being physically and/or sexually abused by a dating partner and nearly 70 percent of sexual assaults on women between the ages of 18 and 29 were date rapes (Silverman et al. 2001).

Emotional abuse is the undermining of an individual's sense of self-worth and/or self-esteem. This may include, but is not limited to, constant criticism, diminishing one's abilities, name-calling, or damaging one's relationship with one's children. Psychological abuse is causing fear by intimidation, threatening physical harm to self, partner, children, or partner's family or friends, destruction of pets or property, and forcing isolation from family, friends, or school and work. This can also include stalking, which is a complicated crime. All states and the District of Columbia have stalking laws, however, there is variation. Stalking is a consistent conduct that may involve acts that alone may seem benign.

Economic abuse occurs when a person maintains total control over financial resources, withholding access to money, or forbidding one to attend school or employment (US Department of Justice 2014). The victims of economic abuse can be intimate partners and the elderly. The actual number of elders abused is unknown because of reluctance to report for fear of retaliation, a lack of physical and/or cognitive ability to report, or because they do not want to get their abuser in trouble (90 percent of whom are family members; Comijs et al. 1999). Elder abuse and neglect can also occur in nursing homes or long-term care facilities. In fact, there is a 300 percent higher risk of death, psychological distress, and lower perceived self-efficacy among abused elderly compared with older adults who were not victimized (Comijs et al. 1999).

Multiple models including psychiatric, social-psychological, and sociocultural attempt to explain the complexity of domestic violence. The psychiatric model examines factors such as substance abuse, personality disorders and mental illness, and how they trigger violent behavior toward family members and intimate partners. The social-psychological model includes theories such as social learning, exchange theory, frustration-aggression, ecological, and sociobiology/evolutionary. Factors such as modeling and reinforcement are identified as primary reasons for learned violent behavior within the social learning theory, while the exchange theory is based on a system of punishments and rewards. The frustration-aggression theory states that if a person views a family member or intimate partner as an obstacle to getting what s/he wants then violence may occur. The environment and systems that influence the family are the basis for the ecological theory. The sociobiology/evolutionary theory examines the emotional and biological bond between parent and child, and presents that if the child is not biologically connected or an emotional bond is not created, then there is a higher likelihood of abuse. The sociocultural model considers the roles of males and females, economic status, and the cultural attitudes toward sex and violence. The overarching commonality across all of the discussed theories is one person is exercising power over another.

SEE ALSO: Child Sexual Abuse and Trauma; Elder Abuse and Gender; Intimate Partner Abuse; Rape Culture; Sexual Assault/Sexual Violence

REFERENCES

Avis, J. 1992. "Where Are All the Family Therapists? Abuse and Violence within Families and Family Therapy's Response." *Journal of Marital and Family Therapy*, 18(3): 225–232.

Bragg, H. L. 2003. *Child Protection in Families Experiencing Domestic Violence*, 1–101. Washington, DC: US Department of Health and Human Services Administration for Children and Families Administration on Children, Youth and Families Children's Bureau: Office on Child Abuse and Neglect.

Catalano, S. 2007. Intimate Partner Violence in the United States. US Department of Justice, Office of Justice Programs Bureau of Justice Statistics. Accessed August 14, 2015, at http://www.bjs.gov/content/pub/pdf/ipvus.pdf.

Coker, A., et al. 2002. "Physical and Mental Health Effects of Intimate Partner Violence for Men and Women." *American Journal of Preventive Medicine*, 23(4): 260–268.

Comijs, H. C., B. W. J. H. Penninx, K. P. M. Knipscheer, and W. van Tilburg. 1999. "Psychological Distress in Victims of Elder Mistreatment: The Effects of Social Support and Coping." *The Journals of Gerontology: Series B: Psychological Sciences and Social Sciences*, 54B(4): 240–245.

National Center for Injury Prevention and Control. 2003. *Costs of Intimate Partner Violence against Women in the United States*. Atlanta: Centers for Disease Control and Prevention.

Silverman, J., A. Raj, L. Mucci, and J. E. Hathaway. 2001. "Dating Violence against Adolescent Girls and Associated Substance Use, Unhealthy Weight Control, Sexual Risk Behavior, Pregnancy, and Suicidality." *Journal of the American Medical Association*, 286(5): 572–279.

US Department of Justice. 2014. "Special Report: Nonfatal Domestic Violence, 2003–2012," 1–21. *Office of Justice Programs Bureau of Justice Statistics*.

"Don't Ask, Don't Tell" Policy in the United States

TAMMY S. SCHULTZ
Marine Corps War College, Virginia, and Georgetown University, USA

After his campaign promise to allow homosexuals to serve openly in the US armed forces, President Bill Clinton's administration issued Department of Defense Directive 1304.26 on December 21, 1993, or what became known as "Don't Ask, Don't Tell" (DADT). The law took effect on February 28, 1994, and Clinton envisioned DADT essentially as a compromise between allowing open service by homosexuals and discharging homosexuals by discerning their sexual preference through questioning. The Obama administration repealed DADT and allowed members to serve openly on September 20, 2011. The Department of Defense (DoD) discharged more than 13,000 service members under DADT.

On the campaign trail and as President-elect, Bill Clinton promised to lift the ban on gays serving in the military, stating, "I don't think status alone, in the absence of some destructive behavior, should disqualify people." Since sodomy had been a dischargeable offense since the American Revolutionary War, Clinton's promise signaled a huge change for the US military. Upon assuming office, however, he faced stiff opposition from the Hill and within DoD.

Among the most vocal critics in the Senate was Sam Nunn (D-Georgia), who said, "We've got to consider not only the rights of homosexuals but also the rights of those who are not homosexual and who give up a great deal of their privacy when they go into the military. … If you did it [lifting the ban on gays in the military] overnight, I fear for the lives of people in the military." All the Joint Chiefs of Staff were against allowing gays to serve openly, including Chairman of the Joint Chiefs Colin Powell (October 1, 1989 – September 30, 1993), Acting Chief David Jeremiah (October 1, 1993 – October 24, 1993), and General John Shalikashvili (October 25, 1993 – September 30, 1997).

Congress included language similar to that in a 1982 total ban on gays in the military in the National Defense Authorization Act for Fiscal Year 1994 (FY1994 NDAA), which essentially funds the DoD. President Clinton followed this law up with Defense Directive 1304.26, holding that military members could not be asked about their sexual orientation. Military sociologist Charles Moskos referred to the new policy as "Don't Ask, Don't Tell," meaning that the military could not ask about sexual orientation, but members were also not supposed to tell.

The FY1994 NDAA's language lays out the opposition to gays in the military, stating that gays serving openly "would create an unacceptable risk to the high standards of morale, good order and discipline, and unit cohesion that are the essence of military capability." According to this argument, the military relies so much on unit cohesion for military readiness, and gays and lesbians would undermine readiness by corroding unit cohesion. Straight troops would not be comfortable sharing close quarters and foxholes with gays and lesbians, so the argument goes, which would negatively impact the troops' ability to fight together as one unit. For these individuals, DADT went too far in allowing for the possibility of closeted homosexuals to serve at all.

For others, DADT did not go far enough. When DADT took effect, Rep. Barney Frank (D-Massachusetts) indicated, "There's something about being a homosexual that means you get kicked out anyway ... That's the untenable aspect of this compromise. ... Even the military opponents of lifting the ban never argued security ... sexual orientation is irrelevant to security concerns." These critics pointed to US military and other studies that measured homosexuals' impact on unit cohesion and found no effect on military effectiveness. Those who disagreed with DADT felt that the discharge rates of gay military members showed that even if one did not tell, he/she could be thrown out of the ranks. Indeed, under DADT, the discharge trend line generally increased until 2001, when the United States became involved in the war in Afghanistan, and continued to drop after the start of the war in Iraq (Table 1).

DADT's opponents launched a multifront challenge to the law, through the courts of public opinion and law. According to Pew Research Center and CNN Opinion Research Poll data, when DADT first became law, 41–45 percent of the public did not believe that gays and lesbians should be allowed to serve openly in the military. By the end of 2010, when DADT was repealed, that number had dropped to 23–27 percent. In other words, unlike desegregation, where the military's policy of integrating African Americans was ahead of public opinion, the public was ahead of the military with the desire to allow gays to serve openly.

The military's reticence to change policy prompted several court cases to overturn DADT. Before essentially being overturned by *Log Cabin Republicans v. The United States* in 2010, five federal Courts of Appeal and the Supreme Court upheld DADT. In the *Log Cabin* case, Judge Virginia A. Phillips ruled that DADT violated gays' first and fifth constitutional amendments rights. Although the Obama administration agreed with this finding, it asked for a stay in order to study the impact and develop a plan to jettison DADT.

The resulting study, *Report of the Comprehensive Review of the Issues Associated with a Repeal of "Don't Ask, Don't Tell"* issued November 30, 2010, included results from one of the largest studies ever conducted by the DoD. The report found that "the risk of repeal of DADT to overall military effectiveness is low." Wholly 70 percent of those military members surveyed predicted DADT's repeal would have a positive, mixed, or no effect.

Additionally, unlike previous hearings involving the military's top leaders where all were against the repeal, the opinions of the

Table 1 Homosexual conduct administrative separation discharge statistics

Fiscal year	Total number of homosexual discharges	Percentage of total active force
1980	1754	0.086
1981	1817	0.088
1982	1998	0.095
1983	1815	0.085
1984	1822	0.085
1985	1660	0.077
1986	1643	0.076
1987	1380	0.063
1988	1101	0.051
1989	996	0.047
1990	941	0.046
1991	949	0.048
1992	730	0.040
1993	682	0.040
1994	617	0.038
1995	757	0.050
1996	858	0.058
1997	997	0.069
1998	1145	0.081
1999	1034	0.075
2000	1212	0.088
2001	1227	0.089
2002	885	0.063
2003	770	0.054
2004	653	0.046
2005	726	0.052
2006	612	0.044
2007	635	0.046
2008	634	0.045
2009	428	0.030

Source: Burrelli (2010).

Joint Chiefs of Staff proved mixed this time around. The Marine Corps Commandant James F. Amos, Army Chief of Staff George W. Casey Jr., and Air Force Chief of Staff Norton A. Schwartz testified against the repeal; however, Chairman Mike Mullen, Vice Chairman James E. Cartwright, and Coast Guard Commandant Robert J. Papp Jr. all supported allowing gays to serve openly. Indeed, Chairman Mullen said, "No matter how I look at the issue, I cannot escape being troubled by the fact that we have in place a policy which forces young men and women to lie about who they are in order to defend their fellow citizens." Having former Chairmans Powell and Shalikashvili also state their support for the repeal proved helpful to the repeal process too.

On December 22, 2010, President Obama signed DADT's repeal, with the policy officially ending on September 20, 2011. At the ceremony, President Obama proclaimed:

Valor and sacrifice are no more limited by sexual orientation than they are by race or by gender or by religion or by creed. ... This law I'm about to sign will strengthen our national security and uphold the ideals that our fighting men and women risk their lives to defend. No longer will our country be denied the service of thousands of patriotic Americans who were forced to leave the military – regardless of their skills, no matter their bravery or their zeal, no matter their years of exemplary performance – because they happen to be gay. No longer will tens of thousands of Americans in uniform be asked to live a lie, or look over their shoulder, in order to serve the country that they love.

SEE ALSO: Coming Out; Employment Discrimination; Fundamentalism and Public Policy; Heterosexism and Homophobia; Lesbian and Gay Movements; Nationalism and Sexuality; Personal is Political; Sexual Identity and Orientation; Sodomy Law in Comparative Perspective

REFERENCES

Burrelli, D.F. 2010. "Don't Ask, Don't Tell": The Law and Military Policy on Same-Sex Behavior. Congressional Research Service's Report to Congress.

Department of Defense (DoD). 2010. *Report of the Comprehensive Review of the Issues Associated with a Repeal of "Don't Ask, Don't Tell"*. Washington, DC: Department of Defense. Accessed July, 20, 2015, at http://www.defense.gov/home/features/2010/0610_dadt/DADTReport_FINAL_20101130(secure-hires).pdf.

FURTHER READING

Belkin, Aaron, Morten G. Ender, Nathaniel Frank, et al. 2013. "Readiness and DADT Repeal: Has the New Policy of Open Service Undermined the Military?" *Armed Forces & Society*, 39(4): 587–601.

Dyer, Kate, ed. 1990. *Gays in Uniform: The Pentagon's Secret Reports*. Boston: Alyson Publications.

Huffman, J. Ford, and Tammy S. Schultz, eds. 2012. *The End of Don't Ask Don't Tell: The Impact in Studies and Personal Essays by Service Members and Veterans*. Quantico: Marine Corps University Press.

Parco, James E., and David A. Levy, eds. 2010. *Attitudes Aren't Free: Thinking Deeply About Diversity in the U.S. Armed Forces*. Maxwell: Air University Press.

Shilts, Randy. 1993. *Conduct Unbecoming: Gays and Lesbians in the U.S. Military*. New York: St. Martin's Press.

Double Standard

SANDRA L. FAULKNER and JING JIANG
Bowling Green State University, USA

The sociocultural standards for sexual behavior differ for women and men (Fine 2005). North American mainstream culture, among others, socializes individuals to advocate for a pleasure-centered or recreational focus on sexuality for men and a person-centered or relational orientation toward sexuality for women (DeLamater 1987). Though premarital sex and sexual intercourse outside of a committed relationship are more acceptable for both men and women now, the current rules and roles for sexual conduct in specific situations and sexual conversation do not apply evenly by sex (Bordini and Sperb 2013). Traditional double standards expect women to be conservative and to set limits for or even refuse sex, while men have more liberty to initiate a date and sexual intercourse and to be sexually experienced.

Those who adhere to a sexual double standard endorse different sexual behavior for women and men, whereby women are expected to confine sexual behavior to the context of a committed relationship and men are expected to engage in sexual behavior in all kinds of relationships. Some explanations for the existence of sexual double standards stem from an evolutionary perspective in which reproductive success relies on different mating strategies for men and women, whereas other explanations focus on sociocultural issues related to gender expectations. Reiss (1967) first operationalized the double standard as differing standards of sexual permissiveness for women and men. Bordini and Sperb (2013) define the sexual double standard as the use of different criteria to evaluate men and women's sexual behavior. That is, the idea that males who engage in casual sexual behavior are rewarded and considered to be "studs," whereas women who engage in casual sexual behavior and/or less common sexual behavior such as threesomes are evaluated negatively and considered to be "sluts" (Jonason and Marks 2009). The double standard remains in place through the "acceptable" number of lifetime sexual partners for men and women, the sex of the person who suggests condom or other contraceptive use (Hynie and Lydon 1995), who should initiate sexual activity (DeLamater 1987), the type of sexual activity considered to be appropriate and desirable, and the expectation that "good/moral" women do not discuss sexual matters openly (Faulkner and Mansfield 2002).

Evidence for a heterosexual double standard is demonstrated when individuals endorse different amounts or levels of sexual activity as acceptable for women and men in heterosexual relationships (Greene and Faulkner 2005). Thus, some women deny or underreport the extent of their sexual experience. In fact, women are more likely than men to use rough approximations of the number of lifetime sexual partners rather than enumeration (Brown and Sinclair 1999). Double standards may become evident in responses to questions about specific behaviors (e.g., it is less acceptable for a woman to have sex on a first encounter). They may also become evident in responses about the context, conditions, or motives for sexual activity (e.g., it is less acceptable for women to have sex without affection, at an early age, or for selfish motives). Double standards may appear not just for heterosexual intercourse, but for other sexual behaviors as well (e.g., sexual initiation).

Although demonstrated by many researchers, sexual double standards are not evident in some research (Fugère et al. 2008). Studies show that sexual double standards are influenced by situational and interpersonal factors (e.g., the target's age, level of relationship commitment, and number of partners), and that double standards are local constructions, differing across ethnic and cultural groups (Crawford and Popp 2003) and peer groups (Lyons et al. 2011). For example, in many studies US men reported greater endorsement and enforcement of double standards than did US women (Sprecher 1989). Men appear to enforce the sexual double standard more than women, as evidenced in advice given to friends (i.e., male friends are encouraged to engage in casual sex and female friends are cautioned against casual sex), though both men and women believe women should not engage in casual sex due to stigma and rape risk (Rudman, Fetterolf, and Sanchez 2013). Another study found that adolescent girls in similar situations with similar sexual experience were more supportive and acted as a buffer against negative assessments at a larger cultural level (Lyons et al. 2011).

Adherence to sexual double standards may put both women and men at risk for HIV and other sexually transmitted infections (STIs), with men feeling pressured to push for sexual opportunities regardless of safety concerns, and women feeling distanced from their own sexual needs, or finding it difficult to negotiate a male partner's insistence on unprotected sexual encounters effectively (Dworkin, Beckford, and Ehrhardt 2007). In one study, women who endorsed less traditional attitudes about the sexual double standard indicated more sexual assertiveness in terms of initiation, refusal of unwanted sexual activity, and ability to engage in sexual talk (Greene and Faulkner 2005). Those individuals who do not believe in traditional sexual double standards for women and men may be able to discuss more effectively sexual issues such as HIV, and to initiate and refuse sexual activity.

Double standards have negative impacts not only on women's sexual health, but also on women's sexual identity. Sexual double standards may lead women to sacrifice their sexual autonomy in exchange for social desirability. Girls learn to look sexy but say no, to be feminine but not sexual, and to attract boys' desire but not to satisfy their own (Fine 2005). Women may form a negative sexual identity because of conflicts between expressing sexuality and controlling sexual urges and resisting sexual desire, the fear of being labeled a slut, and by saving their reputation but sacrificing sexual autonomy (Katz and Farrow 2000). Women are forced to conform to social sex norms; otherwise they might be socially rejected and perceived as culpable for sexual violence. If the victim of a rape initiates physical contact on a date, she may be judged more responsible for the rape (Muehlenhard and MacNaughton 1988), and if the victim is described as sexually experienced, the victim receives more blame than the perpetrator (L'Armand and Pepitone 1982).

SEE ALSO: Rape and Re-Victimization, Treatment of; Sexual Instinct and Sexual Desire; Sexual Scripts

REFERENCES

Bordini, Sagebin G., and Tania M. Sperb. 2013. "Sexual Double Standard: A Review of the Literature between 2001 and 2010." *Sexuality & Culture*, 17(4): 686–704. DOI: 10.1007/s12119-012-9163-0.

Brown, Norman R., and Robert C. Sinclair. 1999. "Estimating Number of Lifetime Sexual Partners: Men and Women Do It Differently." *Journal of Sex Research*, 36(3): 292–297. DOI: 10.1080/00224499909551999.

Crawford, Mary, and Danielle Popp. 2003. "Sexual Double Standards: A Review and Methodological Critique of Two Decades of Research." *Journal of Sex Research*, 40(1): 13–26. DOI: 10.1080/00224490309552163.

DeLamater, John. 1987. "Gender Differences in Sexual Scenarios." In *Females, Males, and Sexuality*, edited by Kathryn Kelley, 127–139. Albany: SUNY Press.

Dworkin, Shari L., Sharlene T. Beckford, and Anke A. Ehrhardt. 2007. "Sexual Scripts of Women: A Longitudinal Analysis of Participants in a Gender-Specific HIV/STD Prevention Intervention." *Archives of Sexual Behavior*, 36(2): 269–279. DOI: 10.1007/s10508-006-9092-9.

Faulkner, Sandra L., and Phyllis K. Mansfield. 2002. "Reconciling Messages: The Process of Sexual Talk for Latinas." *Qualitative Health Research*, 12(3): 310–328. DOI: 10.1177/104973202129119919.

Fine, Michelle. 2005. "Desire: The Morning (and 15 Years) After." *Feminism & Psychology*, 15(1): 54–60. DOI: 10.1177/0959353505049708.

Fugère, Madeleine A., Carlos Escoto, Alita J. Cousins, Matt L. Riggs, and Paul Haerich. 2008. "Sexual Attitudes and Double Standards: A Literature Review Focusing on Participant Gender and Ethnic Background." *Sexuality & Culture*, 12(3): 169–182. DOI: 10.1007/s12119-008-9029-7.

Greene, Kathryn, and Sandra L. Faulkner. 2005. "Gender, Belief in the Sexual Double Standard, and Sexual Talk in Heterosexual Dating Relationships." *Sex Roles*, 53(3–4): 239–251.

Hynie, Michaela, and John E. Lydon. 1995. "Women's Perceptions of Female Contraceptive Behavior: Experimental Evidence of the Sexual Double Standard." *Psychology of Women Quarterly*, 19(4): 563–581. DOI: 10.1111/j.1471-6402.1995.tb00093.x.

Jonason, Peter K., and Michael J. Marks. 2009. "Common vs. Uncommon Sexual Acts: Evidence for the Sexual Double Standard." *Sex Roles*, 60(5): 357–365. DOI: 10.1007/s11199-008-9542-z.

Katz, Jennifer, and Sherry Farrow. 2000. "Discrepant Self-Views and Young Women's Sexual and Emotional Adjustment." *Sex Roles*, 42(9): 781–805. DOI: 10.1023/A:1007051131544.

L'Armand, Kathleen, and Albert Pepitone. 1982. "Judgments of Rape: A Study of Victim–Rapist Relationship and Victim Sexual History." *Personality and Social Psychology Bulletin*, 8(1): 134–139. DOI: 10.1177/0146167282810 21.

Lyons, Heidi, Peggy C. Giordano, Wendy D. Manning, and Monica A. Longmore. 2011. "Identity, Peer Relationships, and Adolescent Girls' Sexual Behavior: An Exploration of the Contemporary Double Standard." *Journal of Sex Research*, 48(5): 437–449.

Muehlenhard, Charlene L., and Jennifer S. MacNaughton. 1988. "Women's Beliefs about Women Who 'Lead Men On'." *Journal of Social and Clinical Psychology*, 7(1)7: 65–79. DOI: 10.1521/jscp.1988.7.1.65.

Reiss, Ira L. 1967. *The Social Context of Premarital Sexual Permissiveness*. New York: Holt, Rinehart & Winston.

Rudman, Laurie A., Janell C. Fetterolf, and Diana T. Sanchez. 2013. "Motives for the Sexual Double Standard: A Test of Female Control Theory." Rutgers University. Accessed July 29, 2015, at http://www.spsptalks.wordpress.com/2013/06/20/motives-for-the-sexual-double-standard-a-test-of-female-control-theory/.

Sprecher, Susan. 1989. "Premarital Sexual Standards for Different Categories of Individuals." *Journal of Sex Research*, 26(2): 232–248. DOI: 10.1080/00224498909551508.

FURTHER READING

Byers, Sandra E. 1996. "How Well Does the Traditional Sexual Script Explain Sexual Coercion? Review of a Program of Research." *Journal of Psychology and Human Sexuality*, 8(1–2): 7–25. DOI: 10.1300/J056v08n01_02.

Gagnon, John H. 1990. "The Explicit and Implicit Use of the Scripting Perspective in Sex Research." *Annual Review of Sex Research*, 1(1): 1–43. DOI: 10.1080/10532528.1990.10559854.

Dowry and Bride-Price

JOHN A. CONTEH
Wright State University, USA

Dowry is the transfer of wealth, an invaluable component of bridal wealth (Botticini and Siow 2003). This is an important responsibility on the part of parents to ensure daughters are given due inheritance rights during the time of marriage. Historically, the term dowry implies the transfer of a large wealth of goods and services to parents of the bride during marriage. The practice of dowry is contemporarily popular in South Asia, particularly given high demand in the twentieth century. Dowry giving was historically popular in the Near East, Europe, East Asia, South Asia, and some parts of the Americas (Botticini and Siow 2003). In South Asia the term groom price can be used in place of dowry since payment is typically to the groom and family. Dowries exist in societies where group interests value the nature of wealth, and rights are negotiated and transferred (Fleising 2003). Dissemination of wealth and inheritance is a cooperate responsibility dominated by males which further contributes to inequality and disparity of resource distribution.

Bride-price is payment to the family of the bride. Depending on the economic status of the groom, payment is typically done by the groom. However, family members of the groom can sometimes be collectively accommodating in helping the groom meet the cost of payment. Historically, bride-price is more common in subsistence economies where horticultural or pastoral farming practices exist. For instance, in Uganda, bride-price can involve payment of money as well as goods such as cows and goats to the family of the bride. The totality of the exchange whether in cash or goods and services as compensation to the family of the bride constitutes bride-price. Women and child labor are indispensable contributions in such societies. Gaulin and Boster (1990) suggested prevalence of bride-price in predominantly agricultural labor-intensive societies where the contribution of women and children is highly valued.

The complexity of societies that practice bride-price is typical in the West African country of Sierra Leone where there are variations across tribal groups regarding bride-price. In Sierra Leone, there are cases where part of the bride-price payment may be used by the family of the bride to pay for the cost of marital expenses. Since the society is still male dominated, in many cases, the money for the bride-price payment is used by the male elders of the bride's family. There are cases when both the bride and groom families offer wealth by way of providing land or other valuables to the bride and groom to establish their new family (this depends on the wealth status of both families).

In the early 1970s Goody and Tambiah (1973) presented an elaborate description of bridewealth and dowry practices in Africa and Eurasia. In the same publication, Tambiah presented a treatise of dowry and bridewealth in relation to property rights of women in South Asia. In medieval Europe, for instance, dowry was used as a form of political connectedness and alliance (Barker 2003). In India, social stratification impacts how much dowry is paid given the anticipated improved status of the woman after marriage. A plausible explanation for stratification is due to resource disparity among men and women. There are few alternatives for women hence marriage decisions are a familial venture as is typically done in arranged marriages.

Geographical variations about where dowry and bride-price are practiced are presented in the literature and research. Some espoused that dowry and bride-price are cultural and traditional practices predominantly done in Asia and Africa (Maitra 2008), while others indicated that dowries are common in the Near East, Europe, East Asia, South Asia, and parts of the Americas (Botticini and Siow 2003). In dowry systems, the concept of a daughter leaving home to unite with a husband comes along with transfer of wealth, goods, and services to the bride's family as a form of compensation for the absence of a family member. In monogamous virilocal economies where agriculture is predominant, children are valued assets and the need to remain in the family is a daunting reality.

Technically, leaving home means that the daughter can no longer contribute to the wealth of the parents or family. Sons primarily receive inheritance while daughters receive theirs in the form of dowries (Goody and Tambiah 1973; Botticini and Siow 2003). Botticini and Siow (2003) predicted and justified the transfer of property rights and dowry in virilocal societies where married daughters are expected to leave home. However, the exception to this was contemporary sub-Saharan Africa where even though many economies are virilocal, bride-prices are preferred. However, in some contemporary sub-Saharan African countries, bride-prices are more prevalent than dowries. Botticini and Siow (2003) examined previous research done by Murdoch (1967) indicating that 7 percent of African societies with bride-prices are collectivistic instead of individualistic in terms of property rights. The study revealed 66 percent of cultures practice bride-price while only 3 percent practice the dowry system. Therefore the favored type of marital exchange practice is that of bride-price since wealth is owned by the family and cannot be transferred, regardless of gender. In certain parts of Africa, depending on the type of agricultural practices, bride-prices may be favored over dowries. For example, non-plow agriculture requires more labor, while plow agriculture requires less, hence the role and contributions of women to the labor force are more highly valued in the former than the latter. It is therefore not surprising that bride-price is common in a non-plow system while dowry is favored in plow economies.

Botticini and Siow (2003) presented a theory of dotal versus virilocal societies. The former is a historical replica of the European pattern of modern society while the latter refers to traditional agricultural societies. Historically, the existence of dotal marriages was impacted by immigration patterns as well as capitalism in North America. It makes sense economically that dowries would be exchanged in traditionally rooted societies since children are regarded as part of the family wealth. The departure of a daughter can therefore be compensated due to loss of family in replacement for a dowry. In dotal (dowry giving) societies, the demand for labor replaced by modernization brought about the disappearance of dowry and bride-price. Individual wealth is more important than collective wealth, hence the absence of a dowry and bride-price in such economies as the United States. The significance of individual investment as dictated by market forces prevails over wealth accumulation within the larger family context of the bride.

The dowry system is a complex process in stratified societies (Harrell and Dickey 1985; Fleising 2003). In India, the connection between dowry and social stratification is clearly discussed in the research literature (Goody and Tambiah 1973; Gaulin and Boster 1990). Researchers have commented that whether a dowry exists or not is not really the issue, rather the focus can be shifted on the role of income disparity and inequality prevalent in societies where dowry is practiced.

According to Gaulin and Boster (1990), dowry creates a form of female competition ensuring brides attain the fittest male for their continued survival. Families therefore compete to have their daughters married to the groom who can ensure the most stable conditions for their daughter. In such a case, families of the bride gather resources to support the continued survival of their kindred under the most favorable conditions. One rationale for this model is social stratification in monogamous societies, which contribute to women and their families bidding for the wealthiest or most suitable male with the anticipated outcome of all inheritance to be in the control of the woman and offspring. This supports one plausible explanation for the existence of dowry in such societies.

There are implications for dowry and bride-price in contemporary research and literature. For example, the burden of responsibility for dowry payments has debilitating consequences for women, such as bride burning in India. In the context of a public health and women's sexual reproductive health perspective, some advocates of women's rights suggest the voices of women in sub-Saharan Africa denounce bride-price due to potential compromise of reproductive health (Wendo 2004). In 2004, the International Conference on Bride-price held in Kampala, Uganda, became the platform to muster support from other African countries. Bride-price practice has been widely criticized as the acquisition of wealth but the terms of who benefits from such wealth are more familial than representative of the couples themselves. The woman has no control over the number of children to have, nor of sexual reproductive health after the bride payment is made. In retrospect, men's control over women's bodies becomes a perception of property.

Advocates suggest that since the system of marriage is more polygamous than monogamous, many parts of Africa risk the potential spread of HIV/AIDS. In certain cases, the bride payment is returned when the woman leaves the relationship. This has potential consequences for domestic violence. In Uganda, there is the possibility of bride recall when the bride-price is not completely paid off as in the case of cohabiting couples. Advocates focus more on behavior change toward women and the ability of women to negotiate their sexual rights. On the other hand, some advocates prefer reform rather than abolish bride-price. Critics of bride-price infer the process has considerable financial burden on families (Fortunato, Holden, and Mace 2006).

Dowry and bride-price as invaluable cultural elements of marriage deserve a treatise of diversity consideration. Both practices present strong semblance of continued male dominance and control. There are already challenges defining, mapping, and assessing dowry and bride-price practices. This implies that there are cultural values that will be ambiguous when compared with Western systems. Understanding cultural systems such as dowry and bride-price can be very challenging given the complex nature of the societies in which they occur. Similarly, since multicultural literature and research is vastly expanding in a global context, it would be important to further expand research geared toward nuances among cultures. Such expansion warrants advocates to further examine the existing implications of custom and traditional practices of other cultures. More advocates are challenging the dowry system and bride burning in India. This signals the need for a universal advocacy appeal given the potential associated public health and mental health concerns.

Barker (2003) and Gaulin and Boster (1990) suggested consideration of a diversity approach to the dowry system and that there is need for within-culture or within-societal examination of the dowry system. Advocates of gender inequality should focus their attention on ways to collaborate with cultural, sociopolitical, and economic dimensions of societies that practice dowry and bride-price as a way of bridging the gap of disparity of wealth distribution. A more radical approach would be increased advocacy for the education of women in societies where dowry and bride-price are prevalent. This may potentially increase possibilities for independence and control of resources. Researchers have suggested more forms of autonomy for marriage and career choice to potentially increasing economic security and independence for women.

Navigating multicultural nuances can certainly present challenges. Researchers have highlighted that diversity of languages and dialects in various parts of Africa indicates one example of how difficult it would be to make clear distinctions between dowry and bride-price practices. Rather, it would be reasonable to discuss practices of cultures in context based on linguistic and semantic presentation within a given geographical location. Therefore, given the advocacy need for women as an underrepresented group faced with historical, economic, political, social, public health, and mental health inequalities, gender audit of dowry and bride-price is a much more serious concern than ever before. Dowry and bride-price are practices to compensate for lost services, goods, and human capital. Marriage and its material components are considered a reciprocal transaction. Definitions and discussions of dowry and bride-price will continue to vary as long as there are various economies around the world. The reality is that marriage payments in the form of dowry and bride-price have implications for both families of bride and groom. Loss or gain for either group can be difficult to determine.

SEE ALSO: Kinship

REFERENCES

Barker, John. 2003. "Dowry." In *International Encyclopedia of Marriage and Family*, edited by James J. Ponzetti, vol. 1, 495–496. New York: Macmillan Reference USA.

Botticini, Maristella, and Aloysius Siow. 2003. "Why Dowries?" *The American Economic Review*, 93: 1385–1398. DOI: 10.1257/000282803769206368.

Fleising, Usher. 2003. "Bride-price." In *International Encyclopedia of Marriage and Family*, edited by James J. Ponzetti, vol. 1, 175–176. New York: Macmillan Reference USA.

Fortunato, Laura, Clare Holden, and Ruth Mace. 2006. "From Bridewealth to Dowry?" *Human*

Nature, 17: 355–376. DOI: 10.1007/s12110-006-1000-4.

Gaulin, Steven J. C., and James S. Boster. 1990. "Dowry as Female Competition." *American Anthropologist*, 92: 994–1005. DOI: 10.1525/aa.1990.92.4.02a00080.

Goody, Jack, and Stanley J. Tambiah. 1973. *Bridewealth and Dowry*. Cambridge: Cambridge University Press.

Harrell, Stevan, and Sara A. Dickey. 1985. "Dowry Systems in Complex Societies." *Ethnology*, 24: 105–120. DOI: 10.2307/3773553.

Maitra, Sudeshna. 2008. "Dowry and Bride Price." In *International Encyclopedia of the Social Sciences*, edited by William A. Darity, vol. 2, 2nd ed., 440–442. Detroit: Macmillan Reference USA.

Murdoch, George Peter. 1967. *Ethnographic Atlas*. Pittsburgh: University of Pittsburgh Press.

Wendo, Charles. 2004. "African Women Denounce Bride Price: Campaigners Claim Payment for Wives Damages Sexual Health and Contributes to AIDS Spread." *Lancet*, 363(9410): 716. DOI: 10.1016/S0140-6736(04)15674-2.

FURTHER READING

Tambiah, Stanley J. 1989. "Bridewealth and Dowry Revisited: The Position of Women in Sub-Saharan Africa and North India." *Current Anthropology*, 30(4): 413–435.

Dowry Deaths

VINDHYA UNDURTI
Tata Institute of Social Sciences, India

The phenomenon of dowry deaths – of violence against young married women by their husbands and families related to extortion for gifts – was vital in activating the women's movement in post-independence India in the 1980s. Although the historical and traditional meaning of dowry has changed over the centuries, the evolution of the practice from possibly customary inheritance to extortion and violence is embedded in an increasingly consumerist society and capitalist economy. Highlighted initially by the women's movement as a symbol of devaluation of women and leading to major legal reform, analysis of the criminal justice system's response to dowry deaths revealed that they obscured other causes of gender-based inequalities and violence against women which are not peculiar to India alone.

The term "dowry deaths" or "dowry murders," as the women's movement in India referred to this phenomenon, is used to indicate deaths of young, married women due to abuse centered on dowry demands by their husbands and their families. This phenomenon first burst onto the center stage of public consciousness in India in the early 1980s with media reports of instances of young brides being burned to death. Captured by the evocative term "bride burning," it was this form of violence against women that was a key issue to trigger the women's movement in post-independence India. While different forms of violence against women are now recognized as near universal and a global phenomenon, the linkage of dowry extortion to marital violence is seen as a "cultural crime" peculiar to India (Oldenburg 2010).

The custom of dowry – of gifts of property, cash, and goods – given at the time of marriage by the bride's parents to the bridegroom and his family is an old one and was largely associated with the upper castes in northern India. It is only in the last four decades or so that demands for dowry and the continued pressure on the woman's natal family for gifts at the time of marriage and subsequently became intertwined with extortion. This signaled a clear message about the worth of women: the continuing practice of dowry reflected the woman's status as a liability in the sense that the new family must be paid off for accepting the woman. Further, she also becomes a hostage to her husband and in-laws' desire for a continued flow of gifts.

The practice of dowry has now spread to almost all regions and across caste groups. In south India, where the practice of dowry was virtually non-existent a little more than half a century ago except in the numerically small upper caste of Brahmins, the current spread of the practice and its growing identification with investible capital is seen as an expression of upward mobility through marriage in an increasingly capitalist market economy. The demand and spread for dowry in this region are seen as equated with rising aspirations of modernity wherein the bridegroom's worth and accomplishments in terms of education and employment are assessed through the dowry price that he can command. It is this evolving and dynamic meaning of dowry across time and across regions – south and north – in India that accounts for the persistence of the phenomenon.

Feminist scholars note that the intersectional links of commercialization of marriage transactions and dowry violence with the current socioeconomic context are evident in increasing consumerism, economic marginalization, and rising costs of living, rendering dowry extortion a living symbol of "private patriarchy" in India today (Kapadia 2002).

Therefore, far from being an obsolete residue of departed times, and despite the diversity of marriage practices between regions and caste groups in the country, the practice of dowry and the related coercion culminating in different forms of violence against the bride has been grafted onto an increasingly consumerist society. Despite the legal prohibition of giving and taking of dowry as declared in the Dowry Prohibition Act in 1961 and its subsequent amendment in 1984, the practice of dowry in fact continues to receive implicit social sanction.

Some have argued (e.g., Kishwar 1988) that the practice of dowry ensures a woman's share and inheritance of the family wealth and provides her with some resource of her own when she enters the marital home. However, it is the coercive nature that the practice has acquired and its relationship to harassment and abuse of the wife that became more central to the campaigns of the women's movement.

Media reports in cities, in particular, of young married women being abused for not fulfilling dowry demands received increasing visibility in the 1980s. Protest campaigns launched by the newly emerging women's groups regarded dowry murders as emblematic of the devaluation of women and demanded responsiveness of the criminal justice system to these deaths. Questioning the gendered nature and application of laws, the women's movement was instrumental in interrogating the power relations within the family structure and in introducing legal reform to combat the problem of dowry violence. As a consequence of these campaigns, amendments to the Indian Penal Code – Section 498A ("mental and physical cruelty to wives on account of dowry demands") and Section 304B ("dowry death") – were made in 1983 and 1986 respectively. These amendments represented the recognition of marital violence for the first time in the legal history of women's rights, and the campaigns of the women's movement resulted in the visibility of such violence as a political issue. However, what soon became apparent was that dowry demands obscured other causes of unnatural deaths of married women. In what became subsequently evident as a classic no-win situation, analysis of the criminal justice system's handling of dowry death cases showed that a majority of them resulted in acquittal of the accused as on the one hand, dowry payments being customary were difficult to prove, and on the other, violence due to any other reason apart from dowry was normalized within the legal system (Agnes 1995; Vindhya 2000). It was only later that the focus of causes of violence expanded to include other than those related to dowry extortion. Domestic violence, which by no means is peculiar to India alone, eventually came to be recognized as a separate crime with the enactment of Protection of Women from Domestic Violence Act in 2005.

SEE ALSO: Domestic Violence in the United States; Dowry and Bride-Price; Women's and Feminist Activism in Southeast Asia; Women's and Feminist Organizations in South Asia

REFERENCES

Agnes, Flavia. 1995. *State, Gender, and the Rhetoric of Law Reform*. Bombay: Research Centre for Women's Studies, Shreemati Nathibai Damodar Thackersey Women's University.

Kapadia, Karin. 2002. "Translocal Modernities and Transformations of Gender and Caste." In *The Violence of Development*, edited by Karin Kapadia. New Delhi: Kali for Women.

Kishwar, Madhu. 1988. "Rethinking Dowry Boycott." *Manushi*, 48: 3–7.

Oldenburg, Veena. 2010. *Dowry Murder: Reinvestigating a Cultural Whodunit*. New Delhi: Penguin.

Vindhya, U. 2000. "'Dowry Deaths' in Andhra Pradesh, India: Response of the Criminal Justice System." *Violence against Women*, 6: 1085–1108.

FURTHER READING

Agnihotri, Indu. 2003. "The Expanding Dimensions of Dowry." *Indian Journal of Gender Studies*, 10: 307–319.

Gangoli, Geetanjali. 2007. *Indian Feminisms: Law, Patriarchies and Violence in India*. Hampshire: Ashgate.

Dowry Prohibition Act

NIDA SAJID
Rutgers University, USA

The Dowry Prohibition Act officially outlaws the practice of marriage dowry in India. The term dowry in the Indian context broadly refers to the cash, consumer goods, jewelry, and/or property that the parents of a bride give to a groom's family. A long-standing Indian custom, dowry evolved into an elaborate system of transferring wealth during weddings in the second half of the twentieth century. Though initially confined to upper-caste Hindus, the practice spread at an alarming rate through different castes, classes, religions, and regions across India. By the late 1950s, dowry came to be identified as a serious social problem because of the rising number of cases where the groom's family harassed the bride and her family with outrageous demands for either money or property during marriage negotiations. As a corollary of these demands, newly wed women were frequently subjected to physical torture and psychological abuse. Dowry-related violence escalated over the decades, resulting in dowry deaths and "bride-burning" cases in many parts of India.

Recognizing the prevalence of dowry and its violent consequences, the Indian parliament passed legislation explicitly banning this practice in the Dowry Prohibition Act of 1961. This Act prohibits the request, payment, or acceptance of a dowry "as consideration for the marriage," where "dowry" is defined as a gift demanded or given as a precondition for marriage. The Act did not aim to entirely abolish the custom of giving gifts upon marriage, and the statutorily proscribed dowry excluded gratuitous gifts of *stridhan*, traditionally representing a woman's share of her parent's wealth. Therefore, items meant for the personal use of the bride or gifts given for common use in the home were permissible gifts, but cash or property given directly to the husband or his family were considered dowry, both prohibited and punishable by the Act. By making a distinction between the Hindu concept of *stridhan* and the relatively modern practice of demanding dowry, the Act intended to reform the dowry system into its antecedent form where *stridhan* constituted a woman's only inalienable property in the absence of inheritance rights.

In analyzing the Dowry Prohibition Act of 1961 as a legislative attempt to end the practice of dowry in India, it became apparent that the statutory language of the Act and its enforcement proved to be inadequate in preventing violence against women. Human rights activists and women's groups began documenting evidence of dowry-related deaths in the late 1970s after newspapers began reporting a series of deaths due to burning, in which newly wed women were depicted as victims of "kitchen accidents." Women's organizations became vigilant and undertook vigorous anti-dowry campaigns in the 1980s, demanding more efficient legislative measures to deal with this particularly gruesome form of gendered violence.

In order to make the Dowry Prohibition Act of 1961 more effective and to reduce incidents of death and torture by criminalizing dowry-related violence, the Indian government enacted amendments to the Act. Following the recommendations of the Joint Parliamentary Committee and the Law Commission of India, the Act was amended in 1984 with a change in vocabulary to widen the definition of dowry. Different sections of the Act enhanced punishment, and dowry-related offenses were made cognizable for the purposes of investigation. The Act underwent further amendments in 1986 to broaden the classification of dowry, provide a minimum sentence, and ban certain aspects of matrimonial advertisement. New sections were also added to shift the burden of proof and for the appointment of dowry prohibition officers. The amendments of 1984 and 1986, together, made dowry-related offenses discernible, non-compoundable, and non-bailable.

The amendments to the Dowry Prohibition Act were accompanied by necessary changes to the Indian Penal Code, the Code of Criminal Procedure, and the Indian Evidence Act to specifically address the issues of dowry death and domestic violence against married women by their in-laws. Since the amended Act required more stringent criminal laws for efficient reinforcement, the Indian Penal Code mandated punishment for dowry-related cruelty by the husband or his relatives, providing a sentence of seven years to life for dowry death. The government amended the Code of Criminal Procedure to require a police investigation of suicides or deaths in suspicious circumstances, particularly if the death occurs within seven years of marriage. The Indian Evidence Act was also amended to create a presumption of dowry death where the woman had been subjected to cruelty or harassment for dowry soon before her death.

The Dowry Prohibition Act, with the amendments and other ancillary measures, continues to remain ineffectual in curbing dowry-related violence or addressing the social mechanisms responsible for the ubiquity of dowry practices across India. The reformist stance of the legislation toward dowry does not clearly distinguish custom from coercion, obscuring the distinction between voluntary gifts and exploitative demands in Indian marriages. Another important consequence of the Dowry Prohibition Act has been the narrowing down of the definition of gendered violence in the process of criminalizing dowry, forcing women's rights organizations to work under the ordinance of the Indian legal system. Lack of enforcement by the police and the courts also contributes to the ineffectiveness of the Act. The multiplicity of social and cultural attitudes surrounding women in India, specifically the predominance of gender hierarchies and patriarchal ideologies, further encumbers emphatic implementation of legislative laws.

SEE ALSO: Dowry and Bride-Price; Dowry Deaths; Suttee (Sati); Women's and Feminist Organizations in South Asia

FURTHER READING

Basu, Srimati, ed. 2005. *Dowry and Inheritance.* New Delhi: Women Unlimited.

Beri, Justice B. P. 1988. *Commentaries on the Dowry Prohibition Act, 1961.* Lucknow: Eastern Book.

Bhatnagar, J. P. 1988. *Cases and Materials on Dowry Prohibition Act, 1961 (Amended by Act No. 43 of 1986), along with Dowry Death and Bride Burning Cases.* Allahabad: Ashoka Law House.

Bradley, Tamsin, Emma Tomalin, and Mangala Subramaniam, eds. 2009. *Dowry: Bridging the Gap between Theory and Practice.* London: Zed Books.

Butalia, Subhadra. 2002. *The Gift of a Daughter: Encounters with Victims of Dowry.* New Delhi: Penguin.

Menski, Werner, ed. 1999. *South Asians and the Dowry Problem.* New Delhi: Vistaar.

Oldenburg, Veena, 2002. *Dowry Murder: The Imperial Origins of a Cultural Crime.* New York: Oxford University Press.

Drag

SHAELEYA MILLER
California State University, USA

Drag commonly refers to the practice of temporarily adopting cross-gender attire and mannerisms for the purpose of entertainment. The most popular categories of drag include drag queens, typically cisgender men (men assigned male at birth) performing femininity, and drag kings, typically cisgender women performing masculinity. However, drag can describe a wide variety of gender performances by cisgender and transgender people, from hypermasculine to hyperfeminine and everything in between.

Although cross-gender performances occur around the globe, drag is a distinctly Western concept often used to "make sense" of gender and sexual practices in non-Western contexts. In some cases, third-gender people who embody femininity and perform onstage may be read as drag queens from a Western perspective when they have distinctly different local meanings. Because globalization has led to the increased incorporation of Western styles of drag within cross-gender performances, the boundaries between what does and does not constitute drag have consequently been blurred.

Even in Western contexts, not all people who embody cross-gender attire or mannerisms identify as drag queens or drag kings. There are butch women (usually lesbian) who wear masculine attire, effeminate men (usually gay) who wear feminine attire, and cross-dressers (formerly called "transvestites"), who are usually heterosexual men dressing in women's attire for non-performance reasons. Transgender people may display and embrace gender identities different from the categories they were assigned at birth, or may actively blur the boundaries of gender for political or individual, rather than performance-related, purposes.

Drag performers' gender and sexual identities vary greatly. Despite a strong connection between non-heterosexual orientation and drag, heterosexual-identified people also perform in drag. Some performers describe their drag personas as an extension of their gender identities, but most do not identify as transgender. Even performers who alter their bodies generally maintain the gender they were assigned at birth. "Titty queens," for example, are drag queens who acquire breasts through hormones or implants to augment their performances, but have no desire to live as women in their daily lives (Rupp and Taylor 2003). Individuals may also perform in drag that embellishes the gender they were assigned at birth. This is the case for "faux queens" or "bio queens," who are lesbian, heterosexual, or queer-identified cisgender women who perform femininity onstage.

HISTORY OF DRAG IN THE UNITED STATES

Despite the primary associations of drag with the stage, modes of embodiment that contradict gender and sexual norms also have a long history offstage. Historical records indicate that female-bodied people have long used cross-gender attire and mannerisms to convey sexual orientation or to navigate cultural gender constraints. However, it is possible that these accounts include people we would now consider to be transgender men (Rupp 2009). In late-seventeenth-century England, men who expressed same-sex desires through effeminate modes of dress and behavior in their daily lives were known as "mollies" or "queens." These men differed in their intent and modes of expression from the early-nineteenth-century "dame comedians" who performed onstage femininity to elicit laughter. It was not until the mid-nineteenth century that the term "drag" was used to describe comedic cross-gender performances as well as more glamorous female impersonators appearing in serious venues. Because women were barred from the stage, female impersonators who performed both male and female roles were granted a degree of legitimacy during this period.

It was not until the 1930s that the term "drag queen" was first used to describe female impersonators with the added implication that the performer was homosexual. This shift followed the expansion of drag performances beyond the realm of the theater and into bars, particularly in the United States, during the 1920s and 1930s. As a strategy for attracting both homosexual and heterosexual audiences into Prohibition speakeasies, drag performances became a central component of bar cultures where mixed working- and middle-class patrons comingled to watch the shows. Harlem performances also attracted mixed African American and white crowds. At public drag balls, homosexual men could dress in women's attire and dance with other men in mixed homosexual and heterosexual crowds. Through the first financially tenuous years of the Great Depression, drag continued to thrive as business owners tried to attract customers by featuring female impersonators in their establishments.

People flocked to New York City's Times Square to see drag shows during a "pansy craze," which ended abruptly with the repeal of Prohibition in 1933. Under new governmental regulations, liquor-serving businesses were subjected to laws forbidding homosexual behavior. With the return to standards of respectable citizenry, homosexuals and drag queens were forced out of mainstream bars, but heterosexual audiences continued to seek out performances in gay and lesbian bars. The first bars catering specifically to gay and lesbian patrons were established at this time and played an integral role in the development of new non-heterosexual subcultures and communities throughout subsequent years (Chauncey 1994).

During World War II, cross-gender performances made a sanctioned appearance in the US and Canadian armed services, where soldiers performing as female impersonators provided morale boosts for their comrades. Some even warranted romantic attention from their peers, but there is little evidence to suggest that any of these soldiers received reprimands. It was not until women were allowed into the armed services at the end of World War II that drag fell out of favor in the military (Halladay 2004). Under postwar conditions, drag remained tenuous. It was illegal to wear drag attire on the streets, and performers were required to carry cabaret cards to prove their legitimacy. Over time, the character of drag shifted away from high-skill performances toward the use of prerecorded music and lip-synching. By the mid-twentieth century, this newly accessible form of female impersonation allowed for large numbers of amateur and street performers to enter the drag scene.

Explicitly political drag emerged during the US Gay Liberation Movement of the 1960s and 1970s, as drag performers used their skills to garner public attention about gay rights and continued police harassment. By 1979, the radical faeries, a group of anti-assimilationist gay men, had joined drag queens and butch lesbians in their pursuit of gender equality within the gay and lesbian movement. That same year, gay men in San Francisco founded The Sisters of Perpetual Indulgence, whose members wore nun's habits and heavy make-up, and used comedic drag to highlight the absurdity of religious gender and sexual mores excluding gays and lesbians.

DRAG IN QUEER COMMUNITIES

As transgender visibility in the United States increased during the 1980s and 1990s, many gay and lesbian activists distanced themselves from gender non-conformity. As a result, drag queens and other gender non-conformists were marginalized in mainstream gay and lesbian politics (McNeal 1999; Berkowitz and Belgrave 2010). Still, drag has remained a staple of US lesbian, gay, bisexual, transgender, and queer (LGBTQ) communities in subsequent decades.

With increasing globalization, Western styles of drag have been incorporated within gay communities in multiple contexts to express non-binary gender identities or as a space of sexual negotiation. In a number of cultures, heterosexual men are the desired or actual sexual partners of gay or third-gender male-bodied people, and dressing and performing in drag offer opportunities to attract potential sexual partners. Mapping the concept of drag onto non-US contexts can be a tricky matter, however, since the distinctly binary conceptions of gender and sexuality do not necessarily hold in cross-cultural contexts. Manalansan (2003) demonstrated this in his study of Filipino *baklâ* living in New York. *Baklâ* are male-bodied, third-gender people who wear feminine attire, exhibit feminine mannerisms, have relationships with heterosexual men, and may perform onstage. However, they do not conceive of themselves as dressing in drag in the Western sense and in some cases (but not all) they identify as women. *Baklâ* is thus a distinct gender and sexual identity that does not translate to the US context, and includes a number of community-based practices, including gay lingo in the form of *swardspeak*.

In their role as performers, drag artists are often able to expand their communities through fundraisers and through other gay and lesbian performance venues. In South Africa, where gay identity is explicitly feminine, drag performances provide gay men of color (regionally referred to as *moffies*, *siskansa*, and *istanbe*) with opportunities to demonstrate publicly their femininity for heterosexual-identified, masculine men (Swarr 2004). In the Cook Islands, *laelae* is a third-gender category that describes male-bodied people who desire non-*laelae* men, may or may not embody femininity, may or may not identify as women, and may or may not see themselves as both male and female (Alexeyef 2008). *Laelae* who have developed transnational networks or who are exposed to gender and sexual norms from other places through television and other forms of media may incorporate gender and sexual signifiers from other contexts within their performances. Although they are highly regarded for their talents and often perform at fundraising events, Alexeyef finds that when they incorporate the highly sexualized components of Western drag into their performances they are less positively received because *laelae* is considered to be more about gender than about sexuality in that local sphere.

Drag communities may also offer supportive enclaves for gender non-conforming people. Since they generally perform in troupes, drag king communities provide affirming spaces for some masculine women and transgender men. Made up of "houses" developed by primarily black and Latino youth who have been rejected by their families of origin, ballroom culture originated in New York over 50 years ago, allowing gay men and transgender women to develop alternative family structures headed by a "mother" (and sometimes a "father") who cares for the children and trains them in the art of drag. At drag balls, these houses compete against one another for prestige, staging performances that challenge race, class, and gender categories (Bailey 2009).

While stigma clings to queens in the United States who perform for pleasure, professional queens may increase their prestige by establishing names for themselves through pride celebrations, drag competitions, and television appearances. *RuPaul's Drag Race* renewed the mainstream popularity of drag performances when it aired in the United States and Canada in 2009. Many queens achieved celebrity status by appearing on the reality TV show, where they competed for the title of "America's next drag superstar." Contestants' weekly challenges mocked gender and sexual norms and created new possibilities for disrupting sexual conventions, although the ultimate emphasis on performing "realness" constrained the multifaceted potential of drag (Edgar 2011).

THE POLITICS OF DRAG

Although drag queens and trans women were some of the most militant protesters against police brutality during the US Gay Liberation Movement, scholars have paid little attention to the political potential of gender-nonconformity until recent years. As trans people became more visible in the 1990s, queer theory and gender studies flourished. Within these fields, some theorists began to suggest that drag performances could offer a productive medium for destabilizing gender and sexual norms by disrupting the notion that specific genders are attached only to particular bodies (Butler 1990). That drag performers often elicit desires transcending the professed sexual orientations of audience members further advanced this claim, particularly when performers take pause, calling attention to their "real" gender in the face of adoring onlookers (Rupp and Taylor 2003).

The understated quality of masculinity makes it difficult for drag kings to parody masculinity in the ways that drag queens parody femininity. Drag kings, most of whom are female bodied, generally lack the sexual privilege that provides male-bodied drag queens a degree of authority during shows. Drag queens often use this autonomy to antagonize audience members while maintaining an amicable rapport. In some cases queens exert superiority over women by suggesting they perform femininity better than the "real women" who make up a bulk of their audiences (Rupp and Taylor 2003). As a result, drag performances may alternatively be viewed as undermining gender norms (Butler 1990) or as reinforcing gender stereotypes and demeaning femininity (Schacht 2002).

Although transgender and drag identity are not the same, performers sometimes suggest that drag has facilitated shifts in their sexual or gender identities (Rupp and Taylor 2003). This is less common among drag queens than among drag kings, who start out as masculine women, genderqueers, or transgender men (Rupp, Taylor, and Shapiro 2010). On college campuses, drag kings may incorporate queer theory in their discussions of drag, and some have played a pivotal role in raising awareness of transgender rights by highlighting gender politics on- and offstage (Shapiro 2007). Drag kings' tendencies toward gender and sexual multiplicity are usually reflected in their performances. Whereas queens tend to perform solo, kings often interact with one another to perform a wide range of sexual scenes onstage. Performances of gay male, butch/femme, and butch/butch sexualities reflect the varied sexual dynamics present in contemporary lesbian communities, allowing performers and audience members to explore their own gender embodiment and desires (Pauliny 2003).

Gender performances inherently draw upon class, race, and sexual categories to make them resonant. White drag queens enacting excessive, trashy, and hypersexualized "camp" femininity illustrate the constructedness of white, middle-class womanhood (Rhyne 2004), and when white drag kings exaggerate white masculinities onstage they may reveal the farce of dominant masculinities. But the cultural invisibility of white masculinity leads many drag kings of all races to adopt black masculinities onstage in order to make visible their gendered performances. However, kings of color are more likely than white kings to perform "softer" masculinities that challenge hypersexualized, racist discourses about men of color (Volcano and Halberstam 1999). Thus, drag kings and queens of color may incorporate their own racial and ethnic experiences to challenge white-normative gender standards and to expose how multiple intersecting identities create unique meanings of masculinity and femininity for people of color (Muñoz 1999).

The politics of drag can transcend the stage in challenging prohibitive gender regulations. In 2014, drag queens played a pivotal role in online activism when Facebook informed users that it would enforce its "real-name" policy by deactivating noncompliant accounts. Drag queens, many of whom used Facebook as a professional networking tool, used their notoriety to challenge the policy through public statements both on- and offline. Alongside other queer activists, including transgender people for whom the issue was especially critical, drag queens led what some people referred to as the "great gay exodus" from Facebook onto other social media sites. Within weeks Facebook had issued a retraction and reinstated the accounts in question.

Everyday instances of drag can also be political. The Sisters of Perpetual Indulgence now occupy houses in multiple locations around the world, using religious iconography and extreme drag during street protests. While glamorous drag queens hold a level of high prestige in the cosmopolitan gay culture of Berlin, *Tunten* are a marginalized subcultural community of gay men who exhibit both mundane and trashy femininity onstage and in their daily lives to explicitly protest normative gender expectations (Balzer 2004). More discreetly, Diane Torr's "Man for a Day" workshops train lesbians, heterosexual women, homosexual men, and trans men in the subtle nuances of masculinity, unmasking its power by showing that literally anyone can do it (Torr and Bottoms 2013).

CONCLUSION

The rich history and culture of drag, both on- and offstage, suggests that the uses, meanings, and methods of drag vary greatly across time and place. As a method for navigating gender norms, a performance technique, or a political strategy for resisting assimilation, drag offers a unique window into the function of gender and sexual norms in various cultures. As a visible marker of queerness, drag can also provide insights about the dynamics and content of queer community spaces.

Whereas some performers emphasize the sheer entertainment value of drag, others consider the medium to be explicitly political. In an increasingly globalized world, the content and methods of drag activism have shifted to incorporate both online interventions and multinational networks of performers across the world. Whatever the intent behind the performance, queer theory and gender studies suggest that drag can have social, political, and ideological implications for sex and gender systems in multiple settings. If nothing else, the cross-gender quality of drag in its multiple iterations allows us to trace the contours of gender and sexual norms as they shift contextually. Through recognition of which representations elicit shock and awe at specific geographic and historical sites, drag can offer alternative imaginings of what it means to be a sexual and gendered being.

SEE ALSO: Butch/Femme; Camp; Cross-Dressing; Gender Performance; Gender Transgression; Lesbian and Gay Movements; Lesbian Performance; Queer Performance; Queer Theory; Transgender Movements in the United States

REFERENCES

Alexeyef, Kalissa. 2008. "Globalizing Drag in the Cook Islands: Friction, Repulsion, and Abjection." *The Contemporary Pacific*, 20(1): 143–161.

Bailey, Marlon. 2009. "Performance as Intervention: Ballroom Culture, and the Politics of HIV/AIDS in Detroit." *Souls: A Critical Journal of Black Politics, Culture and Society*, 11(3): 253–274. DOI: 10.1080/10999940903088226.

Balzer, Carsten. 2004. "The Beauty and the Beast." *Journal of Homosexuality*, 46(3/4): 55–71. DOI: 10.1300/J082v46n03_04.

Berkowitz, Dana, and Linda Belgrave. 2010. "'She Works Hard for the Money': Drag Queens and the Management of Their Contradictory Status of Celebrity and Marginality." *Journal of Contemporary Ethnography*, 39(2): 159–186. DOI: 10.1177/0891241609342193.

Butler, Judith. 1990. *Gender Trouble: Feminism and the Subversion of Identity*. New York: Routledge.

Chauncey, George. 1994. *Gay New York: Gender, Urban Culture, and the Making of the Gay Male World, 1890–1940*. New York: Basic Books.

Edgar, Eir-Anne. 2011. "Xtravaganza!: Drag Representation and Articulation in *RuPaul's Drag Race*." *Studies in Popular Culture*, 34(1): 133–146.

Halladay, Laurel. 2004. "A Lovely War: Male to Female Cross-Dressing and Canadian Military Entertainment in World War II." *Journal of Homosexuality*, 46(3/4): 19–34. DOI: 10.1300/J082v46n03_02.

Manalansan, Martin F., IV. 2003. *Global Divas: Filipino Gay Men in the Diaspora*. Durham, NC: Duke University Press.

McNeal, Kevin E. 1999. "Behind the Make-Up: Gender Ambivalence and the Double-Bind of Gay Selfhood in Drag Performance." *Ethos*, 27(3): 344–378. DOI: 0.1525/eth.1999.27.3.344.

Muñoz, José Esteban. 1999. *Disidentifications: Queers of Color and the Performance of Politics*. Minneapolis: University of Minnesota Press.

Pauliny, Tara. 2003. "Erotic Arguments and Persuasive Acts: Discourses of Desire and Rhetoric of Female-to-Male Drag." *Journal of Homosexuality*, 43(3/4): 221–249. DOI: 10.1300/J082v43n03_14.

Rhyne, Ragan. 2004. "Racializing White Drag." *Journal of Homosexuality*, 46(3): 181–194. DOI: 10.1300/J082v46n03_11.

Rupp, Leila J. 2009. *Sapphistries: A Global History of Love Between Women*. New York: New York University Press.

Rupp, Leila J., and Verta Taylor. 2003. *Drag Queens at the 801 Cabaret*. Chicago: University of Chicago Press.

Rupp, Leila J., Verta Taylor, and Eve L. Shapiro. 2010. "Drag Queens and Drag Kings: The Difference Gender Makes." *Sexualities*, 13(3): 275–294. DOI: 10.1177/1363460709352725.

Schacht, Steven P. 2002. "Four Renditions of Doing Female Drag: Feminine Appearing Conceptual Variations of a Masculine Theme." In *Gendered Sexualities: Advances in Gender Research*, edited by Patricia Gagné and Richard Tewksbury, 157–180. Boston: Elsevier.

Shapiro, Eve. 2007. "Drag Kinging and the Transformation of Gender Identities." *Gender*

& *Society*, 21(2): 250–271. DOI: 10.1177/ 0891243206294509.

Swarr, Amanda L. 2004. "Moffies, Artists, and Queens: Race and the Production of South African Gay Male Drag." *Journal of Homosexuality*, 46(3/4): 181–194. DOI: 10.1300/ J082v46n03_05.

Torr, Diane, and Stephen Bottoms. 2013. *Sex, Drag and Male Roles: Investigating Gender as Performance*. Ann Arbor: University of Michigan Press.

Volcano, Del LaGrace, and Judith "Jack" Halberstam. 1999. *The Drag King Book*. London: Serpent's Tail.

FURTHER READING

Taylor, Verta, and Leila Rupp. 2004. "Chicks with Dicks, Men in Dresses: What it means to be a Drag Queen." *Journal of Homosexuality*, 46(3/4): 113–133.

Drug and Alcohol Abuse

KEITH KLOSTERMANN and DAVID FORSTADT
Medaille College, USA

Research in the field of sexual orientation and substance abuse indicates that substance abuse is predominantly higher in lesbian, gay, and bisexual (LGB) populations compared to those who identify as heterosexual (Green and Feinstein 2012). Data from the Center of Substance Abuse Treatment support these claims; they note that individuals in the LGB community are more likely to use alcohol and drugs than the general population, have higher rates of substance abuse, are less likely to abstain from use, and are more likely to continue heavy drinking into later adulthood (CSAT 2001). They also note that in comparison to the heterosexual population, 20 to 25 percent of gay men and lesbians are heavy alcohol users, compared to 3 to 10 percent of the heterosexuals (CSAT 2001). Early research exploring the prevalence of substance use in LGB individuals has shown a disparity in data due to methodological errors when assessing both substance use and sexual orientation (Green and Feinstein 2012). As a result, it is challenging to evaluate whether previous research is truly representative of the LGB population due to early trends in sampling, which have established stereotypical paradigms of substance use. For example, in past research, LGB participants were recruited in bars and other environments conducive to substance use behavior with no comparison groups to account for discrepancies (Green and Feinstein 2012). Currently, studies that assess sexual orientation on a nationwide level remain infrequent and do little to differentiate the level of risk of substance use behavior across sexual minority status and gender (McCabe et al. 2009).

Similar to the disparities in the measurement of sexual orientation, the construct of substance use behavior demonstrates similar variability across studies. Researchers either focus on substance use over a specific period of time, specific types of maladaptive substance use, or idiosyncratic operationalizations (e.g., abstinence from substance use, amount of substance consumed). Studies regarding substance use rarely address sexual orientation, and studies addressing sexual minority populations only discuss implications of substance use on occasion (McCabe et al. 2009). Also, LGB-identified individuals who have an addiction may experience social pressures and stigma associated with being both a sexual minority and addicted to drugs and/or alcohol, decreasing the likelihood of seeking treatment for their substance use problems (Green and Feinstein 2012). This may have implications on understanding the prevalence of substance use in LGB populations due to limited sampling opportunities in substance use facilities.

Most researchers agree that sexual orientation includes behavioral, affective (attraction or desire), and cognitive (identity) dimensions (Hughes and Eliason 2002; McCabe et al. 2005). Despite this, studies that address the dimensions of sexual orientation do so in an inconsistent manner, skewing the construct and the standardization of terminology, thus making comparisons across studies difficult (McCabe et al. 2005). When addressing sexual orientation, most research has only explored sexual behavior as a measure of orientation, ignoring both cognitive and affective dimensions.

Sell (1997) discussed multiple concerns with the methods utilized in the past for assessing sexual orientation. First, he stresses concern over the unsatisfactory nature of using dichotomous scales when evaluating orientation because sexual preference cannot be defined in discrete categories. For example, studies either exclude or blend bisexual individuals into either gay or lesbian categories (McCabe et al. 2009), and as a result, research is lacking studies specific to bisexual individuals (Hughes and Eliason 2002). Cabaj (1996) also clarifies concerns with measuring sexual orientation, which include poor or absent control groups, unrepresentative sampling, limited generalizability, and inconsistent sexual orientation terminology. Scales that force individuals to make "tradeoffs" between sexual orientation classifications do not allow for valid and reliable representation of individual preference (Sell 1997). Finally, only utilizing physical and affectional preference in classifying orientation can be deemed "oversimplified or inappropriate" (Sell 1997). Points made by Sell emphasize past research's tendency to define sexual orientation in concrete labels (i.e., gay/lesbian/bisexual). The effects of this perpetuate a one-dimensional approach in defining sexual orientation and influence the ability to understand its relationship with substance use behavior.

A study conducted by Weber (2008) sought to examine the relationship between heterosexist events, internalized homophobia, and substance use and abuse among 824 LGB individuals. Participants were asked to complete the Schedule for Heterosexist Events (SHE), Internalized Homophobia Scale (IHP), Alcohol Use Disorders Identification Test (AUDIT), and the Drug Abuse Screening Test (DAST). These tests' interscale correlation coefficients were then evaluated. Results suggested that participants who were classified as having at least one alcohol or drug use disorder also reported that they experienced more internalized homophobia than those who were not classified as having an alcohol or drug use disorder (Weber 2008). Also, a positive relationship was found between exposure to heterosexist events and drug use and abuse, and between internalized homophobia and both alcohol and drug use and abuse (Weber 2008). Weber notes limitations to the study, which include small correlations that may not have statistical significance. Research like Weber's solidifies the need for better sampling when defining sexual orientation in order to clarify the influence of substance use and heterosexist and homophobic behaviors across multi-dimensions of sexual orientation.

The orientation of bisexuality demonstrates a thorough representation of the influence of external factors on sexual identity. Individuals who identify as bisexual may be at great risk of discrimination from both the heterosexual and homosexual community, significantly reducing social supports (Green and Feinstein 2012). As a result, bisexual individuals experience increased minority stress around the disconnection between sexual identity and sexual behavior. This can be attributed to the inability to identify with a social group of individuals that share similar characteristics. Extreme situations of this variable can be seen in the concept of bi-negativity (the denial of bisexuality as a legitimate orientation), a position held by those who are monosexist, and believe that sexuality must be directed toward one gender over another. In studies that have differentiated between sexual minority statuses, whether defined by identity, attraction, or behavior, bisexual adults appear to be at the greatest risk for substance use behavior compared to both heterosexual and homosexual groups (McCabe et al. 2005, 2009). For example, women who identified as mostly homosexual or bisexual reported greater substance use than those who reported only heterosexual identity (McCabe et al. 2005). In comparison to men, it was assumed heterosexual orientation would demonstrate greater reports of substance use, but equal patterns of use were found in bisexual populations as well (McCabe et al. 2005). This increased risk may be related to experiences of prejudice and discrimination from both heterosexual and lesbian/gay communities (Israel and Mohr 2004; Green and Feinstein 2012). These findings may also be related to reports of lower social support of bisexual individuals compared to both heterosexual and lesbian/gay individuals (Green and Feinstein 2012), or the effect of incongruence between sexual identity and sexual behavior (Green and Feinstein 2012).

McCabe and colleagues (2009) conducted one of the first nationwide studies that explored the relationship of substance use behavior across all dimensions of sexual orientation and gender. Results of the study indicate that the prevalence of substance use varied little across each dimension of heterosexual orientation, but varied significantly across dimensions of sexual orientation of LGB individuals. The relationship of minority status and substance use appeared more prevalent in women who either identified as lesbian or bisexual (McCabe et al. 2009). More specifically, women who identified as bisexual had the highest rates of substance use compared to men of minority status across all dimensions of sexual orientation who typically have higher base rates of substance use (McCabe et al. 2009). Recently, in their review of research associated with the relationship between substance use and sexual orientation, Green and Feinstein (2012) found that lesbian and bisexual women were at greater risk for alcohol and drug use disorders and related problems compared to heterosexual women. In regard to gay and bisexual men, studies appear inconsistent. In some studies, gay men appeared more likely to use alcohol and illicit drugs compared to heterosexual men, while other studies report that gay and heterosexual men do not differ in their substance use behavior (Green and Feinstein 2012). The few studies that addressed the relationship between sexual identity and substance use indicated that women and men who identified as non-heterosexual were at greater risk for substance use behaviors compared to those who identify as heterosexual (McCabe et al. 2009). Individuals who identified as a sexual minority may have experienced greater exposure to discrimination and other forms of minority stress compared to those who engaged in same-sex behavior or attraction, but did not identify as a sexual minority (McCabe et al. 2009).

There continues to be minimal research that addresses substance use in LGB individuals, and even less exists on the substance use and abuse patterns for bisexual individuals (Hughes and Eliason 2002). Previous issues in construct design and sampling have made it challenging to fully understand the relationship between substance use and sexual orientation. Continuing to define sexual orientation as a multi-dimensional construct will not only better represent the diversity of those who make up the LGB population, but will also act as a more effective measurement when assessing orientation. Allowing for inclusion of the "gray area" of sexual orientation will help researchers better understand the relationship between variables such as substance abuse, gender, and homonegativity on the LBG population. Current research has begun to debunk early beliefs that all LBG individuals experience higher rates of substance abuse compared to the heterosexual population. By decompartmentalizing LGB individuals out of one clumped group, researchers will be able to assess better the impact of substance abuse across all variables that define sexual orientation.

SEE ALSO: Bisexuality; Health, Healthcare, and Sexual Minorities; Heteronormativity and Homonormativity; Heterosexism and Homophobia; Sexual Addiction

REFERENCES

Cabaj, R. P. 1996. "Substance Abuse in Gay Men, Lesbians, and Bisexuals." In *Textbook of Homosexuality and Mental Health*, edited by R. P. Cabaj and T. S. Stein, 783–799. Washington, DC: American Psychiatric Press.
Center for Substance Abuse Treatment (CSAT). 2001. "A Provider's Introduction to Substance Abuse Treatment for Lesbian, Gay, Bisexual, and Transgender Individuals," *DHHS Publication No. (SMA) 01-3498*. Rockville, MD: CSAT.
Green, K. E., and B. A. Feinstein. 2012. "Substance Use in Lesbian, Gay, and Bisexual Populations: An Update On Empirical Research and Implications for Treatment." *Psychology of Addictive Behaviors*, 26(2): 265–278.
Hughes, T. L., and M. Eliason. 2002. "Substance Use and Abuse in Lesbian, Gay, Bisexual and Transgender Populations." *The Journal of Primary Prevention*, 22: 263–298.
McCabe, S. E., T. L. Hughes, W. B. Bostwick, and C. J. Boyd. 2005. "Assessment of Difference in Dimensions of Sexual Orientation: Implications for Substance Use Research in a College-Age Population." *Journal of Studies on Alcohol and Drugs*, 66(5): 620–629.
McCabe, S. E., T. L. Hughes, W. B. Bostwick, B. T. West, and C. J. Boyd. 2009. "Sexual Orientation, Substance Use Behaviors and Substance Dependence in the United States." *Addiction*, 104: 1333–1345. DOI: 10.1111/j.1360-0443.2009.02596.x.
Sell, Randall. 1997. "Defining and Measuring Sexual Orientation: A Review." *Archives of Sexual Behavior*, 26(6).
Weber, G. 2008. "Using to Numb the Pain: Substance Use and Abuse among Lesbian, Gay, and Bisexual Individuals." *Journal of Mental Health Counseling*, 30(1): 31–48.

FURTHER READING

American Psychological Association. 2008. Answers To Your Questions: For a Better Understanding of Sexual Orientation and Homosexuality. Washington, DC: Author. Accessed August 14, 2015 at www.apa.org/topics/sorientation.pdf.

Dual Labor Market

ANDRZEJ KLIMCZUK
Warsaw School of Economics, Poland

MAGDALENA KLIMCZUK-KOCHAŃSKA
University of Warsaw, Poland

The dual labor market theory is one of the primary explanations for the gender differences in earnings. It shows that gender inequality and stereotypes lead to employment of men and women in different segments of the labor market and occupational gender segregation. These differences result in the overrepresentation of women in low-paying, low-status occupations compared with men. This theory is based on the hypothesis that such markets are divided into segments, which are divided by a separate system of rules, job behavior requirements, and different skills.

The dual labor market theory was introduced by American institutional economists, especially by Peter B. Doeringer and Michael J. Piore (1971), in their research on programs for combating poverty, unemployment, and discrimination. Programs were aimed to increase education and mobility of employees. Analysis of the results showed their low efficiency and the presence of rather isolated areas of the labor market. The employees had a particularly unfavorable situation (unstable jobs, low wages, lack of promotion opportunities, lack of links between a chance to work, and efficiency and education). Explaining such labor division is the assumption that it is the result of employee characteristics that define their work environment and lifestyle (such as gender, age, and race). For example, human resources policies include the preferences for recruiting of white male workers to managerial positions by offering training, financial bonuses, promotion, and job security.

The dual labor market theory allows the analysis of various issues. For example, barriers of satisfying the structural labor demand by women and teenagers, availability of unstable and low productivity jobs in advanced economies, employment of immigrants in jobs not attractive to local workers, barriers to promote the unattractive jobs by market mechanisms such as raising wages, and acceptance of unattractive jobs by social vulnerable groups (Kogan 2007).

Differences between the labor markets include availability of jobs for job seekers, the received and proposed remuneration, the level of employment stability, and opportunity for professional development. The dual labor market theory divides the economy into primary (internal) and secondary (external) segments (Loveridge and Mok 1979; Garz 2013).

Internal labor markets traditionally dominated by white males ensure institutions and rules that provide promotion systems for employees and extensive career ladders (the distinction between the upper-tier, white-collar, and lower-tier blue-collar ladders). Wages are based here on job evaluations and firm-specific skills that support long-term relationships between employers and employees with stable and permanent employment. The primary segment is, therefore, characterized by high wages, attractive working conditions, employees who actively identify with the companies, jobs in large companies with a strong market position and importance for the economy, voluntary payments, employment stability, opportunities for advancement, and the strong position of mainly male trade unions in their efforts to respect the rights and privileges of employees. The unemployment of workers from the primary segment is characterized as an involuntary condition. Such workers do not focus on job seeking but tend to wait or accept less attractive work temporarily. They trust that changes in the economy or the industry will lead to regaining the clearly identified positions from which they have been laid off.

External labor markets are closer to the assumptions of the neoclassical theory, dominated by women and minorities, and contain low-paying and low-status jobs. Such markets are in some respect created by discrimination ("the glass ceiling"). Key features are less attractive jobs (care and domestic work, the helping professions), lower wages that are often poverty level or below (the gender gap in earnings), the filling of vacancies by the market rather than by internal promotions, a requirement of general skills that can be easily replaced by easy hiring and firing, poor working conditions, fewer opportunities to advance, and high absenteeism. Workers may quit because of a dislike of a particular supervisor and may show little respect for the company goals and values. Such markets exist mainly in general industries and serve as buffer stocks in concentrated industries during expansionary periods of business cycles.

There are several reasons for the labor market duality and barriers that prevent mobility between segments (Doeringer and Piore 1971; Luck 1991; Martin 1992). First, it is supported by strategies of firms to maximize profits with little opportunity for mobility between the segments. Second, jobs in a particular sector provide individuals' histories, attitudes, levels of aspirations, expectations, and orientations to work that distinguish them from the workers in other markets. Third, disadvantaged start in the labor market begins with socialization by family and school and different social expectations, for example, to pursue traditional women's domains such as motherhood and to avoid science and authority. Fourth, there are various forms of labor supply such as flexible work arrangements and part-time work that may maintain employment in the external labor markets by prioritizing childcare, education, or other non-occupational activities.

SEE ALSO: Division of Labor, Gender; Employment Discrimination; Gender Wage Gap; Glass Ceiling and Glass Elevator; Occupational Segregation; Work–Family Balance

REFERENCES

Doeringer, Peter B., and Michael J. Piore. 1971. *Internal Labor Markets and Manpower Analysis*. Lexington, MA: Heath.

Garz, Marcel. 2013. "Labour Market Segmentation: Standard and Non-Standard Employment in Germany." *German Economic Review*, 14(3): 349–371.

Kogan, Irena. 2007. *Working Through Barriers: Host Country Institutions and Immigrant Labour Market Performance in Europe*. London: Springer.

Loveridge, Ray, and Albert L. Mok. 1979. *Theories of Labour Market Segmentation: A Critique*. The Hague: Martinus Nijhoff Social Sciences Division.

Luck, Maura. 1991. "Gender and Library Work: The Limitations of Dual Labour Market Theory." In *Working Women: International Perspectives on Labour and Gender Ideology*, edited by Nanneke Redclift and M. Thea Sinclair, 25–40. London: Routledge.

Martin, Patricia Y. 1992. "Gender, Interaction, and Inequality in Organizations." In *Gender, Interaction, and Inequality*, edited by Cecilia L. Ridgeway, 208–231. New York: Springer.

FURTHER READING

Ghilarducci, Teresa, and Mary Lee. 2005. "Female Dual Labour Markets and Employee Benefits." *Scottish Journal of Political Economy*, 52(1): 18–37.

Hirsch, Eric. 1980. "Dual Labor Market Theory: A Sociological Critique." *Sociological Inquiry*, 50(2): 133–145.

Meyer, Christine S., and Swati Mukerjee. 2007. "Investigating Dual Labor Market Theory for Women." *Eastern Economic Journal*, 33(3): 301–316.